A-Level
Biology
Exam Board: OCR A

Everyone knows that life is complicated. As a Biology student, you'll know that life is *really* complicated... and you have to understand how it all works for the exams.

Never mind — at least this CGP book will make your revision a whole lot simpler. It has everything you'll need for a top grade in the OCR A A-Level course, including crystal-clear study notes, realistic exam questions (with answers) and more!

There's also a free Online Edition you can read on your computer or tablet, so you don't even have to strain your myofibrils by carrying the book around.

How to access your free Online Edition

This book includes a free Online Edition to read on your PC, Mac or tablet. You'll just need to go to **cgpbooks.co.uk/extras** and enter this code:

4089 4889 5041 3819

By the way, this code only works for one person. If somebody else has used this book before you, they might have already claimed the Online Edition.

CGP

A-Level revision? It has to be CGP!

Published by CGP

From original material by Richard Parsons.

Editors:
Daniel Fielding, Andy Park, Rachael Rogers, Camilla Simson.

Contributors:
Sophie Anderson, Gloria Barnett, James Foster, Paddy Gannon, Barbara Green, Derek Harvey, David Martindill, Adrian Schmit.

ISBN: 978 1 78908 035 3

With thanks to Philip Armstrong, Lauren Burns, Charlotte Burrows, Ellen Burton, Janet Cruse-Sawyer, Emily Forsberg, Sarah Pattison and Hayley Thompson for the proofreading.
With thanks to Jan Greenway for the copyright research.

Cover image © duncan1890/iStockphoto.com

With thanks to Science Photo Library for permission to reproduce the images on pages
17, 61, 76, 105, 141, 150, 152 and 166.

Data for graph showing glucose concentration vs absorbance on page 31 was obtained
using a Mystrica colorimeter © Mystrica Ltd. www.mystrica.com

Clipart from Corel®
Illustrations by: Sandy Gardner Artist, email sandy@sandygardner.co.uk
Printed by Elanders Ltd, Newcastle upon Tyne.

Contents

If you're revising for the **AS exams**, you'll need to revise Modules 1-4.
If you're revising for the **A-level exams**, you'll need to revise the **whole book**.

Specification Map

This specification map tells you where each part of the OCR specification that you'll need for your exams is covered in this book.

Specification Map

The Scientific Process

'How Science Works' is all about the scientific process — how we develop and test scientific ideas. It's what scientists do all day, every day (well, except at coffee time — never come between a scientist and their coffee).

Scientists Come Up with **Theories** — Then **Test Them...**

Science tries to explain **how** and **why** things happen — it **answers questions**. It's all about seeking and gaining **knowledge** about the world around us. Scientists do this by **asking** questions and **suggesting** answers and then **testing** them, to see if they're correct — this is the **scientific process**.

1) **Ask** a question — make an **observation** and ask **why or how** it happens. E.g. why do plants grow faster in glasshouses than outside?

2) **Suggest** an answer, or part of an answer, by forming a **theory** (a possible **explanation** of the observations), e.g. glasshouses are warmer than outside and plants grow faster when it's warmer because the rate of photosynthesis is higher. (Scientists also sometimes form a **model** too — a **simplified picture** of what's physically going on.)

3) Make a **prediction** or **hypothesis** — a **specific testable statement**, based on the theory, about what will happen in a test situation. E.g. the rate of photosynthesis will be faster at 20 °C than at 10 °C.

4) Carry out a **test** — to provide **evidence** that will support the prediction (or help to disprove it). E.g. measure the rate of photosynthesis at various temperatures.

Simone predicted her hair would be worse for the school year photos tomorrow, based on the theory of sod's law.

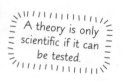

A theory is only scientific if it can be tested.

...Then They **Tell** Everyone About Their **Results...**

The results are **published** — scientists need to let others know about their work. Scientists publish their results in **scientific journals**. These are just like normal magazines, only they contain **scientific reports** (called papers) instead of the latest celebrity gossip.

1) Scientific reports are similar to the **lab write-ups** you do in school. And just as a lab write-up is **reviewed** (marked) by your teacher, reports in scientific journals undergo **peer review** before they're published.

2) The report is sent out to **peers** — other scientists that are experts in the **same area**. They examine the data and results, and if they think that the conclusion is reasonable it's **published**. This makes sure that work published in scientific journals is of a **good standard**.

3) But peer review **can't guarantee** the science is **correct** — other scientists still need to **reproduce** it.

4) Sometimes **mistakes** are made and bad work is published. Peer review **isn't perfect** but it's probably the best way for scientists to self-regulate their work and to publish **quality reports**.

...Then **Other Scientists** Will **Test** the Theory Too

Other scientists read the published theories and results, and try to **test the theory** themselves. This involves:

• Repeating the **exact same experiments**.

• Using the theory to make **new predictions** and then testing them with **new experiments**.

If the **Evidence** Supports a Theory, It's **Accepted** — for **Now**

1) If all the experiments in all the world provide good evidence to back it up, the theory is thought of as **scientific 'fact'** (for now).

2) But it will never become **totally indisputable** fact. Scientific **breakthroughs or advances** could provide new ways to question and test the theory, which could lead to **new evidence** that **conflicts** with the current evidence. Then the testing starts all over again...

And this, my friend, is the **tentative nature of scientific knowledge** — it's always **changing** and **evolving**.

The Scientific Process

So scientists need evidence to back up their theories. They get it by carrying out experiments, and when that's not possible they carry out studies. But why bother with science at all? We want to know as much as possible so we can use it to try and improve our lives (and because we're nosy).

Evidence Comes from Lab Experiments...

1) Results from controlled experiments in laboratories are great.
2) A lab is the easiest place to control variables so that they're all kept constant (except for the one you're investigating).
3) This means you can draw meaningful conclusions.

> For example, if you're investigating how light intensity affects the rate of photosynthesis you need to keep everything but the light intensity constant, e.g. the temperature, the concentration of carbon dioxide etc.

...and Well-Designed Studies

1) There are things you can't investigate in a lab, e.g. whether using a pesticide on farmland affects the number of non-pest species. You have to do a study instead.
2) You still need to try and make the study as controlled as possible to make it valid. But in reality it's very hard to control all the variables that might be having an effect.
3) You can do things to help, like having a control — e.g. an area of similar farmland nearby where the pesticide isn't applied. But you can't easily rule out every possibility.

Having a control reduced the effect of exercise on the study.

Society Makes Decisions Based on Scientific Evidence

1) Lots of scientific work eventually leads to important discoveries or breakthroughs that could benefit humankind.
2) These results are used by society (that's you, me and everyone else) to make decisions — about the way we live, what we eat, what we drive, etc.
3) All sections of society use scientific evidence to make decisions, e.g. politicians use it to devise policies and individuals use science to make decisions about their own lives.

Other factors can influence decisions about science or the way science is used:

Economic factors

- Society has to consider the cost of implementing changes based on scientific conclusions — e.g. the NHS can't afford the most expensive drugs without sacrificing something else.
- Scientific research is expensive so companies won't always develop new ideas — e.g. developing new drugs is costly, so pharmaceutical companies often only invest in drugs that are likely to make them money.

Social factors

- Decisions affect people's lives — E.g. scientists may suggest banning smoking and alcohol to prevent health problems, but shouldn't we be able to choose whether we want to smoke and drink or not?

Environmental factors

- Scientists believe unexplored regions like remote parts of rainforests might contain untapped drug resources. But some people think we shouldn't exploit these regions because any interesting finds may lead to deforestation and reduced biodiversity in these areas.

So there you have it — how science works...

Hopefully these pages have given you a nice intro to how science works, e.g. what scientists do to provide you with 'facts'. You need to understand this, as you're expected to know how science works — for the exam and for life.

Planning an Experiment

Experiments are pretty cool — much more exciting than revising anyway. Before you start planning an experiment, you need to be really clear on what you're trying to find out — you should start off with a prediction or hypothesis (see p. 2).

A **Good Experiment** Gives **Results** that are...

Precise results are sometimes referred to as reliable results.

1) **Precise** — precise results **don't vary much** from the **mean**. Precision is reduced by **random error** (the unpredictable way in which all measurements vary).

2) **Repeatable and reproducible** — repeatable means that if the same person repeats the experiment using the same methods and equipment, they will get the same results. Reproducible means that if someone different does the experiment, using a slightly different method or piece of equipment, the results will still be the same.

3) **Valid** — valid results **answer** the **original question**. To get valid results you need to **control all the variables** (see below) to make sure you're only testing the thing you want to.

4) **Accurate** — accurate results are **really close** to the true answer. **Human interpretation** of a measurement (e.g. determining a colour change) can **reduce** the accuracy of results.

Here are some things you need to consider when designing a good experiment:

1) **Only one variable should be changed** — Variables are **quantities** that have the **potential to change**, e.g. pH. In an experiment you usually **change one variable** and **measure its effect** on another variable.
   - The variable that you **change** is called the **independent variable**.
   - The variable that you **measure** is called the **dependent variable**.

2) **All the other variables should be controlled** — When you're investigating a variable you need to keep everything else that could affect it **constant**. This means you can be sure that **only** your **independent** variable is **affecting** the thing you're measuring (the dependent variable).

3) **Negative controls should be used** — Negative controls are used to **check** that only the independent variable is affecting the dependent variable. Negative controls **aren't expected** to have **any effect** on the experiment.

4) **The experiment should be repeated at least three times and a mean should be calculated** — this reduces the effect of **random error** on your experiment, which makes your results **more precise**. Doing repeats and getting **similar results** each time also shows that your data is **repeatable** and makes it more likely to be **reproducible**.

EXAMPLE: Investigating the effect of **light intensity** on **rate of photosynthesis** of **Canadian pondweed**.
1) Light intensity is the **independent** variable.
2) Rate of photosynthesis is the **dependent** variable.
3) pH, temperature and the time the pondweed is left should all **stay the same** (and the quantities should be recorded to allow someone else to reproduce the experiment).
4) The experiment should be **repeated** at least **three times** for each light intensity used.
5) A **negative control**, in which the experiment is carried out in the **dark**, should also be used. No photosynthesis should happen with this control.

Select Appropriate **Apparatus, Equipment** and **Techniques**

1) When you're **planning** an experiment you need to decide what it is you're going to **measure** and **how often** you're going to take measurements. E.g. if you're investigating the **rate of respiration**, you could either measure the volume of **oxygen used** over time or the volume of **carbon dioxide produced** over time. You could take measurements at, e.g. 30 second intervals or 60 second intervals.

2) Then you need to choose the most **appropriate** apparatus, equipment and techniques for the experiment. E.g.
   - The measuring apparatus you use has to be sensitive enough to measure the changes you're looking for. E.g. if you need to measure changes of 1 cm³ you need to use a measuring cylinder that can measure in 1 cm³ increments. It'd be no good trying with one that only measures 10 cm³ increments — it wouldn't be sensitive enough. And if you need to measure small changes in pH, a pH meter (which can measure pH to several decimal places) would be more sensitive than indicator paper.
   - The equipment and apparatus you choose has to be appropriate for the function it needs to perform. E.g. if you're trying to separate photosynthetic pigments using thin layer chromatography (see page 176), you need to use the right solvent otherwise they won't separate.
   - The technique you use has to be the most appropriate one for your experiment. E.g. if you're growing a culture of microorganisms, you need to use aseptic techniques to prevent contamination (see p. 234).

Examiners love getting you to **suggest improvements** to **methods** — for example, how a method could be improved to make the results more precise. So make sure you really know how to **design** a **good experiment**.

Planning an Experiment

Use **Apparatus** and **Techniques Correctly** to Obtain **Precise Results**

1) Once you've chosen the best apparatus and techniques to use in your experiment, you need to make sure you can **use them correctly**. In the exams, you could be asked about a **whole range** of different apparatus and techniques — make sure you know how to use all the ones you've come across in class. Here are just a few examples:

- **Pipettes** — Graduated pipettes have a **scale** so you can measure specific volumes — make sure you read the **meniscus** at **eye level**.

- **Water baths** — Make sure you **allow time** for water baths to **heat up** before starting your experiment. Don't forget that your **solutions** will need **time** to get to the **same temperature** as the water before you start the experiment too.

- **Data logger** — Decide **what** you are **measuring** and what **type** of **data logger** you will need, e.g. temperature, pH. Connect an **external sensor** to the data logger if you need to. Decide **how often** you want the data logger to take readings depending on the **length** of the **process** that you are measuring.

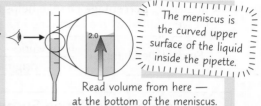

The meniscus is the curved upper surface of the liquid inside the pipette.

Read volume from here — at the bottom of the meniscus.

2) Make sure you're measuring things using **appropriate units**. E.g. if you're measuring time, it might be better to use seconds rather than minutes — when you come to processing your results, it'll be easier to work with a result of 73 seconds than a result of 1.217 minutes. Also, make sure you **record** your **units properly**, e.g. if you're measuring the length of something and accidently write cm instead of mm, any **calculations** you do will be **affected** and your **conclusions** may be **wrong**.

3) Make sure you **perform** all **techniques carefully** and that any **apparatus** is **set up correctly** — this will help to **minimise errors** which would affect your results.

Risk Assessments Help You to **Work Safely**

1) When you're planning an experiment, you need to carry out a **risk assessment**. To do this, you need to identify:
   - All the **dangers** in the experiment, e.g. any hazardous chemicals, microorganisms or naked flames.
   - **Who** is at **risk** from these dangers.
   - What can be done to **reduce** the **risk**, such as wearing goggles or gloves or working in a fume cupboard.

2) You also need to consider any **ethical issues** in your experiment. For example, if you're using **living animals** (e.g. insects) you must treat them with **respect**. This means **handling them carefully** and keeping them away from **harmful chemicals**, **extreme heat sources** and other things that might cause them **physical discomfort**.

Record Your **Data** in a **Table**

It's a good idea to draw a table to **record** the **results** of your experiment in.

1) When you draw a table, make sure you **include** enough **rows** and **columns** to **record all of the data** you need to. You might also need to include a column for **processing** your data (e.g. working out an average).

2) Make sure each **column** has a **heading** so you know what's going to be recorded where.

3) The **units** should be in the **column** heading, not the table itself.

Farm	Length of hedgerows (km)	Number of species
1	49	21
2	90	28
3	155	30

data · heading · units · column · row

Watch Out for **Anomalous Results**

Doing repeats makes it easier to spot anomalous results.

When you look at all the **data** in your **table**, you may notice that you have a result that **doesn't seem to fit in** with the rest at all. These results are called **anomalous results**. You should **investigate** anomalous results — if you can work out what happened (e.g. you measured something totally wrong) you can **ignore** them when **processing** your results. However, you can't just ignore a result because you don't like the look of it.

My best apparatus is the pommel horse...

It's not really, I just like the word pommel. Scientists are rightfully fussy about methods and equipment — I mean if you're going to bother doing an experiment, you should at least make sure it's going to give you results you can trust.

Processing and Presenting Data

Once you've collected your data you really need to do something with it so you can use it....

Processing the Data Helps You to Interpret it

You Need to be Able to Calculate Percentage Change

Calculating **percentage change** helps to **quantify** how much something has changed, e.g. the percentage of plants that were killed with a herbicide in a particular year compared to the previous year. To **calculate** it you use:

$$\text{Percentage change} = \frac{\text{final value} - \text{original value}}{\text{original value}} \times 100$$

A **positive** value is a percentage **increase** and a **negative** value is a percentage **decrease**.

Averages and the Range Summarise Your Data

When you've done **repeats** of an experiment you should always calculate the **mean**. To do this **add together** all the data values and **divide** by the **total** number of values in the sample.

You could also be asked to calculate the median (the middle number when you put all your data in numerical order) or the mode (the number that appears most often in a set of data).

Test tube	Repeat (g) 1	Repeat (g) 2	Repeat (g) 3	Mean (g)	Range (g)
A	28	37	32	(28 + 37 + 32) ÷ 3 = 32.3	37 − 28 = 9
B	47	51	60	(47 + 51 + 60) ÷ 3 = 52.7	60 − 47 = 13
C	68	70	70	(68 + 70 + 70) ÷ 3 = 69.3	70 − 68 = 2

You might also need to calculate the **range** (how **spread out** the data is). To do this find the **largest** data value and **subtract** the **smallest** data value from it.

Standard deviation can be more useful than the **range** because it tells you how **values** are spread about the **mean** rather than just the **total spread** of data. A **small standard deviation** means the repeated results are all **close** to the mean — so the results are all **similar**, i.e. **precise**. There's more on standard deviation on pages 123-124.

You Need to be Able to Use Statistical Tests to Analyse Data

Examples:

1) The **Student's t-test** (see page 161). You can use the Student's t-test when you have two sets of **data** that you want to **compare**. It tests whether there is a **significant difference** in the **means** of the two data sets. The value obtained is compared to a **critical value**, which helps you decide how likely it is that the results or 'differences in the means' were **due to chance**. If the value obtained from the t-test is **greater than** the critical value at a **probability (P value)** of **5% or less** (≤ 0.05), then you can be 95% confident that the difference is significant and not due to chance. This is called a **95% confidence limit** — which is good enough for most biologists to **reject** the **null hypothesis**. A null hypothesis is a special type of hypothesis used with statistical tests. It states that there's no significant difference between the things you're measuring.

2) The **Chi-squared test** (see page 206-207). You can use the Chi-squared test when you have **categorical** (grouped) **data** and you want to compare whether your **observed results** are **statistically different** from your **expected results**. You compare your result to a **critical value** — if it's **larger** than the critical value at **P = 0.05**, you can be **95%** certain the difference is significant.

Watch Out For Significant Figures...

You need to be familiar with the symbols < (less than), > (more than), << (much less than) and >> (much greater than).

When you're processing your data you may well want to round any **really long numbers** to a certain number of **significant figures**. E.g. **0.6878976** rounds to **0.69** to **2 s.f.**. When you're doing **calculations** using numbers given to a certain number of significant figures, you should always give your **answer** to the **lowest number** of significant figures that was used in the calculation. For example:

$$1.2 \div 1.85 = 0.648648648... \quad = 0.65$$

2 s.f. 3 s.f. Answer should be rounded to 2 s.f.

Round the last digit up to 5.

...and Standard Form

When you're processing data you might also want to change **very big** or **very small numbers** that have **lots of zeros** into something more manageable — this is called **standard form**. E.g. 1 000 000 can be written 1×10^6 and 0.017 can be written 1.7×10^{-2}. To do this you just need to **move the decimal point** left or right. The number of places the decimal point moves is then represented by a **power of 10** — this is positive for big numbers, and negative for numbers smaller than 1. For example:

$16\,500 = 1.65 \times 10^4$ — *The decimal point has moved four places to the left, so the power of 10 is +4.*

$0.000362 = 3.62 \times 10^{-4}$ — *The decimal point has moved four places to the right, so the power of 10 is −4.*

Processing and Presenting Data

Choose a Suitable **Graph** or **Chart** to Present Your Data

Graphs and charts are a great way of **presenting data** — they can make results much **easier to interpret**.

1) When you have **qualitative** data (non-numerical data, e.g. blood group) or **discrete** data (numerical data that can only take certain values in a range, e.g. shoe size) you can use **bar charts** or **pie charts**.

2) When you have **continuous** data (data that can take any value in a range, e.g. height or weight) you can use **histograms** or **line graphs.**

Make sure that you know how to construct one of these graphs.

3) When you want to plot **one variable against the other** you can use a **scatter graph.**

You Need to be Able to **Use Logarithms**

1) It's tricky to plot graphs with **very small** and **very large** numbers (e.g. both 0.1 and 1000) on the **same axis**.

2) We can make it easier by converting values to their **logarithms** and plotting them on a **logarithmic scale** (e.g. a $\log_{10}$ scale).

You need to be able to read off a logarithmic scale on a graph.

3) On a **$\log_{10}$ scale**, each value is **ten times larger** than the value before. This means the numbers 1, 2, 3 and 4 on a **$\log_{10}$ scale** represent 10, 100, 1000 and 10 000 on a **linear (normal) scale.**

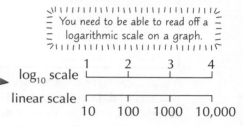

4) To calculate logarithms, you need to use the **log button** on your calculator. On most calculators 'log' will stand for $\log_{10}$, but different calculators work differently, so make sure you know how to use yours.

Find the **Rate** By Finding the **Gradient**

Rate is a **measure** of how much something is **changing over time**. Calculating a rate can be useful when analysing your data, e.g. you might want to the find the **rate of a reaction**. Rates are easy to work out from a graph:

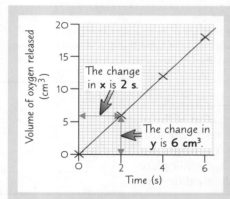

For a **linear** graph you can calculate the **rate** by finding the **gradient of the line**:

$$\text{Gradient} = \frac{\text{Change in Y}}{\text{Change in X}}$$

So in this **example**:

$$\text{rate} = \frac{6 \text{ cm}^3}{2 \text{ s}} = 3 \text{ cm}^3 \text{ s}^{-1}$$

cm³ s⁻¹ means the same as cm³/s (centimetres cubed per second)

The **equation** of a **straight line** can always be written in the form **y = mx + c**, where **m** is the **gradient** and **c** is the **y-intercept** (this is the **value of y** when the line crosses the **y-axis**). In this example, the equation of the line is **y = 3x + 0** (or just **y = 3x**). Knowing the equation of the line allows you to estimate results not plotted on the graph. E.g. in this case, when x (the time) is **20 s**, y (the volume of oxygen released) will be 3x = 3 × 20 = **60 cm³**.

For a **curved** (non-linear) graph you can find the **rate** by drawing a **tangent**:

1) Position a ruler on the graph at the **point** where you want to know the **rate**.

2) **Angle** the **ruler** so there is **equal space** between the **ruler** and the **curve** on **either** side of the point.

3) **Draw a line** along the ruler to make the tangent.
   Extend the line right across the graph — it'll help to make your **gradient** **calculation easier** as you'll have **more points** to choose from.

4) **Calculate** the **gradient** of the **tangent** to find the **rate**.

Gradient = 55 m² ÷ 4.4 years = 12.5 m² year⁻¹

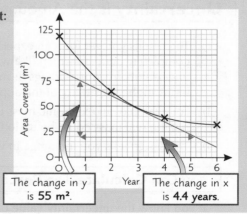

*The change in y is **55 m²**.*   *Year*   *The change in x is **4.4 years**.*

Significant figures — a result of far too many cream cakes...

Graphs and charts are great for seeing what's going on in your results. Don't get confused if you need to find the rate of something from a graph — you just have to find the gradient of the line. And if you haven't got a straight line, draw one.

Drawing Conclusions and Evaluating

So once you've processed your data you'll want to see what conclusions you can come to. Evaluations are important too so you can assess your experiment and think about how you could do things differently next time.

You Need to **Draw Conclusions** From Your **Data**

1) Conclusions need to be **valid**. A conclusion can only be considered as valid if it answers the original question (see page 4).

2) You can often draw conclusions by looking at the relationship (**correlation**) between two variables:

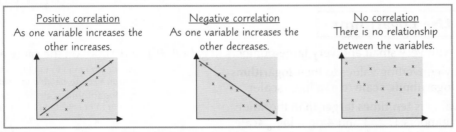

Positive correlation
As one variable increases the other increases.

Negative correlation
As one variable increases the other decreases.

No correlation
There is no relationship between the variables.

There is no correlation between the colour of your tights and the proportion of your life you spend upside down.

3) A statistical test called **Spearman's rank correlation coefficient** allows you to work out the **degree** to which **two** sets of **data** are **correlated**. It is given as value between 1 and –1. A value of 1 indicates a **strong positive correlation**, 0 means there is **no correlation** and –1 is a **strong negative correlation**. You can then compare your result to a critical value to find out whether or not the correlation is significant.

4) You have to be very **careful** when **drawing conclusions** from data like this because a **correlation** between two variables **doesn't** always mean that a **change** in one variable **causes** a **change** in the other (the correlation could be due to **chance** or there could be a **third variable** having an effect).

5) If there's a relationship between two variables and a change in one variable **does** cause a change in the other it's called a **causal relationship**.

6) It can be **concluded** that a **correlation** is a **causal relationship** if every other variable that could possibly affect the result is **controlled**.

   In reality this is very hard to do — correlations are generally accepted to be causal relationships if lots of studies have found the same thing, and scientists have figured out exactly how one factor causes the other.

7) When you're making a conclusion you **can't** make broad **generalisations** from data — you have to be very specific. You can only **conclude** what the results show and **no more**.

> **Example**
>
> The graph shows the results from a study into the effect of concentration of the plant growth hormone gibberellin on the height of Plant Species A. The only conclusion you can draw is that as the concentration of gibberellin increases, the height of Plant Species A increases. You can't conclude that this is true for any other plant hormone or any other plant species — the results could be completely different.
>
> *Height of Plant Species A*
>
> *Concentration of gibberellin*

Uncertainty is the Amount of **Error** Your **Measurements** Might Have

1) The results you get from an experiment won't be completely perfect — there'll always be a **degree of uncertainty** in your readings or measurements due to limits in the **sensitivity** of the apparatus you're using.

   A reading is when you make a judgement about one value, e.g. when you read a value off a mass balance. A measurement is when you judge two values and find the difference, e.g. when you measure length with a ruler.

2) For example, an electronic mass balance might measure to the **nearest 0.01 g**, but the real mass could be up to **0.005 g smaller or larger**. It has an **uncertainty value of ± 0.005 g**.

3) The ± sign tells you the **range** in which the **true value** lies. The range is called the **margin of error**.

You Can **Calculate** The **Percentage Error** of Your **Measurements**

If you know the **uncertainty value** of your measurements, you can calculate the **percentage error** using this formula:

$$\text{percentage error} = \frac{\text{uncertainty}}{\text{reading}} \times 100$$

Example

50 cm³ of HCl is measured with an uncertainty value of ± 0.05 cm³.

$$\text{percentage error} = \frac{0.05}{50} \times 100 = \mathbf{0.1\%}$$

Drawing Conclusions and Evaluating

You Can **Minimise** the **Errors** in Your **Measurements**

1) One obvious way to **reduce errors** in your measurements is to buy the most **sensitive equipment** available. In real life there's not much you can do about this one — you're stuck with whatever your school or college has got. But there are other ways to **lower the uncertainty** in experiments.

2) For example, you can plan your experiment so you **measure** a **greater amount** of something:

> If you use a **500 cm³** cylinder that goes up in **5 cm³** increments, each reading has an uncertainty of ± **2.5 cm³**.
>
> So using a 500 cm³ cylinder to measure **100 cm³** of liquid will give you a percentage error of:
>
> But if you measure **200 cm³** in the same cylinder, the percentage error is:
>
> $$\frac{2.5}{100} \times 100 = \mathbf{2.5\%}$$
>
> $$\frac{2.5}{200} \times 100 = \mathbf{1.25\%}$$
>
> Hey presto — you've just **halved** the uncertainty.

You Need to **Sum Up** Your Experiment in an **Evaluation**

1) In an **evaluation** you need to assess the following things about your **experiment** and the **data** you gathered:
   - **Repeatability**: Did you take enough repeat readings or measurements? Would you do more repeats if you were to do the experiment again? Do you think you'd get similar data if you did the experiment again?
   - **Reproducibility**: Have you compared your results with other people's results? Were your results similar? Could other scientists gain data showing the same relationships that are shown in your data?
   - **Validity**: Does your data answer the question you set out to investigate?

2) Make sure you **evaluate** your **method**. Is there anything you could have done to make your results more **precise** or **accurate**? Were there any **limitations** in your method, e.g. should you have taken measurements more **frequently**? Were there any **sources** of **error** in your experiment? Could you have used more sensitive **apparatus** or **equipment**? Think about how you could **refine** and **improve** your experiment if you did it again.

3) Once you've thought about these points you can decide how much **confidence** you have in your **conclusion**. For example, if your results are **repeatable**, **reproducible** and **valid** and they back up your conclusion then you can have a **high degree** of **confidence** in your conclusion.

Warm-Up Questions

Q1 Why is it important to control all the variables in an experiment?
Q2 What is a negative control?
Q3 Name one type of graph you could use to plot continuous data.

Exam Question

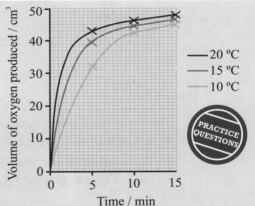

Q1 An experiment was conducted to investigate the effect of temperature on the rate of photosynthesis. The rate of photosynthesis in Canadian pondweed was measured at three different temperatures by measuring the volume of oxygen produced. All other variables were kept constant. The results are shown in the graph above.

a) Give one variable that should have been controlled in this experiment and explain how you would control it. [1 mark]

b) Calculate the rate of photosynthesis at 10 °C at 2.5 minutes. Give your answer in cm³ s⁻¹. [2 marks]

c) The mean rate of photosynthesis between 0 and 5 minutes at 15 °C was 0.13 cm³ s⁻¹. At 20 °C it was 0.14 cm³ s⁻¹. What statistical test would you use to determine whether these results are statistically significant? Explain your answer. [2 marks]

d) The volume of oxygen produced was measured with a measuring cylinder that has an uncertainty of ± 1 cm³.
   i) Calculate the percentage error for the reading at 20 °C at 15 minutes. [1 mark]
   ii) Suggest one way to reduce this error. [1 mark]

e) What conclusions can be drawn from the results of the experiment? [2 marks]

Correlation Street — my favourite programme...

Don't ever, ever assume that correlation means cause. There, I've told you again. No excuses now. A good evaluation is a sign that you really understand what makes a good experiment, so make sure your evaluation-writing-skills are top notch.

Eukaryotic Cells and Organelles

Ah, cells. Where would we be without them? There are two types of cell — prokaryotic and eukaryotic. This topic is about eukaryotic cells and their organelles (all the tiny bits and bobs that you can only see in detail with a fancy microscope)...

Organisms can be **Prokaryotes** or **Eukaryotes**

1) Prokaryotic organisms are **prokaryotic cells** (i.e. they're single-celled organisms) and eukaryotic organisms are made up of **eukaryotic cells**.

2) Both types of cells contain **organelles**. Organelles are **parts** of cells — each one has a **specific function**.

1) Eukaryotic cells are **complex** and include all **animal** and **plant cells**.

2) Prokaryotic cells are **smaller** and **simpler**, e.g. bacteria. See page 15 for more.

Plant and **Animal** Cells are Both **Eukaryotic**

Eukaryotic cells are generally a **bit more complicated** than prokaryotic cells. You've probably been looking at **animal** and **plant cell** diagrams for years, so hopefully you'll be familiar with some of the bits and pieces...

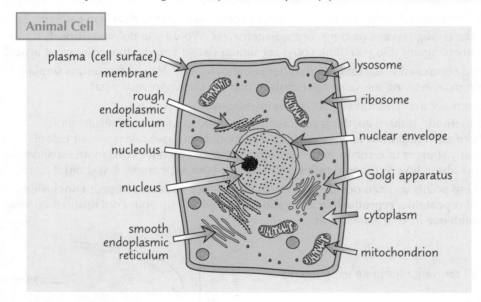

Animal Cell

plasma (cell surface) membrane
rough endoplasmic reticulum
nucleolus
nucleus
smooth endoplasmic reticulum

lysosome
ribosome
nuclear envelope
Golgi apparatus
cytoplasm
mitochondrion

You're expected to be able to interpret photos of cells and their organelles, taken through different types of microscope — so make sure you learn to recognise all the structures on pages 11-13.

Plant Cell

Plant cells have all the **same organelles** as animal cells, but with a few **added extras**:

• a **cell wall** with **plasmodesmata** ('channels' for exchanging substances with adjacent cells),

• a **vacuole** (compartment that contains cell sap),

• and of course good old **chloroplasts**.

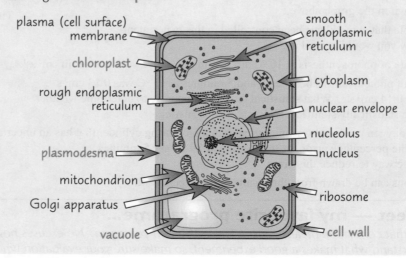

plasma (cell surface) membrane
chloroplast
rough endoplasmic reticulum
plasmodesma
mitochondrion
Golgi apparatus
vacuole

smooth endoplasmic reticulum
cytoplasm
nuclear envelope
nucleolus
nucleus
ribosome
cell wall

Eukaryotic Cells and Organelles

Different Organelles have Different Functions

This giant table contains a big list of organelles — you need to know the **structure** and **function** of them all. Sorry. Most organelles are surrounded by **membranes**, which sometimes causes confusion — don't make the mistake of thinking that a diagram of an organelle is a diagram of a whole cell. They're not cells — they're **parts of** cells.

ORGANELLE	DIAGRAM	DESCRIPTION	FUNCTION
Plasma (cell surface) membrane	plasma membrane, cytoplasm	The membrane found on the **surface** of **animal cells** and just inside the cell wall of **plant cells** and **prokaryotic cells**. It's made mainly of **lipids** and **protein**.	**Regulates the movement** of substances into and out of the cell. It also has **receptor molecules** on it, which allow it to respond to chemicals like hormones.
Cell wall	plasma membrane, cell wall, cytoplasm	A rigid structure that surrounds **plant cells**. It's made mainly of the carbohydrate **cellulose**.	**Supports** plant cells.
Nucleus	nuclear envelope, nucleolus, nuclear pore, chromatin	A large organelle surrounded by a **nuclear envelope** (double membrane), which contains many **pores**. The nucleus contains **chromatin** (which is made from **DNA** and proteins) and a structure called the **nucleolus**.	The nucleus **controls the cell's activities** (by controlling the transcription of DNA — see page 40). **DNA** contains instructions to make proteins — see page 38. The **pores** allow substances (e.g. RNA) to move between the nucleus and the cytoplasm. The **nucleolus** makes **ribosomes** (see below).
Lysosome		A **round organelle** surrounded by a **membrane**, with no clear internal structure.	Contains **digestive enzymes**. These are kept separate from the cytoplasm by the surrounding membrane, and can be used to **digest invading cells** or to **break down** worn out components of the cell.
Ribosome	small subunit, large subunit	A **very small organelle** that either **floats free** in the cytoplasm or is attached to the **rough endoplasmic reticulum**. It's made up of **proteins** and RNA (see page 34). It's **not** surrounded by a membrane.	The **site where proteins** are made.

Eukaryotic Cells and Organelles

ORGANELLE	DIAGRAM	DESCRIPTION	FUNCTION
Rough Endoplasmic Reticulum (RER)	*ribosome* *fluid*	A system of membranes enclosing a fluid-filled space. The surface is **covered with ribosomes**.	**Folds** and **processes proteins** that have been made at the ribosomes.
Smooth Endoplasmic Reticulum (SER)		Similar to rough endoplasmic reticulum, but with no **ribosomes**.	**Synthesises** and **processes lipids**.
Vesicle	*cell's plasma membrane* *vesicle*	A small **fluid-filled sac** in the cytoplasm, surrounded by a membrane.	**Transports substances** in and out of the cell (via the plasma membrane) and between organelles. Some are formed by the Golgi apparatus or the endoplasmic reticulum, while others are formed at the cell surface.
Golgi Apparatus	*vesicle*	A group of fluid-filled, membrane-bound, **flattened sacs**. Vesicles are often seen at the edges of the sacs.	It **processes** and **packages** new lipids and proteins. It also **makes lysosomes**.
Mitochondrion	*outer membrane* *inner membrane* *crista* *matrix*	They're usually oval-shaped. They have a **double membrane** — the inner one is folded to form structures called **cristae**. Inside is the **matrix**, which contains enzymes involved in respiration.	The **site of aerobic respiration**, where **ATP** is produced. They're found in large numbers in cells that are very **active** and require a lot of **energy**.
Chloroplast	*stroma* *two membranes* *granum (plural = grana)* *lamella (plural = lamellae)*	A small, **flattened** structure found in **plant cells**. It's surrounded by a **double membrane**, and also has membranes inside called **thylakoid membranes**. These membranes are stacked up in some parts of the chloroplast to form **grana**. Grana are linked together by lamellae — thin, flat pieces of thylakoid membrane.	The **site** where **photosynthesis** takes place. Some parts of photosynthesis happen in the **grana**, and other parts happen in the **stroma** (a thick fluid found in chloroplasts).

Eukaryotic Cells and Organelles

ORGANELLE	DIAGRAM	DESCRIPTION	FUNCTION
Centriole	microtubule	Small, **hollow cylinders**, made of **microtubules** (tiny protein cylinders). Found in animal cells, but only some plant cells.	Involved with the **separation of chromosomes** during cell division (see p. 60-62).
Cilia	side cross-section	Small, **hair-like structures** found on the surface membrane of some **animal cells**. In cross-section, they have an outer membrane and a ring of nine pairs of **protein microtubules** inside, with two microtubules in the middle.	The microtubules allow the cilia to **move**. This movement is used by the cell to **move substances along the cell surface**. *This is known as the '9 + 2' formation.*
Flagellum		Flagella on eukaryotic cells are **like cilia** but longer. They **stick out** from the cell surface and are surrounded by the plasma membrane. Inside they're like cilia too — two **microtubules** in the centre and nine pairs around the edge.	The microtubules **contract** to make the flagellum **move**. Flagella are used like **outboard motors** to propel cells forward (e.g. when a **sperm cell** swims).

Warm-Up Questions

Q1 How does the structure of rough endoplasmic reticulum differ from that of smooth endoplasmic reticulum?

Q2 Describe the function of vesicles.

Q3 What is the function of chloroplasts?

Q4 What is the function of the centrioles?

PRACTICE QUESTIONS

Exam Questions

Q1 Which of the following describes a structure found in plant cells but not in animal cells?

    A A system of membranes enclosing a fluid-filled space.

    B A flattened structure surrounded by a double membrane. Internal membranes are stacked up in places to form grana.

    C A small organelle consisting of two subunits. It is not surrounded by a membrane.

    D A round, membrane-bound organelle containing digestive enzymes.   [1 mark]

Q2 a) Identify these two organelles from their descriptions as seen in an electron micrograph.

    i) An oval-shaped organelle surrounded by a double membrane. The inner membrane is folded and projects into the inner space, which is filled with a grainy material.   [1 mark]

    ii) A collection of flattened membrane 'sacs' arranged roughly parallel to one another. Small, circular structures are seen at the edges of these 'sacs'.   [1 mark]

  b) State the function of the two organelles that you have identified.   [2 marks]

That's enough talk of fluid-filled sacs for my liking. Scientists eh...

'Organelle' is a very pretty-sounding name for all those blobs. Actually, under a microscope some of them are really quite fetching — well I think so anyway, but then my mate finds sheep fetching, so there's no accounting for taste. Anyway, you need to know the names and functions of all the organelles and also what they look like.

Organelles Working Together

After that endless list of organelles, you might need a few minutes to regain consciousness... Then you can read this lovely page about how they work together to produce proteins. And there's some stuff on cytoskeletons too...

Organelles are Involved in Protein Production

1) Proteins are made at the **ribosomes**.

2) The ribosomes on the **rough endoplasmic reticulum (ER)** make proteins that are **excreted** or attached to the **cell membrane**. The free ribosomes in the **cytoplasm** make proteins that **stay in the cytoplasm**.

3) New proteins produced at the rough ER are **folded** and **processed** (e.g. sugar chains are added) in the rough ER.

4) Then they're **transported** from the ER to the **Golgi apparatus** in vesicles.

5) At the Golgi apparatus, the proteins may undergo **further processing** (e.g. sugar chains are trimmed or more are added).

6) The proteins enter more **vesicles** to be transported around the cell. E.g. glycoproteins (found in **mucus**) move to the cell surface and are **secreted**.

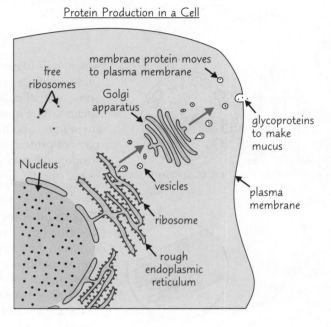

Protein Production in a Cell

The Cytoskeleton has Several Functions

1) The organelles in cells are surrounded by the **cytoplasm**. The cytoplasm is more than just a solution of chemicals though — it's got a **network of protein threads** running through it. These protein threads are called the **cytoskeleton**.

2) In eukaryotic cells the protein threads are arranged as **microfilaments** (small solid strands) and **microtubules** (tiny protein cylinders).

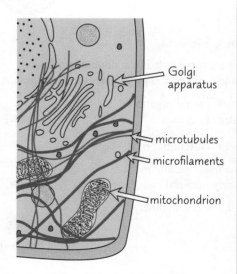

The cytoskeleton has **four main functions**:

1) The microtubules and microfilaments **support** the cell's organelles, keeping them **in position**.

2) They also help to **strengthen** the cell and **maintain its shape**.

3) As well as this, they're responsible for the **movement of materials** within the cell. For example, the movement of **chromosomes** when they separate during cell division depends on contraction of microtubules in the spindle (see pages 60-62 for more on cell division).

4) The proteins of the cytoskeleton can also cause the cell to **move**. For example, the movement of **cilia** and **flagella** is caused by the cytoskeletal protein filaments that run through them. So in the case of single cells that have a flagellum (e.g. sperm cells), the cytoskeleton propels the **whole cell**.

The cytoskeleton is dynamic (constantly changing), which allows it to respond to changes in the cell and carry out its functions.

The assembly of microtubules and microfilaments, and the movement of materials along them, requires energy from respiration. So microtubules and microfilaments can be prevented from functioning using respiratory inhibitors.

Module 2: Section 1 — Cell Structure

Prokaryotic Cells

Prokaryotes are a Different Kind of Cell

You need to be able to compare and contrast prokaryotic and eukaryotic cells. This big orange table should help...

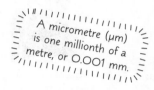

A micrometre (µm) is one millionth of a metre, or 0.001 mm.

PROKARYOTES	EUKARYOTES
Extremely small cells (less than 2 µm diameter)	Larger cells (about 10-100 µm diameter)
DNA is circular	DNA is linear
No nucleus — DNA free in cytoplasm	Nucleus present — DNA is inside nucleus
Cell wall made of a polysaccharide, but not cellulose or chitin	No cell wall (in animals), cellulose cell wall (in plants) or chitin cell wall (in fungi)
Few organelles and no membrane-bound organelles, e.g. no mitochondria	Many organelles — mitochondria and other membrane-bound organelles present
Flagella (when present) made of the protein flagellin, arranged in a helix	Flagella (when present) made of microtubule proteins arranged in a '9 + 2' formation
Small ribosomes	Larger ribosomes
Example: *E. coli* bacterium	**Example:** Human liver cell

Bacterial Cells are Prokaryotic

1) Prokaryotes like bacteria are roughly a tenth the size of eukaryotic cells.

2) This means that normal microscopes aren't really powerful enough to look at their internal structure.

3) The diagram shows a bacterial cell as seen under an electron microscope (see page 17).

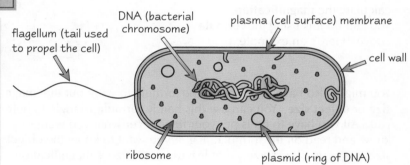

DNA (bacterial chromosome)
flagellum (tail used to propel the cell)
plasma (cell surface) membrane
cell wall
ribosome
plasmid (ring of DNA)

Warm-Up Questions

Q1 An unidentified cell is found to contain mitochondria. Is it prokaryotic or eukaryotic?

Q2 How is a prokaryotic cell wall different to a eukaryotic cell wall?

PRACTICE QUESTIONS

Exam Questions

Q1 Some mucus-secreting cells were immersed in a solution of radioactive amino acids.
Every five seconds, some of the cells were removed and their organelles were separated and analysed.
The radioactivity in the different organelles was measured for each five second interval.

When answering the first two questions below, use organelles from this list —
Golgi apparatus, ribosomes, rough endoplasmic reticulum, vesicles.

a) In which of these organelles would you expect radioactivity to appear first? Explain your answer. [2 marks]

b) After 5 minutes, the Golgi apparatus had become radioactive.
Which other organelle(s) would be radioactive by this time? [2 marks]

c) The researchers were particularly interested in the cells' vesicles. What is the function of vesicles? [1 mark]

Q2 Give three functions of a cell's cytoskeleton. [3 marks]

A cell without a nucleus — it's like a Yorkshire pud without gravy...

Prokaryotes are way, way older than eukaryotes. In fact, most cellular biologists think that mitochondria and chloroplasts are remnants of ancient prokaryotes that lived inside the first eukaryotes and eventually just became part of them. Mad.

Studying Cells — How Microscopes Work

If you were born over a century ago then you wouldn't have had to learn all this stuff about organelles because people wouldn't have known anything about them. But then better microscopes were invented and here we are.

Magnification is Size, Resolution is Detail

We all know that microscopes produce a **magnified image** of a sample, but **resolution** is just as important...

1) MAGNIFICATION is how much **bigger** the image is than the specimen (the sample you're looking at). It's calculated using this formula:

$$\text{magnification} = \frac{\text{image size}}{\text{object size}}$$

2) RESOLUTION is how **detailed** the image is. More specifically, it's how well a microscope **distinguishes** between **two points** that are **close together**. If a microscope lens can't separate two objects, then increasing the magnification won't help.

Georgina didn't believe in the need for microscopes — she had her trusty varifocals.

You Need to be Able to **Calculate** the **Magnification** of an Image

In the exam, you might be told the actual and magnified size of an object and then be asked to calculate the **magnification**. You can do this using the **formula** above. Here's an example...

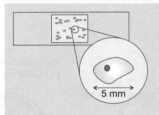

5 mm

You have a magnified image that's 5 mm wide. Your specimen is 50 µm wide. First, get everything into the same units:
1 mm = 1000 µm
so 50 µm ÷ 1000 = 0.05 mm
Now calculate the magnification:
5 ÷ 0.05 = **× 100**

÷ 1000
µm → mm
× 1000

You might also have to rearrange the formula to work out the **image size** or **object size**. You can use this handy **formula triangle** to help you. All you have to do is put your finger over what you want to know and read off the formula. E.g. if you want to know the object size, cover up object size. That leaves image size ÷ magnification.

image size
magnification × object size

A micrometre (µm) is three orders of magnitude smaller than a millimetre (1 µm = 0.001 mm). To convert from µm to mm, divide by 1000.

You Need to Know About **Three Types** of **Microscope**

1) Light microscopes

1) **Light microscopes** use light (no surprises there).
2) They have a **lower resolution** than electron microscopes — they have a maximum resolution of about **0.2 micrometres** (µm). So they're usually used to look at **whole cells** or **tissues**.
3) The maximum useful **magnification** of a light microscope is about **× 1500**.

2) Laser Scanning Confocal Microscopes (a special type of light microscope)

1) **Laser Scanning Confocal Microscopes** use **laser beams** (intense beams of light) to **scan** a specimen, which is usually tagged with a **fluorescent** dye.
2) The laser causes the dye to **fluoresce** — **give off light**. This light is then **focused** through a **pinhole** onto a **detector**. The detector is hooked up to a computer, which generates an image. The image can be **3D**.
3) The pinhole means that any **out-of-focus light** is **blocked**, so these microscopes produce a much **clearer image** than a normal light microscope.
4) They can be used to look at objects at **different depths** in **thick specimens**.

This is not how a Laser Scanning Confocal Microscope works. Sadly.

Studying Cells — How Microscopes Work

3) Electron microscopes

Electron microscopes use electrons instead of light to form an image. They have a higher resolution than light microscopes so give more detailed images. There are two kinds of electron microscope:

1) Transmission electron microscope (TEM) — use electromagnets to focus a beam of electrons, which is then transmitted through the specimen. Denser parts of the specimen absorb more electrons, which makes them look darker on the image you end up with. TEMs are good because they provide high resolution images (so they can be used to look at a range of organelles) but they can only be used on thin specimens. A TEM image of a mitochondrion is shown above on the right.

2) Scanning electron microscope (SEM) — scan a beam of electrons across the specimen. This knocks off electrons from the specimen, which are gathered in a cathode ray tube to form an image. The images produced show the surface of the specimen and can be 3D. But they give lower resolution images than TEMs. Here's an SEM image of a mitochondrion.

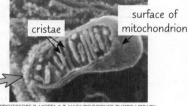

TEM image of a mitochondrion

cristae

matrix

K.R. PORTER/SCIENCE PHOTO LIBRARY

SEM image of a mitochondrion

surface of mitochondrion

cristae

PROFESSORS P. MOTTA & T. NAGURO/SCIENCE PHOTO LIBRARY

The angle at which specimens are cut can affect how they appear (e.g. a mitochondrion cut at a different angle might appear circular).

You Need to be Able to Compare Magnification and Resolution

There are quite a lot of facts and figures about microscopes here. You need to know about the magnification and resolution of light microscopes and both types of electron microscope. So I've put all the important numbers in this table 'cos I'm nice like that.

	light microscope	TEM	SEM
maximum resolution	0.2 µm	0.0002 µm	0.002 µm
maximum magnification	× 1500	can be more than × 1 000 000	usually less than × 500 000

TEMs have the highest resolution because they can distinguish between the smallest objects (or objects that are only 0.0002 µm apart).

Warm-Up Questions

Q1 What is the formula for calculating the magnification of an image?

Q2 What is meant by a microscope's resolution?

Q3 Which has a higher resolution: a light microscope, TEM or SEM?

PRACTICE QUESTIONS

Exam Questions

Q1 An insect is 0.5 mm long. In a book, a picture of the insect is 8 cm long. Calculate the magnification of the image. [2 marks]

Q2 A light micrograph shows a human cheek cell at × 100 magnification. The actual diameter of the cell is 59 µm. What is the diameter of the cell in the image? [2 marks]

Q3 The table shows the dimensions of some different organelles found in animal cells.

a) Name those organelles in the table that would be visible using a good quality light microscope. Explain your answer. [3 marks]

b) Which organelles would be visible using an SEM? Explain your answer. [2 marks]

organelle	diameter / µm
lysosome	0.1
mitochondrion	2
nucleus	5
ribosome	0.02
vesicle	0.05

A light microscope is better than a heavy one — for your back anyway...

OK, there's quite a bit of info on these pages, but the whole magnification thing isn't all that bad once you've given it a go. Make sure you can define resolution — that's a bit trickier. You also need to have a good grasp of the images produced by each of the different types of microscope — light, Laser Scanning Confocal, TEM and SEM. Phew.

Studying Cells — Using Microscopes

The thing about Biology is — it's a practical subject. Not only do you need to know how microscopes work in theory, you also have to know how to actually use one. Time to roll up your sleeves and get stuck in...

You Need to **Stain** Your **Samples**

1) In light microscopes and TEMs, the beam of light (or electrons) **passes through the object** being viewed. An image is produced because some parts of the object **absorb more light** (or electrons) than others.

2) Sometimes the object being viewed is completely **transparent**. This makes the whole thing look **white** because the light rays (or electrons) just pass **straight through**.

3) To get round this, the object can be **stained**:

Staining samples for light microscopes:

• For the light microscope, this means using some kind of **dye**. Common stains include **methylene blue** and **eosin**.

• The stain is taken up by some parts of the object more than others — the **contrast** makes the different parts show up.

• **Different stains** are used to make **different things** show up. For example, **eosin** is used to stain **cell cytoplasms**. **Methylene blue** stains **DNA**.

• **More than one** stain can be used at once.

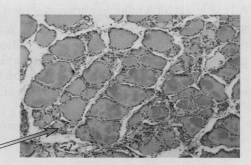

An eosin stained specimen, as seen through a light microscope.

Staining samples for electron microscopes:

For the electron microscope, objects are dipped in a solution of **heavy metals** (like **lead**). The metal ions scatter the electrons, again creating **contrast** — some parts of the object show up **darker** than others.

Electron micrograph images are always black and white even when stained, but colour can be added artificially after the image has been made.

You Need to Know How to **Prepare** a **Microscope Slide**

1) If you want to look at a specimen under a **light microscope**, you need to stick it on a **slide** first.

2) A slide is a strip of **clear glass** or **plastic**. Slides are usually **flat**, but some of them have a small **dip** or **well** in the centre (useful if your specimen's particularly big or a liquid).

3) There are **two main ways** of preparing a microscope slide:

Dry Mount

• Your specimen needs to let **light** through it for you to be able to see it clearly under the microscope. So if you've got quite a **thick specimen**, you'll need to take a **thin slice** to use on your slide.

• Use **tweezers** to pick up your specimen and put it in the **middle** of a clean slide.

• Pop a **cover slip** (a square of thin, transparent plastic or glass) **on top**.

Cover slip
Specimen
Slide

Wet Mount

• Start by pipetting a small **drop of water** onto the slide. Then use **tweezers** to place your specimen on top of the water drop.

• To put the **cover slip** on, stand the slip **upright** on the slide, next to the water droplet. Then carefully **tilt** and lower it so it covers the specimen. Try **not** to get any **air bubbles** under there — they'll obstruct your view of the specimen.

• Once the cover slip is in position, you can add a **stain**. Put a drop of stain next to one edge of the cover slip. Then put a bit of **paper towel** next to the opposite edge. The stain will get **drawn** under the slip, **across** the **specimen**.

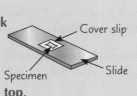

Cover slip
Water droplet

Wet mounts are good for looking at tiny organisms that live in water.

Studying Cells — Using Microscopes

Here's How to Use a **Light Microscope**...

You're expected to be able to use a light microscope to view a specimen.

1) Start by clipping the **slide** containing the specimen you want to look at onto the **stage**.

2) Select the **lowest-powered objective lens** (i.e. the one that produces the lowest magnification).

3) Use the **coarse adjustment knob** to bring the stage up to just below the objective lens.

4) Look down the **eyepiece** (which contains the **ocular lens**). Use the **coarse adjustment knob** to move the stage downwards, away from the objective lens until the image is **roughly in focus**.

5) Adjust the **focus** with the **fine adjustment knob**, until you get a **clear image** of what's on the slide.

6) If you need to see the slide with **greater magnification**, swap to a **higher-powered objective lens** and refocus.

> If you're asked to draw what you can see under the microscope, make sure you write down the magnification the specimen was viewed under. You'll also need to label your drawing.

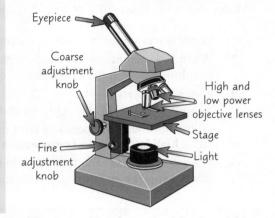

...and an **Eyepiece Graticule** and **Stage Micrometer**

1) Sometimes, you might want to know the **size** of your specimen. And that's where the **eyepiece graticule** and **stage micrometer** come in — they're a bit like **rulers**.

2) An **eyepiece graticule** is fitted onto the **eyepiece**. It's like a transparent ruler with **numbers**, but **no units**.

3) The **stage micrometer** is placed on the **stage** — it is a microscope slide with an **accurate scale** (it has units) and it's used to work out the **value** of the divisions on the **eyepiece graticule** at a **particular magnification**.

4) This means that when you take the stage micrometer away and replace it with the slide containing your specimen, you'll be able to **measure** the size of the specimen. Here's an **example**:

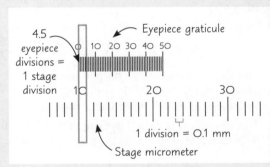

1) Line up the eyepiece graticule and the stage micrometer.

2) Each **division** on the stage micrometer is **0.1 mm** long.

3) At this magnification, **1 division** on the **stage micrometer** is the same as **4.5 divisions** on the **eyepiece graticule**.

4) To work out the size of **1 division** on the **eyepiece graticule**, you need to divide 0.1 by 4.5:

1 division on eyepiece graticule = 0.1 ÷ 4.5 = **0.022 mm**

5) So if you look at an object under the microscope at this magnification and it's **20 eyepiece divisions** long, you know it measures: 20 × 0.022 = **0.44 mm**

> Remember: at a different magnification, 1 division on the stage micrometer will be equal to a different number of divisions on the eyepiece graticule — so the eyepiece graticule will need to be re-calibrated.

Warm-Up Question

Q1 Why is it sometimes necessary to stain an object before viewing it through a microscope?

Exam Question

Q1 a) A microscope is set up with an eyepiece graticule and a stage micrometer. Each division on a stage micrometer is 10 μm long. At ×10 magnification, 1 division of the stage micrometer is equal to 6.5 divisions on the eyepiece graticule. Calculate the size of 1 division on the eyepiece graticule. Give your answer to the nearest 0.1 μm.

[2 marks]

b) A specimen is viewed under this microscope at ×10 magnification. It is 14 eyepiece divisions long. Use your answer to part a) to calculate the specimen's length. Give your answer to the nearest μm. [2 marks]

'Staining your samples' — a common problem at the start of exams...

Wow — I bet you never realised there was so much to know about using a microscope. Still, staining is straightforward and so's preparing a slide. Using a graticule, etc. is trickier, but once you get your head round it you'll be fine.

Water

Your body needs all sorts of different molecules to stay alive, and this section covers all the major groups.
Life can't exist without water — in fact, everyday water is one of the most important substances on the planet.

Water is Vital to Living Organisms

Water makes up about 80% of a cell's contents. It has loads of important **functions**, inside and outside cells:

1) Water is a **reactant** in loads of important **chemical reactions**, including **hydrolysis reactions** (see page 22).
2) Water is a **solvent**, which means some substances **dissolve** in it. Most biological reactions take place **in solution** (e.g. in the **cytoplasm** of eukaryotic and prokaryotic cells) so water's pretty essential.
3) Water **transports** substances. The fact that it's a **liquid** and a **solvent** means it can easily transport all sorts of materials, like glucose and oxygen, around plants and animals.
4) Water helps with **temperature control** because it has a **high specific heat capacity** and a **high latent heat of evaporation** (see below).
5) Water is a **habitat**. The fact that it helps with **temperature control**, is a **solvent** and becomes **less dense** when it **freezes** (see next page) means many organisms can survive and reproduce in it.

Water Molecules have a Simple Structure

Examiners like asking you to relate **structure** to **properties** and **function**, so make sure you know the structure of water.

1) A molecule of **water (H_2O)** is **one atom** of oxygen (O) joined to **two atoms** of hydrogen (H_2) by **shared electrons**.
2) Because the **shared negative** hydrogen electrons are **pulled towards** the oxygen atom, the other side of each hydrogen atom is left with a **slight positive charge**.
3) The **unshared** negative electrons on the oxygen atom give it a **slight negative charge**.
4) This makes water a **polar** molecule — it has a **partial negative ($\delta-$)** charge on one side and a **partial positive ($\delta+$)** charge on the other.

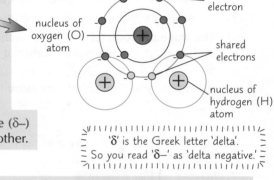

nucleus of oxygen (O) atom
unshared electron
shared electrons
nucleus of hydrogen (H) atom

'δ' is the Greek letter 'delta'. So you read '$\delta-$' as 'delta negative.'

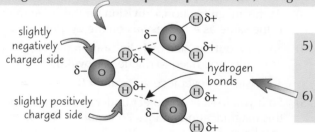

slightly negatively charged side
slightly positively charged side
hydrogen bonds

5) The slightly negatively-charged **oxygen atoms attract** the slightly positively-charged **hydrogen atoms** of other water molecules.
6) This attraction is called **hydrogen bonding** and it gives water some of its useful properties.

Water's Structure is Related to its Properties and Functions

Hydrogen Bonds Give Water a High Specific Heat Capacity

1) Specific heat capacity is the **energy** needed to **raise the temperature** of 1 gram of a substance by 1 °C.
2) The **hydrogen bonds** between water molecules can **absorb** a **lot** of energy. So water has a **high** specific heat capacity — it takes a lot of energy to heat it up.
3) This means water **doesn't** experience **rapid temperature changes**, which is one of the properties that makes it a **good habitat** — the temperature under water is likely to be more stable than it is on land.

Hydrogen Bonds Also Give Water a High Latent Heat of Evaporation

1) It takes a lot of **energy** (**heat**) to **break** the hydrogen bonds between water molecules.
2) So water has a **high latent heat of evaporation** — a lot of energy is used up when water **evaporates**.
3) This is useful for living organisms because it means water's great for **cooling** things. This is why some **mammals**, like us, **sweat** when they're **too hot**. When sweat evaporates, it **cools** the **surface** of the **skin**.

Water

Water's **Polarity** Makes it **Very Cohesive**

1) Cohesion is the **attraction** between molecules of the same type (e.g. two water molecules). Water molecules are **very cohesive** (they tend to stick together) because they're **polar**.

2) This helps water to **flow**, making it great for **transporting substances**. It also helps water to be transported up **plant stems** in the **transpiration stream** (see page 91).

Water's **Polarity** Also Makes it a **Good Solvent**

1) A lot of important substances in biological reactions are **ionic** (like **salt**, for example). This means they're made from **one positively-charged** atom or molecule and **one negatively-charged** atom or molecule (e.g. salt is made from a positive sodium ion and a negative chloride ion).

2) Because water is polar, the **slightly positive end** of a water molecule will be attracted to the **negative ion**, and the **slightly negative end** of a water molecule will be attracted to the **positive ion**.

3) This means the ions will get **totally surrounded** by water molecules — in other words, they'll **dissolve**.

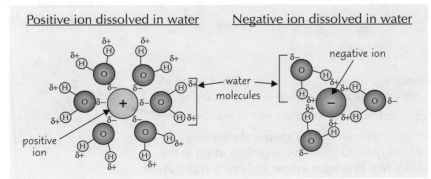

The polar nature of bears sometimes results in unexpected hydrogen bonding.

4) Water's **polarity** makes it useful as a **solvent** in living organisms. E.g. in **humans**, important **ions** (see p. 29) can dissolve in the water in **blood** and then be transported around the body.

Water's **Less Dense When it's Solid**

1) At **low temperatures** water **freezes** — it turns from a liquid to a solid.

2) Water molecules are held **further apart** in **ice** than they are in liquid water because each water molecule forms **four hydrogen bonds** to other water molecules, making a **lattice** shape. This makes ice **less dense** than liquid water — which is why **ice floats**.

3) This is useful for living organisms because, in cold temperatures, ice forms an **insulating layer** on top of water — the water below **doesn't freeze**. So organisms that live in water, like **fish**, **don't freeze** and can still **move around**.

Warm-Up Questions

Q1 Briefly describe the structure of a water molecule.
Q2 Briefly describe what is meant by a polar molecule.
Q3 State five properties of water that make it useful for living organisms.
Q4 Why is water's high specific heat capacity useful for living organisms?

Exam Question

Q1 In hot temperatures, elephants commonly spray themselves with water. With reference to the structure of water, explain why this behaviour acts as a cooling mechanism for the elephant. [3 marks]

Pssssssssssssssssssssssssssssssssssssssssssss — need the loo yet?

Water is pretty darn useful really. It looks so, well, dull — but in fact it's scientifically amazing. It's essential for all kinds of jobs — keeping cool, transporting things, enabling reactions, etc. You need to learn all of its properties and functions, and be able to say how they relate to its structure. Right, I'm off — when you gotta go, you gotta go.

Carbohydrates

Carbohydrates are important biological molecules — for a start they're the main energy supply in living organisms.

Carbohydrates are Made from Monosaccharides

1) Most carbohydrates are **polymers**. A polymer is a molecule made up of **many similar**, **smaller molecules** (called **monomers**) bonded together.

2) The monomers that make up carbohydrates are called **monosaccharides**.

3) **Glucose** is a monosaccharide with **six carbon** atoms — this means it's a **hexose** monosaccharide.

4) There are **two forms** of glucose — **alpha** (α) and **beta** (β). They both have a **ring structure**:

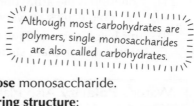

Although most carbohydrates are polymers, single monosaccharides are also called carbohydrates.

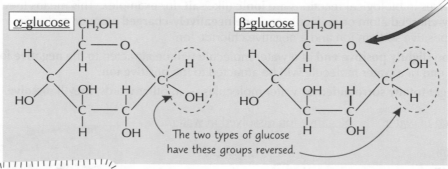

The two types of glucose have these groups reversed.

5) Glucose's **structure** is related to its **function** as the main **energy source** in animals and plants. Its structure makes it **soluble** so it can be **easily transported**. Its chemical bonds contain **lots of energy**.

Ribose is the sugar component of RNA nucleotides (see p. 34).

6) **Ribose** is a monosaccharide with **five carbon** atoms — this means it's a **pentose** monosaccharide.

7) You need to know its **structure**:

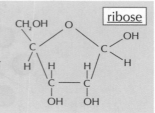

ribose

8) All carbohydrates are made up of the same **three chemical elements** — **carbon** (**C**), **hydrogen** (**H**) and **oxygen** (**O**). For every **carbon atom** in the carbohydrate there are usually **two hydrogen atoms** and **one oxygen atom**.

Monosaccharides Join Together to Form Disaccharides and Polysaccharides

1) Monosaccharides are **joined together** by **glycosidic bonds**.

2) During **synthesis**, a **hydrogen** atom on one monosaccharide bonds to a **hydroxyl** (OH) group on the other, **releasing** a molecule of **water**. This is called a **condensation** reaction.

3) The **reverse** of this synthesis reaction is **hydrolysis**. A molecule of water reacts with the glycosidic bond, **breaking it apart**.

Sugar is a general term for monosaccharides and disaccharides.

4) A **disaccharide** is formed when **two monosaccharides** join together:

For example, two α-glucose molecules are joined together by a **glycosidic bond** to form **maltose**:

α-glucose   +   α-glucose   synthesis ⇌ hydrolysis   maltose   + H_2O

H_2O is removed   glycosidic bond

Other disaccharides are formed in a similar way. **Sucrose** is a disaccharide formed when α–**glucose** and **fructose** join together. **Lactose** is a disaccharide formed by the joining together of either α–**glucose** or β–**glucose** and **galactose**.

5) A **polysaccharide** is formed when **more than two monosaccharides** join together:

Lots of α-glucose molecules are joined together by **glycosidic bonds** to form **amylose**.

glycosidic bonds

α-glucose   α-glucose   α-glucose   α-glucose   α-glucose

Carbohydrates

You Need to Learn About **Three Polysaccharides**

You need to know about the relationship between the **structure** and **function** of three polysaccharides:

1) Starch — the main **energy storage material** in **plants**

Amylose

1) Cells get **energy** from **glucose**. Plants **store** excess glucose as **starch** (when a plant **needs more glucose** for energy it **breaks down** starch to release the glucose).

2) Starch is a mixture of **two** polysaccharides of **alpha-glucose** — **amylose** and **amylopectin**:

- **Amylose** — a long, **unbranched chain** of α–glucose. The angles of the glycosidic bonds give it a **coiled structure**, almost like a cylinder. This makes it **compact**, so it's really **good for storage** because you can **fit more in** to a small space.

one alpha-glucose molecule

- **Amylopectin** — a long, **branched chain** of α–glucose. Its **side branches** allow the **enzymes** that break down the molecule to get at the **glycosidic bonds easily**. This means that the glucose can be **released quickly**.

Amylopectin

3) Starch is **insoluble** in water, so it **doesn't** cause water to enter cells by **osmosis** (see p. 58) which would make them swell. This makes it good for **storage**.

Glycogen

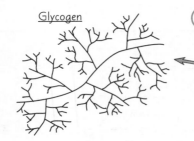

2) Glycogen — the main **energy storage material** in **animals**

1) Animal cells get **energy** from **glucose** too. But animals **store** excess glucose as **glycogen** — another polysaccharide of **alpha-glucose**.

2) Its structure is very similar to amylopectin, except that it has **loads** more **side branches** coming off it. Loads of branches means that stored glucose can be **released quickly**, which is **important for energy release** in animals.

3) It's also a very **compact** molecule, so it's good for storage.

3) Cellulose — the major component of **cell walls in plants**

one cellulose molecule

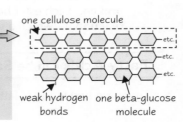

1) Cellulose is made of **long, unbranched** chains of **beta-glucose**.

2) When **beta–glucose** molecules **bond**, they form **straight** cellulose chains.

3) The cellulose chains are linked together by **hydrogen bonds** to form strong fibres called **microfibrils**. The strong fibres mean cellulose provides **structural support** for cells (e.g. in plant cell walls).

weak hydrogen bonds   one beta-glucose molecule

Warm-Up Questions

Q1 What is the structural difference between an alpha-glucose molecule and a beta-glucose molecule?

Q2 Describe how glycosidic bonds are formed and broken in living organisms.

Q3 Briefly describe the structure of starch.

Q4 What is the function of cellulose?

PRACTICE QUESTIONS

Exam Questions

Q1 Mannose is a hexose monosaccharide.
Which of the following is most likely to give the chemical formula of a mannose molecule?

A $C_5H_{10}O_5$ B $C_6H_{12}O_6$ C $C_6H_{12}N_6$ D $C_5H_5O_{10}$ [1 mark]

Q2 State the function of glycogen and explain how the structure of glycogen is linked to its function.   [3 marks]

Mmmm, starch... Tasty, tasty chips and beans... *dribble*. Ahem, sorry.

Remember that condensation and hydrolysis reactions are the reverse of each other. You need to learn how maltose, sucrose and lactose are formed and broken down by these reactions. And don't forget that starch is composed of two different polysaccharides... and that glucose exists in two forms... so many reminders, so little space...

Lipids

On to lipids, or 'fatty oily things' to you and me. Some of them are just straightforward fats, but others have extra bits stuck to them. You need to know about three types of lipid — triglycerides, phospholipids and cholesterol.

Triglycerides are a **Kind** of **Lipid**

1) Triglycerides are **macromolecules** — they're **complex molecules** with a relatively **large molecular mass**.

2) Like **all lipids**, they contain the chemical elements **carbon**, **hydrogen** and **oxygen**.

3) Triglycerides have **one** molecule of **glycerol** with **three fatty acids** attached to it.

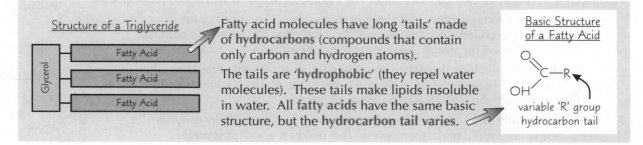

Fatty acid molecules have long 'tails' made of **hydrocarbons** (compounds that contain only carbon and hydrogen atoms).

The tails are '**hydrophobic**' (they repel water molecules). These tails make lipids insoluble in water. All **fatty acids** have the same basic structure, but the **hydrocarbon tail varies**.

Triglycerides Contain **Ester Bonds**

1) Triglycerides are **synthesised** by the formation of an **ester bond** between each **fatty acid** and the **glycerol molecule**.

2) Each ester bond is formed by a **condensation reaction** (in which a water molecule is released).

3) The process in which triglycerides are synthesised is called **esterification**.

4) Triglycerides **break down** when the ester bonds are **broken**. Each ester bond is broken in a **hydrolysis reaction** (in which a water molecule is used up).

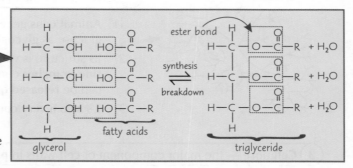

Fatty Acids can be **Saturated** or **Unsaturated**

There are **two** kinds of fatty acids — **saturated** and **unsaturated**. The difference is in their **hydrocarbon tails**.

Saturated fatty acids **don't** have any **double bonds** between their **carbon atoms**. The fatty acid is 'saturated' with hydrogen.

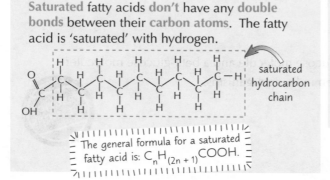

The general formula for a saturated fatty acid is: $C_nH_{(2n+1)}COOH$.

Unsaturated fatty acids have **at least one** double bond between **carbon atoms**, which cause the chain to kink.

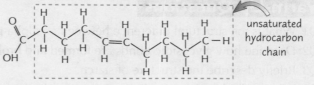

Phospholipids are **Similar** to **Triglycerides**

1) **Phospholipids** are also **macromolecules**. They're pretty similar to triglycerides except one of the fatty acid molecules is replaced by a **phosphate group**.

2) The phosphate group is **hydrophilic** (it attracts water molecules) and the fatty acid tails are **hydrophobic**.

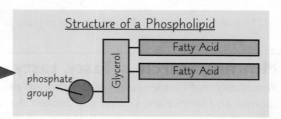

Lipids

The **Structures** of Lipids Relate to Their **Functions**

You need to know how the **properties** of **triglycerides**, **phospholipids** and **cholesterol** are related to their **functions**:

TRIGLYCERIDES

In **animals** and **plants**, triglycerides are mainly used as **energy storage molecules**. Some **bacteria** (e.g. *Mycobacterium tuberculosis*) use triglycerides to store both **energy** and **carbon**. Triglycerides are good for storage because:

1) The **long hydrocarbon tails** of the fatty acids contain lots of **chemical energy** — a load of energy is **released** when they're **broken down**. Because of these tails, lipids contain about **twice** as much energy per gram as carbohydrates.

2) They're **insoluble**, so they don't cause water to enter the cells by **osmosis** (see p. 58) which would make them swell. The triglycerides bundle together as **insoluble droplets** in cells because the fatty acid tails are **hydrophobic** (water-repelling) — the tails **face inwards**, shielding themselves from water with their glycerol heads.

PHOSPHOLIPIDS

Phospholipids are found in the **cell membranes** of all eukaryotes and prokaryotes. They make up what's known as the **phospholipid bilayer** (see p. 50). Cell membranes **control** what **enters and leaves a cell**.

1) Phospholipid heads are **hydrophilic** and their tails are **hydrophobic**, so they form a **double** layer with their heads facing **out** towards the water on either side.

2) The **centre** of the bilayer is **hydrophobic**, so water-soluble substances **can't** easily pass through it — the membrane acts as a **barrier** to those substances.

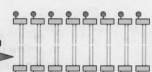

CHOLESTEROL

Cholesterol is another type of lipid — it has a **hydrocarbon ring** structure attached to a **hydrocarbon tail**. The ring structure has a **polar hydroxyl (OH) group** attached to it. In **eukaryotic cells**, cholesterol molecules help to **regulate the fluidity** of the cell membrane by **interacting** with the **phospholipid bilayer**.

'Polar' means it has a slightly negatively charged bit and a slightly positively charged bit — see p. 20.

1) Cholesterol has a **small size** and **flattened shape** — this allows cholesterol to fit **in between** the phospholipid molecules in the membrane.

2) At **higher temperatures**, they bind to the hydrophobic tails of the phospholipids, causing them to **pack more closely together**. This helps to make the membrane **less fluid** and **more rigid**.

3) At **lower temperatures**, cholesterol **prevents** phospholipids from packing too close together, and so **increases membrane fluidity**.

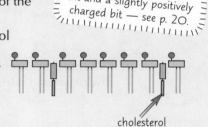

cholesterol

Warm-Up Questions

Q1 What are triglycerides composed of?

Q2 What is the difference between a saturated fatty acid and an unsaturated fatty acid?

Q3 Sketch the structure of a phospholipid.

PRACTICE QUESTIONS

Exam Questions

Q1 Explain how phospholipid molecules arrange themselves in cell membranes and relate this to their structure. [3 marks]

Q2 Explain how each of these features of lipids is important for their function in living things:

a) Cholesterol molecules have a flattened shape. [2 marks]

b) Triglycerides have a hydrophobic tail. [2 marks]

Hydrocarbon tails, phospho-thingies... Whatever happened to just lard?

You don't get far in life without extensive lard knowledge, so learn all the details on this page good and proper. Lipids pop up in other sections, so make sure you know the basics about how their structure gives them some quite groovy properties. Right, all this lipids talk is making me hungry — chips time...

Proteins

There are millions of different proteins. They're the most abundant molecules in cells, making up 50% or more of a cell's dry mass — now that's just plain greedy. Like carbohydrates and lipids, proteins are essential for life.

Proteins are Made from Long Chains of Amino Acids

1) Just like carbohydrates (see page 22), proteins are **polymers**.
2) Amino acids are the **monomers** in proteins.
3) A **dipeptide** is formed when **two** amino acids join together.
4) A **polypeptide** is formed when **more than two** amino acids join together.
5) **Proteins** are made up of **one or more polypeptides**.

Different Amino Acids Have Different Variable Groups

1) All amino acids have the same general structure — a **carboxyl group** (-COOH) and an **amino group** (-NH$_2$) attached to a **carbon** atom. The **difference** between different amino acids is the **variable** group (**R** on diagram) they contain.

Structure of an Amino Acid

E.g. Structure of Glycine

Glycine is the smallest amino acid — the R group is a hydrogen atom.

2) All amino acids contain the chemical elements **carbon**, **oxygen**, **hydrogen** and **nitrogen**. Some also contain **sulfur**.

Amino Acids are Joined Together by Peptide Bonds

1) Amino acids are linked together by **peptide bonds** to form dipeptides and polypeptides.
2) A molecule of **water** is **released** during the reaction — it's a **condensation** reaction.
3) The **reverse** of this reaction **adds** a molecule of water to **break** the peptide bond — it's a **hydrolysis** reaction.

a molecule of water is formed during synthesis.

Proteins

Proteins Have **Four Structural Levels**

Proteins are **big**, **complicated** molecules. They're much easier to explain if you describe their structure in four 'levels'. These levels are a protein's **primary**, **secondary**, **tertiary** and **quaternary** structures.

<u>Primary Structure</u> — this is the **sequence** of **amino acids** in the **polypeptide chain**. Different proteins have **different sequences** of amino acids in their primary structure. A change in just one amino acid may change the structure of the whole protein.

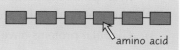
amino acid

<u>Secondary Structure</u> — the polypeptide chain doesn't remain flat and straight. **Hydrogen bonds** form between nearby amino acids in the chain. This makes it automatically **coil** into an **alpha (α) helix** or **fold** into a **beta (β) pleated sheet** — this is the secondary structure.

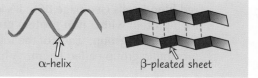
α-helix   β-pleated sheet

<u>Tertiary Structure</u> — the coiled or folded chain of amino acids is often **coiled** and **folded further**. **More bonds** form between different parts of the polypeptide chain. For proteins made from a **single** polypeptide chain, the tertiary structure forms their **final 3D structure**.

<u>Quaternary Structure</u> — some proteins are made of **several different polypeptide chains** held together by **bonds**. The **quaternary structure** is the way these polypeptide chains are assembled together. E.g. **haemoglobin** is made of **four** polypeptide chains, bonded together. For proteins made from **more than one** polypeptide chain, the quaternary structure is the protein's **final 3D structure**.

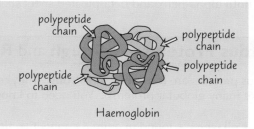
polypeptide chain
polypeptide chain
polypeptide chain
polypeptide chain
Haemoglobin

Computer modelling can create **3D interactive images** of proteins. This is really handy for **investigating** the **different levels of structure** in a protein molecule.

Different Bonds Hold Different **Structural Levels** Together

The four structural levels of a protein are held together by **different kinds** of **bonds**:

1) **Primary structure** — held together by the **peptide bonds** between amino acids.

2) **Secondary structure** — held together by **hydrogen bonds** (see above).

3) **Tertiary structure** — this is affected by a few different kinds of bonds:

- **Ionic bonds**. These are **attractions** between **negatively-charged** R groups and **positively-charged** R groups on different parts of the molecule.

- **Disulfide bonds**. Whenever two molecules of the amino acid **cysteine** come close together, the **sulfur atom** in one cysteine bonds to the sulfur in the other cysteine, forming a disulfide bond.

- **Hydrophobic** and **hydrophilic interactions**. When **hydrophobic** (water-repelling) R groups are close together in the protein, they tend to **clump together**. This means that **hydrophilic** (water-attracting) R groups are more likely to be pushed to the **outside**, which affects how the protein **folds up** into its final structure.

Heating a protein to a high temperature will break up its ionic and hydrophobic/hydrophilic interactions and hydrogen bonds. In turn this will cause a change in the protein's 3D shape.

- **Hydrogen bonds** — these weak bonds form between slightly **positively-charged hydrogen atoms** in some R groups and **slightly negatively-charged** atoms in other R groups on the polypeptide chain.

4) **Quaternary structure** — this tends to be determined by the **tertiary structure** of the individual polypeptide chains being bonded together. Because of this, it can be influenced by **all the bonds** mentioned above.

Proteins

Globular Proteins Are Round and Compact

1) In a globular protein, the **hydrophilic R groups** on the amino acids tend to be pushed to the **outside** of the molecule. This is caused by the **hydrophobic** and **hydrophilic interactions** in the protein's **tertiary structure** (see previous page).

2) This makes globular proteins **soluble**, so they're **easily transported** in fluids.

3) Globular proteins have a **range of functions** in living organisms. For example:

Dean did a great impression of a globular protein.

HAEMOGLOBIN is a globular protein that carries **oxygen** around the body in **red blood cells** (see page 86). It's known as a **conjugated protein** — this means it's a protein with a **non-protein group** attached. The non-protein part is called a **prosthetic group**. Each of the four polypeptide chains in haemoglobin has a prosthetic group called **haem**. A haem group contains **iron**, which oxygen binds to.

haem group

INSULIN is a **hormone** secreted by the **pancreas**. It helps to regulate the **blood glucose level**. Its **solubility** is important — it means it can be **transported** in the **blood** to the tissues where it acts. An insulin molecule consists of **two polypeptide chains**, which are held together by **disulfide bonds**.

AMYLASE is an **enzyme** (see page 42) that catalyses the breakdown of **starch** in the digestive system. It is made of a **single chain** of amino acids. Its secondary structure contains **both** alpha-helix and beta-pleated sheet sections. **Most enzymes are globular proteins.**

Fibrous Proteins Are Tough and Rope-Shaped

Fibrous proteins are **insoluble** and **strong**. They're **structural** proteins and are fairly **unreactive** (unlike many globular proteins). You need to know about these **three** fibrous proteins:

- **Collagen** — found in animal **connective tissues**, such as bone, skin and muscle. It is a very **strong** molecule. **Minerals** can bind to the protein to increase its **rigidity**, e.g. in bone.  *The Structure of a Collagen Molecule*

- **Keratin** — found in many of the **external structures** of animals, such as skin, hair, nails, feathers and horns. It can either be **flexible** (as it is in skin) or **hard and tough** (as it is in nails).

- **Elastin** — found in **elastic connective tissue**, such as skin, large blood vessels and some ligaments. It is **elastic**, so it allows tissues to return to their original shape after they have been stretched.

Warm-Up Questions

Q1 Describe the general structure of an amino acid.

Q2 Name the bond that joins amino acids together in proteins.

Q3 What is a conjugated protein?

(PRACTICE QUESTIONS)

Exam Questions

Q1 Suggest which of the following proteins is most abundant in a tortoise's shell.

   A Collagen   B Elastin   C Alpha-amylase   D Keratin   [1 mark]

Q2* HSA is a globular protein, which transports other molecules such as fatty acids around the bloodstream. The molecule consists of 585 amino acids, several of which are cysteine.

   Describe the bonds that could be present in the tertiary structure of HSA and suggest how its structure makes it suited for its role of transporting molecules in the blood.   [6 marks]

* You will be assessed on the quality of your written response in this question.

The name's Bond — Peptide Bond...

Quite a lot to learn on these pages — proteins are annoyingly complicated. Not happy with one, or even two structural levels, they can have four of the things — and you need to learn 'em all. Remember that condensation and hydrolysis reactions are the reverse of each other. And as for all that nasty stuff about disulfide bonds and ionic interactions... Urgh.

Inorganic Ions

Inorganic ions are just teeny tiny little things, but they're essential for many biological processes.

Inorganic Ions Have an Electric Charge

1) An **ion** is an atom (or group of atoms) that has an **electric charge**.
2) An ion with a **positive charge** is called a **cation**.
3) An ion with a **negative charge** is called an **anion**.
4) An **inorganic** ion is one which **doesn't contain carbon** (although there are a few exceptions to this rule).
5) Inorganic ions are really important in **biological processes**. Here are the ones you need to know about:

	Name of ion	Chemical Symbol	Example(s) of roles in biological processes
Cations	Calcium	Ca^{2+}	Involved in the transmission of **nerve impulses** and the release of **insulin** from the pancreas. Acts as a **cofactor** for many **enzymes** (see p. 47), e.g. those involved in blood clotting. Is important for **bone formation**.
	Sodium	Na^+	Important for generating **nerve impulses**, for **muscle contraction** and for **regulating fluid balance** in the body.
	Potassium	K^+	Important for generating **nerve impulses**, for **muscle contraction** and for **regulating fluid balance** in the body. Activates essential **enzymes** needed for **photosynthesis** in plant cells.
	Hydrogen	H^+	Affects the **pH** of substances (**more H^+ ions** than OH^- ions in a solution creates an **acid**). Also important for **photosynthesis reactions** that occur in the thylakoid membranes inside chloroplasts (see p. 12).
	Ammonium	NH_4^+	Absorbed from the **soil** by **plants** and is an important source of **nitrogen** (which is then used to make, e.g. amino acids, nucleic acids).
Anions	Nitrate	NO_3^-	Absorbed from the **soil** by **plants** and is an important source of **nitrogen** (which is then used to make, e.g. amino acids, nucleic acids).
	Hydrogencarbonate	HCO_3^-	Acts as a **buffer**, which helps to maintain the **pH** of the blood.
	Chloride	Cl^-	Involved in the 'chloride shift' which helps to maintain the **pH** of the blood during gas exchange (see p. 87). Acts as a **cofactor** for the enzyme amylase (see p. 47). Also involved in some nerve impulses.
	Phosphate	PO_4^{3-}	Involved in photosynthesis and respiration reactions. Needed for the synthesis of many biological molecules, such as nucleotides (including ATP), phospholipids, and calcium phosphate (which strengthens bones).
	Hydroxide	OH^-	Affects the **pH** of substances (more OH^- ions than H^+ ions in a solution creates an alkali).

Warm-Up Questions

Q1 What is the difference between a cation and an anion?
Q2 Write the chemical symbols for the following ions: calcium, ammonium, nitrate, phosphate, hydroxide.

Exam Question

Q1 Carbonic acid (H_2CO_3) is a weak acid present in the blood.
A reaction with water causes a hydrogen ion to dissociate from the carbonic acid molecule.
Name the anion that's formed in this reaction and write its chemical symbol. [2 marks]

Stop all that texting and get revising — I've got my ion you...

Well, who doesn't love a big table to brighten up Biology? Make sure you know the difference between a cation and an anion for starters. Then get learning all the names and chemical symbols from the table — you'll definitely meet some of these inorganic ions again in your Biology studies, so it's a good idea to make friends with them now.

Biochemical Tests for Molecules

Here's a bit of light relief for you — two pages on how you test for the different molecules you've just read about...

Use the **Benedict's Test** for **Sugars**

Sugar is a general term for **monosaccharides** and **disaccharides**. All sugars can be classified as **reducing** or **non-reducing**. The **Benedict's test** tests for sugars — it **differs** depending on the **type** of sugar you are testing for.

REDUCING SUGARS

1) Reducing sugars include **all monosaccharides** (e.g. glucose) and **some disaccharides** (e.g. maltose and lactose).

2) You add **Benedict's reagent** (which is **blue**) to a sample and **heat it** in a water bath that's been brought to the **boil**.

> *Always use an excess of Benedict's solution — this makes sure that all the sugar reacts.*

The colour of the precipitate changes from:

blue ⟹ **green** ⟹ **yellow** ⟹ **orange** ⟹ **brick red**

3) If the test's **positive** it will form a **coloured precipitate** (solid particles suspended in the solution).

4) The higher the concentration of reducing sugar, the further the colour change goes — you can use this to **compare** the amount of reducing sugar in different solutions. A more accurate way of doing this is to **filter** the solution and **weigh the precipitate**.

NON-REDUCING SUGARS

1) If the result of the reducing sugars test is **negative**, there could still be a non-reducing sugar present. To test for **non-reducing sugars**, like sucrose, first you have to break them down into monosaccharides.

2) You do this by getting a new sample of the test solution, adding **dilute hydrochloric acid** and carefully heating it in a water bath that's been brought to the **boil**. You then **neutralise** it with **sodium hydrogencarbonate**. Then just carry out the **Benedict's test** as you would for a reducing sugar.

3) If the test's **positive** it will form a **coloured precipitate** (as for the reducing sugars test). If the test's **negative** the solution will **stay blue**, which means it **doesn't contain any sugar** (either reducing or non-reducing).

Use **Test Strips** for **Glucose**

Glucose can also be tested for using **test strips** coated in a **reagent**. The strips are dipped in a test solution and **change colour** if glucose is **present**. The colour change can be compared to a **chart** to give an indication of the concentration of glucose present. The strips are useful for testing a person's **urine** for glucose, which may indicate they have **diabetes**.

Use the **Iodine Test** for **Starch**

Just add **iodine dissolved in potassium iodide solution** to the test sample.
- If starch **is present**, the sample changes from **browny-orange** to a dark, **blue-black** colour.
- If there's **no starch**, it stays browny-orange.

> *Make sure you always talk about iodine in potassium iodide solution, not just iodine.*

Use the **Biuret Test** for **Proteins**

There are **two stages** to this test.
1) The test solution needs to be **alkaline**, so first you add a few drops of **sodium hydroxide solution**.
2) Then you add some **copper(II) sulfate solution**.
   - If protein **is** present the solution turns **purple**.
   - If there's **no protein**, the solution will **stay blue**.

Negative result   Positive result

test solution, sodium hydroxide and copper(II) sulfate solution

solution staying blue indicates no protein

purple colour indicates protein

> *The colours are pale, so you need to look carefully.*

Use the **Emulsion Test** for **Lipids**

Shake the test substance with **ethanol** for about a minute, then **pour** the solution into **water**.
- If lipid **is present**, the solution will turn **milky**.
- The **more lipid** there is, the **more noticeable** the milky colour will be.
- If there's **no lipid**, the solution will **stay clear**.

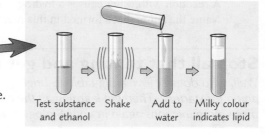

Test substance and ethanol   Shake   Add to water   Milky colour indicates lipid

Module 2: Section 2 — Biological Molecules

Biochemical Tests for Molecules

Colorimetry is Used to Determine the Concentration of a Glucose Solution

1) You can use **Benedict's reagent** and a **colorimeter** to get a **quantitative estimate** of **how much** glucose (or other reducing sugar) there is in a solution.

2) A colorimeter is a device that measures the **strength** of a **coloured solution** by seeing how much **light** passes through it.

3) A colorimeter measures **absorbance** (the amount of light absorbed by the solution). The **more concentrated** the **colour** of the solution, the **higher** the **absorbance** is.

4) It's easiest to measure the concentration of the **blue Benedict's solution** that's **left** after the test (the **paler** the solution, the **more glucose** there was). So, the **higher** the glucose concentration, the **lower** the absorbance of the solution.

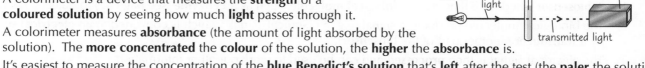

This is How You Do it:

Initially you need to make up several glucose solutions of different, known concentrations. You can do this using a serial dilution technique:

> You don't have to dilute solutions by a factor of 2. E.g. to dilute by a factor of 10, take 1 cm³ from your original sample and add it to 9 cm³ of water.

This is how you'd make **five serial dilutions** with a **dilution factor of 2**, starting with an initial glucose concentration of **40 mM**...

1) Line up five **test tubes** in a rack.

2) Add **10 cm³** of the initial **40 mM glucose solution** to the first test tube and **5 cm³ of distilled water** to the other four test tubes.

3) Then, using a pipette, draw **5 cm³** of the solution from the **first** test tube, add it to the distilled water in the **second** test tube and **mix** the solution **thoroughly**. You now have **10 cm³** of solution that's **half as concentrated** as the solution in the first test tube (it's **20 mM**).

4) Repeat this process **three more times** to create solutions of **10 mM**, **5 mM** and **2.5 mM**.

transfer 5cm³, then mix

20 mM | 10 mM | 5 mM | 2.5 mM

10 cm³ of 40 mM glucose solution   5 cm³ of distilled water

Once you've got your glucose solutions, you need to make a calibration curve. Here's how:

1) Do a Benedict's test on each solution (plus a negative control of pure water). Use the same amount of Benedict's solution in each case.

2) Remove any precipitate — either leave for 24 hours (so that the precipitate settles out) or centrifuge them.

3) Use a colorimeter (with a red filter) to measure the absorbance of the Benedict's solution remaining in each tube.

4) Use the results to make the calibration curve, showing absorbance against glucose concentration.

Then you can test the unknown solution in the same way as the known concentrations and use the calibration curve to find its concentration.

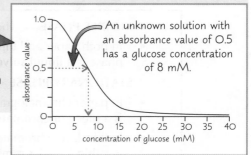

An unknown solution with an absorbance value of 0.5 has a glucose concentration of 8 mM.

Warm-Up Questions

Q1 Describe how you would test a solution for starch.

Q2 Describe how you would test for lipids in a solution.

PRACTICE QUESTIONS

Exam Question

Q1 Equal volumes of three different sugar solutions (A, B and C) were each tested with the same large volume of Benedict's solution. Later, the concentrations of Benedict's solution in each test tube were compared, using a colorimeter. The table shows the absorbance of each solution.

solution	absorbance
A	1.22
B	0.68
C	0.37

a) Which original solution contained the highest concentration of reducing sugar? [1 mark]

b) Suggest two factors that should be kept constant when carrying out this test. [2 marks]

The Anger Test — annoy test subject. If it goes red, anger is present...

Make sure you know the ins and outs of all the biochemical tests on the previous page — don't get mixed up between the different colour changes. Then get your head round this colorimetry thingy-me-bob too — that's a bit more exciting.

Biochemical Tests and Separating Molecules

If you haven't had enough of finding out what biochemical molecules solutions contain, you're in luck. Biosensors and chromatography now — you've probably tried chromatography before with a spot of ink on a piece of filter paper.

Biosensors Can Detect Chemicals in a Solution

1) A **biosensor** is a device that uses a **biological molecule**, such as an **enzyme** (see page 42) to detect a **chemical**.

2) The biological molecule produces a **signal** (e.g. a **chemical** signal), which is converted to an **electrical signal** by a **transducer** (another part of the **biosensor**).

3) The electrical signal is then **processed** and can be used to work out other information.

Example: Glucose Biosensors

1) A **glucose biosensor** is used to determine the **concentration** of **glucose** in a solution.

2) It does this using the enzyme **glucose oxidase** and **electrodes**.

3) The enzyme catalyses the **oxidation** of glucose at the electrodes — this creates a **charge**, which is converted into an **electrical signal** by the electrodes (the transducer).

4) The electrical signal is then **processed** to work out the **initial glucose concentration**.

Chromatography is Good for Separating and Identifying Things

1) Chromatography is used to **separate** stuff in a mixture — once it's separated out, you can often **identify** the components.

2) For example, chromatography can be used to separate out and identify biological molecules such as **amino acids**, **carbohydrates**, **vitamins** and **nucleic acids**.

3) There are quite a few different types of chromatography — you only need to know about **paper chromatography** and **thin-layer chromatography**.

You Need to Understand How Chromatography Works

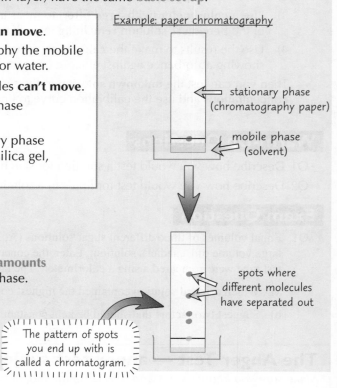

1) All types of chromatography (including paper and thin-layer) have the same basic set up:

> 1) A **MOBILE PHASE** — where the molecules **can move**.
>   - In both paper and thin-layer chromatography the mobile phase is a **liquid solvent**, such as ethanol or water.
> 2) A **STATIONARY PHASE** — where the molecules **can't move**.
>   - In paper chromatography the stationary phase is a piece of **chromatography paper**.
>   - In thin-layer chromatography the stationary phase is a **thin** (0.1-0.3 mm) **layer of solid**, e.g. silica gel, on a **glass or plastic plate**.

Example: paper chromatography

stationary phase (chromatography paper)

mobile phase (solvent)

spots where different molecules have separated out

2) And they all use the same basic principle:

- The mobile phase moves through or over the stationary phase.
- The components in the mixture spend different amounts of time in the mobile phase and the stationary phase.
- The components that spend longer in the mobile phase travel faster or further.
- The time spent in the different phases is what separates out the components of the mixture.

The pattern of spots you end up with is called a chromatogram.

Biochemical Tests and Separating Molecules

Paper Chromatography is used to Identify Unknown Amino Acids

In the exam you might be asked how chromatography can be used to identify the **biological molecules in a mixture**. Below is an example of how **paper chromatography** can be used to identify **amino acids** in a **mixture**. If you're trying to identify **different biological molecules**, the **method** will **vary slightly** (e.g. a different solvent might be used) but the basic principle will be the same.

Here's what you'd do:

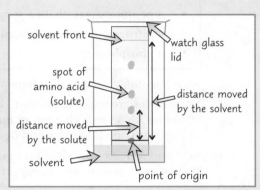

1) Draw a **pencil line** near the bottom of a piece of **chromatography paper** and put a **concentrated spot** of the mixture of amino acids on it. It's best to carefully roll the paper into a **cylinder** with the spot on the outside so it'll stand up.

2) Add a small amount of prepared **solvent** (a mixture of **butan-1-ol**, **glacial ethanoic acid** and **water** is usually used for amino acids) to a beaker and dip the **bottom** of the **paper** into it (not the spot). This should be done in a **fume cupboard**. Cover with a **lid** to stop the solvent evaporating.

3) As the solvent spreads up the paper, the different amino acids (solutes) move with it, but at **different rates**, so they separate out.

4) When the solvent's **nearly** reached the top, take the paper out and **mark** the **solvent front** with pencil. Then you can leave the paper to **dry out** before you analyse it (see below).

> The substances in the sample mixture dissolve as the solvent passes over it, so they are called solutes.

5) Amino acids **aren't coloured**, which means you **won't be able to see them** on the paper. So before you can analyse them, you have to spray the paper with **ninhydrin solution** to turn the amino acids **purple**. This should also be done in a **fume cupboard** and **gloves** should be worn. (Note: you can't use ninhydrin to detect all biological molecules, only proteins and amino acids.)

6) You can then use **R_f values** to **identify** the separated molecules:

An **R_f value** is the ratio of the distance travelled by a solute to the distance travelled by the solvent. You can calculate it using this formula:

$$R_f \text{ value of amino acid} = \frac{\text{distance travelled by solute}}{\text{distance travelled by solvent}}$$

When you're measuring how far a solute has travelled, you measure from the **point of origin** to the **vertical centre** of the spot.

You can work out what was in a mixture by calculating an R_f value for each solute and looking each R_f value up in a **database**, or **table**, of **known values**.

> You could also compare your chromatogram to the chromatogram of a known mixture and identify the components that way — if two solutes have travelled the same distance in the solvent, they will be the same molecule.

Warm-Up Questions

Q1 What is a biosensor?
Q2 What is chromatography used for?
Q3 Why would you use ninhydrin solution when using chromatography to identify amino acids in a mixture?

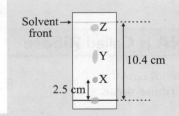

Sugar	R_f value
Glucose	0.20
Fructose	0.24
Xylose	0.30

Exam Question

Q1 The paper chromatogram above shows the separation of three sugars from a solution.

a) Briefly describe the method used to produce this chromatogram. [3 marks]

b) Explain why the solutes have ended up in different positions on the chromatogram. [1 mark]

c) Calculate the R_f value of solute X and use your answer to identify which sugar it is. [3 marks]

I'm afraid you can't read anymore of this page — it's been bio-censored...

Well, these two pages aren't that bad really. There's all that clever, technical biosensor gubbins at the beginning and then the rest is fun stuff about spots appearing in chromatography. And even better, it's the end of another section.

Nucleotides

You might not have heard of them, but nucleotides are pretty vital for life. These two pages will tell you more.

Nucleotides are Used to Make Nucleic Acids

1) A **nucleotide** is a type of biological molecule. It's made from:

- a **pentose sugar** (that's a sugar with **5** carbon atoms),
- a **nitrogenous** (nitrogen-containing) **base**,
- a **phosphate** group.

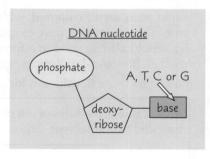

Nucleotide

All nucleotides contain the elements **C**, **H**, **O**, **N** and **P**.

2) Nucleotides are really **important**. For a start, they're the **monomers** (see p. 22) that make up **DNA** and **RNA**. DNA and RNA are both types of **nucleic acid**. DNA is used to **store genetic information** — the instructions an organism needs to grow and develop. **RNA** is used to make **proteins** from the instructions in DNA.

3) **ADP** and **ATP** are **special types** of nucleotide (see next page). They're used to **store** and **transport energy** in **cells**.

The Sugar in DNA is Called Deoxyribose

1) The **pentose sugar** in a **DNA nucleotide** is called **deoxyribose**. (DNA stands for **d**eoxyribo**n**ucleic **a**cid.)

2) Each DNA nucleotide has the **same sugar** and a **phosphate group**. The **base** on each nucleotide can **vary** though.

3) There are **four** possible bases — adenine (**A**), thymine (**T**), cytosine (**C**) and guanine (**G**).

4) **A**denine and **g**uanine are a type of base called a **purine**. **C**ytosine and **t**hymine are a type of base called a **pyrimidine**.

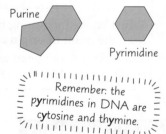

DNA nucleotide

- A **purine** base contains **two carbon-nitrogen rings** joined together.
- A **pyrimidine** base only has **one carbon-nitrogen ring**. So a pyrimidine base is **smaller** than a purine base.

5) A **molecule** of DNA contains two **polynucleotide** chains — each chain is made up of lots of **nucleotides** joined together. There's more on how polynucleotides form on page 36.

Purine

Pyrimidine

Remember: the pyrimidines in DNA are cytosine and thymine.

The Sugar in RNA is Called Ribose

1) **RNA** (**r**ibo**n**ucleic **a**cid) contains nucleotides with a **ribose sugar** (not deoxyribose).

2) Like DNA, an RNA nucleotide also has a **phosphate group** and one of **four** different **bases**.

3) In RNA though, **uracil** (a **pyrimidine**) replaces **thymine** as a base.

4) An RNA molecule is made up of a **single polynucleotide chain**.

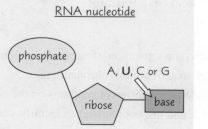

RNA nucleotide

Mary didn't care if it was ribose or deoxyribose, she just wanted her cuppa.

Nucleotides

ADP and ATP are Phosphorylated Nucleotides

1) To **phosphorylate** a nucleotide, you **add** one or more **phosphate** groups to it.
2) **ADP** (adenosine **di**phosphate) contains the base **adenine**, the sugar **ribose** and **two phosphate groups**.
3) **ATP** (adenosine **tri**phosphate) contains the base adenine, the sugar ribose and **three** phosphate groups.

- **ATP** provides **energy** for **chemical reactions** in the cell.
- ATP is **synthesised** from **ADP** and **inorganic phosphate** (P_i) using the **energy** from an energy-releasing reaction, e.g. the breakdown of glucose in respiration. The **ADP** is **phosphorylated** to form **ATP** and a **phosphate bond** is formed.
- Energy is **stored** in the phosphate bond. When this energy is needed by a cell, ATP is **broken back down** into ADP and inorganic phosphate (P_i). **Energy** is **released** from the phosphate bond and used by the cell.

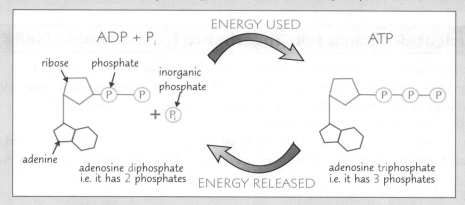

ENERGY USED

ADP + P_i

ribose
phosphate
inorganic phosphate

+ P_i

adenine

adenosine diphosphate
i.e. it has 2 phosphates

ENERGY RELEASED

ATP

adenosine triphosphate
i.e. it has 3 phosphates

Warm-Up Questions

Q1 What are the three main components of nucleotides?

Q2 What sugar is found in DNA nucleotides?

Q3 Which sugar do RNA nucleotides contain?

Q4 What is the name of the base in ATP?

PRACTICE QUESTIONS

Exam Questions

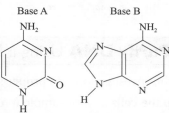

Base A

Base B

NH_2

NH_2

Q1 The structures of two nitrogen-containing bases are shown on the right.
 a) Which base, **A** or **B**, is adenine and which is cytosine?
  Explain your answer. [3 marks]
 b) Apart from nitrogen, name a chemical element present in base **A**. [1 mark]

Q2 ADP is made up of the molecule AMP and an inorganic phosphate.
 a) Suggest the chemical composition of AMP. [3 marks]
 b) Name the process by which one or more phosphate groups are added to a molecule. [1 mark]

Q3 After a heart attack ATP levels in the heart are low. Studies have been carried out to find whether ribose supplements could help the heart to replenish ATP supplies after a heart attack.
 Suggest why scientists think ribose supplements have the potential to be used in this way. [2 marks]

I prefer my tides on a beach...

There are a lot of long, dull scientific words in this topic, but all-in-all it's not too bad. It's really just a case of making sure you learn all the facts (including all the long, dull scientific words) so you can reproduce them in the exam. So go on then. Get a highlighter out. Make some notes. Or better yet, flashcards. Just make sure you learn it all.

Polynucleotides and DNA

Right, by now you should know what a nucleotide is (see the previous two pages if not).
Well now you need to learn how they come together to form polynucleotides — like DNA.

Nucleotides Join Together to Form Polynucleotides

1) The nucleotides join up between the **phosphate** group of one nucleotide and the **sugar** of another via a **condensation reaction**. This forms a **phosphodiester bond** (consisting of the phosphate group and two ester bonds).

2) The chain of sugars and phosphates is known as the **sugar-phosphate backbone**.

3) **Polynucleotides** can be **broken down** into nucleotides again by breaking the phosphodiester bonds (using **hydrolysis reactions**).

There's more on condensation and hydrolysis reactions involving ester bonds on p.24.

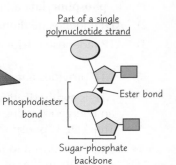

Part of a single polynucleotide strand

Phosphodiester bond

Ester bond

Sugar-phosphate backbone

Two Polynucleotide Strands Join Together to Form a Double-Helix

1) **Two DNA** polynucleotide strands join together by **hydrogen bonding** between the bases.

2) Each base can only join with one particular partner — this is called **complementary base pairing**.

3) **Adenine** always pairs with **thymine (A - T)** and **cytosine** always pairs with **guanine (C - G)**. A **purine** (A or G) always pairs with a **pyrimidine** (T or C).

4) **Two** hydrogen bonds form between **A and T**, and **three** hydrogen bonds form between **C and G**.

5) Two **antiparallel** (running in opposite directions) polynucleotide strands **twist** to form the **DNA double-helix**.

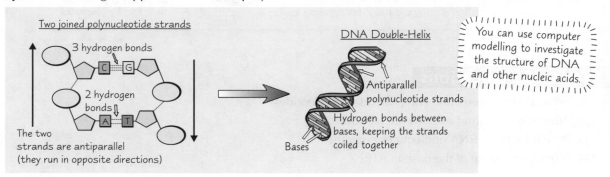

Two joined polynucleotide strands

3 hydrogen bonds

2 hydrogen bonds

The two strands are antiparallel (they run in opposite directions)

DNA Double-Helix

Antiparallel polynucleotide strands

Hydrogen bonds between bases, keeping the strands coiled together

Bases

You can use computer modelling to investigate the structure of DNA and other nucleic acids.

You Can Purify DNA Using a Precipitation Reaction

PRACTICAL SKILLS

I really like this investigation. It's **proper science**, with **green bubbly stuff** (detergent) and everything...

1) **Break up the cells** in your sample (probably a bit of **onion** or something). You can do this using a **blender**.

2) Make up a solution of **detergent** (a dilute washing-up liquid will do), **salt** (sodium chloride) and **distilled water**.

3) Add the broken-up cells to a beaker containing the detergent solution. Incubate the beaker in a **water bath** at **60 °C** for **15 minutes**.

The detergent in the mixture breaks down the cell membranes. The salt binds to the DNA and causes it to clump together. The temperature of the water bath should stop enzymes in the cells from working properly and breaking down the DNA.

4) Once incubated, put your beaker in an **ice bath** to **cool** the mixture down. When it's cooled, **filter** the mixture. Transfer a sample of your mixture to a clean boiling tube.

5) Add **protease enzymes** to the filtered mixture. These will **break down** some **proteins** in the mixture, e.g. proteins bound to the DNA. Adding **RNase enzymes** will break down any **RNA** in the mixture.

There's more on enzymes on pages 42 - 49.

6) Slowly dribble some **cold ethanol** down the side of the tube, so that it forms a **layer** on top of the DNA-detergent mixture.

7) If you leave the tube for a few minutes, the DNA will form a **white precipitate** (solid), which you can remove from the tube using a glass rod.

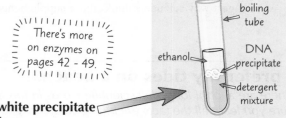

boiling tube

ethanol

DNA precipitate

detergent mixture

Polynucleotides and DNA

DNA can Copy Itself — Self-Replication

DNA copies itself before **cell division** (see page 60) so that each new cell has the full amount of DNA.

1) **DNA helicase** (an enzyme) **breaks** the **hydrogen bonds** between the two **polynucleotide** DNA strands. The helix **unzips** to form two single strands.

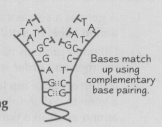

Helicase breaks hydrogen bonds

DNA helix

2) Each **original** single strand acts as a **template** for a new strand. Free-floating DNA nucleotides join to the **exposed bases** on each original template strand by **complementary base pairing** — A with T and C with G.

Bases match up using complementary base pairing.

3) The nucleotides of the new strand are **joined together** by the enzyme **DNA polymerase**. This forms the **sugar-phosphate backbone**. **Hydrogen bonds** form between the bases on the original and new strand. The strands twist to form a **double-helix**.

DNA polymerase joins the nucleotides. Hydrogen bonds form between the strands.

4) Each new DNA molecule contains **one strand** from the **original** DNA molecule and **one new strand**.

New strand

Original DNA strand

1) This type of copying is called **semi-conservative replication** because **half** of the strands in each new DNA molecule are from the **original** piece of DNA (i.e. the new molecule contains one **old** strand and one **new** strand).

2) DNA replication is really **accurate** — it has to be, to make sure **genetic information** is **conserved** (stays the same) **each time** the DNA in a cell is replicated.

3) Every so often though, a **random**, **spontaneous mutation** occurs. A mutation is any **change** to the **DNA base sequence**. Mutations don't always have an effect, but they can **alter** the **sequence of amino acids** in a **protein** (see next page). This can cause an **abnormal protein** to be produced. The abnormal protein might function **better** than the normal protein — or it might **not work at all**.

Warm-Up Questions

Q1 Name the type of bond formed between nucleotides in a polynucleotide chain.
Q2 Which DNA bases pair together in complementary base pairing?

Exam Questions

Q1 a) Describe how nucleotides are joined together in DNA. [3 marks]
b) Describe how two single polynucleotide strands are joined to make a double helix. [3 marks]

Q2 A student is extracting DNA from peas. He adds ground-up peas to a solution containing detergent and salt.
a) Explain the purpose of the detergent. [1 mark]
b) The student incubates the mixture, then cools it. He adds cold ethanol to a sample of the mixture and a white precipitate is formed. His teacher tells him that the precipitate will be a mixture of nucleic acids and not pure DNA. Suggest what the student could have done to obtain a pure sample of DNA. [2 marks]

Q3* Describe the method of semi-conservative DNA replication. [6 marks]

* You will be assessed on the quality of your written response in this question.

Give me a D, give me an N, give me an A! What d'you get? Confused...

So now you know all the DNA basics — what it's made from, its structure, how to get it out of a biological sample and how it goes about making more of itself. Phew. You still need to know what it does though. Time to turn over...

Genes and Protein Synthesis

You need to know how DNA is used to carry information — and how that information gets turned into proteins.
Luckily for you, it's all here over the next few pages...

DNA Contains **Genes** Which are **Instructions** for **Making Proteins**

1) A **gene** is a sequence of **DNA nucleotides** that codes for a **polypeptide** — the sequence of **amino acids** in a polypeptide forms the **primary structure** of a **protein** (see page 27).

2) Different proteins have a **different number** and **order** of amino acids.

3) It's the **order** of **nucleotide bases** in a gene that determines the **order of amino acids** in a particular **protein**.

4) Each amino acid is coded for by a sequence of **three bases** (called a **triplet**) in a gene.

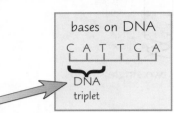

5) **Different sequences** of bases code for **different amino acids**. So the **sequence of bases** in a section of DNA is a **template** that's used to make **proteins** during **protein synthesis**.

DNA is **Copied** into **RNA** for **Protein Synthesis**

1) DNA molecules are found in the **nucleus** of the cell, but the organelles that make proteins (**ribosomes**, see page 11) are found in the **cytoplasm**.

2) DNA is **too large** to move out of the nucleus, so a section is **copied** into **mRNA** (see below). This process is called **transcription** (see page 40).

3) The mRNA **leaves** the nucleus and joins with a ribosome in the cytoplasm, where it can be used to synthesise a protein. This process is called **translation** (see page 41).

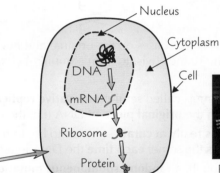

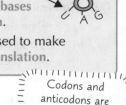

Rita Some knew how to synthesise some great tunes.

There are **Three Main Types** of **RNA**

Remember, RNA is a **single** polynucleotide strand and it contains **uracil** (**U**) as a base instead of thymine (see page 34). Uracil **always pairs** with **adenine** during protein synthesis. RNA isn't all the same though. You need to know about:

Messenger RNA (mRNA)
- Made in the **nucleus**.
- **Three adjacent bases** are called a **codon**.
- It **carries the genetic code** from the DNA in the **nucleus** to the **cytoplasm**, where it's used to make a **protein** during **translation**.

Transfer RNA (tRNA)

- Found in the **cytoplasm**.
- It has an **amino acid binding site** at one end and a **sequence** of **three bases** at the other end called an **anticodon**.
- It **carries** the amino acids that are used to make **proteins** to the **ribosomes** during **translation**.

Codons and anticodons are sometimes referred to as triplets.

Ribosomal RNA (rRNA)
- Forms the two **subunits** in a **ribosome** (along with proteins).
- The ribosome **moves along** the **mRNA strand** during protein synthesis. The rRNA in the ribosome helps to **catalyse** the formation of **peptide bonds** between the amino acids.

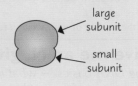

Genes and Protein Synthesis

The **Genetic Code** is **Non-Overlapping**, **Degenerate** and **Universal**

1) The genetic code is the **sequence of base triplets (codons)** in **DNA** or **mRNA**, which **codes** for **specific amino acids**.

2) In the genetic code, each base triplet is **read** in sequence, **separate** from the triplet **before** it and **after** it. Base triplets **don't share** their **bases** — the code is **non-overlapping**.

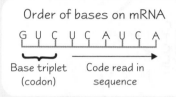 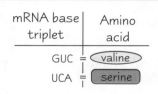 

Order of bases on mRNA

G U C U C A U C A

Base triplet (codon)   Code read in sequence

mRNA base triplet	Amino acid
GUC =	valine
UCA =	serine

Order of amino acids in a protein

valine — serine — serine

3) The genetic code is also **degenerate** — there are **more** possible combinations of **triplets** than there are amino acids (20 amino acids but 64 possible triplets). This means that some **amino acids** are coded for by **more than one** base triplet, e.g. tyrosine can be coded for by UAU or UAC.

4) Some triplets are used to tell the cell when to **start** and **stop** production of the protein — these are called **start** and **stop** signals (or start and stop **codons**). They're found at the **beginning** and **end** of the gene. E.g. UAG is a stop signal.

5) The genetic code is also **universal** — the **same** specific base triplets code for the **same** amino acids in **all living things**. E.g. UAU codes for tyrosine in all organisms.

Warm-Up Questions

Q1 What is a gene?

Q2 What is the function of mRNA?

Q3 Why is the genetic code described as degenerate?

Q4 Why is the genetic code described as universal?

PRACTICE QUESTIONS

Exam Questions

Q1 Which of the following is **not** a correct description of tRNA?

 A   It has an amino acid binding site.

 B   It contains the bases adenine, guanine, cytosine and uracil.

 C   It catalyses the formation of peptide bonds between amino acids.

 D   It carries amino acids to the ribosomes during translation.   [1 mark]

Q2 A piece of mRNA has the sequence: GUGUGUCGCGCA.

 a) How many amino acids does this sequence code for?   [1 mark]

 b) Using the table on the right, write down the
    amino acid sequence it codes for.   [2 marks]

mRNA codon	amino acid
UGU	Cysteine
CGC	Arginine
GGG	Glycine
GUG	Valine
GCA	Alanine
UUG	Leucine
UUU	Phenylalanine

Q3 An artificial mRNA was synthesized to code for a particular protein. Part of the mRNA sequence was: UUGUGUGGGUUUGCAGCA. This produced the following sequence of amino acids: Leucine–Cysteine–Glycine–Phenylalanine–Alanine–Alanine. Use the table above to help you answer the following questions.

 a) Explain how the result suggests that the genetic code is based on triplets of nucleotides in mRNA.   [2 marks]

 b) Explain how the result suggests that the genetic code is non-overlapping.   [2 marks]

Genes contain instructions — wash at 40 °C...

You really need to get your head around how DNA and RNA work together to produce proteins or the next two pages are going to be a teeny weeny bit tricky. Don't say I didn't warn you. Turn over too quickly at your own peril...

Transcription and Translation

Time to find out how RNA works its magic to make proteins. It gets a bit complicated but bear with it.

First Stage of Protein Synthesis — Transcription

During transcription an **mRNA copy** of a gene
(a section of DNA) is made in the **nucleus**:

1) Transcription starts when **RNA polymerase** (an **enzyme**) **attaches** to the **DNA** double-helix at the **beginning** of a **gene**.

2) The **hydrogen bonds** between the two DNA strands in the gene **break**, **separating** the strands, and the DNA molecule **uncoils** at that point.

3) One of the strands is then used as a **template** to make an **mRNA copy**.

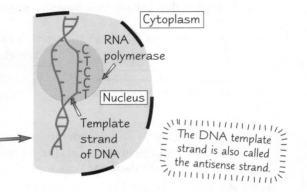

The DNA template strand is also called the antisense strand.

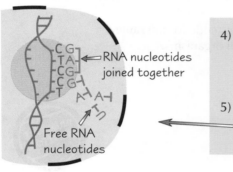

RNA nucleotides joined together

Free RNA nucleotides

4) The RNA polymerase **lines up** free **RNA nucleotides** alongside the template strand. **Complementary base pairing** means that the mRNA strand ends up being a **complementary copy** of the DNA template strand (except the base **T** is replaced by **U** in **RNA**).

5) Once the RNA nucleotides have **paired up** with their **specific bases** on the DNA strand they're **joined together**, forming an **mRNA** molecule.

| DNA triplet | A | T | C |
| codon on mRNA | U | A | G |

In eukaryotes, it's actually a complex of proteins including a DNA helicase that separates the strands. RNA polymerase just assembles the mRNA strand.

6) The RNA polymerase moves **along** the DNA, separating the strands and **assembling** the mRNA strand.

7) The **hydrogen bonds** between the uncoiled strands of DNA **re-form** once the RNA polymerase has passed by and the strands **coil back into a double-helix**.

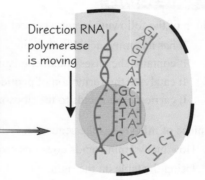

Direction RNA polymerase is moving

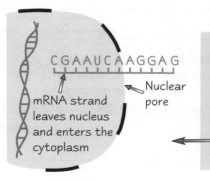

mRNA strand leaves nucleus and enters the cytoplasm

Nuclear pore

8) When RNA polymerase reaches a **stop codon** (see previous page) it stops making mRNA and **detaches** from the DNA.

9) The **mRNA** moves **out** of the **nucleus** through a **nuclear pore** and attaches to a **ribosome** in the cytoplasm, where the next stage of protein synthesis takes place (see next page).

Transcription and Translation

Second Stage of Protein Synthesis — Translation

Translation occurs at the **ribosomes** in the **cytoplasm**. During **translation**, **amino acids** are **joined together** to make a **polypeptide chain** (protein), following the sequence of **codons** carried by the mRNA.

1) The **mRNA attaches** itself to a **ribosome** and **transfer RNA** (**tRNA**) molecules **carry amino acids** to the ribosome.

2) A tRNA molecule, with an **anticodon** that's **complementary** to the **start codon** on the mRNA, attaches itself to the mRNA by **complementary base pairing**.

3) A second tRNA molecule attaches itself to the **next codon** on the mRNA in the **same way**.

4) **Ribosomal RNA** (**rRNA**) in the ribosome **catalyses** the formation of a **peptide bond** between the two amino acids attached to the tRNA molecules. This **joins** the amino acids together. The first tRNA molecule **moves away**, leaving its amino acid behind.

5) A third tRNA molecule binds to the **next codon** on the mRNA. Its amino acid **binds** to the first two and the second tRNA molecule **moves away**.

6) This process continues, producing a chain of linked amino acids (a **polypeptide chain**), until there's a **stop codon** on the mRNA molecule.

7) The polypeptide chain **moves away** from the ribosome and translation is complete.

> anticodon on tRNA U A C
> codon on mRNA A U G

Protein synthesis is also called polypeptide synthesis as it makes a polypeptide.

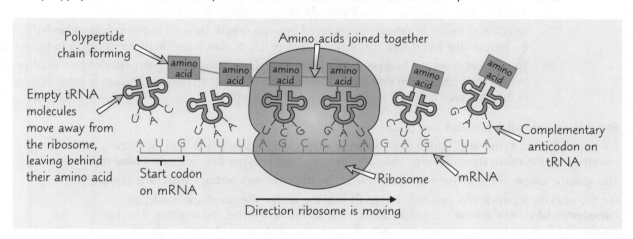

Polypeptide chain forming — amino acid

Amino acids joined together

Empty tRNA molecules move away from the ribosome, leaving behind their amino acid

Start codon on mRNA

Ribosome

mRNA

Complementary anticodon on tRNA

Direction ribosome is moving

Warm-Up Questions

Q1 What are the two stages of protein synthesis called?

Q2 Where does the first stage of protein synthesis take place?

Q3 When does RNA polymerase stop making mRNA?

Q4 Where does the second stage of protein synthesis take place?

PRACTICE QUESTIONS

Exam Questions

Q1 A DNA sequence is GCGAAGTCCATG.
  a) Write down the complementary mRNA sequence. [1 mark]
  b) Write down the sequence of the tRNA anticodons. [1 mark]

Q2 A drug that inhibits cell growth is found to be able to bind to DNA, preventing RNA polymerase from binding. Explain how this drug will affect protein synthesis. [2 marks]

Q3 A polypeptide chain (protein) from a eukaryotic cell is 10 amino acids long. Predict how long the mRNA for this protein would be in nucleotides. Explain your answer. [2 marks]

I could do with a translation for this page...

So you start off with DNA, lots of cleverness happens and bingo... you've got a protein. Only problem is you need to know the cleverness bit in quite a lot of detail. So scribble it down, recite it to yourself, explain it to your best mate or do whatever else helps you remember the joys of protein synthesis. And then think how clever you are to know it all.

Action of Enzymes

Enzymes crop up loads in Biology — they're really useful 'cos they make reactions work more quickly.

Enzymes are Biological Catalysts

> A catalyst is a substance that speeds up a chemical reaction without being used up in the reaction itself.

1) Enzymes **speed up chemical reactions** by acting as **biological catalysts**. They catalyse **metabolic reactions** — both at a **cellular level** (e.g. **respiration**) and for the **organism** as a **whole** (e.g. **digestion** in mammals).

2) Enzymes can affect **structures** in an organism (e.g. enzymes are involved in the production of **collagen**, an important protein in the **connective tissues** of animals) as well as **functions** (like **respiration**).

3) Enzyme action can be **intracellular** — **within** cells, or **extracellular** — **outside** cells.

> **Intracellular Enzyme Example — Catalase**
>
> 1) **Hydrogen peroxide** (H_2O_2) is the **toxic by-product** of several cellular reactions. If left to build up, it can **kill cells**.
>
> 2) **Catalase** is an enzyme that works **inside cells** to catalyse the breakdown of hydrogen peroxide to **harmless oxygen** (O_2) and **water** (H_2O).

> **Extracellular Enzyme Examples — Amylase and Trypsin**
>
> 1) Amylase and trypsin both work **outside cells** in the human **digestive system**.
>
> 2) **Amylase** is found in **saliva**. It's **secreted** into the **mouth** by cells in the **salivary glands**. It catalyses the **hydrolysis** (breakdown, see p. 22) of **starch** into **maltose** (a sugar) in the mouth.
>
> 3) **Trypsin** catalyses the hydrolysis of **peptide bonds** — turning **big polypeptides** into **smaller ones** (which then get broken down into amino acids by other enzymes). Trypsin is produced by cells in the **pancreas** and secreted into the **small intestine**.

4) Enzymes are **globular proteins** (see p. 28).

5) Enzymes have an **active site**, which has a **specific shape**. The active site is the part of the enzyme that the **substrate** molecules (the substance that the enzyme interacts with) **bind to**.

6) The specific shape of the active site is determined by the enzyme's **tertiary structure** (see p. 27).

7) For the enzyme to work, the substrate has to **fit into** the **active site** (its shape has to be **complementary**). If the substrate shape doesn't match the active site, the reaction won't be catalysed. This means that enzymes work with very few substrates — usually only one.

Enzymes Reduce Activation Energy

1) In a chemical reaction, a certain amount of energy needs to be supplied to the chemicals before the reaction will start. This is called the **activation energy** — it's often provided as **heat**.

2) Enzymes **reduce** the amount of activation energy that's needed, often making reactions happen at a **lower temperature** than they could without an enzyme. This **speeds** up the **rate of reaction**.

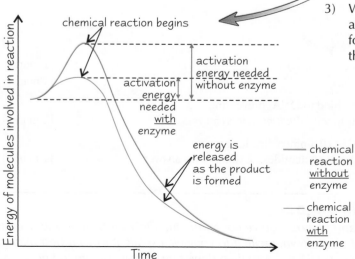

3) When a substance binds to an enzyme's active site, an **enzyme-substrate complex** is formed. It's the formation of the enzyme-substrate complex that **lowers** the **activation energy**. Here are two reasons why:

> 1) If two substrate molecules need to be **joined**, attaching to the enzyme holds them **close together**, **reducing** any **repulsion** between the molecules so they can bond more easily.
>
> 2) If the enzyme is catalysing a **breakdown reaction**, fitting into the active site puts a **strain** on bonds in the substrate. This strain means the substrate molecule **breaks up** more easily.

Action of Enzymes

The 'Lock and Key' Model is a Good Start...

Enzymes are a bit picky. They only work with **substrates** that fit their active site. Early scientists studying the action of enzymes came up with the **'lock and key'** model. This is where the **substrate fits** into the **enzyme** in the same way that a **key fits** into a **lock**.

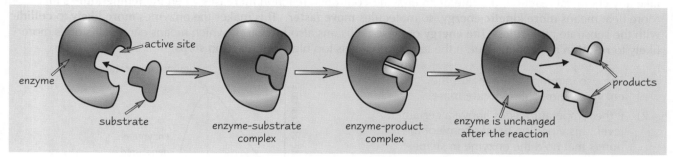

Scientists soon realised that the lock and key model didn't give the full story. The enzyme and substrate do have to fit together in the first place, but new evidence showed that the **enzyme-substrate complex changed shape** slightly to complete the fit. This **locks** the substrate even more tightly to the enzyme. Scientists modified the old lock and key model and came up with the **'induced fit'** model.

...but the 'Induced Fit' Model is a **Better Theory**

The **'induced fit'** model helps to explain why enzymes are so **specific** and only bond to one particular substrate.

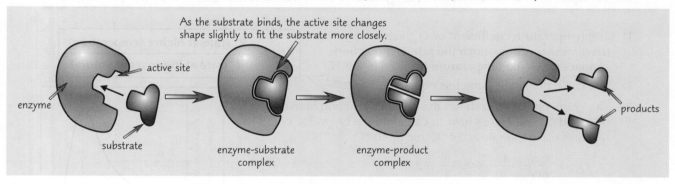

The substrate doesn't only have to be the right shape to fit the active site, it has to make the active site **change shape** in the right way as well. This is a prime example of how a widely accepted theory can **change** when **new evidence** comes along. The 'induced fit' model is still widely accepted — for now, anyway.

Warm-Up Questions

Q1 What is an enzyme?

Q2 What is the name given to the amount of energy needed to start a reaction?

Q3 What is an enzyme-substrate complex?

Q4 Explain why enzymes are specific.

Exam Question

Q1 Dextranase is an enzyme that catalyses the breakdown of specific bonds in dextran (a polysaccharide).

Use the induced fit model of enzyme action to explain why dextranase catalyses the breakdown of dextran, but not amylose (another polysaccharide). [3 marks]

But why is the enzyme-substrate complex?

OK, nothing too tricky here. The main thing to remember is that every enzyme has a specific shape, so it only works with specific substrates that fit the active site. The induced fit model is a newer theory that explains this.

Factors Affecting Enzyme Activity

Now you know what enzymes are and how they work, it's time to take a look at what makes them tick. There are four main factors affecting enzyme activity that you need to know about...

1) **Temperature** has a **Big Influence** on Enzyme Activity

Like any chemical reaction, the **rate** of an enzyme-controlled reaction **increases** when the **temperature's increased**. More heat means **more kinetic energy**, so molecules **move faster**. This makes the enzymes **more likely** to **collide** with the substrate molecules. The **energy** of these collisions also **increases**, which means each collision is more likely to **result** in a **reaction**. But, if the temperature gets too high, the **reaction stops**.

1) The rise in temperature makes the enzyme's molecules **vibrate more**.

2) If the temperature goes above a certain level, this vibration **breaks** some of the **bonds** that hold the enzyme in shape.

3) The **active site changes shape** and the enzyme and substrate **no longer fit together**.

4) At this point, the enzyme is **denatured** — it no longer functions as a catalyst.

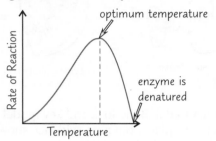

Every enzyme has an optimum temperature. For most human enzymes it's around 37 °C but some enzymes, like those used in biological washing powders, can work well at 60 °C.

The **Temperature Coefficient (Q_{10})** Shows How **Rate Changes** with **Temperature**

1) The **temperature coefficient** or Q_{10} value for a reaction shows **how much** the **rate** of a **reaction changes** when the **temperature** is **raised** by **10 °C**.

2) You can calculate it using this **equation**:

$$Q_{10} = \frac{R_2 \text{ (rate at higher temperature)}}{R_1 \text{ (rate at lower temperature)}}$$

3) The graph on the right shows the **rate** of a reaction between 0 °C and 50 °C. Here's how to **calculate** the Q_{10} value of the reaction using the rate at **30 °C** and at **40 °C**:

$$Q_{10} = \frac{\text{rate at 40 °C}}{\text{rate at 30 °C}} = \frac{8}{4} = 2$$

4) At temperatures **before** the **optimum**, a Q_{10} value of **2** means that the **rate doubles** when the temperature is raised by 10 °C. A Q_{10} value of **3** would mean that the **rate trebles**.

5) Most **enzyme-controlled reactions** have a Q_{10} value of **around 2**.

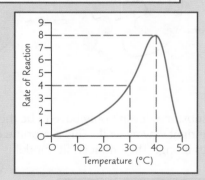

2) **pH** Also Affects Enzyme Activity

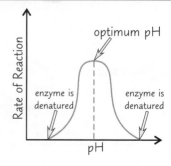

1) All enzymes have an optimum pH value. Most human enzymes work best at pH 7 (neutral), but there are exceptions. **Pepsin**, for example, works best at acidic pH 2, which is useful because it's found in the stomach.

2) Above and below the optimum pH, the H^+ and OH^- ions found in acids and alkalis can mess up the ionic bonds and hydrogen bonds that hold the enzyme's tertiary structure in place. This makes the active site change shape, so the enzyme is denatured.

Factors Affecting Enzyme Activity

3) **Enzyme Concentration** Affects the Rate of Reaction

1) The **more enzyme molecules** there are in a solution, the more likely a substrate molecule is to **collide** with one and form an **enzyme-substrate complex**. So increasing the concentration of the enzyme **increases** the **rate of reaction**.

2) But, if the amount of **substrate** is **limited**, there comes a point when there's more than enough enzyme molecules to deal with all the available substrate, so adding more enzyme has **no further effect**.

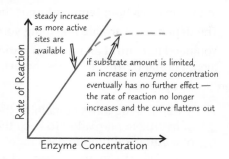

steady increase as more active sites are available

if substrate amount is limited, an increase in enzyme concentration eventually has no further effect — the rate of reaction no longer increases and the curve flattens out

4) **Substrate Concentration** Affects the Rate of Reaction **Up to a Point**

1) The higher the substrate concentration, the faster the reaction — more substrate molecules means a collision between substrate and enzyme is more likely and so more active sites will be used.

2) This is only true up until a 'saturation' point though. After that, there are so many substrate molecules that the enzymes have about as much as they can cope with (all the active sites are full), and adding more substrate makes no difference to the rate of reaction.

3) Substrate concentration decreases with time during a reaction (unless more substrate is added to the reaction mixture), so if no other variables are changed, the rate of reaction will decrease over time too. This makes the initial rate of reaction (the reaction rate right at the start of the reaction, close to time 0) the highest rate of reaction.

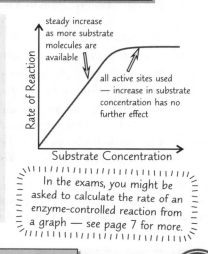

steady increase as more substrate molecules are available

all active sites used — increase in substrate concentration has no further effect

In the exams, you might be asked to calculate the rate of an enzyme-controlled reaction from a graph — see page 7 for more.

You can **Measure** the **Rate** of an **Enzyme-Controlled** Reaction

You need to know how the effects of **pH**, **temperature**, **enzyme concentration** and **substrate concentration** can be investigated **experimentally**. Here are two ways of measuring the **rate** of an enzyme-controlled reaction:

Example 1

You can measure **how fast** the **product** of the reaction **appears**. The diagram on the right shows how to measure this with the enzyme **catalase**. Catalase catalyses the **breakdown** of **hydrogen peroxide** into **water** and **oxygen**. It's easy to collect the oxygen produced and measure **how fast** it's given off.

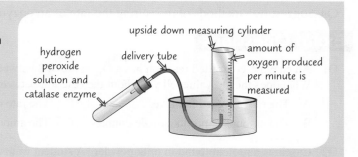

upside down measuring cylinder

delivery tube

hydrogen peroxide solution and catalase enzyme

amount of oxygen produced per minute is measured

Example 2

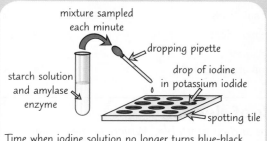

mixture sampled each minute

dropping pipette

drop of iodine in potassium iodide

starch solution and amylase enzyme

spotting tile

Time when iodine solution no longer turns blue-black is noted — starch has then been broken down.

You can also measure the **disappearance** of the **substrate** rather than the appearance of the product and use this to **compare the rate** of reaction under different conditions. For example, the enzyme **amylase** catalyses the breakdown of **starch** to **maltose** (see p. 42). It's easy to detect starch using a solution of potassium iodide and iodine. You can **time** how long it takes for the starch to disappear by **regularly sampling** the starch solution. You can then **alter** the **conditions** of the reaction and compare rates.

Factors Affecting Enzyme Activity

Example: Investigating the Effect of Temperature on Catalase Activity

1) In this investigation, **temperature** is the **independent variable** — the thing you **change**.
2) The **dependent variable** (the thing you **measure**) will be the **volume of oxygen** produced.
3) You need to **control** all the **other variables** that could affect the outcome of the investigation (i.e. keep them constant). That includes the **pH**, the **enzyme concentration**, the **substrate concentration**, etc.

Here's what you do:

1) Set up boiling tubes containing the **same volume** and **concentration** of **hydrogen peroxide**. To keep the pH constant, add **equal volumes** of a **buffer solution** to each tube. (A buffer solution is able to resist changes in pH when small amounts of acid or alkali are added.)

> Different buffer solutions have different pHs. You'd need to use one with the optimum pH for the enzyme you're testing here.

2) Set up the **apparatus** to measure the **volume** of oxygen produced from each boiling tube. For example, use a delivery tube and upside down measuring cylinder, as shown on the previous page.
3) Put each boiling tube in a **water bath** set to a different temperature (e.g. 10 °C, 20 °C, 30 °C and 40 °C) along with another tube containing **catalase** (wait 5 minutes before moving on to the next step to allow the enzyme to reach the set temperature).
4) Use a pipette to add the **same volume** and **concentration** of **catalase** to each boiling tube.
5) **Record** how much oxygen is produced in the **first 60 seconds** of the reaction. Use a **stopwatch** to measure the time.

> A negative control reaction, i.e. a boiling tube not containing catalase, should also be carried out at each temperature.

6) **Repeat** the experiment at each temperature three times, and use the results to find the **mean volume of oxygen produced** at each temperature.
7) **Calculate** the **mean rate of reaction** at each temperature by dividing the volume of oxygen produced by the time taken (i.e. 60 s). The **unit** for the **rate of reaction** here will be cm³/second or $cm^3 \, s^{-1}$.

It's easy to **alter** this experiment to investigate the effect of a **different variable** on catalase activity. E.g. if you wanted to investigate the effect of **substrate concentration**, you'd keep the **temperature** of the reaction the **same**, but prepare boiling tubes with **different concentrations** of **hydrogen peroxide** (this could be done using **serial dilutions** — see page 31). To investigate the effect of **pH**, you could add a **buffer solution** with a **different pH** to each tube.

Warm-Up Questions

Q1 What does it mean if an enzyme is denatured?
Q2 Explain why increasing the concentration of an enzyme doesn't always increase the rate of reaction.
Q3 Explain the effect of increasing substrate concentration on the rate of an enzyme-catalysed reaction.
Q4 Suggest two methods of measuring the rate of an enzyme-catalysed reaction.

Exam Questions

Q1 An enzyme-controlled reaction has a Q_{10} value of 2 between 10 °C and 30 °C.
What does the Q_{10} value tell you about the reaction between these two temperatures?

A   The rate of reaction halves.   C   The rate of reaction doubles.

B   The amount of product made doubles.   D   The amount of product made halves.   [1 mark]

Q2 Casein is a protein found in milk powder. A student wants to investigate the effect of varying pH on the rate of casein breakdown by the enzyme trypsin. She intends to add trypsin to a series of solutions containing milk powder at different pHs and time how long it takes for each solution to turn from cloudy to translucent.

a) Suggest how the student could vary the pH of the milk powder solutions.   [1 mark]

b) Give one variable that the student will need to control in this experiment.   [1 mark]

c) The student has read that the optimum pH for trypsin is pH 8.
Describe and explain what will happen to the rate of the reaction above this pH.   [4 marks]

Factors affecting my activity — laziness, lack of sleep...

Enzymes are pretty fussy — they'll only work best when they are nice and comfortable. Which, come to think of it, is when I work best too. Make sure you're comfortable, then learn how temperature, pH, enzyme concentration and substrate concentration affect enzyme activity — and how to investigate their effects on the rate of a reaction.

Cofactors and Enzyme Inhibition

Cofactors are substances that enzymes need to work. Enzyme inhibitors, yep you guessed it, inhibit their action. Some inhibitors are poisons, but they're not all bad — we use some of them as medicinal drugs.

Cofactors and Coenzymes are Essential for Enzymes to Work

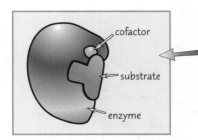

Some enzymes will only work if there is another **non-protein** substance bound to them. These non-protein substances are called **cofactors**.

1) Some cofactors are **inorganic** molecules or ions. They work by helping the enzyme and substrate to **bind together**. They don't directly participate in the reaction so aren't **used up** or **changed** in any way. For example, **chloride ions (Cl⁻)** are **cofactors** for the enzyme **amylase**.

2) Some cofactors are **organic** molecules — these are called **coenzymes**. They participate in the reaction and are **changed** by it (they're just like a second substrate, but they aren't called that). They often act as **carriers**, moving **chemical groups** between different enzymes. They're **continually recycled** during this process. **Vitamins** are often **sources** of coenzymes.

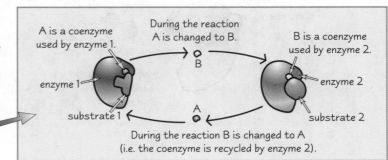

3) If a cofactor is **tightly bound** to the enzyme, it's known as a **prosthetic group**. For example, **zinc ions (Zn²⁺)** are a prosthetic group for **carbonic anhydrase** (an enzyme in red blood cells, which catalyses the production of carbonic acid from water and carbon dioxide). The zinc ions are a **permanent part** of the enzyme's **active site**.

You need to learn the Cl⁻ and Zn²⁺ examples for the exam.

Enzyme Activity can be Inhibited

Enzyme activity can be prevented by **enzyme inhibitors** — molecules that **bind to the enzyme** that they inhibit. Inhibition can be **competitive** (see below) or **non-competitive** (see next page).

COMPETITIVE INHIBITION

1) **Competitive inhibitor** molecules have a **similar shape** to that of the **substrate** molecules.
2) They **compete** with the substrate molecules to **bind** to the **active site**, but **no reaction** takes place.
3) Instead they **block** the active site, so **no substrate** molecules can **fit** in it.

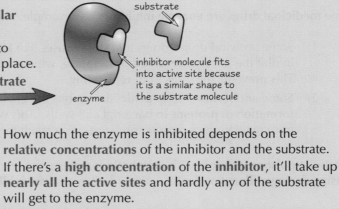

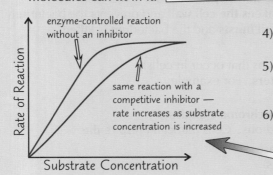

4) How much the enzyme is inhibited depends on the **relative concentrations** of the inhibitor and the substrate.
5) If there's a **high concentration** of the **inhibitor**, it'll take up **nearly all** the **active sites** and hardly any of the substrate will get to the enzyme.
6) But if there's a **higher concentration** of **substrate**, then the substrate's chances of getting to an active site before the inhibitor **increase**. So **increasing** the concentration of **substrate** will **increase** the **rate of reaction** (up to a point).

Cofactors and Enzyme Inhibition

NON-COMPETITIVE INHIBITION

1) **Non-competitive inhibitor** molecules bind to the enzyme **away from its active site**. The site they bind to is known as the enzyme's **allosteric site**.

2) This causes the active site to **change shape** so the substrate molecules can **no longer bind** to it.

3) They **don't 'compete'** with the substrate molecules to bind to the active site because they are a **different shape**.

4) **Increasing** the concentration of **substrate won't** make any difference to the reaction rate — enzyme activity will still be inhibited.

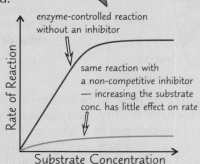

inhibitor molecules fits into allosteric site of enzyme

substrate molecule can no longer fit into active site

enzyme

inhibitor causes changes that alter active site

enzyme-controlled reaction without an inhibitor

same reaction with a non-competitive inhibitor — increasing the substrate conc. has little effect on rate

Rate of Reaction

Substrate Concentration

Inhibitors Can Be **Reversible** or **Non-Reversible**

Which one they are depends on the **strength of the bonds** between the enzyme and the inhibitor.

1) If they're strong, covalent bonds, the inhibitor can't be removed easily and the inhibition is irreversible.

2) If they're weaker hydrogen bonds or weak ionic bonds, the inhibitor can be removed and the inhibition is reversible.

The hockey team had strong bonds. Especially after they accidentally glued their kits together.

Some **Drugs** and **Metabolic Poisons** are **Enzyme Inhibitors**

Some **medicinal drugs** are **enzyme inhibitors**, for example:

1) Some **antiviral** drugs (drugs that stop **viruses** like **HIV**) — e.g. **reverse transcriptase inhibitors** inhibit the enzyme **reverse transcriptase**, which catalyses the **replication** of **viral DNA**. This **prevents** the virus from **replicating**.

2) Some **antibiotics** — e.g. **penicillin** inhibits the enzyme **transpeptidase**, which **catalyses** the **formation** of **proteins** in bacterial cell walls. This **weakens the cell wall** and prevents the bacterium from regulating its osmotic pressure. As a result the cell **bursts** and the bacterium is **killed**.

Metabolic **poisons interfere** with **metabolic reactions** (the reactions that occur in cells), causing **damage**, **illness** or **death** — they're often **enzyme inhibitors**. For example:

1) Cyanide is an irreversible inhibitor of cytochrome c oxidase, an enzyme that catalyses respiration reactions. Cells that can't respire die.

2) Malonate inhibits succinate dehydrogenase (which also catalyses respiration reactions).

3) Arsenic inhibits the action of pyruvate dehydrogenase, another enzyme that catalyses respiration reactions.

Cofactors and Enzyme Inhibition

Metabolic Pathways are Regulated by End-Product Inhibition

1) A **metabolic pathway** is a series of **connected metabolic reactions**. The **product** of the **first reaction** takes part in the **second reaction** — and so on. Each reaction is catalysed by a **different enzyme**.

2) Many enzymes are **inhibited** by the **product** of the reaction they catalyse. This is known as **product inhibition**.

3) **End-product inhibition** is when the **final product** in a **metabolic pathway** inhibits an enzyme that acts **earlier on** in the pathway.

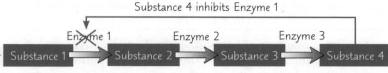

Substance 4 inhibits Enzyme 1

Enzyme 1 — Enzyme 2 — Enzyme 3

Substance 1 → Substance 2 → Substance 3 → Substance 4

4) End-product inhibition is a nifty way of **regulating** the pathway and **controlling** the amount of end-product that gets made. For example:

- **Phosphofructokinase** is an enzyme involved in the metabolic pathway that **breaks down glucose** to make **ATP**.
- ATP **inhibits** the action of phosphofructokinase — so a **high level** of ATP **prevents** more ATP from being made.

5) Both product and end-product inhibition are **reversible**. So when the level of product starts to **drop**, the level of inhibition will start to fall and the enzyme can start to **function again** — this means that **more product** can be made.

Enzyme Inhibition Can Help to Protect Cells

1) Enzymes are sometimes synthesised as **inactive precursors** in **metabolic pathways** to prevent them causing damage to cells. For example, some **proteases** (which **break down proteins**) are synthesised as inactive precursors to stop them **damaging proteins** in the cell in which they're made.

2) Part of the precursor molecule **inhibits** its action as an enzyme. Once this part is **removed** (e.g. via a chemical reaction) the enzyme becomes **active**.

A sense of inhibition might have protected Dan from his dress sense.

Warm-Up Questions

Q1 What are cofactors, coenzymes and prosthetic groups?
Q2 What's the difference between competitive and non-competitive enzyme inhibitors?
Q3 Name one metabolic poison and describe how it works.
Q4 Why are some enzymes synthesised as inactive precursors?

Exam Questions

Q1 In bacteria, lactose is broken down into glucose and galactose by the enzyme ß-galactosidase. Galactose inhibits ß-galactosidase by binding to the active site. Which one of the following statements is correct?

A Galactose is a cofactor of ß-galactosidase.
B The inhibition of ß-galactosidase by galactose is irreversible.
C Galactose binds to ß-galactosidase via weak hydrogen bonds.
D Galactose is a non-competitive inhibitor of ß-galactosidase. [1 mark]

Q2 During an experiment hexokinase (an enzyme that catalyses reactions important in respiration) was found to work only in the presence of magnesium ions and to work slower when aluminium ions were also present.
a) Suggest a possible reason why hexokinase only works when magnesium ions are present. [2 marks]
b) Suggest a possible reason why hexokinase works slower when aluminium ions are present. [2 marks]
c) Explain why aluminium ions are a metabolic poison. [1 mark]

Q3 HIV uses protease enzymes to catalyse the breakdown of proteins. It uses the products of the reaction to replicate new viruses. Ritonavir is a drug used to treat HIV. Its molecules have a similar shape to the protein molecules which are the substrate for HIV protease. Suggest how Ritonavir will affect HIV. Explain your answer. [3 marks]

Enzymes are easily inhibited — they're very shy you know...

Crikey, it's like a rubbish soap or something — one minute the enzymes are trying to kill us, the next they're bringing us back to life, and all the while there are some things trying to stop them, and others trying to help them — if you can follow the ins, outs, ups and downs of some crazy soap then you can follow this. Everybody needs good en-zymes...

Cell Membranes

You might remember a bit about cell membranes from that giant pink table of fun back in Module 2 Section 1. Well now it's time to delve a little deeper and see exactly what they do — lucky you.

Membranes Control What Passes Through Them

Cells, and many of the **organelles** inside them, are surrounded by **membranes**, which have a **range of functions**:

Membranes at the **surface of cells** (PLASMA membranes)

1) They are a **barrier** between the **cell** and its **environment**, controlling **which substances enter and leave** the cell. They're **partially permeable** — they let some molecules through but not others. Substances can move across the plasma membrane by **diffusion**, **osmosis** or **active transport** (see pages 54-59).

2) They allow **recognition** by other cells, e.g. the cells of the **immune system** (see p. 102).

3) They allow **cell communication** (sometimes called **cell signalling**) — see p. 52.

Partially permeable membranes can be useful at sea.

Membranes **within cells**

1) The membranes around **organelles divide** the cell into different **compartments** — they act as a **barrier** between the **organelle** and the **cytoplasm**. This makes different **functions more efficient**, e.g. the substances needed for **respiration** (like enzymes) are kept together inside **mitochondria**.

2) They can form **vesicles** to **transport** substances between different areas of the cell (see p. 57).

3) They control **which substances enter and leave** the organelle, e.g. RNA (see p. 38) leaves the nucleus via the nuclear membrane. They are also **partially permeable**.

4) You can also get membranes **within organelles** — these act as **barriers** between the membrane contents and the rest of the organelle, e.g. thylakoid membranes in chloroplasts (see p. 12).

5) Membranes within cells can be the **site** of **chemical reactions**, e.g. the **inner membrane** of a mitochondrion contains **enzymes** needed for **respiration**.

Cell Membranes have a 'Fluid Mosaic' Structure

The **structure** of all membranes is basically the same. They're composed of **lipids** (mainly phospholipids), **proteins** and **carbohydrates** (usually attached to proteins or lipids).

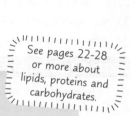

See pages 22-28 or more about lipids, proteins and carbohydrates.

1) In 1972, the **fluid mosaic model** was suggested to describe the **arrangement** of **molecules** in the membrane.

2) In the model, **phospholipid molecules** form a continuous, double layer (**bilayer**).

3) This bilayer is 'fluid' because the phospholipids are **constantly moving**.

4) **Cholesterol** molecules are present within the bilayer (see next page).

5) **Protein molecules** are scattered through the bilayer, like tiles in a **mosaic**.

6) Some **proteins** have a **polysaccharide** (carbohydrate) **chain** attached — these are called **glycoproteins**.

7) Some **lipids** also have a **polysaccharide chain** attached — these are called **glycolipids**.

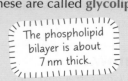

The phospholipid bilayer is about 7 nm thick.

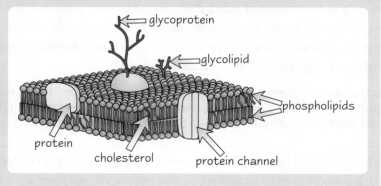

glycoprotein

glycolipid

phospholipids

protein

cholesterol

protein channel

Cell Membranes

The **Different Components** of Cell Membranes have **Different Roles**

Phospholipids Form a Barrier to Dissolved Substances

1) **Phospholipid molecules** have a 'head' and a 'tail'.
2) The **head** is **hydrophilic** — it **attracts water**.
3) The **tail** is **hydrophobic** — it **repels water**.
4) The molecules automatically **arrange** themselves into a **bilayer** — the **heads face out** towards the water on either side of the membrane.
5) The **centre** of the bilayer is **hydrophobic** so the membrane **doesn't** allow **water-soluble substances** (like ions) through it — it acts as a **barrier** to these dissolved substances. (But **fat-soluble substances**, e.g. fat-soluble vitamins, can **dissolve** in the bilayer and pass directly through the membrane.)

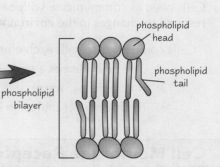

phospholipid head

phospholipid tail

phospholipid bilayer

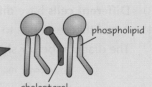

See p. 25 for more on phospholipids and cholesterol.

Cholesterol Gives the Membrane Stability

1) **Cholesterol** is a type of lipid.
2) It's present in **all** cell membranes (except bacterial cell membranes).
3) Cholesterol molecules fit **between** the phospholipids. They bind to the hydrophobic tails of the phospholipids, causing them to pack **more closely together**. This makes the membrane **less fluid** and **more rigid**.
4) At **lower temperatures**, cholesterol **prevents** phospholipids from packing **too close together** and so **increases membrane fluidity**.

phospholipid

cholesterol

Proteins Control What Enters and Leaves the Cell

1) Some proteins form **channels** in the membrane (see p. 56) — these allow **small** or **charged** particles **through**.
2) Other proteins (called **carrier proteins**) **transport molecules** and **ions** across the membrane by **active transport** and **facilitated diffusion** (see p. 56).
3) Proteins also act as **receptors** for molecules (e.g. hormones) in **cell signalling** (see next page). When a molecule **binds** to the protein, a **chemical reaction** is triggered inside the cell.

Glycolipids and Glycoproteins act as Receptors for Messenger Molecules

1) Glycolipids and glycoproteins **stabilise** the membrane by forming **hydrogen bonds** with surrounding **water molecules**.
2) They're also sites where **drugs**, **hormones** and **antibodies** bind.
3) They act as **receptors** for **cell signalling** (see next page).
4) They're also **antigens** — cell surface molecules involved in the immune response (see p. 102).

Warm-Up Questions

Q1 Give two functions of membranes at the cell surface and two functions of membranes within the cell.
Q2 Give three molecules that are present in animal cell membranes.

PRACTICE QUESTIONS

Exam Questions

Q1 Explain why the plasma membrane can be described as having a fluid mosaic structure. [2 marks]

Q2 State two functions of proteins in cell membranes. [2 marks]

Fluid Mosaic Model — think I saw one being sold at a craft fair...

It's weird to think that cells are surrounded by a layer that's 'fluid' — it's a good job it is though, 'cause if cell membranes were rigid a cell wouldn't be able to change shape or stretch without bursting. It's also a good job that the membrane's partially permeable — so that it can let oxygen into the cell and carbon dioxide out of the cell. Phew.

Cell Membranes

Cells like to have a good chat with one another every so often. To do this they use a process called cell signalling.

Cell Signalling is How Cells Communicate with Each Other

Cells need to communicate with each other to **control processes** inside the body and to **respond** to **changes** in the **environment**.

> Cells communicate with each other using **messenger molecules**:
>
> 1) One cell **releases** a messenger molecule (e.g. a **hormone**).
> 2) This molecule **travels** (e.g. in the blood) to another cell.
> 3) The messenger molecule is detected by the cell because it **binds** to a **receptor** on its **cell membrane**.

Cell Membrane Receptors Play an Important Role in Cell Signalling

1) **Proteins** in the cell membrane act as **receptors** for messenger molecules. These are called 'membrane-bound receptors'.
2) Receptor proteins have **specific shapes** — only **messenger molecules** with a **complementary shape** can **bind** to them.
3) **Different cells** have **different types** of receptors — they respond to **different messenger molecules**.
4) A cell that responds to a particular messenger molecule is called a **target cell**.

   The diagram below shows how messenger molecules bind to target cells.

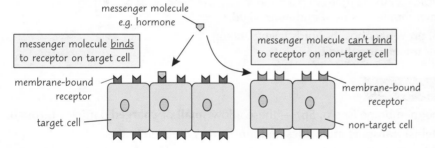

Example: Glucagon

Glucagon is a **hormone** that's **released** when there **isn't enough glucose** in the **blood**. It **binds** to **receptors** on **liver cells**, causing the liver cells to **break down** stores of **glycogen** to glucose.

Drugs Also Bind to Cell Membrane Receptors

1) Many **drugs** work by **binding** to **receptors** in cell membranes.
2) They either **trigger** a **response** in the cell, or **block** the receptor and **prevent** it from **working**.

Example: Antihistamines

Cell damage causes the release of **histamine**. Histamine binds to receptors on the surface of other cells and causes **inflammation**. **Antihistamines** work by **blocking histamine receptors** on cell surfaces. This **prevents** histamine from binding to the cell and **stops inflammation**.

The Permeability of the Cell Membrane can be Investigated in the Lab

PRACTICAL SKILLS

The permeability of cell membranes is affected by **different conditions**, e.g. **temperature**, **solvent type** and **solvent concentration**. You can investigate how these things affect permeability by doing an experiment using **beetroot**. Beetroot cells contain a **coloured pigment** that **leaks out** — the **higher** the **permeability** of the membrane, the **more pigment** leaks out of the cell.

> Here's how you could investigate how temperature affects beetroot membrane permeability:
>
> 1) Cut five equal sized pieces of beetroot and rinse them to remove any pigment released during cutting.
> 2) Place the five pieces in five different test tubes, each with 5 cm³ of water.
> 3) Place each test tube in a water bath at a different temperature, e.g. 10°C, 20°C, 30°C, 40°C, 50°C, for the same length of time.
> 4) Remove the pieces of beetroot from the tubes, leaving just the coloured liquid.
> 5) Now you need to use a colorimeter — a machine that passes light through the liquid and measures how much of that light is absorbed (see p. 31). The higher the permeability of the membrane, the more pigment is released, so the higher the absorbance of the liquid.

Cell Membranes

Increasing the Temperature Increases Membrane Permeability

Experiments like the one on the previous page have shown that membrane permeability **changes** with temperature:

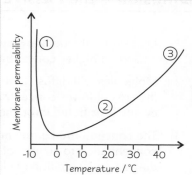

① **Temperatures below 0 °C**
The phospholipids don't have much energy, so they can't move very much. They're **packed closely together** and the membrane is **rigid**. But **channel proteins** and **carrier proteins** in the membrane **deform**, **increasing** the **permeability** of the membrane. **Ice crystals** may form and **pierce** the membrane making it **highly permeable** when it thaws.

② **Temperatures between 0 and 45 °C**
The phospholipids can **move** around and **aren't** packed as tightly together — the membrane is **partially permeable**. As the temperature **increases** the phospholipids **move more** because they have more energy — this **increases** the **permeability** of the membrane.

③ **Temperatures above 45 °C**
The phospholipid bilayer starts to **melt** (break down) and the membrane becomes more **permeable**. **Water** inside the cell **expands**, putting pressure on the membrane. **Channel proteins** and **carrier proteins** **deform** so they can't control what enters or leaves the cell — this increases the **permeability** of the membrane.

Changing the Solvent Affects Membrane Permeability

Different solvents and their **concentration** can affect the **permeability** of cell membranes.

1) Surrounding cells in a **solvent** (such as ethanol) **increases** the **permeability** of their cell membranes.

2) This is because solvents **dissolve** the **lipids** in a cell membrane, so the membrane **loses** its **structure**.

3) Some solvents **increase** cell **permeability** more than others, e.g. **ethanol** increases cell permeability more than **methanol**.

4) You could **investigate** the effects of different solvents by doing an experiment using **beetroot** like the one on the previous page.

5) **Increasing** the **concentration** of the solvent will also **increase** membrane **permeability**. For example, this graph shows the effect of alcohol concentration on membrane permeability.

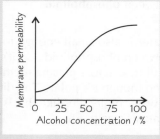

Warm-Up Questions

Q1 Describe, using an example, how cells communicate with one another.

Q2 Describe how the permeability of a cell membrane changes as the temperature increases.

Exam Question

Q1 The table on the right shows the results of an investigation into the effect of alcohol concentration on the permeability of beetroot cell membranes.

a) Suggest a suitable method that could have been used to obtain these results. [4 marks]

b) What conclusion can be drawn from the results? [2 marks]

c) Suggest an explanation for the results. [1 mark]

Alcohol concentration / %	Absorbance
0	0.14
25	0.22
50	0.49
75	1.03
100	1.28

Perm-eability — it's definitely decreased since the 80s...

Messenger molecules are released by different cells in your body. They travel round and bind to receptors on other cells, causing some kind of response. This signalling fine-tunes all the body's processes and keeps us working properly.

Transport Across Cell Membranes

The beauty of cell membranes is that they're partially permeable — they'll only let certain substances enter and leave. Some substances move across cell membranes by passive transport, which means no energy is involved in the process. Passive transport processes include diffusion, facilitated diffusion (see p. 56) and osmosis (see p. 58).

Diffusion is the Passive Movement of Particles

1) Diffusion is the **net movement** of particles (molecules or ions) from an area of **higher concentration** to an area of **lower concentration**.

2) Molecules will diffuse **both ways**, but the **net movement** will be to the area of **lower concentration**. This continues until particles are **evenly distributed** throughout the liquid or gas.

3) The **concentration gradient** is the path from an area of higher concentration to an area of lower concentration. Particles diffuse **down** a concentration gradient.

4) Diffusion is a **passive process** — **no energy** is needed for it to happen.

Diffusion — not good in a swimming pool.

Small, Non-Polar Molecules Diffuse Through Cell Membranes

- **Small**, **non-polar** molecules such as **oxygen** and **carbon dioxide** are able to **diffuse** easily through spaces between **phospholipids**.

- **Water** is also **small** enough to fit between phospholipids, so it's able to **diffuse** across **plasma membranes** even though it's **polar**. The diffusion of water molecules like this is called **osmosis** (see p. 58).

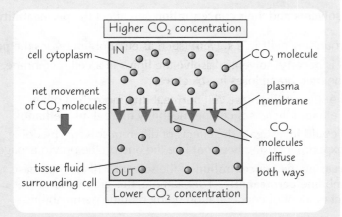

The Rate of Diffusion Depends on Several Factors

1) The concentration gradient — the higher it is, the faster the rate of diffusion.

2) The thickness of the exchange surface — the thinner the exchange surface (i.e. the shorter the distance the particles have to travel), the faster the rate of diffusion.

3) The surface area — the larger the surface area (e.g. of a cell membrane), the faster the rate of diffusion.

4) The temperature — the warmer it is, the faster the rate of diffusion because the particles have more kinetic energy so they move faster.

Transport Across Cell Membranes

You Can **Investigate Diffusion** in **Model Cells**

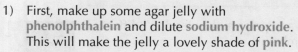

Phenolphthalein is a **pH indicator** — it's **pink** in alkaline solutions and **colourless** in acidic solutions.
You can use it to investigate **diffusion** in **agar jelly**:

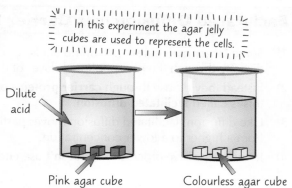

In this experiment the agar jelly cubes are used to represent the cells.

1) First, make up some agar jelly with phenolphthalein and dilute sodium hydroxide. This will make the jelly a lovely shade of pink.

2) Then fill a beaker with some dilute hydrochloric acid. Using a scalpel, cut out a few cubes from the jelly and put them in the beaker of acid.

3) If you leave the cubes for a while they'll eventually turn colourless as the acid diffuses into the agar jelly and neutralises the sodium hydroxide.

Dilute acid

Pink agar cube   Colourless agar cube

Using this experiment you can **investigate factors** that affect the **rate of diffusion**. For example:

SURFACE AREA — Cut the agar jelly into **different sized** cubes and work out their **surface area to volume ratio** (see p. 70). Time how long it takes each cube to go **colourless** when placed in the **same concentration** of hydrochloric acid. You would expect the cubes with the **largest surface area to volume ratio** to go colourless **fastest**.

CONCENTRATION GRADIENT — Prepare test tubes containing **different concentrations** of hydrochloric acid. Put an equal-sized cube of the agar jelly in each test tube and time how long it takes each one to turn **colourless**. You would expect the cubes in the **highest concentration** of hydrochloric acid to go colourless **fastest**.

TEMPERATURE — Prepare several boiling tubes containing the same concentration of hydrochloric acid and put the tubes into water baths of **varying temperatures**. Put an equal-sized cube of the agar jelly into each boiling tube and time how long it takes each cube to go **colourless**. You would expect the cubes in the **highest temperature** to go colourless **fastest**.

Don't increase the temperature above 65 °C or the agar jelly will start to melt.

Warm-Up Questions

Q1 Diffusion is a passive transport process. What does this mean?

Q2 Other than concentration gradient, give three factors that affect the rate of diffusion.

Q3 Describe an experiment you could use to investigate the effect of concentration gradient on the rate of diffusion.

Exam Question

Q1 A student carried out an experiment with gelatine blocks containing cresol red, a pH indicator that changes from red to yellow when it comes into contact with acid. She cut cubes into three different sizes and placed each cube into a hydrochloric acid solution. She observed when each cube turned yellow and recorded the time taken. She repeated the experiment four times for each size of cube. Her results are shown in the table.

Size of cube (mm)	Surface area to volume ratio	Time taken for cube to become yellow (s)			
		Trial 1	Trial 2	Trial 3	Trial 4
5 × 5 × 5	1.2:1	174	167	177	182
7 × 7 × 7	0.9:1	274	290	284	292
10 × 10 × 10	0.6:1	835	825	842	838

a) Give two variables that should have been controlled during the experiment. [2 marks]

b) What conclusion about the rate of diffusion can be drawn from the results of the experiment? [1 mark]

c) Suggest one reason why the results of the experiment might not be very precise. [1 mark]

All these molecules moving about — you'd think they'd get tired...

Diffusion is simple really — it's just particles spreading themselves out evenly. Make sure you learn the different factors that can affect the rate of diffusion and know how you can investigate the rate of diffusion in the lab.

Transport Across Cell Membranes

Facilitated diffusion is another passive transport process, but there's also an active transport process involving energy, which is imaginatively named 'active transport'. Facilitated diffusion and active transport are actually quite similar though — they both involve proteins.

Facilitated Diffusion uses Carrier Proteins and Channel Proteins

1) Some **larger molecules** (e.g. amino acids, glucose), **ions** and **polar molecules don't diffuse directly through** the phospholipid bilayer of the cell membrane.

2) Instead they diffuse through **carrier proteins** or **channel proteins** in the cell membrane — this is called **facilitated diffusion**.

3) Like diffusion, facilitated diffusion moves particles **down** a **concentration gradient**, from a higher to a lower concentration.

4) It's also a passive process — it **doesn't** use **energy**.

Andy needed all his concentration for this particular gradient...

Carrier proteins move **large molecules** into or out of the cell, down their concentration gradient. **Different carrier proteins** facilitate the diffusion of **different molecules**.

1) First, a large molecule **attaches** to a carrier protein in the membrane.

2) Then, the protein **changes shape**.

3) This **releases** the molecule on the **opposite side** of the membrane.

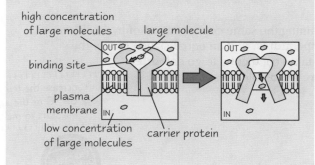

Channel proteins form **pores** in the membrane for **charged particles** to diffuse through (down their concentration gradient). **Different channel proteins** facilitate the diffusion of **different charged particles**.

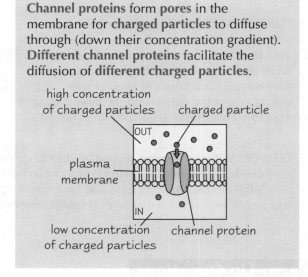

Active Transport Moves Substances Against a Concentration Gradient

Active transport uses **energy** to move **molecules** and **ions** across plasma membranes, **against** a **concentration gradient**. This process involves **carrier proteins**.

1) The process is pretty similar to facilitated diffusion — a molecule **attaches** to the carrier protein, the protein **changes shape** and this moves the molecule **across** the membrane, **releasing it** on the other side.

2) The only difference is that **energy** is used (from **ATP** — a common source of energy used in the cell), to move the solute against its concentration gradient.

3) The diagram on the right shows the active transport of **calcium ions** (Ca^{2+}).

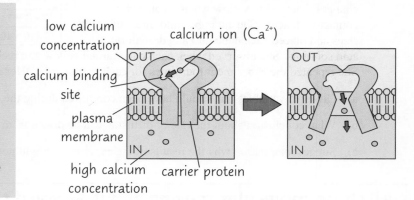

Transport Across Cell Membranes

Cells can **Take in** Substances by **Endocytosis**

1) Some molecules are way too **large** to be taken into a cell by carrier proteins, e.g. proteins, lipids and some carbohydrates.

2) Instead a cell can **surround** a substance with a **section** of its **plasma membrane**.

3) The membrane then **pinches off** to form a **vesicle** inside the cell containing the **ingested substance** — this is **endocytosis**.

4) Some cells also take in much **larger objects** by endocytosis — for example, some **white blood cells** (mainly phagocytes, see p. 102) use endocytosis to take in things like **microorganisms** and **dead cells** so that they can destroy them.

5) Like active transport, (see previous page), this process also uses **ATP** for **energy**.

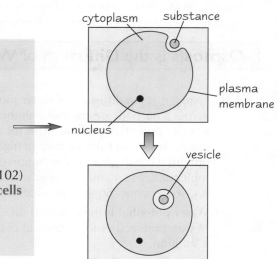

Cells can **Secrete** Substances by **Exocytosis**

1) Some substances produced by the cell (e.g. digestive enzymes, hormones, lipids) need to be released from the cell — this is done by exocytosis.

2) **Vesicles** containing these substances **pinch off** from the sacs of the **Golgi apparatus** (see p. 12) and **move towards** the plasma membrane.

3) The vesicles **fuse** with the **plasma membrane** and **release** their contents **outside** the cell.

4) Some substances (like membrane proteins) **aren't** released outside the cell — instead they are **inserted** straight into the plasma membrane.

5) Exocytosis uses **ATP** as an **energy source**.

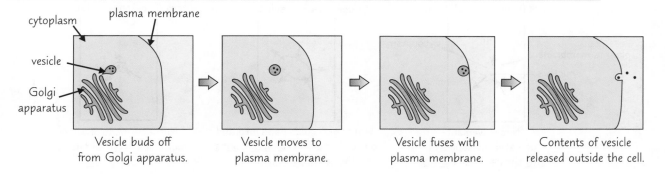

| Vesicle buds off from Golgi apparatus. | Vesicle moves to plasma membrane. | Vesicle fuses with plasma membrane. | Contents of vesicle released outside the cell. |

Warm-Up Questions

Q1 When would facilitated diffusion take place rather than simple diffusion?

Q2 What is active transport?

Q3 Which molecule provides the energy for active transport?

Exam Questions

Q1 Describe the role of membrane proteins in facilitated diffusion. [3 marks]

Q2 Explain the difference between endocytosis and exocytosis. [4 marks]

Revision — like working against a concentration gradient...

Wouldn't it be great if you could revise by endocytosis — you could just stick this book on your head and your brain would slowly surround it and take it in... actually when I put it like that it sounds a bit gross. Maybe just stick to the good old 'closing the book and scribbling down the diagrams till you know them off by heart' method.

Transport Across Cell Membranes

Here is the last bit on molecules crossing cell membranes. These pages are entirely about the movement of water molecules. Don't worry though — if you've mastered diffusion (see p. 54) you'll nail this in no time.

Osmosis is the Diffusion of Water Molecules

1) Osmosis is the **diffusion** of **water molecules** across a **partially permeable membrane** down a **water potential gradient**. This means water molecules move from an area of **higher water potential** (i.e. higher concentration of water molecules) to an area of **lower water potential** (i.e. lower concentration of water molecules).

2) **Water potential** is the potential (likelihood) of water molecules to diffuse out of or into a solution.

3) **Pure water** has the **highest water potential**. All solutions have a **lower** water potential than pure water.

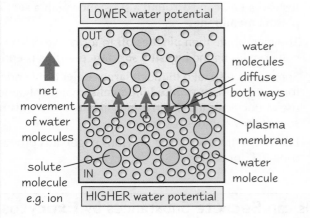

Cells are Affected by the Water Potential of the Surrounding Solution

Water moves **in** or **out** of a cell by osmosis. **How much** moves in or out depends on the **water potential** of the **surrounding solution**. Animal and plant cells behave differently in different solutions.

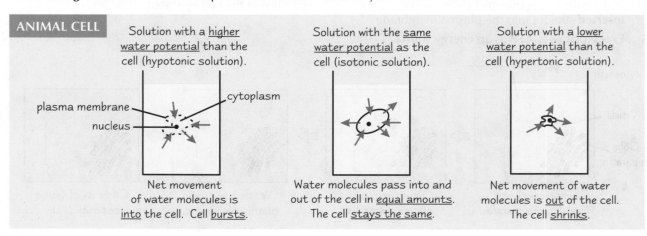

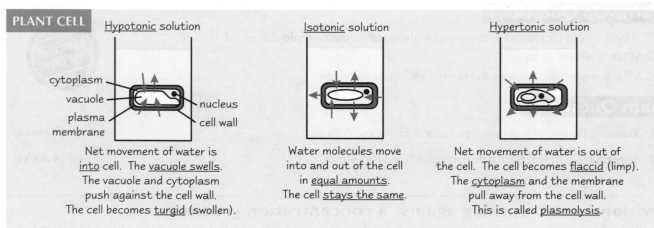

Transport Across Cell Membranes

You can do **Experiments** to Investigate **Water Potential**

You can do a simple **experiment**, using potato cylinders, to find out the **water potential** of **plant tissue**. This experiment involves putting potato cylinders into **different concentrations** of sucrose solution — remember, the **higher** the sucrose **concentration**, the **lower** the water **potential**.

1) Prepare **sucrose solutions** of the following concentrations:
   0.0 M, 0.2 M, 0.4 M, 0.6 M, 0.8 M, 1.0 M.

2) Use a cork borer or chip maker to cut **potatoes** into **the same sized** pieces. (They need to be about 1 cm in diameter.)

3) Divide the chips into **groups of three** and use a **mass balance** to measure the **mass** of each **group**.

4) Place **one group** in each solution.

5) **Leave** the chips in the solution for **as long as possible** (making sure that they all get the **same amount of time**). Try to leave them for at least 20 minutes.

6) **Remove** the chips and pat dry **gently** with a paper towel.

7) **Weigh** each **group** again and record your results.

8) Calculate the **% change in mass** for each group.

9) Plot your results on a **graph** like this:

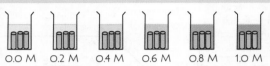

You might also see M written as mol dm⁻³.

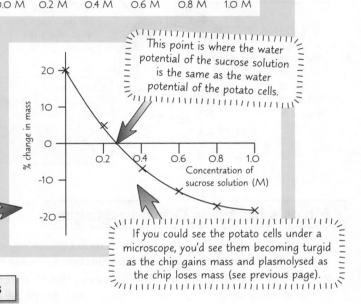

This point is where the water potential of the sucrose solution is the same as the water potential of the potato cells.

If you could see the potato cells under a microscope, you'd see them becoming turgid as the chip gains mass and plasmolysed as the chip loses mass (see previous page).

You can do a **Similar Experiment** with **Eggs**

You can carry out a **similar experiment** using chickens' eggs that have had their **shells dissolved**. The remaining **membrane** is **partially permeable**, so it's a good **model** for showing the effects of **osmosis** in **animal tissue**.

Warm-Up Questions

Q1 Define osmosis.

Q2 What happens to an animal cell if it is placed in a solution with the same water potential as the cell?

Q3 What happens to a plant cell if it is placed in a solution with a higher water potential than the cell?

Exam Question

Q1 Pieces of potato of equal mass were put into different concentrations of sucrose solution for 24 hours. The difference in mass for each is recorded in the table.

Concentration of sucrose / %	1	2	3	4
Mass difference / g	0.4	0.2	0	– 0.2

a) Explain why the pieces of potato in 1% and 2% sucrose solutions gained mass. [3 marks]

b) Suggest a reason why the mass of the piece of potato in 3% sucrose solution stayed the same. [1 mark]

c) What would you expect the mass difference for a potato in a 5% solution to be? Explain your answer. [2 marks]

I always knew that glass of water had potential...

Osmosis is just a fancy name for the diffusion of water molecules. But whether water moves in or out of a cell depends on the water potential of the surrounding solution. Water potential can be pretty confusing — if you can't make head nor tail of an exam question about it try replacing the word 'potential' with 'concentration' and it'll become clearer.

The Cell Cycle and Mitosis

Ever wondered how you grow from one tiny cell to a complete whole person?
No, oh... well it's because your cells replicate and you need to learn the processes involved.

The **Cell Cycle** is the Process of **Cell Growth** and **Division**

The **cell cycle** is the process that all body cells in **multicellular organisms** use to **grow** and **divide**.

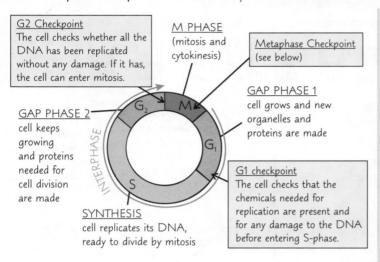

G2 Checkpoint
The cell checks whether all the DNA has been replicated without any damage. If it has, the cell can enter mitosis.

M PHASE (mitosis and cytokinesis)

Metaphase Checkpoint (see below)

GAP PHASE 1
cell grows and new organelles and proteins are made

GAP PHASE 2
cell keeps growing and proteins needed for cell division are made

G1 checkpoint
The cell checks that the chemicals needed for replication are present and for any damage to the DNA before entering S-phase.

SYNTHESIS
cell replicates its DNA, ready to divide by mitosis

1) The cell cycle **starts** when a cell has been produced by cell division and **ends** with the cell dividing to produce two identical cells.

2) The cell cycle consists of a period of **cell growth** and **DNA replication**, called **interphase**, and a period of **cell division**, called **M phase**. M phase involves **mitosis** (nuclear division) and **cytokinesis** (cytoplasmic division).

3) **Interphase** (cell growth) is subdivided into three separate growth stages. These are called G_1, **S** and G_2.

4) The cell cycle is regulated by **checkpoints**. Checkpoints occur at key points during the cycle to make sure it's **OK** for the **process** to **continue**.

Mitosis has **Four Division Stages**

1) Mitosis is needed for the **growth** of multicellular organisms (like us) and for **repairing damaged tissues**. It is also a method of **asexual reproduction** for some plants, animals and fungi.

2) Mitosis is really one **continuous process**, but it's described as a series of **division stages** — prophase, metaphase, anaphase and telophase.

3) **Interphase** comes **before** mitosis in the cell cycle. It's when cells grow and replicate their DNA ready for division.

Interphase — The cell carries out normal functions, but also prepares to divide. The cell's **DNA** is unravelled and **replicated**, to double its genetic content. The **organelles** are also **replicated** so it has spare ones, and its ATP content is increased (ATP provides the energy needed for cell division).

Cell
Chromosome
Cytoplasm
Nucleus
Centriole
Homologous pair
Interphase
Unravelled DNA containing two copies of each chromosome

1) **Prophase** — The **chromosomes condense**, getting shorter and fatter. Tiny bundles of protein called **centrioles** start moving to opposite ends of the cell, forming a network of protein fibres across it called the **spindle**. The **nuclear envelope** (the membrane around the nucleus) **breaks down** and chromosomes lie free in the cytoplasm.

Nuclear envelope starts to break down
Centrioles move to opposite ends of the cell
Centromere

As mitosis begins, the chromosomes are made of two strands joined in the middle by a centromere. The separate strands are called chromatids.

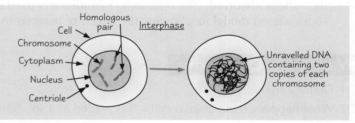

One chromatid
Centromere
Sister chromatids

There are two strands because each chromosome has already made an identical copy of itself during interphase. When mitosis is over, the chromatids end up as one-strand chromosomes in the new daughter cells.

2) **Metaphase** — The chromosomes (each with two chromatids) **line up** along the middle of the cell and become **attached** to the **spindle** by their **centromere**. At the **metaphase checkpoint**, the cell **checks** that all the **chromosomes** are **attached** to the **spindle** before **mitosis** can continue.

Spindle fibres
Centromeres on spindle equator

The Cell Cycle and Mitosis

3) <u>Anaphase</u> — The centromeres divide, **separating** each pair of sister **chromatids**. The spindles contract, pulling chromatids to opposite ends of the cell, centromere first.

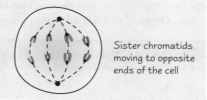

Sister chromatids moving to opposite ends of the cell

4) <u>Telophase</u> — The chromatids reach the **opposite poles** on the spindle. They uncoil and become long and thin again. They're now called **chromosomes** again. A **nuclear envelope** forms around each group of chromosomes, so there are now **two nuclei**.

Centriole

Nuclear envelopes form

Cytokinesis — The **cytoplasm divides**. In animal cells, a **cleavage furrow** forms to **divide** the **cell membrane**. There are now **two daughter cells** that are **genetically identical** to the original cell and to each other. **Cytokinesis** usually begins in **anaphase** and ends in **telophase**. It's a **separate** process to **mitosis**.

Centriole

Cleavage furrow

You can **Observe** the **Cell Cycle** and **Mitosis** by **Staining Chromosomes**

PRACTICAL SKILLS

You can **stain chromosomes** so you can see them under a **microscope**. This means you can watch what happens to them **during mitosis** — and it makes high-adrenaline viewing, I can tell you. These are some **plant root cells** shown under a **light microscope** at different stages of the **cell cycle** and mitosis. You need to be able to **recognise**, **draw** and **label** each stage.

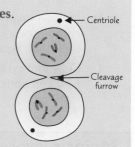

Prophase

Anaphase

Telophase

Metaphase

Interphase

HERVE CONGE, ISM/SCIENCE PHOTO LIBRARY

These plant roots cells are being viewed on a 'squash' microscope slide. In other words, they've been deliberately squashed beneath the cover slip. This makes it easier to see the chromosomes.

You can recognise cells in interphase because the chromosomes will be spread out and not condensed.

Warm-Up Questions

Q1 What happens during interphase?

Q2 List in order the four stages of mitosis.

Q3 At what stage in mitosis does the nuclear envelope break down?

PRACTICE QUESTIONS

Exam Question

Q1 The diagrams show cells at different stages of mitosis.

a) Which of the cells, A, B or C, is undergoing anaphase? Give a reason for your answer.

[2 marks]

b) Name the structures labelled X, Y and Z in cell B.

[3 marks]

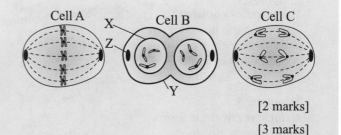

Cell A   X   Cell B   Cell C

Z

Y

Doctor, Doctor, I'm getting short and fat — don't worry, it's just a phase...

Quite a lot to learn in this topic — but it's all dead important stuff, so no slacking. Most body cells undergo mitosis — it's needed for cells to multiply so organisms like us can grow and develop. Remember that chromosomes during mitosis are made up of two sister chromatids joined by a centromere. Nice to know family values are important to genetic material too.

Sexual Reproduction and Meiosis

Ahh, now on to some really exciting stuff — the production of gametes (sex cells to you and me).
This is how we end up different from our parents and our siblings — and yet, in some ways, strangely alike...

Meiosis Produces Gametes for Sexual Reproduction

1) In sexual reproduction two **gametes** (an egg and a sperm) join together at **fertilisation** to form a **zygote**. The zygote then divides and develops into a **new organism**.

2) **Meiosis** is a type of **cell division** that happens in the reproductive organs to **produce gametes**.

3) Meiosis involves a **reduction division**. Cells that divide by meiosis have the **full number** of chromosomes to start with, but the cells that are formed from meiosis have **half the number**. Cells with half the normal number of chromosomes are called **haploid cells**.

4) Cells formed by meiosis are all **genetically different** because each new cell ends up with a **different combination** of chromosomes.

> *Without meiosis, you'd get double the number of chromosomes when the gametes fused. Not good.*

Meiosis Involves Two Divisions

1) **Meiosis** involves two divisions: **meiosis I** and **meiosis II**. **Meiosis I** is the **reduction division** (it halves the chromosome number).

2) Like **mitosis** (see previous two pages) meiosis I and meiosis II are each split into **prophase**, **metaphase**, **anaphase** and **telophase** stages.

The whole of meiosis begins with **interphase**. During interphase, the DNA **unravels** and **replicates** to produce double-armed chromosomes called **sister chromatids** (see page 60).

> *You need to learn what homologous chromosomes are.*

Meiosis I (first division)

Prophase I
The **chromosomes condense**, getting shorter and fatter. The chromosomes then arrange themselves into **homologous pairs** (see yellow box) and **crossing-over** occurs (see next page). Just like in mitosis, **centrioles** start moving to opposite ends of the cell, forming the **spindle fibres**. The **nuclear envelope breaks down**.

Metaphase I
The **homologous pairs line up** across the **centre** of the cell and **attach** to the **spindle fibres** by their **centromeres**.

Anaphase I
The **spindles contract**, separating the **homologous pairs** — one chromosome goes to **each end** of the cell.

Telophase I
A **nuclear envelope** forms around each group of chromosomes.

Cytokinesis (division of the cytoplasm) occurs and **two haploid daughter cells** are produced.

A Note About Homologous Pairs:
Humans have <u>46 chromosomes</u> in total — <u>23 pairs</u>. One chromosome in each pair came from mum and one from dad, e.g. there are two number 1's (one from mum and one from dad), two number 2's etc. The chromosomes that make up each pair are the <u>same size</u> and have the <u>same genes</u>, although they could have <u>different versions</u> of those genes (called <u>alleles</u>). These pairs of chromosomes are called <u>homologous pairs</u>.

Meiosis II (second division)

The two daughter cells undergo **prophase II**, **metaphase II**, **anaphase II**, **telophase II** and **cytokinesis** — which are a lot like the stages in **mitosis**.

In **anaphase II**, the pairs of **sister chromatids** are **separated** — each **new** daughter cell inherits **one chromatid** from **each chromosome**. **Four (genetically different) haploid** daughter cells are produced — these are the **gametes**.

Homologous pair — Nuclear envelope — Nucleus — Cytoplasm — Cell — Prophase I — Centrioles — Metaphase I — Spindle fibres — Anaphase I — Telophase I — Chromosome number is halved

End of meiosis I = two haploid daughter cells

STAGES OF MEIOSIS II

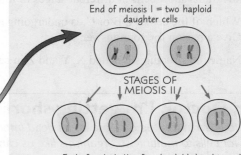

End of meiosis II = four haploid daughter cells

Sexual Reproduction and Meiosis

Chromatids **Cross Over** in **Prophase I**

During prophase I of meiosis I, **homologous pairs** of chromosomes come together and pair up. The chromatids twist around each other and bits of **chromatids** swap over. The chromatids still contain the **same genes** but now have a different combination of **alleles**.

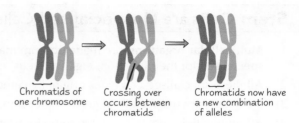

Chromatids of one chromosome

Crossing over occurs between chromatids

Chromatids now have a new combination of alleles

Meiosis Produces Cells that are **Genetically Different**

There are two main events during meiosis that lead to **genetic variation**:

1 Crossing over of chromatids

The **crossing over** of chromatids in meiosis I means that each of the **four daughter cells** formed from meiosis contains chromatids with **different alleles**:

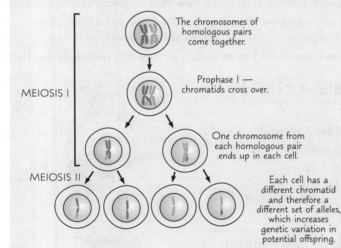

The chromosomes of homologous pairs come together.

MEIOSIS I

Prophase I — chromatids cross over.

One chromosome from each homologous pair ends up in each cell.

MEIOSIS II

Each cell has a different chromatid and therefore a different set of alleles, which increases genetic variation in potential offspring.

2 Independent assortment of chromosomes

1) Each **homologous pair** of chromosomes in your cells is made up of **one chromosome** from your mum (**maternal**) and **one chromosome** from your dad (**paternal**).

2) When the homologous pairs **line up** in **metaphase I** and are **separated** in **anaphase I**, it's completely **random** which chromosome from each pair ends up in which daughter cell.

3) So the **four daughter cells** produced by meiosis have completely **different combinations** of those **maternal** and **paternal chromosomes**.

4) This is called **independent assortment** (separation) of the chromosomes.

5) This '**shuffling**' of chromosomes leads to **genetic variation** in any **potential** offspring.

Paternal   Maternal   OR

MEIOSIS I

Possible combinations in daughter cells

Warm-Up Questions

Q1 Explain what is meant by the term haploid.

Q2 What happens to homologous pairs of chromosomes during meiosis I?

Q3 How many cells does meiosis produce?

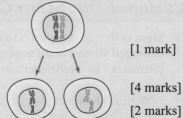

PRACTICE QUESTIONS

Exam Question

Q1 *Drosophila* (fruit flies) only have four chromosomes.
The diagram on the right summarises one of the meiotic divisions in *Drosophila*.

a) Does the diagram show meiosis I or meiosis II? Give a reason for your answer. [1 mark]

b) Crossing over does not occur very frequently in male *Drosophila*.
Explain what crossing over is and how it leads to genetic variation. [4 marks]

c) Explain how independent assortment leads to genetic variation. [2 marks]

Reproduction isn't as exciting as some people would have you believe...

These pages are quite tricky, so use the diagrams to help you understand — they might look evil, but they really do help. The key thing to understand is that meiosis produces four genetically different haploid daughter cells. And that the genetic variation in the daughter cells occurs because of two processes — crossing over and independent assortment.

Stem Cells and Differentiation

If I had to choose a favourite type of cell, I'd choose a stem cell and here's why...

Stem Cells are Unspecialised Cells

1) **Multicellular organisms** are made up from many **different** cell types that are **specialised** for their function, e.g. liver cells, muscle cells, white blood cells.

2) **All** these specialised cell types originally came from **stem cells**.

3) Stem cells are **unspecialised** cells — they can develop into **different types** of cell.

4) **All** multicellular organisms have some form of **stem cell**.

5) In **humans**, stem cells are found in **early embryos** and in a few places in **adults**. Stem cells in **early embryos** can develop into **any type** of human cell. Stem cells in **adults** can only develop into a **limited range** of cells.

Tina, Joe and Bex knew their cells were specialised — specialised to look good.

Stem Cells Differentiate into Specialised Cells

1) Stem cells **divide** to become **new cells**, which then become **specialised**.

2) The process by which a cell becomes specialised for its job is called **differentiation**.

3) In animals, adult stem cells are used to replace **damaged cells**, e.g. to make **new skin** or **blood cells** (see below).

4) **Plants** are always growing, so stem cells are needed to make **new shoots** and **roots** throughout their lives. Stem cells in plants can **differentiate** into various plant tissues including **xylem and phloem** (see below).

5) Stem cells are also able to **divide** to produce **more** undifferentiated **stem cells**, i.e. they can **renew** themselves.

Cells in the Bone Marrow Differentiate into Blood Cells

1) **Bones** are living organs, containing nerves and **blood vessels**.

2) The main bones of the body have **marrow** in the **centres**.

3) Here, **adult stem cells** divide and **differentiate** to replace worn out blood cells — **erythrocytes** (red blood cells) and **neutrophils** (white blood cells that help to fight infection).

Cells in the Meristems Differentiate into Xylem and Phloem

1) In plants, **stem cells** are found in the **meristems** (parts of the plant where growth can take place).

2) In the root and stem, stem cells of the **vascular cambium** divide and **differentiate** to become **xylem vessels** and **phloem sieve tubes**.

There's more about the function of xylem and phloem on p. 88.

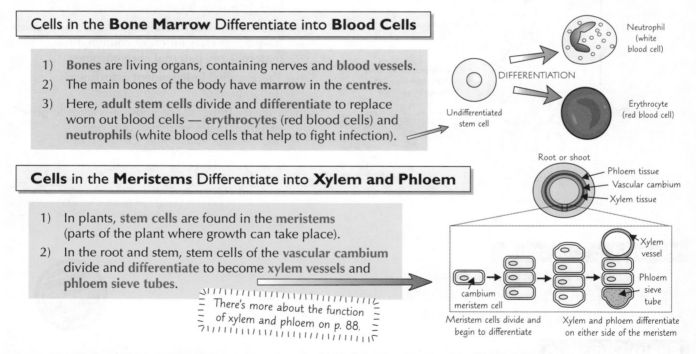

It's Hoped That Stem Cells Might Cure Diseases Like Parkinson's

1) **Stem cells** can develop into **different specialised cell types**, so scientists think they could be used to **replace damaged tissues** in a **range** of **diseases**. For example, it might be possible to use **stem cells** to treat **neurological disorders** like **Alzheimer's** and **Parkinson's**:

With **Alzheimer's**, **nerve cells** in the brain **die** in increasing numbers. This results in severe **memory loss**. Researchers are hoping to use stem cells to **regrow healthy nerve cells** in people with Alzheimer's.

Patients with **Parkinson's** suffer from **tremors** that they can't control. The disease causes the loss of a particular type of **nerve cell** found in the **brain**. These cells release a **chemical** called **dopamine**, which is needed to **control movement**. **Transplanted stem cells** may help to **regenerate** the dopamine-producing cells.

2) Stem cells are also used by scientists researching **developmental biology**, i.e. how organisms **grow** and **develop**. Studying stem cells can help us to understand more about things like **developmental disorders** and **cancer**.

Module 2: Section 6 — Cell Division and Cellular Organisation

Stem Cells and Differentiation

Cells are **Specialised** for their Particular Function

Once cells **differentiate**, they have a **specific function**. Their **structure** is **adapted** to perform that function. You need to **know** how the following cell types are specialised for their functions:

Animal cells

1) **Neutrophils** (a type of white blood cell) defend the body against disease. Their **flexible shape** allows them to **engulf** foreign particles or pathogens (see p. 102). The many **lysosomes** in their cytoplasm contain **digestive enzymes** to **break down** the engulfed particles.

2) **Erythrocytes** (red blood cells) carry oxygen in the blood. The **biconcave** disc shape provides a **large surface area** for gas exchange. They have **no nucleus** so there's more room for **haemoglobin** (see p. 86), the protein that carries oxygen.

3) **Epithelial cells** cover the surfaces of organs. The cells are **joined** by **interlinking** cell membranes and a membrane at their base. **Ciliated** epithelia (e.g. in the **airways**) have **cilia** that beat to move particles away. **Squamous** epithelia (e.g. in the **lungs**) are very thin to allow **efficient diffusion** of **gases**.

4) **Sperm cells** (male sex cells) have a **flagellum** (tail) so they can **swim** to the egg (female sex cell). They also have lots of **mitochondria** to provide the **energy** to swim. The **acrosome** contains **digestive enzymes** to enable the sperm to **penetrate** the surface of the egg.

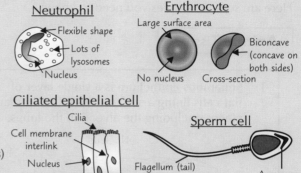

Plant cells

1) **Palisade mesophyll cells** in leaves do most of the **photosynthesis**. They contain **many chloroplasts**, so they can absorb a lot of sunlight. The walls are **thin**, so carbon dioxide can **easily diffuse** into the cell.

2) **Root hair cells** absorb water and mineral ions from the soil. They have a **large surface area** for absorption and a **thin**, permeable cell wall, for entry of water and ions. The cytoplasm contains **extra mitochondria** to provide the **energy** needed for **active transport** (see p. 56).

3) **Guard cells** are found in pairs, with a gap between them to form a **stoma**. This is one of the tiny **pores** in the surface of the leaf used for **gas exchange**. In the **light**, guard cells **take up water** and become **turgid**. Their **thin outer walls** and **thickened inner walls** force them to bend outwards, **opening** the stomata. This allows the leaf to exchange gases for photosynthesis.

Warm-Up Questions

Q1 What are stem cells?

Q2 Stem cells in bone marrow can differentiate into other cell types. Name two of these cell types.

Q3 Describe how stem cells might be used to treat Parkinson's.

Exam Questions

Q1 Describe how a palisade cell is adapted for its role in photosynthesis. [2 marks]

Q2 Describe, with an example, the role of stem cells in adult mammals. [3 marks]

And you thought differentiation was just boring maths stuff...

Stem cells are pretty amazing when you think about it — they can differentiate to become any cell in the whole body. Scientists are excited about them because they could be used to repair damaged cells, like nerve cells in the brain.

Tissues, Organs and Systems

Multicellular organisms are made up of lots of different cell types, which are organised to work together — cells that carry out the same job are organised into tissues (e.g. epithelium), different tissues are organised into organs (e.g. the lungs) and organs work together as organ systems (e.g. the respiratory system).

Similar Cells are Organised into Tissues

A **tissue** is a group of cells (plus any **extracellular material** secreted by them) that are specialised to **work together** to carry out a **particular function**. A tissue can contain **more than one** cell type.

Here are some examples you need to know:

Animal Tissues

1) <u>Squamous epithelium</u> is a **single layer** of **flat cells** lining a surface. It's found in many places, including the alveoli in the lungs.

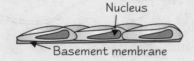

Nucleus

Basement membrane

2) <u>Ciliated epithelium</u> is a layer of cells covered in **cilia** (see page 13). It's found on surfaces where things need to be **moved** — in the trachea for instance, where the cilia waft mucus along.

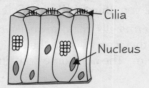

Cilia

Nucleus

3) <u>Muscle tissue</u> is made up of bundles of elongated cells called **muscle fibres**. There are three **different** types of muscle tissue: **smooth** (e.g. found lining the **stomach wall**), **cardiac** (found in the **heart**) and **skeletal** (which you use to **move**). They're all slightly different in structure. Here's what **skeletal muscle tissue** looks like:

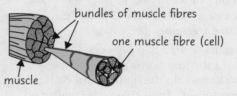

bundles of muscle fibres

one muscle fibre (cell)

muscle

4) <u>Cartilage</u> is a type of **connective tissue** found in the **joints**. It also **shapes** and **supports** the **ears**, **nose** and **windpipe**. It's formed when cells called chondroblasts **secrete** an extracellular **matrix** (a jelly-like substance containing protein **fibres**), which they become **trapped inside**.

two cells trapped together

fibre-filled matrix

Plant Tissues

1) <u>Xylem tissue</u> is a plant tissue with two jobs — it **transports water** around the plant, and it **supports** the plant. It contains hollow **xylem vessel cells**, which are dead, and living **parenchyma cells**.

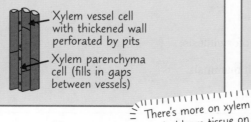

Xylem vessel cell with thickened wall perforated by pits

Xylem parenchyma cell (fills in gaps between vessels)

There's more on xylem and phloem tissue on pages 88-89.

2) <u>Phloem tissue</u> transports **sugars** around the plant. It's arranged in **tubes** and is made up of **sieve cells**, **companion cells**, and some **ordinary** plant cells. Each sieve cell has end walls with **holes** in them, so that sap can move easily through them. These end walls are called **sieve plates**.

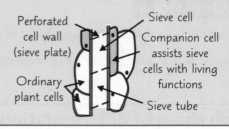

Perforated cell wall (sieve plate)

Ordinary plant cells

Sieve cell

Companion cell assists sieve cells with living functions

Sieve tube

Tissues, Organs and Systems

Different Tissues Make up an Organ

An **organ** is a group of different tissues that **work together** to perform a particular function. Examples include:

- The **lungs** — they contain **squamous epithelial tissue** (in the alveoli) and **ciliated epithelial tissue** (in the bronchi, etc.). They also have **elastic connective tissue** and **vascular tissue** (in the blood vessels).
- **Leaves** — they contain **palisade tissue** for photosynthesis, as well as **epidermal** tissue (to prevent water loss from the leaf), and **xylem** and **phloem** tissues in the veins.

Different Organs Make up an Organ System

Organs work together to form **organ systems** — each system has a **particular function**.
Yup, you've guessed it, more examples:

1) The **respiratory system** is made up of all the organs, tissues and cells involved in **breathing**.
   The lungs, trachea, larynx, nose, mouth and diaphragm are all part of the respiratory system.

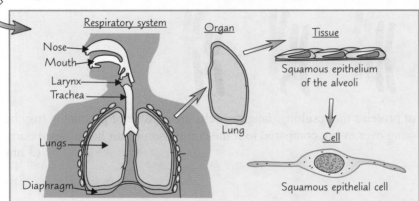

John and Fido —
working together as part
of an organ system.

2) The **circulatory system** is made up of the organs involved in **blood supply**.
   The heart, arteries, veins and capillaries are all parts of this system.

Warm-Up Questions

Q1 Define what is meant by a tissue.

Q2 Briefly describe squamous epithelium.

Q3 What is the difference between the functions of xylem and phloem tissues?

Q4 Name one organ found in plants and one organ found in animals.

PRACTICE QUESTIONS

Exam Questions

Q1 The liver is made of hepatocyte cells that form the main tissue, blood vessels to
provide nutrients and oxygen, and connective tissue that holds the liver together.
Is the liver best described as a tissue, organ or an organ system? Explain your answer.   [2 marks]

Q2 Phloem tissue is found in plants. Which of the following statements correctly describe phloem tissue?

Statement 1: Phloem tissue is arranged in tubes.

Statement 2: Phloem tissue contains sieve cells.

Statement 3: Phloem tissue contains squamous epithelial cells.

Answer: A   Statement 1 to 3   C   Statements 2 and 3 only
            B   Statement 1 and 2 only   D   Statement 1 only   [1 mark]

Soft and quilted — the best kind of tissues...

So, similar cells group together to form tissues. Then, because they love being so helpful, tissues work together in an organ to perform a particular function. But even organs are better together — along comes the organ system. Lovely.

Extra Exam Practice

You're almost done with <u>Module 2</u> — just give these practice questions a try before you tick it off.

- Have a look at this example of how to answer a tricky exam question.
- Then check how much you've understood from Module 2 by having a go at the questions that follow.

There are synoptic questions covering the whole course on pages 258-265 — give these a go when you've mastered all the modules in this book.

1 Meiosis is a type of cell division that occurs in cells in the reproductive organs.

(a) Some chemicals can break down the microtubules of the cytoskeleton in cells. Suggest why the breakdown of microtubules during meiosis I could result in daughter cells inheriting the incorrect number of chromosomes.

(2 marks)

During meiosis I, homologous chromosome pairs normally align with their centromeres in line with one another. However, sometimes the chromosome pairs can misalign. **Figure 1** shows two chromatids of a misaligned chromosome pair crossing over during prophase I.

Figure 1

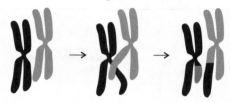

(b) Explain why the number of proteins the resulting daughter cells are capable of producing may be altered following this crossing over event, compared to if the chromosome pair had aligned normally.

(3 marks)

When faced with a question on cell division, it might help to sketch yourself a quick diagram of the process — sometimes questions are easier to get your head around when you can visualise what's going on.

1(a)

The contraction of microtubules in spindles pulls chromosomes to opposite ends of the cell during anaphase I. If the microtubules have been broken down then the homologous chromosome pairs may not be separated, which could result in one daughter cell inheriting more chromosomes than normal and the other inheriting fewer chromosomes than normal.

1(b)

Because the homologous chromosome pair failed to align normally, one chromatid may now have a **greater number of genes** than it had previously and one may have a **smaller number of genes** than it had previously. Each of these chromatids would be inherited by a different daughter cell following meiosis. As **genes code for proteins**, the cell that inherits the chromatid with more genes may be able to produce more proteins than the cell that inherits the chromatid with fewer genes.

Each chromatid is made from tightly wound DNA, so they each contain many genes — you need to mention that chromatids contain genes to be able to link your answer to protein production.

2 Lactose is a sugar found in milk. **Figure 2** shows the structure of lactose.

Figure 2

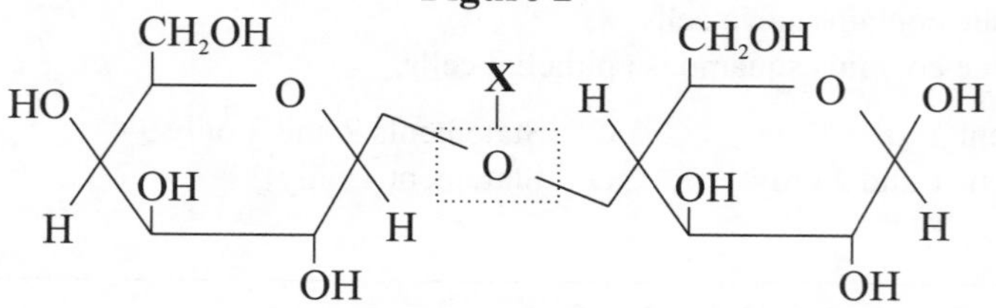

CH_2OH　　　　　　　CH_2OH

HO　　　　O　　　**X**　　　H　　　　O　　　OH

OH　　　　　　　　　　O　　　　　OH

H　　　　　　　H　　　　　　　　　　　H

　　　　OH　　　　　　　　OH

(a) (i) Identify the bond labelled **X** in **Figure 2**.

(1 mark)

Extra Exam Practice

(ii) Using the information in **Figure 2**, draw the structure of a galactose molecule.

(1 mark)

(b) Lactase is an enzyme that catalyses the breakdown of lactose. Some people do not produce this enzyme, so they cannot digest milk and are lactose-intolerant. Lactose-free milk is an alternative for people who are lactose-intolerant and can be produced using the process shown in **Figure 3**.

Figure 3

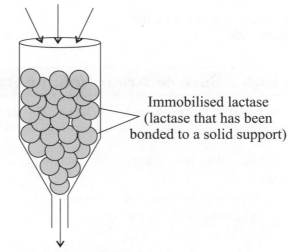

Milk is added at the
top of the column

Immobilised lactase
(lactase that has been
bonded to a solid support)

Lactose-free milk flows out
of the bottom of the column

Studies have shown that galactose can be a competitive inhibitor of lactase. Using this information, explain why the rate of flow of milk through the column should be controlled.

(3 marks)

(c) Free lactase is lactase which has not been immobilised. It can also be used to produce lactose-free milk. A group of students investigated the effect of temperature on the yield of glucose produced by both free lactase and immobilised lactase, relative to the yield produced at the optimum temperature for lactase. The results of their investigation are shown in **Table 1**.

Table 1

Temperature / °C	Relative yield of glucose from free lactase / %	Relative yield of glucose from immobilised lactase / %
40	100	100
50	65	90
60	20	60
70	0	25

(i) State **one** factor that the students should have controlled in this investigation.

(1 mark)

(ii) One of the students suggested that immobilisation strengthens the tertiary structure of the enzyme. Explain how the results shown in **Table 1** support this suggestion.

(3 marks)

Specialised Exchange Surfaces

Exchanging things with the environment is pretty easy if you're a single-celled organism, but if you're multicellular it all gets a bit more complicated... and it's all down to this 'surface area to volume ratio' malarkey.

Organisms Need to **Exchange Substances** with their **Environment**

Every organism, whatever its size, needs to exchange things with its environment.

1) Cells need to take in things like oxygen and glucose for aerobic respiration and other metabolic reactions.

2) They also need to excrete waste products from these reactions — like carbon dioxide and urea.

Raj was glad he'd exchanged his canoe for a bigger boat.

How easy the exchange of substances is depends on the organism's **surface area to volume ratio** (SA:V).

Smaller Animals have Higher **Surface Area : Volume Ratios**

A mouse has a bigger surface area **relative to its volume** than a hippo. This can be hard to imagine, but you can prove it mathematically. Imagine these animals as cubes:

The hippo could be represented by a block measuring 2 cm × 4 cm × 4 cm.

Its **volume** is 2 × 4 × 4 = **32 cm³**

Its **surface area** is 2 × 4 × 4 = 32 cm² (top and bottom surfaces of cube)

$\qquad\qquad$ + 4 × 2 × 4 = 32 cm² (four sides of the cube)

Total surface area = **64 cm²**

So the hippo has a **surface area : volume ratio** of 64 : 32 or **2 : 1**.

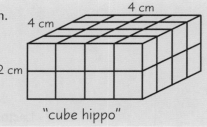

"cube hippo"

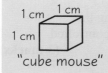

"cube mouse"

Compare this to a mouse cube measuring 1 cm × 1 cm × 1 cm

Its **volume** is 1 × 1 × 1 = **1 cm³**

Its **surface area** is 6 × 1 × 1 = **6 cm²**

So the mouse has a **surface area : volume ratio** of **6 : 1**.

The cube mouse's surface area is six times its volume, but the cube hippo's surface area is only twice its volume. Smaller animals have a bigger surface area compared to their volume.

To calculate the surface area to volume ratio you just **divide** the **surface area** by the **volume**. Easy.

Multicellular Organisms Need **Exchange Surfaces**

An organism needs to supply **every one of its cells** with substances like **glucose** and **oxygen** (for respiration). It also needs to **remove waste products** from every cell to avoid damaging itself.

1) In single-celled organisms, these substances can diffuse directly into (or out of) the cell across the cell surface membrane. The diffusion rate is quick because of the small distances the substances have to travel (see p. 54).

2) In multicellular animals, diffusion across the outer membrane is too slow, for several reasons:

- Some cells are deep within the body — there's a big distance between them and the outside environment.

- Larger animals have a low surface area to volume ratio — it's difficult to exchange enough substances to supply a large volume of animal through a relatively small outer surface.

- Multicellular organisms have a higher metabolic rate than single-celled organisms, so they use up oxygen and glucose faster.

So rather than using straightforward diffusion to absorb and excrete substances, multicellular animals need specialised **exchange surfaces** — like the **alveoli** in the **lungs**...

Specialised Exchange Surfaces

Exchange Surfaces Have **Special Features** to **Improve** their **Efficiency**

Most Exchange Surfaces Have A **Large Surface Area**...

Example — ROOT HAIR CELLS

1) The cells on plant roots grow into long '**hairs**' which stick out into the soil. Each branch of a root will be covered in **millions** of these microscopic hairs.

2) This gives the roots a **large surface area**, which helps to **increase** the **rate** of **absorption** of **water** (by osmosis) and **mineral ions** (by active transport) from the soil.

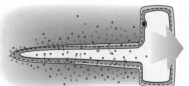
A root hair cell

...They're also **Thin**...

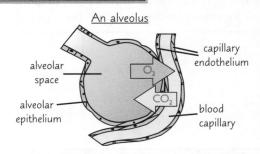

An alveolus

alveolar space
alveolar epithelium
O_2
CO_2
capillary endothelium
blood capillary

Example — the ALVEOLI

1) The **alveoli** are the **gas exchange surface** in the **lungs**.

2) Each alveolus is made from a **single layer** of **thin, flat cells** called the **alveolar epithelium**.

3) O_2 **diffuses out** of the alveolar space into the blood. CO_2 diffuses in the **opposite direction**.

4) The thin alveolar epithelium helps to **decrease the distance** over which O_2 and CO_2 diffusion takes place, which **increases** the **rate of diffusion** (see p. 54).

...And They Have a **Good Blood Supply** and/or **Ventilation**

Example 1 — ALVEOLI

1) The alveoli are surrounded by a large capillary network, giving each alveolus its own blood supply. The blood constantly takes oxygen away from the alveoli, and brings more carbon dioxide.

2) The lungs are also ventilated (you breathe in and out — see page 74) so the air in each alveolus is constantly replaced.

3) These features help to maintain concentration gradients of O_2 and CO_2.

There's more on how a concentration gradient is maintained in fish gills on page 76.

Example 2 — FISH GILLS

1) The gills are the gas exchange surface in fish. In the gills, O_2 and CO_2 are exchanged between the fish's blood and the surrounding water.

2) Fish gills contain a large network of capillaries — this keeps them well-supplied with blood. They're also well-ventilated — fresh water constantly passes over them. These features help to maintain a concentration gradient of O_2 — increasing the rate at which O_2 diffuses into the blood.

Warm-Up Questions

Q1 Name four substances an organism needs to exchange with its environment.

Q2 How do the surface area to volume ratios of large and small organisms differ?

Exam Questions

Q1 Give two ways in which the alveoli are adapted for efficient gas exchange. [2 marks]

Q2 Nutrients such as amino acids are absorbed into the bloodstream in the small intestine. Cells in the wall of the small intestine are covered in microvilli. Microvilli are tiny extensions of the plasma membrane. Suggest how microvilli increase the efficiency of nutrient absorption in the small intestine. [2 marks]

Cube hippos... very Picasso...

I know you've just got to the end of a page, but it would be a pretty smart idea to have another look at diffusion on page 54. It'll help these pages make much more sense — all I can think about at the moment is cube hippos.

The Gaseous Exchange System in Mammals

The gaseous exchange system in mammals consists of the lungs, plus a few related tubes, muscles, etc., all enclosed in a protective ribcage. You need to know how it all works...

In Mammals the **Lungs** are **Exchange Organs**

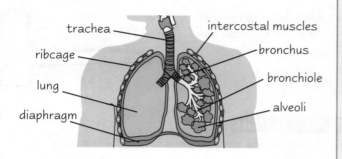

trachea
ribcage
lung
diaphragm
intercostal muscles
bronchus
bronchiole
alveoli

1) As you breathe in, air enters the trachea (windpipe).

2) The trachea splits into two bronchi — one bronchus leading to each lung.

3) Each bronchus then branches off into smaller tubes called bronchioles.

4) The bronchioles end in small 'air sacs' called alveoli (see previous page) where gases are exchanged.

5) The ribcage, intercostal muscles and diaphragm all work together to move air in and out (see page 74).

There are actually three layers of intercostal muscles. You need to know about two of them (the internal and external intercostal muscles — see p. 74) for your exam. We've only shown one layer here for simplicity.

Structures in the **Gaseous Exchange System** Have Different **Functions**

The gaseous exchange system is made up of different **cells** and **tissues**.
These help it to exchange gases **efficiently**.

1) **Goblet cells** (lining the airways) secrete mucus. The mucus traps microorganisms and dust particles in the inhaled air, stopping them from reaching the alveoli.

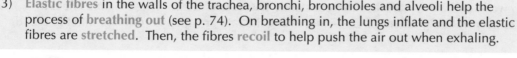

goblet cell   cilia

2) **Cilia** (on the surface of cells lining the airways) **beat** the **mucus**. This **moves** the mucus (plus the trapped microorganisms and dust) upward away from the alveoli towards the throat, where it's swallowed. This helps **prevent lung infections**.

3) **Elastic fibres** in the walls of the trachea, bronchi, bronchioles and alveoli help the process of **breathing out** (see p. 74). On breathing in, the lungs inflate and the elastic fibres are **stretched**. Then, the fibres **recoil** to help push the air out when exhaling.

Derek was quickly mastering efficient gaseous exchange.

4) **Smooth muscle** in the walls of the trachea, bronchi and bronchioles allows their **diameter to be controlled**. During exercise the smooth muscle **relaxes**, making the tubes **wider**. This means there's **less resistance** to airflow and air can move in and out of the lungs more easily.

5) **Rings of cartilage** in the walls of the trachea and bronchi **provide support**. It's strong but flexible — it stops the trachea and bronchi **collapsing** when you breathe in and the pressure drops (see p. 74).

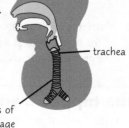

trachea

rings of cartilage

The Gaseous Exchange System in Mammals

The Different **Parts** are Found in **Different Places** in the System

Part of the lung	Cross section	Cartilage	Smooth muscle	Elastic fibres	Goblet cells	Epithelium
trachea	smooth muscle / elastic fibres / c-shaped cartilage / ciliated epithelium	large C-shaped pieces	✓	✓	✓	ciliated
bronchi	smooth muscle / small cartilage pieces / elastic fibres / ciliated epithelium	smaller pieces	✓	✓	✓	ciliated
larger bronchiole	smooth muscle and elastic fibres / ciliated epithelium	none	✓	✓	✓	ciliated
smaller bronchiole		none	✓	✓	✗	ciliated
smallest bronchiole		none	✗	✓	✗	no cilia
alveoli	blood capillary / elastic fibres / alveolar epithelium	none	✗	✓	✗	no cilia

Warm-Up Questions

Q1 What is the function of goblet cells in the mammalian gas exchange system?

Q2 Describe the distribution of smooth muscle in the mammalian gas exchange system.

Q3 Describe the distribution of ciliated epithelium in the mammalian gas exchange system.

PRACTICE QUESTIONS

Exam Questions

Q1 A student is observing a dissection of a pig's lungs.

a) The student is given the pig's trachea, a bronchus and a larger bronchiole. Apart from the differences in size, explain how the student will be able to tell the trachea, bronchus and bronchiole apart. [3 marks]

b) The student is given two tissue samples. One was taken from one of the smallest bronchioles and one was taken from a larger bronchiole. The student looks at each sample under the microscope. Suggest one way in which the student will be able to tell the two samples apart. [1 mark]

Q2 a) Smoking destroys the elastic fibres in the walls of the alveoli. Suggest and explain what effect this will have on the process of breathing out. [2 marks]

b) Smoking also destroys cilia in the gaseous exchange system. Suggest two problems this could cause. [2 marks]

Rings of cartilage — I prefer mine in gold... with diamonds...

There's a fair bit to learn on these two pages. Copying out my beautiful blue table will help — and then you can write out what the function of each part is. You won't be coughing and spluttering in the exam once you know this lot.

Ventilation in Mammals

If you're in need of inspiration then there's plenty on this page... sadly I'm only talking about the kind of inspiration that gets air into your lungs — if you want the other sort head over to the Grand Canyon.

Ventilation in Mammals is Breathing In and Out

Ventilation consists of **inspiration** (breathing in) and **expiration** (breathing out). It's controlled by the **movements** of the **diaphragm**, **internal** and **external intercostal muscles** and **ribcage**.

> Ventilation can also mean 'changing air' in general. Fish gills are ventilated, but fish don't breathe in and out like we do.

Inspiration

1) The external intercostal and diaphragm muscles contract.

2) This causes the ribcage to move upwards and outwards and the diaphragm to flatten, increasing the volume of the thorax (the space where the lungs are).

3) As the volume of the thorax increases the lung pressure decreases (to below atmospheric pressure).

4) This causes air to flow into the lungs.

5) Inspiration is an active process — it requires energy.

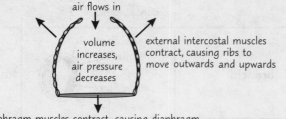

air flows in

volume increases, air pressure decreases

external intercostal muscles contract, causing ribs to move outwards and upwards

diaphragm muscles contract, causing diaphragm to move downwards and flatten

Expiration

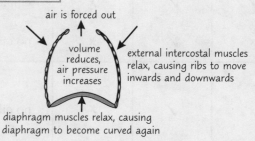

air is forced out

volume reduces, air pressure increases

external intercostal muscles relax, causing ribs to move inwards and downwards

diaphragm muscles relax, causing diaphragm to become curved again

1) The external intercostal and diaphragm muscles relax.

2) The ribcage moves downwards and inwards and the diaphragm becomes curved again.

3) The thorax volume decreases, causing the air pressure to increase (to above atmospheric pressure).

4) Air is forced out of the lungs.

5) Normal expiration is a passive process — it doesn't require energy.

6) Expiration can be forced though (e.g. if you want to blow out the candles on your birthday cake). During forced expiration, the internal intercostal muscles contract, to pull the ribcage down and in.

Tidal Volume is the Volume of Air in a Normal Breath

Here are some terms that you need to know about breathing:

1) **Tidal volume (TV)** — the volume of air in **each breath** — usually about **0.4 dm³**.

2) **Vital capacity** — the **maximum** volume of air that can be breathed **in** or **out**.

3) **Breathing rate** — **how many** breaths are taken — usually in a minute.

4) **Oxygen consumption** or **oxygen uptake** — the rate at which an organism **uses up** oxygen (e.g. the number of dm³ used per minute).

> dm³ is short for decimetres cubed — it's the same as litres.

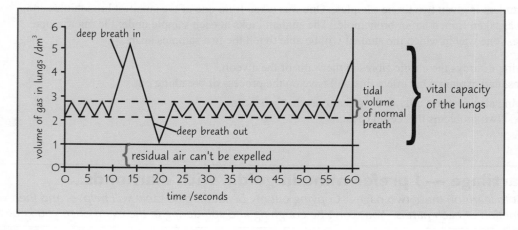

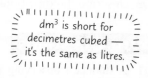

deep breath in

deep breath out

residual air can't be expelled

tidal volume of normal breath

vital capacity of the lungs

volume of gas in lungs /dm³

time /seconds

Ventilation in Mammals

Spirometers Can be Used to Investigate Breathing

A spirometer is a machine that can give readings of **tidal volume**, **vital capacity**, **breathing rate** and **oxygen uptake**.

1) A spirometer has an **oxygen-filled** chamber with a **movable lid**.

2) The person breathes through a **tube** connected to the oxygen chamber.

3) As the person breathes in and out, the lid of the chamber moves **up and down**.

4) These movements can be recorded by a **pen** attached to the lid of the chamber — this writes on a **rotating drum**, creating a **spirometer trace**. Or the spirometer can be hooked up to a **motion sensor** — this will use the movements to produce **electronic signals**, which are picked up by a **data logger**.

5) The **soda lime** in the tube the subject breathes into absorbs **carbon dioxide**.

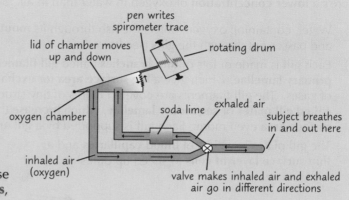

The **total volume of gas** in the chamber **decreases** over time. This is because the air that's breathed out is a **mixture** of oxygen and carbon dioxide. The carbon dioxide is absorbed by the **soda lime** — so there's **only oxygen** in the chamber which the subject inhales from. As this oxygen gets **used up** by respiration, the **total volume decreases**.

You Need to be Able to Analyse Data from a Spirometer

> This graph looks different to the one on the previous page because it shows the volume of air in the spirometer, not in the lungs.

In the exam, you might have to work out **breathing rate**, **tidal volume**, **vital capacity** and **oxygen consumption** from a spirometer trace. For example:

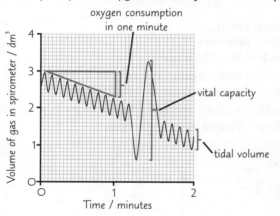

1) In this trace, the breathing rate in the first minute is **10 breaths per minute** (there are 10 'peaks' in the first minute).

2) The tidal volume may change from time to time, but in this trace it's about **0.5 dm³**.

3) The graph shows a vital capacity of **2.65 dm³**.

4) Oxygen consumption is the decrease in the volume of gas in the spirometer chamber. It can be read from the graph by taking the average slope of the trace. In this case, it drops by 0.7 dm³ in the first minute — so, oxygen consumption is **0.7 dm³/min**.

Warm-Up Questions

Q1 What is meant by tidal volume and vital capacity?

Q2 Describe how a spirometer can be used to measure oxygen uptake.

PRACTICE QUESTIONS

Exam Question

Q1 Describe the changes that take place in the human thorax during inspiration.

[5 marks]

Investigate someone's breathing — make sure they've had a mint first...

I thought spirometers were those circular plastic things you draw crazy patterns with... apparently not. I know the graphs don't look that approachable, but it's important you understand what the squiggly lines show, and the four terms used when investigating breathing — I'd bet my right lung there'll be a question on spirometer graphs in the exam.

Ventilation in Fish and Insects

If you're squeamish, you might want to brace yourself for this topic. You do need to know it all though...

Fish Use a Counter-Current System for Gas Exchange

There's a **lower concentration** of oxygen in water than in air. So **fish** have special **adaptations** to get enough of it.

1) Water, containing oxygen, enters the fish through its **mouth** and passes out through the **gills** (see below).

2) Each gill is made of lots of **thin branches** called **gill filaments** or **primary lamellae**, which give a **big surface area** for **exchange** of **gases**. The gill filaments are covered in lots of tiny structures called **gill plates** or **secondary lamellae**, which **increase** the **surface area** even more. Each gill is supported by a **gill arch**.

3) The gill plates have lots of **blood capillaries** and a **thin surface layer of cells** to speed up diffusion.

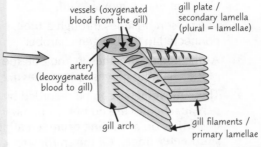

4) **Blood** flows through the gill plates in one direction and **water** flows over in the opposite direction. This is called a **counter-current system**. It maintains a **large concentration gradient** between the water and the blood. The **concentration of oxygen** in the **water** is always **higher** than that in the **blood**, so as much oxygen as possible diffuses from the water into the blood.

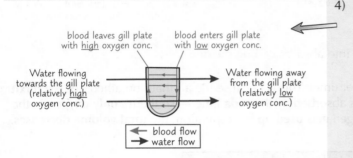

You Need to Know How Fish Gills are Ventilated

Here's how the gills are usually ventilated in **bony fish**:

Bony fish include salmon and cod. Unsurprisingly, they have a skeleton made of bone — not all fish do.

1) The fish **opens** its **mouth**, which **lowers** the **floor** of the **buccal cavity** (the space inside the mouth). The **volume** of the buccal cavity **increases**, **decreasing** the **pressure** inside the cavity. **Water** is then **sucked in** to the cavity.

2) When the fish **closes** its **mouth**, the **floor** of the **buccal cavity** is **raised again**. The **volume** inside the cavity **decreases**, the **pressure increases**, and **water** is **forced out** of the cavity **across the gill filaments**.

3) Each gill is covered by a **bony flap** called the **operculum** (which protects the gill). The **increase** in **pressure** forces the operculum on each side of the head to **open**, allowing **water** to **leave the gills**.

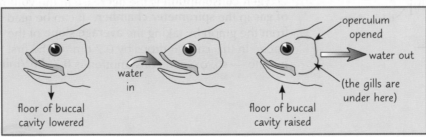

In some bony fish, the operculum bulges out (increasing the volume of the cavity behind the operculum) just after the floor of the buccal cavity lowers. This contributes to the decrease in pressure that causes water to enter the fish's mouth.

You Need to Know How to Dissect Fish Gills

1) First up, fish dissection is **messy** so make sure you're wearing an **apron** or **lab coat**, and **gloves**.

2) Place your chosen fish (something like a perch or salmon works well) in a **dissection tray** or on a **cutting board**.

3) **Push back** the **operculum** and use **scissors** to carefully **remove the gills**. Cut each **gill arch** through the bone at the **top** and **bottom**. They should look a bit like this:

4) If you look closely, you should be able to see the **gill filaments**.

5) Finish off by **drawing** the gill and **labelling** it.

A single gill arch

gill filaments

Ventilation in Fish and Insects

Insects use **Tracheae** to **Exchange Gases**

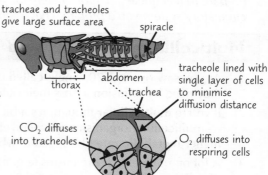

tracheae and tracheoles give large surface area

spiracle

tracheole lined with single layer of cells to minimise diffusion distance

thorax   abdomen   trachea

CO_2 diffuses into tracheoles

O_2 diffuses into respiring cells

1) Insects have microscopic air-filled pipes called **tracheae** which they use for gas exchange.

'Tracheae' is the plural of 'trachea'.

2) Air moves into the tracheae through pores on the insect's surface called **spiracles**.

3) **Oxygen** travels down the **concentration gradient** towards the **cells**. **Carbon dioxide** from the cells moves down its own concentration gradient towards the **spiracles** to be **released** into the atmosphere.

4) The tracheae branch off into smaller **tracheoles** which have **thin**, **permeable walls** and go to individual cells. The tracheoles also contain **fluid**, which oxygen **dissolves** in.

5) The oxygen then **diffuses** from this fluid **into body cells**. **Carbon dioxide** diffuses in the **opposite direction**.

6) Insects use **rhythmic abdominal movements** to **change** the **volume** of their bodies and **move air in** and **out** of the spiracles. When larger insects are **flying**, they use their **wing movements** to **pump** their **thoraxes** too.

You Can **Dissect** the **Gaseous Exchange System** in **Insects** too

PRACTICAL SKILLS

Big insects like **grasshoppers** or **cockroaches** are usually **best** for dissecting because they're easier to handle. For dissection, you'll need to use an insect that's been **humanely killed** fairly recently.

1) First fix the insect to a **dissecting board**. You can put **dissecting pins** through its legs to hold it in place.

2) To examine the **tracheae**, you'll need to carefully **cut** and **remove** a piece of **exoskeleton** (the insect's hard outer shell) from along the length of the insect's **abdomen**.

3) Use a syringe to fill the abdomen with **saline solution**. You should be able to see a network of **very thin**, **silvery-grey tubes** — these are the **tracheae**. They look silver because they're **filled** with **air**.

4) You can examine the tracheae under a **light microscope** using a **wet mount slide** (see page 18). Again, the tracheae will appear silver or grey. You should also be able to see **rings of chitin** in the walls of the **tracheae** — these are there for **support** (like the rings of cartilage in a human trachea).

Some live insects, e.g. grasshoppers, can cause allergic reactions in some people. They need to be handled carefully.

Warm-Up Questions

PRACTICE QUESTIONS

Q1 What is the function of the gill filaments and gill plates in fish gills?

Q2 What is the advantage to fish of having a counter-current exchange system in their gills?

Q3 Name the structures on an insect's surface that allow air to enter the tracheae.

Q4 Describe the structure of an insect's tracheoles.

Exam Questions

Q1 A student is examining grasshopper tracheae under the microscope.

    a) The tracheae were taken from a preserved grasshopper specimen. The grasshopper was killed some time ago and kept in a liquid preservative. The tracheae do not appear silver under the microscope, instead they are a dark grey. Suggest why this is the case.   [1 mark]

    b) The tracheae are surrounded by rings of chitin. What is their function?   [1 mark]

Q2 Salmon are bony fish. Explain how water is drawn into the salmon's mouth during ventilation.   [4 marks]

Keep revising and you'll be on the right trachea...

Ventilation in fish is actually a lot like ventilation in mammals. In fish, when the volume of the buccal cavity is increased, the pressure drops and water rushes in. In mammals, it's the volume of the lungs that's increased, and they fill with air instead of water, but the principle is the same. Lucky for you really because it should make all this easier to learn.

Circulatory Systems

Right then, this section's all about blood and hearts and veins and things, so if that's not up your street, then prepare to feel queasy. Unfortunately for you, it's all really important for the exams. And besides, without a circulatory system you'd probably have some issues when it comes to things like... ooh I dunno... living.

Multicellular Organisms need Transport Systems

1) As you saw on page 70, **single-celled** organisms can get substances that they need by **diffusion** across their outer membrane.

2) If you're **multicellular** though, it's a bit **harder** to supply all your cells with everything they need — multicellular organisms are relatively **big**, they have a **low surface area to volume ratio** and a **higher metabolic rate** (the speed at which chemical reactions take place in the body).

3) A lot of multicellular organisms (e.g. mammals) are also **very active**. This means that a **large number of cells** are all **respiring very quickly**, so they need a constant, rapid supply of glucose and oxygen.

4) To make sure that every cell has a good enough supply, multicellular organisms need a **transport system**.

5) In mammals, this is the **circulatory system**, which uses **blood** to carry glucose and oxygen around the body. It also carries hormones, antibodies (to fight disease) and waste (like CO_2).

Fish and Mammals have Different Circulatory Systems

Not all organisms have the same type of circulatory system — **fish** have a **single circulatory system** and **mammals** have a **double circulatory system**.

1) In a **single** circulatory system, blood only passes through the heart **once** for each complete circuit of the body.

2) In a **double** circulatory system, the blood passes through the heart **twice** for each complete circuit of the body.

Fish

In **fish**, the **heart** pumps blood to the **gills** (to pick up oxygen) and then on through the **rest of the body** (to deliver the oxygen) in a single circuit.

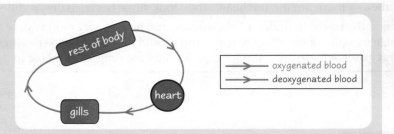

Single you say? How interesting. Now pass us the tartare sauce...

Mammals

In **mammals**, the heart is **divided** down the middle, so it's really like **two** hearts joined together.

1) The **right side** of the heart pumps blood to the **lungs** (to pick up oxygen).

2) From the lungs it travels to the **left side** of the heart, which pumps it to the rest of the **body**.

3) When blood **returns** to the heart, it enters the right side again.

The right and left sides of the heart are reversed in the diagram because it's the right and left of the person the heart belongs to.

So, our circulatory system is really two linked loops. One sends blood to the lungs — this is called the **pulmonary** system, and the other sends blood to the rest of the body — this is called the **systemic** system.

An **advantage** of the mammalian double circulatory system is that the heart can give the blood an **extra push** between the lungs and the rest of the body. This makes the blood travel **faster**, so oxygen is delivered to the tissues **more quickly**.

Circulatory Systems

Circulatory Systems can be Open or Closed

All vertebrates (e.g. fish and mammals) have **closed circulatory systems** — the blood is **enclosed** inside **blood vessels**.

1) The heart pumps blood into arteries. These branch out into millions of capillaries (see p. 80).
2) Substances like oxygen and glucose diffuse from the blood in the capillaries into the body cells, but the blood stays inside the blood vessels as it circulates.
3) Veins take the blood back to the heart.

Some invertebrates (e.g. insects) have an **open circulatory system** — blood **isn't enclosed** in blood vessels all the time. Instead, it flows freely through the **body cavity**.

1) The heart is segmented. It contracts in a wave, starting from the back, pumping the blood into a single main artery.
2) That artery opens up into the body cavity.
3) The blood flows around the insect's organs, gradually making its way back into the heart segments through a series of valves.

The circulatory system supplies the insect's cells with nutrients, and transports things like hormones around the body. It doesn't supply the insect's cells with oxygen though — this is done by a system of tubes called the tracheal system (see p. 77 for more).

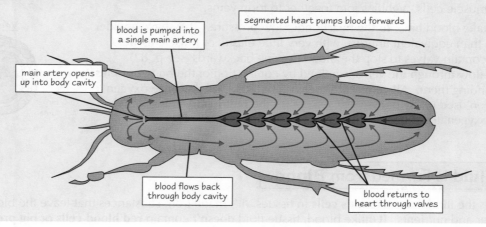

blood is pumped into a single main artery

segmented heart pumps blood forwards

main artery opens up into body cavity

blood flows back through body cavity

blood returns to heart through valves

Warm-Up Questions

Q1 Give three reasons why multicellular organisms usually need a transport system, but unicellular organisms don't.
Q2 Explain why the mammalian circulatory system is described as a double circulatory system.
Q3 What is an open circulatory system?

PRACTICE QUESTIONS

Exam Questions

Q1 Explain why the circulatory system of a trout is described as being closed. [1 mark]

Q2 Briefly describe the circulatory system of a beetle. [2 marks]

Q3 The Atlantic salmon (*Salmo salar*) and the red fox *(Vulpes vulpes)* have circulatory systems. Describe one way in which the circulatory system of the Atlantic salmon is:

a) similar to that of the red fox. [1 mark]

b) different from that of the red fox. [1 mark]

OK, open circulatory systems are officially grim. Body cavities?! Bleurgh...

After reading this page, we can all finally put to rest the idea that the Earth will eventually be overrun by giant insects. Their circulatory system just isn't up to it you see... All the nutrients and stuff in their blood have to diffuse through the whole body cavity, so if they were giant they wouldn't be able to supply all their organs and bits and pieces properly...

Blood Vessels

Watch out — now you need to learn about all the bits and bobs that make up that useful circulatory system of yours...

Blood Vessels Transport Substances Round the Body

The five types of blood vessel that you need to know about are **arteries**, **arterioles**, **capillaries**, **venules** and **veins**:

1) **Arteries** carry blood **from** the heart **to** the rest of the body. Their walls are thick and **muscular** and have elastic tissue to **stretch** and **recoil** as the heart beats, which helps maintain the **high pressure**. The inner lining (**endothelium**) is **folded**, allowing the artery to **expand** — this also helps it to maintain the high pressure. All arteries carry **oxygenated** blood except for the **pulmonary arteries**, which take deoxygenated blood to the lungs.

2) Arteries branch into **arterioles**, which are **much smaller** than arteries. Like arteries, arterioles have a layer of **smooth muscle**, but they have less elastic tissue. The **smooth muscle** allows them to **expand** or **contract**, thus controlling the amount of blood flowing to tissues.

3) Arterioles branch into **capillaries**, which are the **smallest** of the blood vessels. Substances like glucose and oxygen are exchanged between cells and capillaries, so they're adapted for **efficient diffusion**, e.g. their walls are only **one cell thick**.

4) Capillaries connect to **venules**, which have very **thin walls** that can contain some muscle cells. Venules join together to form veins.

5) **Veins** take blood **back to the heart** under low pressure. They have a **wider lumen** than equivalent arteries, with very little elastic or muscle tissue. Veins contain **valves** to stop the blood flowing backwards (see p. 82). Blood flow through the veins is helped by contraction of the **body muscles** surrounding them. All veins carry **deoxygenated** blood (because oxygen has been used up by body cells), except for the **pulmonary veins**, which carry oxygenated blood to the heart from the lungs.

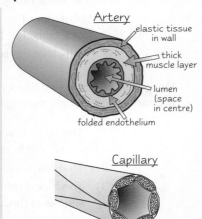

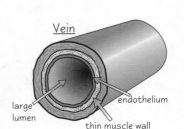

Tissue Fluid is Formed from Blood

Tissue fluid is the fluid that **surrounds cells** in tissues. It's made from substances that leave the blood plasma, e.g. oxygen, water and nutrients. (Unlike blood, tissue fluid **doesn't** contain **red blood cells** or **big proteins**, because they're **too large** to be pushed out through the capillary walls.) Cells take in oxygen and nutrients from the tissue fluid, and release metabolic waste into it. In a **capillary bed** (the network of capillaries in an area of tissue), substances move out of the capillaries, into the tissue fluid, by **pressure filtration**:

1) At the **start** of the capillary bed, nearest the arteries, the **hydrostatic (liquid) pressure** inside the capillaries is **greater** than the hydrostatic pressure in the tissue fluid. This difference in hydrostatic pressure **forces fluid out** of the **capillaries** and into the **spaces** around the cells, forming tissue fluid.

2) As fluid leaves, the hydrostatic pressure reduces in the capillaries — so the hydrostatic pressure is much **lower** at the **end** of the capillary bed that's nearest to the venules.

3) There is another form of pressure at work here called **oncotic pressure** — this is generated by **plasma proteins** present in the capillaries which lower the water potential. At the venule end of the capillary bed, the water potential in the capillaries is **lower** than the water potential in the tissue fluid due to the **fluid loss** from the capillaries and the **high oncotic pressure**. This means some **water re-enters** the capillaries from the tissue fluid at the venule end by **osmosis**.

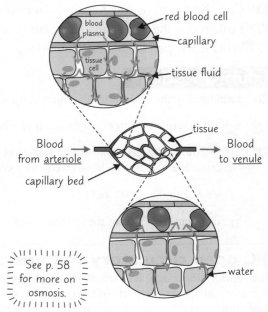

See p. 58 for more on osmosis.

Blood Vessels

Excess Tissue Fluid Drains into the Lymph Vessels

Not all of the tissue fluid **re-enters** the capillaries at the venule end of the capillary bed
— some **excess tissue fluid** is left over. This extra fluid eventually gets returned to the blood
through the **lymphatic system** — a kind of **drainage** system, made up of **lymph vessels**.

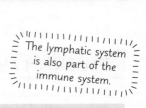
The lymphatic system
is also part of the
immune system.

1) The smallest lymph vessels
are the **lymph capillaries**.

2) Excess tissue fluid passes into
lymph vessels. Once inside,
it's called **lymph**.

3) **Valves** in the lymph vessels stop
the lymph going **backwards**.

4) Lymph gradually moves towards
the main lymph vessels in the
thorax (chest cavity). Here, it's
returned to the **blood**, near the **heart**.

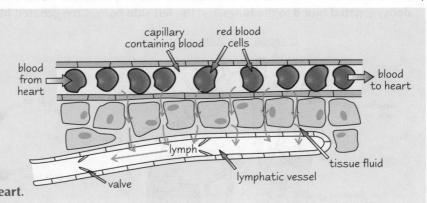

You Need to Know the Differences Between Blood, Tissue Fluid and Lymph

Blood, tissue fluid and lymph are all quite **similar** — **tissue fluid** is formed from **blood**, and **lymph** is formed from
tissue fluid. The main differences are shown in the table.

	blood	tissue fluid	lymph	comment
red blood cells	✓	✗	✗	Red blood cells are too big to get through capillary walls into tissue fluid.
white blood cells	✓	very few	✓	Most white blood cells are in the lymph system. They only enter tissue fluid when there's an infection.
platelets	✓	✗	✗	Only present in tissue fluid if the capillaries are damaged.
proteins	✓	very few	only antibodies	Most plasma proteins are too big to get through capillary walls.
water	✓	✓	✓	Tissue fluid and lymph have a higher water potential than blood.
dissolved solutes	✓	✓	✓	Solutes (e.g. salt) can move freely between blood, tissue fluid and lymph.

Warm-Up Questions

Q1 Is the blood pressure highest in veins or arteries?

Q2 Explain the differences between blood, tissue fluid and lymph.

PRACTICE QUESTIONS

Exam Questions

Q1 The diameter of different types of
blood vessel are shown on the right.
Select the row that shows the most
appropriate diameter for each type of
blood vessel.

Type of blood vessel and its diameter			
	Artery	Arteriole	Capillary	Vein
A	13 mm	8 µm	2 cm	200 µm
B	8 µm	2 cm	200 µm	13 mm
C	200 µm	13 mm	2 cm	8 µm
D	2 cm	200 µm	8 µm	13 mm

[1 mark]

Q2 At the arteriole end of a capillary bed the hydrostatic pressure is 5.1 kPa in a capillary and 0.13 kPa in the space
around the cells. Explain the effect this has on the movement of fluid between the capillary and cell space. [2 marks]

Tissue fluid... Imagine draining the fluid out of a used tissue. Urrrgh.

*That table looks a bit terrifying, but a lot of it's pretty obvious when you think about it — there can't be any red blood
cells floating around loose in your tissues, otherwise you'd be bright red. And platelets are the bits that cause blood
clots, so they're going to be in your blood... In fact, proteins and white blood cells are the only tricky bits.*

The Heart

You saw on page 78 that mammals have a double circulatory system — well that means that our hearts have to be a bit more complicated than just a big old pump.

The **Heart** Consists of **Two Muscular Pumps**

The diagrams below show the **internal** and **external structure** of the heart. The **right side** of the heart pumps **deoxygenated blood** to the **lungs** and the **left side** pumps **oxygenated blood** to the **rest of the body**.

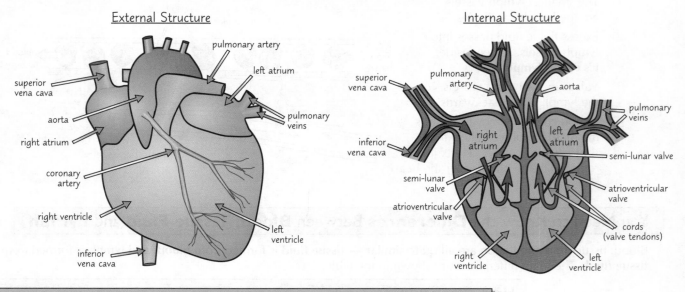

External Structure

Internal Structure

Valves in the Heart **Prevent** Blood Flowing the **Wrong Way**

The **atrioventricular valves** link the atria to the ventricles, and the **semi-lunar** valves link the ventricles to the pulmonary artery and aorta — they all stop blood flowing the **wrong way**. Here's how they work:

1) The **valves** only open one way — whether they're open or closed depends on the **relative pressure** of the heart chambers.

2) If there's higher pressure **behind** a valve, it's **forced open**.

3) If pressure is higher **in front** of the valve, it's **forced shut**.

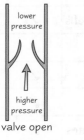

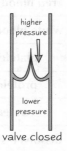

You Need to be Able to Carry Out a **Heart Dissection**

Equipment: You'll need a **pig or cow's heart**, a **dissecting tray**, a **scalpel**, an **apron** and **lab gloves**.

External examination: Look at the outside of the heart and try to identify the **four main vessels** attached to it. **Feel inside** the vessels to help you — remember arteries are thick and rubbery, whereas veins are much thinner.

Identify the right and left **atria**, the right and left **ventricles** and the **coronary arteries**. Draw a **sketch** of the outside of the heart with labels.

Internal examination: **Cut** along the lines shown on the diagram to **look inside** each ventricle. **Measure** and **record** the **thickness** of the ventricle walls and note any **differences** between them.

Cut open the **atria** and **look inside** them too. Note whether the **atria walls** are thicker or thinner than the ventricle walls.

Find the **atrioventricular valves**, followed by the **semi-lunar valves**. Look at the **structure** of the valves.

Draw a **sketch** to show the valves and the inside of the ventricles and atria.

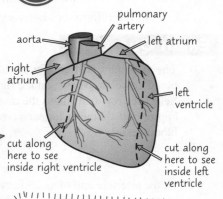

The left ventricle wall is thicker and more muscular than the right, to push blood all the way round the body. Also, the ventricles have thicker walls than the atria because they have to push blood out of the heart.

The Heart

The **Cardiac Cycle** Pumps Blood Round the Body

The cardiac cycle is an ongoing sequence of **contraction** and **relaxation** of the atria and ventricles that keeps blood **continuously circulating** round the body. The **volumes** of the atria and ventricles **change** as they contract and relax, altering the **pressure** in each chamber. This causes **valves** to open and close, which directs the **blood flow** through the heart. The cardiac cycle can be simplified into three stages:

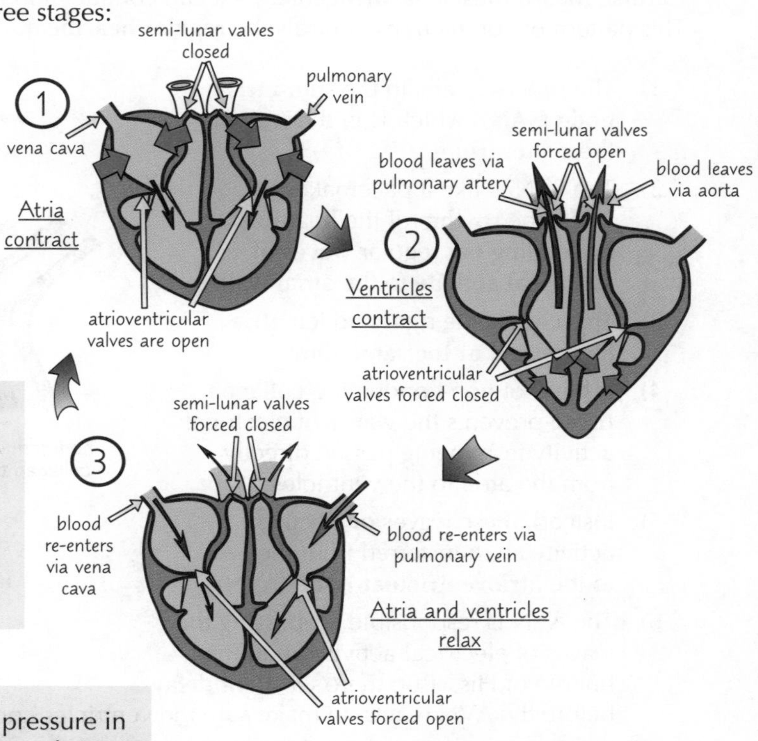

1 Ventricles relax, atria contract

The **ventricles are relaxed**. The **atria contract**, which decreases their volume and **increases** their **pressure**. This **pushes** the blood into the ventricles through the **atrioventricular valves**. There's a slight **increase** in **ventricular pressure** and **volume** as the **ventricles receive the ejected blood** from the contracting atria.

2 Ventricles contract, atria relax

The **atria relax**. The **ventricles contract** (decreasing their volume), **increasing** their **pressure**. The pressure becomes **higher** in the ventricles than the atria, which forces the **atrioventricular valves shut** to prevent back-flow. The high pressure in the ventricles **opens** the semi-lunar valves — blood is forced out into the **pulmonary artery** and **aorta**.

3 Ventricles relax, atria relax

The **ventricles and the atria both relax**. The higher pressure in the pulmonary artery and aorta causes the semi-lunar valves to **close**, preventing back-flow. The **atria fill** with blood (**increasing** their **pressure**) due to the higher pressure in the vena cava and pulmonary vein. As the ventricles continue to **relax**, their **pressure falls below the pressure in the atria**. This causes the **atrioventricular valves** to **open** and blood flows **passively** (without being pushed by atrial contraction) into the ventricles from the atria. The atria contract, and the whole process begins again.

Diagram labels:
semi-lunar valves closed
pulmonary vein
vena cava
Atria contract
atrioventricular valves are open
blood leaves via pulmonary artery
semi-lunar valves forced open
blood leaves via aorta
Ventricles contract
atrioventricular valves forced closed
semi-lunar valves forced closed
blood re-enters via vena cava
blood re-enters via pulmonary vein
Atria and ventricles relax
atrioventricular valves forced open

In the exam you could be asked to calculate **cardiac output**. This is the **volume of blood** pumped by the heart **per minute** (measured in cm^3 min^{-1}). It's calculated using the formula: **cardiac output = heart rate × stroke volume**.

Heart rate is the number of beats per minute (bpm) and stroke volume is the volume of blood pumped during each heartbeat in cm^3.

Warm-Up Question

Q1 Which chamber of the heart receives blood from the lungs?

PRACTICE QUESTIONS

Exam Question

Q1 The graph shows the pressure changes in the left side of the heart during one heartbeat.

a) At which labelled point (A-H) on the graph does:

   i) the semi-lunar valve open? [1 mark]

   ii) the atrioventricular valve close? [1 mark]

b) On the diagram, sketch the graph that you would expect for the right ventricle. [2 marks]

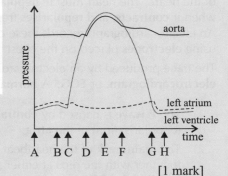

Graph labels: pressure; aorta; left atrium; left ventricle; time; A B C D E F G H

Apparently an adult heart is the size of two fists. Two whole fists! Huge!

If you listen to a heartbeat you'll hear a 'lub-dub' sound. The first 'lub' sound is caused by the atrioventricular valves closing (stage 2). The second 'dub' sound is caused by the semi-lunar valves closing (stage 3). How very interesting.

Heart Activity

You don't have to think about making your heart beat — your body does it for you.
So you couldn't stop it beating even if for some strange reason you wanted to. Which is nice to know.

Cardiac Muscle Controls the Regular Beating of the Heart

Cardiac (heart) muscle is 'myogenic' — it can contract and relax without receiving signals from nerves.
This pattern of contractions controls the regular heartbeat.

1) The process starts in the sino-atrial node (SAN), which is in the wall of the right atrium.

2) The SAN is like a pacemaker — it sets the rhythm of the heartbeat by sending out regular waves of electrical activity to the atrial walls.

3) This causes the right and left atria to contract at the same time.

4) A band of non-conducting collagen tissue prevents the waves of electrical activity from being passed directly from the atria to the ventricles.

5) Instead, these waves of electrical activity are transferred from the SAN to the atrioventricular node (AVN).

6) The AVN is responsible for passing the waves of electrical activity on to the bundle of His. But, there's a slight delay before the AVN reacts, to make sure the ventricles contract after the atria have emptied.

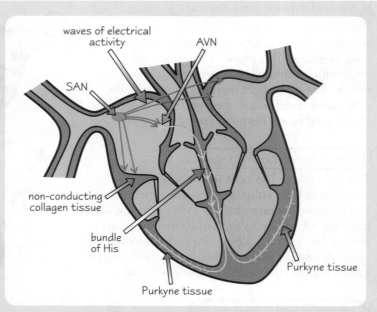

7) The bundle of His is a group of muscle fibres responsible for conducting the waves of electrical activity to the finer muscle fibres in the right and left ventricle walls, called the Purkyne tissue.

8) The Purkyne tissue carries the waves of electrical activity into the muscular walls of the right and left ventricles, causing them to contract simultaneously, from the bottom up.

An Electrocardiograph Records the Electrical Activity of the Heart

A doctor can check someone's heart function using an electrocardiograph — a machine that records the electrical activity of the heart. The heart muscle depolarises (loses electrical charge) when it contracts, and repolarises (regains charge) when it relaxes. An electrocardiograph records these changes in electrical charge using electrodes placed on the chest.

When Ed did that special thing to her beak, Polly's heart activity increased 10-fold.

The trace produced by an electrocardiograph is called an electrocardiogram, or ECG. A normal ECG looks like this:

1) The P wave is caused by contraction (depolarisation) of the atria.

2) The main peak of the heartbeat, together with the dips at either side, is called the QRS complex — it's caused by contraction (depolarisation) of the ventricles.

3) The T wave is due to relaxation (repolarisation) of the ventricles.

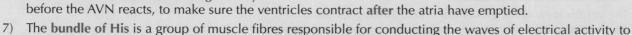

4) The height of the wave indicates how much electrical charge is passing through the heart — a bigger wave means more electrical charge, so (for the P and R waves) a bigger wave means a stronger contraction.

Heart Activity

Doctors use ECGs to Diagnose Heart Problems

Doctors **compare** their patients' ECGs with a **normal trace**. This helps them to diagnose any heart problems.

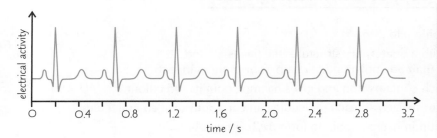

This heartbeat is **too fast** — around 120 beats per minute. It's called **tachycardia**. That might be OK during **exercise**, but at **rest** it shows that the heart **isn't pumping blood efficiently**. A heartbeat can also be **too slow** — below 60 beats per minute at rest. This is called **bradycardia**.

The 5th heartbeat on this ECG is an **ectopic heartbeat** — an 'extra' heartbeat. Here it's caused by an **earlier contraction of the atria** than in the previous heartbeats (you can see that the P wave is different and that it comes earlier than it should). However, it can be caused by **early contraction of the ventricles** too. Occasional ectopic heartbeats in a healthy person don't cause a problem.

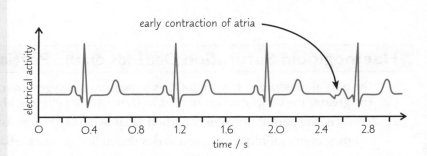

early contraction of atria

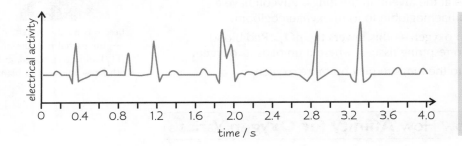

This is **fibrillation** — a really **irregular heartbeat**. The atria or ventricles completely **lose their rhythm** and **stop contracting properly**. It can result in anything from chest pain and fainting to lack of pulse and death.

Warm-Up Questions

Q1 What prevents impulses from the atria travelling straight into the ventricles?

Q2 What is the name of the structure that picks up impulses from the atria and passes them on to the ventricles?

Q3 What causes the QRS part of an ECG trace?

Exam Questions

Q1 Describe the function of:

   a) the sino-atrial node.   [1 mark]

   b) the Purkyne tissue.   [1 mark]

Q2 Suggest the cause of an ECG which has a QRS complex that is not as high as normal.   [2 marks]

The cardiac cycle — a bewilderingly complicated pump-action bicycle...

It's pretty incredible that your heart manages to go through all those stages in the right order, at exactly the right time, without getting it even slightly wrong. It does it perfectly, about 70 times every minute. That's about 100 800 times a day. If only my brain was that efficient. I'd have all this revision done in five minutes, then I could go and watch TV...

Haemoglobin

Aaagh, complicated topic alert. Don't worry though, because your poor, over-worked brain cells will recover from the brain-strain of these pages thanks to haemoglobin. So the least you can do is learn how it works.

Oxygen is Carried Round the Body as Oxyhaemoglobin

1) **Red blood cells** contain **haemoglobin** (Hb).

2) Haemoglobin is a large **protein** with a **quaternary** structure (see pages 27 and 28 for more) — it's made up of **more than one** polypeptide chain (**four** of them in fact).

'Affinity' for oxygen means tendency to combine with oxygen.

3) Each chain has a **haem group** which contains **iron** and gives haemoglobin its **red** colour.

4) Haemoglobin has a **high affinity for oxygen** — each molecule can carry **four oxygen molecules**.

5) In the lungs, oxygen **joins** to the **iron** in haemoglobin to form **oxyhaemoglobin**.

6) This is a **reversible reaction** — when oxygen leaves oxyhaemoglobin (**dissociates** from it) near the body cells, it turns back to haemoglobin.

$$Hb \; + \; 4O_2 \; \rightleftharpoons \; HbO_8$$

haemoglobin + oxygen $\rightleftharpoons$ oxyhaemoglobin

Haemoglobin Saturation Depends on the Partial Pressure of Oxygen

1) The **partial pressure** of **oxygen** (**pO_2**) is a measure of **oxygen concentration**. The **greater** the concentration of dissolved oxygen in cells, the **higher** the partial pressure.

2) Similarly, the **partial pressure** of **carbon dioxide** (**pCO_2**) is a measure of the concentration of CO_2 in a cell.

3) Haemoglobin's **affinity** for oxygen **varies** depending on the **partial pressure** of **oxygen**:

> Oxygen **loads onto** haemoglobin to form oxyhaemoglobin where there's a **high pO_2**. Oxyhaemoglobin **unloads** its oxygen where there's a **lower pO_2**.

4) Oxygen enters blood capillaries at the **alveoli** in the **lungs**. Alveoli have a **high pO_2** so oxygen **loads onto** haemoglobin to form oxyhaemoglobin.

5) When **cells respire**, they use up oxygen — this **lowers** the **pO_2**. Red blood cells deliver oxyhaemoglobin to respiring tissues, where it unloads its oxygen.

6) The haemoglobin then returns to the lungs to pick up more oxygen.

There was no use pretending — the partial pressure of CH_4 had just increased, and Keith knew who was to blame.

Dissociation Curves Show How Affinity for Oxygen Varies

An oxygen **dissociation curve** shows how **saturated** the haemoglobin is with oxygen at any given partial pressure.

100% saturation means every haemoglobin molecule is carrying the maximum of 4 molecules of oxygen.

0% saturation means none of the haemoglobin molecules are carrying any oxygen.

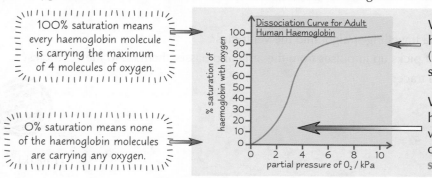

Where pO_2 is high (e.g. in the lungs), haemoglobin has a **high affinity** for oxygen (i.e. it will **readily combine** with oxygen), so it has a **high saturation** of oxygen.

Where pO_2 is low (e.g. in respiring tissues), haemoglobin has a **low affinity** for oxygen, which means it **releases oxygen** rather than combines with it. That's why it has a **low saturation** of oxygen.

1) The graph is 'S-shaped' because when haemoglobin (Hb) combines with the **first O_2 molecule**, its **shape alters** in a way that makes it **easier** for other molecules to join too.

2) But as the Hb starts to become saturated, it gets **harder** for more oxygen molecules to join.

3) As a result, the curve has a **steep** bit in the middle where it's really easy for oxygen molecules to join, and **shallow** bits at each end where it's harder. When the curve is steep, a **small change in pO_2** causes a **big change** in the **amount of oxygen** carried by the Hb.

Haemoglobin

Fetal Haemoglobin has a Higher Affinity for Oxygen than Adult Haemoglobin

Adult haemoglobin and fetal haemoglobin have different affinities for oxygen. Fetal haemoglobin has a **higher affinity** for oxygen (the fetus's blood is **better at absorbing** oxygen than its mother's blood) at the **same partial pressure** of oxygen. This is really important:

1) The fetus gets oxygen from its mother's blood across the placenta.

2) By the time the mother's blood reaches the placenta, its oxygen saturation has decreased (because some has been used up by the mother's body).

3) For the fetus to get enough oxygen to survive its haemoglobin has to have a higher affinity for oxygen (so it takes up enough).

4) If its haemoglobin had the same affinity for oxygen as adult haemoglobin its blood wouldn't be saturated enough.

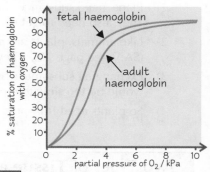

Carbon Dioxide Concentration Affects Oxygen Unloading

To complicate matters, haemoglobin gives up its oxygen **more readily** at **higher partial pressures of carbon dioxide** (pCO_2). It's a cunning way of getting more oxygen to cells during activity. When cells respire they produce carbon dioxide, which raises the pCO_2, increasing the rate of oxygen unloading. The reason for this is linked to how CO_2 affects blood pH.

1) Most of the CO_2 from respiring tissues diffuses into red blood cells. Here it reacts with water to form carbonic acid, catalysed by the enzyme carbonic anhydrase. (The rest of the CO_2, around 10%, binds directly to haemoglobin and is carried to the lungs.)

2) The carbonic acid dissociates (splits up) to give hydrogen (H^+) ions and hydrogencarbonate (HCO_3^-) ions.

3) This increase in H^+ ions causes oxyhaemoglobin to unload its oxygen so that haemoglobin can take up the H^+ ions. This forms a compound called haemoglobinic acid. (This process also stops the hydrogen ions from increasing the cell's acidity.)

4) The HCO_3^- ions diffuse out of the red blood cells and are transported in the blood plasma. To compensate for the loss of HCO_3^- ions from the red blood cells, chloride (Cl^-) ions diffuse into the red blood cells. This is called the chloride shift and it maintains the balance of charge between the red blood cell and the plasma.

5) When the blood reaches the lungs the low pCO_2 causes some of the HCO_3^- and H^+ ions to recombine into CO_2 (and water).

6) The CO_2 then diffuses into the alveoli and is breathed out.

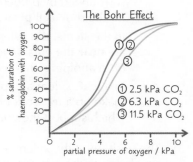

When carbon dioxide levels increase, the dissociation curve 'shifts' right, showing that more oxygen is released from the blood (because the lower the saturation of haemoglobin with O_2, the more O_2 is released). This is called the Bohr effect.

Warm-Up Questions

Q1 How many oxygen molecules can each haemoglobin molecule carry?

Q2 What is carbon dioxide converted to in red blood cells?

Exam Question

Q1 Which statement correctly describes the Bohr effect?

A When pCO_2 increases, less O_2 is released from the blood and the O_2 dissociation curve shifts right.

B When pCO_2 increases, more O_2 is released from the blood and the O_2 dissociation curve shifts right.

C When pCO_2 increases, less O_2 is released from the blood and the O_2 dissociation curve shifts left.

D When pCO_2 increases, more O_2 is released from the blood and the O_2 dissociation curve shifts left. [1 mark]

The Bore effect — it's happening right now...

Dissociation graphs can be a bit confusing — but basically, when tissues contain lots of oxygen (i.e. pO_2 is high), haemoglobin readily combines with the oxygen, so the blood has a high saturation of oxygen (and vice versa when pO_2 is low). Simple. Also, make sure you get the lingo right, like 'partial pressure' and 'affinity' — hey, I'm hip, I'm groovy.

Xylem and Phloem

A whole section on transport in plants... just what I always dreamed of...

Multicellular Plants Need Transport Systems

Plants also need carbon dioxide, but this enters at the leaves (where it's needed).

1) Plants need substances like **water**, **minerals** and **sugars** to live. They also need to **get rid of waste substances**.

2) Like animals, plants are **multicellular** — so they have a **small surface area : volume ratio** (SA:V, see page 70). They're also relatively **big** with a relatively **high metabolic rate**.

3) Exchanging substances by **direct diffusion** (from the outer surface to the cells) would be **too slow** to meet their metabolic needs.

4) So plants **need transport systems** to move substances to and from individual cells **quickly**.

Two Types of Tissue are Involved in Transport in Plants

1) **Xylem tissue** transports **water** and **mineral ions** in solution. These substances move **up** the plant from the roots to the leaves. **Phloem tissue** mainly transports **sugars** (also in solution) both **up and down** the plant.

2) Xylem and phloem make up a plant's **vascular system**. They are found **throughout** a plant and **transport materials** to all parts. **Where** they're found in each part is connected to the **xylem's** other function — **support**:

- In a **root**, the xylem is in the **centre** surrounded by phloem to **provide support** for the root as it **pushes** through the soil.
- In the **stems**, the xylem and phloem are **near the outside** to provide a sort of 'scaffolding' that reduces bending.
- In a **leaf**, xylem and phloem make up a **network of veins** which support the thin leaves.

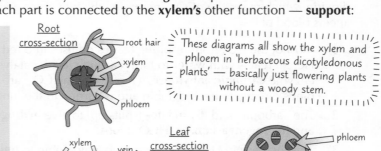

These diagrams all show the xylem and phloem in 'herbaceous dicotyledonous plants' — basically just flowering plants without a woody stem.

Root cross-section — root hair, xylem, phloem

Leaf cross-section — xylem, vein, phloem

Stem cross-section — phloem, xylem

3) The position of the xylem and phloem in the root, leaf and stem are shown in these **transverse cross-sections**. Transverse means the sections cut through each structure at a **right angle** to its **length**.

4) You can also get **longitudinal** cross-sections. These are taken **along the length** of a structure. For example, this cross-section shows where the **xylem** and **phloem** are located in a **typical stem**.

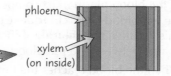

phloem, xylem (on inside)

Xylem Vessels are Adapted for Transporting Water and Mineral Ions

Xylem is a **tissue** made from several **different cell types** (see page 66). You need to learn about **xylem vessels** — the part of xylem tissue that actually transports the water and ions. Xylem vessels are adapted for their **function**:

1) Xylem vessels are very **long, tube-like** structures formed from cells (**vessel elements**) joined end to end.

2) There are **no end walls** on these cells, making an **uninterrupted tube** that allows water to pass up through the middle easily.

3) The cells are **dead**, so they contain **no cytoplasm**.

4) Their walls are **thickened** with a **woody** substance called **lignin**, which helps to **support** the xylem vessels and stops them **collapsing inwards**. Lignin can be deposited in xylem walls in different ways, e.g. in a **spiral** or as **distinct rings**.

5) The amount of lignin **increases** as the cell gets **older**.

6) **Water** and **ions** move **into** and **out of** the vessels through **small pits** in the walls where there's **no lignin**.

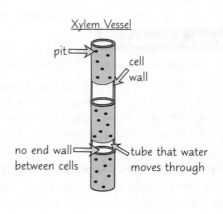

Xylem Vessel — pit, cell wall, no end wall between cells, tube that water moves through

Xylem and Phloem

Phloem Tissue is Adapted for Transporting Solutes

1) Phloem tissue transports **solutes** (dissolved substances), mainly sugars like sucrose, round plants.
2) Like xylem, phloem is formed from cells arranged in **tubes**.
   But, unlike xylem, it's purely a **transport tissue** — it **isn't** used for support as well.
3) Phloem tissue contains **phloem fibres**, **phloem parenchyma**, **sieve tube elements** and **companion cells**.
4) **Sieve tube elements** and **companion cells** are the most important cell types in phloem for **transport**:

① Sieve tube elements

1) These are **living cells** that form the tube for **transporting solutes** through the plant.
2) They are joined **end to end** to form **sieve tubes**.
3) The 'sieve' parts are the **end walls**, which have lots of **holes** in them to allow **solutes** to pass through.
4) Unusually for living cells, sieve tube elements have **no nucleus**, a **very thin** layer of **cytoplasm** and **few organelles**.
5) The cytoplasm of adjacent cells is **connected** through the holes in the sieve plates.

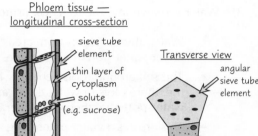

Phloem tissue — longitudinal cross-section

sieve tube element
thin layer of cytoplasm
solute (e.g. sucrose)
sieve plate
companion cell

Transverse view
angular sieve tube element
companion cell

② Companion cells

1) The **lack** of a **nucleus** and **other organelles** in sieve tube elements means that they **can't survive** on their own. So there's a **companion cell** for **every** sieve tube element.
2) Companion cells carry out the living functions for **both** themselves and their sieve cells. For example, they provide the **energy** for the **active transport** of solutes.

The active transport of solutes requires energy (see p. 56).

You Need to be Able to Dissect Plant Stems

You can **look at plant tissue** (e.g. part of a plant stem) under a **microscope**, and then **draw** it. But first you need to **dissect** the plant and **prepare** a section of the tissue. You can do this using the following method:

1) Use a scalpel (or razor blade) to cut a cross-section of the stem (transverse or longitudinal).
   Cut the sections as thinly as possible — thin sections are better for viewing under a microscope.
2) Use tweezers to gently place the cut sections in water until you come to use them. This stops them from drying out.
3) Transfer each section to a dish containing a stain, e.g. toluidine blue O (TBO), and leave for one minute. TBO stains the lignin in the walls of the xylem vessels blue-green. This will let you see the position of the xylem vessels and examine their structure.
4) Rinse off the sections in water and mount each one onto a slide (see page 18).

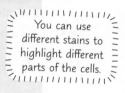

You can use different stains to highlight different parts of the cells.

Warm-Up Questions

Q1 Why do multicellular plants need transport systems?
Q2 What is the name of the substance that thickens the walls of xylem vessels?
Q3 What is the function of companion cells?

Exam Question

Q1 Explain two ways in which the structure of the xylem vessels makes them well-adapted to their function.   [4 marks]

Sieve tube — WLTM like-minded cell for long-term companionship...

Sieve tube elements sound a bit feeble to me — not being able to survive on their own, and all that. Anyway, some of the structures and functions of the cell types covered here are quite similar, so it's important you learn them properly. You don't want to mix up your sieve tube elements with your vessel elements in the exam — you'd never forgive yourself...

Water Transport

Water enters a plant through its roots and eventually, if it's not used, exits via the leaves. "Ah-ha", I hear you say, "but how does it flow upwards, against gravity?" Well that, my friends, is a mystery that's about to be explained...

Water Enters a Plant through its Root Hair Cells

Cross-Section of a Root

1) Water has to get from the **soil**, through the **root** and into the **xylem** to be transported around the plant.

2) Water enters through **root hair cells** and then passes through **the root cortex**, including the **endodermis**, to reach the xylem (see below).

3) Water is drawn into the roots via **osmosis**. This means it travels down a **water potential gradient**:

- Water always moves from areas of **higher water potential** to areas of **lower water potential** — it goes down a **water potential gradient**.
- The **soil** around roots generally has a **high water potential** (i.e. there's lots of water there) and **leaves** have a **lower water potential** (because water constantly **evaporates** from them).
- This creates a water potential gradient that keeps water moving through the plant in the right direction, **from roots** (high) to **leaves** (low).

Remember: osmosis is the diffusion of water molecules across a partially permeable membrane, from an area of higher water potential to an area of lower water potential — see p. 58.

Water Moves Through the Root into the Xylem...

Water travels through the **roots** (via the **root cortex**) into the **xylem** by **two** different paths:

1) The **symplast pathway** — goes through the **living** parts of cells — the **cytoplasm**. The cytoplasms of neighbouring cells connect through **plasmodesmata** (small channels in the cell walls). Water moves through the symplast pathway via **osmosis**.

2) The **apoplast pathway** — goes through the **non-living** parts of the cells — the **cell walls**. The walls are very absorbent and water can simply **diffuse** through them, as well as pass through the spaces between them. The water can carry **solutes** and move from areas of **high hydrostatic pressure** to areas of **low hydrostatic pressure** (i.e. along a pressure gradient). This is an example of **mass flow** (see page 94).

The prison had been strangely quiet ever since plasmodesmata were installed.

- When water in the apoplast pathway gets to the endodermis cells in the root, its path is blocked by a waxy strip in the cell walls, called the Casparian strip. Now the water has to take the symplast pathway.
- This is useful, because it means the water has to go through a cell membrane. Cell membranes are partially permeable and are able to control whether or not substances in the water get through (see p. 50).
- Once past this barrier, the water moves into the xylem.

3) Both pathways are used, but the main one is the **apoplast pathway** because it provides the **least resistance**.

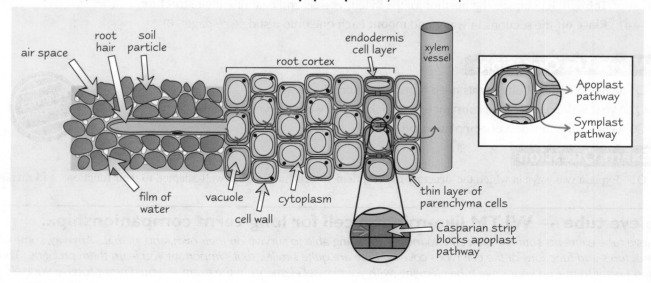

Water Transport

...then **Up** the **Xylem** and **Out** at the **Leaves**

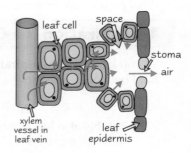

1) **Xylem vessels** transport the water **all around** the plant.
2) At the **leaves**, water leaves the xylem and moves into the cells mainly by the **apoplast pathway**.
3) Water **evaporates** from the cell walls into the **spaces** between cells in the leaf.
4) When the **stomata** (tiny pores in the surface of the leaf) open, the water **diffuses** out of the leaf (down the **water potential gradient**) into the **surrounding air**.
5) The loss of water from a plant's surface is called **transpiration** (see next page).

Water Moves **Up** a Plant **Against** the Force of **Gravity**

The movement of water from **roots to leaves** is called the **transpiration stream**. The **mechanisms** that **move** the water include **cohesion**, **tension** and **adhesion**.

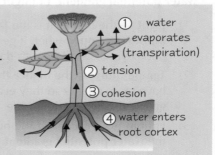

Cohesion and **tension** help water move up plants, from roots to leaves, **against** the force of gravity.

1) Water **evaporates** from the **leaves** at the 'top' of the xylem (**transpiration**).
2) This creates a **tension** (**suction**), which pulls more water into the leaf.
3) Water molecules are **cohesive** (they **stick together**) so when some are pulled into the leaf others follow. This means the whole **column** of water in the **xylem**, from the leaves down to the roots, **moves upwards**.
4) **Water** enters the stem through the **root cortex cells**.

Adhesion is also partly responsible for the **movement of water**.

1) As well as being attracted to each other, water molecules are **attracted to the walls** of the xylem vessels.
2) This helps water to **rise up** through the xylem vessels.

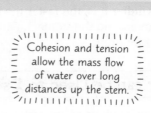

Cohesion and tension allow the mass flow of water over long distances up the stem.

Warm-Up Questions

Q1 In terms of water potential, why does water move into the roots from the soil?
Q2 Describe how water moves through a plant root via the symplast pathway.
Q3 What is the Casparian strip?
Q4 How does adhesion help to move water through a plant?

Exam Questions

Q1 Explain the role of cohesion and tension in the loss of water from the leaves of plants. [4 marks]

Q2 Plants that are infected by a pathogen are able to block their plasmodesmata. This is thought to be an attempt to reduce the spread of the pathogen. Suggest how this would affect the way that water travels through a plant. [2 marks]

So many routes through the roots...

As you've probably noticed, there are lots of impressive biological words on these pages that you can amaze your friends with. Go over the pages again, and whenever you see a word like plasmodesmata, stop and check you know exactly what it means. (Personally I think they should just call them cell wall channels, but nobody ever listens to me.)

Transpiration

Plants can't sing, juggle or tap dance (as you will hopefully be aware). But they can exchange gases — how exciting. What makes it all the more thrilling though is that they lose water vapour as they do it. Gripping stuff.

Transpiration is a Consequence of Gas Exchange

So you know that **transpiration** is the evaporation of **water** from a plant's surface, especially the **leaves**. But I bet you didn't know it happens as a result of **gas exchange**. Read on...

1) A plant needs to open its stomata to let in carbon dioxide so that it can produce glucose (by photosynthesis).
2) But this also lets water out — there's a higher concentration of water inside the leaf than in the air outside, so water moves out of the leaf down the water potential gradient when the stomata open.
3) So transpiration's really a side effect of the gas exchange needed for photosynthesis.

Four Main Factors Affect Transpiration Rate

Temperature, humidity and wind all alter the **water potential gradient**, but **light** is a bit different:

Water moves from areas of higher water potential to areas of lower water potential — it moves down the water potential gradient.

1) <u>Light</u> — the **lighter** it is the **faster** the **transpiration rate**. This is because the **stomata open** when it gets **light**, so CO_2 can diffuse into the leaf for photosynthesis. When it's **dark** the stomata are usually **closed**, so there's little transpiration.

2) <u>Temperature</u> — the **higher the temperature** the **faster the transpiration rate**. Warmer water molecules have more energy so they **evaporate** from the cells inside the leaf **faster**. This **increases the water potential gradient** between the inside and outside of the leaf, making water **diffuse** out of the leaf **faster**.

3) <u>Humidity</u> — the <u>lower</u> the **humidity**, the **faster** the **transpiration rate**. If the air around the plant is **dry**, the **water potential gradient** between the leaf and the air is **increased**, which increases transpiration.

4) <u>Wind</u> — the **windier** it is, the **faster** the **transpiration rate**. Lots of air movement **blows away** water molecules from around the stomata. This **increases** the water potential gradient, which increases the rate of transpiration.

A Potometer can be Used to Estimate Transpiration Rate

PRACTICAL SKILLS

A **potometer** is a special piece of apparatus used to **estimate transpiration rates**. It actually measures **water uptake** by a plant, but it's **assumed** that water uptake by the plant is **directly related** to **water loss** by the **leaves**. You can use it to estimate how different factors **affect** the transpiration rate.

A potometer

Reservoir of water used to return bubble to start for repeats.

As the plant takes up water, the air bubble moves along the scale.

water moves this way

Tap is shut off during experiment.

capillary tube with a scale

bubble moves this way

beaker of water

The air bubble is sometimes called the air-water meniscus.

Here's what you'd do:

1) **Cut** a **shoot underwater** to prevent air from entering the xylem. Cut it at a **slant** to increase the surface area available for water uptake.

2) Assemble the potometer **in water** and insert the shoot **underwater**, so no air can enter.

3) Remove the apparatus from the water but keep the **end of the capillary tube submerged** in a beaker of water.

4) Check that the apparatus is **watertight** and **airtight**.

5) **Dry** the leaves, allow time for the shoot to **acclimatise**, and then **shut the tap**.

6) Remove the end of the capillary tube from the beaker of water until **one air bubble** has formed, then put the end of the tube back into the water.

7) Record the **starting position** of the **air bubble**.

8) Start a **stopwatch** and record the **distance** moved by the bubble **per unit time**, e.g. per hour. The **rate of air bubble movement** is an estimate of the **transpiration rate**.

9) Remember, only change **one variable** (e.g. temperature) at a time. All other **conditions** (e.g. light, humidity) must be kept **constant**.

Module 3: Section 3 — Transport in Plants

Transpiration

Xerophytic Plants are Adapted to Reduce Water Loss

Xerophytes are plants like **cacti** and **marram grass** (which grows on sand dunes). They're **adapted** to live in **dry climates**. Their adaptations prevent them **losing too much water** by **transpiration**...

1) Marram grass has stomata that are sunk in pits, so they're sheltered from the wind. This helps to slow transpiration down.

2) It also has a layer of 'hairs' on the epidermis — this traps moist air round the stomata, which reduces the water potential gradient between the leaf and the air, slowing transpiration down.

3) In hot or windy conditions marram grass plants roll their leaves — again this traps moist air, slowing down transpiration. It also reduces the exposed surface area for losing water and protects the stomata from wind.

4) Both marram grass and cacti have a thick, waxy layer on the epidermis — this reduces water loss by evaporation because the layer is waterproof (water can't move through it).

5) Cacti have spines instead of leaves — this reduces the surface area for water loss.

6) Cacti also close their stomata at the hottest times of the day when transpiration rates are the highest.

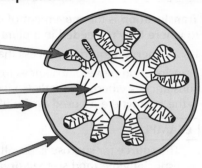

Cross-section through a marram grass leaf.

Cacti spines   Marram grass

Hydrophilic Plants are Adapted to Survive in Water

Hydrophytes are plants like **water lilies**, which live in **aquatic habitats**. As they **grow in water**, they **don't need** adaptations **to reduce water loss** (like xerophytes), but they do need adaptations to help them cope with a **low oxygen level**. Here are some adaptations of hydrophytes...

1) **Air spaces** in the tissues help the plants to **float** and can act as a **store of oxygen** for use in respiration. For example, **water lilies** have **large air spaces** in their **leaves**. This allows the leaves to **float on the surface** of the water, **increasing** the amount of **light** they receive. Air spaces in the **roots** and **stems** allow **oxygen** to move from the floating leaves down to parts of the plant that are **underwater**.

2) **Stomata** are usually only present on the **upper surface** of **floating leaves**. This helps **maximise gas exchange**.

3) Hydrophytes often have **flexible leaves and stems** — these plants are **supported** by the **water** around them, so they don't need rigid stems for support. Flexibility helps to **prevent damage** by water currents.

Warm-Up Questions

Q1 Explain why transpiration is a consequence of gaseous exchange.
Q2 Name a piece of apparatus used to measure transpiration.
Q3 What is a hydrophyte?

PRACTICE QUESTIONS

Exam Question

Q1 The diagram shows a section of a leaf of a xerophytic plant. Describe and explain two ways, visible in the picture, in which this leaf is adapted to reduce water loss.   [4 marks]

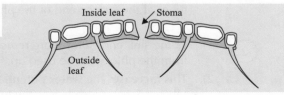

Inside leaf   Stoma

Outside leaf

Xerophytes — an exciting word for a boring subject...

Actually, that's unfair. It's taken millions of years for plants to evolve those adaptations, and here I am slagging them off. When I've managed to develop a thick waxy cuticle on my leaves and stems, then I can comment, and not before.

Translocation

Translocation is the movement of dissolved solutes through a plant. Annoyingly, translocation sounds a lot like transpiration. Or is that just me? Make sure you don't get them confused.

Translocation is the Movement of Dissolved Substances

1) **Translocation** is the **movement** of dissolved substances (e.g. sugars like sucrose, and amino acids) to **where they're needed** in a plant. Dissolved substances are sometimes called **assimilates**.

2) It's an **energy-requiring** process that happens in the **phloem** (see p.89 for more on the phloem).

3) Translocation moves substances from 'sources' to 'sinks'. The **source** of a substance is **where it's made** (so it's at a **high concentration** there). The **sink** is the area where it's **used up** (so it's at a **lower concentration** there).

> *Sugars are transported as sucrose because sucrose is both soluble and metabolically inactive — so it doesn't get used up during transport.*

> **EXAMPLE**
>
> The source for sucrose is usually the leaves (where it's made), and the sinks are the other parts of the plant, especially the food storage organs and the meristems (areas of growth) in the roots, stems and leaves.

4) Some parts of a plant can be both a **sink** and a **source**.

> **EXAMPLE**
>
> Sucrose can be stored in the roots. During the growing season, sucrose is transported from the roots to the leaves to provide the leaves with energy for growth. In this case, the roots are the source and the leaves are a sink.

Reeta liked a bit of translocation in her spare time.

5) **Enzymes** maintain a **concentration gradient** from the source to the sink by **changing** the dissolved substances at the **sink** (e.g. by breaking them down or making them into something else). This makes sure there's always a **lower concentration** at the sink than at the source.

> **EXAMPLES**
>
> In potatoes, sucrose is converted to starch in the sink areas, so there's always a lower concentration of sucrose at the sink than inside the phloem. This makes sure a constant supply of new sucrose reaches the sink from the phloem. In other sinks, enzymes such as invertase break down sucrose into glucose (and fructose) for use by the plant — again this makes sure there's a lower concentration of sucrose at the sink.

The Mass Flow Hypothesis Best Explains Phloem Transport

Scientists still aren't certain **exactly how** the dissolved substances (solutes) are transported from source to sink by **translocation**. The best supported theory is the **mass flow hypothesis**:

(1)

1) Active transport is used to **actively load** the solutes (e.g. sucrose from photosynthesis) into the **sieve tubes** of the phloem at the **source** (e.g. the **leaves**). There's more on this on the next page.

2) This **lowers** the **water potential** inside the **sieve tubes**, so **water** enters the tubes by **osmosis** from the **xylem** and **companion cells**.

3) This creates a **high pressure** inside the sieve tubes at the **source end** of the phloem.

(2)

1) At the **sink** end, **solutes** are removed from the phloem to be used up.

2) This **increases** the **water potential** inside the sieve tubes, so water also leaves the tubes by **osmosis**.

3) This **lowers the pressure** inside the sieve tubes.

(3)

1) The result is a **pressure gradient** from the **source** end to the **sink** end.

2) This gradient pushes solutes along the sieve tubes to where they're needed.

① SOURCE
low water potential, high pressure

Water enters from xylem

water flow
solute flow

sieve plate

plasmodesma

Water flows to xylem

companion cell

HIGH
Pressure gradient forces sap down.
LOW

solute (e.g. sucrose)

② SINK
high water potential, low pressure

Translocation

Substances Enter the Phloem at the Source by Active Loading

1) Active loading is used to move substances into the **companion cells** from **surrounding tissues**, and from the companion cells into the **sieve tubes**, **against** a **concentration gradient**.

2) The **concentration** of **sucrose** is usually **higher** in the **companion cells** than the **surrounding tissue cells**, and **higher** in the **sieve tube cells** than the companion cells.

3) So sucrose is moved to where it needs to go using **active transport** and **co-transporter proteins**. Here's how it works:

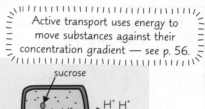
Active transport uses energy to move substances against their concentration gradient — see p. 56.

- In the companion cell, ATP is used to actively transport hydrogen ions (H⁺) out of the cell and into surrounding tissue cells.

- This sets up a concentration gradient — there are more H⁺ ions in the surrounding tissue than in the companion cell.

- An H⁺ ion binds to a co-transport protein in the companion cell membrane and re-enters the cell (down the concentration gradient).

- A sucrose molecule binds to the co-transport protein at the same time. The movement of the H⁺ ion is used to move the sucrose molecule into the cell, against its concentration gradient.

- Sucrose molecules are then transported out of the companion cells and into the sieve tubes by the same process.

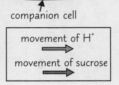
sucrose

companion cell

| movement of H⁺ | |
| movement of sucrose | |

ATP is one of the products of **respiration**. The **breakdown** of **ATP** supplies the initial **energy** needed for the **active transport** of the H⁺ ions.

Warm-Up Questions

Q1 Explain the terms source and sink in connection with translocation.

Q2 Explain how the process of active loading increases the concentration of sucrose in companion cells.

PRACTICE QUESTIONS

Exam Question

Q1 A student has set up an experimental model of mass flow as shown in the diagram.

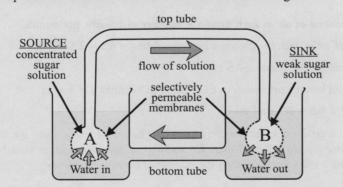

top tube

SOURCE
concentrated sugar solution

flow of solution

SINK
weak sugar solution

selectively permeable membranes

A

B

Water in

bottom tube

Water out

a) Explain how the concentrated sugar solution is forced to flow along the top tube. [3 marks]

b) i) What part of a plant does the top tube represent? [1 mark]

   ii) The bottom tube only transports water. What part of the plant does this tube represent? [1 mark]

Human mass flow — running out of the hall at the end of an exam...

The mass flow hypothesis is just the best theory that scientists have come up with so far. If other evidence came along, a different theory could be developed based on the new findings (see p. 2). However, that doesn't mean that there's no point in learning about it — it could be in your exam. Don't look so sad — what else would you do with your time...

Extra Exam Practice

Time for some questions that link ideas from <u>Module 3</u> together. These questions might seem daunting, but doing them will help you to check what you've learnt from the last few (cough, twenty-six) pages.

- Have a look at this example of how to answer a tricky exam question.
- Then check how much you've understood from Module 3 by having a go at the questions on the next page.

1   Hyperventilation is very fast and deep breathing. **Figure 1** shows the volume of air in the lungs of a person at rest, who begins hyperventilating after 10 seconds.

Figure 1

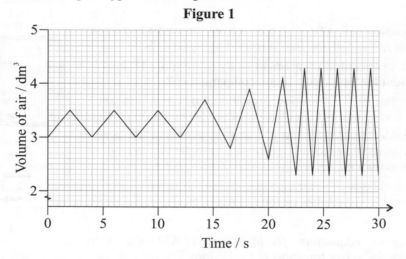

(a)   The pulmonary ventilation rate (PVR) is the volume of air inspired or expired in one minute. Calculate the maximum PVR of the person while they were hyperventilating, in dm^3 min^{-1}. Show your working.

(3 marks)

(b)   Using **Figure 1** and your knowledge of the Bohr effect, suggest how hyperventilation when at rest can result in body cells being unable to obtain sufficient oxygen from red blood cells.

(4 marks)

Start by working out what you need to calculate and think about how you can use the information from the graph to do it.

1(a)

PVR = **volume of air in each breath × number of breaths per minute**

Volume of air in each breath when hyperventilating = 4.3 − 2.3 = 2 dm^3

Time taken for one breath = 1.5 s

Number of breaths per minute = 60 ÷ 1.5 = 40 breaths per minute

PVR = 2 × 40 = **80 dm^3 min^{-1}**

Here you'd get 3 marks for the correct answer. But, don't worry, if you got the answer wrong you'd still get 1 mark for working out the volume of air in each breath and 1 mark for calculating the number of breaths per minute.

It's a good idea to use a ruler to draw lines to the axes when you're reading values from a graph — this helps to make sure the values you read off are accurate.

From your knowledge of the Bohr effect, you should know that an increase in the partial pressure of carbon dioxide reduces the affinity of haemoglobin for oxygen — here you need to think what would happen in the opposite situation.

1(b)

A **greater amount of CO_2 would be exhaled during hyperventilation**, due to the increased breathing rate and volume of air in each breath. Because the person is at rest, the respiration rate of the body cells is not increased, so there is no increase in the amount of CO_2 entering the blood. This causes a reduction in the partial pressure of CO_2, which **increases the affinity of haemoglobin for oxygen**. This reduces the rate of oxygen unloading from red blood cells, meaning the body cells may be unable to obtain sufficient oxygen.

You've been asked to use your knowledge of the Bohr effect, so you need to think about how hyperventilation could affect the partial pressure of carbon dioxide.

Extra Exam Practice

2 Insects are very important organisms in many different ecosystems.

(a) **Figure 2** shows the circulatory system of an insect. The arrows indicate the direction of blood flow. Blood is pumped through each segment of the insect's heart in a wave of contractions. The blood then enters the body cavity and flows around the insect's organs before re-entering the heart through a series of valves.

Figure 2

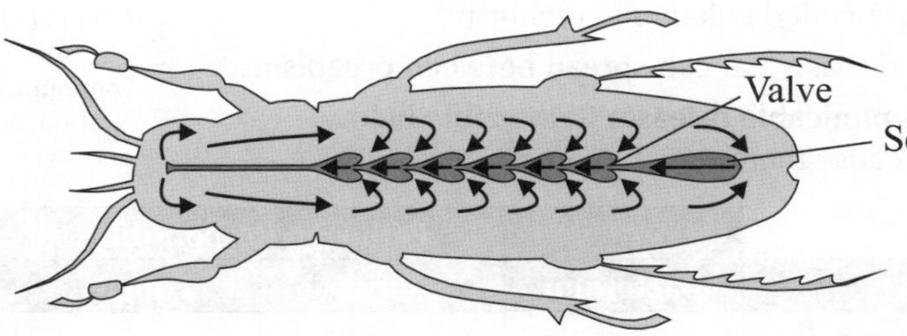

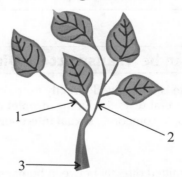

An insect's circulatory system has similarities and differences to that of a mammal.

(i) Using your knowledge of valves in the mammalian heart, suggest why blood from the body cavity does not re-enter segments of the insect heart while they are contracting.

(2 marks)

(ii) Haemoglobin has an important role in the mammalian circulatory system. Suggest why most insects do not require haemoglobin.

(2 marks)

(b) Some insects feed on the phloem sap of plants to obtain nutrients, such as sucrose. They do this using a long, sharp mouthpiece called a stylet, which is used to pierce the stem of the plant and then draw up the phloem sap. A scientist investigated translocation in a plant using insects that feed with a stylet. She selected insects that were feeding at three different sites on a plant, as shown in **Figure 3**. She removed each insect from the plant but left the stylets in place. She then collected the sap excreted through each stylet over 30 minutes.

Figure 3

(i) Assuming the plant is not in a growing season, explain how the water potential inside the sieve tubes will change between sites **2** and **3**.

(2 marks)

(ii) The volume of sap collected at site **2** was greater than at site **1**. Suggest an explanation for this.

(4 marks)

(iii) Sucrose can move into the companion cells of the phloem from cells in the leaves via the symplast pathway.
Suggest the route that sucrose takes when moving between cells via the symplast pathway.

(1 mark)

Pathogens and Communicable Diseases

Coughs and sneezes spread diseases, as they say. Well now it's time to find out why...

Pathogens Can Cause Communicable Diseases

1) **Disease** is a **condition** that **impairs** the **normal functioning** of an **organism**. Both **plants** and **animals** can get diseases.

2) A **pathogen** is an organism that causes **disease**. Types of pathogen include **bacteria**, **viruses**, **fungi** and **protoctista** (a type of single-celled eukaryotic organism).

3) A **communicable disease** is a disease that can **spread between organisms**.

4) You need to **learn all** the **communicable diseases** in the table below, as well as the **pathogens** that cause them:

You might have heard communicable diseases referred to as infectious diseases.

Disease:	Affects:	Pathogen Responsible:			
		Bacterium	Virus	Fungus	Protoctist
Tuberculosis (TB)	Animals, typically humans and cattle	✔			
Bacterial meningitis	Humans	✔			
Ring rot	Potatoes, tomatoes	✔			
HIV/AIDS	Humans		✔		
Influenza	Animals, including humans		✔		
Tobacco mosaic virus	Plants		✔		
Black sigatoka	Banana plants			✔	
Ringworm	Cattle			✔	
Athlete's foot	Humans			✔	
Potato/tomato late blight	Potatoes/tomatoes				✔
Malaria	Animals, including humans				✔

Communicable Diseases Can be Transmitted Directly or Indirectly

1) **Direct transmission** is when a disease is transmitted **directly** from one organism to another. Direct transmission can happen in several ways, including: **droplet infection** (**coughing** or **sneezing** tiny droplets of mucus or saliva directly onto someone), **sexual intercourse**, or **touching** an infected organism.

> Examples:
> - **HIV** can be transmitted directly between humans via sexual intercourse.
> - **Athlete's foot** can be spread via touch.

2) **Indirect transmission** is when a disease is transmitted from one organism to another **via an intermediate**. Intermediates include **air**, **water**, **food** or **another organism** (known as a **vector**).

Spores are the cells that some organisms use to reproduce asexually, including some protoctista and all fungi.

> Examples:
> - **Potato/tomato late blight** is spread when **spores** are carried between plants — first in the **air**, then in **water**.
> - **Malaria** is spread between humans (and other animals) via **mosquitoes** — insects that feed on blood. The mosquitoes act as **vectors** — they don't cause malaria themselves, they just spread the protoctista that cause it.

Pathogens and Communicable Diseases

Living Conditions, Climate and Social Factors Affect Disease Transmission

1) **Overcrowded** living conditions **increase** the **transmission** of many communicable diseases.

> **Example:**
>
> TB is spread directly via droplet infection (see previous page). It's also spread indirectly because the bacteria can remain in the air for long periods of time and infect new people. The risk of TB infection is increased when lots of people live crowded together in a small space.

2) **Climate** can also affect the spread of communicable diseases.

> **Examples:**
>
> - **Potato/tomato late blight** is especially common during **wet summers** because the **spores** need **water** to **spread** (see previous page).
> - **Malaria** is most common in **tropical countries**, which are **humid** and **hot**. This is because these are the **ideal conditions** for **mosquitoes** (the malaria **vectors**) to **breed**.

3) In **humans**, **social factors** can increase the transmission of communicable diseases.

> **Example:**
>
> The risk of HIV infection is high in places where there's limited access to:
> - good healthcare — people are less likely to be diagnosed and treated for HIV, and the most effective anti-HIV drugs are less likely to be available, so the virus is more likely to be passed on to others.
> - good health education — to inform people about how HIV is transmitted and how it can be avoided, e.g. through safe-sex practices like using condoms.

Warm-Up Questions

Q1 What is a communicable disease?

Q2 Name a virus that affects plants.

Q3 What type of pathogen causes malaria?

Q4 Give one way in which a disease can be transferred directly.

Q5 Give one example of how climate can affect the spread of a disease.

Exam Questions

Q1 Which of the following pathogens is responsible for causing black sigatoka?

    A bacterium   B virus   C fungus   D protoctista   [1 mark]

Q2 The most common way for the tobacco mosaic virus to be transferred between garden plants is via gardeners' hands and tools.

    a) Is this an example of direct or indirect disease transmission? Explain your answer.   [1 mark]

    b) Suggest one thing that gardeners could do to try to prevent transmission of the tobacco mosaic virus between plants.   [1 mark]

Q3 There are more deaths from tuberculosis in low-income countries than in high-income countries.

    a) What type of pathogen causes tuberculosis?   [1 mark]

    b) Suggest two reasons why more deaths from tuberculosis occur in low-income countries compared to wealthier countries.   [2 marks]

My computer has a virus — I knew I shouldn't have sneezed on it...

You need to learn all the communicable diseases in the big table, as well as the type of pathogen that causes each one. You also need to learn how diseases can be transmitted, as well as the factors that affect disease transmission. Phew.

Defence Against Pathogens

Well, all that stuff about disease is making me feel a bit on edge. Luckily both animals and plants have a few tricks up their sleeves to defend themselves against pathogen invasion...

Animals Have Several Barriers to Prevent Infection

1) **Pathogens** need to **enter** an **organism** in order to **cause disease**.

2) So most **animals**, including **humans**, have a range of **primary**, **non-specific defences** to help **prevent** this from happening. These include:

> *Non-specific means they work in the same way for all pathogens. There's more on non-specific and specific responses on page 102.*

Skin — this acts as a **physical barrier**, **blocking pathogens** from **entering** the body. It also acts as a **chemical barrier** by producing **chemicals** that are **antimicrobial** and can **lower pH**, **inhibiting** the **growth** of pathogens.

Mucous membranes — these **protect body openings** that are **exposed** to the **environment** (such as the mouth, nostrils, ears, genitals and anus). Some membranes **secrete mucus** — a sticky substance that **traps pathogens** and contains **antimicrobial enzymes**.

Blood clotting — a blood clot is a mesh of **protein (fibrin) fibres**. Blood clots **plug wounds** to **prevent pathogen entry** and **blood loss**. They're formed by a series of **chemical reactions** that take place when **platelets** (fragments of cells in the blood) are exposed to **damaged blood vessels**.

Inflammation — the signs of inflammation include **swelling**, **pain**, **heat** and **redness**. It can be triggered by **tissue damage** — the damaged tissue releases **molecules**, which **increase** the **permeability** of the **blood vessels**, so they start to **leak fluid** into the surrounding area. This causes **swelling** and helps to **isolate any pathogens** that may have entered the damaged tissue. The molecules also cause **vasodilation** (widening of the blood vessels), which **increases blood flow** to the affected area. This makes the area **hot** and brings **white blood cells** to the area to fight off any pathogens that may be present.

Wound repair — the **skin** is able to repair itself in the event of **injury** and **re-form** a barrier against pathogen entry. The surface is repaired by the **outer layer of skin cells dividing** and **migrating** to the edges of the wound. The **tissue below the wound** then **contracts** to bring the edges of the wound closer together. It is repaired using **collagen fibres** — too many collagen fibres and you'll end up with a **scar**.

It was all going so beautifully 'til Josie felt an expulsive reflex coming on.

Expulsive reflexes — e.g. **coughing** and **sneezing**. A **sneeze** happens when the **mucous membranes** in the **nostrils** are **irritated** by things such as **dust** or **dirt**. A **cough** stems from **irritation** in the **respiratory tract**. Both coughing and sneezing are an attempt to **expel foreign objects**, including **pathogens**, from the body. They happen **automatically**.

If pathogens make it past these defences, they'll have the animal's **immune system** to deal with — see pages 102-105.

Defence Against Pathogens

Plants Have Physical Defences Against Pathogens...

Like animals, **plants** have **physical defences** against infection by **pathogens**.

1) Most plant leaves and stems have a **waxy cuticle**, which provides a **physical barrier** against pathogen entry. It may also **stop water** collecting on the leaf, which could reduce the risk of infection by pathogens that are transferred between plants in water.

2) Plant cells themselves are surrounded by **cell walls**. These form a **physical barrier** against pathogens that make it past the waxy cuticle.

3) Plants produce a **polysaccharide** called **callose**. Callose gets **deposited** between **plant cell walls** and **plasma membranes** during times of **stress**, e.g. **pathogen invasion**. Callose deposition may make it **harder** for **pathogens** to **enter cells**. Callose deposition at the **plasmodesmata** (small channels in the cell walls) may **limit the spread** of **viruses** between cells.

...as Well as Chemical Ones

1) Plants don't just rely on physical defences. They also produce antimicrobial chemicals (including antibiotics, see page 108) which kill pathogens or inhibit their growth.

> **Examples:**
> - Some plants produce chemicals called saponins. These are thought to destroy the cell membranes of fungi and other pathogens.
> - Plants also produce chemicals called phytoalexins, which inhibit the growth of fungi and other pathogens.

2) Other chemicals secreted by plants are toxic to insects — this reduces the amount of insect-feeding on plants and therefore reduces the risk of infection by plant viruses carried by insect vectors.

Warm-Up Questions

Q1 Give two ways in which skin helps defend animals against infection by pathogens.
Q2 What is the function of the mucous membranes?
Q3 What are expulsive reflexes?
Q4 Give one example of a plant chemical defence against pathogens.

Exam Question

Q1 The tobacco mosaic virus is a virus that affects plants.

a) The virus usually infects plants that have been damaged by feeding insects.
Suggest why damaged plant cells are more susceptible to infection by the virus than normal cells. [2 marks]

b) Suggest one way a plant may respond to limit the spread of infection once the tobacco mosaic virus enters a plant. [1 mark]

Hiding under the duvet — a student's primary defence against revision...

Plant defences against pathogens are the "absolute bomb", or so says a colleague of mine. He's very excited by them. You don't need to be excited by them (although it's fine if you are), but you do need to learn them. And all those animal primary defences too. You've got your immune system to learn next. What an absolute treat...

The Immune System

If a pathogen enters the body, the immune system will respond. Bad luck pathogens...

Foreign Antigens Trigger an Immune Response

1) **Antigens** are **molecules** (usually proteins or polysaccharides) found on the **surface** of **cells**.

2) When a pathogen (like a bacterium) **invades** the body, the antigens on its cell surface are **identified as foreign**, which **activates cells** in the **immune system**.

3) The immune response involves **specific** and **non-specific** stages. The **non-specific** response happens in the **same way** for **all microorganisms** — whatever foreign antigens they have. The **specific** response is **antigen-specific** — it is aimed at **specific pathogens**. It involves **white blood cells** called **T** and **B lymphocytes**.

There are Four Main Stages in the Immune Response

1) Phagocytes Engulf Pathogens

A **phagocyte** is a type of **white blood cell** that carries out **phagocytosis** (engulfment of pathogens). They're found in the **blood** and in **tissues** and carry out a **non-specific** immune response. Here's how they work:

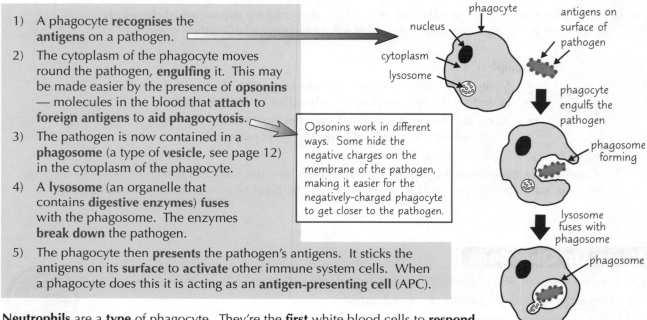

1) A phagocyte **recognises** the **antigens** on a pathogen.

2) The cytoplasm of the phagocyte moves round the pathogen, **engulfing** it. This may be made easier by the presence of **opsonins** — molecules in the blood that **attach** to **foreign antigens** to **aid phagocytosis**.

Opsonins work in different ways. Some hide the negative charges on the membrane of the pathogen, making it easier for the negatively-charged phagocyte to get closer to the pathogen.

3) The pathogen is now contained in a **phagosome** (a type of **vesicle**, see page 12) in the cytoplasm of the phagocyte.

4) A **lysosome** (an organelle that contains **digestive enzymes**) **fuses** with the phagosome. The enzymes **break down** the pathogen.

5) The phagocyte then **presents** the pathogen's antigens. It sticks the antigens on its **surface** to **activate** other immune system cells. When a phagocyte does this it is acting as an **antigen-presenting cell** (APC).

Neutrophils are a **type** of phagocyte. They're the **first** white blood cells to **respond** to a pathogen inside the body. Neutrophils **move towards** a **wound** in response to signals from **cytokines** (proteins that act as messenger molecules — see page 52). The cytokines are released by cells at the site of the wound.

2) Phagocytes Activate T lymphocytes

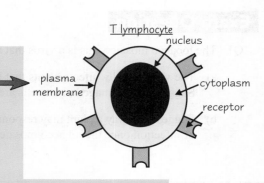

1) A **T lymphocyte** is another type of **white blood cell**.

2) Their surface is covered with **receptors**.

3) The receptors **bind to antigens** presented by APCs.

4) Each T lymphocyte has a **different receptor** on its surface.

5) When the receptor on the surface of a T lymphocyte meets a **complementary antigen**, it binds to it — so each T lymphocyte will bind to a **different antigen**.

6) This **activates** the T lymphocyte — the process is called **clonal selection**.

7) The T lymphocyte then undergoes **clonal expansion** — it **divides** to produce **clones** of itself. **Different types** of T lymphocytes carry out **different functions** — see next page.

The Immune System

Different types of activated T lymphocytes include:

1) **T helper cells** — these **release substances** to **activate B lymphocytes** (see below) and **T killer cells**.

2) **T killer cells** — these **attach** to and **kill cells** that are infected with a **virus**.

3) **T regulatory cells** — these **suppress** the **immune response** from **other white blood cells**. This helps to stop immune system cells from mistakenly attacking the host's body cells.

Some activated T lymphocytes become **memory cells** (see next page).

3) T lymphocytes **Activate B lymphocytes**, Which Divide Into **Plasma Cells**

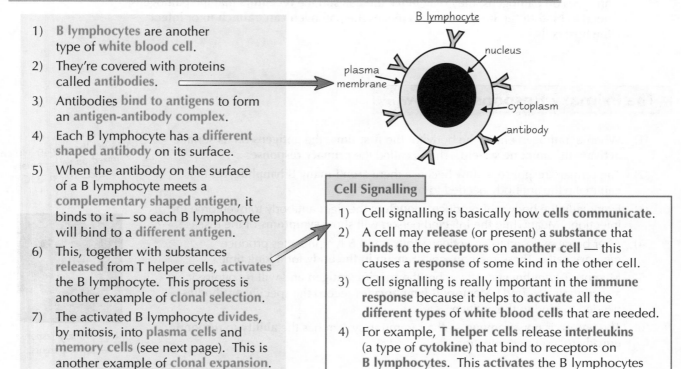

1) **B lymphocytes** are another type of **white blood cell**.

2) They're covered with proteins called **antibodies**.

3) Antibodies **bind to antigens** to form an **antigen-antibody complex**.

4) Each B lymphocyte has a **different shaped antibody** on its surface.

5) When the antibody on the surface of a B lymphocyte meets a **complementary shaped antigen**, it binds to it — so each B lymphocyte will bind to a **different antigen**.

6) This, together with substances **released** from T helper cells, **activates** the B lymphocyte. This process is another example of **clonal selection**.

7) The activated B lymphocyte **divides**, by mitosis, into **plasma cells** and **memory cells** (see next page). This is another example of **clonal expansion**.

B lymphocyte

nucleus
plasma membrane
cytoplasm
antibody

Cell Signalling

1) Cell signalling is basically how **cells communicate**.

2) A cell may **release** (or present) a **substance** that **binds to the receptors** on **another cell** — this causes a **response** of some kind in the other cell.

3) Cell signalling is really important in the **immune response** because it helps to **activate** all the **different types** of **white blood cells** that are needed.

4) For example, **T helper cells** release **interleukins** (a type of **cytokine**) that bind to receptors on **B lymphocytes**. This **activates** the B lymphocytes — the T helper cells are signalling to the B lymphocytes that there's a pathogen in the body.

See p. 52 for more on cell signalling.

4) **Plasma Cells** Make More **Antibodies** to a Specific **Antigen**

1) Plasma cells are **clones** of the B lymphocyte (they're **identical** to the B lymphocyte).

2) They secrete **loads** of the **antibody**, specific to the antigen, into the blood.

3) These antibodies will bind to the antigens on the surface of the pathogen to form **lots** of **antigen-antibody complexes**.

4) You need to **learn** the **structure** of antibodies:

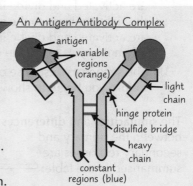

An Antigen-Antibody Complex

antigen
variable regions (orange)
light chain
hinge protein
disulfide bridge
heavy chain
constant regions (blue)

- Antibodies are **glycoproteins** made of **four polypeptide chains** — two **heavy** chains and two **light** chains. Each chain has a **variable region** and a **constant region**.

- The **variable regions** of the antibody form the **antigen binding sites**. The **shape** of the variable region is **complementary** to a particular antigen. The variable regions **differ** between antibodies.

- The **hinge region** allows **flexibility** when the antibody binds to the antigen.

- The **constant regions** allow binding to **receptors** on **immune system cells**, e.g. phagocytes. The constant region is the **same** (i.e. it has the same sequence of amino acids) **in all** antibodies.

- **Disulfide bridges** (a type of bond) hold the polypeptide chains of the protein together.

The Immune System

Antibodies **help** to **clear** an **infection** by:

1) <u>Agglutinating pathogens</u> — each antibody has two binding sites, so an antibody can **bind** to two pathogens at the same time — the pathogens become clumped together. Phagocytes then bind to the antibodies and phagocytose a lot of pathogens all at once. Antibodies that behave in this way are known as agglutinins.

2) <u>Neutralising toxins</u> — like antigens, toxins have different shapes. Antibodies called anti-toxins can bind to the toxins produced by pathogens. This prevents the toxins from affecting human cells, so the toxins are neutralised (inactivated). The toxin-antibody complexes are also phagocytosed.

3) <u>Preventing the pathogen binding to human cells</u> — when antibodies bind to the antigens on pathogens, they may block the cell surface receptors that the pathogens need to bind to the host cells. This means the pathogen can't attach to or infect the host cells.

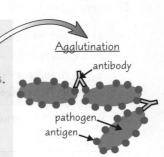

<u>Agglutination</u>

antibody

pathogen

antigen

The **Primary Response** is **Slow**...

1) When a pathogen enters the body for the first time, the antigens on its surface activate the immune system. This is called the primary response.

2) The primary response is slow because there aren't many B lymphocytes that can make the antibody needed to bind to it.

3) Eventually the body will produce enough of the right antibody to overcome the infection. Meanwhile the infected person will show symptoms of the disease.

4) After being exposed to an antigen, both T and B lymphocytes produce memory cells. These memory cells remain in the body for a long time.

5) Memory T lymphocytes remember the specific antigen and will recognise it a second time round. Memory B lymphocytes record the specific antibodies needed to bind to the antigen.

6) The person is now immune — their immune system has the ability to respond quickly to a second infection.

Don't get the primary response mixed up with primary defences (see p. 100).

Neil's primary response — to his parents.

...the **Secondary Response** is **Faster**

1) If the same pathogen enters the body again, the immune system will produce a quicker, stronger immune response — the secondary response.

2) Clonal selection happens faster. Memory B lymphocytes are activated and divide into plasma cells that produce the right antibody to the antigen. Memory T lymphocytes are activated and divide into the correct type of T lymphocytes to kill the cell carrying the antigen.

3) The secondary response often gets rid of the pathogen before you begin to show any symptoms.

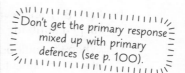

1st exposure to antigen

primary response

secondary response

2nd exposure to antigen

Concentration of the right antibody in the blood.

10   20   30   long interval

Time / days

The **similarities** and **differences** between the primary and secondary responses are summarised in the table:

	Primary response	Secondary response
Pathogen	Enters for 1st time	Enters for 2nd time
Speed of response	Slow	Fast
Cells activated	B and T lymphocytes	Memory cells
Symptoms	Yes	No

Module 4: Section 1 — Disease and the Immune System

The Immune System

You Need to be Able to **Examine** and **Draw Blood Smears**

1) As the name suggests, a **blood smear** is a sample of blood smeared over a **microscope slide**.

2) **Stains** are added to the sample to make the **different cells** easy to see (see page 18 for more on staining microscope images).

3) When looking at a blood smear you're likely to see **red blood cells**, **white blood cells** and **platelets** (tiny fragments of cells involved in blood clotting). Some types of white blood cells have **granules** in their cytoplasm (so they look **grainy**) and other types don't.

4) Here's an **example** of what a blood smear looks like:

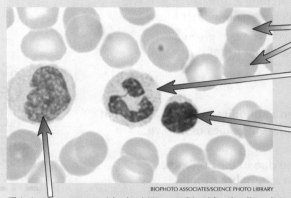

Most of the cells are <u>red blood cells</u> (see page 65). They're easy to spot because they <u>don't have a nucleus</u>.

This is a <u>neutrophil</u>. Its <u>nucleus</u> looks like three <u>interconnected blobs</u> — the posh way of saying this is that the nucleus is '<u>multi-lobed</u>'. The <u>cytoplasm</u> of a neutrophil is <u>grainy</u>.

This is a <u>lymphocyte</u>. It's much <u>smaller</u> than the neutrophil. The <u>nucleus takes up most of the cell</u> and there's <u>very little cytoplasm</u> to be seen (it's not grainy either). You can't tell whether this is a T lymphocyte or a B lymphocyte under a light microscope.

BIOPHOTO ASSOCIATES/SCIENCE PHOTO LIBRARY

This is a <u>monocyte</u>. It's the <u>biggest white blood cell</u> and a type of <u>phagocyte</u>. It has a <u>kidney-bean shaped nucleus</u> and a <u>non-grainy cytoplasm</u>.

Warm-Up Questions

Q1 What are antigens?

Q2 What structures are found on the surface of T lymphocytes?

Q3 Draw and label the structure of a B lymphocyte.

Q4 Draw and label the structure of an antibody.

Q5 Give two differences between the primary and secondary response.

Exam Questions

Q1 Three types of white blood cell are shown in the table.

Select the row in the table that correctly describes the function of each type of cell.

[1 mark]

		Neutrophil	T helper cell	B lymphocyte
	A	Releases interleukins to activate other cells	Divides to form plasma cells	Engulfs pathogens
	B	Engulfs pathogens	Divides to form plasma cells	Releases interleukins to activate other cells
	C	Releases interleukins to activate other cells	Engulfs pathogens	Divides to form plasma cells
	D	Engulfs pathogens	Releases interleukins to activate other cells	Divides to form plasma cells

Q2 IgG is a type of antibody, as well as an agglutinin and opsonin. Suggest how IgG works. [2 marks]

Q3 A scientist is looking at a blood smear under the microscope.
Explain how she will be able to tell the difference between a neutrophil and a B lymphocyte. [3 marks]

Q4 A person had chickenpox as a child. She was exposed to the virus that causes it again as a teenager, but did not experience any symptoms. Explain why. [5 marks]

The student-revision complex — only present the night before an exam...

Memory cells are still B and T lymphocytes, but they're the ones that stick around for a long time. So if a pathogen is stupid enough to invade the body again, these cells can immediately divide into more of themselves, and release antibodies specifically against the pathogen or bind to the pathogen and destroy it. Ha ha (evil laugh).

Immunity and Vaccinations

Immunity is the ability to respond quickly to an infection — because your immune system recognises the foreign antigens. There are different types of immunity though and different ways of developing it. And sometimes your immune system gets a bit mixed up, leading to autoimmunity...

Immunity can be Active or Passive

ACTIVE IMMUNITY

This is the type of immunity you get when **your immune system makes its own antibodies** after being **stimulated** by an **antigen**. There are **two** different types of active immunity:

1) **Natural** — this is when you become immune after **catching a disease**. E.g. if you have measles as a child, you shouldn't be able to catch it again in later life.

2) **Artificial** — this is when you become immune after you've been given a **vaccination** containing a harmless dose of antigen (see next page).

PASSIVE IMMUNITY

This is the type of immunity you get from being given antibodies made by a different organism — your immune system doesn't produce any antibodies of its own. Again, there are two types:

1) Natural — this is when a baby becomes immune due to the antibodies it receives from its mother, through the placenta and in breast milk.

2) Artificial — this is when you become immune after being injected with antibodies from someone else. E.g. If you contract tetanus you can be injected with antibodies against the tetanus toxin, collected from blood donations.

Claire was grateful for her mum's antibodies. She was less grateful for the dress.

Learn the Similarities and Differences Between Active and Passive Immunity

This handy summary table should help:

Active immunity	Passive immunity
Requires exposure to antigen	No exposure to antigen
It takes a while for protection to develop	Protection is immediate
Protection is long-term	Protection is short-term
Memory cells are produced	Memory cells aren't produced

Autoimmune Diseases Involve an Abnormal Immune Response

1) Sometimes, an organism's immune system **isn't able** to **recognise self-antigens** — the antigens present on the organism's **own cells**.

2) When this happens, the immune system treats the self-antigens as **foreign antigens** and launches an **immune response** against the organism's **own tissues**.

3) A disease resulting from this abnormal immune response is known as an **autoimmune disease**.

Examples of autoimmune diseases:

- **Lupus** — caused by the immune system attacking cells in the **connective tissues**. This **damages** the tissues and causes painful **inflammation** (see page 100). Lupus can affect the **skin** and **joints**, as well as **organs** such as the **heart** and **lungs**.

- **Rheumatoid arthritis** — caused by the immune system attacking cells in the **joints**. Again this causes **pain** and **inflammation**.

4) Autoimmune diseases are usually **chronic** (long-term). They can often be **treated**, but **not cured**.

Immunity and Vaccinations

Vaccines Help to Control Disease and Prevent Epidemics

1) While your B lymphocytes are busy **dividing** to build up their numbers to deal with a pathogen (i.e. the **primary response** — see p. 104), you **suffer** from the disease. **Vaccination** can help avoid this.

2) Vaccines contain substances that cause your body to **produce memory cells** against a particular pathogen, **without** the pathogen **causing disease**. This means you become **immune** without getting any **symptoms**.

3) **Epidemics** (mass outbreaks of disease) can be **prevented** if a large percentage of the population is **vaccinated**. That way, even people who haven't been vaccinated are **unlikely** to get the disease, because there's no one to catch it from. This is called **herd immunity**

4) The substances in a vaccine may be **antigens**, which could be free or attached to a **dead** or **attenuated** (weakened) **pathogen**. The substances can also be other molecules, such as **mRNA** (see p.38), designed to **code for antigens** found on a pathogen. When the mRNA enters the body cells, it provides the instructions needed for cells to produce these antigens, which triggers **memory cells** to be made.

5) Sometimes **booster** vaccines are given later on (e.g. after several years) to **make sure** memory cells are produced.

6) **Vaccination** is **not the same** as **immunisation**. Vaccination is the **administration** of a substance designed to **stimulate** the **immune system**. **Immunisation** is the **process** by which you **develop immunity**. Vaccination **causes** immunisation.

Vaccines may be injected, or taken orally or in an aerosol.

> **Routine vaccines** are offered to everybody. They include:
>
> - the MMR — protects against **measles**, **mumps** and **rubella**. The MMR is usually given to **children** as an **injection** at around a year old, and again before they start school. It contains **attenuated measles**, **mumps** and **rubella viruses**.
>
> - the Meningitis C vaccine — protects against the **bacteria** that cause **Meningitis C**. It is first given as an **injection** to babies at **3 months**. **Boosters** are then given to **1-year-olds** and **teenagers**.

Vaccines and Vaccination Programmes Change — EXAMPLE: the Influenza Vaccine

1) The influenza (flu) vaccine changes every year. That's because the antigens on the surface of the influenza virus change regularly, forming new strains of the virus.

2) Memory cells produced from vaccination with one strain of the flu will not recognise other strains with different antigens. The strains are immunologically distinct.

3) Every year there are different strains of the influenza virus circulating in the population, so a different vaccine has to be made.

4) Laboratories collect samples of these different strains, and organisations, such as the WHO (World Health Organisation) and CDC (Centre for Disease Control), test the effectiveness of different influenza vaccines against them.

5) New vaccines are developed and one is chosen every year that is the most effective against the recently circulating influenza viruses.

6) Governments and health authorities then implement a programme of vaccination using the most suitable vaccine. Sometimes people are given a vaccine that protects them from a strain causing an epidemic in another country — this helps to stop the strain spreading globally.

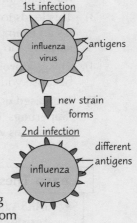

1st infection

influenza virus — antigens

new strain forms

2nd infection

influenza virus — different antigens

Warm-Up Questions

Q1 What is the difference between active and passive immunity?

Q2 What are autoimmune diseases? Give an example.

Q3 Explain how vaccines help prevent epidemics.

PRACTICE QUESTIONS

Exam Question

Q1 Influenza is caused by a virus that constantly changes its antigens.
Explain why a new influenza vaccine is made every year.

[2 marks]

An injection of dead bugs — roll on my next vaccine...

The influenza virus is so clever that it would almost make you think it had a mind of its own. I mean, as soon as we catch up with it and develop a vaccine, off it goes and changes its surface antigens again. Influenza virus 1: humans 0.

Antibiotics and Other Medicines

Our immune systems aren't always enough to fight off an infection by pathogens.
Sometimes we need a bit of extra help from medicines like antibiotics.

Antibiotics are Extremely Useful

1) **Antibiotics** are **chemicals** that **kill** or **inhibit** the **growth** of **bacteria**.

2) They're **used** by humans as **drugs** to **treat bacterial infections**. They're useful because they can usually **target** bacterial cells **without damaging** human body cells.

3) **Penicillin** was the **first antibiotic** to be **isolated** (by Alexander Fleming, in 1928).

4) Antibiotic use became **widespread** from the **mid-twentieth century** — partly thanks to the successful treatment of soldiers with penicillin in the Second World War.

5) For the **past few decades**, we've been able to deal with bacterial infections **pretty easily** using **antibiotics**. As a result of this, the **death rate** from **infectious bacterial disease** has **fallen dramatically**.

6) Despite their usefulness, there are **risks** to using antibiotics. For example, they can cause **side effects** and even **severe allergic reactions** in some people. Perhaps the **biggest risk** though, is from **antibiotic resistance**...

Antibiotics are used to treat bacterial infections in animals too.

Antibiotic Resistance is a Big Problem

1) There is **genetic variation** in a population of bacteria. Genetic **mutations** make some bacteria **naturally resistant** to an **antibiotic**.

2) For the bacterium, this ability to **resist an antibiotic** is a big **advantage**. It's better able to **survive**, even in a host who's being treated with antibiotics to get rid of the infection, and so it lives for longer and **reproduces** many more times.

3) This leads to the **allele** for **antibiotic resistance** being **passed on** to lots of **offspring**. It's an example of **natural selection** — see page 127. This is how antibiotic resistance **spreads** and becomes **more common** in a population of bacteria over time.

An allele is a version of a gene — see page 123.

4) This is a **problem** for people who become **infected** with these bacteria, because you **can't easily get rid of them** with antibiotics.

5) **Increased use** of antibiotics means that **antibiotic resistance** is **increasing**. 'Superbugs' that are resistant to **most known antibiotics** are becoming **more common**. This means we are **less able to treat** some **potentially life-threatening** bacterial **infections**.

Learn These Examples of Antibiotic-Resistant Bacteria:

- **MRSA** (meticillin-resistant *Staphylococcus aureus*) causes **serious wound infections** and is **resistant** to **several antibiotics**, including **meticillin** (which used to be called methicillin).

- *Clostridium difficile* infects the **digestive system**, usually causing problems in people who have **already been treated** with **antibiotics**. It is thought that the **harmless bacteria** that are **normally present** in the digestive system are **killed** by the antibiotics, which *C. difficile* is **resistant** to. This allows *C. difficile* to **flourish**. *C. difficile* produces a **toxin**, which causes severe **diarrhoea**, **fever** and **cramps**.

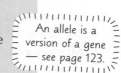

MRSA and Clostridium difficile *infections are most common in hospitals, where many antibiotics are used and patients who are already ill have weakened immune systems.*

Developing new antibiotics and **modifying** existing ones are two ways of **overcoming** the current problem of antibiotic resistance. This isn't easy though.

To reduce the likelihood of antibiotic resistance developing in the first place, **doctors** are being encouraged to **reduce** their **use of antibiotics**, e.g. **not** to prescribe them for **minor infections** and **not** to prescribe them to **prevent infections** (except in patients with already weak immune systems, e.g. the elderly or people with HIV). **Patients** are advised to take **all** of the antibiotics they're **prescribed** to make sure the infection is fully cleared and all the bacteria have been killed (which reduces the likelihood of a population of antibiotic-resistant bacteria developing).

Antibiotics and Other Medicines

Possible **Sources** of **Medicines** Need to be **Protected**

1) Many **medicinal drugs** are manufactured **using natural compounds** found in **plants, animals** or **microorganisms**. E.g. **penicillin** is obtained from a **fungus**, some **cancer drugs** are made using **soil bacteria**, and **daffodils** are now grown to produce a drug used to treat **Alzheimer's disease**.

2) Only a **small proportion** of organisms have been **investigated** so far, so it's possible that plants or microorganisms **exist** that contain compounds that could be used to treat **currently incurable** diseases, such as AIDS. Others may produce **new antibiotics**.

3) Possible **sources of drugs** need to be **protected** by **maintaining** the **biodiversity** (the variety of different species) on Earth. If we **don't** protect them, some species could **die** out before we get a **chance** to study them.

4) Even organisms that have **already** been studied could still prove to be **useful** sources of medicines as **new techniques** are developed for identifying, purifying and testing compounds.

The **Future** of **Medicine** Looks Pretty **High-Tech**

Personalised Medicines

1) Your **genes** determine how your body **responds** to certain **drugs**. **Different people** respond to the **same drug** in **different ways** — which makes certain drugs **more effective** for **some people** than others. This is where **personalised medicines** come in.

2) Personalised medicines are medicines that are **tailored** to an **individual's DNA**. The theory is that if doctors have your **genetic information**, they can use it to **predict** how you will respond to different drugs and only prescribe the ones that will be **most effective** for you.

3) Scientists hope that by studying the **relationship** between someone's genetic make-up and their responsiveness to drugs, **more effective drugs** can be produced in the future.

Synthetic biology

1) Synthetic biology involves using technology to design and make things like artificial proteins, cells and even microorganisms.

2) It has applications in lots of different areas, including medicine. For example, scientists are looking at engineering bacteria to destroy cancer cells, while leaving healthy body cells intact.

Not an example of synthetic biology.

Warm-Up Questions

Q1 What are antibiotics?

Q2 Name two strains of antibiotic-resistant bacteria.

Q3 Why is protecting biodiversity important for the development of new medicines?

Exam Question

Q1 MRSA bacteria are resistant to several antibiotics, including meticillin.
Suggest how *Staphylococcus aureus* bacteria developed resistance to the antibiotic meticillin. [4 marks]

The Market Research Society of Australia — not a deadly bacterium...

In 2014, the World Health Organisation (WHO) released a report on the worldwide threat posed by antibiotic resistance — and it's not good news. Unless we take action now, relatively minor bacterial infections (that we've been able to treat successfully with antibiotics for decades) will once again become life-threatening illnesses. So we need to work on stopping the spread of antibiotic resistance and developing new antibiotics as soon as possible.

Studying Biodiversity

Bet you've noticed how there are loads of different living things in the world — well that's biodiversity in a nutshell.

Biodiversity is the Variety of Organisms

Before you can sink your teeth into the real meat of biodiversity, there are a few definitions you need to know:

1) **Biodiversity** — the **variety** of **living organisms** in an **area**.
2) **Species** — a group of **similar organisms** able to **reproduce** to give **fertile offspring**.
3) **Habitat** — the **area inhabited** by a species. It includes the **physical** factors, like the soil and temperature range, and the **living** (biotic) factors, like availability of food or the presence of predators.

Pete wasn't sure that the company's new increased biodiversity policy would be good for productivity.

Areas with a **high** biodiversity are those with lots of **different species**.

Biodiversity Can be Considered at Different Levels

1) **Habitat diversity** — the number of **different habitats** in an **area**. For example, a particular area could contain many different habitats — sand dunes, woodland, meadows, streams, etc.
2) **Species diversity** — the number of **different species** (species richness) and the **abundance** of each species (species evenness) in an **area**. For example, a woodland could contain many different species of plants, insects, birds and mammals.

Alleles are different versions of genes.

3) **Genetic diversity** — the variation of **alleles** within a species (or a population of a species). For example, the variation of alleles within the dog species gives rise to different breeds, such as a Labrador or poodle.

Sampling Can be Used to Measure Biodiversity

In most cases it'd be **too time-consuming** to count every individual organism in a habitat. Instead, a **sample** of the population is taken. **Estimates** about the whole habitat are based on the sample. Here's what sampling involves:

1) **Choose** an **area** to **sample** — a small area within the habitat being studied.
2) **Count** the number of individuals of **each species** (see below).
3) **Repeat** the process — take as many samples as possible. This gives a better indication of the **whole habitat**.
4) Use the results to **estimate** the total number of individuals or the total number of different species in the habitat being studied.
5) When sampling **different habitats** and comparing them, always use the **same sampling technique**.

You could **investigate** the **impact** of **mowing** on the **biodiversity** of your school playing field by sampling a mowed and an un-mowed field. Calculate the biodiversity for each field using Simpson's Index (see next page).

Different Organisms Require Different Sampling Techniques

How you find out **how many individuals** are in your **sample area** depends on the **organism** you are studying. E.g.

1) For **crawling ground insects** you could use a **pitfall trap** (a small pit that insects can't get out of) or a **pooter** (a device that allows you to safely suck small insects through a tube into a jar).
2) For **small organisms** that live in **soil** or **leaf litter** you could use a **Tullgren funnel** — this is where a soil or leaf litter sample is put on a mesh filter at the top of a funnel and a light is shone down onto it. Organisms move away from the heat created by the light and fall out of the funnel and into a collecting beaker.
3) For some **aquatic organisms** you could use **kick sampling** (you gently kick the bottom of a stream then use a net to collect the organisms that have been disturbed).
4) For organisms living in **long grass** you could use a **sweep net** (a net lined with strong cloth on a pole).

Sampling Can be Random or Non-Random

1) To avoid **bias** in your results, the **sample** should be **random**. For example, if you were looking at plant species in a field, you could pick random sample sites by dividing the field into a **grid** using **measuring tapes** and using a **random number generator** to select **coordinates**.
2) However, sometimes it's **necessary** to take a **non-random sample**. E.g. when there's a lot of variety in the distribution of species in the habitat and you want to make sure all the different areas are sampled.

Studying Biodiversity

There are **three** types of **non-random** sample:

1) **Systematic** — This is when samples are taken at **fixed intervals**, often along a **line**. E.g. if you were counting plant species in a field, **quadrats** (frames which you place on the ground) could be placed along a line (called a **transect**) from an area of shade in the corner to the middle of the field. **Each quadrat** would be a **sample site**.

2) **Opportunistic** — This is when samples are **chosen** by the **investigator**. It's used because it is **simple** to carry out, but the data will be **biased**.

3) **Stratified** — This is when **different areas** in a habitat are **identified** and **sampled** separately in **proportion** to their part of the **habitat** as a **whole**. E.g. a heathland may have patches of gorse in it — the heath and gorse areas would be sampled separately according to how much of each there was in the habitat.

Species Richness and Species Evenness Affect Biodiversity

The **greater** the **species richness** and **species evenness** in an area, the **higher** the biodiversity.

1) **Species richness** is the number of **different species** in an area. The **higher** the number of species, the **greater** the species richness. It's measured by taking random samples of a habitat (see previous page) and counting the number of different species.

2) **Species evenness** is a measure of the **relative abundance** of **each species** in an area. The **more similar** the **population size** of each species, the **greater** the species evenness. It's measured by taking random samples of a habitat, and counting the **number of individuals** of each different species.

Diversity is Measured using Simpson's Index of Diversity

1) Species present in a habitat in very **small** numbers shouldn't be treated the same as those with **bigger** populations.

2) **Simpson's Index of Diversity** takes into account both **species richness** and **species evenness**.

3) Simpson's Index of Diversity (**D**) can be calculated using this formula.

4) Simpson's Index of Diversity is always a value **between 0 and 1**. The **closer to 1** the index is, the **more diverse** the habitat. The greater the species richness and evenness, the higher the number.

$$D = 1 - \left(\sum \left(\frac{n}{N} \right)^2 \right)$$

n = **Total number** of individuals of **one** species
N = **Total number** of organisms of **all** species
∑ = **'Sum of'** (i.e. added together)

Here's a simple example of the index of diversity in a field:

There are 3 different species of flower in this field — a red species, a white and a blue.
There are 11 organisms altogether, so N = 11.
There are 3 of the red species, 5 of the white and 3 of the blue.
So the index of diversity for this field is:

$$D = 1 - \left(\left(\frac{3}{11} \right)^2 + \left(\frac{5}{11} \right)^2 + \left(\frac{3}{11} \right)^2 \right) = 1 - 0.36 = 0.64$$

You need to work out the (n/N)² bit for each different species then add them all together.

The field has an index of diversity of 0.64, which is fairly high.

Warm-Up Questions

Q1 What is meant by habitat diversity, species diversity and genetic diversity?

Q2 What is stratified sampling?

	Field A	Field B
Species A	80	20
Species B	110	50
Species C	210	330
Total	**400**	**400**

Exam Question

Q1 A group of students is investigating the diversity of millipedes (small ground insects) in a habitat. They sampled two fields (A and B) and counted the number of millipedes of different species, as shown in the table above.

Calculate Simpson's Index of Diversity for each field. Give your answers to two decimal places. [2 marks]

Species richness — goldfish and money spiders top the list...

Make sure you know the definitions of species richness and species evenness and can describe how you'd measure them. As for Simpson's Index of Diversity — be prepared to use it and to say what the numbers it churns out actually mean.

More on Biodiversity

Advances in genetics mean we can now assess genetic diversity. This helps us to understand the human impacts on global biodiversity (the total number of species on Earth). You'll need to learn all about this for your exam...

Genetic Diversity Can be Assessed

1) You know from page 110 that genetic diversity is the variation of alleles within a species (or within a population of a species).

2) You can do calculations to work out the genetic diversity of a population.

3) This is important because if a population has low genetic diversity, they might not be able to adapt to a change in the environment and the whole population could be wiped out by a single event (e.g. a disease).

4) Populations in which genetic diversity may be low include isolated populations such as those bred in captivity (e.g. in zoos, and pedigree animals and rare breeds).

5) Calculations can be used to monitor the genetic diversity of these populations over time and efforts can be made to increase the genetic diversity of the population if needed. E.g. breeding programmes in zoos are very closely managed to maximise genetic diversity.

A pedigree animal is one that has been bred purely from animals of the same breed. A rare breed is usually a breed of farm animal that's not used in large-scale farming.

Genetic Polymorphism is Used to Measure Genetic Diversity

1) You know that alleles are different versions of a gene.

2) Alleles of the same gene are found at the same point (called a locus) on a chromosome.

3) Polymorphism describes a locus that has two or more alleles.

4) Working out the proportion of polymorphic gene loci in an organism (i.e. those points on a chromosome which can have more than one allele) gives you a measure of genetic diversity.

different alleles at the same locus

B   b

Loci is the plural of locus.

5) There's a nifty formula you can use:

$$\text{proportion of polymorphic gene loci} = \frac{\text{number of polymorphic gene loci}}{\text{total number of loci}}$$

If you multiply the proportion of polymorphic gene loci in a sample by 100, you'll get the percentage of genes in the sample that have alleles.

Example:
If 40 of the genes sampled in a population are polymorphic out of 100 genes sampled in total, then the proportion of polymorphic gene loci $= \frac{40}{100} = 0.4$.

Factors Affecting Global Biodiversity Include...

1) Human Population Growth

The human population of the planet has grown hugely in the last couple of centuries and is continuing to rise. This is decreasing global biodiversity because of the following factors:

1) Habitat loss — human development is destroying habitats, e.g. there is deforestation in the Amazon to make way for grazing and agriculture. This decreases habitat diversity.

2) Over-exploitation — a greater demand for resources (such as food, water and energy) means a lot of resources are being used up faster than they can be replenished. E.g. industrial fishing can deplete the populations of certain fish species and may even cause extinction (a species to die out). This decreases genetic diversity within populations, as well as decreasing species diversity (as a result of extinction).

3) Urbanisation — sprawling cities and major road developments can isolate species, meaning populations are unable to interbreed and genetic diversity is decreased.

4) Pollution — high amounts of pollutants can kill species or destroy habitats, e.g. high levels of fertiliser flowing into a river can lead to a decrease in fish species in that river. This decreases biodiversity.

More on Biodiversity

2) Increased Use of Monoculture in Agriculture

In order to **feed** an ever growing number of **people**, **large areas** of land are devoted to **monoculture** — the growing of a **single variety** of a **single crop**. E.g. in Africa, large areas of land are used for palm oil plantations. This leads to a **decline** in **global biodiversity** because of the following factors:

1) **Habitats** are **lost** as **land** is **cleared** to make way for the large fields, **reducing habitat diversity**.

2) **Local** and naturally occurring **plants** and **animals** are seen as **weeds** and **pests**, and so are destroyed with **pesticides** and **herbicides**, **reducing species diversity**.

3) **Heritage** (traditional) **varieties** of crops are **lost** because they **don't make enough money** and so are not **planted** any more, which **reduces species diversity**.

3) Climate Change

1) **Climate change** is the **variation** in the Earth's climate, e.g. things like changes in **temperature** and **rainfall patterns**.

2) It occurs **naturally**, but the **scientific consensus** is that the climate change we're **experiencing at the moment** is **caused** by **humans** increasing emissions of **greenhouse gases** (such as **carbon dioxide**).

3) Greenhouse gases cause **global warming** (**increasing global average temperature**), which causes **other types** of climate change, e.g. changing rainfall patterns.

4) Climate change will affect **different areas** of the world in **different ways** — some places will get **warmer**, some **colder**, some **wetter** and others **drier**. All of these are likely to **affect global biodiversity**:

- Most species need a particular **climate** to survive.
- A change in climate may mean that an area that was previously **inhabitable** becomes **uninhabitable** (and **vice versa**).
- This may cause an **increase** or **decrease** in the **range** of some species (the area in which they live). This could increase or decrease biodiversity.
- Some species may be forced to **migrate** to a more suitable area, causing a change in **species distribution**. Migrations usually **decrease** biodiversity in the areas the species migrate from, and **increase** biodiversity in the areas they migrate to.
- If there isn't a suitable habitat to migrate to, the species is a plant and **can't migrate**, or if the change is **too fast**, the species may become **extinct**. This will **decrease** biodiversity.

Range change example

The southern **range** limit of the **Sooty Copper Butterfly** has **moved** 60 miles north in recent decades.

Extinction example

Corals die if water temperature **changes** by just one or two degrees. In 1998 a coral reef near Panama was badly damaged because the water **temperature** had **increased** — at least one species of coral became **extinct** as a result.

Warm-Up Questions

Q1 What is the formula used to work out the proportion of polymorphic gene loci?

Q2 Give two ways in which climate change affects global biodiversity.

PRACTICE QUESTIONS

Exam Questions

Q1 In a population of Species A, a sample of 80 gene loci were tested for polymorphism. 36 of the genes were found to be polymorphic.
What is the proportion of polymorphic gene loci in this sample? [1 mark]

Q2* Describe how human population growth and monoculture during the last 30 years could have decreased global biodiversity. [6 marks]

* You will be assessed on the quality of your written response in this question.

Extinction — coming soon to a habitat near you...

All of this makes the future look a bit bleak — deforestation, loads of different species dying out and climate change. Now you know why biodiversity's at risk, it's time to take a look at why it's so important and worth saving...

Importance of Biodiversity

You're probably wondering what all this fuss about biodiversity is for. Well, it turns out that everything is connected, so if you eliminate even just one species you might just end up with all sorts of problems you'd never even thought of.

Maintaining Biodiversity is Important for Ecological Reasons...

The ecological reasons for maintaining biodiversity are all down to the **complex relationships** between **organisms** and their **environments**.

1) To Protect Species, Including **Keystone Species**

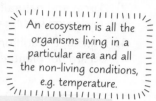

An ecosystem is all the organisms living in a particular area and all the non-living conditions, e.g. temperature.

Organisms in an ecosystem are **interdependent** — they depend on each other to survive. This means that the loss of **just one species** can have pretty **drastic effects** on an ecosystem, such as:

1) **Disruption** of **food chains**, e.g. some species of bear feed on salmon, which feed on herring. If the number of herring decline it can affect **both** the salmon and the bear populations.

2) **Disruption** of **nutrient cycles**, e.g. decomposers like worms improve the **quality of soil** by recycling nutrients. If worm numbers decline, soil quality will be affected. This will affect the **growth** of plants and the **amount of food** available to animals.

There are some species on which many of the other species in an ecosystem **depend** and without which the ecosystem would **change dramatically** — these are called **keystone species**. Keystone species are often **predators** — keeping the population of prey in check, but can also be **modifiers** — maintaining the environment needed for the ecosystem (e.g. beavers building dams), or **hosts** — plants that provide a particular environment, such as palm trees.

Example: The **wolf** is a **keystone species** in America. **Wolf populations** were **eliminated** in most American states during the 20th century. Without the wolves to hunt them, **elk populations increased**, leading to **overgrazing**. This led to the **loss of plant species**, as well as the loss of species that depend on those plants such as **beavers** and **songbirds**. The situation has since been reversed in some national parks.

2) To Maintain **Genetic Resources**

Genetic resources refer to any **material** from **plants**, **animals** or **microorganisms**, containing **genes**, that we find **valuable**. Genetic resources could be crops, plants used for medicines, micro-organisms used in industrial processes, or animal breeds. We need to **maintain** genetic resources for the following reasons:

1) Genetic resources provide us with a **variety** of **everyday products**, such as:

- **Food** and **drink** — plants and animals are the source of almost all **food** and some **drinks**.
- **Clothing** — a lot of **fibres** and **fabrics** are made from plants and animals (e.g. cotton from plants and leather from animals).
- **Drugs** — many are made from plant compounds (e.g. the painkiller **morphine** is made from **poppies**).
- **Fuels** — we use a number of organisms to produce **renewable** fuels, including ethanol and biogas. Fossil fuels are **non-renewable** (they'll run out), so other sources are of **major economic importance**.
- **Other industrial materials** — a huge variety of other materials are produced from plant and animal species, including **wood**, **paper**, **dyes**, **adhesives**, **oils**, **rubber** and chemicals such as **pesticides**.

Many genetic resources are important to the **global economy**. Products derived from plant and animal species are traded on a local and global scale.

2) Genetic resources allow us to **adapt** to **changes in the environment**. For example, **climate change** (see page 113) may mean that some crops won't be able to grow in the same areas as they do now, e.g. there might be **droughts** in those areas. However, we may be able to use **genes** from a plant that's **resistant** to droughts to genetically engineer a **drought-resistant crop** — that's if we have such genetic resources to choose from.

Importance of Biodiversity

...Economic Reasons...

To Reduce Soil Depletion

1) **Monoculture** is growing a **single variety** of a **single crop** (see p. 113).
2) **Continuous monoculture** involves planting the **same crop** in the **same field** without interruption.
3) Continuous monoculture causes **soil depletion** because the **nutrients** required by the crop are gradually **used up**. (In more traditional farming methods crops are rotated with other types of crops, so that the **nutrients** and **organic** matter are **replaced**.)
4) The **economic costs** of soil depletion include **increased spending** on **fertilisers** (to artificially replace nutrients) and **decreased yields** (in the long run and if fertilisers are not used).

'Yield' is the amount of a crop produced.

...and Aesthetic Reasons

Some people believe we should conserve biodiversity because it brings **joy** to millions of people.

1) Areas **rich** in biodiversity provide pleasant, **attractive landscapes** that people can enjoy. By maintaining biodiversity we **protect** these beautiful **landscapes**.
2) The more biodiversity in an area the more **visitors** the area is likely to **attract** — this also has economic advantages.

There are lots of aesthetic reasons for maintaining biodiversity... this isn't one of them.

Warm-Up Questions

Q1 What is meant when we say that organisms in an ecosystem are 'interdependent'?
Q2 What is a genetic resource?
Q3 Give two reasons why it's important to maintain genetic resources.
Q4 Give an economic reason for the conservation of biodiversity.
Q5 Give an aesthetic reason for the conservation of biodiversity.

PRACTICE QUESTIONS

Exam Questions

Q1 Sea otters live in the Pacific northwest. Part of their food web is shown below.

kelp (seaweed) $\longrightarrow$ sea urchin $\longrightarrow$ sea otter

Sea otters are described as a keystone species.
a) What is a keystone species? [1 mark]
b) Use the information above to give one reason why the otter is a keystone species. [1 mark]

Q2 Explain why reducing biodiversity through continuous monoculture can come at an economic cost. [4 marks]

All biodiversity is important — even spider diversity...

So, it turns out biodiversity is pretty important. Without it, not only would your life lack its little luxuries, like tissues with aloe vera, and designer clothes, just surviving would be tricky — there'd be nothing to eat and fewer drugs to treat you when you're ill. Make sure you learn all the reasons for maintaining biodiversity — they might just crop up in the exam.

Conservation and Biodiversity

Places like zoos and botanic gardens help preserve biodiversity through conservation — they help species that are endangered get out of the woods, or back into the woods, depending how you look at it...

In Situ Conservation Keeps Species in Their **Natural Habitat**

In situ conservation means **on site** conservation — it involves protecting species in their **natural habitat**. Conservation is important to **ensure the survival** of **endangered species** — species which are at risk of **extinction** because of a **low** population, or a **threatened habitat**. Methods of *in situ* conservation include:

1) Establishing **protected areas** such as **national parks** and **wildlife reserves** (also known as nature reserves) — habitats and species are protected in these areas by **restricting urban development**, **industrial development** and **farming**. A similar idea has been introduced to **sea ecosystems** with **Marine Conservation Zones**, where human activities (like fishing) are **controlled**.

2) **Controlling** or **preventing the introduction** of species that **threaten** local biodiversity. For example, grey squirrels are not native to Britain. They **compete** with the native red squirrel and have caused a population **decline**. So they're controlled in some areas.

3) **Protecting habitats** — e.g. controlling water levels to conserve wetlands and coppicing (trimming trees) to conserve woodlands. This allows organisms to **continue living** in their **natural habitat**.

4) **Promoting** particular species — this could be by protecting **food sources** or **nesting sites**.

5) Giving **legal protection** to **endangered species**, e.g. making it illegal to kill them (see next page).

Jim reckoned he'd seen the last of those red squirrels — but he hadn't counted on their friends turning up.

One advantage of *in situ* conservation is that often both the **species** and their **habitat** are conserved. **Larger populations** can be protected and it's **less disruptive** than removing organisms from their habitats. The chances of the population **recovering** are **greater** than with *ex situ* methods (see below).

But it can be **difficult to control** some factors that are **threatening** a species (such as poaching, predators, disease or climate change).

Ex Situ Conservation **Removes** Species from Their **Natural Habitat**

Ex situ conservation means **off site** conservation — it involves protecting a species by **removing** part of the population from a **threatened habitat** and placing it in a **new location**. *Ex situ* conservation is often a **last resort**. Methods of *ex situ* conservation include:

1) Relocating an organism to a safer area, e.g. five white rhinos were recently relocated from the Congo to Kenya because they were in danger from poachers who kill them for their ivory.

2) Breeding organisms in captivity then reintroducing them to the wild when they are strong enough, e.g. sea eagles have been reintroduced to Britain through a captive breeding programme. Breeding is carried out in animal sanctuaries and zoos.

3) Botanic gardens are controlled environments used to grow a variety of rare plants for the purposes of conservation, research, display and education. Endangered plant species as well as species that are extinct in the wild can be grown and reintroduced into suitable habitats.

4) Seed banks — seeds can be frozen and stored in seed banks for over a century without losing their fertility. Seed banks provide a useful source of seeds if natural reserves are destroyed, for example by disease or other natural disasters.

The advantages of *ex situ* conservation are that it can be used to protect individual animals in a **controlled environment** — things like predation and hunting can be managed more easily. It can also be used to **reintroduce** species that have **left an area**.

But, there are disadvantages — usually only a **small number** of individuals can be cared for. It can be **difficult** and **expensive** to create and **sustain** the **right environment**. In fact, animals that are habituated (used to) human contact may be less likely to exhibit natural behaviour and may be more likely to catch a disease from humans. *Ex situ* conservation is usually **less successful** than *in situ* methods — many species can't **breed successfully** in captivity, or don't **adapt** to their new environment when moved to a new location.

Conservation and Biodiversity

International Cooperation is Important in Species Conservation

Information about threats to biodiversity needs to be shared and countries need to decide on conservation methods and implement them together. Here are a couple of examples of successful international cooperation:

Rio Convention on Biological Diversity (CBD)

1) It aims to **develop international strategies** on the conservation of biodiversity and how to use animal and plant resources in a **sustainable** way.

2) The convention made it part of **international law** that conserving biodiversity is **everyone's responsibility**.

3) It also provides **guidance** to governments on how to conserve biodiversity.

CITES Agreement

1) CITES (**Convention** on **International Trade** in **Endangered Species**) is an agreement designed to increase **international cooperation** in **regulating trade** in wild animal and plant specimens.

2) The member countries all agreed to make it **illegal** to **kill** endangered species.

3) The agreement helps to **conserve** species by **limiting** trade through **licensing**, and by making it **illegal** to trade in products made from endangered animals (such as rhino ivory and leopard skins).

4) It's also designed to **raise awareness** of threats to biodiversity through **education**.

International cooperation is really **important** — it'd be pointless making hunting endangered species illegal in one country if poachers could just go and hunt them in another country.

Local Conservation Agreements Protect Special Areas in the UK

Whilst international cooperation is important, schemes at the **local** level are vital too. Here is an example from the UK:

The Countryside Stewardship Scheme (CSS)

1) The Countryside Stewardship Scheme was introduced in 1991. Some of its aims were to conserve wildlife and biodiversity, and to improve and extend wildlife habitats by promoting specific management techniques to landowners.

2) The Government offered 10-year agreements to **pay landowners** who followed the **management techniques** they were suggesting. For example, to **regenerate hedgerows**, to leave **grassy margins** around the edges of fields where **wildflowers** could grow, and to **graze upland** areas to keep down **bracken**.

3) In the year 2000, there were 10 000 agreements in England. Since the introduction of the scheme, various **species** have begun to rebuild in numbers, including **birds** such as the **stone curlew**, **black grouse** and **bittern**.

Warm-Up Questions

Q1 Describe how botanic gardens and seed banks help in the conservation of biodiversity.

Q2 What is CITES and how does it help to conserve endangered species?

Q3 What is the Countryside Stewardship Scheme and how does it help to conserve endangered species?

PRACTICE QUESTIONS

Exam Question

Q1 The hawksbill turtle is an endangered species of sea turtle threatened by hunting and loss of nesting sites. They have slow reproductive, growth and development rates and their numbers are in rapid decline. The hawksbill turtle could be conserved using *in situ* or *ex situ* methods.

a) Suggest how the hawksbill turtle could be conserved by *in situ* methods. [3 marks]

b) Describe the disadvantages of using *ex situ* conservation methods. [4 marks]

The path of true conservation ne'er did run smooth...

I'm sure the animals being forcibly removed from their homes are just as bemused as you are right now but I'm afraid it's another case of having to learn the facts. Don't be put off by things like 'in' or 'ex' situ — that's just a way of saying 'on' or 'off' site that makes people feel clever when they say them. In fact, I'm feeling rather clever right now.

Classification Basics

For hundreds of years people have been putting organisms into groups to make it easier to recognise and name them. For example, my brother is a member of the species Idioto bigearian (Latin for idiots with big ears).

Classification is All About **Grouping Together Similar Organisms**

Classification is the act of **arranging organisms** into **groups** based on their **similarities** and **differences**. This makes it **easier** for scientists to **identify** them and to **study** them. **Taxonomy** is the **study** of classification. There are a few different classification systems in use, but they all involve placing organisms into groups in a **taxonomic hierarchy**:

1) There are **eight levels** of groups (called taxonomic groups) used in classification.

2) **Similar organisms** are first sorted into one of **three** very **large groups** called **domains**, e.g. animals, plants and fungi are in the Eukarya domain.

There's more on domains on page 121.

3) **Similar organisms** are then sorted into **slightly smaller groups** called **kingdoms**, e.g. all animals are in the animal kingdom.

4) **Similar** organisms from that kingdom are then grouped into a **phylum**. **Similar** organisms from each phylum are then grouped into a **class**, and **so on** down the eight levels of the taxonomic hierarchy.

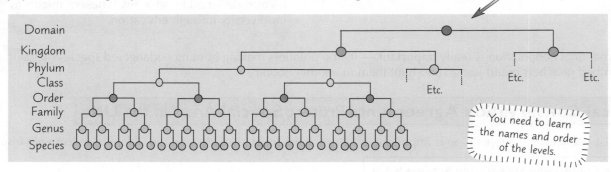

Domain
Kingdom
Phylum
Class
Order
Family
Genus
Species

Etc.   Etc.   Etc.

You need to learn the names and order of the levels.

5) As you move **down** the hierarchy, there are **more groups** at each level but **fewer organisms** in each group.

6) The hierarchy **ends** with **species** — the groups that contain only **one type** of organism (e.g. humans, dog, *E. coli* and about 50 million other living species).

Organisms Can be Placed into One of **Five Kingdoms**

The **five kingdom classification system** is a bit old now (see page 121), but you still need to **learn** these five kingdoms and the **general characteristics** of the organisms in each of them:

KINGDOM	EXAMPLES	FEATURES
Prokaryotae	bacteria	prokaryotic, unicellular (single-celled), no nucleus, less than 5 μm
Protoctista	algae, protozoa	eukaryotic cells, usually live in water, single-celled or simple multicellular organisms
Fungi	moulds, yeasts, mushrooms	eukaryotic, chitin cell wall, saprotrophic (absorb substances from dead or decaying organisms), single-celled or multicellular organisms
Plantae	mosses, ferns, flowering plants	eukaryotic, multicellular, cell walls made of cellulose, can photosynthesise, contain chlorophyll, autotrophic (produce their own food)
Animalia	nematodes (roundworms), molluscs, insects, fish, reptiles, birds, mammals	eukaryotic, multicellular, no cell walls, heterotrophic (consume plants and animals)

Plants are also known as photoautotrophs — they produce their own food using light.

Classification Basics

The **Binomial Naming System** is Used in **Classification**

1) The **nomenclature** (**naming system**) used for classification is called the **binomial system** — all organisms are given **one** internationally accepted scientific **name** in **Latin** that has **two parts**.

2) The **first part** of the name is the **genus** name and has a capital letter. The **second part** is the **species** name and begins with a lower case letter. E.g. using the binomial system humans are *Homo sapiens*. Names are always written in *italics* (or they're <u>underlined</u> if they're **handwritten**).

3) The binomial system helps to avoid the **confusion** of using **common names**. E.g. over 100 different plant species are called **raspberries** and one species of buttercup has over 90 different common names.

Phylogeny Tells Us About the **Evolutionary History** of Organisms

1) **Phylogeny** is the study of the **evolutionary history** of groups of **organisms**. Phylogeny tells us **who's related** to whom and how **closely related** they are.

2) All organisms have **evolved** from shared **common ancestors** (relatives). This can be shown on a **phylogenetic tree**, like this one.

First branch point

Orangutan
Human
Chimpanzee
Bonobo
Gorilla

3) This tree shows the **relationship** between members of the Hominidae family (great apes and humans). The **first branch point** represents a **common ancestor** of **all** the family members. This ancestor is now **extinct**. **Orangutans** were the first group to **diverge** (evolve to become a different species) from this common ancestor.

4) Each of the following branch points represents **another common ancestor** from which a **different group diverged**. Gorillas diverged next, then humans, closely followed by bonobos and chimpanzees.

5) According to phylogenetics, a **species** is the **smallest group** that shares a **common ancestor** — in other words, the **end of a branch** on a phylogenetic tree.

This is known as the phylogenetic species concept.

6) Closely related species **diverged** away from each other **most recently**. E.g. humans and **chimpanzees** are **closely** related, as they diverged very **recently**. You can see this because their branches are **close** together. Humans and orangutans are more **distantly** related, as they diverged longer ago, so their branches are **further** apart.

Classification systems now take into account **phylogeny** when arranging organisms into **groups**. Classifying organisms in this way is known as **cladistics**.

Warm-Up Questions

Q1 List the taxonomic hierarchy in order, starting at the top.
Q2 Give two features of the kingdom Fungi.

PRACTICE QUESTIONS

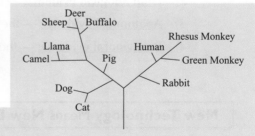

Exam Questions

Q1 The brown trout is part of the Salmonidae family.
   Its Latin name is *Salmo trutta*. It is part of the kingdom Animalia.
   a) What genus does the brown trout belong to? [1 mark]
   b) Give two features that the brown trout must have to place it in the kingdom Animalia. [2 marks]

Q2 The phylogenetic tree above shows the evolutionary history of some mammalian species.
   a) Which species shown on the tree is most closely related to humans? Explain how you know this. [2 marks]
   b) On the tree, circle the most recent common ancestor of both camels and deer. [1 mark]

Snozcumber kingdom features — long, thin, green, filled with snot...

Make sure that you really understand all the basics on these pages before delving any deeper into this section. Learning the order of the levels in the taxonomic hierarchy is about as easy as licking your elbow... try making up a mnemonic to help (like 'Dopey King Prawns Can't Order Fried Green Sausages' for Domain, Kingdom, Phylum, Class, Order, Family, etc).

Evolution of Classification Systems

Classification systems and the groups organisms are placed in aren't set in stone. New technology and new evidence can lead to changes in these systems and the reclassification of organisms.

Classification Systems are now Based on a Range of Evidence

Observable Features aren't Always Enough

1) Early classification systems **only** used **observable features** (things you can see) to place organisms into groups, e.g. whether they lay eggs, can fly or can cook a mean chilli...

2) But this method has **problems**. Scientists don't always agree on the **relative importance** of different features and groups based **solely** on **physical features** may not show how **related** organisms are.

EXAMPLE

Sharks and **whales look** quite similar and they both **live** in the sea. But they're **not** actually **closely related**. Whales are **mammals** and sharks are **cartilaginous fish** — two completely **different classes**.

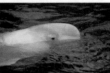

It's not all about looks, you know.

Other Evidence Shows How Similar Organisms are

1) Classification systems are **now** based on observable features **along** with **other evidence**.

2) The **more similar** organisms are, the **more related** they are. We now use a wide range of evidence to see **how similar**, and therefore how related, organisms are.

> **EXAMPLES**
>
> 1) <u>Molecular evidence</u> — the similarities in **proteins** and **DNA**. **More closely related** organisms will have **more similar** molecules.
>   - You can **compare** things like how **DNA** is **stored** and the **sequence** of DNA bases (see page 128 for more). E.g. the **base sequence** for human and chimpanzee **DNA** is about 94% the **same**.
>   - You can also compare the **sequence** of **amino acids** in **proteins** from different organisms. E.g. **cytochrome C** is a short protein found in many species. The more **similar** the **amino acid sequence** of cytochrome C in two different species, the **more closely related** the species are likely to be.
>
> 2) <u>Embryological evidence</u> — the similarities in the **early stages** of an organism's **development**.
>
> 3) <u>Anatomical evidence</u> — the similarities in **structure** and **function** of different body parts.
>
> 4) <u>Behavioural evidence</u> — the similarities in **behaviour** and **social organisation** of organisms.

New Technology Means New Discoveries

1) **New technologies** (e.g. new **DNA** techniques, better **microscopes**) can result in **new discoveries** being made and the **relationships** between organisms being **clarified**.

2) Scientists can share their new discoveries in **meetings** and **scientific journals** (see p. 2). How organisms are **classified** is **continually revised** to take account of any **new findings** that scientists **discover**.

EXAMPLE

Skunks **were** classified in the family **Mustelidae** until **molecular evidence** revealed their **DNA sequence** was significantly different to other members of that family. So they were reclassified into the family **Mephitidae**.

Evolution of Classification Systems

The **five kingdom classification system** shown on page 118 has now been replaced with the **three domain system**:

1) In the older system the **largest groups** were the **five kingdoms** — all organisms were placed into **one** of these groups.

2) In 1990, the **three domain system** was proposed. This new system has three domains — **large superkingdoms** that are **above** the kingdoms in the **taxonomic hierarchy** (see p. 118).

3) In the three domain system, organisms that were in the kingdom **Prokaryotae** (which contains unicellular organisms **without a nucleus**) are separated into two domains — the **Archaea** and **Bacteria**.

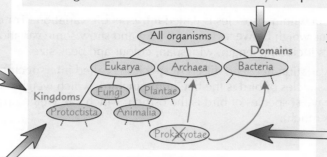

4) Organisms with cells that **contain a nucleus** are placed in the domain **Eukarya** (this includes four of the five kingdoms).

5) The **lower** hierarchy stays the **same** — Kingdom, Phylum, Class, Order, Family, Genus, Species.

Molecular Evidence Led to the Proposal of the Three Domain System

1) The three domain system was proposed because of **new evidence**, mainly molecular. E.g. the **Prokaryotae** were **reclassified** into **two domains** because new evidence showed **large differences** between the Archaea and Bacteria. The new evidence included:

- Molecular evidence — The enzyme **RNA polymerase** (needed to make RNA) is **different** in Bacteria and Archaea. **Archaea**, but **not Bacteria**, have similar **histones** (proteins that bind to DNA) to **Eukarya**.
- Cell membrane evidence — The **bonds** of the **lipids** (see p. 24) in the **cell membranes** of Bacteria and Archaea are **different**. The **development** and composition of **flagellae** (see p. 13) are also **different**.

2) Most scientists now **agree** that Archaea and Bacteria **evolved separately** and that Archaea are **more closely related** to Eukarya than Bacteria. The three domain system reflects how **different** the Archaea and Bacteria are.

3) The development of the three domain system is an example of how **scientific knowledge** is always **changing** and **improving** (see page 2).

Warm-Up Questions

Q1 What evidence were the first classification systems solely based on?

Q2 Give three types of evidence currently used to classify organisms.

Q3 What is meant by a domain?

PRACTICE QUESTIONS

Exam Questions

Q1 A gibbon is a type of ape. Describe one way in which scientists could use molecular evidence to determine how closely gibbons are related to humans. [2 marks]

Q2 The three domain system of classification places Cyanobacteria in the domain Bacteria. Describe three differences between organisms in the Bacteria and Archaea domains. [3 marks]

Five kingdoms, three domains — all the makings of a great TV series...

So there you have it — lots of exciting new discoveries. Molecular evidence in particular has a lot to answer for — imagine thinking you were a Prokaryote, then waking up one morning and discovering you were an archaeon. It's enough to give anyone issues. Make sure you learn why the three domain system was proposed and what it replaced.

Variation

Ever wondered why no two people are exactly alike? No, well nor have I actually, but it's time to start thinking about it. This variation is partly genetic and partly due to differences in the environment.

Variation Exists Between **All Individuals**

Variation is the **differences** that exist between **individuals**. Every individual organism is **unique** — even **clones** (such as identical twins) show some **variation**. It can occur:

Here's how I remember which is which — Int-*er* means diff-*er*-ent species.

1) <u>Within species</u> — Variation within a species is called **intraspecific** variation. For example, **individual** European robins weigh **between** 16 g and 22 g and show some variation in many other characteristics including length, wingspan, colour and beak size.

2) <u>Between species</u> — The variation between **different species** is called **interspecific** variation. For example, the **lightest** species of bird is the bee hummingbird, which weighs around 1.6 g on average. The **heaviest** species of bird is the ostrich, which can weigh up to 160 kg (100 000 times as much).

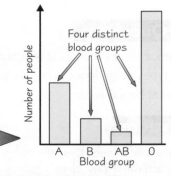

No matter what anyone said, Omar knew size was important.

Variation can be **Continuous...**

Continuous variation is when the **individuals** in a population vary **within a range** — there are **no distinct categories**, e.g. **humans** can be **any height** within a range (139 cm, 175 cm, 185.9 cm, etc.), **not just** tall or short. Here are some more examples:

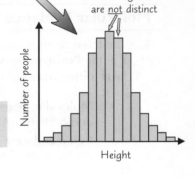

The categories are <u>not</u> distinct

| Animals |

1) **Milk yield** — e.g. cows can produce any volume of milk within a range.
2) **Mass** — e.g. humans can be any mass within a range.

| Plants |

1) **Number of leaves** — e.g. a tree can have any number of leaves within a range.
2) **Mass** — e.g. the mass of the seeds from a flower head varies within a range.

| Microorganisms |

1) **Width** — e.g. the width of *E. coli* bacteria varies within a range.
2) **Length** — e.g. the length of the flagellum (see p. 13) can vary within a range.

...or **Discontinuous**

Discontinuous variation is when there are two or more **distinct categories** — each individual falls into **only one** of these categories, there are **no intermediates**. Here are some examples:

Four distinct blood groups

| Animals |

Blood group — e.g. humans can be group A, B, AB or O.

| Plants |

1) **Colour** — e.g. courgettes are either yellow, dark green or light green.
2) **Seed shape** — e.g. some pea plants have smooth seeds and some have wrinkled seeds.

| Microorganisms |

1) **Antibiotic resistance** — e.g. bacteria are either resistant or not.
2) **Pigment production** — e.g. some types of bacteria can produce a coloured pigment, some can't.

Module 4: Section 3 — Classification and Evolution

Variation

Variation can be Caused by Genes, the Environment, or Both

Variation can be caused by **genetic factors**, **environmental factors** or a combination of **both**:

1) Genetic factors

1) **Different species** have **different genes**.
2) Individuals of the **same species** have the **same genes**, but **different versions** of them (called **alleles**).
3) The genes and alleles an organism has make up its **genotype**.
4) The differences in **genotype** result in **variation** in **phenotype** — the **characteristics** displayed by an organism.
5) Examples of variation caused **only** by genetic factors include **blood group** in humans (O, A, B or AB) and **antibiotic resistance** in bacteria.
6) You **inherit** your genes from your parents. This means variation caused by genetic factors is **inherited**.

2) Environmental factors

1) Variation can also be caused by **differences in the environment**, e.g. climate, food, lifestyle.
2) Characteristics controlled by environmental factors can **change** over an organism's life.
3) Examples of variation caused **only** by environmental factors include **accents** and whether people have **pierced ears**.

3) Both

Genetic factors determine the characteristics an organism's **born with**, but **environmental factors** can **influence** how some characteristics **develop**. For example:

1) **Height** — **genes** determine how tall an organism **can grow** (e.g. tall parents tend to have tall children). But **diet or nutrient availability** affect how tall an organism **actually grows**.
2) **Flagellum** — genes determine if a microorganism **can grow** a flagellum, but some will only **start to grow** them in **certain environments**, e.g. if metal ions are present.

You Can Use the Mean to Look for Variation Between Samples

1) To **investigate variation** you usually take **samples** of a population (see page 110).
2) The **mean** is an **average** of the values collected in a sample. It can be used to tell if there is **variation between samples**. For example:

> The **mean height** of a species of **tree** in woodland A = **26 m**, in woodland B = **32 m** and in woodland C = **35 m**. So the **mean height varies**.

3) Most samples will include values **either side** of the **mean**, so you end up with a **bell**-shaped graph — this is called a **normal distribution**. A normal distribution is **symmetrical** about the mean.

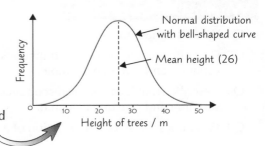

The Standard Deviation Tells You About Variation Within a Sample

1) The standard deviation tells you how much the values in a single sample vary. It's a measure of the spread of values about the mean.
2) Sometimes you'll see the mean written as, e.g. **9 ± 3**. This means that the mean is **9** and the standard deviation is **3**, so most of the values are spread between **6** and **12**.
3) A large standard deviation means the values in the sample vary a lot. A small standard deviation tells you that most of the sample data is around the mean value, so varies little.

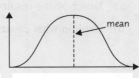

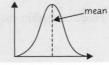

Here, all the values are similar and close to the mean, so the graph is steep and the standard deviation is small.

Here, the values vary a lot, so the graph is fatter and the standard deviation is large.

Variation

You Can Find the **Standard Deviation** Using the **Formula**

This is the formula for finding the standard deviation of a group of values:

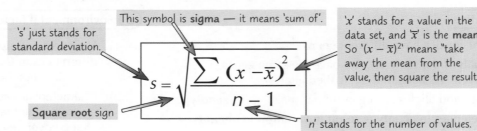

This symbol is **sigma** — it means 'sum of'.

'x' stands for a value in the data set, and '$\bar{x}$' is the **mean**. So '$(x - \bar{x})^2$' means "take away the mean from the value, then square the result."

's' just stands for standard deviation.

$$s = \sqrt{\dfrac{\sum (x - \bar{x})^2}{n - 1}}$$

Square root sign

'n' stands for the number of values.

Example:

The table shows the height of four different trees in a forest. To find the **standard deviation**:

Tree	Height (m)
A	22
B	27
C	26
D	29

1 Write out the **equation**. $s = \sqrt{\dfrac{\sum (x - \bar{x})^2}{n - 1}}$

2 Work out the **mean** height of the trees, $\bar{x}$. $(22 + 27 + 26 + 29) \div 4 = \mathbf{26}$

3 Work out $(x - \bar{x})^2$ for each value of x.
For each tree height in the table, you need to take away the mean, then square the answer.

A: $(22 - 26)^2 = (-4)^2 = \mathbf{16}$ B: $(27 - 26)^2 = 1^2 = \mathbf{1}$
C: $(26 - 26)^2 = 0^2 = \mathbf{0}$ D: $(29 - 26)^2 = 3^2 = \mathbf{9}$

4 Add up all these numbers to find $\sum(x - \bar{x})^2$. $16 + 1 + 0 + 9 = \mathbf{26}$

5 **Divide** this number by the number of values, n, minus 1. Then take the **square root** to get the answer.

$26 \div 3 = 8.66...$
$\sqrt{8.66...} = \mathbf{2.94}$ **to 3 s.f.**

Warm-Up Questions

Q1 What is variation?

Q2 Describe what is meant by continuous variation and give one example.

Q3 Describe what is meant by discontinuous variation and give one example.

Q4 What does the standard deviation of a set of data tell us?

PRACTICE QUESTIONS

Exam Question

Q1 The graph shows the results of an investigation into the effects of temperature on the length of time it took for ladybird larvae to emerge as adults. Two species of ladybird were investigated, species A and species B.

a) Describe the results of the study.   [2 marks]

b) Explain what causes the variation within each species.   [1 mark]

Environmental Factor — the search is on for the most talented environment...

It's amazing to think how many factors and genes influence the way we look and behave. It's the reason why every single organism is unique. My parents have often said they're glad they'll never have another child as 'unique' as me.

Adaptations

All the variation between and within species means that some organisms are better adapted to their environment than others...

Adaptations make Organisms **Well Suited** to Their **Environment**

1) Being adapted to an environment means an organism has features that increase its chances of survival and reproduction, and also the chances of its offspring reproducing successfully.

2) These features are called adaptations and can be behavioural, physiological and anatomical (see below).

3) Adaptations develop because of evolution by natural selection (see page 127).

4) In each generation, the best-adapted individuals are more likely to survive and reproduce — passing their adaptations on to their offspring. Individuals that are less well adapted are more likely to die before reproducing.

Adaptations can be **Behavioural**, **Physiological** and **Anatomical**

Behavioural adaptations

Ways an organism **acts** that increase its chance of survival. For example:

- **Possums** sometimes '**play dead**' — if they're being threatened by a **predator** they play dead to **escape attack**. This **increases** their chance of **survival**.
- **Scorpions dance** before **mating** — this makes sure they attract a mate of the **same species**, increasing the likelihood of **successful mating**.

Bob and Sue were well adapted to hiding in candyfloss shops.

Physiological adaptations

Processes inside an organism's body that increase its chance of survival. For example:

- **Brown bears hibernate** — they **lower their rate of metabolism** (all the chemical reactions taking place in their body) over **winter**. This **conserves energy**, so they don't need to look for **food** in the months when it's scarce — **increasing** their chance of **survival**.
- **Some bacteria** produce **antibiotics** — these **kill** other species of bacteria in the area. This means there's **less competition**, so they're **more likely** to **survive**.

Anatomical (structural) adaptations

Structural features of an organism's body that increase its chance of survival. For example:

- **Otters** have a **streamlined shape** — making it easier to **glide** through the **water**. This makes it easier for them to **catch prey** and **escape predators**, increasing their chance of **survival**.
- **Whales** have a **thick layer** of **blubber** (fat) — this helps to keep them **warm** in the cold sea. This increases their chance of survival in places where their **food** is found.

Different Taxonomic Groups May Have **Similar Features**

1) Organisms from **different** taxonomic groups may have **similar** features even though they're **not closely related** — for example, whales and sharks (see page 120).

2) This is usually because the organisms have **evolved** in **similar environments** and to fill **similar ecological niches**.

3) The example you need to learn for your exam is of **marsupial** and **placental moles** — see next page.

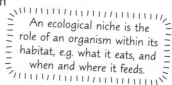

An ecological niche is the role of an organism within its habitat, e.g. what it eats, and when and where it feeds.

Adaptations

Marsupial and Placental Mammals Have Evolved Separately

1) There are **three different groups** of mammals. Most mammals are **placental mammals**, while some are **marsupials** (and a very few are egg-laying monotremes).

2) Marsupials are found mainly in **Australia** and the **Americas**. They **diverged** from placental mammals many **millions of years ago** and have been **evolving separately** ever since.

Marsupial mammals (e.g. kangaroos):
- have a **short gestation period** (pregnancy).
- don't develop a **full placenta**.
- are born **early** in their development and climb into their mother's **pouch**. Here they become attached to a **teat** and receive milk while they **continue** to **develop**.

Placental mammals (e.g. humans):
- have a **longer gestation period**.
- develop a **placenta** during pregnancy, which allows the **exchange of nutrients** and **waste products** between the fetus and the mother.
- are born more **fully developed**.

Marsupial and Placental Moles Look Alike But Aren't Closely Related

1) **Marsupial** moles and **placental** moles **aren't closely related** — they **evolved independently** on different **continents**.

2) They do share **similar anatomical features** though (i.e. they look alike). That's because they've both evolved to live in **similar environments**:

When two species evolve similar characteristics independently of one another (because they've adapted to live in similar environments) it's called convergent evolution.

Both types of mole live in tunnels in the ground. They burrow to reach their food supply (e.g. earthworms, insects and other invertebrates). Their adaptations to this lifestyle include:
- Small or nonexistent eyes because they don't need to be able to see underground.
- No external ears, to keep a streamlined head for burrowing.
- Scoop-shaped and powerful front paws, which are good for digging.
- Claws that are specialised for digging.
- A tube shaped body and cone shaped head, which makes it easier to push through sand or soil.

Warm-Up Questions

Q1 What is meant by the term adaptation?

Q2 Describe the differences between behavioural, physiological and anatomical adaptations.

Q3 Explain why marsupial moles and placental moles share similar anatomical features, even though they are not closely related.

Q4 Give two anatomical features marsupial and placental moles have in common.

Exam Question

Q1 a) Both whales and sharks have developed a streamlined body and fins, despite being from different taxonomic groups. Suggest why. [1 mark]

b) Like humans, whales are mammals. This means they can't breathe underwater and have to come to the surface for air. However, whales have developed the ability to exchange up to 90% of the oxygen in their lungs compared to the human average of 10-15%.

Suggest why humans haven't developed the same oxygen-exchanging ability as whales. [1 mark]

I'm perfectly adapted — for staying in bed...

Adaptations are features that make an organism more likely to survive and reproduce. Repetitive? Yes, but that's why it's so easy to learn. Adaptations develop because of evolution by natural selection, which is on the next page. Lucky you.

The Theory of Evolution

Evolution is the slow and continual change of organisms from one generation to the next. It explains how advantageous adaptations become common within a population of organisms...

Darwin Published his Theory of Evolution by Natural Selection in 1859

Darwin made **four** key observations about the world around him.

Observations:

1) Organisms produce **more offspring** than **survive**.

2) There's **variation** in the characteristics of members of the **same species**.

3) Some of these characteristics can be **passed on** from one generation to the next.

4) Individuals that are **best adapted** to their environment are more likely to **survive**.

Darwin wrote his theory of **evolution by natural selection** to **explain** his observations:

Natural selection is one process by which evolution occurs.

Theory:

1) Individuals within a population **show variation** in their **phenotypes** (their characteristics).

2) **Selection pressures** (environmental factors such as **predation**, **disease** and **competition**) create a **struggle for survival**.

3) Individuals with **better adaptations** (characteristics that give a selective advantage, e.g. being able to run away from predators faster) are **more likely** to **survive** and have **reproductive success** — in other words, they **reproduce** and **pass on** their advantageous adaptations to their **offspring**.

4) Over time, the **proportion** of the population possessing the **advantageous adaptations increases**.

The opposite is also true — organisms without these adaptations are less likely to survive and have reproductive success.

5) Over generations this leads to **evolution** as the favourable adaptations become **more common** in the population.

1) We now know that **genes** determine many of an organism's **characteristics** and that individuals show variations in their **phenotypes** partly as a result of **genetic variation**, i.e. the different **alleles** they have.

2) When an organism with advantageous characteristics **reproduces**, the **alleles** that determine those characteristics may be passed on to its **offspring**.

Wallace Contributed to the Theory of Evolution

Alfred Russel Wallace, a scientist working at the **same time** as Darwin, played an important part in developing the **theory of evolution by natural selection**.

- He **independently** came up with the idea of **natural selection** and wrote to Darwin about it.

- He and Darwin **published** their **papers** on evolution **together** and acknowledged each other's work — although they **didn't always agree** about the mechanisms involved in natural selection.

- Wallace's **observations** provided lots of **evidence** to **support** the theory of evolution by natural selection. For example, he realised that **warning colours** are used by some species (e.g. butterflies) to deter predators from eating them and that this was an example of an **advantageous adaptation** that had evolved by natural selection.

1) Unfortunately for Wallace, it wasn't until Darwin published his famous book **'On the Origin of Species'** that other **scientists** began to pay **attention** to the theory.

2) In this book Darwin gave lots of **evidence** to support the theory and expanded on it. For example, he wrote about all the **species** that he had **observed** during his voyage to South America and the Galápagos Islands in the 1830s.

3) The book is partly why **Darwin** is usually **better remembered** than Wallace — even though **Wallace helped** to come up with the **theory**.

The Theory of Evolution

There's **Plenty of Evidence** to **Support Evolution**

Fossil Record Evidence

Fossils are the **remains** of organisms **preserved in rocks**.
By arranging fossils in chronological (date) order, **gradual changes** in organisms can be observed that provide **evidence** of evolution.

Example — The fossil record of the **horse** shows a **gradual change** in characteristics, including increasing **size** and **hoof** development.

DNA Evidence

1) The theory of evolution suggests that all organisms have **evolved** from shared **common ancestors**.

2) Closely related species **diverged** (evolved to become different species) **more recently**.

3) Evolution is caused by **gradual changes** in the **base sequence** of an organisms' DNA.

4) Organisms that diverged away from each other more recently, should have **more similar DNA**, as **less time** has passed for changes in the DNA sequence to occur. This is exactly what scientists have found.

See p. 38 for more on the DNA base sequence.

Example — Humans, chimps and mice all evolved from a common ancestor. Humans and mice diverged a **long time ago**, but humans and chimps diverged **quite recently**. The **DNA base sequence** of humans and chimps is 94% the same, but human and mouse DNA is only 85% the same.

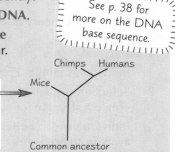

In **eukaryotes**, **most DNA** is found in the **cell nucleus**. But scientists don't just analyse **nuclear DNA** to find out about **evolutionary relationships**. Eukaryotic organisms also have DNA in their **mitochondria**, so scientists can also look at **differences in mitochondrial DNA** to see how **closely related** organisms are.

Molecular Evidence

In addition to DNA, the similarities in **other molecules** provide evidence.
Scientists compare the **sequence** of amino acids in **proteins**, and compare **antibodies**.
Organisms that diverged away from each other **more recently** have **more similar molecules**, as **less time** has passed for changes in proteins and other molecules to occur.

Populations of **Insects** can **Evolve Resistance** to **Pesticides**

Pesticides are chemicals that **kill pests** (e.g. insects that damage crops). Scientists have observed the evolution of **pesticide resistance** in many species of insect.

For example, some populations of **mosquito** have **evolved resistance** to the pesticide **DDT**. Some populations of **pollen beetles** (which damage the crop oilseed rape) are resistant to **pyrethroid** pesticides.

Janet was resistant to DDT but not to Malcolm's smooth talking.

The evolution of **pesticide resistance** can be explained by **natural selection**:

1) There is **variation** in a population of insects. **Genetic mutations** create **alleles** that make some insects naturally **resistant** to a pesticide.

2) If the population of insects is exposed to that pesticide only the individuals with resistance will **survive** to **reproduce**.

3) The **alleles** which cause the pesticide resistance will be **passed on** to the next generation, and so the population will **evolve** — more individuals will carry the allele than in the previous generation.

The pesticide acts as a selection pressure — without a selection pressure, natural selection won't take place.

The Theory of Evolution

The Evolution of **Pesticide Resistance** has **Implications** for **Humans**

1) Crop infestations with pesticide-resistant insects are harder to control — some insects are resistant to lots of different pesticides. It takes farmers a while to figure out which pesticide will kill the insect and in that time all the crop could be destroyed. If the insects are resistant to specific pesticides (ones that only kill that insect), farmers might have to use broader pesticides (those that kill a range of insects), which could kill beneficial insects.

2) If disease-carrying insects (e.g. mosquitoes) become pesticide-resistant, the spread of disease could increase.

3) A population of insects could evolve resistance to all pesticides in use. To prevent this new pesticides need to be produced. This takes time and costs money.

The Evolution of **Drug Resistance** Has **Implications** for **Humans** Too

1) You might remember from page 108 that scientists have observed the **evolution** of **antibiotic resistance** in many species of **bacteria**, e.g. **MRSA**.

2) **Other pathogens** have **evolved resistance** to specific **drugs** too. For example, some of the **protoctists** that cause **malaria** (see page 98) are **resistant** to several drugs used to treat malaria.

3) **Infections** caused by drug-resistant microorganisms are **harder** to **treat** — especially if the microorganism is resistant to **lots of different drugs**. It can take doctors a while to figure out which drugs will get rid of the infection, and in that time the **patient** could become **very ill** or **die**.

4) There could come a point where a pathogen has become resistant to **all the drugs** we currently use against it. To prevent this, **new drugs** need to be **developed**. This takes **time** and costs a lot of **money**.

Warm-Up Questions

Q1 What four key observations did Darwin make?
Q2 Give one way in which Wallace contributed to the theory of evolution.
Q3 Briefly describe how fossil evidence supports the theory of evolution.
Q4 Describe how DNA evidence supports the theory of evolution.

PRACTICE QUESTIONS

Exam Questions

Q1 Tawny owls show variation in colour. There are light grey owls and darker brown owls. Before the 1970s there were more grey owls than brown owls in Finland. Since then, climate change has been causing a decrease in the amount of snowfall in Finland. During this period, the darker brown owls have become more common.

a) Suggest why the brown owls are better adapted to living in an area with less snowfall than the grey owls. [2 marks]

b) Explain how the brown owls have become more common. [3 marks]

Q2 The diamondback moth is a pest of many crops. In 1953 it became resistant to the pesticide DDT and by 1981 it had become resistant to 36 other pesticides.

a) Explain how the diamondback moth populations could have developed DDT resistance. [4 marks]

b) Describe two possible implications of the diamondback moth developing resistance to pesticides. [2 marks]

The fossil record — it rocks...

Evolution by natural selection isn't that bad really... just remember that any adaptation that increases the chances of an organism surviving (e.g. by avoiding being killed by antibiotics) or reproducing will increase in the population due to the process of natural selection. Now I know why mullets have disappeared... so unattractive...

Extra Exam Practice

...and <u>Module 4</u> bites the dust. You might have made your way through that meaty module, but you've still got some practice questions to try. It's the only way to really make sure you're ready for the exams.

- Have a look at this example of how to answer a tricky exam question.
- Then check how much you've understood from Module 4 by having a go at the questions on the next page.

The questions at the end of each module are great practice (even if I do say so myself) but make sure you try the questions on pages 258-265 too — they'll test your knowledge of the whole course.

1 **Figure 1** shows how the number of copies of HIV and antibodies complementary to HIV vary over time in the blood of a person who has been infected with HIV.

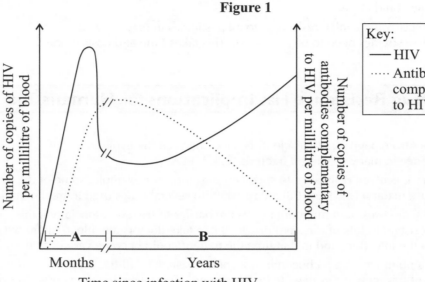

(a) Explain how B lymphocytes are involved in the rise in the number of copies of antibodies complementary to HIV, during time period **A** in **Figure 1**.

(4 marks)

(b) HIV infects, and eventually kills, T helper cells.
Using this information and **Figure 1**, explain why the number of copies of antibodies complementary to HIV falls during time period **B**.

(3 marks)

The graph here looks pretty complicated — it has two y-axes with separate labels, a split x-axis and a key. But don't let that put you off answering the questions — once you've taken the time to read all the labels you'll see that the information shown on the graph is actually pretty straightforward.

You've been asked specifically about B lymphocytes so don't be tempted to write everything you know about the immune response, e.g. don't write about T lymphocytes here — they're not relevant.

1(a)

Some **B lymphocytes** have antibodies on their surface that are a complementary shape to the HIV antigens. When these antibodies bind to the HIV antigens, it activates the B lymphocytes in a process called clonal selection. The activated B lymphocytes then divide by mitosis in a process called clonal expansion, and differentiate into plasma cells that secrete lots of antibodies complementary to the HIV antigens, causing the rise shown in Figure 1.

1(b)

During time period B, the number of copies of HIV in the blood rises, suggesting that more T helper cells are being infected and killed during this time. T helper cells release **interleukins**, which activate B lymphocytes. Therefore, if the number of T helper cells falls then fewer B lymphocytes are activated, so fewer plasma cells are produced. As plasma cells secrete antibodies, the number of copies of complementary antibodies to HIV in the blood also falls.

Always use scientific terms where you can in your answers — it could help you to pick up marks.

Extra Exam Practice

2 **Figure 2** shows part of a phylogenetic tree for some aquatic organisms.

Figure 2

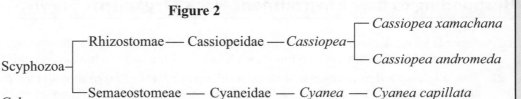

(a) Using **Figure 2**, name the order that *Cassiopea andromeda* belongs to.

(1 mark)

(b) The DNA base sequences of *Cassiopea xamachana* and *Cassiopea andromeda* are likely to be more similar to one another than they are to *Cyanea capillata*.
Explain how this could provide evidence to support the theory of evolution by natural selection.

(3 marks)

(c) *Physalia physalis* is an aquatic species that has many similar features to organisms in the taxonomic group Scyphozoa.
Explain why *Physalia physalis* may have similar features to scyphozoans, despite being from a different taxonomic group.

(1 mark)

3 Ecologists conducted a survey to assess whether the biodiversity of insect larvae in an area of a park changed between 2016 and 2017. The data they collected is shown in **Table 1**.

Table 1

Species	No. of individuals found in July 2016	No. of individuals found in July 2017
Hemerobius micans	18	2
Hemerobius stigma	15	3
Hemerobius alpestris	11	9
Forficula auricularia	22	19
Simpson's Index of Diversity		0.58

(a) **(i)** Suggest **two** variables the ecologists should have controlled when collecting the two different sets of data.

(2 marks)

(ii) With reference to the data in **Table 1**, explain the difference between species richness and Simpson's Index of Diversity and use these measures to make a conclusion for the study.
You should use the following formula in your answer:

$$D = 1 - \left(\sum \left(\frac{n}{N} \right)^2 \right)$$ where n = total number of organisms in one species and N = total number of all organisms

Show your working and give your answer to **two** significant figures.

(4 marks)

(b) The park contains many different types of habitat for the species studied.
The ecologists plan to collect data on the biodiversity of the species across the whole park.
Explain why using stratified sampling may provide more valid results than using a random sampling method when collecting this data.

(3 marks)

Communication and Homeostasis Basics

Ah, homeostasis. What a lovely topic — all about your body making sure that everything is just right.

Responding to their Environment Helps Organisms Survive

1) **Animals increase** their **chances** of **survival** by **responding** to **changes** in their **external environment**, e.g. by **avoiding harmful environments** such as places that are too hot or too cold.

2) They also **respond** to **changes** in their **internal environment** to make sure that the **conditions** are always **optimal** for their **metabolism** (all the chemical reactions that go on inside them).

3) **Plants** also **increase** their **chances** of **survival** by **responding** to **changes** in their **environment** (see p. 168).

4) Any **change** in the internal or external **environment** is called a **stimulus**.

Receptors Detect Stimuli and Effectors Produce a Response

1) **Receptors detect stimuli**.

2) Receptors are **specific** — they only **detect one particular stimulus**, e.g. light or pressure.

3) There are **many different types** of receptor that each detect a **different type of stimulus**.

4) Some receptors are **cells**, e.g. photoreceptors are receptor cells that connect to the nervous system. Some receptors are **proteins** on **cell surface membranes**, e.g. glucose receptors are proteins found in the cell membranes of some pancreatic cells.

5) **Effectors** are cells that bring about a **response** to a **stimulus**, to produce an **effect**. Effectors include **muscle cells** and cells found in **glands**, e.g. the **pancreas**.

Communication can Occur Between Adjacent and Distant Cells

1) To produce a **response**, **receptors** need to **communicate** with **effectors** and effectors may need to communicate with **other cells**.

This communication makes sure that the activities of different organs are coordinated to keep the organism working effectively.

2) This happens via **cell signalling**.

3) Cell signalling can occur between **adjacent** (nearby) cells or between **distant** cells. For example, cells in the **nervous system** communicate by secreting **chemicals** called **neurotransmitters**, which send signals to **adjacent** cells, such as other nerve cells or muscle cells. The **hormonal** system works by cells releasing **chemicals** called **hormones**, which travel in the blood and act as signals to **distant** cells.

The nervous system and hormonal system are 'communication systems'.

4) **Cell-surface receptors** allow cells to **recognise** the chemicals involved in cell signalling.

Homeostasis is the Maintenance of a Constant Internal Environment

1) **Changes** in your **external environment** can affect your **internal environment** — the blood and tissue fluid that surrounds your cells.

2) **Homeostasis** involves **control systems** that keep your **internal environment** roughly **constant** (within **certain limits**).

3) **Keeping** your internal environment **constant** is vital for cells to **function normally** and to **stop** them being **damaged**.

4) It's particularly important to **maintain** the right **core body temperature**. This is because temperature affects **enzyme activity**, and enzymes **control** the **rate** of **metabolic reactions**:

- If **body temperature** is **too high** (e.g. 40 °C) enzymes may become **denatured**. The enzyme's molecules **vibrate too much**, which **breaks** the **hydrogen bonds** that hold them in their **3D shape**. The **shape** of the enzyme's **active site** is **changed** and it **no longer works** as a **catalyst**. This means **metabolic reactions** are **less efficient**.

- If body temperature is **too low** enzyme activity is **reduced**, **slowing** the rate of **metabolic reactions**.

- The **highest rate** of **enzyme activity** happens at their **optimum temperature** (about **37 °C** in humans).

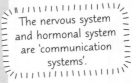

There's more about control of body temperature on p. 142-143 and control of blood glucose on p. 144-145.

5) It's also important to **maintain** the right **concentration** of **glucose** in the **blood**, so there's always enough available for respiration.

Communication and Homeostasis Basics

Homeostatic Systems Detect a Change and Respond by Negative Feedback

1) Homeostatic systems involve **receptors**, a **communication system** and **effectors** (see the previous page).

2) Receptors detect when a level is **too high** or **too low**, and the information's communicated via the **nervous** system or the **hormonal** system to **effectors**.

3) The effectors respond to **counteract** the change — bringing the level **back** to **normal**.

4) The mechanism that **restores** the level to **normal** is called a **negative feedback** mechanism.

5) Negative feedback **keeps** things around the **normal** level, e.g. body temperature is usually kept **within 0.5 °C** above or below **37 °C**.

6) Negative feedback only works within **certain limits** though — if the change is **too big** then the **effectors** may **not** be able to **counteract** it, e.g. a huge drop in body temperature caused by prolonged exposure to cold weather may be too large to counteract.

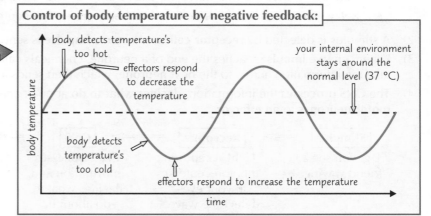

Control of body temperature by negative feedback:

body detects temperature's too hot

effectors respond to decrease the temperature

your internal environment stays around the normal level (37 °C)

body detects temperature's too cold

effectors respond to increase the temperature

body temperature

time

Positive Feedback Mechanisms Amplify a Change from the Normal Level

1) Some changes trigger a **positive feedback** mechanism, which **amplifies** the change.

2) The effectors respond to **further increase** the level **away** from the **normal** level.

3) Positive feedback is useful to **rapidly activate** something, e.g. a **blood clot** after an injury:

- **Platelets** become **activated** and release a **chemical** — this triggers **more platelets** to be activated, and so on.
- Platelets **very quickly** form a **blood clot** at the injury site.
- The process **ends** with **negative feedback**, when the body detects the **blood clot** has been **formed**.

4) Positive feedback **isn't** involved in **homeostasis** because it **doesn't** keep your internal environment **constant**.

Warm-Up Questions

Q1 Why do organisms respond to changes in their environment?

Q2 What is a stimulus?

Q3 Give two types of effector.

Q4 What is cell signalling?

Q5 What is a negative feedback mechanism?

Q6 What type of mechanism amplifies a change from the normal level?

PRACTICE QUESTIONS

Exam Question

Q1 a) Define homeostasis. [1 mark]

b) Describe the role of receptors, communication systems and effectors in homeostasis. [3 marks]

Responding to questions in an exam helps you to pass...

Multicellular organisms respond to internal changes so that they can keep conditions just right for all their bodily reactions. Maintaining this constant internal environment is called homeostasis — basically you just need to remember that if one thing goes up too high the body responds to bring it down, and vice versa.

Receptors and Neurones

The nervous system helps organisms to respond to the environment, so you need to know a bit more about it...

The **Nervous System** Sends Information as **Nerve Impulses**

1) The **nervous system** is made up of a **complex network** of cells called **neurones**. There are **three main types**:

- **Sensory neurones** transmit nerve impulses from **receptors** to the **central nervous system** (CNS) — the **brain** and **spinal cord**.
- **Motor neurones** transmit nerve impulses from the **CNS** to **effectors**.
- **Relay neurones** transmit nerve impulses **between** sensory neurones and motor neurones.

Nerve impulses are electrical impulses. They're also called action potentials.

2) A stimulus is detected by **receptor cells** and a **nerve impulse** is sent along a **sensory neurone**.

3) When a **nerve impulse** reaches the end of a neurone, chemicals called **neurotransmitters** take the information across to the **next neurone**, which then sends a **nerve impulse** (see p. 138).

4) The **CNS processes** the information, **decides what to do** about it and sends impulses along **motor neurones** to an **effector**.

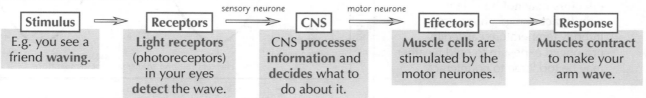

Stimulus		Receptors		CNS		Effectors		Response
E.g. you see a friend **waving**.	⟹ sensory neurone	**Light receptors** (photoreceptors) in your eyes **detect** the wave.	⟹	**CNS processes information** and **decides** what to do about it.	⟹ motor neurone	**Muscle cells** are stimulated by the motor neurones.	⟹	**Muscles contract** to make your arm **wave**.

Sensory Receptors Convert **Stimulus Energy** into **Nerve Impulses**

1) **Different stimuli** have **different forms** of **energy**, e.g. light energy or chemical energy.
2) But your **nervous system** only sends information in the form of **nerve impulses** (electrical impulses).
3) **Sensory receptors convert** the energy of a **stimulus** into **electrical energy**.
4) So, sensory receptors act as **transducers** — something that **converts** one form of energy into another.
5) Here's a bit more about how receptor cells that communicate information via the **nervous system** work:

- When a nervous system receptor is in its **resting state** (not being stimulated), there's a **difference in charge** between the **inside** and the **outside** of the cell — this is generated by ion pumps and ion channels. This means there's a **voltage** across the membrane. Voltage is also known as **potential difference**.

- The **potential difference** when a cell is at **rest** is called its **resting potential**. When a stimulus is detected, the cell membrane is **excited** and becomes **more permeable**, allowing **more ions** to move **in** and **out** of the cell — **altering** the potential difference. The **change** in **potential difference** due to a stimulus is called the **generator potential**.

- A **bigger stimulus** excites the membrane more, causing a **bigger movement** of ions and a **bigger change** in potential difference — so a **bigger generator potential** is produced.

- If the **generator potential** is **big enough** it'll trigger an **action potential** (nerve impulse) along a neurone. An action potential is only triggered if the generator potential reaches a certain level called the **threshold** level.

- If the stimulus is **too weak** the generator potential **won't reach** the **threshold**, so there's **no action potential**.

Example — Pacinian corpuscles

Pacinian corpuscles are **mechanoreceptors** — they detect **mechanical stimuli**, e.g. **pressure** and **vibrations**. They're found in your **skin**. They contain the end of a **sensory neurone**, called a **sensory nerve ending**. The sensory nerve ending is **wrapped** in lots of layers of connective tissue called **lamellae**.

When a Pacinian corpuscle is **stimulated**, e.g. by a tap on the arm, the lamellae are **deformed** and **press** on the **sensory nerve ending**. This causes **deformation** of **stretch-mediated sodium channels** in the sensory neurone's cell membrane. The sodium ion channels **open** and **sodium ions diffuse into** the cell, creating a **generator potential**. If the **generator potential** reaches the **threshold**, it triggers an **action potential**.

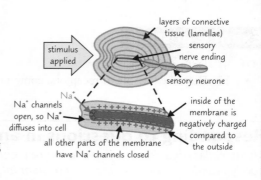

layers of connective tissue (lamellae)
sensory nerve ending
sensory neurone
stimulus applied
Na⁺ channels open, so Na⁺ diffuses into cell
all other parts of the membrane have Na⁺ channels closed
inside of the membrane is negatively charged compared to the outside

Receptors and Neurones

You Need to **Learn** the **Structure** of **Sensory, Motor** and **Relay Neurones...**

All neurones have a **cell body** with a **nucleus** (plus **cytoplasm** and all the other **organelles** you usually get in a cell). The cell body has **extensions** that **connect** to **other neurones** — dendrites and **dendrons** carry nerve impulses **towards** the **cell body**, and **axons** carry nerve impulses **away** from the **cell body**.

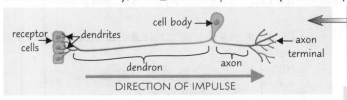

receptor cells → dendrites
cell body
axon terminal
dendron
axon
DIRECTION OF IMPULSE

Sensory neurones have **short dendrites** and **one long dendron** to carry nerve impulses from **receptor cells** to the **cell body**, and **one short axon** that carries impulses from the **cell body** to the **CNS**.

Motor neurones have **many short dendrites** that carry nerve impulses from the **central nervous system (CNS)** to the **cell body**, and **one long axon** that carries nerve impulses from the **cell body** to **effector cells**.

axon terminal (end of the axon)
cell body
axon
effector cells
dendrites
DIRECTION OF IMPULSE

This is a non-myelinated motor neurone — see p. 137 for the structure of a myelinated one.

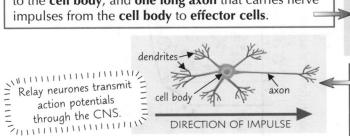

dendrites
cell body
axon
DIRECTION OF IMPULSE

Relay neurones transmit action potentials through the CNS.

Relay neurones have **many short dendrites** that carry nerve impulses from **sensory neurones** to the **cell body**, and **one axon** that carries nerve impulses from the **cell body** to **motor neurones**.

Neurone **Cell Membranes** are **Polarised** at **Rest**

1) In a neurone's **resting state** (when it's not being stimulated), the **outside** of the membrane is **positively charged** compared to the **inside**. This is because there are **more positive ions outside** the cell than inside.

2) So the membrane is **polarised** — there's a **difference in charge**. The voltage across the membrane when it's at rest is called the **resting potential** — it's about **–70 mV**.

3) The resting potential is created and maintained by **sodium-potassium pumps** and **potassium ion channels** in a neurone's membrane:

4) The sodium-potassium pumps move **sodium ions out** of the neurone, but the membrane **isn't permeable** to **sodium ions**, so they **can't diffuse back in**. This creates a **sodium ion electrochemical gradient** (a **concentration gradient** of **ions**) because there are **more** positive sodium ions **outside** the cell than inside.

5) The sodium-potassium pumps also move **potassium ions in** to the neurone, but the membrane **is permeable** to **potassium ions** so they **diffuse back out** through potassium ion channels.

6) This makes the **outside** of the cell **positively charged** compared to the inside.

Sodium-potassium pump — These pumps use active transport to move three sodium ions (Na^+) out of the neurone for every two potassium ions (K^+) moved in. ATP is needed to do this.

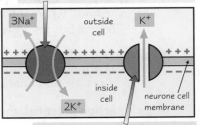

$3Na^+$
outside cell
K^+
inside cell
$2K^+$
neurone cell membrane

Potassium ion channel — These channels allow facilitated diffusion of potassium ions (K^+) out of the neurone, down their concentration gradient.

Warm-Up Questions

Q1 Describe the structures of sensory, motor and relay neurones.
Q2 Describe how resting potential is maintained in a neurone.

PRACTICE QUESTIONS

Exam Question

Q1 Sensory neurones play a key role in the function of Pacinian corpuscles.
a) Explain why Pacinian corpuscles can be described as transducers. [1 mark]
b) Explain how a generator potential is created when a Pacinian corpuscle is stimulated. [4 marks]
c) Describe the pathway of communication from a Pacinian corpuscle to effector cells via the CNS if the generator potential reaches the threshold level. [2 marks]

Sunday afternoons — all resting potential and no action potential...

Blimey, there's a lot on these pages. All the stuff about sensory receptors and resting potentials can be a bit tricky to get your head around. Just take your time and try scribbling it all down a few times till it starts to make some kind of sense.

Action Potentials

Electrical impulses, nerve impulses, action potentials... call them what you will, you need to know how they work.

Neurone **Cell Membranes** Become **Depolarised** when They're **Stimulated**

A **stimulus** triggers **sodium ion channels** in the cell membrane to **open**. If the stimulus is big enough, it'll trigger a **rapid change** in **potential difference**. The sequence of events that happen are known as an **action potential**:

① **Stimulus** — this **excites** the neurone cell membrane, causing **sodium ion channels** to **open**. The membrane becomes **more permeable** to sodium, so **sodium ions diffuse into** the neurone down the sodium ion electrochemical gradient. This makes the **inside** of the neurone **less negative**.

② **Depolarisation** — if the potential difference reaches the **threshold** (around −55 mV), **voltage-gated sodium ion channels open**. **More sodium ions diffuse into** the neurone. This is **positive** feedback (see p. 133).

> Voltage-gated ion channels open at a certain voltage.

③ **Repolarisation** — at a potential difference of around +30 mV the **sodium ion channels close** and **voltage-gated potassium ion channels open**. The membrane is **more permeable** to potassium so **potassium ions diffuse out** of the neurone down the potassium ion concentration gradient. This starts to get the membrane **back** to its **resting potential**. This is **negative** feedback (see p. 133).

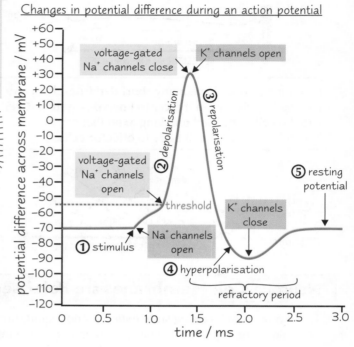

Changes in potential difference during an action potential

④ **Hyperpolarisation** — **potassium ion channels** are **slow to close** so there's a slight **'overshoot'** where too many potassium ions diffuse out of the neurone. The potential difference becomes **more negative** than the **resting potential** (i.e. less than −70 mV).

⑤ **Resting potential** — the ion channels are **reset**. The **sodium-potassium pump** returns the membrane to its **resting potential** and maintains it until the membrane's excited by another stimulus.

After an **action potential**, the neurone cell membrane **can't** be **excited** again straight away. This is because the ion channels are **recovering** and they **can't** be made to **open** — sodium ion channels are **closed** during repolarisation and **potassium ion channels** are **closed** during hyperpolarisation. This period of recovery is called the **refractory period**.

The **Action Potential** Moves **Along** the **Neurone** as a **Wave** of **Depolarisation**

1) When an **action potential** happens, some of the **sodium ions** that enter the neurone **diffuse sideways**.

2) This causes **sodium ion channels** in the **next region** of the neurone to **open** and **sodium ions diffuse into** that part.

3) This causes a **wave of depolarisation** to travel along the neurone.

4) The **wave** moves **away** from the parts of the membrane in the **refractory period** because these parts **can't fire** an action potential.

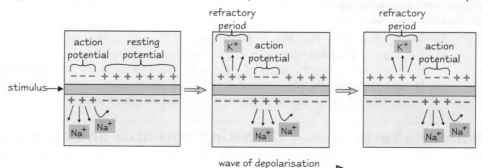

Action Potentials

A **Bigger Stimulus** Causes **More Frequent Impulses**

1) Once the threshold is reached, an action potential will **always fire** with the **same change in voltage**, no matter how big the stimulus is.

2) If the **threshold isn't reached**, an action potential **won't fire**. This is the **all-or-nothing** nature of action potentials.

3) A **bigger stimulus** won't cause a bigger action potential, but it will cause them to fire **more frequently** (so if the brain receives a **high frequency** of action potentials, it interprets this as a **big stimulus** and **responds** accordingly).

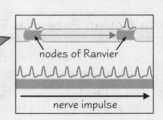

small stimulus

big stimulus

Action Potentials Go Faster in Myelinated Neurones

1) Some neurones are myelinated — they have a **myelin sheath**.

2) The myelin sheath is an **electrical insulator**.

3) In the peripheral nervous system (see p. 158), the myelin sheath is made of a type of cell called a **Schwann cell**.

4) Between the Schwann cells are tiny patches of **bare membrane** called the **nodes of Ranvier**. **Sodium ion channels** are **concentrated** at the nodes.

5) In a **myelinated** neurone, **depolarisation** only happens at the **nodes of Ranvier** (where sodium ions can get through the membrane).

6) The neurone's **cytoplasm conducts** enough electrical charge to **depolarise** the **next node**, so the impulse 'jumps' from node to node.

7) This is called **saltatory conduction** and it's **really fast**.

8) In a **non-myelinated** neurone, the impulse travels as a **wave** along the **whole length** of the **axon membrane**.

9) This is **slower** than saltatory conduction (although it's still pretty quick).

Structure of a myelinated motor neurone

myelin sheath made up of a Schwann cell

node of Ranvier

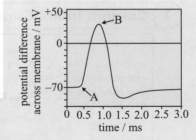

nodes of Ranvier

nerve impulse

Warm-Up Questions

Q1 Briefly describe how an action potential moves along a non-myelinated neurone.

Q2 What are nodes of Ranvier?

PRACTICE QUESTIONS

Exam Questions

Q1 The graph shows an action potential across an axon membrane following the application of a stimulus.

a) Explain what causes the change in potential difference between point A and point B. **[2 marks]**

b) The same stimulus was applied consistently for over one hour. The next action potential fired at 4.5 ms. Calculate how many action potentials fired in one hour. Give your answer in standard form. **[2 marks]**

c) The strength of the stimulus was increased by 50%. Give the maximum potential difference across the membrane that would be experienced with this stronger stimulus. **[1 mark]**

Q2 Multiple sclerosis is a disease of the nervous system characterised by damage to the myelin sheaths of neurones. Explain how this will affect the transmission of action potentials. **[3 marks]**

I'm feeling a bit depolarised after all that...

Action potentials are potentially confusing. Just remember that polarisation is the difference in charge across the cell's membrane — during depolarisation that difference becomes smaller and during repolarisation it gets bigger again.

Synapses

When an action potential arrives at the end of a neurone the information has to be passed on to the next cell — this could be another neurone, a muscle cell or a gland cell.

A **Synapse** is a **Junction** Between a **Neurone** and the **Next Cell**

1) A **synapse** is the junction between a **neurone** and another **neurone**, or between a **neurone** and an **effector cell**, e.g. a muscle or gland cell.

2) The **tiny gap** between the cells at a synapse is called the **synaptic cleft**.

3) The **presynaptic neurone** (the one before the synapse) has a **swelling** called a **synaptic knob**. This contains **synaptic vesicles** filled with **chemicals** called **neurotransmitters**.

4) When an **action potential** reaches the end of a neurone it causes **neurotransmitters** to be **released** into the synaptic cleft. They **diffuse across** to the **postsynaptic membrane** (the one after the synapse) and **bind** to **specific receptors**.

5) When neurotransmitters bind to receptors they might **trigger** an **action potential** (in a neurone), cause **muscle contraction** (in a muscle cell), or cause a **hormone** to be **secreted** (from a gland cell).

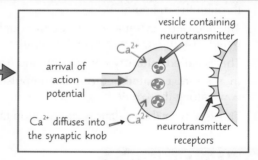

Typical structure of a synapse

6) Neurotransmitters are **removed** from the **cleft** so the **response** doesn't keep happening, e.g. they're taken back into the **presynaptic neurone** or they're **broken down** by **enzymes** (and the products are taken into the neurone).

7) There are many **different** neurotransmitters, e.g. **acetylcholine (ACh)** and **noradrenaline**. Synapses that use acetylcholine are called **cholinergic synapses**. Their structure is exactly the **same** as in the diagram above. They bind to receptors called **cholinergic receptors**, and they're broken down by an enzyme called **acetylcholinesterase (AChE)**.

Here's How **Neurotransmitters Transmit Nerve Impulses Between Neurones**

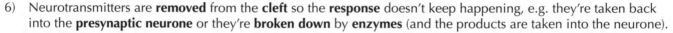

(1) An **Action Potential** Triggers **Calcium Influx**

1) An action potential (see p. 136) arrives at the **synaptic knob** of the **presynaptic neurone**.

2) The action potential stimulates **voltage-gated calcium ion channels** in the **presynaptic neurone** to open.

3) **Calcium ions diffuse into** the synaptic knob. (They're pumped out afterwards by active transport.)

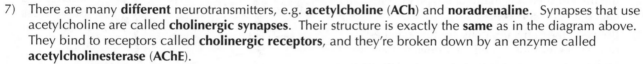

(2) **Calcium Influx** Causes **Neurotransmitter Release**

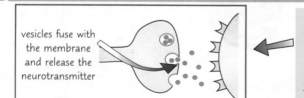

1) The influx of **calcium ions** into the synaptic knob causes the **synaptic vesicles** to **move** to the **presynaptic membrane**. They then **fuse** with the presynaptic membrane.

2) The **vesicles release** the neurotransmitter into the **synaptic cleft** by **exocytosis**.

(3) The **Neurotransmitter Triggers** an **Action Potential** in the **Postsynaptic Neurone**

1) The neurotransmitter **diffuses** across the **synaptic cleft** and **binds** to specific **receptors** on the **postsynaptic membrane**.

2) This causes **sodium ion channels** in the **postsynaptic neurone** to **open**. The **influx** of **sodium ions** into the postsynaptic membrane causes **depolarisation**. An **action potential** on the **postsynaptic membrane** is generated if the **threshold** is reached.

3) The **neurotransmitter** is **removed** from the **synaptic cleft** so the **response** doesn't keep happening.

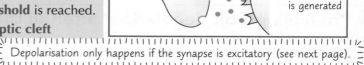

Depolarisation only happens if the synapse is excitatory (see next page).

Synapses

Synapses Play **Vital Roles** in the **Nervous System**

Synapses can be **Excitatory** or **Inhibitory**

1) At an **excitatory** synapse, neurotransmitters **depolarise** the postsynaptic membrane, making it fire an **action potential** if the threshold is reached (see previous page).

2) At an **inhibitory** synapse, when neurotransmitters bind to receptors on the postsynaptic membrane, they **hyperpolarise** the membrane (make the potential difference more negative), **preventing** an action potential from being fired.

Impulses diverge

Impulses converge

Synapses allow **Information** to be **Dispersed** or **Amplified**

1) When one neurone connects to many neurones information can be dispersed to different parts of the body. This is called synaptic divergence.

2) When many neurones connect to one neurone information can be amplified (made stronger). This is called synaptic convergence.

Summation at **Synapses Finely Tunes** the **Nervous Response**

If a stimulus is **weak**, only a **small amount** of **neurotransmitter** will be released from a neurone into the synaptic cleft. This might not be enough to **excite** the postsynaptic membrane to the **threshold** level and stimulate an action potential. **Summation** is where the effect of neurotransmitters can be **combined**. There are two types:

Spatial summation

1) When neurones converge (see above), the small amount of **neurotransmitter** released from **each** neurone can be enough **altogether** to **reach** the **threshold** in the postsynaptic neurone and **trigger an action potential**.

2) If some neurones release an **inhibitory neurotransmitter** then the total effect of all the neurotransmitters might be **no action potential**.

3) Stimuli might arrive from **different sources**. Spatial summation allows signals from **multiple stimuli** to be **coordinated** into a **single response**.

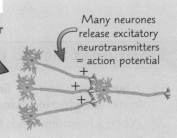

Many neurones release excitatory neurotransmitters = action potential

Temporal summation

Temporal summation is where **two or more** nerve impulses arrive in **quick succession** from the **same presynaptic neurone**. This makes an action potential **more likely** because **more neurotransmitter** is released into the **synaptic cleft**.

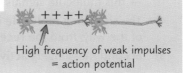

High frequency of weak impulses = action potential

Both types of **summation** mean synapses **accurately process information**, **finely tuning** the response.

Synapses Make Sure **Impulses** are **Transmitted One Way**

Receptors for neurotransmitters are **only** on the **postsynaptic** membranes, so synapses make sure **impulses** can only travel in **one direction**.

Warm-Up Questions

Q1 Give one way that neurotransmitters are removed from the synaptic cleft.

Q2 What neurotransmitter do you find at cholinergic synapses?

Exam Question

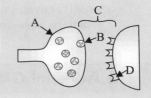

Q1 The diagram on the right shows a synapse. Describe the event that happens at each labelled point following the arrival of an action potential. [4 marks]

Synaptic knobs and clefts — will you stop giggling at the back...

Some more pretty tough pages here — lovely. And lots more diagrams to have a go at drawing and re-drawing. Don't worry if you're not the world's best artist, just make sure you add labels to your drawings to explain what's happening.

The Hormonal System and Glands

Now you've seen how the nervous system helps us respond to our environment, it's on to the hormonal system...

The **Hormonal System** Sends Information as **Chemical Signals**

1) The **hormonal system** is made up of **glands** (called **endocrine glands**) and **hormones**:
   - **Endocrine glands** are groups of cells that are specialised to **secrete hormones**. E.g. the **pancreas** secretes **insulin**.

   The hormonal system is also called the endocrine system.

   - **Hormones** are 'chemical messengers'. Many hormones are **proteins** or **peptides**, e.g. **insulin**. Some hormones are **steroids**, e.g. **progesterone**.
2) **Hormones** are **secreted** when an **endocrine gland** is **stimulated**:
   - Glands can be **stimulated** by a **change** in **concentration** of a specific **substance** (sometimes **another hormone**).
   - They can also be **stimulated** by **electrical impulses**.
3) Hormones **diffuse directly into** the **blood**, then they're **taken** around the body by the **circulatory system**.
4) They **diffuse out** of the blood **all over** the **body** but each hormone will only **bind** to **specific receptors** for that hormone, found on the membranes of some cells, called **target cells**. Tissue that contains target cells is called **target tissue**.
5) The hormones trigger a **response** in the **target cells** (the **effectors**).

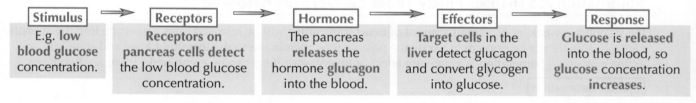

Stimulus	**Receptors**	**Hormone**	**Effectors**	**Response**
E.g. **low blood glucose** concentration.	**Receptors on pancreas cells detect** the low blood glucose concentration.	The pancreas **releases** the hormone **glucagon** into the blood.	**Target cells** in the **liver** detect glucagon and convert glycogen into glucose.	**Glucose is released** into the blood, so **glucose** concentration **increases**.

Hormones Bind to **Receptors** and **Trigger Second Messengers**

1) A **hormone** is called a **first messenger** because it carries the chemical message the **first part** of the way, from the **endocrine gland** to the **receptor** on the **target cells**.
2) When a hormone **binds** to its receptor it **activates** an **enzyme** in the **cell membrane**.
3) The enzyme catalyses the **production** of a **molecule** inside the cell called a **signalling molecule** — this molecule **signals** to **other parts** of the cell to **change** how the cell **works**.
4) The **signalling molecule** is called a **second messenger** because it carries the chemical message the **second part** of the way, from the **receptor** to **other parts** of the **cell**.
5) Second messengers **activate** a **cascade** (a chain of reactions) **inside** the cell. Here's an **example** you need to **learn**:

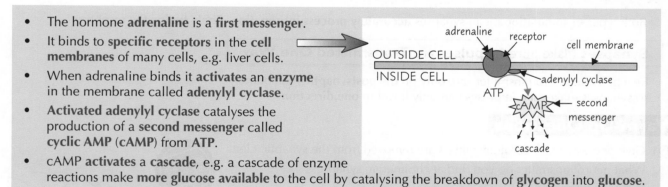

- The hormone **adrenaline** is a **first messenger**.
- It binds to **specific receptors** in the **cell membranes** of many cells, e.g. liver cells.
- When adrenaline binds it **activates an enzyme** in the membrane called **adenylyl cyclase**.
- **Activated adenylyl cyclase** catalyses the production of a **second messenger** called **cyclic AMP (cAMP)** from **ATP**.
- cAMP **activates** a **cascade**, e.g. a cascade of enzyme reactions make **more glucose available** to the cell by catalysing the breakdown of **glycogen** into **glucose**.

The **Adrenal Glands** Secrete **Hormones**

1) The **adrenal glands** are **endocrine glands** that are found just **above** your **kidneys**.
2) Each adrenal gland has an **outer** part called the **cortex** and an **inner** part called the **medulla**.
3) The cortex and the medulla have **different functions** and produce different responses.

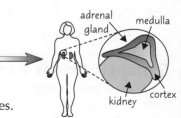

Module 5: Section 1 — Communication and Homeostasis

The Hormonal System and Glands

The **Cortex** and the **Medulla** are Involved in the **Response** to **Stress**

The cortex secretes steroid hormones, e.g. it secretes cortisol and aldosterone when you're stressed. These hormones have a role in both the short-term and the long-term responses to stress. Their effects include:

- stimulating the breakdown of proteins and fats into glucose. This increases the amount of energy available so the brain and muscles can respond to the situation.
- increasing blood volume and pressure by increasing the uptake of sodium ions and water by the kidneys.
- suppressing the immune system.

The medulla secretes catecholamine hormones (modified amino acids), e.g. it secretes adrenaline and noradrenaline when you're stressed. These act to make more energy available in the short-term by:

- increasing heart and breathing rate.
- causing cells to break down glycogen into glucose.
- constricting some blood vessels so that blood is diverted to the brain and muscles.

These effects help to prepare the body for the **'fight or flight'** response (see pages 160-161).

The **Pancreas** has a role as an **Endocrine Gland**

The pancreas is a gland that's found **below** the **stomach**. You need to know about its **endocrine** function:

1) The areas of the pancreas that contain **endocrine tissue** are called the **islets of Langerhans**.
2) They're found in clusters around **blood capillaries**.
3) The islets of Langerhans **secrete hormones** directly into the **blood**.
4) They're made up of **two types** of cell:
   - Alpha (α) **cells** secrete a **hormone** called **glucagon**.
   - Beta (β) **cells** secrete a **hormone** called **insulin**.
5) **Glucagon** and **insulin** help to **control blood glucose concentration** (see p. 144).

PRACTICAL SKILLS

Here's what you might see if you looked at a stained section of **pancreatic tissue** under a **light microscope**:

The purple stained cells are the β cells.

If you look closely you can see pink stained cells — these are α cells.

CNRI/SCIENCE PHOTO LIBRARY

The islets of Langerhans (endocrine tissue) appear as paler patches in amongst all the other cells.

You can only differentiate between α and β cells if a special stain has been used to make them different colours, e.g. chrome haematoxylin and phloxine.

stomach

duodenum

pancreatic duct

blood vessels

pancreas

secretory vesicle containing insulin

mitochondrion

blood capillary

β cell membrane

nucleus

rough endoplasmic reticulum

β cell

α cell

PRACTICE QUESTIONS

Warm-Up Questions

Q1 Name the two hormones secreted by the islets of Langerhans.

Q2 How would you identify endocrine tissue if you examined stained pancreatic tissue under a light microscope?

Exam Questions

Q1 Describe the role of the adrenal gland cortex in the long-term response to stress. [3 marks]

Q2 One physiological effect of the 'fight or flight' response is an increase in the conversion of glycogen to glucose. Explain how stimulation of the adrenal gland's medulla causes this effect. [3 marks]

Islets of Langerhans — sounds like an sxotic beach to me...

All this talk of the "islets of Langerhans" and I can think of nothing else but sun, sea and sand... but it's secretions, second messengers and cyclic AMP for you, until your exams are over and you can start planning any holidays.

Homeostasis — Control of Body Temperature

Homeostasis is responsible for controlling body temperature in mammals like you — stopping you freezing or becoming a hot sweaty mess. Other organisms control their body temperature differently. Read on, oh chosen one, read on...

Temperature is Controlled Differently in Ectotherms and Endotherms

Animals are classed as either **ectotherms** or **endotherms**, depending on how they **control** their body temperature:

Ectotherms — e.g. reptiles, fish	Endotherms — e.g. mammals, birds
Ectotherms **can't control** their body temperature **internally** — they **control** their temperature by **changing** their **behaviour** (e.g. reptiles gain heat by basking in the sun).	Endotherms **control** their body temperature **internally** by homeostasis. They can also control their temperature by **behaviour** (e.g. by finding shade).
Their **internal** temperature **depends** on the **external temperature** (their surroundings).	Their internal temperature is **less affected** by the **external temperature** (within certain limits).
Their **activity** level **depends** on the external temperature — they're **more** active at **higher** temperatures and **less** active at **lower** temperatures.	Their **activity** level is largely **independent** of the **external temperature** — they can be active at any temperature (within certain limits).
They have a **variable metabolic rate** and they **generate** very **little heat** themselves.	They have a constantly **high metabolic rate** and they **generate** a **lot** of **heat** from metabolic reactions.

Mammals have Many Mechanisms to Change Body Temperature

Mechanisms to REDUCE body temperature:

Sweating — **more sweat** is secreted from **sweat glands** when the body's too hot. The water in sweat **evaporates** from the surface of the skin and **takes heat** from the body. The **skin is cooled**.

Hairs lie flat — mammals have a layer of **hair** that provides **insulation** by **trapping air** (air is a poor conductor of heat). When it's hot, **erector pili muscles relax** so the hairs lie flat. **Less air** is trapped, so the skin is **less insulated** and **heat** can be **lost** more easily.

Vasodilation — when it's hot, **arterioles** near the surface of the skin **dilate** (this is called **vasodilation**). **More blood** flows through the **capillaries** in the surface layers of the dermis. This means **more heat** is **lost** from the skin by **radiation** and the **temperature** is **lowered**.

Mechanisms to INCREASE body temperature:

Shivering — when it's cold, **muscles contract** in **spasms**. This makes the body **shiver** and **more heat** is **produced** from **increased respiration**.

Much less sweat — less sweat is secreted from sweat glands when it's cold, reducing the amount of heat loss.

Hairs stand up — erector pili muscles contract when it's cold, which makes the hairs stand up. This traps more air and so prevents heat loss.

Hormones — the body releases adrenaline and thyroxine. These increase metabolism and so more heat is produced.

Vasoconstriction — when it's cold, arterioles near the surface of the skin constrict (this is called vasoconstriction) so less blood flows through the capillaries in the surface layers of the dermis. This reduces heat loss.

epidermis — hair — sweat gland — DERMIS — erector pili muscle — capillary — arteriole

Homeostasis — Control of Body Temperature

The **Hypothalamus Controls** Body Temperature in **Mammals**

1) **Body temperature** in mammals is **maintained** at a **constant level** by a part of the **brain** called the **hypothalamus**.

2) The hypothalamus **receives information** about **temperature** from **thermoreceptors** (temperature receptors):
   - Thermoreceptors in the **hypothalamus** detect **internal temperature** (the temperature of the blood).
   - Thermoreceptors in the **skin** (called **peripheral temperature receptors**) detect **external temperature** (the temperature of the skin).

3) Thermoreceptors send **impulses** along **sensory neurones** to the **hypothalamus**, which sends **impulses** along **motor neurones** to **effectors** (e.g. **skeletal muscles**, or **sweat glands** and **erector pili muscles** in the **skin**).

4) The effectors respond to **restore** the body temperature **back to normal**.
   Here's how it all works:

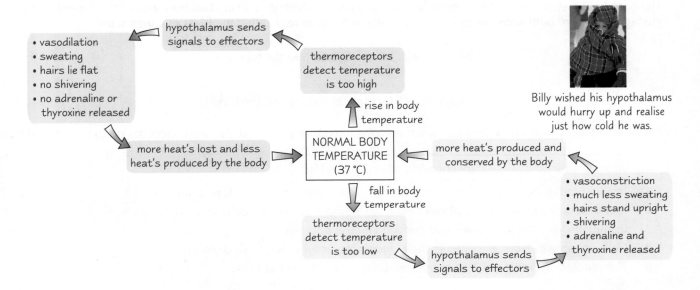

- vasodilation
- sweating
- hairs lie flat
- no shivering
- no adrenaline or thyroxine released

hypothalamus sends signals to effectors

thermoreceptors detect temperature is too high

rise in body temperature

more heat's lost and less heat's produced by the body

NORMAL BODY TEMPERATURE (37 °C)

fall in body temperature

thermoreceptors detect temperature is too low

hypothalamus sends signals to effectors

more heat's produced and conserved by the body

- vasoconstriction
- much less sweating
- hairs stand upright
- shivering
- adrenaline and thyroxine released

Billy wished his hypothalamus would hurry up and realise just how cold he was.

Warm-Up Questions

Q1 Give four differences between ectotherms and endotherms.

Q2 Which type of animal has more control over their body temperature, ectotherms or endotherms?

Q3 How does sweating reduce body temperature?

Q4 How does vasodilation help the body to lose heat?

Q5 Which part of the brain is responsible for maintaining a constant body temperature in mammals?

PRACTICE QUESTIONS

Exam Questions

Q1 Describe and explain how the body detects a high external temperature. [2 marks]

Q2 Snakes are usually found in warm climates. Suggest why they are not usually found in cold climates. Explain your answer. [3 marks]

Q3 Mammals that live in cold climates have thick fur and layers of fat beneath their skin to keep them warm. Describe and explain two other ways they maintain a constant body temperature in cold conditions. [4 marks]

No need to sweat about this page...

The mechanisms that change body temperature are pretty good and can cope with some extreme temperatures, but I reckon I could think up some slightly less embarrassing ways of doing it, instead of getting all red-faced and stinky. Mind you, it seems like ectotherms have got it sussed with their whole sunbathing thing — now that's definitely the life...

Homeostasis — Control of Blood Glucose

These pages are all about how homeostasis helps you to not go totally hyper when you stuff your face with sweets.

Eating and Exercise Change the Concentration of Glucose in your Blood

1) **All cells** need a constant **energy supply** to work — so **blood glucose concentration** must be carefully **controlled**.

2) The **concentration** of **glucose** in the blood is **normally** around **90 mg per 100 cm³** of blood. It's **monitored** by cells in the **pancreas**.

3) Blood glucose concentration **rises** after **eating food** containing **carbohydrate**.

4) Blood glucose concentration **falls** after **exercise**, as **more glucose** is used in **respiration** to **release energy**.

Insulin and Glucagon Control Blood Glucose Concentration

The hormonal system (see p. 140) **controls** blood glucose concentration using **two hormones** called **insulin** and **glucagon**. They're both **secreted** by clusters of cells in the **pancreas** called the **islets of Langerhans**:

> **Beta (β) cells** secrete **insulin** into the blood.

> **Alpha (α) cells** secrete **glucagon** into the blood.

Insulin and glucagon act on **effectors**, which respond to **restore** the blood glucose concentration to the **normal level**:

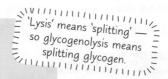
Liver cells are also called hepatocytes.

Insulin lowers blood glucose concentration when it's too high

1) Insulin binds to **specific receptors** on the cell membranes of **liver cells** and **muscle cells**.

2) It **increases** the **permeability** of cell membranes to glucose, so the cells **take up more glucose**.

3) Insulin also **activates enzymes** that convert **glucose** into **glycogen**.

4) Cells are able to **store glycogen** in their cytoplasm, as an **energy source**.

5) The process of **forming glycogen** from glucose is called **glycogenesis**.

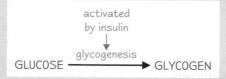

GLUCOSE $\xrightarrow[\text{glycogenesis}]{}$ GLYCOGEN

activated by insulin

'Genesis' means 'making' — so glycogenesis means making glycogen.

6) Insulin also **increases** the **rate** of **respiration** of glucose, especially in muscle cells.

Glucagon raises blood glucose concentration when it's too low

'Lysis' means 'splitting' — so glycogenolysis means splitting glycogen.

1) Glucagon binds to **specific receptors** on the cell membranes of **liver cells**.

2) Glucagon **activates enzymes** that **break down glycogen** into **glucose**.

3) The process of **breaking down glycogen** is called **glycogenolysis**.

4) Glucagon also promotes the formation of glucose from **glycerol** and **amino acids**.

5) The process of **forming glucose** from **non-carbohydrates** is called **gluconeogenesis**.

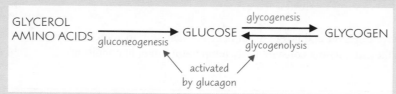

GLYCEROL AMINO ACIDS $\xrightarrow[\text{gluconeogenesis}]{}$ GLUCOSE $\underset{\text{glycogenolysis}}{\overset{\text{glycogenesis}}{\rightleftarrows}}$ GLYCOGEN

activated by glucagon

6) Glucagon **decreases** the **rate** of **respiration** of glucose in cells.

Melvin had finally mastered the ancient "chair-lysis" move.

Homeostasis — Control of Blood Glucose

Negative Feedback Mechanisms Keep Blood Glucose Concentration **Normal**

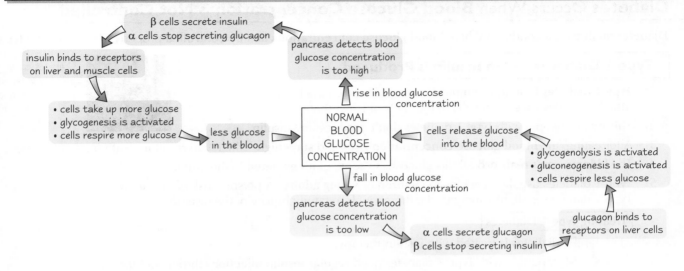

Beta (β) Cells Secrete **Insulin** when they're **Depolarised**

β cells **contain insulin** stored in **vesicles**. β cells **secrete insulin** when they **detect high blood glucose concentration**. Here's how it happens:

1) When blood glucose concentration is **high**, **more glucose enters** the β cells by **facilitated diffusion**.

2) **More glucose** in a β cell causes the rate of **respiration** to **increase**, making **more ATP**.

3) The **rise** in **ATP** triggers the **potassium ion channels** in the β cell plasma membrane to **close**.

4) This means **potassium ions** (K⁺) **can't** get through the membrane — so they **build up inside** the cell.

5) This makes the **inside** of the β cell **less negative** because there are **more positively-charged** potassium ions **inside** the cell — so the plasma membrane of the β cell is **depolarised**.

6) Depolarisation triggers **calcium ion channels** in the membrane to **open**, so **calcium ions diffuse into** the β cell.

7) This causes the **vesicles** to **fuse** with the **β cell plasma membrane**, **releasing insulin** (by **exocytosis**).

Warm-Up Questions

Q1 Why does your blood glucose concentration fall after exercise?

Q2 What's the process of breaking down glycogen into glucose called?

Q3 Give two effects of glucagon on liver cells.

Exam Questions

Q1 The pancreas secretes hormones that control blood glucose concentration.
   a) What type of feedback mechanism is involved in the control of blood glucose concentration? Explain your answer. [1 mark]
   b) Explain the role of insulin in this feedback mechanism. [4 marks]

Q2 Suggest the effect on a ß cell of respiration being inhibited. [2 marks]

My alpha cells detect low glucose — urgent tea and biscuit break needed...

Aaaaargh there are so many stupidly complex names to learn and they all look bnd sound exactly the same to me. You can't even get away with sneakily misspelling them all in your exam — like writing 'glycusogen' or 'gluconesisolysis'. Nope, examiners have been around for centuries, so I'm afraid old tricks like that just won't work on them. Grrrrrrr.

Diabetes

Homeostasis really tries its best to keep everything under control. Unfortunately nothing's perfect...

Diabetes Occurs When **Blood Glucose Concentration** is **Not Controlled**

Diabetes mellitus is a condition where **blood glucose concentration** can't be **controlled** properly. There are two types:

Type 1 Diabetes — **No Insulin** is **Produced**

1) **Type 1 diabetes** is an **auto-immune** disease, in which the body **attacks** and **destroys** the β **cells** in the islets of Langerhans.

2) This means people with Type 1 diabetes **don't produce** any **insulin**.

3) After eating, the **blood glucose concentration rises** and **stays high**, which can result in death if left untreated.

4) The **kidneys can't reabsorb** all this glucose, so some of it's **excreted** in the urine.

5) Type 1 diabetes usually develops in **children** or **young adults**. A person's risk of developing Type 1 diabetes is slightly increased if there's a close family history of the disease.

Diabetes is not a joking matter so here's a picture of a pumpkin on its birthday.

Treating Type 1 Diabetes

1) Type 1 diabetes is treated with insulin therapy:
   - Most people with Type 1 diabetes need regular insulin injections throughout the day.
   - Some people use an insulin pump — this is a machine that continuously delivers insulin into the body via a tube inserted beneath the skin.

2) Some people have been successfully treated by having islet cell transplantation — they receive healthy islet cells from a donor so their pancreas can produce some insulin (although they usually still need some additional insulin therapy).

3) Whatever type of treatment they have, people with Type 1 diabetes need to regularly monitor their blood glucose concentration and think carefully about:
   - Diet — Eating a healthy, balanced diet reduces the amount of insulin that needs to be injected. People with Type 1 diabetes often have a carefully planned diet so that they can manage the amount of glucose they are taking in.
   - Activity — Doing regular exercise reduces the amount of insulin that needs to be injected by using up blood glucose.

Type 2 Diabetes — **Linked** to **Obesity**

1) **Type 2 diabetes** occurs when the β **cells** don't produce **enough insulin** or when the **body's cells** don't **respond properly** to insulin.

2) Cells don't respond properly because the **insulin receptors** on their membranes don't work properly, so the cells don't take up enough glucose.

3) This means the **blood glucose concentration** is **higher** than normal.

4) Type 2 diabetes is usually acquired **later in life** than Type 1, and it's often linked with **obesity**. The risk of developing Type 2 diabetes is also increased in people from certain ethnic groups, e.g. African or Asian, and in people with a close family history of the disease.

Treating Type 2 Diabetes

1) Type 2 diabetes is **initially** managed through **lifestyle** changes. Eating a **healthy, balanced diet**, getting **regular exercise** and **losing weight** if needed can help **prevent** the **onset** of Type 2 diabetes as well as **control** the **effects**.

2) If blood glucose concentration can't be controlled through lifestyle changes alone, then **medication** may be prescribed. Some examples are:
   - **Metformin** — This is usually the first medicine to be prescribed. Metformin acts on **liver cells** to **reduce** the **amount of glucose** that they **release** into the blood. It also acts to **increase** the **sensitivity** of cells to **insulin** so **more glucose** can be **taken up** with the same amount of insulin.
   - **Sulfonylureas** (e.g. gliclazide) — These stimulate the pancreas to **produce more insulin**.
   - **Thiazolidinediones** (e.g. pioglitazone) — These also make the body cells **more sensitive** to **insulin**.

3) In some people with Type 2 diabetes, these types of medication are **not enough** to control blood glucose concentration so **insulin therapy** is used in addition or instead.

Diabetes

Insulin can be Produced by Genetically Modified Bacteria

1) Insulin **used** to be **extracted** from **animal pancreases** (e.g. **pigs** and **cattle**), to treat people with **Type 1** diabetes.
2) But **nowadays**, **human insulin** can be made by **genetically modified** (**GM**) **bacteria** (see p. 232).
3) Using **GM bacteria** to produce insulin is **much better** for many reasons, for example:

- **Producing** insulin using GM bacteria is **cheaper** than extracting it from animal pancreases.
- **Larger quantities** of insulin can be produced using GM bacteria.
- GM bacteria make **human insulin**. This is **more effective** than using **pig** or **cattle insulin** (which is slightly different to human insulin) and it's **less likely** to trigger an **allergic response** or be **rejected** by the **immune system**.
- Some people **prefer** insulin from **GM bacteria** for **ethical** or **religious** reasons. E.g. some **vegetarians** may **object** to the **use** of **animals**, and some **religious people object** to using insulin from **pigs**.

Stem Cells Could be Used to Cure Diabetes

1) Stem cells are **unspecialised cells** — they have the **ability** to **develop** into **any type** of cell.
2) Using stem cells could **potentially cure** diabetes — here's how:

Look back at page 64 if you need to remind yourself about stem cells.

- **Stem cells** could be **grown** into β **cells**.
- The β cells would then be **implanted** into the **pancreas** of a person with **Type 1 diabetes**.
- This means the person would be able to **make insulin as normal**.
- This treatment is **still being developed**. But if it's effective, it'll **cure** people with Type 1 diabetes.

Warm-Up Questions

Q1 What is diabetes?
Q2 What is the cause of Type 1 diabetes?
Q3 Briefly describe how stem cells could be used to cure diabetes.

PRACTICE QUESTIONS

Exam Questions

Q1 Give two advantages of using insulin produced by genetically modified (GM) bacteria over using insulin extracted from animal pancreases. [2 marks]

Q2 A glucose tolerance test can indicate the presence of diabetes. After fasting for 12 hours, a drink containing glucose is consumed. The graph on the right shows how the blood glucose concentration of two people changed in the time after having the drink. Person A has Type 2 diabetes, person B does not have diabetes.

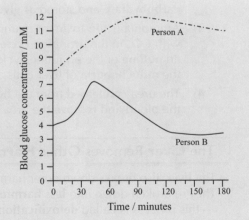

a) Give two pieces of evidence from the graph that suggest person A has diabetes. [1 mark]
b) Person A produces insulin but can't control their blood glucose concentration. Explain why. [2 marks]
c) i) Calculate the rate at which person B's blood glucose concentration is decreasing between 50 and 120 minutes. [1 mark]
   ii) Explain why person A's blood glucose does not decrease at the same rate as person B's. [1 mark]
d) After the test person A started taking Metformin regularly. Explain how this would affect their blood glucose concentration if they were to do the glucose tolerance test again in the future. [3 marks]

And people used to think the pancreas was just a cushion...(true)

Sometimes the hormonal system goes wrong and causes problems, like diabetes. Luckily advances in medical technology (e.g. GM insulin and stem cells) have helped to treat these problems. A healthy diet and regular exercise help too. Congratulations, you've made it to the end of this gigantic section. Have some tea to celebrate.

The Liver and Excretion

Liver — not just what my friend Ted eats with onions. The liver has lots of functions, but the main one you need to know about is its job in excretion. It's great at breaking things down like excess amino acids and other harmful substances.

Excretion is the Removal of Waste Products from the Body

All the **chemical reactions** that happen in your cells make up your **metabolism**. Metabolism produces **waste products** — substances that **aren't needed** by the cells, such as **carbon dioxide** and **nitrogenous** (nitrogen-containing) **waste**. Many of these products are **toxic**, so if they were allowed to **build up** in the body they would cause **damage**, e.g. by affecting other metabolic reactions. This is where **excretion** comes in. Excretion is the **removal** of the **waste products of metabolism** from the body.

For example, **carbon dioxide** is a waste product of **respiration**. **Too much** in the blood is toxic, so it's removed from the body by the **lungs** (e.g. in mammals) or **gills** (e.g. in fish). The lungs and gills act as **excretory organs**.

Excreting waste products from the body **maintains normal metabolism**. It also **maintains homeostasis** by helping to keep the levels of certain substances in the blood **roughly constant**.

You Need to Know About the Functions of the Liver

The liver has important functions in **excretion** and **energy storage**:

Excess Amino Acids are Broken Down by the Liver

One of the liver's most important roles is getting rid of **excess amino acids** produced by eating and **digesting protein**. **Amino acids** contain **nitrogen** in their **amino groups**. **Nitrogenous substances can't** usually be **stored** by the body. This means **excess** amino acids can be **damaging** to the body, so they must be **used** by the body (e.g. to make proteins) or be **broken down and excreted**. Here's how excess amino acids are **broken down** in the **liver**:

1) First, the nitrogen-containing **amino groups** ($-NH_2$) are **removed** from any **excess** amino acids, forming **ammonia** (NH_3) and **organic acids** — this process is called **deamination**.

2) The organic acids can be **respired** to give **ATP** or converted to **carbohydrate** and stored as **glycogen**.

3) Ammonia is **too toxic** for mammals to excrete directly, so it's **combined** with CO_2 in the **ornithine cycle** to create **urea**. The diagram shows an **outline** of the ornithine cycle — the part in **orange** happens in the **mitochondria** of liver cells and the rest happens in the **cytoplasm**.

4) The urea is **released** from the liver into the **blood**. The **kidneys** then **filter** the blood and **remove** the urea as **urine** (see p. 151-152), which is excreted from the body.

The Liver Removes Other Harmful Substances from the Blood

The **liver** also breaks down other harmful substances, like **alcohol**, **drugs** and **unwanted hormones**. They're broken down into **less harmful compounds** that can then be **excreted** from the body — this process is called **detoxification**. Some of the harmful products broken down by the liver include:

1) **Alcohol (ethanol)** — a **toxic** substance that can **damage** cells. It's **broken down** by the liver into **ethanal**, which is then broken down into a **less harmful** substance called **acetic acid**. **Excess** alcohol over a long period can lead to **cirrhosis** of the liver — this is when the cells of the liver **die** and **scar tissue blocks blood flow**.

2) **Paracetamol** — a common painkiller that's **broken down** by the liver. **Excess** paracetamol in the blood can lead to **liver** and **kidney failure**.

3) **Insulin** — a **hormone** that controls **blood glucose concentration**. Insulin is also broken down by the liver as excess insulin can cause problems with blood sugar levels.

The Liver Stores Glycogen

The body needs **glucose** for **energy**. The liver converts **excess glucose** in the blood to **glycogen** and stores it as granules in its cells until the glucose is needed for energy.

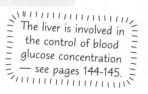
The liver is involved in the control of blood glucose concentration — see pages 144-145.

The Liver and Excretion

You Need to Know the Structure of the Liver

You need to learn all the different **veins**, **arteries** and **ducts** connected to the liver:

1) The **hepatic artery** supplies the liver with **oxygenated blood** from the heart, so the liver has a good supply of **oxygen** for **respiration**, providing plenty of **energy**.

2) The **hepatic vein** takes **deoxygenated blood** away from the liver.

3) The **hepatic portal vein** brings blood from the **duodenum** and **ileum** (parts of the small intestine), so it's rich in the products of **digestion**. This means any ingested harmful substances are **filtered out** and **broken down straight away**.

4) The **bile duct** takes bile (a substance produced by the liver to **emulsify fats**) to the **gall bladder** to be **stored**.

You need to learn about the **structure** of the liver too:

1) The liver is made up of **liver lobules** — **cylindrical** structures made of **cells** called **hepatocytes** that are arranged in rows **radiating** out from the centre.

2) Each lobule has a **central vein** in the middle that connects to the **hepatic vein**. **Many branches** of the **hepatic artery**, **hepatic portal vein** and **bile duct** are also found connected to each lobule (only one of each is shown in the picture).

3) The **hepatic artery** and the **hepatic portal vein** are connected to the **central vein** by **capillaries** called **sinusoids**.

4) Blood runs **through** the sinusoids, past the hepatocytes that **remove harmful substances** and **oxygen** from the blood.

5) The harmful substances are **broken down** by the hepatocytes into **less harmful** substances that then **re-enter** the blood.

6) The blood runs to the **central vein**, and the central veins from all the lobules **connect** up to form the **hepatic vein**.

7) Cells called **Kupffer cells** are also attached to the walls of the sinusoids. They **remove bacteria** and **break down** old **red blood cells**.

8) Hepatocytes produce **bile** and secrete it into tubes called **bile canaliculi**. These tubes drain into the **bile ducts**. The bile ducts from all the lobules eventually **connect up** and leave the liver.

The Liver and Excretion

You Need to be Able to Examine and Draw Sections of Liver Tissue

PRACTICAL SKILLS

1) You need to know what liver tissue looks like under a **light microscope** and be able to **identify** and **draw** the different structures that you see.

2) Before examination, a sample of liver tissue is placed on a **microscope slide**. The sample is **stained** so the cells are **easier to see**.

3) Here's an example of what liver tissue looks like under a light microscope — it shows a section through **one** of the liver's many **lobules**:

Tissue samples to be viewed under a light microscope are commonly stained with haematoxylin and eosin.

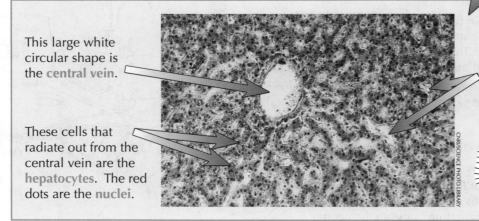

This large white circular shape is the **central vein**.

These cells that radiate out from the central vein are the **hepatocytes**. The red dots are the **nuclei**.

These white spaces are the **sinusoids**.

See the previous page for the functions of all of these structures.

CNRI/SCIENCE PHOTO LIBRARY

Warm-Up Questions

PRACTICE QUESTIONS

Q1 Define excretion.

Q2 Why is excretion needed?

Q3 Briefly describe the liver's role in detoxification.

Q4 Give a function of the liver, other than excretion.

Q5 Which blood vessel brings oxygenated blood to the liver?

Q6 What are liver lobules?

Exam Questions

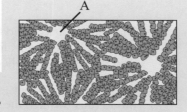

A

Q1 Name the part of the liver labelled A in the diagram on the right. [1 mark]

Q2 Which row in the table below correctly describes the function of each part of the liver?

	Hepatocyte	Kupffer cell	Canaliculus	Sinusoid
A	Removes bacteria and breaks down old red blood cells.	Removes harmful substances and oxygen from the blood.	Drains bile into the bile duct.	Connects the hepatic artery and the hepatic portal vein to the central vein.
B	Removes harmful substances and oxygen from the blood.	Removes bacteria and breaks down old red blood cells.	Drains bile into the bile duct.	Connects the hepatic artery and the hepatic portal vein to the central vein.
C	Drains bile into the bile duct.	Removes bacteria and breaks down old red blood cells.	Removes bacteria and breaks down old red blood cells.	Connects the hepatic artery and the hepatic portal vein to the central vein.
D	Removes harmful substances and oxygen from the blood.	Removes harmful substances and oxygen from the blood.	Connects the hepatic artery and the hepatic portal vein to the central vein.	Drains bile into the bile duct.

[1 mark]

Q3* Explain why the concentration of urea in urine might increase after eating a meal that's rich in protein. [6 marks]

* You will be assessed on the quality of your written response in this question.

Lots of important functions — can't liver without it...

Poor little amino acids, doing no harm then suddenly they're broken down and excreted. As upsetting as it is, however, you need to learn how they're broken down in the liver. It's a heart-wrenching tale of separation — the amino group and the organic acid are torn from each other's life. Right, enough of that nonsense. Learn it and learn it good.

The Kidneys and Excretion

So you've learnt about how the liver does a pretty good job at breaking down stuff for excretion. Now you get to learn that the kidneys like to play a part in this excretion malarkey too...

The **Kidneys** are **Organs** of **Excretion**

One of the main **functions** of the **kidneys** is to **excrete waste products**, e.g. **urea** produced by the **liver**. They also **regulate** the **water potential** of the blood (see p. 154-155). Here's an overview of how they excrete waste products (you need to **learn** the **structure** of the kidneys too):

1) Blood **enters** the kidney through the **renal artery** and then passes through **capillaries** in the **cortex** of the kidneys.

2) As the blood passes through the capillaries, **substances** are **filtered out of the blood** and into **long tubules** that surround the capillaries. This process is called **ultrafiltration** (see below).

3) **Useful substances** (e.g. glucose) are **reabsorbed** back into the blood from the tubules in the **medulla** and **cortex** — this is called **selective reabsorption** (see next page).

4) The remaining **unwanted substances** (e.g. urea) pass along the tubules, then along the **ureter** to the **bladder**, where they're **expelled** as urine.

5) The filtered blood passes out of the kidneys through the **renal vein**.

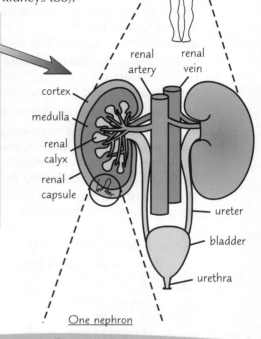

Blood is **Filtered** at the **Start** of the **Nephrons**

The **long tubules** along with the bundle of **capillaries** where the blood is **filtered** are called **nephrons** — there are around **one million** nephrons in each kidney.

1) Blood from the **renal artery** enters smaller **arterioles** in the **cortex**.

2) Each arteriole splits into a structure called a **glomerulus** — a **bundle** of **capillaries** looped inside a hollow ball called the **Bowman's capsule**.

3) This is where **ultrafiltration** takes place.

4) The **arteriole** that takes blood **into** each glomerulus is called the **afferent** arteriole, and the arteriole that takes the filtered blood **away** from the glomerulus is called the **efferent** arteriole.

5) The **efferent** arteriole is **smaller** in **diameter** than the afferent arteriole, so the blood in the glomerulus is under **high pressure**.

6) The high pressure **forces liquid** and **small molecules** in the blood **out** of the **capillary** and **into** the **Bowman's capsule**.

7) The liquid and small molecules pass through **three** layers to get into the Bowman's capsule and **enter** the nephron **tubule** — the **capillary wall**, a membrane (called the **basement membrane**) and the **epithelium** of the Bowman's capsule. Larger molecules like **proteins** and **blood cells** **can't pass through** and **stay** in the blood.

8) The liquid and small molecules, now called **filtrate**, pass along the rest of the nephron and **useful substances** are **reabsorbed** along the way — see next page.

9) Finally, the filtrate flows through the **collecting duct** and passes out of the kidney along the **ureter**.

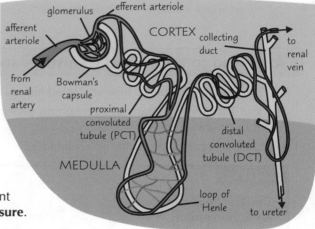

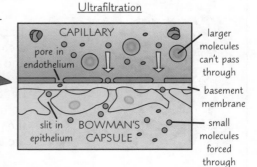

Ultrafiltration

The Kidneys and Excretion

Useful Substances are Reabsorbed Along the Nephron Tubules

1) **Selective reabsorption** takes place as the filtrate flows along the **proximal convoluted tubule (PCT)**, through the **loop of Henle**, and along the **distal convoluted tubule (DCT)**.

2) **Useful substances** leave the tubules of the nephrons and **enter** the capillary network that's **wrapped** around them (see diagram on previous page).

3) The **epithelium** of the wall of the PCT has **microvilli** to provide a **large surface area** for the **reabsorption** of useful materials from the **filtrate** (in the tubules) into the **blood** (in the capillaries).

4) Useful solutes like **glucose**, **amino acids**, **vitamins** and some **salts** are reabsorbed along the PCT by **active transport** and **facilitated diffusion**.

5) Some **urea** is also reabsorbed by **diffusion**.

6) **Water** enters the blood by **osmosis** because the **water potential** of the blood is **lower** than that of the filtrate. Water is reabsorbed from the **loop of Henle**, **DCT** and the **collecting duct** (see page 154).

7) The filtrate that remains is **urine**, which passes along the **ureter** to the **bladder**.

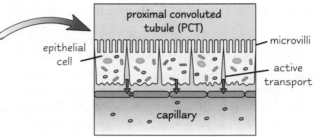

proximal convoluted tubule (PCT)

epithelial cell — microvilli — active transport — capillary

Water potential basically describes the tendency of water to move from one area to another. Water will move from an area of higher water potential to an area of lower water potential — it moves down the water potential gradient.

Urine is usually **made up of**:
- **Water** and **dissolved salts**.
- **Urea**.
- Other substances such as **hormones** and **excess vitamins**.

Urine **doesn't** usually contain:
- **Proteins** and **blood cells** — they're **too big** to be **filtered out** of the blood.
- **Glucose, amino acids** and **vitamins** — they're **actively reabsorbed** back into the blood (see above).

The volume of water in urine varies depending on how much you've drunk (see p. 154). The amount of urea also varies depending on how much protein you've eaten (see p. 148).

You Need to be Able to Examine and Draw Nephrons

PRACTICAL SKILLS

1) You need to be able to look at stained **kidney tissue** under a **light microscope** and **identify** and **draw** what you see.

2) You'll see different parts of the nephron depending on whether you're looking at the **cortex** or the **medulla** region of the kidney.

3) Here's an example of what you might see:

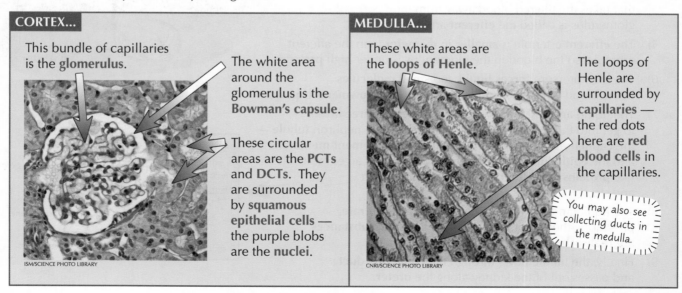

CORTEX...

This bundle of capillaries is the **glomerulus**.

The white area around the glomerulus is the **Bowman's capsule**.

These circular areas are the **PCTs** and **DCTs**. They are surrounded by **squamous epithelial cells** — the purple blobs are the **nuclei**.

ISM/SCIENCE PHOTO LIBRARY

MEDULLA...

These white areas are the **loops of Henle**.

The loops of Henle are surrounded by **capillaries** — the red dots here are **red blood cells** in the capillaries.

You may also see collecting ducts in the medulla.

CNRI/SCIENCE PHOTO LIBRARY

The Kidneys and Excretion

You Need to be Able to do a **Kidney Dissection**

A **kidney dissection** is great for really getting to know the **structure** of the kidney.

Equipment you'll need:

A **mammal's kidney** (e.g. from a sheep, pig or cow), a **dissecting tray**, a **scalpel**, an **apron** and **lab gloves**.

External examination:

1) Look at the outside of the kidney — it's covered with a thin, strong membrane called the **renal capsule**.
2) Beneath the renal capsule is the outside of the **cortex**.
3) You'll notice that part of the kidney is **indented** — this is the **renal hilum** and you'll probably see **tubes** coming from here.
4) Have a look at the tubes and see if you can identify them as the **renal vein**, **renal artery** and **ureter**. You might need to **look inside** the blood vessels to identify them — the wall of the artery will be thicker than the wall of the vein. The ureter is likely to have the most **adipose** (fatty) **tissue** around it.
5) Draw a **sketch** of the outside of the kidney and add clear **labels**.

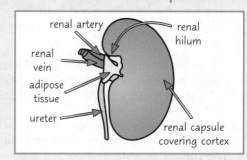

Internal examination:

1) Cut the kidney in half **lengthways** from one side. Split it open and have a look at the structures inside.
2) You should notice that the **cortex** appears **dense** and **grainy** and is a **lighter shade** than the medulla.
3) In the **medulla** you will find many **cone-shaped** structures — these are **renal pyramids**. They appear **stripy** because they contain straight sections of nephrons (loops of Henle and collecting ducts).
4) In-between the pyramids are **renal columns**.
5) You may see **hollow cavities** leading from the base of the renal pyramids — these are the **renal calyces** (singular is a **renal calyx**).
6) These lead to a larger hollow structure called the **renal pelvis**, which connects to the **ureter**.
7) Draw a **sketch** to show the structures you see inside the kidney. Don't forget to add **labels**.

Warm-Up Questions

Q1 Which blood vessel supplies the kidney with blood?

Q2 What are the bundles of capillaries found in the cortex of the kidneys called?

Q3 What is selective reabsorption?

Q4 Why aren't proteins normally found in urine?

Q5 Describe the internal structures you'd expect to see during a kidney dissection.

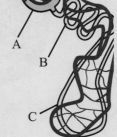

Exam Question

Q1 The diagram on the right shows part of a nephron in a kidney.
   a) From which structure (A-C) is water reabsorbed into the blood? [1 mark]
   b) Would you expect the concentration of glucose to be lower at point B or point C on the diagram? Explain your answer. [1 mark]
   c) Describe and explain the process that occurs at point A on the diagram. [5 marks]

Mmm — it's steak and excretion organ pie for dinner...

Excretion is a pretty horrible sounding word I know, but it's gotta be done. Mind you, I've never been able to eat kidney ever since I learnt all about this urine production business. Shame really — I used to love kidney sarnies for lunch.

Controlling Water Potential

More lovely kidney to gobble up on these pages — this time it's their role in controlling the water potential of the blood. Busy things, these kidneys.

The **Kidneys** Regulate the **Water Potential** of the **Blood**

Water is **essential** to keep the body **functioning**, so the **amount** of water in the **blood** (and so the **water potential** of the blood) needs to be kept **constant**. Mammals excrete **urea** (and other waste products) in **solution**, which means **water** is **lost** during excretion. Water is also lost in **sweat**. The kidneys **regulate** the water potential of the blood (and urine), so the body has just the **right amount** of water:

Brad liked his urine to be dilute.

If the water potential of the blood is too **low** (the body is **dehydrated**), **more** water is **reabsorbed** by osmosis **into** the blood from the tubules of the nephrons (see p. 151-152 for more). This means the urine is **more concentrated**, so **less** water is **lost** during excretion.

If the water potential of the blood is too **high** (the body is too **hydrated**), **less** water is **reabsorbed** by osmosis **into** the blood from the tubules of the nephrons. This means the urine is **more dilute**, so **more** water is **lost** during excretion (see next page).

Regulation of the water potential of the blood takes place in the **middle** and **last parts** of the nephron — the **loop of Henle**, the **distal convoluted tubule** (DCT) and the **collecting duct** (see below). The **volume** of water reabsorbed is controlled by **hormones** (see next page).

The **Loop of Henle** has a **Countercurrent Multiplier Mechanism**

The **loop of Henle** is made up of two 'limbs' — the **descending** limb and the **ascending** limb. They help set up a mechanism called the **countercurrent multiplier mechanism**. It's this mechanism that helps to **reabsorb water** back into the blood. Here's how it **works**:

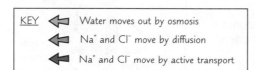

KEY
⇐ Water moves out by osmosis
⇐ Na⁺ and Cl⁻ move by diffusion
⇐ Na⁺ and Cl⁻ move by active transport

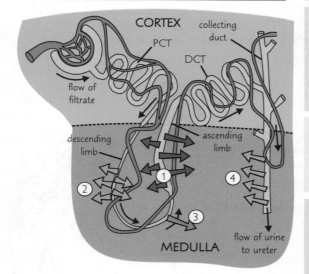

CORTEX
collecting duct
PCT
DCT
flow of filtrate
descending limb
ascending limb
① ② ③ ④
flow of urine to ureter
MEDULLA

① Near the **top** of the **ascending** limb, Na⁺ and Cl⁻ ions are **actively pumped out** into the **medulla**. The ascending limb is **impermeable** to **water**, so the water **stays inside** the tubule. This creates a **low water potential** in the **medulla**, because there's a **high concentration** of ions.

② Because there's a **lower** water potential in the **medulla** than in the descending limb, **water** moves **out** of the **descending limb into** the **medulla** by osmosis. This makes the **filtrate more concentrated** (the ions can't diffuse out — the descending limb isn't permeable to them). The water in the medulla is **reabsorbed** into the **blood** through the **capillary network**.

③ Near the **bottom** of the ascending limb Na⁺ and Cl⁻ ions **diffuse out** into the **medulla**, further **lowering** the **water potential** in the medulla. (The ascending limb is **impermeable** to **water**, so it **stays in the tubule**.)

④ The first three stages massively **increase** the **ion concentration** in the **medulla**, which **lowers** the **water potential**. This causes **water** to **move out** of the **collecting duct** by osmosis. As before, the water in the medulla is **reabsorbed** into the **blood** through the **capillary network**.

The **volume** of water **reabsorbed** from the collecting duct into the capillaries is **controlled** by **changing the permeability** of the **collecting duct** (see next page).

Different animals have **different length loops of Henle**. The **longer** an animal's loop of Henle, the **more water they can reabsorb** from the filtrate. When there's a longer ascending limb, **more ions** are **actively pumped out** into the medulla, which creates a **really low water potential** in the medulla. This means **more water** moves **out** of the nephron and collecting duct **into** the **capillaries**, giving very **concentrated urine**. Animals that live in areas where there's **little water** usually have **long loops** to save as much **water** as possible.

Controlling Water Potential

Water Reabsorption is Controlled by Hormones

1) The water potential of the blood is **monitored** by cells called **osmoreceptors** in a part of the **brain** called the **hypothalamus**.

2) When the osmoreceptors are **stimulated** by **low** water potential in the blood, the hypothalamus sends **nerve impulses** to the **posterior pituitary gland** to release a **hormone** called **antidiuretic hormone** (ADH) into the blood.

3) ADH makes the walls of the DCT and collecting duct **more permeable** to **water**.

4) This means **more water** is **reabsorbed** from these tubules **into** the medulla and into the blood by osmosis. A **small** amount of **concentrated urine** is produced, which means **less water** is **lost** from the body.

It's called antidiuretic hormone because diuresis is when lots of dilute urine is produced, so anti means a small amount of concentrated urine is produced.

Here's how ADH changes the **water content** of the **blood** when it's too **low** or too **high**:

1 Blood ADH Level Rises When You're Dehydrated

Dehydration is what happens when you **lose water**, e.g. by sweating during exercise, so the **water content** of the blood needs to be **increased**:

1) The **water content** of the blood drops, so its **water potential drops**.
2) This is detected by **osmoreceptors** in the **hypothalamus**.
3) The **posterior pituitary gland** is stimulated to release more **ADH** into the blood.
4) More **ADH** means that the DCT and collecting duct are **more permeable**, so **more water** is **reabsorbed** into the blood by osmosis.
5) A **small amount** of **highly concentrated** urine is produced and **less water** is **lost**.

Dehydrated? Me? As if...

2 Blood ADH Level Falls When You're Hydrated

If you're **hydrated**, you've taken in **lots of water**, so the **water content** of the blood needs to be **reduced**:

1) The **water content** of the blood rises, so its **water potential rises**.
2) This is detected by the **osmoreceptors** in the **hypothalamus**.
3) The **posterior pituitary gland** releases less **ADH** into the blood.
4) **Less ADH** means that the DCT and collecting duct are **less permeable**, so **less water** is **reabsorbed** into the blood by osmosis.
5) A **large amount** of **dilute** urine is produced and **more water** is **lost**.

Warm-Up Questions

Q1 In which parts of the nephron does water reabsorption take place?

Q2 Describe what happens along the descending limb of the loop of Henle.

Q3 Which cells monitor the water potential of the blood?

Q4 Which gland releases ADH?

PRACTICE QUESTIONS

Exam Questions

Q1 The level of ADH in the blood rises during strenuous exercise.
   a) Explain the cause of the increase in ADH level.   [3 marks]
   b) Explain the effect the increased ADH level has on kidney function.   [2 marks]

Q2 Gerbils are small rodents. They produce relatively little urine in comparison to other rodents of a similar size, such as mice or rats. Suggest and explain how the nephrons of gerbils differ from those of mice or rats.   [4 marks]

If you don't understand what ADH does, ur-ine trouble...

There are two main things to learn here — how water is reabsorbed from the kidney tubules, and how the water potential of the blood is regulated by osmoreceptors, the hypothalamus and the posterior pituitary gland. Now I need a wee.

Kidney Failure and Detecting Chemicals

Everything's fine while the kidneys are working well, but when they get damaged things don't run quite so smoothly.

Kidney Failure is When the Kidneys Stop Working Properly

Kidney failure is also called renal failure.

Kidney failure is when the kidneys **can't** carry out their **normal functions** because they **don't work properly**. Kidney failure can be **detected** by measuring the **glomerular filtration rate** (**GFR**) — this is the rate at which blood is filtered from the glomerulus into the Bowman's capsule. A rate **lower** than the normal range indicates the kidneys aren't working properly. Kidney failure can be **caused** by many things including:

1) **Kidney infections** — these can cause **inflammation** (swelling) of the kidneys, which can **damage** the cells. This **interferes** with **filtering** in the Bowman's capsules, or with **reabsorption** in the other parts of the nephrons.

2) **High blood pressure** — this can damage the **glomeruli**. The blood in the glomeruli is already under **high pressure** but the **capillaries** can be **damaged** if the blood pressure gets **too high**. This means **larger** molecules like **proteins** can get through the capillary walls and into the **urine**.

Kidney failure causes **lots of problems**, for example:

If the problems caused by kidney failure can't be controlled, it can eventually lead to death.

1) **Waste products** that the kidneys would normally **remove** (e.g. **urea**) begin to **build up** in the blood. **Too much** urea in the blood causes **weight loss** and **vomiting**.

2) **Fluid** starts to **accumulate** in the tissues because the kidneys **can't remove excess water** from the blood. This causes **parts of the body** to **swell**, e.g. the person's legs, face and abdomen can swell up.

3) The balance of **electrolytes** (ions) in the body becomes, well, unbalanced. The blood may become **too acidic**, and an imbalance of calcium and phosphate can lead to **brittle bones**. **Salt build-up** may cause more **water retention**.

4) **Long-term** kidney failure causes **anaemia** — a **lack** of **haemoglobin** in the blood.

Renal Dialysis and Kidney Transplants can be used to Treat Kidney Failure

When the kidneys can no longer **function** (i.e. they've **totally failed**), a person is unable to **survive** without **treatment**. There are **two** main treatment options:

Renal dialysis is where a patient's blood is filtered. There are two types:

1) HAEMODIALYSIS — this is where the patient's blood is passed through a dialysis machine — the blood flows on one side of a partially permeable membrane and dialysis fluid flows on the other side. Waste products and excess water and ions diffuse across the membrane into the dialysis fluid, removing them from the blood. Blood cells and larger molecules like proteins are prevented from leaving the blood. Each dialysis session takes three to five hours, and patients need two or three sessions a week, usually in hospital. Patients can feel increasingly unwell between dialysis sessions because waste products and fluid start to build up in their blood.

2) PERITONEAL DIALYSIS — dialysis fluid is put through a tube that passes from the outside of a patient's abdomen into their abdominal cavity. Waste products diffuse out of the patient's blood into the dialysis fluid across the peritoneum (the membrane the lines the abdominal cavity). After some time, the fluid is drained out via the tube. This dialysis is usually carried out by the patient at home either several times a day or in one long session overnight. However, there's a risk of infection around the site of the tube and the patient doesn't have any dialysis-free days.

There are disadvantages to both types of dialysis, but it can keep a person alive until a transplant is available (see below), and it's a lot less risky than having the major surgery involved in a transplant.

1) A **kidney transplant** is where a **new kidney** is implanted into a patient's body to **replace** a damaged kidney.

2) The new kidney has to be from a person with the **same blood** and **tissue type**. They're often donated from a **living relative**, as people can survive with **only one** kidney. They can also come from **other people** who've recently **died** — organ donors.

3) Transplants have a lot of **advantages** over dialysis — it's **cheaper** to give a person a transplant than keep them on dialysis for a **long time** and it's **more convenient** for a person than regular dialysis sessions.

4) But there are also **disadvantages** to having a kidney transplant: the patient will have to undergo a **major operation**, which is **risky**. The **immune system** may also **reject** the transplant, so the patient has to take **drugs** to **suppress it**.

Kidney Failure and Detecting Chemicals

Urine is used to Test for Pregnancy and Drug Use

Urine is made by **filtering** the **blood**, so you can have a look at what's in a person's blood by **testing** their **urine**. Urine samples can be used to test for **medical problems** such as diabetes, as well as **pregnancy** and **drug use**.

PREGNANCY: Pregnancy tests detect the hormone **human chorionic gonadotropin (hCG)** that's only found in the **urine** of **pregnant women**:

1) A **stick** is used with an **application area** that contains **monoclonal antibodies for hCG** bound to a **coloured bead** (**blue**). Monoclonal antibodies are all **identical** to each other.

2) When urine is applied to the application area any hCG will **bind** to the antibody on the beads.

3) The urine **moves** up to the **test strip, carrying** the **beads** with it.

4) The test strip has **antibodies to hCG** stuck in place (**immobilised**).

5) If there **is hCG present** the test strip turns **blue** because the **immobilised** antibody binds to any **hCG** attached to the **blue** beads, concentrating the **blue beads** in that area. If **no hCG** is present, the beads will **pass through** the test area **without** binding to anything, and so it **won't** go blue.

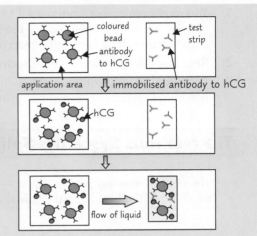

STEROIDS:

1) **Anabolic steroids** (e.g. **testosterone**, Nandrolone) are **drugs** that **build up muscle tissue**.

2) Some **athletes** are **banned** from taking anabolic steroids. This is to try to stop the misuse of steroids that can have **dangerous side-effects**, such as **liver damage**. Also, it's considered **unfair** for some athletes to use steroids.

3) Athletes regularly have their **urine tested** for steroids (or the **products** made when they're **broken down**) by a technique called **gas chromatography/mass spectrometry (GC/MS)**.

4) In gas chromatography the urine sample is **vaporised** (turned into a **gas**) and passed through a column containing a **polymer**. **Different substances** move through the column at **different speeds**, so substances in the urine sample **separate out**. Once the substances have separated out, a **mass spectrometer** converts them into **ions**, then **separates** them depending on their **mass** and **charge**. The results are **analysed** by a computer and by comparing them with the results of **known substances** it's possible to tell which substances were in the urine sample.

RECREATIONAL DRUGS:

1) Sometimes people have their urine tested to see if they've been using recreational drugs such as cannabis, ecstasy or cocaine. For example, some employers can carry out drug tests on their employees.

2) Testing for these drugs usually starts with test strips, which contain antibodies that the drug being tested for will bind to (or the products made when it's broken down). A sample of urine is applied to the test strip and if a certain amount of the drug (or its products) is present a colour change will occur, indicating a positive result.

3) If this first test shows a positive result, a sample of the urine is usually sent for further testing to confirm which drugs have been used. This second test uses GC/MS (just like the test for steroids).

Warm-Up Questions

Q1 Give one effect of kidney failure on the body.
Q2 What substance does a pregnancy test detect in a urine sample?
Q3 Briefly describe how use of recreational drugs, such as cannabis, can be tested for.

Exam Question

Q1 Describe two advantages and two disadvantages of kidney transplants over renal dialysis. [4 marks]

Kidney failure, kidney infections, kidney transplants, kidney beans...

So you can either treat kidney failure with a kidney transplant or you can use haemodialysis or peritoneal dialysis to filter the blood. All treatments come with their advantages and disadvantages, so make sure you can sum them both up.

The Nervous System

The nervous system is so clever that lots of stuff happens without you even having to think about it — digestion, breathing, blinking, yawning... aaaawaaaaawh...

Responding to their Environment Helps Animals Survive

1) You might remember from page 132 that animals need to **respond** to changes in their **external** environment, (e.g. by avoiding places that are too hot or too cold) as well as changes in their **internal** environment, (e.g. by controlling blood glucose concentration). This **increases** their chance of **survival**.

2) **Receptors detect stimuli** and **effectors** bring about a **response** to a **stimulus**.

3) Receptors usually **communicate** with effectors via the **nervous system** or the **hormonal system**, or sometimes using **both**.

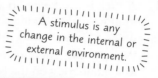
A stimulus is any change in the internal or external environment.

The Nervous System is Split into Two Main Structural Systems

The **central nervous system (CNS)** — made up of the **brain** and the **spinal cord**.

The **peripheral nervous system** — made up of the neurones that connect the CNS to the **rest** of the **body**. It also has two different functional systems:

The **somatic nervous system** controls **conscious** activities, e.g. running and playing video games.

The **autonomic nervous system** controls **unconscious** activities, e.g. digestion. It's got two divisions that have **opposite effects** on the body:

The **sympathetic** nervous system gets the body **ready for action**. It's the 'fight or flight' system. Sympathetic neurones release the neurotransmitter **noradrenaline**.

The **parasympathetic** nervous system **calms** the body down. It's the '**rest and digest**' system. Parasympathetic neurones release the neurotransmitter **acetylcholine**.

The Brain is Part of the Central Nervous System

You need to know the **location** and **function** of these **five brain structures**:

1 Hypothalamus — Controls Body Temperature

1) The hypothalamus is found just beneath the middle part of the brain.

2) The hypothalamus automatically maintains body temperature at the normal level (see p. 143).

3) The hypothalamus produces hormones that control the pituitary gland.

FRONT   BACK

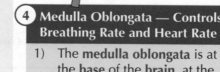

2 Cerebrum — Allows You to See, Hear, Learn and Think

1) The **cerebrum** is the **largest** part of the brain.

2) It's divided into **two halves** called **cerebral hemispheres**.

3) The cerebrum has a thin **outer layer** called the **cerebral cortex**, which is highly **folded**.

4) The cerebrum is involved in **vision, hearing, learning** and **thinking**.

3 Pituitary Gland — Controls Hormone Release by Body Glands

1) The pituitary gland is found beneath the hypothalamus

2) It is controlled by the hypothalamus. It releases hormones and stimulates other glands, e.g. the adrenal glands (see p. 140), to release their hormones.

4 Medulla Oblongata — Controls Breathing Rate and Heart Rate

1) The **medulla oblongata** is at the **base** of the **brain**, at the top of the spinal cord.

2) It automatically controls **breathing rate** and **heart rate**.

5 Cerebellum — Coordinates Muscles, Balance and Posture

1) The **cerebellum** is **underneath** the **cerebrum** and it also has a **folded cortex**.

2) It's important for **muscle coordination, posture** and **coordination of balance**.

The Nervous System

Reflexes are Rapid, Automatic Responses to Stimuli

1) A **reflex** is where the body **responds** to a stimulus **without** making a **conscious decision** to respond. This is because the **pathway** of **communication** doesn't involve **conscious** parts of the **brain**.

2) Because you don't have to **spend time deciding** how to respond, information travels **really fast** from **receptors** to **effectors**.

3) So simple reflexes help organisms to **avoid damage** to the body because they're **rapid**.

4) You need to know about two particular reflexes — the **blinking reflex** and the **knee-jerk reflex**.

The Blinking Reflex

When your body detects something that could **damage** your **eye**, you automatically **blink** — you quickly **close** your **eyelid** to protect your eye, then **open** your eyelid again. For example, you **blink** if your eye is **touched**:

- **Sensory nerve endings** in the cornea (front part of the eye) are stimulated by **touch**.

- A nerve impulse is sent along the **sensory neurone** to a **relay neurone** in the **CNS**.

- The impulse is then passed from the relay neurone to **motor neurones**.

- The **motor neurones** send impulses to the **effectors** — the **orbicularis oculi muscles** that move your eyelids. These muscles **contract** causing your eyelids to **close quickly** and **prevent** your eye from being **damaged**.

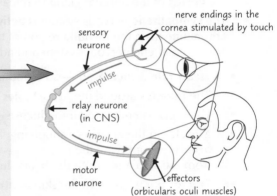

nerve endings in the cornea stimulated by touch

sensory neurone

impulse

relay neurone (in CNS)

impulse

motor neurone

effectors (orbicularis oculi muscles)

See page 135 for more about the structure and function of the different types of neurone.

The Knee-jerk Reflex

The **knee-jerk reflex** works to quickly straighten your leg if the body detects your quadriceps is suddenly stretched. It helps to maintain **posture** and **balance**. For example, if your knees **buckle** after landing from a jump, the reflex causes your quadriceps to **contract** to keep you **upright**. This is how it works:

- **Stretch receptors** in the **quadriceps muscle** detect that the muscle is being **stretched**.

- A nerve impulse is passed along a **sensory neurone**, which communicates directly with a **motor neurone** in the **spinal cord** (there is no relay neurone involved).

- The **motor neurone** carries the nerve impulse to the **effector** (the **quadriceps muscle**) causing it to **contract** so the lower leg **moves forward** quickly.

You can test your knee-jerk reflex by quickly hitting your patellar tendon (just below your kneecap) when your leg is bent.

Warm-Up Questions

Q1 Which part of the nervous system controls unconscious activities?

Q2 What does the sympathetic nervous system do?

Q3 Which part of the brain controls body temperature?

PRACTICE QUESTIONS

Exam Questions

Q1 The diagram on the right shows a cross-section of the brain from front to back.

a) Name structure A on the diagram of the brain. [1 mark]
b) Give two roles of structure B. [1 mark]
c) What effect might damage to structure C have on the body? [1 mark]

Q2 a) State why the knee-jerk reflex is beneficial for humans. [1 mark]
b) Explain how the knee-jerk reflex is coordinated by the body. [4 marks]

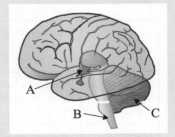

A

B

C

AAAAAAAAAAAAAAAAAAAAAAAAAAAARGH — the reflex response to revision...

You covered a bit about the nervous system at the start of this module. Now you need to learn about how the nervous system is organised and the structure of that big squelchy mess in your skull. Reflexes are automatic responses that keep your body out of all sorts of trouble — make sure you know how the blinking and knee-jerk reflexes work.

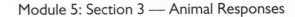

'Fight or Flight' Response and Heart Rate

Woah there. I know this looks scary, but don't run away. There are hormones, racing hearts, exercise... it's gripping stuff.

The **Nervous** and **Hormonal** Systems **Coordinate** 'Fight or Flight'

1) When an organism is **threatened** (e.g. by a predator) it responds by **preparing the body for action** (e.g. for fighting or running away). This **response** is called the **'fight or flight'** response.

2) **Nerve impulses** from **sensory** neurones arrive at the **hypothalamus** (see page 158), activating both the **hormonal system** and the **sympathetic nervous system**.

Harold thought it was about time his sympathetic nervous system took over.

- The **pituitary gland** is stimulated to release a **hormone** called **ACTH**. This causes the **cortex** of the **adrenal gland** to release **steroidal hormones** (see page 141).

- The **sympathetic** nervous system is **activated**, **triggering** the **release** of **adrenaline** from the **medulla** region of the **adrenal gland** (see page 141). The sympathetic nervous system and adrenaline have the following effects:

- **Heart rate** is increased — so blood is pumped around the body **faster** (see below).
- The muscles around the bronchioles relax — so breathing is deeper.
- Glycogen is converted into glucose — so more glucose is available for muscles to respire.
- Muscles in the arterioles supplying the skin and gut constrict, and muscles in the arterioles supplying the heart, lungs and skeletal muscles dilate — so blood is diverted from the skin and gut to the heart, lungs and skeletal muscles.
- Erector pili muscles in the skin contract — this makes hairs stand on end so the animal looks bigger.

> The conversion of glycogen to glucose is called glycogenolysis (see page 144).

The **Control** of **Heart Rate** Involves **Both** the **Nervous** and **Hormonal Systems**

The **nervous system** helps to control heart rate in these ways:

1) The **sinoatrial node** (**SAN**) generates **electrical impulses** that cause the **cardiac muscles** to **contract**.

2) The **rate** at which the SAN fires (i.e. heart rate) is **unconsciously controlled** by a part of the **brain** called the **medulla**.

3) Animals need to **alter** their **heart rate** to **respond** to **internal stimuli**, e.g. to prevent fainting due to low blood pressure or to make sure the heart rate is high enough to supply the body with enough oxygen.

4) **Stimuli** are **detected** by **pressure receptors** and **chemical receptors**:
- There are **pressure receptors** called **baroreceptors** in the **aorta** and the **vena cava**. They're stimulated by **high** and **low blood pressure**.
- There are **chemical receptors** called **chemoreceptors** in the **aorta**, the **carotid artery** (a major artery in the neck) and in the **medulla**. They **monitor** the **oxygen** level in the **blood** and also **carbon dioxide** and **pH** (which are indicators of O_2 level).

5) Electrical impulses from receptors are sent **to the medulla** along **sensory** neurones. The medulla processes the information and sends impulses to the SAN along **motor** neurones. Here's how it all works:

STIMULUS	RECEPTOR	NEURONE	EFFECTOR	RESPONSE
High blood pressure.	Baroreceptors detect high blood pressure.	Impulses are sent to the medulla, which sends impulses along the vagus nerve. This secretes acetylcholine, which binds to receptors on the SAN.	Cardiac muscles	Heart rate slows down to reduce blood pressure back to normal.
Low blood pressure.	Baroreceptors detect low blood pressure.	Impulses are sent to the medulla, which sends impulses along the accelerator nerve. This secretes noradrenaline, which binds to receptors on the SAN.	Cardiac muscles	Heart rate speeds up to increase blood pressure back to normal.
High blood O_2, low CO_2 or high pH levels.	Chemoreceptors detect chemical changes in the blood.	Impulses are sent to the medulla, which sends impulses along the vagus nerve. This secretes acetylcholine, which binds to receptors on the SAN.	Cardiac muscles	Heart rate decreases to return O_2, CO_2 and pH levels back to normal.
Low blood O_2, high CO_2 or low pH levels.	Chemoreceptors detect chemical changes in the blood.	Impulses are sent to the medulla, which sends impulses along the accelerator nerve. This secretes noradrenaline, which binds to receptors on the SAN.	Cardiac muscles	Heart rate increases to return O_2, CO_2 and pH levels back to normal.

The **hormonal system** also helps to control heart rate by releasing adrenaline, e.g. when the 'fight or flight' response is activated. Adrenaline **binds** to **specific receptors** in the **heart**. This causes the cardiac muscle to **contract more frequently** and with **more force**, so **heart rate increases** and the heart **pumps more blood**.

Module 5: Section 3 — Animal Responses

'Fight or Flight' Response and Heart Rate

You Can Investigate The Effect of Exercise on Heart Rate

Before you start, make sure you know how to measure your **heart rate**.
Find your **pulse** in your wrist by placing your index and middle finger where the
base of your thumb meets your forearm. Count the **number** of beats in **15 seconds**
and then **multiply by four** to get the number of **beats per minute**. Then:

1) Measure your heart rate at **rest** and record it in a table.

2) Do some **gentle exercise**, such as stepping on and off a step for about
5 minutes. **Immediately** afterwards, measure your heart rate again.

3) Return to a **resting position**. Measure your heart rate **every minute** until it
returns to the starting rate. Record **how long** it takes to return to normal.

You could use an electrical heart rate monitor instead — these contain sensors which measure your heart rate.

You could also measure other effects on heart rate in a similar way. For example, you could test the effect of a loud noise or the effect of anxiety (by doing something that makes you nervous).

Analyse the Effect of Exercise on Heart Rate Using Student's t-Test

You can test whether **regular, intense exercise** has a **significant** effect on **resting heart rate** by using **Student's t-test**. You
need **two sets of data** — the example below uses two groups of 8 people. One group received **six months** of **endurance
training** (Set 1) and the other group **did not** (Set 2). The **resting heart rates** of both groups were then **measured**.

Student's t-test is used to find out whether there is a **significant difference** in the **means** of the two data sets.
The value obtained is compared to a **critical value**,
which helps you decide how **likely** it is that the results
or 'differences in the means' were due to **chance**.

To carry out the t-test, follow these steps:

$$t = \frac{\bar{x}_1 - \bar{x}_2}{\sqrt{(s_1^2 / n_1) + (s_2^2 / n_2)}}$$

$\bar{x}$ = mean
s = standard deviation
n = number of values in group
$_1$ or $_2$ = group being referred to

There is a different equation that you can use for paired data (data that includes two measurements for each person, e.g. before and after endurance training).

1) **Identify the null hypothesis**. This is always
that the **means** for the two sets of data are
going to be **exactly** the **same**, i.e. there is
no significant difference between them.

2) **Calculate the mean and standard
deviation** for each data set.

3) **Use the formula** in the pink box above
to calculate t.

4) **Calculate the degrees of freedom** by
doing $(n_1 + n_2) - 2$. (Look at the key next
to the formula above to help you here).

5) **Look up the values for t** in a table of
critical values. If the value obtained
from the t-test is **greater** than the **critical
value** at a probability (or P value) of
5% or less (≤ 0.05), then you can be
95% confident that the difference is
significant and not due to chance.
So you'd **reject** the null hypothesis.

If the result of your t-test is greater than the critical value at a P value of less than 2% (< 0.02), or even 1%, you can be even more confident that the difference is significant.

Example

1) Null hypothesis — there is no significant
difference between the mean resting heart
rate of people who received endurance
training and those who did not.

2) $\bar{x}_1 = 69$, $\bar{x}_2 = 78$
$s_1 = 5.7$, $s_2 = 9.9$

3) $t = \dfrac{69 - 78}{\sqrt{(5.7^2 / 8) + (9.9^2 / 8)}}$

$t = -2.2$ (to 1 decimal place) (You can ignore the minus sign.)

4) Degrees of freedom
$= (8 + 8) - 2 = 14$

5) Critical value is 2.145.
The t value of 2.2 is **greater**
— this means that the mean
resting heart rate for the group
that received endurance training
was **significantly lower** after
6 months than for the group
that did not receive training.

Resting heart rate at end of test period (beats min⁻¹)	
Set 1	Set 2
67	89
72	68
65	78
61	70
75	67
78	82
65	94
69	76

degrees of freedom	critical t values			
12	1.356	1.782	2.179	2.681
13	1.350	1.771	2.160	2.650
14	1.345	1.761	2.145	2.624
15	1.341	1.753	2.131	2.602
probability that result is due to chance only	0.2 (20%)	0.1 (10%)	0.05 (5%)	0.02 (2%)

FISHER, STATISTICAL TABLES FOR BIOLOGICAL, AGRICULTURAL, AND MEDICAL RESEARCH, 1st Ed., © 1930, p.46. Reprinted by permission of Pearson Education, Inc., New York, New York

You'll be given a table of critical values in the exam.

Warm-Up Question

Q1 Describe how the hormonal and nervous systems
coordinate the 'fight or flight' response.

Exam Questions

Q1 a) Explain how high blood pressure in the aorta causes the heart rate to slow down. [5 marks]
b) What would be the effect of severing the nerves from the medulla to the sinoatrial node (SAN)? [2 marks]

My heart rate seems to be controlled by the boy next door...

*It's also rising rapidly at the sight of so much to learn. You've got to properly learn it though — it's no good just having a
rough idea. SANs, baroreceptors, chemoreceptors — get it learnt then try to reproduce the table from the previous page.*

Muscle Contraction

Muscles are effectors — they contract so you can respond to your environment. You need to know how they contract, but first you need to know a bit more about them.

The **Central Nervous System** (CNS) **Coordinates Muscular Movement**

1) The **CNS** (**brain** and **spinal cord**) receives **sensory information** and **decides** what kind of **response** is needed.
2) If the response needed is **movement**, the CNS sends signals along **neurones** to tell **skeletal muscles** to **contract**.
3) Skeletal muscle (also called striated, striped or voluntary muscle) is the type of muscle you use to **move**, e.g. the biceps and triceps move the lower arm.

Skeletal Muscle is made up of **Long Muscle Fibres**

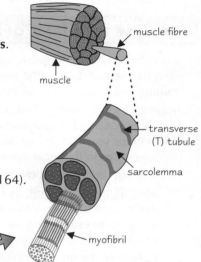

1) Skeletal muscle is made up of **large bundles** of **long cells**, called **muscle fibres**.
2) The cell membrane of muscle fibre cells is called the **sarcolemma**.
3) Bits of the sarcolemma **fold inwards** across the muscle fibre and stick into the **sarcoplasm** (a muscle cell's cytoplasm). These folds are called **transverse (T) tubules** and they help to **spread electrical impulses** throughout the sarcoplasm so they **reach** all parts of the **muscle fibre**.
4) A network of **internal membranes** called the **sarcoplasmic reticulum** runs through the sarcoplasm. The sarcoplasmic reticulum **stores** and **releases calcium ions** that are needed for muscle contraction (see pages 163-164).
5) Muscle fibres have lots of **mitochondria** to **provide** the **ATP** that's needed for **muscle contraction**.
6) They are **multinucleate** (contain many nuclei).
7) Muscle fibres have lots of **long**, **cylindrical organelles** called **myofibrils**. They're made up of proteins and are **highly specialised** for **contraction**.

Myofibrils Contain **Thick Myosin** Filaments and **Thin Actin** Filaments

1) Myofibrils contain bundles of **thick** and **thin myofilaments** that **move past each other** to make muscles **contract**.
 - **Thick myofilaments** are made of the protein **myosin**.
 - **Thin myofilaments** are made of the protein **actin**.
2) If you look at a **myofibril** under a **microscope**, you'll see a pattern of alternating **dark** and **light bands**:
 - **Dark** bands contain the **thick myosin filaments** and some overlapping thin actin filaments — these are called **A-bands**.
 - **Light** bands contain **thin actin filaments** only — these are called **I-bands**.
3) A myofibril is made up of many short units called **sarcomeres**.
4) The **ends** of each **sarcomere** are marked with a **Z-line**.
5) In the **middle** of each sarcomere is an **M-line**. The M-line is the **middle** of the **myosin** filaments.
6) **Around** the M-line is the **H-zone**. The H-zone **only** contains **myosin** filaments.

There's more detail on actin and myosin on pages 163-164.

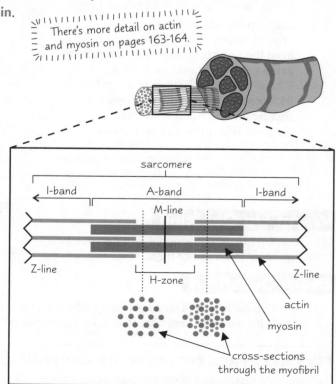

Eric and Susan just loved working their myofibrils. Oh yeah.

Muscle Contraction

Muscle Contraction is Explained by the Sliding Filament Theory

1) **Myosin** and **actin** filaments **slide** over one another to make the **sarcomeres contract** — the myofilaments themselves **don't** contract.

2) The **simultaneous contraction** of lots of **sarcomeres** means the **myofibrils** and **muscle fibres contract**.

3) Sarcomeres return to their **original length** as the muscle **relaxes**.

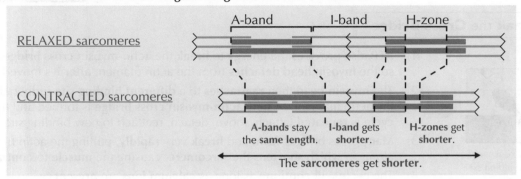

RELAXED sarcomeres

CONTRACTED sarcomeres

A-band   I-band   H-zone

A-bands stay the same length.   **I-band** gets shorter.   **H-zones** get shorter.

The **sarcomeres** get **shorter**.

Myosin Filaments Have Globular Heads and Binding Sites

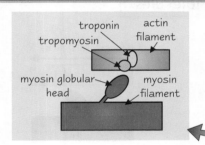

troponin   actin filament
tropomyosin
myosin globular head   myosin filament

1) **Myosin filaments** have **globular heads** that are **hinged**, so they can move **back** and **forth**.

2) Each myosin head has a **binding site** for actin and a **binding site** for ATP.

3) **Actin filaments** have **binding sites** for **myosin heads**, called **actin-myosin** binding sites.

4) Two other **proteins** called **tropomyosin** and **troponin** are found between actin filaments. These proteins are **attached** to **each other** and they **help** myofilaments **move** past each other.

Binding Sites in Resting Muscles are Blocked by Tropomyosin

1) In a **resting** (unstimulated) muscle the **actin-myosin binding site** is **blocked** by **tropomyosin**, which is held in place by **troponin**.

2) So **myofilaments can't slide** past each other because the **myosin heads can't bind** to the actin-myosin binding site on the actin filaments.

tropomyosin blocks the binding site

Muscle Contraction is Triggered by an Action Potential

1) The Action Potential Triggers an Influx of Calcium Ions

1) When an action potential from a motor neurone **stimulates** a muscle cell, it **depolarises** the **sarcolemma**. Depolarisation **spreads** down the **T-tubules** to the **sarcoplasmic reticulum** (see previous page).

2) This causes the **sarcoplasmic reticulum** to **release** stored **calcium ions** (Ca^{2+}) into the **sarcoplasm**.

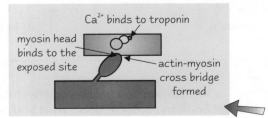

Ca^{2+} binds to troponin
myosin head binds to the exposed site   actin-myosin cross bridge formed

3) Calcium ions **bind** to **troponin**, causing it to **change shape**. This **pulls** the attached **tropomyosin out** of the **actin-myosin binding site** on the actin filament.

4) This **exposes** the **binding site**, which allows the **myosin head** to **bind**.

5) The bond formed when a **myosin head** binds to an **actin filament** is called an **actin-myosin cross bridge**.

Muscle Contraction

2) ATP Provides the Energy Needed to Move the Myosin Head...

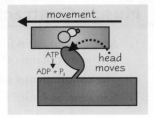

movement

1) **Calcium** ions also **activate** the enzyme **ATPase**, which **breaks down ATP** (into ADP + P$_i$) to **provide** the **energy** needed for muscle contraction.

2) The **energy** released from ATP **moves** the **myosin head**, which **pulls** the **actin filament** along in a kind of **rowing action**.

3) ...and to Break the Cross Bridge

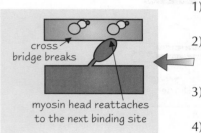

cross bridge breaks

myosin head reattaches to the next binding site

1) **ATP** also provides the **energy** to **break** the **actin-myosin cross bridge**, so the **myosin head detaches** from the actin filament **after** it's moved.

2) The **myosin head** then **reattaches** to a **different binding site** further along the actin filament. A **new actin-myosin cross bridge** is formed and the **cycle** is **repeated** (attach, move, detach, reattach to new binding site...).

3) **Many** cross bridges **form** and **break** very **rapidly**, pulling the actin filament along — which **shortens** the **sarcomere**, causing the **muscle** to **contract**.

4) The cycle will **continue** as long as **calcium ions** are **present** and **bound** to **troponin**.

When **Excitation Stops, Calcium Ions Leave** Troponin Molecules

1) When the muscle **stops** being **stimulated**, **calcium ions leave** their **binding sites** on the **troponin** molecules and are moved by **active transport** back into the **sarcoplasmic reticulum** (this needs **ATP** too).

2) The **troponin** molecules return to their **original shape**, pulling the attached **tropomyosin** molecules with them. This means the **tropomyosin** molecules **block** the actin-myosin **binding sites** again.

3) Muscles **aren't contracted** because **no myosin heads** are **attached** to **actin** filaments (so there are no actin-myosin cross bridges).

4) The **actin** filaments **slide back** to their **relaxed** position, which **lengthens** the **sarcomere**.

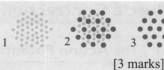

actin filaments slide back

tropomyosin blocks the binding sites again

Warm-Up Questions

Q1 Name the two proteins that make up myofibrils.

Q2 What happens to sarcomeres as a muscle relaxes?

Q3 Which molecule blocks the actin-myosin binding site in resting muscles?

Q4 What's the name of the bond that's formed when a myosin head binds to an actin filament?

PRACTICE QUESTIONS

Exam Questions

Q1 A muscle myofibril was cut through the M-line and then examined under an electron microscope. State which of the cross-section drawings (1-3) you would expect to see and explain why. **[3 marks]**

Q2 Describe how the lengths of the different bands in a myofibril change during muscle contraction. **[2 marks]**

Q3 Rigor mortis is the stiffening of muscles in the body after death. It happens when ATP reserves are exhausted. Explain why a lack of ATP leads to muscles being unable to relax. **[3 marks]**

Q4 Bepridil is a drug that blocks calcium ion channels. Describe and explain the effect this drug will have on muscle contraction. **[3 marks]**

What does muscle contraction cost? 80p...

Sorry, that's my favourite sciencey joke so I had to fit it in somewhere — a small distraction before you revisit this page. It's tough stuff but you know the best way to learn it. That's right, shut the book and scribble down what you can remember — if you can't remember much, read it again till you can (then read it again anyway, just to be sure).

Muscle Contraction

Keep going, you've almost got muscles done and dusted — just a few more bits and pieces to learn about them.

ATP and CP Provide the Energy for Muscle Contraction

So much **energy** is **needed** when muscles contract that **ATP** gets **used up very quickly**.
ATP has to be **continually generated** so exercise can continue — this happens in **three main ways**:

① Aerobic respiration

- Most **ATP** is generated via **oxidative phosphorylation** in the cell's **mitochondria**.
- **Aerobic** respiration only works when there's **oxygen** so it's good for **long periods** of **low-intensity exercise**, e.g. walking or jogging.

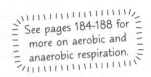
See pages 184-188 for more on aerobic and anaerobic respiration.

② Anaerobic respiration

- **ATP** is made **rapidly** by **glycolysis**.
- The **end product** of glycolysis is **pyruvate**, which is converted to **lactate** by **lactate fermentation**.
- Lactate can **quickly build up** in the muscles and cause **muscle fatigue** (where the muscles can't contract as forcefully as they could do previously).
- Anaerobic respiration is good for **short periods** of **hard exercise**, e.g. a **400 m sprint**.

Many activities use a combination of these systems.

③ ATP-Creatine Phosphate (CP) System

- **ATP** is made by **phosphorylating ADP** — adding a phosphate group taken from **creatine phosphate (CP)**.
- **CP** is **stored** inside cells and the ATP-CP system **generates ATP** very **quickly**.
- **CP runs out** after a few seconds so it's used during **short bursts** of **vigorous exercise**, e.g. a tennis serve.
- The ATP-CP system is **anaerobic** (it doesn't need oxygen) and it's **alactic** (it doesn't form any lactate).

$$\begin{array}{ccc} ADP & & ATP \\ + & \rightarrow & + \\ CP & & C \text{ (creatine)} \end{array}$$

Neuromuscular Junctions are Synapses Between Neurones and Muscles

1) A **neuromuscular junction** is a **synapse** between a **motor neurone** and a **muscle cell**.
2) Neuromuscular junctions use the neurotransmitter **acetylcholine (ACh)**, which binds to receptors called **nicotinic cholinergic receptors**.
3) Neuromuscular junctions **work** in the **same way** as **synapses between neurones** — they **release neurotransmitter**, which triggers **depolarisation** in the **postsynaptic cell** (see pages 138-139).
4) Depolarisation of a muscle cell always causes it to **contract** (if the **threshold level** is reached).
5) **Acetylcholinesterase (AChE)** stored in clefts on the postsynaptic membrane is released to **break down** acetylcholine after use.

presynaptic membrane

postsynaptic membrane (also called motor end plate)

nicotinic cholinergic receptors

AChE stored in clefts

motor neurone

ACh

AChE breaks down ACh

- Sometimes a chemical (e.g. a drug) may block the release of the neurotransmitter or affect the way it binds to the receptors on the postsynaptic membrane. This may prevent the action potential from being passed on to the muscle, so the muscle won't contract.
- This can be fatal if it affects the muscles involved in breathing, e.g. the diaphragm and intercostal muscles. If they can't contract, ventilation can't take place and the organism can't respire aerobically.

Muscle Contraction

There are **Three Types** of **Muscle**

You need to learn the differences between the **structure** and **function** of each different muscle type.

1 Skeletal muscle (also called voluntary muscle)

1) **Skeletal** muscle contraction is controlled **consciously** (you have to voluntarily decide to contract it).
2) It's made up of **many muscle fibres** that have **many nuclei**. The muscle fibres can be **many centimetres long**.
3) You can see regular **cross-striations** (a **striped pattern**) under a **microscope** (see below).
4) Some muscle fibres **contract very quickly** — they're used for **speed** and **strength** but **fatigue** (get tired) **quickly**.
5) Some muscle fibres **contract slowly and fatigue slowly** — they're used for **endurance and posture**.

You need to know how to examine a **stained** section of skeletal muscle under a **light microscope** or examine a **photomicrograph** of one. Here's an example of what you might see:

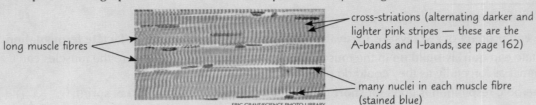

long muscle fibres

cross-striations (alternating darker and lighter pink stripes — these are the A-bands and I-bands, see page 162)

many nuclei in each muscle fibre (stained blue)

ERIC GRAVE/SCIENCE PHOTO LIBRARY

PRACTICAL SKILLS

2 Involuntary muscle (also called smooth muscle)

1) **Involuntary** muscle contraction is controlled **unconsciously** (it'll contract automatically without you deciding).
2) It's also called **smooth muscle** because it **doesn't** have the **striped appearance** of voluntary muscle.
3) It's found in the **walls** of your **hollow internal organs**, e.g. the **gut**, the **blood vessels**. Your **gut smooth muscles contract** to **move food along** (peristalsis) and your **blood vessel smooth muscles contract** to **reduce** the **flow** of blood.
4) Each muscle fibre has **one nucleus**. The muscle fibres are **spindle-shaped** with **pointed ends**, and they're only about **0.2 mm long**.
5) The muscle fibres **contract slowly** and **don't fatigue**.

nucleus

spindle-shaped muscle fibre

3 Cardiac muscle (heart muscle)

1) **Cardiac** muscle **contracts** on its **own** — it's **myogenic** (but the **rate** of contraction is controlled involuntarily by the **autonomic nervous system**).
2) It's found in the **walls** of your **heart**.
3) It's made of muscle fibres **connected** by **intercalated discs**, which have **low electrical resistance** so nerve impulses pass **easily** between cells.
4) The muscle fibres are **branched** to allow **nerve impulses** to **spread quickly** through the whole muscle.
5) Each muscle fibre has **one nucleus**. The muscle fibres are shaped like **cylinders** and they're about **0.1 mm long**.
6) You can see **some cross-striations** but the striped pattern **isn't** as **strong** as it is in voluntary muscle.
7) The muscle fibres **contract rhythmically** and **don't fatigue**.

intercalated discs

some cross-striations

nucleus

branched muscle fibre

John liked to put his skeletal muscle to the test by holding up ancient monuments.

Muscle Contraction

Electrical Signals Can be Used to Monitor Muscle Fatigue

Bill and Bob felt they were perfect candidates for the experiment.

If you have access to specialist equipment you may be able to investigate **muscle contraction** and **fatigue** by **monitoring** the **electrical activity** that occurs.

1) Muscles **contract** in **response** to nervous impulses — these are **electrical signals**.

2) Electrical signals in muscles can be **detected** by **electrodes** (sensors) placed on the **skin**. The electrodes are connected to a **computer** to allow the electrical signals to be monitored. The procedure is called **electromyography** and the reading it generates is called an **electromyogram**.

To carry out the procedure:

1) First of all you need to **attach** two **electrodes** to places on the **muscle** that you want to record from — in this example we will use the **biceps** muscle in the arm. A third electrode goes on an **inactive** point (such as the bony wrist area) to act as a **control**.

2) Switch off any other **electrical** equipment that you don't need as this generates 'noise' that **interferes** with the **electrical signal** from the **muscle**.

3) **Connect** the electrodes to an **amplifier** and a **computer**. (An amplifier increases the strength of the electrical signals from the muscle.)

4) Keep the muscle **relaxed**. You should see a **straight line** on the electromyogram.

5) Then **contract** the **muscle** by bending your arm. You should see **spikes** in the graph as **motor units** are activated to contract the muscle.

6) If you then **lift** a weight, the **amplitude** of the trace on the graph will **increase** — there are more electrical signals because **more motor units** are required to lift the weight.

7) If you **continue** to **hold** the **weight**, your muscle will begin to **fatigue**. On the electromyogram you will see the **amplitude** of the trace **increase** further. This is because your brain is trying to activate **more motor units** to generate the **force** needed to hold the weight up.

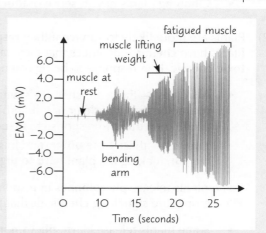

A motor unit is made up of a motor neurone and all the muscle fibres that it connects to.

Warm-Up Questions

Q1 What is a neuromuscular junction?
Q2 Describe the role of AChE at a neuromuscular junction.
Q3 How does the function of involuntary muscle differ from skeletal muscle?
Q4 Describe the structure of cardiac muscle.
Q5 Briefly describe how you could use electrical signals to monitor muscle fatigue.

Exam Questions

Q1 During exercise the supply of ATP stored in the body is very quickly used up.
　a) How does creatine phosphate maintain the supply of ATP so that exercise can continue? [2 marks]
　b) What type of exercise does the ATP-creatine phosphate system provide energy for? Give a reason for your answer. [2 marks]

Q2 Myasthenia gravis is a neuromuscular disease in which antibodies can damage or block the nicotinic cholinergic receptors at neuromuscular junctions. A symptom of myasthenia gravis is muscle fatigue. Suggest why this is the case. [4 marks]

Smooth muscle — it has a way with the ladies...

Blimey, what a section. Neuromuscular junctions are synapses that are specific to muscle cells so make sure you learn the names of the neurotransmitters and the receptors involved here. You also need to learn the structure and function of the three different types of muscle so cover and scribble 'til you're sure you've got it. Then that's it for muscles. Happy days.

Plant Responses

You might not think that plants do much, but they respond to stimuli just like us. OK, not just like us (I can't picture a daisy boogying to cheesy music), but their responses are important all the same.

Plants Need to Respond to Stimuli

1) Plants, like animals, **increase** their chances of **survival** by **responding** to changes in their **environment**, e.g.

- They sense the direction of **light** and **grow** towards it to **maximise** light absorption for **photosynthesis**.
- They can sense **gravity**, so their roots and shoots **grow** in the **right direction**.
- **Climbing** plants have a sense of **touch**, so they can find things to climb and **reach** the **sunlight**.

2) Plants are more likely to survive if they **respond** to **herbivory** — **being eaten** by **animals** (including insects). Plants have **chemical defences** that they can use against herbivory. For example, they can produce **toxic chemicals** in response to being eaten. Examples of these chemicals include:

Herbivores are animals that eat plants.

- **Alkaloids** — these are chemicals with **bitter tastes, noxious smells** or **poisonous characteristics** that deter or kill herbivores, e.g. **tobacco plants** produce the alkaloid **nicotine** in response to tissue damage. Nicotine is **highly poisonous** to many insects.
- **Tannins** — these **taste bitter**, and in some herbivores (e.g. cattle, sheep) they can **bind to proteins** in the **gut**, making the plant **hard to digest**. Both of these things **deter animals** from eating the plant.

Some plants release **pheromones** in response to herbivory.
Pheromones are **signalling chemicals** that produce a **response** in other **organisms**, e.g.

- Some plants release **alarm pheromones** into the air in response to herbivore grazing. This can cause **nearby plants** that detect these chemicals to start making chemical defences such as **tannins**.
- When **corn plants** are being eaten by **caterpillars**, they can produce **pheromones** which **attract parasitic wasps**. These wasps then lay their eggs in the caterpillars (eww), which eventually kills them.

Other plants are able to **fold up** in response to being **touched**, e.g.

If a single leaflet (a mini leaf-shaped structure that makes up part of a leaf) of the plant *Mimosa pudica* is touched, a signal spreads through the whole leaf, causing it to quickly fold up. It's thought that this could help **protect** *Mimosa pudica* **against herbivory** in a variety of ways, e.g. it may help to **knock off** any **small insects** feeding on the plant. It may also **scare off** animals trying to eat it (I'd certainly be scared if my dinner moved mid-meal).

3) Plants are more likely to survive if they **respond** to **abiotic stress** — anything **harmful** that's **natural** but **non-living**, like a **drought**. E.g. some plants respond to **extreme cold** by **producing** their own form of **antifreeze**:

Carrots produce antifreeze proteins at low temperatures — the proteins bind to ice crystals and lower the temperature that water freezes at, stopping more ice crystals from growing.

A Tropism is a Plant's Growth Response to an External Stimulus

1) A **tropism** is the **response** of a plant to a **directional stimulus** (a stimulus coming from a particular direction).
2) Plants respond to stimuli by **regulating** their **growth**.
3) A **positive tropism** is growth **towards** the stimulus.
4) A **negative tropism** is growth **away** from the stimulus.

Phototropism is the growth of a plant in response to **light**.
- **Shoots** are **positively phototropic** and grow **towards** light.
- **Roots** are **negatively phototropic** and grow **away** from light.

Unidirectional light

Shoots →

Unidirectional light

→ Roots

Geotropism is the growth of a plant in response to **gravity**.
- **Shoots** are **negatively geotropic** and grow **upwards**.
- **Roots** are **positively geotropic** and grow **downwards**.

The men's gymnastics team were positively phototropic.

Plant Responses

Other tropisms you might come across include:

- **Hydrotropism** — plant growth in response to **water**. **Roots are positively hydrotropic.**
- **Thermotropism** — plant growth in response to **temperature**.
- **Thigmotropism** — plant growth in response to **contact with an object**.

Responses are Brought About by Growth Hormones

1) Plants **respond** to some stimuli using growth hormones — chemicals that speed up or slow down plant growth.

2) Growth hormones are produced in the growing regions of the plant (e.g. shoot tips, leaves) and they move to where they're needed in the other parts of the plant.

3) A growth hormone called gibberellin stimulates seed germination, stem elongation, side shoot formation and flowering.

4) Growth hormones called auxins stimulate the growth of shoots by cell elongation — this is where cell walls become loose and stretchy, so the cells get longer.

5) High concentrations of auxins inhibit growth in roots though.

Growth hormones are also called growth substances.

Indoleacetic Acid (IAA) is an Important Auxin

1) **Auxins** are produced in the **tips** of **shoots** in flowering plants (see p. 171). One important example of an auxin is **indoleacetic acid** (**IAA**) which, like other auxins, works by stimulating **cell elongation**.

2) IAA is **moved** around the plant to **control tropisms** — it moves by **diffusion** and **active transport** over short distances, and via the **phloem** over long distances.

3) This results in **different parts** of the plants having **different amounts** of IAA. The **uneven distribution** of IAA means there's **uneven growth** of the plant, e.g.:

Phototropism — IAA moves to the more **shaded** parts of the **shoots** and **roots**, so there's uneven growth.

shoot — IAA moves to this side — cells elongate and the shoot bends towards the light

IAA moves to this side — growth is inhibited so the root bends away from the light — root

Geotropism — IAA moves to the **underside** of **shoots** and **roots**, so there's uneven growth.

shoot — IAA moves to this side — cells elongate so the shoot grows upwards

IAA moves to this side — growth is inhibited so the root grows downwards — root

You Can Carry Out Practical Investigations into Phototropism

This investigation can be done to show how **plant shoots** respond to **light**.

1) Take **nine wheat shoots**. The shoots should be planted in **individual pots** in the **same type** of soil. The shoots should be roughly **equal in height**.

2) Cover the **tips of three shoots** with a **foil cap**. Leave **three shoots without foil**. Wrap the **base** of the final **three shoots** with **foil**, leaving only the **tip exposed**.

3) Set up the shoots in front of a **light source** and **leave them for two days**. The shoots should all be the **same distance** from the light source and experience the **same intensity** of light. **All other variables**, including **temperature** and **exposure to moisture**, should be **controlled**.

4) By the end of the experiment, the plants should look a bit like this. The shoots with **exposed tips** should have **grown towards the light source** (positive phototropism). **Covering the tip** with a foil cap **prevents growth towards the light** — it's the **tip** (where IAA is produced) that's **most sensitive** to light and because it's covered the shoot should have continued to grow straight up. **Covering the base** of the shoot with foil should still **allow the tip to grow towards the light**.

5) Recording the **amount of growth** (in mm), as well as the **direction** of growth, will give you quantitative results.

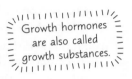

foil

light

A   B   C
Experimental set up

light

A   B   C
Results

foil

Plant Responses

You Can Carry Out **Practical Investigations** into **Geotropism** too

There are lots of ways you could investigate geotropism. Here's one of them:

1) Line **three Petri dishes** with **moist** (but not soaking wet) **cotton wool**. You should use the **same volume** of **water** and the same amount of cotton wool in each dish.

2) Space out **10 cress seeds** on the surface of the cotton wool in each dish, then push each one into the wool.

3) Tape a **lid** onto each dish and **wrap** each one in **foil** (this will prevent any light reaching the seeds and affecting your results).

4) Choose somewhere you can leave the dishes where the **temperature** is likely to be **warmish** and **pretty constant**, e.g. a cupboard.

5) Prop one dish **upright**, at a **90° angle** — **label it** and mark which way is 'up' (or down). Place another dish on a **slope** at a **45° angle**. Place the third dish on a **flat, horizontal surface**. You need to **label** the dishes **carefully**, so you know **which way up** each one was when you come to unwrap the dishes at the end of the experiment.

6) Leave the seeds for **4 days**. Then take a look at their **shoot** and **root growth**.

7) You should find that **whatever** the **angle** the dishes were placed at, the **shoots** have all **grown away** from **gravity** (negative geotropism) and the **roots** have grown **towards gravity** (positive geotropism).

8) To get quantitative results, **measure** the **amount** of growth of the shoots and roots and the **angle** of growth.

Warm-Up Questions

Q1 Why is it important for plants to respond to stimuli?

Q2 Give two examples of chemical defences produced by plants in response to herbivory.

Q3 What is a tropism?

Q4 What is hydrotropism?

Q5 How does the movement of IAA control geotropism in roots?

Exam Question

Q1 An experiment was carried out to investigate the role of auxin in shoot growth. Eight shoots, equal in height and mass, had their tips removed. Sponges soaked in glucose and either auxin or water were then placed where the tip should be. This is shown in the diagram on the right.

☐ Sponge soaked in auxin and glucose
■ Sponge soaked in water and glucose

Four shoots were then placed in the dark (experiment A) and the other four shoots were exposed to a light source directed at them from the right (experiment B).

A B C D ← Shoot minus the tip

After two days, the amount of growth (in mm) and direction of growth was recorded. The results are shown in the table.

a) Why were the tips of the shoots removed before the experiment began? [1 mark]

b) Suggest why glucose was added to the sponges. [1 mark]

c) Explain why two of the sponges were soaked in water and glucose rather than auxin and glucose. [2 marks]

d)* Explain the results for shoots A-C in each experiment. [6 marks]

	Growth			
	Shoot A	**Shoot B**	**Shoot C**	**Shoot D**
Experiment A (dark)	6 mm, right	6 mm, left	6 mm, straight	1 mm, straight
Experiment B (light)	8 mm, right	8 mm, right	8 mm, right	3 mm, straight

* You will be assessed on the quality of your written response in this question.

IAA Productions — do you have the growth factor — with Simon Trowel...

Remember a tropism is a plant growth response to a directional stimulus — the bit before 'tropism' gives you a clue as to what that stimulus is, e.g. 'photo' = light, 'hydro' = water, 'thermo' = temperature, etc. Tropisms increase a plant's chances of survival, e.g. shoots need light to photosynthesise, so they grow towards light to help the plant survive.

The Effects of Plant Hormones

Plant hormones are responsible for all sorts — like your roses getting the hump and not keeping their pot tidy.

Auxins are Involved in Apical Dominance

1) The **shoot tip** at the top of a flowering plant is called the **apical bud**.

2) Auxins **stimulate** the **growth** of the **apical bud** and **inhibit** the **growth** of **side shoots** from **lateral buds**. This is called **apical dominance** — the apical bud is **dominant** over the lateral buds.

3) Apical dominance prevents side shoots from growing — this **saves energy** and prevents side shoots from the same plant **competing** with the shoot tip for light.

4) Because energy **isn't** being used to grow side shoots, apical dominance allows a **plant** in an area where there are **loads of other plants** to **grow tall very fast**, past the smaller plants, to **reach** the **sunlight**.

5) If you **remove** the apical bud then the plant **won't produce auxins**, so the **side shoots** will **start growing** by **cell division** and **cell elongation**.

6) However, if you replace the tip with a **source of auxin**, side shoot development is **inhibited**. This demonstrates that apical dominance is **controlled by auxin**.

7) Auxins become **less concentrated** as they **move away** from the apical bud to the rest of the plant. If a plant grows **very tall**, the bottom of the plant will have a **low auxin concentration** so side shoots will start to grow near the bottom.

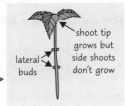

shoot tip grows but side shoots don't grow

lateral buds

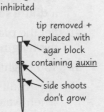

tip removed

side shoots no longer inhibited

tip removed + replaced with agar block containing <u>auxin</u>

side shoots don't grow

The Role of Auxins in Apical Dominance Can be Investigated

PRACTICAL SKILLS

Scientists have **demonstrated** the **role of auxins** in **apical dominance** in **experiments** like the one below. You could also do this experiment yourself:

1) Plant **30 plants** (e.g. **pea plants**) that are a **similar age**, **height** and **weight** in pots.

2) **Count** and **record** the number of **side shoots** growing from the main stem of **each plant**.

3) For **10 plants**, **remove** the **tip** of the **shoot** and apply a **paste containing auxins** to the **top of the stem**.

4) For another 10 plants, remove the tip of the shoot and apply a **paste without auxins** to the top of the stem.

5) Leave the final 10 plants as they are — these are your untreated **controls**. These are needed for **comparison** so that you know the **effect** you see is **likely** to be due to the **hormone** and **not any other factor**.

6) Let each group **grow** for **six days**. You need to keep all the plants in the **same conditions** — the same **light intensity**, **water**, etc. This makes sure any **variables** that may affect your results are **controlled**, which makes your experiment **valid**.

7) After six days, **count** the number of **side shoots** growing from the main stem of **each** of your **plants**.

8) The results in the **table** show that **removing** the **tips** of shoots caused **extra side shoots** to **grow**, but removing tips **and** applying **auxins prevented** extra side shoots from growing.

9) The results suggest auxins **inhibit** the **growth** of side shoots — suggesting that auxins are involved in **apical dominance**.

	average no. of side shoots per plant	
	start of experiment	end of experiment
untreated plants (control group)	4	5
tips removed, auxin paste applied	4	5
tips removed, paste without auxins applied	4	9

Gibberellins are Another Type of Plant Hormone

1) **Gibberellins** are produced in **young leaves** and in **seeds**. They stimulate **seed germination**, **stem elongation**, **side shoot formation** and **flowering**.

2) Gibberellins **stimulate** the **stems** of plants to **grow** by **stem elongation** — this helps plants to grow **very tall**. If a **dwarf variety** of a plant is treated with gibberellin, it will grow to the **same height** as the **tall variety**. Unlike auxins, gibberellins **don't inhibit** plant growth in any way.

3) Gibberellins stimulate **seed germination** by triggering the **breakdown** of **starch** into **glucose** in the seed. The **plant embryo** in the seed can then use the glucose to begin **respiring** and **release** the **energy** it needs to **grow**. Gibberellins are **inhibited** (and so seed germination is prevented) by the hormone **abscisic acid**.

The Effects of Plant Hormones

The Role of Gibberellins can be Investigated

Scientists have done lots of experiments to provide **evidence** for the role of **gibberellins** in plant growth.

> For example, scientists have produced **genetically altered** seeds that are **unable** to **produce gibberellins**. These seeds are **unable to germinate** unless they are given gibberellins.

Here's an example of how you could investigate the role of gibberellins in **stem elongation**:

1) Plant **40 plants** (e.g. dwarf pea plants) that are a similar **age**, **height** and **mass** in pots.

2) **Leave 20** plants as they are to grow, **watering** them **all** in the **same way** and keeping them **all** in the **same conditions** — these are your **controls**.

3) **Leave the other 20 plants** to grow in the **same conditions**, **except** water them with a **dilute solution** of gibberellin (e.g. **100 mg dm⁻³** gibberellin).

4) Let the plants grow for about **28 days** and **measure** the **lengths** of all the **stems once each week**.

5) You might get **results** a bit like these:

6) The results in the **table** show that stems **grow more** when watered with a dilute solution of **gibberellin**.

7) The results suggest **gibberellin stimulates stem elongation**.

8) You might have to **calculate** the **rate of growth** of the plants in your exam, e.g:

time / days	average stem length / cm	
	plants watered normally	plants watered with gibberellin
O	14	14
7	15	17
14	18	27
21	19	38
28	23	46

- In **28 days** the plants **watered normally** grew an **average** of **9 cm** (23 cm – 14 cm), so they grew at an average **rate** of 9 ÷ 28 = **0.32 cm/day** or **0.32 cm day⁻¹**.

- In **28 days** the plants **watered with gibberellin** grew an **average** of **32 cm** (46 cm – 14 cm), so they grew at an average **rate** of 32 ÷ 28 = **1.14 cm day⁻¹**.

Gibberellins and Auxins can Work Together to Affect Plant Growth

Auxins and gibberellins are often **synergistic** — this means that they **work together** to have a really **big effect**. E.g. auxins and gibberellins work together to help plants grow **very tall**.

Auxins and gibberellins are sometimes **antagonistic** — this means they **oppose** each other's actions. E.g. **gibberellins stimulate** the growth of **side shoots** but **auxins inhibit** the growth of side shoots.

Hormones are Involved in Leaf Loss in Deciduous Plants

1) **Deciduous plants** are plants that **lose** their **leaves** in **winter**.

2) Losing their leaves helps plants to **conserve water** (lost from leaves) during the cold part of the year, when it might be **difficult** to **absorb water** from the **soil** (the soil water may be **frozen**), and when there's **less light** for **photosynthesis**.

> The technical term for leaf loss is abscission.

3) Leaf loss is **triggered** by the **shortening day length** in the autumn.

4) Leaf loss is **controlled** by hormones:

- **Auxins inhibit** leaf loss — auxins are produced by **young leaves**. As the leaf gets **older**, **less auxin** is produced, leading to **leaf loss**.

> Auxins are antagonistic to ethene.

- **Ethene stimulates** leaf loss — ethene is produced by **ageing leaves**. As the leaves get **older**, **more ethene** is produced. A **layer of cells** (called the **abscission layer**) develops at the **bottom** of the **leaf stalk** (where the leaf joins the stem). The abscission layer **separates** the leaf from the rest of the plant. Ethene **stimulates** the cells in the abscission layer to **expand**, **breaking** the **cell walls** and causing the **leaf** to **fall off**.

The Effects of Plant Hormones

Hormones are Involved in Stomatal Closure

1) Plants need to be able to close their **stomata** in order to **reduce water loss** through **transpiration** (see page 92).
2) They do this using **guard cells**. Guard cells are found either side of a stomatal pore. When the guard cells are **full of water**, they are plump and **turgid** and the pore is **open**. When the guard cells **lose water**, they become **flaccid**, making the pore **close**.
3) The plant hormone **abscisic acid** (ABA) is able to **trigger stomatal closure**.
4) ABA **binds** to receptors on the **guard cell membranes**. This causes specific **ion channels** to **open**, which allows **calcium ions** to enter the **cytosol** from the vacuole. The increased concentration of calcium ions in the cytosol causes **other ion channels** to **open**. These ion channels allow ions (such as potassium ions) to **leave** the guard cells, **raising** the **water potential** of the cells. **Water** then **leaves** the guard cells by **osmosis**. The guard cells become **flaccid** and the **stomata close**.

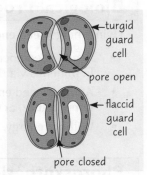
turgid guard cell
pore open
flaccid guard cell
pore closed

Plant Hormones have Many Commercial Uses

1) The **fruit industry** uses different **plant hormones** to **control** how different fruits develop, e.g.

Ethene stimulates enzymes that **break down cell walls**, **break down chlorophyll** and convert **starch** into **sugars**. This makes the fruit **soft**, **ripe** and **ready to eat**. E.g. **bananas** are harvested and transported **before** they're **ripe** because they're **less likely** to be **damaged** this way. They're then **exposed** to **ethene** on arrival so they **all ripen** at the **same time** on the **shelves** and in people's **homes**.

2) **Auxins** are also used **commercially** by **farmers** and **gardeners**, for example:

Auxins are used in selective weedkillers (herbicides) — auxins make weeds produce long stems instead of lots of leaves. This makes the weeds grow too fast, so they can't get enough water or nutrients, so they die.

Auxins are used as rooting hormones (e.g. in rooting powder) — auxins make a cutting (part of the plant, e.g. a stem cutting) grow roots. The cutting can then be planted and grown into a new plant. Many cuttings can be taken from just one original plant and treated with rooting hormones, so lots of the same plant can be grown quickly and cheaply from just one plant.

Warm-Up Questions

Q1 Name the type of plant hormone that controls apical dominance.
Q2 Apart from controlling seed germination, give one function of gibberellins in a plant.

Exam Questions

Q1 Which of the following hormones inhibits leaf loss in deciduous plants?
A auxins   B gibberellins   C ethene   D abscisic acid   [1 mark]

Q2 A tomato grower wants all her tomatoes to ripen at the same time, just before she sells them at a market.
a) Name a plant hormone she could use to make the tomatoes ripen. [1 mark]
b) Explain how the hormone you named in part a) makes tomatoes ripen. [1 mark]
c) Suggest a commercial advantage of being able to pick and transport tomatoes before they're ripe. [1 mark]

Q3 Drought conditions stimulate plants to produce the hormone abscisic acid (ABA). Suggest how this helps plants to survive when there is little or no water available. [2 marks]

The weeping willow — yep, that plant definitely has hormones...

Just wait till the next time you're in a supermarket — I bet you can't get round the whole shop without commenting on why the bananas are ripe. And you're going to be great fun when all the leaves start dropping off the trees in autumn. Make sure you know the roles of all the plant hormones mentioned on pages 171-173 or there'll be trouble.

Photosynthesis and Respiration

OK, this isn't the easiest topic in the world, but 'cos I'm feeling nice today we'll take it slowly, one bit at a time...

Biological Processes Need Energy

Living things **need energy** for biological processes to occur:

- **Plants** need energy for things like **photosynthesis**, **active transport** (e.g. to take in minerals via their roots), **DNA replication**, **cell division** and **protein synthesis**.
- **Animals** need energy for things like **muscle contraction**, maintenance of **body temperature**, **active transport**, **DNA replication**, **cell division** and **protein synthesis**.
- Without energy, these biological processes would **stop** and the plant or animal would **die**.

Microorganisms need energy for things like DNA replication, cell division, protein synthesis and sometimes motility (movement).

Photosynthesis Stores Energy in Glucose

1) **Plants** can **make** their **own food** (**glucose**). They do this using **photosynthesis**.
2) **Photosynthesis** is the process where **energy** from **light** is used to **make glucose** from H_2O and CO_2 (the light energy is **converted** to **chemical energy** in the form of glucose).
3) Photosynthesis occurs in a **series** of **reactions**, but the overall equation is:

$$6CO_2 + 6H_2O + Energy \longrightarrow C_6H_{12}O_6 \text{ (glucose)} + 6O_2$$

4) So, energy is **stored** in the **glucose** until the plants **release** it by **respiration**.
5) **Animals can't make** their **own food**. So, they obtain glucose by **eating plants** (or **other animals**), then respire the glucose to release energy.

Cells Release Energy from Glucose by Respiration

1) **Living** cells **release energy** from **glucose** — this process is called **respiration**.
2) This energy is used to power all the **biological processes** in a cell.
3) There are two types of respiration:
   - **Aerobic respiration** — respiration **using oxygen**.
   - **Anaerobic respiration** — respiration **without oxygen**.
4) Aerobic respiration produces **carbon dioxide** and **water**, and releases **energy**.

The glucose made in photosynthesis by plants is needed for use in respiration in both plants and animals.

The overall equation is:

$$C_6H_{12}O_6 \text{ (glucose)} + 6O_2 \longrightarrow 6CO_2 + 6H_2O + Energy$$

You Need to Know Some Basics Before You Start

There are some pretty confusing terms in this section (and the next) that you need to get your head around:

- **Metabolic pathway** — a **series** of **small reactions** controlled by **enzymes**, e.g. **respiration** and **photosynthesis**.
- **Phosphorylation** — **adding phosphate** to a molecule, e.g. **ADP** is phosphorylated to **ATP**.
- **Photophosphorylation** — **adding phosphate** to a molecule using **light**.
- **Photolysis** — the **splitting** (lysis) of a molecule using **light** (photo) energy.
- **Hydrolysis** — the **splitting** (lysis) of a molecule using **water** (hydro).
- **Decarboxylation** — the **removal** of **carbon dioxide** from a molecule.
- **Dehydrogenation** — the **removal** of **hydrogen** from a molecule.
- **Redox reactions** — reactions that involve **oxidation** and **reduction**.

Remember redox reactions:

1) If something is **reduced** it has **gained electrons** (e^-), and may have **gained hydrogen** or lost oxygen.
2) If something is **oxidised** it has **lost electrons**, and may have **lost hydrogen** or gained oxygen.
3) Oxidation of one molecule **always** involves reduction of another molecule.

One way to remember electron and hydrogen movement is OILRIG. Oxidation Is Loss, Reduction Is Gain.

Photosynthesis and Respiration

Photosynthesis and Respiration Involve Coenzymes

1) As you know from Module 2, a **coenzyme** is a molecule that **aids** the **function** of an **enzyme**.

2) They usually work by **transferring** a **chemical group** from one molecule to another.

3) A coenzyme used in **photosynthesis** is **NADP**. NADP transfers **hydrogen** from one molecule to another — this means it can **reduce** (give hydrogen to) or **oxidise** (take hydrogen from) a molecule.

4) Examples of coenzymes used in **respiration** are: **NAD**, **coenzyme A** and **FAD**.
   - NAD and FAD transfer **hydrogen** from one molecule to another — this means they can **reduce** (give hydrogen to) or **oxidise** (take hydrogen from) a molecule.
   - **Coenzyme A** transfers **acetate** between molecules (see page 185).

When hydrogen is transferred between molecules, electrons are transferred too.

Photosynthesis Takes Place in the Chloroplasts of Plant Cells

1) **Chloroplasts** are **small, flattened organelles** found in **plant cells**. They're the **location** for **photosynthesis** in plant cells.

2) They have a **double membrane** called the **chloroplast envelope**.

3) **Thylakoids** (fluid-filled sacs) are **stacked up** in the chloroplast into structures called **grana** (singular = **granum**). The grana are **linked** together by bits of thylakoid membrane called **lamellae** (singular = **lamella**).

4) Chloroplasts contain **photosynthetic pigments** (e.g. **chlorophyll a**, **chlorophyll b** and **carotene**). These are **coloured substances** that **absorb** the **light energy** needed for photosynthesis. The pigments are found in the **thylakoid membranes** — they're attached to **proteins**. The protein and pigment is called a **photosystem**.

5) A photosystem contains **two types** of photosynthetic pigments — **primary** pigments and **accessory** pigments. Primary pigments are **reaction centres**, where **electrons** are **excited** during the light-dependent reaction (see pages 176-177). **Accessory pigments** make up **light-harvesting systems**. These **surround** reaction centres and **transfer light energy** to them to boost the energy available for electron excitement to take place.

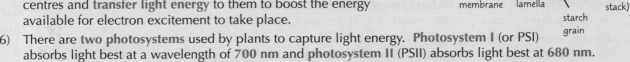

outer membrane of envelope · inner membrane of envelope · circular DNA · stroma · thylakoid · thylakoid membrane · lamella · granum (thylakoid stack) · starch grain

6) There are **two photosystems** used by plants to capture light energy. **Photosystem I** (or PSI) absorbs light best at a wavelength of **700 nm** and **photosystem II** (PSII) absorbs light best at **680 nm**.

7) Contained within the inner membrane of the chloroplast and **surrounding** the thylakoids is a gel-like substance called the **stroma**. It contains **enzymes**, **sugars** and **organic acids**.

8) Chloroplasts have their own **DNA**. It's found in the **stroma** and is often **circular**. There can be **multiple copies** in **each** chloroplast.

9) Carbohydrates produced by photosynthesis and not used straight away are stored as **starch grains** in the **stroma**.

Warm-Up Questions

Q1 Write down three biological processes in animals that need energy.

Q2 Give the name of a coenzyme involved in respiration.

Q3 What are photosynthetic pigments?

PRACTICE QUESTIONS

Exam Question

Q1 Which one of these statements about chloroplasts is correct?

A The thylakoids are stacked up into structures called lamellae.

B The photosynthetic pigments are located in the chloroplast envelope.

C The stroma is a gel-like substance that contains enzymes, sugars and organic acids.

D Chloroplasts don't contain any DNA.

[1 mark]

Oh dear, I've used up all my energy on these two pages...

Well, I won't beat about the bush, this stuff is pretty tricky... nearly as hard as a cross between Hugh Jackman and concrete. With a little patience and perseverance (and plenty of [chocolate] [coffee] [marshmallows] — delete as you wish), you'll get there. Once you've got these pages straight in your head, the next ones will be easier to understand.

Photosynthesis

Right, pen at the ready. Check. Brain switched on. Check. Cuppa piping hot. Check. Sweets on standby. Check. Okay, I think you're all sorted to look at the light-dependent stage of photosynthesis. Here we go...

Photosynthesis can be Split into **Two Stages**

There are actually **two stages** that make up **photosynthesis**:

See p. 178 for loads more information on the Calvin cycle.

1) The Light-Dependent Reaction

1) As the name suggests, this reaction **needs light energy**.

2) It takes place in the **thylakoid membranes** of the chloroplasts.

3) Here, light energy is absorbed by **photosynthetic pigments** in the **photosystems** and converted to **chemical energy**.

4) The light energy is used to add a phosphate group to ADP to form **ATP**, and to reduce NADP to form **reduced NADP**. (Reduced NADP is an **energy-rich molecule** because it can transfer hydrogen, and so electrons, to other molecules.) **ATP transfers energy** and reduced **NADP transfers hydrogen** to the light-independent reaction.

5) During the process **H₂O** is **oxidised** to **O₂**.

2) The Light-Independent Reaction

1) This is also called the **Calvin cycle** and as the name suggests it **doesn't use light energy** directly. (But it does **rely on the products** of the light-dependent reaction).

2) It takes place in the **stroma** of the chloroplasts.

3) Here, the **ATP** and **reduced NADP** from the light-dependent reaction supply the **energy** and **hydrogen** to make **glucose** from **CO₂**.

Thin Layer Chromatography can Separate Photosynthetic Pigments

The **photosynthetic pigments** in plants can be **separated** using **thin layer chromatography** (**TLC**). Like all types of chromatography, TLC involves a **mobile phase** (in this case a liquid solvent) and a **stationary phase** (in this case a solid, e.g. glass, plate with a thin layer of gel, e.g. silica gel, on top — called a **chromatography plate**).

1) **Grind** up several leaves (spinach works nicely) with some **anhydrous sodium sulfate** and some **propanone**.

2) **Transfer** the **liquid** to a test tube, add some **petroleum ether** and gently shake the tube. **Two distinct layers** will form in the liquid — the **top layer** is the **pigments** mixed in with the petroleum ether.

It's best to do steps 2 and 5 in a fume cupboard as the chemicals used are volatile (evaporate easily) and the vapours are hazardous.

3) Transfer some of the liquid from the **top layer** into a second test tube with some **anhydrous sodium sulfate**.

4) Draw a horizontal **pencil line** near the bottom of a **chromatography plate**. Build up a single **concentrated spot** of the liquid from step 3) on the line by applying several drops and ensuring each one is **dry** before the next is added. This is the **point of origin**.

5) Once the point of origin is completely dry, put the plate into a glass beaker with some prepared **solvent** (e.g. a mixture of **propanone**, **cyclohexane** and **petroleum ether**) — just enough so that the **point of origin** is a little bit **above** the solvent. Put a **lid** on the beaker and leave the plate to develop. As the solvent spreads up the plate, the different **pigments** move with it, but at **different rates** — so they **separate**.

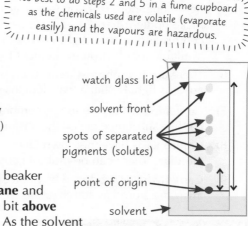

watch glass lid

solvent front

spots of separated pigments (solutes)

point of origin

solvent

6) When the solvent has **nearly** reached the top, take the plate out and **mark** the **solvent front** (the furthest point the solvent has reached) with a **pencil** and leave the plate to dry in a well-ventilated place.

7) There should be **several** new coloured spots on the chromatography plate between the **point of origin** and the **solvent front**. These are the separated **pigments** (solutes). You can calculate their **R_f values** and look them up in a database to **identify** what the pigments are.

$$R_f \text{ value} = \frac{\text{distance travelled by solute}}{\text{distance travelled by solvent}}$$

In the **Light-Dependent Reaction**, ATP is Made by **Photophosphorylation**

In the light-dependent reaction, the **light energy** absorbed by the photosystems is used for **three** things:

1) Making ATP from ADP and inorganic phosphate. This reaction is called photophosphorylation (see p. 174).

2) Making reduced NADP from NADP.

3) Splitting water into protons (H⁺ ions), electrons and oxygen. This is called photolysis (see p. 174).

The light-dependent reaction actually includes **two types** of **photophosphorylation** — **non-cyclic** and **cyclic**. Each of these processes has **different products**.

Photosynthesis

Non-cyclic Photophosphorylation Produces **ATP**, Reduced **NADP** and **O₂**

To understand the process you need to know that the photosystems (in the thylakoid membranes) are **linked** by **electron carriers**. Electron carriers are **proteins** that **transfer electrons**. The photosystems and electron carriers form an **electron transport chain** — a **chain** of **proteins** through which **excited electrons flow**. All the processes in the diagrams are happening together — I've just split them up to make it easier to understand.

1 **Light energy excites electrons in chlorophyll**

- **Light energy** is absorbed by **PSII**.

- The light energy **excites electrons** in **chlorophyll**.

- The electrons move to a **higher energy level** (i.e. they have more energy).

- These high-energy electrons **move along** the **electron transport chain** to **PSI**.

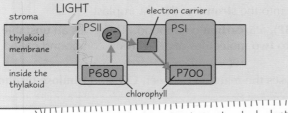

If too much light energy has been absorbed, plants release some of the excess energy by emitting fluorescent light. This is called chlorophyll fluorescence.

2 **Photolysis of water produces protons (H⁺ ions), electrons and O₂**

- As the excited electrons **from chlorophyll leave PSII** to **move along** the electron transport chain, they must be **replaced**.

- **Light** energy splits **water** into **protons** (H⁺ ions), **electrons** and **oxygen**. (So the O_2 in photosynthesis comes from water.)

- The reaction is: $H_2O \rightarrow 2H^+ + \frac{1}{2}O_2$

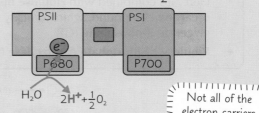

Not all of the electron carriers are shown in these diagrams.

3 **Energy from the excited electrons makes ATP...**

- The excited electrons **lose energy** as they **move along** the **electron transport chain**.

- This energy is used to **transport protons into** the **thylakoid**, via membrane proteins called **proton pumps**, so that the thylakoid has a **higher concentration** of protons than the stroma. This forms a **proton gradient** across the membrane.

- Protons move **down** their concentration gradient, into the stroma, **via an enzyme** called **ATP synthase**. The energy from this movement combines **ADP** and **inorganic phosphate** (P$_i$) to form **ATP**.

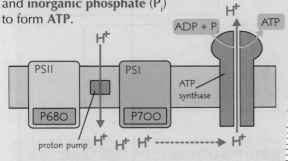

4 **...and generates reduced NADP.**

- Light energy is **absorbed** by PSI, which excites the electrons again to an **even higher** energy level.

- Finally, the electrons are **transferred** to NADP, along with a **proton** (H⁺ ion) from the **stroma**, to form **reduced NADP**.

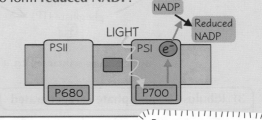

Remember a 'proton' is just another word for a hydrogen ion (H⁺).

The process of electrons flowing down the electron transport chain and creating a proton gradient across the membrane to drive ATP synthesis is called chemiosmosis. It's described by the chemiosmotic theory.

Cyclic Photophosphorylation Only Produces **ATP**

Cyclic photophosphorylation **only uses PSI**. It's called 'cyclic' because the electrons from the chlorophyll molecule **aren't** passed onto NADP, but are **passed back** to PSI via electron carriers. This means the electrons are **recycled** and can repeatedly flow through PSI. This process doesn't produce any reduced NADP or O₂ — it **only produces** small amounts of **ATP**.

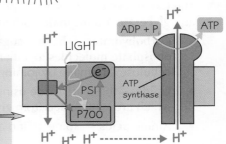

Photosynthesis

Don't worry, you're over the worst of photosynthesis now. Instead of electrons flying around, there's a nice cycle of reactions to learn. What more could you want from life? Money, fast cars and nice clothes have nothing on this...

The **Light-Independent** Reaction is also called the **Calvin Cycle**

1) **The Calvin cycle** takes place in the **stroma** of the chloroplasts. (The Calvin cycle is also known as **carbon dioxide fixation** because **carbon** from CO_2 is 'fixed' into an **organic molecule**.)

2) It makes a molecule called **triose phosphate** from CO_2 and **ribulose bisphosphate** (a 5-carbon compound). Triose phosphate can be used to make **glucose** and other **useful organic substances** (see below).

3) There are a few steps in the cycle, and it needs **ATP** and **H^+ ions** to keep it going.

4) The reactions are linked in a **cycle**, which means the starting compound, **ribulose bisphosphate**, is **regenerated**.

Here's what happens at each stage in the cycle:

> **1) Carbon dioxide is combined with ribulose bisphosphate to form two molecules of glycerate 3-phosphate**

- CO_2 enters the leaf through the stomata and diffuses into the stroma of the chloroplast.
- Here, it's combined with **ribulose bisphosphate (RuBP)**, a **5-carbon** compound. This gives an **unstable 6-carbon** compound, which quickly breaks down into **two** molecules of a **3-carbon** compound called **glycerate 3-phosphate (GP)**.
- **Ribulose bisphosphate carboxylase (RuBisCO)** catalyses the reaction between CO_2 and ribulose bisphosphate.

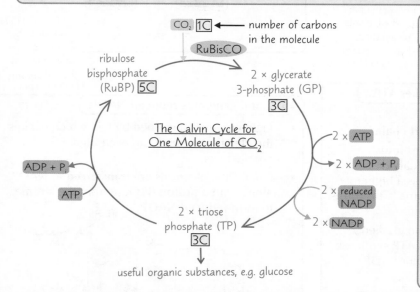

> **2) ATP and reduced NADP are required for the reduction of GP to triose phosphate**

- Now **ATP**, from the **light-dependent** reaction, **provides energy** to turn the **3-carbon** compound, **GP**, into a **different** 3-carbon compound called **triose phosphate (TP)**.
- This reaction also requires **H^+ ions**, which come from **reduced NADP** (also from the **light-dependent reaction**). Reduced NADP is **recycled** to **NADP** (for use in the light-dependent reaction again).
- **Triose phosphate** is then converted into many **useful organic compounds**, e.g. glucose (see below).

> **3) Ribulose bisphosphate is regenerated**

- **Five** out of every **six** molecules of **TP** produced in the cycle aren't used to make hexose sugars, but to **regenerate RuBP**.
- Regenerating RuBP uses the **rest** of the **ATP** produced by the **light-dependent reaction**.

TP and **GP** are **Converted** into **Useful Organic Substances** like **Glucose**

The **Calvin cycle** is the starting point for making **all** the organic substances a plant needs. **Triose phosphate** (TP) and **glycerate 3-phosphate** (GP) molecules are used to make **carbohydrates**, **lipids** and **amino acids**:

- **Carbohydrates** — hexose sugars (e.g. glucose) are made by joining **two triose phosphate molecules** together and **larger** carbohydrates (e.g. sucrose, starch, cellulose) are made by joining **hexose sugars** together in **different ways**.
- **Lipids** — these are made using **glycerol**, which is synthesised from **triose phosphate**, and **fatty acids**, which are synthesised from **glycerate 3-phosphate**.
- **Amino acids** — some amino acids are made from **glycerate 3-phosphate**.

Photosynthesis

The **Calvin Cycle** Needs to Turn **Six Times** to Make **One Hexose Sugar**

1) **Three turns** of the cycle produces **six** molecules of **triose phosphate** (TP), because two molecules of TP are made for every one CO_2 molecule used.

2) **Five** out of **six** of these TP molecules are used to **regenerate ribulose bisphosphate** (RuBP).

3) This means that for **three turns** of the cycle only **one TP** is produced that's used to make a **hexose sugar**.

4) A hexose sugar has **six carbons** though, so **two TP** molecules are needed to form one hexose sugar.

5) This means the cycle must turn **six times** to produce **two molecules** of TP that can be used to make **one hexose sugar**.

6) Six turns of the cycle need **18 ATP** and **12 reduced NADP** from the light-dependent reaction.

Warm-Up Questions

Q1 Where in the chloroplasts does the light-independent reaction occur?

Q2 Name one method that can be used to separate photosynthetic pigments in plants.

Q3 What is the equation to work out an R_f value?

Q4 What three substances does non-cyclic photophosphorylation produce?

Q5 What is an electron carrier?

Q6 Describe the role of water in the light-dependent reaction.

Q7 Which photosystem is involved in cyclic photophosphorylation?

Q8 Name the two products from the light-dependent reaction that are used in the light-independent reaction.

Q9 Name two organic substances made from triose phosphate.

Q10 How many CO_2 molecules need to enter the Calvin cycle to make one hexose sugar?

These questions cover pages 176-179.

Exam Questions

Q1 The diagram below shows the light-dependent reaction of photosynthesis.

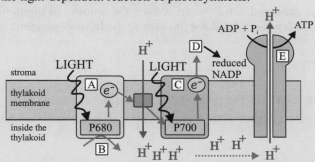

a) Where precisely in a plant does the light-dependent reaction of photosynthesis occur? [1 mark]

b) What is A? [1 mark]

c) Describe process B and explain its purpose. [4 marks]

d) What is reactant D? [1 mark]

Q2 RuBisCO is an enzyme that catalyses the first reaction of the Calvin cycle.
CA1P is an inhibitor of RuBisCO.

a)* Describe how triose phosphate is produced in the Calvin cycle. [6 marks]

b) Briefly explain how ribulose bisphosphate (RuBP) is regenerated in the Calvin cycle. [2 marks]

c) Explain the effect that CA1P would have on glucose production. [3 marks]

* You will be assessed on the quality of your written response in this question.

Calvin cycles — bikes made by people that normally make pants...

Next thing we know there'll be people swanning about in their pants riding highly fashionable bikes. Sounds awful I know, but let's face it, anything would look better than cycling shorts. Anyway, it would be a good idea to go over these pages a couple of times — I promise you, there's still room left in your head for more information...

Limiting Factors in Photosynthesis

Now you know what photosynthesis is it's time to find out what conditions make it speedy and what slows it down. I'd start by making sure you have the best conditions for revision — oodles of biscuits and your thinking cap on.

There are **Optimum Conditions** for Photosynthesis

The **ideal conditions** for photosynthesis vary from one plant species to another.
Most plants in temperate climates, like in the UK, would be happy with the conditions below:

1. High light intensity of a certain wavelength

- Light is needed to provide the energy for the light-dependent reaction — the higher the intensity of the light, the more energy it provides.
- Only certain wavelengths of light are used for photosynthesis. The photosynthetic pigments chlorophyll a, chlorophyll b and carotene only absorb the red and blue light in sunlight. (Green light is reflected, which is why plants look green.)

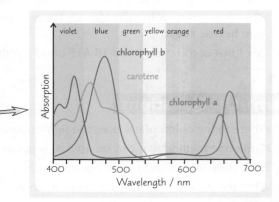

2. Temperature around 25 °C

- Photosynthesis involves enzymes (e.g. ATP synthase, RuBisCO). If the temperature falls below 10 °C, the enzymes become inactive, but if the temperature is more than 45 °C they may start to denature.
- Also, at high temperatures:

  1) Stomata close to avoid losing too much water. This causes photosynthesis to slow down because less CO_2 enters the leaf when the stomata are closed.

  The width of the opening of stomata is called the stomatal aperture.

  2) The thylakoid membranes may be damaged. This could reduce the rate of the light-dependent stage reactions by reducing the number of sites available for electron transfer.

  3) The membranes around the chloroplasts could be damaged, which could cause enzymes important in the Calvin cycle to be released into the cell. This would reduce the rate of the light-independent stage reactions.

  4) Chlorophyll could be damaged. This would reduce the amount of pigment that can absorb light energy, which would reduce the rate of the light-dependent stage reactions.

3. Carbon dioxide at 0.4%

- Carbon dioxide makes up 0.04% of the gases in the atmosphere.
- Increasing this to 0.4% gives a higher rate of photosynthesis, but any higher and the stomata start to close.

Light, Temperature and CO_2 can all Limit Photosynthesis

1) **All three** of these things need to be at the **right level** to allow a plant to photosynthesise as quickly as possible.

2) If any **one** of these factors is **too low** or **too high**, it will **limit photosynthesis** (slow it down). Even if the other two factors are at the perfect level, it won't make **any difference** to the speed of photosynthesis as long as that factor is at the wrong level.

3) On a warm, sunny, windless day, it's usually CO_2 that's the limiting factor, and at night it's the **light intensity**.

4) However, **any** of these factors could become the limiting factor, depending on the **environmental conditions**.

All that Murray and Fraser knew was that limiting photosynthesis was a tasty business...

Limiting Factors in Photosynthesis

You Might Have to **Interpret Graphs** About **Limiting Factors**

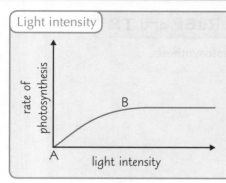

Between points A and B, the rate of photosynthesis is limited by the **light intensity**. So as the light intensity **increases**, so can the rate of photosynthesis. Point B is the **saturation point** — increasing light intensity after this point makes no difference, because **something else** has become the limiting factor. The graph now **levels off**.

The saturation point is where a factor is no longer limiting the reaction — something else has become the limiting factor.

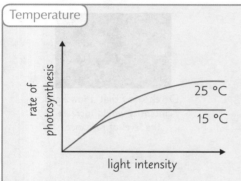

Both these graphs level off when **light intensity** is no longer the limiting factor. The graph at **25 °C** levels off at a **higher point** than the one at **15 °C**, showing that **temperature** must have been a limiting factor at **15 °C**.

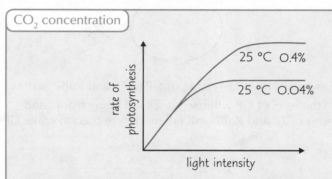

Again, both these graphs level off when **light intensity** is no longer the limiting factor. The graph at **0.4% CO_2** levels off at a **higher point** than the one at **0.04%**, so **CO_2 concentration** must have been a limiting factor at **0.04% CO_2**. The limiting factor here **isn't temperature** because it's the **same** for both graphs (25 °C).

Water Stress Can Also Affect **Photosynthesis**

When plants **don't** have **enough water**, their **stomata** will **close** to preserve what little water they do have, leading to **less CO_2** entering the leaf for the Calvin cycle and **slowing** photosynthesis down.

Warm-Up Questions

Q1 Why is a high light intensity an optimum condition for photosynthesis?

Q2 What is the optimum concentration of carbon dioxide for photosynthesis?

Q3 What are the possible likely limiting factors for photosynthesis on a warm, sunny day?

Q4 Explain how a lack of water slows down photosynthesis in a plant.

Exam Question

Q1 An experiment was carried out to investigate how temperature affects photosynthesis.
The rate of photosynthesis was measured at 10 °C, 25 °C and 45 °C.
At which temperature would the rate of photosynthesis have been greatest? Explain your answer. [4 marks]

I'm a whizz at the factors that limit revision...

... watching Hollyoaks, making tea, watching EastEnders, walking the dog... not to mention staring into space. These pages aren't that bad though. You just need to learn how light, CO_2, temperature and water stress affect the rate of photosynthesis. Try shutting the book and writing down what you know — you'll be amazed at what you remember.

Limiting Factors in Photosynthesis

Well, I hope you didn't think we'd finished covering limiting factors.... ohhhhhh no, I could write a whole book on them. But just for you I've added an experiment to spice things up a bit. It's time to polish your test tubes.

Light, Temperature and CO_2 Affect the Levels of GP, RuBP and TP

Light intensity, temperature and CO_2 concentration all affect the rate of photosynthesis, which means they affect the levels of GP, RuBP and TP in the Calvin cycle.

1. Light intensity

- In **low light intensities**, the products of the light-dependent stage (**reduced NADP and ATP**) will be in **short supply**.

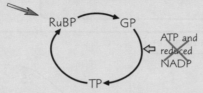

- This means that **conversion of GP to TP and RuBP is slow**.
- So the level of **GP** will **rise** (as it's still being made) and levels of **TP** and **RuBP** will **fall** (as they're used to make GP).

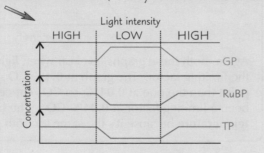

Derek knew that a low light intensity would increase the level of romance.

2. Temperature

- All the reactions in the Calvin cycle are catalysed by **enzymes** (e.g. RuBisCO).
- At **low temperatures**, all of the reactions will be **slower** as the enzymes work more **slowly**.

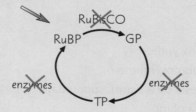

- This means the levels of **RuBP, GP** and **TP** will **fall**.
- GP, TP and RuBP are affected in the same way at **very high temperatures**, because the **enzymes** will start to **denature**.

3. Carbon Dioxide concentration

- At **low CO_2 concentrations**, **conversion of RuBP** to GP is also **slow** (as there's less CO_2 to combine with RuBP to make GP).

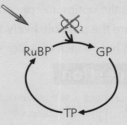

- So the level of **RuBP** will **rise** (as it's still being made) and levels of **GP** and **TP** will **fall** (as they're used up to make RuBP).

Limiting Factors in Photosynthesis

Limiting Factors can be Investigated using Pondweed

PRACTICAL SKILLS

1) **Canadian pondweed** (*Elodea*) can be used to measure the effect of light intensity, temperature and CO_2 concentration on the **rate of photosynthesis**.

2) The rate at which **oxygen** is **produced** by the pondweed can be easily **measured** and this **corresponds** to the rate of photosynthesis.

Remember photosynthesis produces glucose and oxygen (see page 174).

3) For example, the **apparatus** below is used to **measure** the **effect** of **light intensity** on photosynthesis.

- A **test tube** containing the **pondweed** and **water** is connected to a **capillary tube** full of water.
- The tube of water is connected to a **syringe**.
- A **source of white light** is placed at a **specific distance** from the pondweed.
- The pondweed is left to photosynthesise for a **set** amount of **time**. As it photosynthesises, the **oxygen released** will **collect** in the **capillary tube**.
- At the end of the experiment, the syringe is used to **draw** the gas **bubble** in the tube **up** alongside a **ruler** and the **length** of the gas bubble is **measured**. This is proportional to the volume of O_2 produced.
- Any **variables** that could affect the results should be **controlled**, e.g. temperature, the time the weed is left to photosynthesise.
- The experiment is **repeated** and the **average** length of gas bubble is calculated, to make the results **more precise**.
- The whole experiment is then **repeated** with the **light source** placed at **different distances** from the pondweed.

light source

ruler

O_2 bubble   water in capillary tube

clamp

small O_2 bubbles

Canadian pondweed

water

ruler to vary distance from plant

To work out the exact volume of O_2 produced, you also need to know the radius of the capillary tube.

The volume of O_2 can also be measured by counting the number of small O_2 bubbles released by the pondweed, but this is less accurate.

4) The apparatus above can be adapted to **measure** the **effect** of **temperature** on photosynthesis — the test tube of pondweed is put in a **beaker of water** at a **set temperature** (then the experiment's repeated with different temperatures of water).

Warm-Up Questions

Q1 How does a low CO_2 concentration in the air affect the level of TP in a plant?

Q2 In an experiment on the rate of photosynthesis, how can light intensity be varied?

Q3 In the experiment above, give two variables that must be controlled.

PRACTICE QUESTIONS

Exam Questions

Q1 A scientist was investigating the effect of different conditions on the levels of GP, TP and RuBP in a plant. Predict the results of his experiment under the following conditions. Explain your answers.
   a) Low light intensity, optimum temperature and optimum CO_2 concentration.   [3 marks]
   b) Low temperature, optimum light intensity and optimum CO_2 concentration.   [3 marks]

Q2* Briefly describe the apparatus and method you would use to investigate how temperature affects photosynthesis in Canadian pondweed.   [6 marks]

   * You will be assessed on the quality of your written response in this question.

Aah, Canadian pondweed — a biology student's best friend...

Well... sometimes — usually you end up staring endlessly at it while it produces lots of tiny bubbles. Thrilling. If you have to describe an experiment in the exam make sure you include details about the apparatus, the method and the variables you'd keep constant to make your results accurate, precise, valid, repeatable and reproducible.

Aerobic Respiration

From the last gazillion pages you know that plants make their own glucose. Unfortunately, that means now you need to learn how plant and animal cells release energy from glucose. It's not the easiest thing in the world to understand, but it'll make sense once you've gone through it a couple of times.

There are **Four Stages** in **Aerobic Respiration**

1) The four stages in aerobic respiration are **glycolysis**, the **link reaction**, the **Krebs cycle** and **oxidative phosphorylation**.

2) The **first three** stages are a **series of reactions**. The **products** from these reactions are **used** in the **final stage** to produce loads of ATP.

3) The **first** stage happens in the **cytoplasm** of cells and the **other three** stages take place in the **mitochondria**. You might want to refresh your memory of mitochondrion structure before you start.

4) All cells use **glucose** to **respire**, but organisms can also **break down** other **complex organic molecules** (e.g. fatty acids, amino acids), which can then be respired.

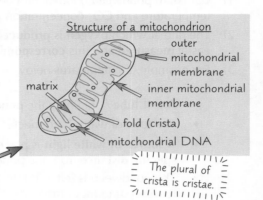

Structure of a mitochondrion
outer mitochondrial membrane
matrix
inner mitochondrial membrane
fold (crista)
mitochondrial DNA

The plural of crista is cristae.

Stage 1 — **Glycolysis** Makes **Pyruvate** from **Glucose**

1) Glycolysis involves splitting **one molecule** of glucose (with 6 carbons — 6C) into **two** smaller molecules of **pyruvate** (3C).

2) The process happens in the **cytoplasm** of cells.

3) Glycolysis is the **first stage** of both aerobic and anaerobic respiration and **doesn't need oxygen** to take place — so it's an **anaerobic** process.

Respiration Map
Glycolysis — You are here
Link Reaction
Krebs Cycle
Oxidative Phosphorylation

There are **Two Stages** in Glycolysis — **Phosphorylation** and **Oxidation**

First, **ATP** is **used** to **phosphorylate glucose** to triose phosphate. Then **triose phosphate** is **oxidised**, releasing ATP. Overall there's a **net gain** of **2 ATP**.

(1) Stage One — Phosphorylation

1) Glucose is **phosphorylated** by adding **2 phosphates** from 2 molecules of **ATP**.

2) This creates 1 molecule of **hexose bisphosphate** and 2 molecules of **ADP**.

3) Then, **hexose bisphosphate** is **split up** into **2** molecules of **triose phosphate**.

(2) Stage Two — Oxidation

1) Triose phosphate is **oxidised** (loses hydrogen), forming **2** molecules of **pyruvate**.

2) **NAD** collects the hydrogen ions, forming **2 reduced NAD**.

3) **4 ATP are produced**, but 2 were used up in stage one, so there's a **net gain** of **2 ATP**.

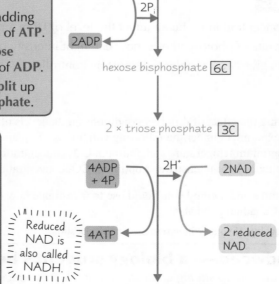

glucose 6C ← number of carbons in the molecule
2ATP
2Pᵢ
2ADP
hexose bisphosphate 6C
2 × triose phosphate 3C
4ADP + 4Pᵢ
2H⁺
2NAD
4ATP
2 reduced NAD
2 × pyruvate 3C

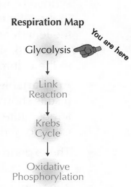
Reduced NAD is also called NADH.

You're probably wondering what now happens to all the products of glycolysis...

1) The **two** molecules of **reduced NAD** go to the **last stage** (oxidative phosphorylation — see page 187).

2) The **two pyruvate** molecules are **actively transported** into the **matrix** of the **mitochondria** for the **link reaction** (see the next page).

Aerobic Respiration

Stage 2 — The **Link Reaction** Converts **Pyruvate** to **Acetyl Coenzyme A**

The **link reaction** takes place in the **mitochondrial matrix**:

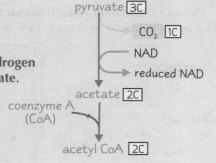

1) **Pyruvate is decarboxylated**
   — **one carbon atom** is **removed**
   from pyruvate in the form of CO_2.

2) **NAD** is **reduced** to **NADH** — it collects **hydrogen**
   from pyruvate, changing **pyruvate** into **acetate**.

3) **Acetate** is combined with
   coenzyme A (CoA) to form
   acetyl coenzyme A (acetyl CoA).

4) **No ATP** is produced in this reaction.

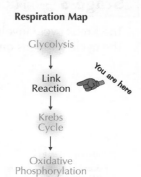

Respiration Map

The **Link Reaction** Occurs **Twice** for Every **Glucose Molecule**

Two pyruvate molecules are made for **every glucose molecule** that enters glycolysis. This means the **link reaction** and the third stage (the **Krebs cycle**) happen **twice** for every glucose molecule. So for each glucose molecule:

- **Two** molecules of acetyl coenzyme A go into the Krebs cycle (see next page).
- **Two CO_2 molecules** are released as a waste product of respiration.
- **Two** molecules of reduced NAD are formed and go to the last stage (oxidative phosphorylation, see page 187).

Warm-Up Questions

Q1 In the mitochondrial structure, what is a crista?

Q2 Where in the cell does glycolysis occur?

Q3 Is glycolysis an anaerobic or aerobic process?

Q4 How many ATP molecules are used up in glycolysis?

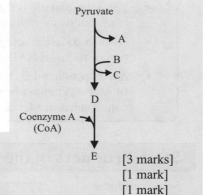

Exam Questions

Q1 The diagram on the right shows a stage of aerobic respiration.
  a) Identify compounds A, D and E. [3 marks]
  b) What is the role of compound B in this reaction? [1 mark]
  c) Where does this reaction happen in the cell? [1 mark]

Q2 Which of the following best describes acetyl coenzyme A?
  A A 6-carbon molecule formed during the first stage of glycolysis.
  B A 3-carbon molecule that is a product of glycolysis and the first reactant in the link reaction.
  C A 2-carbon molecule that is the product of the link reaction and feeds into the Krebs cycle.
  D A 3-carbon molecule formed by the splitting of hexose bisphosphate in the first stage of glycolysis. [1 mark]

Q3 Aerobic respiration involves several different steps. Which of the following statement(s) is/are true?
  Statement 1: One glucose molecule is broken down into two molecules of pyruvate during glycolysis.
  Statement 2: In glycolysis, there is an overall gain of 4 ATP molecules.
  Statement 3: In aerobic respiration, the link reaction immediately follows the Krebs cycle.
  A 1, 2 and 3 / B Only 1 and 2 / C Only 2 and 3 / D Only 1 [1 mark]

Q4* Describe how a 6-carbon molecule of glucose is converted to pyruvate. [6 marks]

* You will be assessed on the quality of your written response in this question.

No ATP was harmed during this reaction...

Ahhhh... too many reactions. I'm sure your head hurts now, 'cause mine certainly does. Just think of revision as like doing exercise — it can be a pain while you're doing it (and maybe afterwards too), but it's worth it for the well-toned brain you'll have. Just keep going over and over it, until you get the first two stages of respiration straight in your head.

Aerobic Respiration

As you've seen, glycolysis produces a net gain of two ATP. Pah, we can do better than that.
The Krebs cycle and oxidative phosphorylation are where it all happens — ATP galore.

Stage 3 — The **Krebs Cycle** Produces **Reduced Coenzymes** and **ATP**

The Krebs cycle involves a series of **oxidation-reduction reactions**, which take place in the **matrix** of the **mitochondria**.
The cycle happens **once** for **every pyruvate** molecule, so it goes round **twice** for **every glucose** molecule.

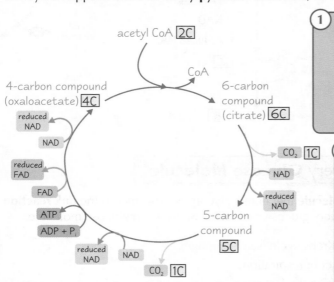

1
- The **acetyl group** from **acetyl CoA** (produced in the link reaction) combines with **oxaloacetate** to form **citrate** (citric acid). This is catalysed by citrate synthase.
- **Coenzyme A** goes back to the **link reaction** to be used again.

2
- The **6C citrate molecule** is converted to a **5C molecule**.
- **Decarboxylation** occurs, where CO_2 is **removed**.
- **Dehydrogenation** also occurs, where **hydrogen** is **removed**.
- The hydrogen is used to **produce reduced NAD** from NAD.

Respiration Map

Glycolysis

Link Reaction — You are here

Krebs Cycle

Oxidative Phosphorylation

3
- The **5C molecule** is then converted to a **4C molecule**. (There are some intermediate compounds formed during this conversion, but you don't need to know about them.)
- **Decarboxylation** and **dehydrogenation** occur, producing **one molecule** of **reduced FAD** and **two** of **reduced NAD**.
- **ATP is produced** by the **direct transfer** of a **phosphate** group from an **intermediate** compound **to ADP**. When a phosphate group is directly transferred from one molecule to another it's called **substrate-level phosphorylation**. **Citrate** has now been **converted** into **oxaloacetate**.

Some **Products** of the **Krebs Cycle** are Used in **Oxidative Phosphorylation**

Some products are **reused**, some are **released** and others are used for the **next stage** of respiration:

Product from one Krebs cycle	Where it goes
1 coenzyme A	Reused in the next link reaction
Oxaloacetate	Regenerated for use in the next Krebs cycle
2 CO_2	Released as a waste product
1 ATP	Used for energy
3 reduced NAD	To oxidative phosphorylation
1 reduced FAD	To oxidative phosphorylation

Respiration Map

Glycolysis

Link Reaction

Krebs Cycle

Oxidative Phosphorylation — You are here

Stage 4 — **Oxidative Phosphorylation** Produces **Lots** of **ATP**

1) Oxidative phosphorylation is the process where the **energy** carried by **electrons**, from **reduced coenzymes** (reduced NAD and reduced FAD), is used to **make ATP**.
   (The whole point of the previous stages is to make reduced NAD and reduced FAD for the final stage.)

2) Oxidative phosphorylation takes place in the **inner mitochondrial membrane**.
   A description of the process is on the next page.

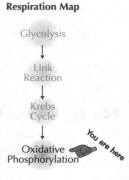

Aerobic Respiration

Protons are Pumped Across the Inner Mitochondrial Membrane

So now on to how **oxidative phosphorylation** actually **works**:

The regenerated coenzymes are reused in the Krebs cycle.

1) **Hydrogen atoms** are released from **reduced NAD** and **reduced FAD** as they're oxidised to NAD and FAD. The H atoms **split** into **protons (H⁺)** and **electrons (e⁻)**.

2) The **electrons** move along the **electron transport chain** (made up of three **electron carriers**), **losing energy** at each carrier. (The electron transport chain is located in the **inner mitochondrial membrane**. This membrane is folded into **cristae**, which **increases** the membrane's **surface area** to maximise respiration.)

3) This energy is used by the electron carriers to **pump protons** from the **mitochondrial matrix into** the **intermembrane space** (the space **between** the inner and outer **mitochondrial membranes**).

4) The **concentration** of **protons** is now **higher** in the **intermembrane space** than in the mitochondrial matrix — this forms an **electrochemical gradient** (a **concentration gradient** of **ions**).

5) Protons **move down** the **electrochemical gradient**, back into the mitochondrial matrix, via **ATP synthase**. This **movement** drives the synthesis of **ATP** from **ADP** and **inorganic phosphate** (P$_i$).

6) This process of ATP production driven by the movement of H⁺ ions across a membrane (due to electrons moving down an electron transport chain) is called **chemiosmosis** (which is described by the **chemiosmotic theory**).

7) In the mitochondrial matrix, at the end of the transport chain, the **protons**, **electrons** and **O₂** (from the blood) combine to form **water**. Oxygen is said to be the final **electron acceptor**.

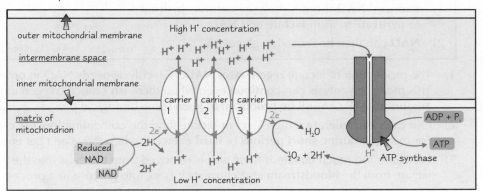

32 ATP Can be Made from One Glucose Molecule

As you know, **oxidative phosphorylation makes ATP** using energy from the reduced coenzymes — **2.5 ATP** are made from each **reduced NAD** and **1.5 ATP** are made from each **reduced FAD**. The table on the right shows **how much** ATP a cell can make from **one molecule** of **glucose** in **aerobic respiration**. (Remember, one molecule of glucose produces 2 pyruvate, so the link reaction and Krebs cycle happen twice.)

Stage of respiration	Molecules produced	Number of ATP molecules
Glycolysis	2 ATP	2
Glycolysis	2 reduced NAD	2 × 2.5 = 5
Link Reaction (×2)	2 reduced NAD	2 × 2.5 = 5
Krebs cycle (×2)	2 ATP	2
Krebs cycle (×2)	6 reduced NAD	6 × 2.5 = 15
Krebs cycle (×2)	2 reduced FAD	2 × 1.5 = 3
		Total ATP = 32

Warm-Up Questions

Q1 Where in the cell does the Krebs cycle occur?

Q2 How many times does decarboxylation happen during one turn of the Krebs cycle?

Q3 What do the electrons lose as they move along the electron transport chain in oxidative phosphorylation?

Exam Question

Q1 Carbon monoxide inhibits the final electron carrier in the electron transport chain.
   a) Explain how this affects ATP production via the electron transport chain. [2 marks]
   b) Explain how this affects ATP production via the Krebs cycle. [2 marks]

The electron transport chain isn't just a FAD with the examiners...

Oh my gosh, I didn't think it could get any worse... You may be wondering how to learn these pages of crazy chemistry. Basically, you have to put in the time and go over and over it. Don't worry though, it WILL pay off and before you know it, you'll be set for the exam. And once you know this section you'll be able to do anything, e.g. world domination.

Anaerobic Respiration and RQs

If you need a little extra ATP, but there's not enough oxygen to increase your aerobic respiration, anaerobic respiration has got your back. Even in low oxygen conditions, your cells can still produce a little bit of ATP.

There are **Two Types** of **Anaerobic Respiration**

1) **Anaerobic** respiration **doesn't use oxygen**.

2) It **doesn't** involve the **link reaction**, the **Krebs cycle** or **oxidative phosphorylation**.

3) There are **two types** of anaerobic respiration — **alcoholic fermentation** and **lactate fermentation**.

4) These two processes are **similar**, because they both take place in the **cytoplasm** and they both **start** with **glycolysis** (which produces pyruvate).

5) They **differ** in **which organisms** they occur in and what happens to the **pyruvate** (see below).

Lactate Fermentation Occurs in **Mammals** and Produces **Lactate**

1) **Reduced NAD** (from glycolysis) transfers **hydrogen** to **pyruvate** to form **lactate** and **NAD**.

2) **NAD** can then be reused in **glycolysis**.

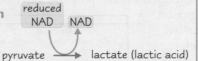

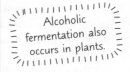
Some bacteria carry out lactate fermentation.

1) The production of lactate **regenerates NAD**. Glycolysis needs NAD in order to take place. This means **glycolysis** can **continue** even when there **isn't** much oxygen around, so a **small amount of ATP** can still be **produced** to keep some biological process going.

2) Our cells can **tolerate** a high level of lactate (and the coinciding **low pH** conditions) for **short periods** of time. For example during **short periods** of **hard exercise**, when they can't get **enough ATP** from aerobic respiration.

3) However, too much lactate is toxic and is removed from the cells into the bloodstream. The **liver** takes up lactate from the **bloodstream** and **converts** it back into **glucose** in a process called **gluconeogenesis** (see p. 144).

Alcoholic Fermentation Occurs in **Yeast Cells** and Produces **Ethanol**

1) **CO₂** is **removed** from **pyruvate** to form **ethanal**.

2) **Reduced NAD** (from glycolysis) transfers **hydrogen** to **ethanal** to form **ethanol** and **NAD**.

3) **NAD** can then be reused in **glycolysis**.

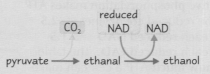

Alcoholic fermentation also occurs in plants.

The production of ethanol also **regenerates NAD** so **glycolysis** can **continue** when there isn't much oxygen around.

Anaerobic Respiration Releases Less Energy than Aerobic Respiration

1) The **ATP yield** from **anaerobic** respiration is **always lower** than from **aerobic** respiration.

2) This is because **anaerobic** respiration **only** includes **one energy-releasing stage (glycolysis)**, which only produces **2 ATP** per glucose molecule.

3) The energy-releasing reactions of the **Krebs cycle** and **oxidative phosphorylation** need **oxygen**, so they **can't** occur during anaerobic respiration.

Cells Can Respire Different Substrates

1) Cells **respire glucose**, but they also respire **other carbohydrates**, **lipids** and **proteins**.

2) Any **biological molecule** that can be **broken down** in **respiration** to **release energy** is called a **respiratory substrate**.

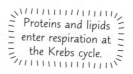
Proteins and lipids enter respiration at the Krebs cycle.

Anaerobic Respiration and RQs

Different Respiratory Substrates Have Different Energy Values

Respiratory Substrate	Average Energy Value (kJ g⁻¹)
Carbohydrates	15.8
Lipids	39.4
Proteins	17.0

1) **Different respiratory substrates** release different amounts of **energy** when they're **respired**. **Lipids** have the **highest energy value**, followed by **proteins**, then **carbohydrates**.

2) This is because **most ATP** is made in **oxidative phosphorylation**, which requires **hydrogen atoms** from **reduced NAD** and **reduced FAD**. This means that respiratory substrates that contain **more hydrogen atoms per unit of mass** cause **more ATP** to be produced when respired. **Lipids** contain the **most** hydrogen atoms per unit of mass, followed by proteins and then carbohydrates.

The Respiratory Quotient Can be Calculated Using a Formula

1) When an organism respires a specific **respiratory substrate**, the **respiratory quotient** (RQ) can be **worked out**.

2) The **respiratory quotient** is the volume of **carbon dioxide** produced when that **substrate** is **respired, divided** by the volume of **oxygen consumed**, in a set period of **time**.

$$RQ = \frac{\text{Volume of CO}_2 \text{ released}}{\text{Volume of O}_2 \text{ consumed}}$$

3) For example, you can work out the **RQ** for cells that **only respire glucose**:
   - The basic equation for aerobic respiration using glucose is: $C_6H_{12}O_6 + 6O_2 \rightarrow 6CO_2 + 6H_2O + \text{energy}$
   - The RQ of glucose = molecules of **CO₂ released** ÷ molecules of **O₂ consumed** = **6 ÷ 6 = 1**.

4) Respiratory quotients have been worked out for the respiration of **other respiratory substrates**. **Lipids** and **proteins** have an RQ value **lower than one** because **more oxygen** is needed to oxidise fats and lipids than to oxidise carbohydrates.

Respiratory Substrate	RQ
Lipids (triglycerides)	0.7
Proteins or amino acids	0.9
Carbohydrates	1

The Respiratory Quotient tells you what Substrate is being Respired

1) The **respiratory quotient** for an organism is **useful** because it tells you **what kind** of **respiratory substrate** an organism is respiring and what **type** of **respiration** it's using (aerobic or anaerobic).

2) For example, under **normal conditions** the **usual RQ** for humans is between **0.7** and **1.0**. An RQ in this range shows that some **fats (lipids)** are being used for respiration, as well as **carbohydrates** like glucose. Protein **isn't** normally used by the body for respiration unless there's **nothing else**.

3) **High RQs** (greater than 1) mean that an organism is **short** of **oxygen**, and is having to respire **anaerobically** as well as aerobically.

4) **Plants** sometimes have a **low RQ**. This is because the CO_2 **released** in respiration is **used** for **photosynthesis** (so it's not measured).

Warm-Up Questions

Q1 What molecule is made when CO_2 is removed from pyruvate during alcoholic fermentation?

Q2 Does anaerobic respiration release more or less energy per glucose molecule than aerobic respiration?

Q3 What is a respiratory substrate?

Exam Questions

Q1 A culture of mammalian cells was incubated with glucose, pyruvate and antimycin C. Antimycin C inhibits an electron carrier in the electron transport chain of aerobic respiration. Explain why these cells can still produce lactate. [1 mark]

Q2 This equation shows the aerobic respiration of a fat called triolein: $C_{57}H_{104}O_6 + 80O_2 \rightarrow 52H_2O + 57CO_2$ Calculate the respiratory quotient for this reaction. Show your working. [2 marks]

My little sis has an RQ of 157 — she's really clever...

I know, I'm really pushing the boundary between humour and non-humour here. Oh well, make sure that you know the benefits of anaerobic respiration and the two different types. Also, you really need to be able to work out RQs...

Respiration Experiments

These pages give you some examples of experiments you could carry out to measure the rate of respiration...

Aerobic and Anaerobic Respiration Rates in Yeast can be Investigated

Yeast can respire **aerobically** when **plenty** of **oxygen** is **available** and **anaerobically** when **oxygen isn't available**. Both aerobic and anaerobic respiration in yeast produce CO_2. So the **rate of CO_2 production** gives an indication of the yeast's **respiration rate**. One way to measure CO_2 production is by using a **gas syringe** to collect the CO_2 as shown in the methods below:

Aerobic Respiration

1) Put a **known volume** and **concentration** of **substrate solution** (e.g. glucose) in a test tube.

2) Add a **known volume** of buffer solution to keep the **pH constant**. (Choose the optimum pH for the yeast you're testing — usually 4-6).

3) Place the test tube in a **water bath** set to 25 °C. This ensures that the temperature stays **constant** throughout the experiment. Leave it there for **10 minutes** to allow the temperature of the **substrate** to **stabilise**.

4) Add a **known mass** of **dried yeast** (e.g. *Saccharomyces cerevisiae*) to the test tube and **stir** for two minutes.

5) After the yeast has dissolved into the solution, put a **bung** with a **tube attached** to a **gas syringe** in the top of the test tube. The **gas syringe** should be set to **zero**.

6) **Start** a **stop watch** as soon as the bung has been put in the test tube.

7) As the yeast **respire**, the CO_2 **formed** will travel up the tube and into the **gas syringe**, which is used to measure the **volume** of CO_2 **released**.

8) At **regular time intervals** (e.g. every minute), record the **volume** of CO_2 that is **present** in the **gas syringe**. Do this for a set amount of time (e.g. 10 minutes).

9) A **control** experiment should also be set up, where **no yeast** is present. **No CO_2** should be formed without the yeast.

10) **Repeat** the experiment three times. Use your data to **calculate** the **mean rate of CO_2 production**.

bung with tube *gas syringe (held by stand and clamp)*
test tube
water bath
yeast culture and substrate solution

The yeast will only respire aerobically until the oxygen trapped in the tube is all used up. If you wanted to run the experiment for more time or with more yeast or glucose, you could use a conical flask that can trap more oxygen.

Anaerobic Respiration

1) Set up the apparatus according to **steps 1-4** of the experiment above.

2) After the yeast has dissolved into the substrate solution, trickle some **liquid paraffin** down the **inside** of the test tube so that it **settles** on and **completely covers** the **surface** of the solution. This will **stop oxygen** getting in, which will force the yeast to respire **anaerobically**.

3) Put a **bung**, with a **tube attached** to a **gas syringe**, in the top of the test tube. The **gas syringe** should be set to **zero**.

4) Perform **steps 6-10** from the method above.

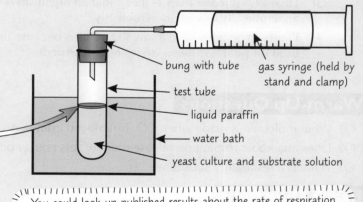

bung with tube *gas syringe (held by stand and clamp)*
test tube
liquid paraffin
water bath
yeast culture and substrate solution

You could look up published results about the rate of respiration in yeast and see how they compare to yours. If there are any differences, you could try and work out what caused them and how you could improve the way you carried out your own experiment.

The **only** difference between these experiments is the **presence** or **absence** of **oxygen**, so you can directly **compare** your **results** for both experiments with **each other** to find out how the **respiration rate** of yeast under **aerobic** and **anaerobic** conditions **differs**.

You can also easily **adapt** these methods to investigate the **effects** of **variables**, such as **temperature**, **substrate concentration** and the use of **different respiratory substrates** (e.g. sucrose), on the **respiration rate**. For example, to investigate the effect of **different temperatures** on the respiration rate, you could perform the experiment with the test tubes in **water baths** set at **different temperatures**.

Respiration Experiments

The Rate of Respiration can be Measured using a Respirometer

Respirometers can be used to indicate the **rate** of **aerobic respiration** by measuring the **amount** of **oxygen consumed** by an organism over a **period** of **time**. The example below shows how a respirometer can be used to measure the respiration rate of **woodlice**. You could also use it to measure the respiration rate of other small organisms or of plant seeds.

- The apparatus is set up as shown on the right.
- **Each tube** contains **potassium hydroxide** solution (or soda lime), which **absorbs carbon dioxide**.
- The **control tube** is set up in exactly the **same way** as the test tube, but **without** the **woodlice**, to make sure the **results** are **only** due to the woodlice **respiring** (e.g. it contains beads that have the same mass as the woodlice).
- **Coloured fluid** is added to the **manometer** by dipping the **end** of the **capillary tube** into a **beaker** of **fluid**. Capillary action will make the fluid **move into** the tube. The **syringe** is then used to set the **fluid** to a **known level**.
- The apparatus is **left** for a **set period of time** (e.g. 20 minutes).
- During that time there'll be a **decrease** in the **volume** of the **air** in the test tube, due to **oxygen consumption** by the **woodlice** (all the CO_2 produced is absorbed by the potassium hydroxide).
- The decrease in the volume of the air will **reduce the pressure** in the tube and cause the **coloured liquid** in the manometer to **move towards** the test tube.
- The **distance moved** by the **liquid** in a **given time** is **measured**. This value can then be used to **calculate** the **volume of oxygen** taken in by the woodlice **per minute**. (You also need to know the **diameter** of the **capillary tube** in the manometer to do this.)
- Any **variables** that could **affect** the results are **controlled**, e.g. temperature, volume of potassium hydroxide solution in each test tube.
- To produce more **precise** results, the experiment is **repeated** and a **mean volume** of O_2 is calculated.

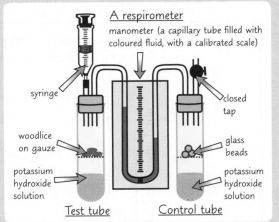

A respirometer

manometer (a capillary tube filled with coloured fluid, with a calibrated scale)

syringe

closed tap

woodlice on gauze

glass beads

potassium hydroxide solution

potassium hydroxide solution

Test tube   Control tube

This experiment has some limitations. For example, it can be difficult to accurately read the meniscus of the fluid in the manometer.

You can use a respirometer to investigate the effect of different factors on the rate of respiration by changing the independent variable.

Respirometers can be set up with an electronic **oxygen sensor** to measure the **oxygen concentration** inside the **respirometer chamber** at set intervals and also with **data loggers** to **automatically** record the data measured by the sensor. Using technology like this reduces the chance of human error when it comes to recording data. The data collected by the data logger can be put into **data analysis software**, which can help you to analyse your data and draw **conclusions** from your experiment.

Warm-Up Questions

Q1 Why is CO_2 production a suitable factor to measure when investigating the rate of both aerobic and anaerobic respiration in yeast?

Q2 What does a respirometer measure?

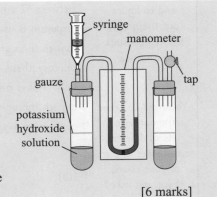

syringe

manometer

gauze

tap

potassium hydroxide solution

Exam Question

Q1* Suggest a suitable method using the respirometer shown above right, as well as any other apparatus that you think is appropriate, that could be used to investigate the effect of temperature on the respiration rate of germinating mung beans.

[6 marks]

* You will be assessed on the quality of your written response in this question.

My results are dodgy — I'm sure the woodlice are holding their breath...

Okay, that wasn't very funny, but these pages don't really give me any inspiration. You probably feel the same way. They're the sort of pages that you just have to plough through. You could try drawing a few pretty diagrams to get the experiments in your head. And after you've got it sorted do something exciting, like trying to stick your toe in your ear...

Extra Exam Practice

Phew! Module 5 sure is a whopper — there's loads of stuff to revise. You've done really well to get this far, so you might as well just exert your cerebrum a little bit more and have a go at these practice exam questions. It's important to make sure that what you've learnt has really sunk in by trying to apply your knowledge — after all, that's what the exams are all about.

- Have a look at this example of how to answer a tricky exam question.
- Then check how much you've understood from Module 5 by having a go at the questions on the next page.

---

1   **Figure 1** shows the mean net oxygen consumption for two organisms (**A** and **B**), over 24 hours, in the UK in spring. Organism **A** is an animal species and organism **B** is a plant species.

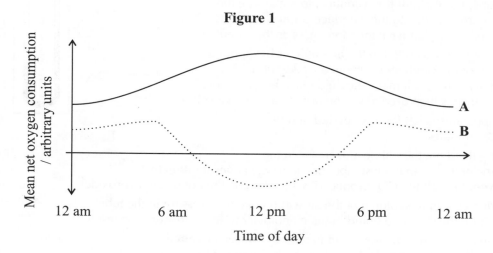

Figure 1

(a)   Explain what the graph shows for organism **B**, between the hours of 12 am and 6 am.

(4 marks)

(b)   Explain how the rate of acetyl coenzyme A production in organism **A** will change between 12 pm and 6 pm.

(2 marks)

Take your time to read all the information and to figure out the graph before you start your answer.

You need to know the names of lots of different substances as part of your course. If you get asked about a specific substance in a question, take time to think about its role and how it relates to what you're being asked.

1(a)

Between 12 am and around 5 am, the mean net oxygen consumption of organism B rises slightly. This is because it's dark so organism B is consuming oxygen through **aerobic respiration** but not producing oxygen through photosynthesis. From around 5 am to 6 am, the mean net oxygen consumption falls. This is because, as the light level increases, organism B starts to produce oxygen through the **light-dependent reaction** of **photosynthesis**, as well as consuming oxygen through aerobic respiration.

1(b)

Acetyl coenzyme A is produced during the **link reaction** of **aerobic respiration**. As the mean net oxygen consumption in organism A falls between 12 pm and 6 pm, this suggests that the rate of aerobic respiration is falling and therefore that the rate of the link reaction and acetyl coenzyme A production is falling too.

This question requires you to use your knowledge of two different processes — respiration and photosynthesis. Make sure you explain how each one affects the graph in your answer.

Extra Exam Practice

2 During exercise, a person contracts their muscles more than when they are at rest.

(a) Explain how the movement of calcium ions lengthens the sarcomere following muscle contraction.

(3 marks)

(b) Exercise can lead to sweating, which can cause a reduction in blood water potential.

(i) Describe the role of the hypothalamus in sweating as body temperature rises.

(2 marks)

(ii) Diabetes insipidus is a condition in which a person secretes lower levels of ADH than normal. Would a person with diabetes insipidus be more or less at risk of dehydration during exercise than a person without the condition? Explain your answer.

(4 marks)

3 Plants have many different hormones which allow them to respond to stimuli. Plants may respond to some abiotic stress factors by producing more of the hormone abscisic acid (ABA).

(a) Explain how an increased concentration of ABA in the leaves could reduce the rate of photosynthesis.

(4 marks)

(b) Gibberellins are inhibited by ABA. Scientists investigated whether an enzyme called OsNCED4 is involved in the synthesis of ABA. The scientists inserted the *OsNCED4* gene into individuals from a strain of plants which do not normally possess this gene. They then measured the rate of seed germination in these genetically modified plants and compared this to the rate of seed germination in plants which had not had this gene inserted.

(i) Suggest **two** variables that the scientists should have controlled in this investigation.

(2 marks)

(ii) Describe and explain the results you would expect the scientists to have seen in this investigation if the OsNCED4 enzyme is involved in the synthesis of ABA.

(3 marks)

4 Diabetes mellitus is a condition that affects millions of people worldwide.

(a) Diabetes is associated with other disorders in the body. These include conditions that affect the nervous system, such as diabetic neuropathy. Some people with diabetic neuropathy can experience an impairment of sensitivity to pain.

(i) Pain can normally be felt following stimulation of receptors called nociceptors. Stimulation of a nociceptor increases the permeability of its membrane to ions. Suggest an explanation for how stimulation of nociceptors leads to the brain rapidly sensing pain.

(3 marks)

(ii) The symptoms of some of the other disorders experienced by people with diabetes may be due to a reduced sensitivity of receptors for the chemical serotonin. Serotonin acts as a first messenger. Suggest an explanation of how this effect on receptors could disrupt cell signalling.

(3 marks)

(b)* Sulfonylureas are a type of drug used to treat Type 2 diabetes. They work by closing potassium ion channels in the plasma membranes of the β cells in the pancreas. One of the main side effects of the drugs is weight gain.
Explain how sulfonylureas work as a treatment for Type 2 diabetes and suggest why the side effects could make doctors reluctant to prescribe the drugs to many patients with Type 2 diabetes.

(6 marks)

* You will be assessed on the quality of your written response in this question.

Regulating Gene Expression

In cells, genes are transcribed and translated into proteins, but it doesn't just happen willy-nilly...

Genes can be Switched On or Off

All the **cells** in an organism carry the **same genes** (DNA) but the **structure** and **function** of different cells **varies**. This is because **not all** the **genes** in a cell are **expressed** (transcribed and used to make a functional protein) — they are selectively switched on or off. Because **cells** show **different gene expression**, **different proteins** are made and these proteins modify the cell — they determine the **cell structure** and control **cell processes** (including the expression of more genes, which produce more proteins).

Gene expression (and therefore protein synthesis) can be controlled at the **transcriptional**, **post-transcriptional** and **post-translational** level. This happens via a number of different mechanisms.

You'll have covered transcription and translation in Module 2.

Transcription Factors Control Gene Expression at the Transcriptional Level

1) **Gene expression** can be **controlled** at the **transcriptional level** by **altering** the rate of **transcription** of genes. E.g. **increased** transcription produces **more mRNA**, which can be used to make **more protein**.

2) This is controlled by **transcription factors** — proteins that **bind** to **DNA** and **switch** genes **on** or **off** by **increasing** or **decreasing** the **rate of transcription**. Factors that **increase** the rate are called **activators** and those that **decrease** the rate are called **repressors**.

3) The **shape** of a transcription factor determines whether it **can bind to DNA** or **not**, and can sometimes be **altered** by the binding of some molecules, e.g. certain hormones and sugars.

4) This means the **amount** of certain **molecules** in an environment or a cell can **control** the **synthesis** of some **proteins** by affecting **transcription factor binding**.

5) In **eukaryotes**, transcription factors bind to **specific DNA sites** near the **start** of their **target genes** — the genes they **control** the **expression** of.

6) In **prokaryotes** control of gene expression often involves transcription factors binding to **operons** (see below).

7) An **operon** is a **section** of **DNA** that contains a cluster of **structural genes**, that are **transcribed together**, as well as **control elements** and sometimes a **regulatory gene**:

- The **structural genes** code for **useful proteins**, such as **enzymes**.
- The **control elements** include a **promoter** (a DNA sequence located **before** the structural genes that **RNA polymerase** binds to) and an **operator** (a DNA sequence that **transcription factors** bind to).
- The **regulatory gene** codes for an **activator** or **repressor**.

8) Here's an example of an operon that you need to learn about:

EXAMPLE: The *lac* operon in *E. coli*

1) *E. coli* is a bacterium that **respires glucose**, but it can use **lactose** if glucose isn't available.

2) The genes that produce the **enzymes** needed to **respire lactose** are found on an operon called the *lac* operon.

3) The *lac* operon has **three structural genes** — **lacZ**, **lacY** and **lacA**, which produce proteins that help the bacteria digest lactose (including β-**galactosidase** and **lactose permease**).

Lactose NOT present

The **regulatory** gene (lacI) produces the **lac repressor**, which is a **transcription factor** that **binds** to the **operator** site when there's **no lactose** present. This **blocks transcription** because RNA polymerase can't bind to the promoter.

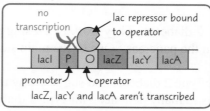

Lactose present

When **lactose is present**, it **binds** to the **repressor**, **changing** the repressor's **shape** so that it can **no longer bind** to the operator site.

RNA polymerase can now begin **transcription** of the structural genes.

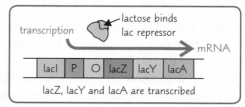

Regulating Gene Expression

mRNA is Edited at a Post-Transcriptional Level

1) Genes in **eukaryotic DNA** contain sections that **don't code** for amino acids.

2) These sections of DNA are called **introns**. All the bits that **do** code for amino acids are called **exons**.

3) During transcription the introns and exons are both **copied** into mRNA. mRNA strands containing introns and exons are called **primary mRNA transcripts** (or pre-mRNA).

4) Introns are **removed** from primary mRNA strands by a process called **splicing** — introns are removed and exons joined, forming mature **mRNA** strands. This takes place in the **nucleus**.

5) The mature mRNA then **leaves** the nucleus for the next stage of protein synthesis (**translation**).

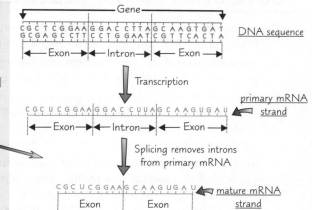

cAMP Activates Some Proteins at the Post-Translational Level

1) Some **proteins** aren't **functional** straight after they have been synthesised — they need to be **activated** to work (become a functional protein).

2) **Protein activation** is controlled by **molecules**, e.g. **hormones** and **sugars**.

3) Some of these molecules work by **binding** to **cell membranes** and **triggering** the production of **cyclic AMP** (**cAMP**) **inside** the **cell**.

4) cAMP then **activates proteins** inside the cell by **altering** their **three-dimensional (3D) structure**.

5) For example, altering the 3D structure can **change** the **active site** of an enzyme, making it become **more** or **less active**.

6) Here is how **cAMP** activates **protein kinase A** (**PKA**):

1) **PKA** is an **enzyme** made of four subunits.

2) When cAMP **isn't bound**, the four units are bound together and are **inactive**.

3) When cAMP **binds**, it causes a **change** in the enzyme's **3D structure**, releasing the active subunits — PKA is now **active**.

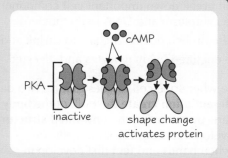

cAMP is a secondary messenger — it relays the message from the control molecule, e.g. the hormone, to the inside of the cell.

Warm-Up Questions

Q1 What does a transcription factor do?

Q2 What is an operon?

Q3 How does cAMP activate a protein?

Exam Questions

Q1 Describe how mRNA is edited at a post-transcriptional level [2 marks]

Q2 Explain how the presence of lactose causes *E. coli* to produce ß-galactosidase and lactose permease. [4 marks]

Genes are a bit like my concentration — they can be switched on or off...

The lac operon is a great example of how gene expression can be controlled at the transcriptional level and it's well worth learning because you might get asked about it in your exam. Don't forget that gene expression can also be controlled post-transcriptionally, by splicing out the introns, and proteins can even be controlled post-translationally.

Regulating Gene Expression

I know these pages look pretty packed, but it's all good stuff. It's about the control of development and mutations.

Some Genes Control the Development of Body Plans

1) A **body plan** is the **general structure** of an organism, e.g. the *Drosophila* fruit fly has various **body parts** (head, abdomen, etc.) that are **arranged** in a **particular way** — this is its body plan.

2) **Proteins control** the **development** of a **body plan** — they help set up the basic body plan so that everything is in the right place, e.g. legs grow where legs should grow.

3) The proteins that control body plan development are **coded for** by genes called **Hox genes**. E.g. two Hox gene clusters control the development of the *Drosophila* body plan — one controls the development of the head and anterior thorax and the other controls the development of the posterior thorax and abdomen.

4) **Similar Hox genes** are found in **animals**, **plants** and **fungi**, which means that **body plan development** is controlled in a **similar way** in flies, mice, humans, etc. Hox genes have **regions** called **homeobox sequences**, which are highly conserved — this means that these sequences have **changed** very little during the **evolution** of different organisms that possess these homeobox sequences.

5) Here's how Hox genes control development:
   - **Homeobox sequences** code for a **part** of the **protein** called the **homeodomain**.
   - The homeodomain **binds** to specific **sites** on **DNA**, enabling the protein to work as a **transcription factor** (see p. 194).
   - The proteins bind to DNA at the **start** of **developmental genes**, **activating** or **repressing transcription** and so altering the production of proteins involved in the development of the body plan.

Apoptosis and Mitosis are Involved in the Development of Body Plans

1) Some cells **die** and **break down** as a **normal** part of **development**.

2) This is a **highly controlled process** called **apoptosis**, or **programmed cell death**.

3) Once **apoptosis** has been **triggered** the **cell** is **broken down** in a series of steps:

   > 1) **Enzymes** inside the cell **break down** important cell components such as **proteins** in the cytoplasm and **DNA** in the nucleus.
   >
   > 2) As the cell's contents are broken down it begins to **shrink** and **breaks up** into **fragments**.
   >
   > 3) The **cell fragments** are **engulfed** by **phagocytes** and **digested**.

4) **Mitosis** (part of the cell cycle where one cell divides to form two daughter cells — see pages 60-61) and **differentiation create** the bulk of the **body parts** and then apoptosis **refines** the parts by **removing** the **unwanted structures**. For example, as tadpoles develop into frogs, their tail cells are removed by apoptosis and when **hands** and **feet** first develop in humans, the **digits** (fingers and toes) are **connected** — they're only **separated** when cells in the **connecting tissue** undergo **apoptosis**.

5) During development, genes that **control** apoptosis and genes that control mitosis are **switched on** and **off** in **appropriate** cells. This means that **some cells die**, whilst **some new cells** are **produced** and the **correct body plan develops**.

Although it sounded daunting, Graham was thankful for apoptosis because he no longer looked like a giant sperm.

Genes that Regulate Apoptosis and the Cell Cycle can Respond to Stimuli

The genes that **regulate apoptosis** and progression through the **cell cycle** (e.g. cells undergoing mitosis) can **respond** to both **internal** and **external stimuli**.

- An **internal** stimulus could be **DNA damage**. If DNA damage is **detected** during the cell cycle, this can result in the expression of genes which cause the cycle to be **paused** and can even trigger **apoptosis**.

- An **external** stimulus, such as **stress** caused by a **lack** of **nutrient availability**, could result in gene expression that prevents cells from undergoing mitosis. Gene expression which leads to **apoptosis** being triggered can also be caused by an external stimulus such as **attack** by a **pathogen**.

Regulating Gene Expression

Mutations are Changes to the Base Sequence of DNA

1) Any change to the **base** (**nucleotide**) **sequence** of DNA is called a **mutation**. Types of mutations include:

   - **Substitution** — one or more bases are swapped for another, e.g. ATGCCT becomes ATTCCT
   - **Deletion** — one or more bases are removed, e.g. ATGCCT becomes ATCT
   - **Insertion** — one or more bases are added, e.g. ATGCCT becomes ATGACCT

2) The **order** of **DNA bases** in a gene determines the **order of amino acids** in a particular **protein**. If a mutation occurs in a gene, the **primary structure** (amino acid chain) of the protein it codes for could be altered.

3) This may **change** the final **3D shape** of the protein so it **doesn't work properly**, e.g. **active sites** in enzymes may not form properly, meaning that **substrates can't bind** to them.

Mutations can be Neutral, Beneficial or Harmful

1) Some mutations can have a **neutral effect** on a protein's **function**. They may have a neutral effect because:

   - The mutation changes a base in a triplet, but the amino acid that the triplet codes for doesn't change. This happens because some amino acids are coded for by more than one triplet. E.g. both TAT and TAC code for tyrosine, so if TAT is changed to TAC the amino acid won't change.
   - The mutation produces a triplet that codes for a different amino acid, but the amino acid is chemically similar to the original so it functions like the original amino acid. E.g. arginine (AGG) and lysine (AAG) are coded for by similar triplets — a substitution mutation can swap the amino acids. But this mutation could have a neutral effect on a protein as the amino acids are chemically similar.
   - The mutated triplet codes for an amino acid not involved with the protein's function, e.g. one that's located far away from an enzyme's active site, so the protein works as it normally does.

2) A **neutral effect** on protein function **won't** affect an **organism** overall.

3) However, some mutations **do** affect a protein's **function** — they can make a protein **more** or **less active**, e.g. by **changing** the **shape** of an enzyme's **active site**.

4) If protein function **is affected** it can have a **beneficial** or **harmful effect** on the **whole organism**:

Mutations with beneficial effects	Mutations with harmful effects
These have an advantageous effect on an organism, i.e. they increase its chance of survival.	These have a **disadvantageous effect** on an organism, i.e. they **decrease** its chance of **survival**.
E.g. some bacterial enzymes break down certain antibiotics. Mutations in the genes that code for these enzymes could make them work on a wider range of antibiotics. This is beneficial to the bacteria because antibiotic resistance can help them to survive.	E.g. **cystic fibrosis** (CF) can be caused by a **deletion** of three bases in the gene that codes for the **CFTR** (cystic fibrosis transmembrane conductance regulator) **protein**. The mutated CFTR protein **folds incorrectly**, so it's **broken down**. This leads to **excess mucus production**, which affects the **lungs** of CF sufferers.

5) Mutations can also affect **whether or not** a protein is **produced**. E.g. if a mutation occurs at the start of a gene, so that **RNA polymerase** can't bind to it and begin transcription, the protein coded for by the gene won't be made. The **loss of production** of a protein can have **harmful effects** — some **genetic disorders** are caused by this.

Warm-Up Question

Q1 Describe the process of apoptosis.

Exam Questions

Q1 Huntington's disease is caused by a mutation in the HTT gene, which results in the nucleotide triplet 'CAG' being repeated an abnormally high number of times, increasing the length of the gene. What name is given to this type of mutation? [1 mark]

Q2 Explain why the genetic control of body plan development is similar in plants, animals and fungi. [2 marks]

Too much revision stimulates apoptosis in your brain...

OK, that's not true. There's lots to learn here and some of it can be quite hard to get your head around. Just take your time and keep going over it until it all makes sense — it will click eventually and you'll be all set for your exam.

Types and Causes of Variation

You might remember learning about variation in Module 4... Well, you need to learn it again for Module 6, but in a bit more detail. Not very varied, I know — but that's revision for you.

Variation Within a Species can be Continuous...

1) **Continuous variation** is when the **individuals** in a population vary **within a range** — there are **no distinct categories**, e.g. **humans** can be **any height** within a range (139 cm, 175 cm, 185.9 cm, etc.), not just tall or short.

2) Some more examples of continuous variation include:

- **Waist circumference** — e.g. humans can have any waist size within a range.
- **Fur length** — e.g. dogs can have any length of fur within a range.

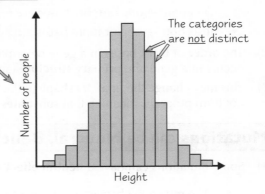

The categories are <u>not</u> distinct

Number of people

Height

...or Discontinuous

1) **Discontinuous variation** is when there are two or more **distinct categories** — each individual falls into **only one** of these categories, there are **no intermediates**.

2) Here are some examples of discontinuous variation:

- **Blood group** — e.g. humans can be group A, B, AB or O.
- **Violet flower colour** — e.g. violets can either be coloured or white.

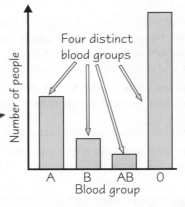

Four distinct blood groups

Number of people

A   B   AB   O
Blood group

Variation — a concept lost on the army.

Variation can be Influenced by Your Genes...

1) **Different species** have **different genes**.

2) Individuals of the **same species** have the **same genes**, but **different versions** of them (called **alleles**).

3) The genes and alleles an organism has make up its **genotype**.

4) **Sexual reproduction** leads to **variation** in genotypes within a species. **Meiosis** makes gametes with a **unique** assortment of **alleles** through **crossing-over** and the **independent assortment** of **chromosomes**. The **random fusion** of gametes during **fertilisation** also increases genetic variation in the offspring.

5) The **differences** in **genotype** result in **variation** in **phenotype** — the **characteristics** displayed by an organism. Variation in phenotype is also referred to as **phenotypic variation**.

> **EXAMPLE** | **Human blood group** — there are **three** different **blood group alleles**, which result in **four different blood groups**.

Meiosis is covered in Module 2.

6) **Inherited** characteristics that show **continuous** variation are usually **influenced** by **many genes** — these characteristics are said to be **polygenic**.

> **EXAMPLE** | **Human skin colour** is **polygenic**— it comes in **loads of different shades** of colour.

7) **Inherited** characteristics that show **discontinuous** variation are usually influenced by only **one gene** (or a **small number** of genes). Characteristics controlled by **only one gene** are said to be **monogenic**.

> **EXAMPLE** | **Violet flower colour** is **monogenic**— can either be **coloured** or **white**.

Types and Causes of Variation

...the **Environment**...

Variation can also be caused by **differences in the environment**, e.g. climate, food, lifestyle. Characteristics controlled by environmental factors can **change** over an organism's life.

EXAMPLES

1) **Etiolation** — this is when plants grow **abnormally long** and **spindly** because they're **not getting** enough **light**.

2) **Chlorosis** — this is when plants **don't produce** enough **chlorophyll** and turn **yellow**. It's caused by several environmental factors, e.g. a **lack of magnesium** in soil.

...or **Both**

Genetic factors determine genotype and the characteristics an organism's **born with**, but **environmental factors** can **influence** how some characteristics **develop**. Most phenotypic variation is caused by the **combination** of genotype and **environmental factors**. Phenotypic variation influenced by both usually shows **continuous variation**.

EXAMPLES

1) **Height of pea plants** — pea plants come in **tall** and **dwarf** forms (**discontinuous** variation), which is determined by **genotype**. However, the **exact height** of the tall and dwarf plants **varies** (**continuous** variation) because of environmental factors (e.g. **light intensity** and **water availability** affect how tall a plant grows).

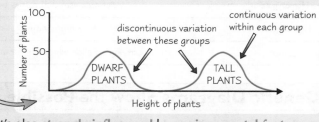

2) **Body mass in animals** — this is **partly genetic**, but it's also **strongly influenced** by **environmental factors**, like **diet**. For example, if your diet doesn't contain enough of the right nutrients, your body mass is likely to be lower than that determined by your genes. Body mass **varies** within a **range**, so it's **continuous** variation.

Warm-Up Questions

Q1 What is a monogenic characteristic?

Q2 Give an example of phenotypic variation in plants that's caused only by the environment.

Exam Question

Q1 The mass and coat colour of 15 Labrador puppies is shown in the table.

Puppy	Mass / kg	Colour	Puppy	Mass / kg	Colour	Puppy	Mass / kg	Colour
1	10.04	yellow	6	10.39	yellow	11	9.25	black
2	10.23	chocolate	7	10.55	chocolate	12	11.06	black
3	15.65	black	8	15.87	chocolate	13	12.45	yellow
4	18.99	black	9	16.99	black	14	14.99	yellow
5	9.45	black	10	10.47	yellow	15	10.93	chocolate

a) Which of the characteristics shown in the table, mass or coat colour, is most likely to be influenced by only a small number of genes? Explain your answer.   [1 mark]

b) Which of the characteristics described in the table is most likely to be influenced by both genotype and the environment? Explain your answer.   [1 mark]

c) Calculate the range of puppy mass.   [1 mark]

Revision boredom shows discontinuous variation — always bored with it...

Remember, continuous variation is usually influenced by many genes. Discontinuous variation is usually influenced by only one or a few genes. Make sure you've learnt some examples of genetic and environmental factors that affect phenotypic variation too — particularly etiolation and chlorosis in plants, and diet in animals.

Inheritance

Nope, this isn't about who gets Mum's best china — we're talking genetic inheritance here...

You **Need to Know** These **Genetic Terms**

'Codes for' means 'contains the instructions for'.

TERM	DESCRIPTION
Gene	A sequence of bases on a DNA molecule that codes for a protein (polypeptide), which results in a characteristic, e.g. a gene for eye colour.
Allele	A different version of a gene. Most plants and animals, including humans, have two alleles of each gene, one from each parent. The order of bases in each allele is slightly different — they code for different versions of the same characteristic. They're represented using letters, e.g. the allele for brown eyes (B) and the allele for blue eyes (b).
Genotype	The alleles an organism has, e.g. BB, Bb or bb for eye colour.
Phenotype	The characteristics the alleles produce, e.g. brown eyes.
Dominant	An allele whose characteristic appears in the phenotype even when there's only one copy. Dominant alleles are shown by a capital letter. E.g. the allele for brown eyes (B) is dominant — if a person's genotype is Bb or BB, they'll have brown eyes.
Recessive	An allele whose characteristic only appears in the phenotype if two copies are present. Recessive alleles are shown by a lower case letter. E.g. the allele for blue eyes (b) is recessive — if a person's genotype is bb, they'll have blue eyes.
Codominant	Alleles that are both expressed in the phenotype — neither one is recessive, e.g. the alleles for haemoglobin.
Locus	The fixed position of a gene on a chromosome. Alleles of a gene are found at the same locus on each chromosome in a pair.
Homozygote	An organism that carries two copies of the same allele, e.g. BB or bb.
Heterozygote	An organism that carries two different alleles, e.g. Bb.
Carrier	A person carrying an allele which is not expressed in the phenotype but that can be passed on to offspring.

Genetic Diagrams Show the **Possible Genotypes** of **Offspring**

The body cells of individuals have **two alleles** for **each gene**. Gametes (sex cells) contain only **one allele** for each gene. When gametes from two parents fuse together, the alleles they contain form the **genotype** of the **offspring** produced. **Genetic diagrams** can be used to **predict** the **genotypes** and **phenotypes** of the offspring produced if two parents are **crossed** (bred).

You need to know how to use genetic diagrams to predict the results of various crosses, including **monogenic crosses**. **Monogenic inheritance** is the inheritance of a **characteristic** controlled by a **single gene**. **Monogenic crosses** show the **likelihood** of the **different alleles** of that gene (and so different versions of the characteristic) being **inherited** by offspring of particular parents. This genetic diagram shows how **wing length** is inherited in fruit flies:

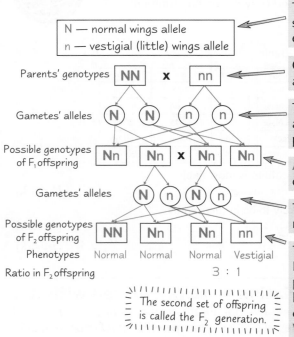

N — normal wings allele
n — vestigial (little) wings allele

Parents' genotypes **NN** x **nn**

Gametes' alleles (N) (N) (n) (n)

Possible genotypes of F₁ offspring **Nn** **Nn** x **Nn** **Nn**

Gametes' alleles (N) (n) (N) (n)

Possible genotypes of F₂ offspring **NN** **Nn** **Nn** **nn**

Phenotypes Normal Normal Normal Vestigial

Ratio in F₂ offspring   3 : 1

The allele for **normal wings** is **dominant**, so it's shown by a **capital** letter N. Any flies that have even one N allele will have normal wings.

One parent is **homozygous** with **normal wings** (NN) and one is **homozygous** with **vestigial wings** (nn).

The normal winged parent **only** produces gametes with the allele for **normal wings** (N). The vestigial winged parent **only** produces gametes with the allele for **vestigial wings** (n).

All F_1 offspring are **heterozygous** (Nn), as one allele is inherited from **each** parent.

The first set of offspring is called the F_1 generation.

The gametes produced by the F_1 offspring may contain the allele for **either normal** (N) or **vestigial wings (n)**.

The second set of offspring is called the F_2 generation.

The F_2 offspring could have **either** normal or vestigial wings. But there's a **75%** chance they'll have the **normal wings phenotype** (genotype of NN or Nn) and a **25%** chance they'll have the **vestigial wings phenotype** (genotype nn). So you'd expect a **3:1** ratio of normal : vestigial wings in the offspring. **Whenever** you do a monogenic cross with **two heterozygous** parents you get a **3:1** ratio of **dominant : recessive** characteristic.

Inheritance

A **Punnett square** is just another way of showing a **genetic diagram** — they're also used to predict the **genotypes** and **phenotypes** of offspring. The Punnett squares below show the same crosses from the previous page:

1) First work out the alleles the **gametes** would have.

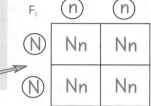

Parents' genotypes NN nn

Gametes' alleles N N n n

2) Next **cross the parents' gametes** to show the possible genotypes of the **F$_1$ generation** — all heterozygous, Nn.

F$_1$

	n	n
N	Nn	Nn
N	Nn	Nn

3) Then **cross the gametes' alleles of the F$_1$ generation** to show the possible **genotypes** of the **F$_2$ generation**. The Punnett square shows a **75%** chance that offspring will have **normal wings** and a **25%** chance that they'll have **vestigial wings**, i.e. a **3:1 ratio**.

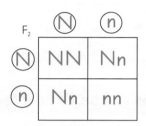

F$_2$

	N	n
N	NN	Nn
n	Nn	nn

1 in 4 chance of offspring having the genotype NN (normal wings)
2 in 4 chance of offspring having the genotype Nn (normal wings)
1 in 4 chance of offspring having the genotype nn (vestigial wings)
So phenotype ratio =
normal : vestigial = 3 : 1

Some **Genes** Have **Codominant Alleles**

Occasionally, alleles show codominance — **both alleles** are expressed in the **phenotype**, **neither one** is recessive. One example in humans is the allele for sickle-cell anaemia:

1) People who are **homozygous** for **normal haemoglobin** (H^NH^N) don't have the disease.

2) People who are **homozygous** for **sickle haemoglobin** (H^SH^S) have **sickle-cell anaemia** — all their **blood cells** are **sickle-shaped** (crescent-shaped).

3) People who are **heterozygous** (H^NH^S) have an **in-between** phenotype, called the **sickle-cell trait** — they have **some** normal haemoglobin and some sickle haemoglobin. The two alleles are **codominant** because they're **both** expressed in the **phenotype**.

4) The **genetic diagram** on the right shows the possible offspring from **crossing** two parents with **sickle-cell trait** (heterozygous).

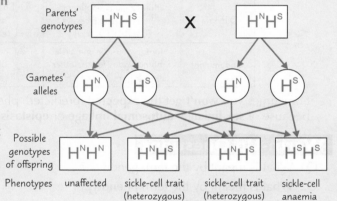

Parents' genotypes H^NH^S X H^NH^S

Gametes' alleles H^N H^S H^N H^S

Possible genotypes of offspring H^NH^N H^NH^S H^NH^S H^SH^S

Phenotypes unaffected sickle-cell trait (heterozygous) sickle-cell trait (heterozygous) sickle-cell anaemia

Some **Genes** Have **Multiple Alleles**

Inheritance is **more complicated** when there are **more than two** alleles of the same gene (**multiple alleles**).

Example In the **ABO blood group system** in humans there are **three alleles** for blood type:

I^O is the allele for blood group **O**. I^A is the allele for blood group **A**. I^B is the allele for blood group **B**.

Allele I^O is **recessive**. Alleles I^A and I^B are **codominant** — people with genotype I^AI^B will have blood group **AB**.

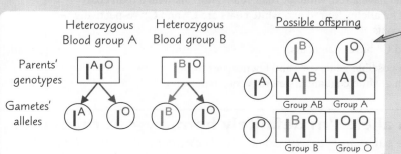

Heterozygous Blood group A   Heterozygous Blood group B   Possible offspring

Parents' genotypes I^AI^O I^BI^O

Gametes' alleles I^A I^O I^B I^O

	I^B	I^O
I^A	I^AI^B Group AB	I^AI^O Group A
I^O	I^BI^O Group B	I^OI^O Group O

The genetic diagram shows a cross between a **heterozygous** person with blood group **A** and a **heterozygous** person with blood group **B**. Any offspring could have one of **four** different blood groups — **A, B, O** or **AB**.

Recessive blood groups are normally really rare, but it just so happens that loads of people in Britain are descended from people who were $I^O I^O$, so O's really common.

Module 6: Section 2 — Patterns of Inheritance

Inheritance

Genetic Diagrams can Show how More Than One Characteristic is Inherited

You can use genetic diagrams to work out the chances of offspring inheriting certain **combinations** of characteristics. **Dihybrid inheritance** is the inheritance of **two characteristics** which are controlled by different genes. You can use a **dihybrid cross** to look at how the **two different genes** are inherited at the **same time**. The diagram below is a **dihybrid cross** showing how seed texture **and** colour are inherited in **pea plants**.

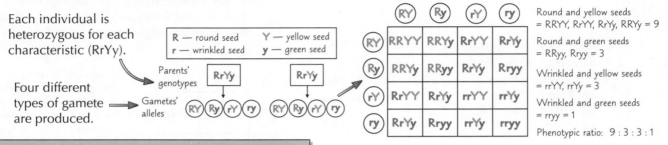

Each individual is heterozygous for each characteristic (RrYy).

Four different types of gamete are produced.

R — round seed   Y — yellow seed
r — wrinkled seed   y — green seed

Parents' genotypes   RrYy   RrYy

Gametes' alleles   RY Ry rY ry   RY Ry rY ry

Round and yellow seeds = RRYY, RrYY, RRYy, RrYy = 9

Round and green seeds = RRyy, Rryy = 3

Wrinkled and yellow seeds = rrYY, rrYy = 3

Wrinkled and green seeds = rryy = 1

Phenotypic ratio: 9 : 3 : 3 : 1

Phenotypic Ratios can be Predicted

The **phenotypic ratio** is the **ratio** of **different phenotypes** in offspring. Genetic diagrams allow you to **predict** the phenotypic ratios in F_1 and F_2 offspring. Here's a handy summary table of ratios for the following crosses:

Type of cross	Parents	Phenotypic ratio in F_1	Phenotypic ratio in F_2
Monogenic	Homozygous dominant × homozygous recessive (e.g. RR × rr)	All heterozygous offspring (e.g. Rr)	3 : 1 dominant : recessive
Dihybrid	Homozygous dominant × homozygous recessive (e.g. RRYY × rryy)	All heterozygous offspring (e.g. RrYy)	9 : 3 : 3 : 1 dominant both : dominant 1st recessive 2nd : recessive 1st dominant 2nd : recessive both
Codominant	Homozygous for one allele × homozygous for the other allele (e.g. H^NH^N × H^SH^S)	All heterozygous offspring (e.g. H^NH^S)	1 : 2 : 1 homozygous for one allele : heterozygous : homozygous for the other allele

Sometimes you **won't** get the **expected** (predicted) phenotypic ratio — it'll be quite different. This can be because of **sex linkage**, **autosomal linkage** or **epistasis** — all of which are covered on pages 203-205.

Warm-Up Questions

Q1 What is meant by the term genotype?

Q2 What is meant by the term phenotype?

Q3 What's dihybrid inheritance?

Q4 In the cross aabb × AABB, what would be the expected phenotypic ratios in the F_1 generation and the F_2 generation?

PRACTICE QUESTIONS

Exam Questions

Q1 In pea plants, seed texture (round or wrinkled) is passed from parent to offspring by monogenic inheritance. The allele for round seeds is represented by R and the allele for wrinkled seeds is represented by r.

Draw a genetic diagram to show the possible genotypes of F_1 offspring produced by crossing a homozygous round seed pea plant with a homozygous wrinkled-seed pea plant.   [3 marks]

Q2 Individuals of a particular breed of cow can have a red, white or roan coat. Animals with a roan coat have patches of both red and white hair. The alleles for red and white coats are C^R and C^W respectively. Heterozygotes for these alleles have roan coats.

a) Explain why heterozygotes for C^W and C^R have roan coats.   [1 mark]

b) Draw a genetic diagram to predict the possible genotypes and phenotypes of the F_1 offspring produced by a parent with a white coat and a heterozygous parent.   [4 marks]

If there's a dominant revision allele I'm definitely homozygous recessive...

OK, so there are a lot of fancy words on these pages and yes, you do need to know them all. Sorry. But don't despair — once you've learnt what the words mean and know how genetic diagrams work it'll all just fall into place.

Linkages and Epistasis

Right, this stuff is fairly hard, so if you don't get it first time don't panic. Make sure you're happy with the genetic diagrams and phenotypic ratios on the previous three pages before you get stuck into this lot.

Some **Characteristics** are **Sex-linked**

1) The genetic information for **biological sex** is carried on two **sex chromosomes**.

2) In mammals, **females** have **two X** chromosomes (XX) and **males** have **one X** and **one Y** chromosome (XY).

3) A **characteristic** is said to be **sex-linked** when the allele that codes for it is located on a **sex chromosome**.

4) The **Y chromosome** is **smaller** than the X chromosome and carries **fewer genes**.
So most genes on the sex chromosomes are **only carried** on the X chromosome (called **X-linked** genes).

5) As **males** only have **one X chromosome**, they often only have **one allele** for sex-linked genes.
So because they **only** have one copy, they **express the characteristic** of this allele even if it's **recessive**.
This makes males **more likely** than females to show **recessive phenotypes** for genes that are sex-linked.

6) Genetic disorders caused by **faulty alleles** on sex chromosomes include **colour blindness** and **haemophilia**.
The faulty alleles for both of these disorders are carried on the X chromosome — they're called **X-linked disorders**.

Example

1) **Colour blindness** is a **sex-linked disorder** caused by a faulty allele carried on the **X chromosome**.

2) As it's sex-linked **both** the chromosome and the allele are **represented** in the **genetic diagram**, e.g. X^n, where **X** represents the **X chromosome** and **n** the **faulty allele** for **colour vision**.

3) The **Y chromosome** doesn't have an allele for colour vision so is **just represented** by **Y**.

4) **Females** would need **two copies** of the **recessive allele** to be colour blind, while **males** only need **one copy**. This means colour blindness is **much rarer** in **women** than **men**.

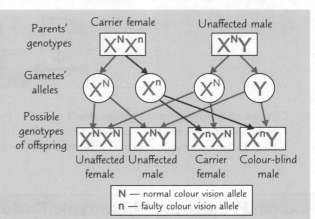

7) In the example above there's a **3 : 1 ratio** of offspring **without** colour blindness : offspring **with** colour-blindness.

8) But when a **female carrier** and a **male without colour-blindness** have children (as in this example), only their **male offspring** are at risk of being colour-blind. So you can also say that there's a predicted **2 : 1 : 1 ratio** — of **female** offspring **without** colour-blindness : **male** offspring **without** colour-blindness : **male** offspring **with** colour-blindness.

9) This ratio will **change** if a female carrier ($X^N X^n$) and a male **with** colour-blindness ($X^n Y$) have children. The predicted ratio will then be **1 : 1** — of offspring **with** colour-blindness : offspring **without** colour-blindness. The ratio will be the **same** for offspring of **each sex**. You only end up with this predicted ratio for a monogenic F_2 cross with a **sex-linked characteristic**.

Some **Autosomal** Genes are **Linked**

1) **Autosome** is the fancy name for any chromosome that **isn't** a sex chromosome. **Autosomal genes** are the genes located on the autosomes.

2) Genes on the **same autosome** are said to be **linked** — because they're on the same autosome they'll stay together during the **independent assortment of chromosomes** in meiosis I, and their alleles will be **passed on to the offspring together**. The only reason this won't happen is if **crossing over** splits them up first.

3) The **closer together** two genes are on the autosome, the **more closely** they are said to be **linked**. This is because **crossing over** is **less likely** to split them up.

4) If two genes are autosomally linked, you **won't get** the phenotypic ratio you expect in the offspring of a cross.

> Crossing over is when two homologous (paired) chromosomes 'swap bits'. It happens in meiosis I before independent assortment. You'll have learnt about this in Year 1 of your course.

Genes A, B and C are all linked.

An autosome

Genes A and B are more closely linked than genes A and C.

5) For example, in the **F₂ generation** of a **dihybrid cross** (see previous page) you'd expect a **9 : 3 : 3 : 1 ratio**. Instead, the phenotypic ratio is more likely to be that expected for the F_2 generation of a **monohybrid cross** (3 : 1) because the two autosomally-linked alleles are **inherited together**. This means that a **higher proportion** of the **offspring** will have their **parents'** (heterozygous) **genotype** and **phenotype**.

6) This allows you to use the **predicted phenotypic ratio** to **identify** autosomal linkage.

Linkages and Epistasis

An **Epistatic Gene Masks** the **Expression** of **Another Gene**

1) **Many different genes** can control the **same** characteristic — they **interact** to form the phenotype.

2) This can be because the **allele** of one gene **masks** (blocks) **the expression** of the alleles of other genes — this is called **epistasis**.

Example 1   In humans a **widow's peak** (see picture) is controlled by one gene and **baldness** by others. If you have the **alleles** that code for baldness, it **doesn't matter** whether you have the allele for a widow's peak or not, as you have **no hair**. The baldness genes are **epistatic** to the widow's peak gene, as the baldness genes **mask** the expression of the widow's peak gene.

Example 2   **Flower pigment** in a plant is controlled by two genes. **Gene 1** codes for a **yellow pigment** (Y is the dominant yellow allele) and **gene 2** codes for an enzyme that **turns** the yellow pigment **orange** (R is the dominant orange allele). If you **don't have** the Y allele it **won't matter** if you have the R allele or not as the flower **will be colourless**. Gene 1 is **epistatic** to gene 2 as it can **mask** the expression of gene 2.

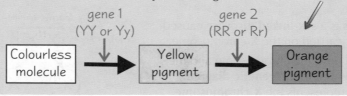

gene 1
(YY or Yy)

gene 2
(RR or Rr)

| Colourless molecule | → | Yellow pigment | → | Orange pigment |

3) **Crosses** involving epistatic genes **don't result** in the **expected phenotypic ratios** given above, e.g. if you cross **two heterozygous orange** flowered plants (YyRr) from the above example you wouldn't get the expected **9 : 3 : 3 : 1** phenotypic ratio for a **normal dihybrid cross**.

You can **Predict** the **Phenotypic Ratios** for Some **Epistatic Genes**

Just as you can **predict** the phenotypic ratios for **normal dihybrid crosses** (see page 202), you can predict the phenotypic ratios for dihybrid crosses involving some **epistatic genes** too:

A dihybrid cross involving a recessive epistatic allele — 9 : 3 : 4

Having **two copies** of the **recessive** epistatic allele **masks** (blocks) the expression of the **other gene**. If you cross a **homozygous recessive** parent with a **homozygous dominant** parent you will get a **9 : 3 : 4** phenotypic ratio of **dominant both : dominant epistatic recessive other : recessive epistatic** in the F$_2$ generation.

E.g. the **flower example above** is an example of a **recessive epistatic allele**. If a plant is **homozygous recessive** for the **epistatic gene** (yy) then it will be **colourless**, **masking** the expression of the orange gene. So if you cross homozygous parents, you should get a **9 : 3 : 4** ratio of **orange : yellow : white** in the F$_2$ **generation**. You can check the **phenotypic ratio** is right **using a genetic diagram**:

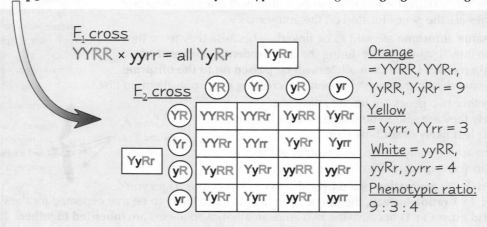

F$_1$ cross
YYRR × yyrr = all YyRr   YyRr

F$_2$ cross

	YR	Yr	yR	yr
YR	YYRR	YYRr	YyRR	YyRr
Yr	YYRr	YYrr	YyRr	Yyrr
yR	YyRR	YyRr	yyRR	yyRr
yr	YyRr	Yyrr	yyRr	yyrr

YyRr

<u>Orange</u>
= YYRR, YYRr,
YyRR, YyRr = 9

<u>Yellow</u>
= Yyrr, YYrr = 3

<u>White</u> = yyRR,
yyRr, yyrr = 4

<u>Phenotypic ratio:</u>
9 : 3 : 4

Linkages and Epistasis

A dihybrid cross involving a dominant epistatic allele — 12 : 3 : 1

Having **at least one** copy of the **dominant epistatic** allele **masks** (**blocks**) the expression of the other gene. Crossing a **homozygous recessive** parent with a **homozygous dominant** parent will produce a **12 : 3 : 1** phenotypic ratio of **dominant epistatic : recessive epistatic dominant other : recessive both** in the F_2 generation.

> E.g. **squash colour** is controlled by two genes — the **colour epistatic gene** (**W/w**) and the **yellow gene** (**Y/y**). The **no-colour, white** allele (**W**) is **dominant** over the **coloured** allele (**w**), so **WW** or **Ww** will be **white** and **ww** will be **coloured**. The yellow gene has the **dominant yellow** allele (**Y**) and the **recessive green** allele (**y**). So if the plant has **at least one W**, then the squash **will be white**, **masking** the expression of the yellow gene. So if you cross **wwyy** with **WWYY**, you'll get a **12 : 3 : 1** ratio of **white : yellow : green** in the F_2 generation. Here's a **genetic diagram** to prove it:

$\underline{F_1 \text{ cross}}$
WWYY × wwyy = all WwYy | WwYy |

$\underline{F_2 \text{ cross}}$

	WY	Wy	wY	wy
WY	WWYY	WWYy	WwYY	WwYy
Wy	WWYy	WWyy	WwYy	Wwyy
wY	WwYY	WwYy	wwYY	wwYy
wy	WwYy	Wwyy	wwYy	wwyy

| WwYy |

White = WWYY,
WWYy, WWyy,
WwYY, WwYy,
Wwyy = 12

Yellow = wwYY,
wwYy = 3

Green = wwyy = 1

Phenotypic ratio:
12 : 3 : 1

Warm-Up Questions

Q1 What is a sex-linked characteristic?

Q2 Two genes are autosomally-linked. What does this mean?

Q3 The cross AaBb x AaBb produces a 3 : 1 ratio of phenotypes in the offspring, instead of the expected 9 : 3 : 3 : 1 ratio. What does this tell you about the two genes involved?

Q4 What is an epistatic gene?

Q5 A dihybrid cross produces the phenotypic ratio 9 : 3 : 4 in the F_2 generation. What does this indicate about the genes involved?

PRACTICE QUESTIONS

Exam Questions

Q1 Haemophilia A is a sex-linked genetic disorder caused by a recessive allele carried on the X chromosome (X^h).

  a) Draw a genetic diagram for a female carrier and a male with haemophilia A to predict the possible genotypes of their offspring. [3 marks]

  b) Explain why haemophilia is more common in males than females. [3 marks]

Q2 Coat colour in mice is controlled by two genes. Gene 1 controls whether fur is coloured (C) or albino (c). Gene 2 controls whether the colour is grey (G) or black (g). Gene 1 is epistatic over gene 2.

  Describe and explain the phenotypic ratio produced in the F_2 generation from a CCGG × ccgg cross. [4 marks]

Q3 Hair type in organism A is controlled by two genes: hair (H bald, h hair) and type (S straight, s curly). The F_2 offspring of a cross are shown in the table on the right.

  State and explain the phenotypic ratio shown by the cross. [3 marks]

Homozygous curly hair (hhss) crossed with a homozygous bald (HHSS)

Phenotypes of the F_2 offspring produced		
Bald	Straight hair	Curly hair
36	9	3

Biology students — 9 : 1 phenotypic ratio normal : geek...

I don't know about you but I think I need a lie-down after these pages. Epistasis is a bit of a tricky topic, but you just need to understand what it is and learn the phenotypic ratios for the two types of epistasis — dominant and recessive.

The Chi-Squared Test

Just when you thought it was safe to turn the page... I stick in some maths. Surprise!

The **Chi-Squared Test** Can Be Used to **Check** the **Results** of **Genetic Crosses**

1) The **chi-squared** (χ^2) **test** is a **statistical test** that's used to see if the **results** of an experiment **support** a **theory**.

2) First, the theory is used to **predict** a **result** — this is called the **expected result**.
   Then, the experiment is carried out and the **actual result** is recorded — this is called the **observed result**.

3) To see if the results support the theory you have to make a **hypothesis** called the **null hypothesis**.

4) The null hypothesis is always that there's **no significant difference** between the observed and expected results (your experimental result will usually be a bit different from what you expect, but you need to know if the difference is just **due to chance**, or because your **theory is wrong**).

5) The χ^2 **test** is then carried out and the **outcome** either **supports** or **rejects** the **null hypothesis**.

6) You can use the χ^2 test in **genetics** to test theories about the **inheritance** of **characteristics**. For example:

Theory: **Wing length** in fruit flies is controlled by a **single gene** with **two alleles** (**monogenic inheritance**). The **dominant allele (N)** gives **normal** wings, and the **recessive allele (n)** gives **vestigial** wings.

Expected results: With monogenic inheritance, if you cross a **homozygous dominant** parent with a **homozygous recessive** parent, you'd expect a **3 : 1 phenotypic ratio** of **normal : vestigial** wings in the F_2 generation (see p. 200).

Observed results: The **experiment** (of crossing a homozygous dominant parent with a homozygous recessive parent) is **carried out** on fruit flies and the **number of F_2 offspring** with normal and vestigial wings is **counted**.

Null hypothesis: There's **no significant difference** between the observed and expected results. (If the χ^2 test shows the observed and expected results are **not significantly different**, then we are **unable to reject** the null hypothesis — the data **supports** the **theory** that wing length is controlled by **monogenic inheritance**.)

In this kind of statistical test, you can never prove that the null hypothesis is true — you can only 'fail to reject it'. This just means that the evidence doesn't give you a reason to think the null hypothesis is wrong.

First, **Work** Out the **Chi-Squared Value...**

Chi-squared (χ^2) is calculated using this formula: where **O** = **observed** result and **E** = **expected** result.

$$\chi^2 = \sum \frac{(O-E)^2}{E}$$

The best way to understand the χ^2 test is to work through an example — here's one for testing the **wing length** of **fruit flies** as explained above:

You don't need to learn the formula for chi-squared — it'll be given to you in the exam.

Homozygous dominant (NN) flies are crossed with homozygous recessive (nn) flies. **160 offspring** are produced in the F_2 generation.

(1) First, the **number of offspring** (out of a total of 160) **expected** for each phenotype is worked out. E for normal wings: 160 (total) ÷ 4 (ratio total) × 3 (predicted ratio for normal wings) = 120. E for vestigial wings: 160 ÷ 4 × 1 = 40.

Phenotype	Ratio	Expected Result (E)	Observed Result (O)
Normal wings	3	120	
Vestigial wings	1	40	

(2) Then the **actual number** of offspring **observed** with each phenotype (out of the 160 offspring) is **recorded**, e.g. 111 with normal wings.

Phenotype	Ratio	Expected Result (E)	Observed Result (O)
Normal wings	3	120	111
Vestigial wings	1	40	49

(3) The results are used to work out χ^2, taking it **one step at a time**:

(a) First calculate **O − E** (subtract the **expected result** from the **observed result**) for each phenotype. E.g. for normal wings: 111 − 120 = −9.

(b) Then the resulting numbers are **squared**, e.g. $9^2 = 81$

(c) These figures are divided by the **expected results**, e.g. 81 ÷ 120 = 0.675.

Phenotype	Ratio	Expected Result (E)	Observed Result (O)	O − E	$(O-E)^2$	$\frac{(O-E)^2}{E}$
Normal wings	3	120	111	−9	81	0.675
Vestigial wings	1	40	49	9	81	2.025

$$\sum \frac{(O-E)^2}{E} = 2.7$$

Remember, you need to work it out for each phenotype first, then add all the numbers together.

(d) Finally, the numbers are **added** together to get χ^2, e.g. 0.675 + 2.025 = **2.7**.

The Chi-Squared Test

...Then **Compare** it to the **Critical Value**

1) To find out if there is a **significant difference** between your observed and expected results you need to **compare** your χ^2 **value** to a **critical value**.

2) The critical value is the value of χ^2 that corresponds to a 0.05 (**5%**) level of **probability** that the **difference** between the observed and expected results is **due to chance**.

3) If your χ^2 value is **larger** than or equal to the critical value then there **is a significant difference** between the observed and expected results (something **other than chance** is causing the difference) — and the **null hypothesis** can be **rejected**.

4) If your χ^2 value is **smaller** than the critical value then there **is no significant difference** between the observed and expected results — the null hypothesis **can't be rejected**. E.g. for the example on the previous page the χ^2 value is **2.7**, which is **smaller** than the critical value of **3.84** (see table below) — there's **no significant difference** between the observed and expected results. We've failed to reject the null hypothesis, so the **theory** that wing length in fruit flies is controlled by **monogenic inheritance** is **supported**.

5) In the exam you might be **given** the **critical value** or asked to **work it out** from a **table**:

Using a χ^2 table:

If you're not given the critical value, you may have to find it yourself from a χ^2 **table** — this shows a range of **probabilities** that correspond to different **critical values** for different **degrees of freedom** (explained below). Biologists normally use a **probability** level of **0.05** (5%), so you only need to look in that column.

- First, the **degrees of freedom** for the experiment are worked out — this is the **number of classes** (number of phenotypes) **minus one**. E.g. 2 – 1 = 1.

- Next, the **critical value** corresponding to a **probability** of 0.05 at **one degree of freedom** is found in the table — here it's **3.84**.

- Then just **compare** your χ^2 value of **2.7** to this critical value, as explained above.

degrees of freedom	no. of classes	Critical values					
1	2	0.46	1.64	2.71	3.84	6.64	10.83
2	3	1.39	3.22	4.61	5.99	9.21	13.82
3	4	2.37	4.64	6.25	7.82	11.34	16.27
4	5	3.36	5.99	7.78	9.49	13.28	18.47
probability that result is due to chance only		0.50 (50%)	0.20 (20%)	0.10 (10%)	0.05 (5%)	0.01 (1%)	0.001 (0.1%)

Abridged from Statistical Tables for Biological Agricultural and Medical Research (6th ed.)
© 1963 R.A Fisher and F. Yates. Reprinted with permission of Pearson Education Limited.

Warm-Up Questions

Q1 What is a χ^2 test used for?

Q2 What can the results of the χ^2 test tell you?

Q3 How do you tell if the difference between your observed and expected results is due to chance?

PRACTICE QUESTIONS

Exam Question

Q1 A scientist is investigating petal colour in a flower. It's thought to be controlled by two separate genes (dihybrid inheritance), the colour gene — B = blue, b = purple, and the spots gene — W = white, w = yellow. A cross involving a homozygous dominant parent and a homozygous recessive parent should give a 9 : 3 : 3 : 1 ratio in the F_2 generation. The scientist observes the number of offspring showing each of four phenotypes in 240 F_2 offspring. Her results are shown in the table.

Her null hypothesis is that there is no significant difference between the observed and expected ratios.

a) Complete the table to calculate χ^2 for this experiment. [3 marks]

b) The critical value for this experiment is 7.82. Explain whether the χ^2 value supports or rejects the null hypothesis. [2 marks]

Phenotype	Ratio	Expected Result (E)	Observed Result (O)	O − E	O − E²	$\frac{(O-E^2)}{E}$
Blue with white spots	9	135	131			
Purple with white spots	3	45	52			
Blue with yellow spots	3	45	48			
Purple with yellow spots	1	15	9			
					$\sum \frac{(O-E)^2}{E} =$	

The expected result of revising these pages — boredom...

...the observed result — boredom (except for the maths geeks among you). Don't worry if you're not brilliant at maths though, you don't have to be to do the chi-squared test — just make sure you know the steps above off by heart.

Evolution by Natural Selection and Genetic Drift

You already know that evolution occurs by natural selection. The twist is that it can also happen by genetic drift.

Evolution is a **Change** in **Allele Frequency**

1) The complete range of **alleles** present in a **population** is called the **gene pool**.
2) **New alleles** are usually generated by **mutations** in **genes**.
3) How **often** an **allele occurs** in a population is called the **allele frequency**.
   It's usually given as a **percentage** of the total population, e.g. 35%, or a **number**, e.g. 0.35.
4) The **frequency** of an **allele** in a population **changes** over time — this is **evolution**.

> A population is a group of organisms of the same species living in a particular area.

Evolution Occurs by **Natural Selection**

You might remember **natural selection** from Module 4. Here's a reminder of how it works:

1) **Individuals** within a population **vary** because they have **different alleles**.
2) **Predation**, **disease** and **competition** (**selection pressures**) create a **struggle for survival**.
3) Because individuals vary, some are **better adapted** to the selection pressures than others.
4) Individuals that have an allele that **increases** their **chance of survival** (an **advantageous** allele) are **more likely** to **survive**, **reproduce** and **pass on** the advantageous allele, than individuals with different alleles.
5) This means that a **greater proportion** of the next generation **inherit** the **advantageous allele**.
6) They, in turn, are **more likely** to **survive**, **reproduce** and **pass on** their genes.
7) So the **frequency** of the advantageous allele **increases** from generation to generation.
8) This process is called **natural selection**.

> Variation is generated by meiosis and mutations.

> A selection pressure is anything that affects an organism's chance of survival and reproduction.

An allele is only advantageous with the right **selection pressure**.
Without a selection pressure, natural selection **won't take place**.

The **Environment** Affects **Which Characteristics Become More Common**

Whether the **environment** is **changing** or **stable** affects **which characteristics are selected for** by natural selection:

When the **environment isn't changing** much, individuals with alleles for characteristics towards the **middle** of the range are more likely to **survive** and **reproduce**. This is called **STABILISING SELECTION** and it **reduces the range** of possible **phenotypes**.
<u>EXAMPLE</u> In any **mammal population** there's a **range** of **fur length**. In a **stable climate**, having fur at the **extremes** of this range **reduces** the **chances** of **surviving** as it's harder to maintain the **right body temperature**. Animals with alleles for **average fur length** are the **most likely** to **survive**, **reproduce** and **pass on** their alleles. So these alleles **increase** in **frequency**. The **proportion** of the **population** with **average fur length increases** and the **range** of fur lengths **decreases**.

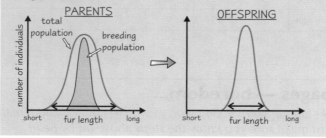

When there's a **change** in the environment, individuals with alleles for characteristics of an **extreme type** are more likely to **survive** and **reproduce**. This is called **DIRECTIONAL SELECTION**.
<u>EXAMPLE</u> If the environment becomes **very cold**, individual mammals with **alleles** for **long fur length** will find it **easier** to **maintain** the **right body temperature** than animals with short fur length. So they're **more likely** to **survive**, **reproduce** and **pass on** their alleles. Over time the **frequency** of alleles for **long fur length increases**.

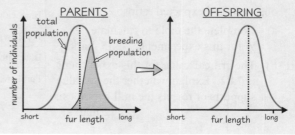

Evolution by Natural Selection and Genetic Drift

Evolution Also Occurs via Genetic Drift

1) **Natural selection** is just **one** process by which **evolution** occurs.

2) Evolution **also** occurs due to **genetic drift** — instead of **environmental factors** affecting which individuals **survive**, **breed** and pass on their alleles, **chance** dictates **which alleles** are **passed on**. Here's how it works:

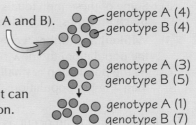

- Individuals within a population show **variation** in their **genotypes** (e.g. A and B).
- By **chance**, the **allele** for **one genotype** (B) is **passed on** to the offspring **more often** than others.
- So the number of individuals with the allele **increases**.
- If by chance the same allele is passed on more often again and again, it can lead to **evolution** as the allele becomes **more common** in the population.

genotype A (4)
genotype B (4)

genotype A (3)
genotype B (5)

genotype A (1)
genotype B (7)

3) Natural selection and genetic drift work **alongside each other** to drive evolution, but one process can drive evolution **more** than the other depending on the **population size**.

4) **Evolution by genetic drift** usually has a **greater effect** in **smaller populations** where **chance** has a **greater influence**. In larger populations any **chance variations** in allele frequency tend to **even out** across the whole population.

5) The evolution of **human blood groups** is a good example of **genetic drift**:

- Different **Native American tribes** show different **blood group frequencies**. For example, **Blackfoot Indians** are mainly **group A**, but **Navajos** are mainly **group O**.
- Blood group doesn't affect **survival** or **reproduction**, so the differences **aren't** due to evolution by natural selection.
- In the past, human populations were much **smaller** and were often found in **isolated groups**. The blood group differences were due to evolution by **genetic drift** — by **chance** the allele for **blood group O** was **passed on more often** in the Navajo tribe, so over time this **allele** and blood group became **more common**.

Genetic Drift Has a Greater Effect if There's a Genetic Bottleneck

A **genetic bottleneck** is an **event** (such as a natural disaster) that causes a **big reduction** in a **population's size**, leading to a **reduction** in the **gene pool**. For example:

> The gene pool is the complete range of alleles in a population.

1) The **mice** in a **large population** are either **black or grey**. The coat colour **doesn't** affect their **survival** or **reproduction**.

2) A **large flood** hits the population and the **only survivors** are **grey** mice and **one black** mouse.

3) **Grey** becomes the **most common colour** due to **genetic drift**.

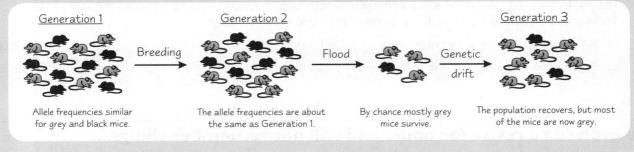

Generation 1

Breeding

Generation 2

Flood

Genetic drift

Generation 3

Allele frequencies similar for grey and black mice.

The allele frequencies are about the same as Generation 1.

By chance mostly grey mice survive.

The population recovers, but most of the mice are now grey.

Evolution by Natural Selection and Genetic Drift

Genetic Drift Also Has a Greater Effect if There's a Founder Effect

The **founder effect** describes what happens when just a **few organisms** from a population **start a new population** and there are only a **small number of different alleles** in the **initial gene pool**:

1) Individuals within a population show **variation** in their **genotypes** (e.g. A and B).
2) Some of these individuals start a **new population**.
   By **chance** these individuals are mostly **one particular genotype** (A).
3) **Without** any further 'gene flow' (i.e. the introduction of new alleles from outside the population) the new population will **grow** with **reduced genetic variation**. As the population is **small**, it's **more heavily influenced** by **genetic drift** than a larger population.

genotype A
genotype B

The founder effect can occur as a result of **migration** leading to geographical **separation** or if a new colony is separated from the original population for **another reason**, such as **religion**.

Example — The Amish

The **Amish population** of North America are all descended from a **small** number of Swiss who **migrated** there. The population shows **little genetic diversity**. They have remained **isolated** from the surrounding population due to their **religious beliefs**, so **few new alleles** have been introduced. The population has an unusually high incidence of certain **genetic disorders**.

Warm-Up Questions

Q1 What is evolution?
Q2 What is allele frequency?
Q3 What is genetic drift?
Q4 Does genetic drift have a greater effect in smaller or larger populations? Why?
Q5 What situation does the founder effect describe?

PRACTICE QUESTIONS

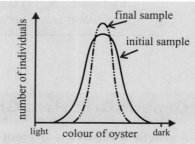

Exam Questions

Q1 Northern elephant seals were hunted by humans in the late 1800s. Their original population was reduced to about 20 seals at their lowest point, which have since reproduced to a population of over 100 000. Southern elephant seals were not hunted to the same extent.

Northern elephant seals now show much less genetic variation than southern elephant seals. Explain why this is the case.

[3 marks]

Q2 A group of scientists monitored how the colour of oyster shells on a beach changed over time. The graph above right shows the colour of the oyster shells in the scientists' initial sample and in their final sample. The oysters were mainly found on the sand, which was a mid-brown colour.

a) What type of selection is shown on the graph? Explain your answer. [3 marks]

b) Suggest how the changes shown in the graph might have taken place. [4 marks]

I've evolved to revise for hours and still not remember things...

The trickiest thing here is tying all the information together in your head. Basically, natural selection and genetic drift drive evolution. And the characteristics selected for in natural selection are determined by what the environment's like. The characteristics that become more common by genetic drift do so purely by chance.

Hardy-Weinberg Principle and Artificial Selection

Now you know what allele frequency is you need to be able to calculate it. So switch your maths brain on now.
Then you can take a breather and learn all about artificial selection.

The **Hardy-Weinberg Principle** Predicts **Allele Frequencies Won't Change**

1) The **Hardy-Weinberg principle** predicts that the **frequencies of alleles** in a population **won't change** from **one generation** to the **next**.

2) But this prediction is **only true** under **certain conditions** — it has to be a **large population** where there's **no immigration, emigration, mutations** or **natural selection**. There also needs to be **random mating** — all possible genotypes can breed with all others.

3) The **Hardy-Weinberg equations** (see below) are based on this principle.
They can be used to **estimate the frequency** of particular **alleles** and **genotypes** within populations.

4) If the allele frequencies **do change** between generations in a large population then immigration, emigration, natural selection or mutations have happened.

The **Hardy-Weinberg Equations** Can be Used to **Predict Allele Frequency...**

You can **figure out** the frequency of one allele if you **know the frequency of the other**, using this equation:

$$p + q = 1$$

Where: **p** = the **frequency** of the **dominant** allele
q = the **frequency** of the **recessive** allele

The total frequency of all possible alleles for a characteristic in a certain population is 1.O. So the frequencies of the individual alleles (the dominant one and the recessive one) must add up to 1.O.

E.g. a species of plant has either **red** or **white** flowers. Allele **R** (red) is **dominant** and allele **r** (white) is **recessive**. If the frequency of **R** is **0.4**, then the frequency of **r** is:
$$1 - 0.4 = 0.6.$$

...and **Genotype Frequency**

You can **figure out** the frequency of one genotype if you **know the frequencies of the others**, using this equation:

$$p^2 + 2pq + q^2 = 1$$

Where: p^2 = the **frequency** of the **homozygous dominant genotype**
$2pq$ = the **frequency** of the **heterozygous genotype**
q^2 = the **frequency** of the **homozygous recessive genotype**

The total frequency of all possible genotypes for one characteristic in a certain population is 1.O. So the frequencies of the individual genotypes must add up to 1.O.

E.g. if there are **two alleles** for **flower colour** (R and r), there are **three possible genotypes** — **RR, Rr** and **rr**.
If the frequency of genotype **RR** (p^2) is **0.34** and the frequency of genotype **Rr** ($2pq$) is **0.27**, the frequency of genotype **rr** (q^2) must be:
$$1 - 0.34 - 0.27 = 0.39.$$

Hardy-Weinberg Principle and Artificial Selection

Sometimes You Need to Use **Both Hardy-Weinberg Equations**

The **frequency** of **cystic fibrosis** (genotype **ff**) in the UK is currently approximately **1 birth in every 2500**. From this information you can estimate the **percentage** of people in the UK that are cystic fibrosis **carriers (Ff)**. To do this you need to find the **frequency** of **heterozygous genotype Ff**, i.e. **2pq**, using **both** equations:

$$p + q = 1 \qquad p^2 + 2pq + q^2 = 1$$

First calculate q:
Frequency of cystic fibrosis
(homozygous recessive, ff) is 1 in 2500
$ff = q^2 = 1 \div 2500 = 0.0004$
So, $q = \sqrt{0.0004} = 0.02$

Next calculate p:
Using $p + q = 1$, $p = 1 - q$
$p = 1 - 0.02 = 0.98$

Then calculate 2pq:
$2pq = 2 \times 0.98 \times 0.02 = 0.039$

The **frequency** of **genotype Ff** is **0.039**, so the **percentage** of the UK population that are **carriers** is **3.9%**.

Artificial Selection Involves **Breeding** Individuals with **Desirable Traits**

Artificial selection is when **humans select individuals** in a population to **breed together** to get **desirable traits**. In can be done in both **animals** and **plants**. Here are **two examples**:

> Artificial selection is also called selective breeding.

Modern Dairy Cattle

Modern **dairy cows** produce **many litres of milk** a day as a result of **artificial selection**:

1) Farmers **select** a **female** with a **very high milk yield** and a **male** whose **mother** had a very high milk yield and **breed** these two **together**.

2) Then they **select** the **offspring** with the **highest milk yields** and **breed** them **together**.

3) This is continued over **several generations** until a **very high milk-yielding cow** is produced.

Bread Wheat

Bread wheat (*Triticum aestivum*) is the plant from which **flour** is produced for **bread-making**. It produces a **high yield** of wheat because of **artificial selection** by **humans**:

1) Wheat plants with a **high wheat yield** (e.g. large ears) are **bred together**.

2) The **offspring** with the **highest yields** are then **bred together**.

3) This is continued over **several generations** to produce a plant that has a **very high yield**.

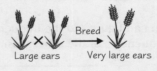

Large ears × × Breed → Very large ears

Artificial Selection **Reduces** the **Gene Pool**

1) Artificial selection means that only organisms with **similar traits** and therefore **similar alleles** are bred together. This leads to a **reduction** in the **number of alleles** in the **gene pool**.

2) A reduced gene pool could cause us **problems** in the **future** — for example, if a **new disease** appears, there's **less chance** of the **alleles** that could offer **resistance** to that disease being present in the population.

3) Artificial selection could also mean that **potentially useful alleles** are **accidentally lost** from the population when other alleles are being selected for.

4) That's why it's important to **maintain resources** of **genetic material** for use in the future, e.g. by **preserving** the original '**wild type**' organisms that haven't undergone any artificial selection.

Hardy-Weinberg Principle and Artificial Selection

Artificial Selection Can Cause Problems for the Organisms Involved

1) Artificial selection can **exaggerate** certain traits, leading to **health problems** for the organisms involved.

Example: Pedigree Dogs...

Modern pedigree dog breeds are all descended from a single wolf-like ancestor. Each breed has gone through **many generations** of **artificial selection** to produce the dogs we know today. Pedigree dogs such as **Pugs** and **French Bulldogs** have been bred to have **flat, squashed up faces**. This trait has become so exaggerated that many of these dogs now suffer **breathing problems** as a result.

2) A reduced gene pool also tends to result in an **increased incidence** of **genetic disease**.

Example continued...

There's a high incidence of **hereditary deafness** in certain dog breeds, e.g. **Dalmatians** and **English Bull Terriers**.

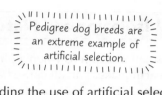

Pedigree dog breeds are an extreme example of artificial selection.

3) Problems like these mean that there are **ethical issues** surrounding the use of artificial selection. For example, many people don't think it's fair to keep artificially selecting traits in dogs that cause them health problems.

Warm-Up Questions

Q1 Which term represents the frequency of the dominant allele in the Hardy-Weinberg equations?

Q2 Which term represents the frequency of the recessive allele in the Hardy-Weinberg equations?

Q3 What is artificial selection?

Q4 Give one ethical issue surrounding artificial selection.

Exam Questions

Q1 Modern beef cattle (raised for meat production) produce a very high meat yield.
Explain how artificial selection by farmers could have led to this. [3 marks]

Q2 A breed of dog has either a black or brown coat. Allele B (black) is dominant and allele b (brown) is recessive. The frequency of the recessive allele is 0.23. The Hardy-Weinberg equations are:

$$p^2 + 2pq + q^2 = 1 \qquad \text{and} \qquad p + q = 1.$$

Find the frequency of the heterozygous (Bb) genotype. [2 marks]

Q3 Cleft chins are controlled by a single gene with two alleles. The allele coding for cleft chin (C) is dominant over the allele coding for a non-cleft chin (c). In a particular population, the frequency of the homozygous dominant genotype for cleft chin is 0.14. The Hardy-Weinberg equations are:

$$p^2 + 2pq + q^2 = 1 \qquad \text{and} \qquad p + q = 1.$$

a) What is the frequency of the recessive allele in the population? [2 marks]

b) What is the frequency of the homozygous recessive genotype in the population? [1 mark]

This stuff's surely not that bad — Hardly worth Weining about...

Not many of you will be thrilled with the maths content on the first two pages of this topic, but don't worry. Make sure you know what to use each Hardy-Weinberg equation for and what the different terms mean, so you can plug the numbers you're given into the right places. Don't forget to take a calculator into the exam with you, either.

Speciation

Evolution leads to the development of lots of different species. I bet you can't guess the name for this process...

Speciation is the Development of a New Species

1) A species is defined as a group of similar organisms that can reproduce to give fertile offspring.

2) Speciation is the development of a new species.

3) It occurs when populations of the same species become reproductively isolated — changes in allele frequencies cause changes in phenotype that mean they can no longer breed together to produce fertile offspring.

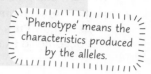
'Phenotype' means the characteristics produced by the alleles.

Geographical Isolation and Natural Selection Lead to Allopatric Speciation

1) Geographical isolation happens when a **physical barrier divides** a population of a species — **floods**, **volcanic eruptions** and **earthquakes** can all cause barriers that isolate some individuals from the main population.

2) **Conditions** on either side of the barrier will be slightly **different**. For example, there might be a **different climate** on each side.

3) Because the environment is different on each side, **different characteristics** will become **more common** due to **natural selection** (because there are **different selection pressures**):

- Because different **characteristics** will be **advantageous** on each side, the **allele frequencies** will change in each population, e.g. if one allele is more advantageous on one side of the barrier, the frequency of that allele on that side will **increase**.

- **Mutations** will take place **independently** in each population, also changing the **allele frequencies**.

- The changes in allele frequencies will lead to changes in **phenotype frequencies**, e.g. the advantageous characteristics (**phenotypes**) will become more common on that side.

4) Eventually, individuals from different populations will have changed so much that they won't be able to breed with one another to produce **fertile** offspring — they'll have become **reproductively isolated**.

5) The two groups will have become separate **species**.

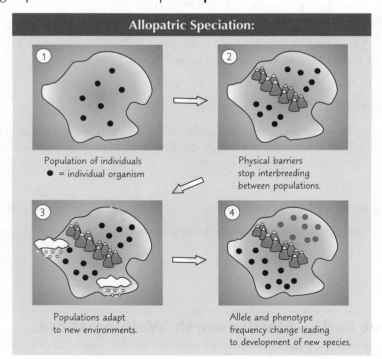

Allopatric Speciation:

Population of individuals
● = individual organism

Physical barriers stop interbreeding between populations.

Populations adapt to new environments.

Allele and phenotype frequency change leading to development of new species.

Allopatric speciation is much more common than sympatric speciation (see next page).

Bill wasn't going to let a mountain get in the way of his reproductive success.

Speciation

Reproductive Isolation Occurs in Many Ways

Reproductive isolation occurs because the **changes** in the alleles and phenotypes of the two populations **prevent** them from **successfully breeding together**. These changes include:

1) **Seasonal changes** — individuals from the same population develop different **flowering** or **mating** seasons, or become **sexually active** at **different times** of the year.

2) **Mechanical changes** — changes in **genitalia** prevent successful mating.

3) **Behavioural changes** — a group of individuals develop **courtship rituals** that **aren't attractive** to the main population.

Janice's courtship ritual was still successful in attracting mates.

Sympatric Speciation Doesn't Require Geographical Isolation

A population **doesn't** have to become **geographically isolated** to become **reproductively isolated**. Random mutations could occur **within a population**, resulting in the changes mentioned above, **preventing** members of that population breeding with other members of the species. Speciation without geographical isolation is called **sympatric speciation**.

Example:

1) Most eukaryotic organisms are **diploid** — they have **two sets** of **homologous** (matched) **chromosomes** in their cells. Sometimes, **mutations** can occur that **increase** the number of **chromosomes**. This is known as **polyploidy**.

2) Individuals with different numbers of chromosomes **can't reproduce** sexually to give **fertile offspring** — so if a polyploid organism emerges in a diploid population, the polyploid organism will be **reproductively isolated** from the diploid organisms.

3) If the polyploid organism then reproduces **asexually**, a **new species** could develop.

4) Polyploidy can only lead to speciation if it **doesn't prove fatal** to the organism and more polyploid organisms can be produced. It's **more common** in **plants** than animals.

Warm-Up Questions

Q1 What is speciation?

Q2 What is the difference between allopatric and sympatric speciation?

PRACTICE QUESTIONS

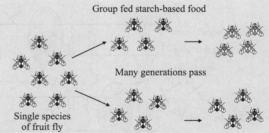

Group fed starch-based food

Many generations pass

Single species of fruit fly

Group fed maltose-based food

Exam Question

Q1 The diagram shows an experiment conducted with fruit flies. One population was split in two and each population was fed a different food. After many generations the two populations were placed together and it was observed that they were unable to breed together.

a) What evidence shows that speciation occurred? [1 mark]

b) Explain why the experiment resulted in speciation. [3 marks]

c) Suggest two possible reasons why members of the two populations were not able to breed together. [2 marks]

d) During the experiment, populations of fruit flies were artificially isolated. Suggest one way that populations of organisms could become isolated naturally. [1 mark]

If they were ever separated, Al and Patrick would be heartbroken...

These gags get better and better... Anyway, it's a bit of a toughie getting your head round the different mechanisms that can produce a new species. The key thing to remember is that both allopatric and sympatric speciation involve reproductive isolation. But only allopatric speciation involves geographical isolation.

Common Techniques

This section is all about techniques used to investigate and fiddle about with genes. So get your deerstalker hat on and your magnifying glass out...

Techniques Used to **Study Genes**

There are lots of **techniques** used to **study genes** and their **function** — you need to learn some of these techniques for the exam. They include:

- The **polymerase chain reaction** (**PCR**) (see below).
- **Gel electrophoresis** (see next page).
- Cutting out DNA fragments using **restriction enzymes** (see page 218).

"Jeans have an important function in politics — they make me look cool..."

These techniques are also used in **DNA profiling** (see page 219), **DNA sequencing** (see page 225), **genetic engineering** (see page 220) and **gene therapy** (see page 224).

Multiple Copies of a **DNA Fragment** can be **Made** Using **PCR**

The **polymerase chain reaction** (PCR) can be used to **select** a fragment of DNA (containing the gene or bit of DNA you're interested in) and **amplify** it to produce **millions of copies** in just a few hours. PCR has **several stages** and is **repeated** over and over to make lots of copies:

1) A reaction mixture is set up that contains the **DNA sample**, **free nucleotides**, **primers** and **DNA polymerase**.
   - **Primers** are short pieces of DNA that are **complementary** to the bases at the **start** of the fragment you want.
   - **DNA polymerase** is an **enzyme** that creates new DNA strands.

2) The DNA mixture is **heated** to **95 °C** to break the **hydrogen bonds** between the two strands of DNA. DNA polymerase **doesn't denature** even at this high temperature — this is important as it means **many cycles** of PCR can be carried out without having to use **new enzymes** each time.

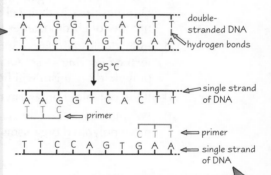

3) The mixture is then **cooled** to between **50** and **65 °C** so that the primers can **bind** (**anneal**) to the strands.

4) The reaction mixture is heated to **72 °C**, so **DNA polymerase** can **work**.

5) The DNA polymerase **lines up** free DNA nucleotides **alongside** each **template strand**. Complementary **base pairing** means **new complementary strands** are formed.

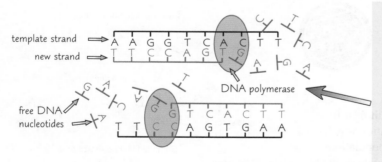

6) **Two new copies** of the fragment of DNA are formed and **one cycle** of PCR is **complete**.

7) The cycle starts again, with the mixture being heated to 95 °C and this time **all four strands** (two original and two new) are used as **templates**.

8) Each PCR cycle **doubles** the amount of DNA, e.g. **1st cycle = 2 × 2 = 4 DNA fragments**, **2nd cycle = 4 × 2 = 8 DNA fragments**, **3rd cycle = 8 × 2 = 16 DNA fragments**, and so on.

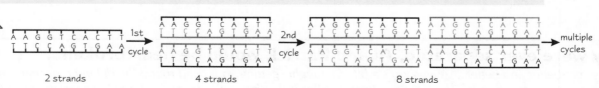

2 strands   4 strands   8 strands

Common Techniques

Electrophoresis Separates DNA Fragments by Size

Electrophoresis is a procedure that uses an **electrical current** to **separate out DNA fragments**, **RNA fragments**, or **proteins** depending on their **size**. Here's how you can carry out electrophoresis in the **lab** using samples of **fragmented DNA** — there are several stages involved...

Firstly you add a **Gel Tray** to a **Gel Box** (or **Tank**)

1) Electrophoresis is commonly performed using **agarose gel** that has been poured into a **gel tray** and left to **solidify**. A **row of wells** is created at **one end** of the gel.

2) To perform electrophoresis, firstly you need to put the **gel tray** into a **gel box** (or tank). You need to make sure the end of the gel tray with the wells is closest to the **negative electrode** on the gel box.

3) Then add **buffer solution** to the **reservoirs** at the **sides** of the **gel box** so that the **surface of the gel** becomes **covered** in the buffer solution.

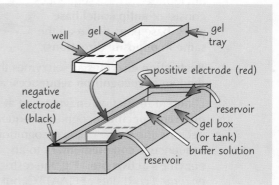

Next **DNA Samples** are Loaded Into the **Wells**

1) Take your fragmented DNA samples and, using a micropipette, add the same volume of **loading dye** to each — loading dye helps the samples to **sink to the bottom** of the wells and makes them **easier to see**.

2) Next add a set volume (e.g. **10 µl**) of a DNA sample to the first well. You have to be **really careful** when adding the samples to the wells — make sure the **tip** of your micropipette is in the **buffer solution** and **just above** the **opening of the well**. **Don't** stick the tip of the micropipette too far into the well or you could **pierce the bottom** of it.

3) Then repeat this process and add the same volume of each of your **other DNA samples** to **other wells** in the gel. Use a **clean micropipette tip** each time.

4) Make sure you **record** which DNA sample you have added to each well.

Then **Electrophoresis** is Carried Out

1) Put the **lid** on the **gel box** and **connect the leads** from the gel box to the **power supply**.

2) **Turn on** the power supply and **set it to the required voltage**, e.g. 100 V. This causes an **electrical current** to be **passed through the gel**.

3) DNA fragments are **negatively charged**, so they'll move through the gel **towards the positive electrode** at the far end of the gel (called the **anode**). **Small** DNA fragments move **faster** and **travel further** through the gel, so the DNA fragments will **separate** according to **size**.

4) Let the gel run for about **30 minutes** (or until the dye is **about 2 cm** from the end of the gel) then **turn off** the power supply.

5) **Remove** the gel tray from the gel box and **tip off** any **excess buffer solution**.

6) Wearing **gloves**, **stain** the DNA fragments by covering the surface of the gel with a **staining solution** then **rinsing** the gel with water. The **bands** of the different **DNA fragments** will now be **visible**. The size of a DNA fragment is **measured** in **bases**, e.g. ATCC = 4 bases or base pairs, 1000 bases is one **kilobase** (**1 kb**).

Electrophoresis can be carried out on **RNA fragments** following the **same basic method** as for **DNA fragments**.

However, proteins can be positively charged or negatively charged, so before they undergo electrophoresis, they're mixed with a chemical that **denatures** the proteins so they all have the **same charge**. Electrophoresis of proteins has **many uses**, e.g. to identify the proteins present in **urine** or **blood** samples, which may help to **diagnose disease**.

Module 6: Section 4 — Manipulating Genomes

Common Techniques

Restriction Enzymes can be Used to Cut Out DNA Fragments

As well as PCR, another way to get a DNA fragment from an organism's DNA is by using **restriction enzymes**:

1) Some sections of DNA have **palindromic** sequences of **nucleotides**. These sequences consist of **antiparallel base pairs** (base pairs that read the **same** in **opposite directions**).

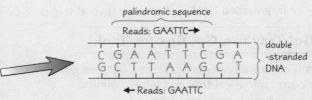

palindromic sequence

Reads: GAATTC→

C G A A T T C G A
G C T T A A G C T

} double-stranded DNA

← Reads: GAATTC

2) **Restriction enzymes** are enzymes that **recognise specific** palindromic sequences (known as **recognition sequences**) and cut (**digest**) the DNA at these places.

3) Different restriction enzymes cut at **different specific** recognition sequences, because the **shape** of the recognition sequence is **complementary** to an enzyme's **active site**. E.g. the restriction enzyme *Eco*RI cuts at GAATTC, but *Hind*III cuts at AAGCTT.

4) If recognition sequences are present at **either side** of the DNA fragment you want, you can use restriction enzymes to **separate** it from the rest of the DNA.

5) The DNA sample is **incubated** with the specific restriction enzyme, which **cuts** the DNA fragment out via a **hydrolysis reaction**.

6) Sometimes the cut leaves **sticky ends** — **small tails** of **unpaired bases** at **each end** of the fragment. Sticky ends can be used to **bind** (**anneal**) the DNA fragment to another piece of DNA that has sticky ends with **complementary sequences**.

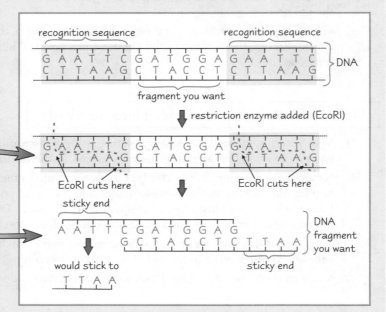

Warm-Up Questions

Q1 What does 'PCR' stand for?

Q2 By what feature does electrophoresis separate DNA fragments?

Q3 During electrophoresis, which electrode do DNA fragments move towards? Explain why.

Q4 Describe how and why the procedure used to separate proteins by electrophoresis is slightly different from the procedure used to separate nucleic acids by electrophoresis.

Q5 What are restriction enzymes?

Exam Question

Q1* In the EU there is a ban on the import and export of any products made from dog fur. Authorities enforcing the ban only need to analyse DNA from a single hair found within a product they suspect to contain dog fur, to identify if the product is illegal.
Describe and explain a procedure that allows scientists to successfully isolate and amplify DNA from such a small original sample.

[6 marks]

* You will be assessed on the quality of your written response in this question.

Sticky ends — for once a name that actually makes sense...

Okay, your eyes might have gone funny from seeing so many nucleotides on these pages. But once you've recovered, it's really important to go over these pages as many times as you need to 'cause examiners love throwing in a few questions about PCR or restriction enzymes. Bless 'em — examiners get excited about the strangest things.

DNA Profiling

It's time to see how some of the techniques used to study genes are used in DNA profiling...

Electrophoresis is Used to Produce DNA Profiles

1) Some of an organism's **genome** (all the genetic material in an organism) consists of **repetitive, non-coding base sequences** — sequences that **don't code** for proteins and **repeat** over and over (sometimes thousands of times).

2) The **number of times** these non-coding sequences are **repeated differs** from person to person, so the **length** of these sequences in nucleotides differs too.

3) The **number** of times a **sequence is repeated** at **different, specific places** (**loci**) in a person's genome (and so the number of nucleotides there) can be analysed using **electrophoresis**. This creates a **DNA profile**.

4) The **probability** of **two individuals** having the **same** DNA profile is **very low** because the **chance of two individuals** having the **same number** of sequence repeats at **each locus** in DNA is **very low**.

DNA Profiling can be Used in Forensic Science...

Forensic scientists use DNA profiling to **compare** samples of **DNA** collected from **crime scenes** (e.g. DNA from **blood, semen, skin cells, saliva, hair** etc.) to samples of DNA from **possible suspects**, to **link them** to crime scenes.

1) The **DNA** is **isolated** from all the collected samples (from the crime scene and from the suspects).

2) **PCR** (see p. 216) is used to amplify multiple areas containing different sequence repeats — primers are used to bind to either side of these repeats and so the whole repeat is amplified.

3) The **PCR products** are run on an **electrophoresis gel** and the DNA profiles produced are **compared** to see if any **match** (i.e. if they have the **same pattern** of bands on the gel).

4) If the samples match, it **links** a **person** to the **crime scene**. E.g. this gel shows that the DNA profile from **suspect C matches** that from the crime scene, **linking** them to the crime scene. All five bands match, so suspect C has the **same number** of repeats (nucleotides) at **five** different places.

Example — DNA Profiles

Crime scene | Suspect A | Suspect B | Suspect C

Electrophoresis could also be used in this way to see if two DNA samples have come from the **same species** (i.e. the more similar the pattern of bands, the more likely the samples are from the same species).

...and Medical Diagnosis

1) In medical diagnosis, a DNA profile can refer to a **unique pattern** of **several alleles**.

2) It can be used to **analyse the risk of genetic disorders**. It's useful when the **specific** mutation **isn't** known or where **several mutations** could have caused the disorder, because it identifies a **broader, altered** genetic pattern.

EXAMPLE
Preimplantation genetic haplotyping (PGH) screens embryos created by IVF for genetic disorders before they're implanted into the uterus. The faulty regions of the parents' DNA are used to produce DNA profiles, which are compared to the DNA profile of the embryo. If the profiles match, the embryo has inherited the disorder. It can be used to screen for cystic fibrosis, Huntington's disease etc.

Warm-Up Questions

Q1 Briefly describe what a DNA profile is.

Q2 Outline how DNA profiling can be used to identify the risk of an IVF baby being born with a genetic disorder.

PRACTICE QUESTIONS

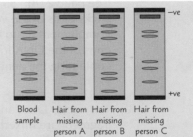

Blood sample | Hair from missing person A | Hair from missing person B | Hair from missing person C

Exam Question

Q1 Forensic detectives have discovered blood at a crime scene. They suspect the blood may belong to one of three local missing people. Using the blood, and hair samples gained from the missing people's personal belongings, they produce the DNA profiles above.

a) Describe how a DNA profile is made. [3 marks]

b) Explain which missing person the blood is most likely to belong to. [1 mark]

The Carpenters and The Doors — that's two bands that match...

DNA profiling is pretty fascinating. It's amazing that scientists have learnt how to chop up DNA, make squillions of copies of it, subject it to an electrical current and use the results to fight crime or identify disease risk. Science is fab*.

*Criminals may disagree.

Genetic Engineering

Genetic engineering — you need to know what it is and how it's done... (unlucky)...

Genetic Engineering is the Manipulation of an Organism's DNA

1) Organisms that have had their DNA altered by genetic engineering are called transformed organisms.

2) These organisms have recombinant DNA — DNA formed by joining together DNA from different sources.

3) Genetic engineering usually involves extracting a gene from one organism and then inserting it into another organism (often one that's a different species).

4) Genes can also be manufactured instead of extracted from an organism.

5) The organism with the inserted gene will then produce the protein coded for by that gene.

6) An organism that has been genetically engineered to include a gene from a different species is sometimes called a transgenic organism.

> Transformed organisms are also known as genetically engineered or genetically modified organisms.

You Need to Know How Genetic Engineering is Carried Out

1 The DNA Fragment Containing the Desired Gene is Obtained

The DNA fragment containing the gene you want is isolated using restriction enzymes (see page 218).

2 The DNA Fragment (with the Gene in) is Inserted into a Vector

The isolated DNA fragment is then inserted into a vector using restriction enzymes and DNA ligase (an enzyme):

1) The DNA fragment is inserted into vector DNA — a vector is something that's used to transfer DNA into a cell. They can be plasmids (small, circular molecules of DNA in bacteria) or bacteriophages (viruses that infect bacteria).

2) The vector DNA is cut open using the same restriction enzyme that was used to isolate the DNA fragment containing the desired gene (see page 218). So the sticky ends of the vector are complementary to the sticky ends of the DNA fragment containing the gene.

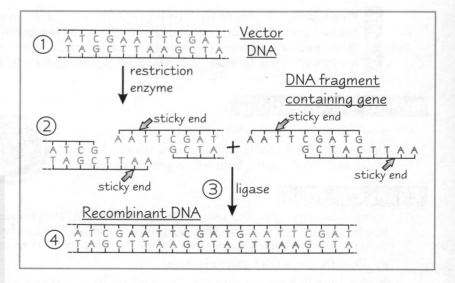

3) The vector DNA and DNA fragment are mixed together with DNA ligase. DNA ligase joins up the sugar-phosphate backbones of the two bits. This process is called ligation.

4) The new combination of bases in the DNA (vector DNA + DNA fragment) is called recombinant DNA.

Genetic Engineering

③ The **Vector Transfers** the **Gene** into the **Bacteria**

1) The **vector** with the **recombinant DNA** is used to **transfer** the gene into the **bacterial cells**.

2) If a **plasmid vector** is used, the bacterial cells have to be **persuaded** to **take in** the plasmid vector and its DNA:

   For example...

   - A suspension of the **bacterial cells** is **mixed** with the **plasmid vector** and placed in a machine called an **electroporator**.
   - The machine is switched on and an **electrical field** is created in the mixture, which increases the **permeability** of the **bacterial cell membranes** and allows them to **take in** the plasmids.
   - This technique is called **electroporation**.

3) With a **bacteriophage** vector, the bacteriophage will **infect** the bacterium by **injecting** its **DNA** into it. The phage DNA (with the desired gene in it) then **integrates** into the bacterial DNA.

4) **Cells** that **take up** the vectors containing the desired gene are genetically engineered, so are called **transformed**.

Warm-Up Questions

Q1 What is the name for an organism that has had its DNA altered?
Q2 What is a vector?
Q3 Other than a plasmid, give an example of a vector.
Q4 Name the type of enzyme that can be used to cut DNA.
Q5 What is the name of the type of DNA formed from vector DNA and an inserted DNA fragment?

Exam Questions

Q1 Genetic engineering involves different enzymes and methods. Which of the following statement(s) is/are true?

Statement 1: DNA ligase is the enzyme used to isolate a DNA fragment from a sample of DNA.
Statement 2: A vector is something that's used to transfer DNA into a cell, e.g. a plasmid.
Statement 3: Electroporation is the technique used to increase the permeability of bacterial cell membranes so they will take up vectors.

A 1, 2 and 3 / B Only 1 and 2 / C Only 2 and 3 / D Only 1   [1 mark]

Q2 A scientist has genetically engineered some bacterial cells to contain the yellow fluorescent protein (YFP) gene, using a plasmid vector. YFP can be visualised under UV light. The cells were grown on an agar plate, which was then studied under a UV light. The results are shown below.

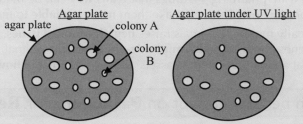

a) Explain why the scientist thinks colony A contains transformed bacterial cells, but colony B doesn't.   [2 marks]
b) Explain how the scientist might have inserted the YFP gene into the plasmid.   [3 marks]
c) Explain how and why the scientist would have used electroporation during the process.   [3 marks]

Transformed parents — made to stop nagging at you to revise...

This stuff might seem tricky the first time you read it, but it's not too bad once you've gone over it a few times. Basically you get the gene you want and bung it in a vector, and the vector gets the gene into the cell (it's kind of like a delivery boy). Easy peasy. Unfortunately you need to know each stage in detail, so get learnin'.

Genetically Modified Organisms

Genetic engineering can be used to benefit humans in loads of different ways. But when scientists are fiddling about with organisms and genes, there are bound to be ethical issues involved...

Genetic Engineering Can be Used to Create Insect-Resistance in Plants

One way in which plants can be **genetically manipulated** is by having a **gene** inserted into their cells which makes them **resistant** to **insect pests**. For example:

1) **Soybeans** are an important food source across the world, but yields of soybeans can be **greatly reduced** by **insect pests** that feed on the soybean plants.

2) Scientists have successfully **genetically modified** soybean plants to include a **gene** originally found in the bacteria *Bacillus thuringiensis* (*Bt*). The gene codes for a **protein** that is **toxic** to some of the **insects** that **feed** on soybean plants.

3) To genetically modify a soybean plant, the **desired gene** can be isolated from *Bt* using **restriction enzymes** and inserted into a **plasmid** taken from the bacterium *Agrobacterium tumefaciens*. The plasmid is put back into *A. tumefaciens* and then soybean plant cells are deliberately **infected** with the transformed bacteria. The desired gene gets inserted into the soybean plant cells' DNA, creating a **genetically modified** (GM) plant.

4) There are **positive ethical issues** concerning GM plants — for example, they will reduce the amount of **chemical pesticides** that farmers use on their crops, which can **harm** the **environment**.

5) But there are also **negative ethical issues** to consider. For example, farming GM soybean plants may encourage **monoculture** (where only one type of crop is planted). Monoculture **decreases biodiversity** and could leave the **whole crop vulnerable** to **disease**, because all the plants are **genetically identical**.

Genetic Engineering Can be Used to Produce Drugs from Animals

1) Many **pharmaceuticals** (**medicinal drugs**) are produced using **genetically modified organisms**, such as animals. This is called '**pharming**'. For example:

- **Hereditary antithrombin deficiency** is a disorder that makes **blood clots** more likely to form in the body. The risk of developing blood clots in people with this disorder can be reduced with **infusions** of the protein **antithrombin**.

- Scientists have developed a way to produce **high yields** of this protein using **goats**.

- Initially, **DNA fragments** that code for production of human antithrombin in the mammary glands are **injected** into a **goat embryo**.

- The embryo is **implanted** into a **female goat**, and when the **offspring** is born it is **tested** to see if it produces the antithrombin protein. If it does, **selective breeding** is used to produce a **herd** of goats that produce antithrombin in their **milk**.

- The protein is **extracted** from the milk and used to produce a **drug** (ATryn®) that can be given to people with hereditary antithrombin deficiency.

2) There are **positive ethical issues** with 'pharming' — drugs made this way can be made in **large quantities** compared to other methods of production. This can make them more **available** to more people.

3) However, the creation of genetically modified animals raises **negative ethical issues**. For example, there is **concern** that manipulating an animal's genes could cause **harmful side-effects** for the animal, and that using an animal in this way is enforcing the idea that animals are merely 'assets' that can be **treated however we choose**.

Genetic Engineering Can be Carried Out on Pathogens for Research

Scientists are carrying out **research** into **genetically engineered pathogens** (microorganisms that cause disease, such as viruses) in order to find **treatments** for **disease**. For example:

1) Scientists found that some tumour cells have receptors on their membranes for the poliovirus — so the poliovirus will recognise and attack them.

2) By genetically engineering the poliovirus to inactivate the genes that cause poliomyelitis, scientists can use it to attack and kill cancer cells without causing disease. This may lead to a treatment for cancer.

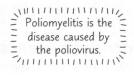
Poliomyelitis is the disease caused by the poliovirus.

Genetically Modified Organisms

Genetic Engineering of **Pathogens** Raises **Ethical Issues**

1) The genetic modification of pathogens to help cure disease has obvious **positive ethical issues** — e.g. it could mean that **previously untreatable** diseases can now be **treated**, reducing the suffering they would cause.

2) However, there are many possible **negative ethical issues** as well. For example, people worry that:

- the scientists researching the pathogens could become **infected** with the live pathogen and potentially cause a **mass outbreak of disease**.
- the genetically modified version of a pathogen could **revert back** to its **original form** and cause an **outbreak of disease**.
- in the wrong hands, knowledge of how to genetically engineer **dangerous pathogens** could be used **maliciously** to create agents for **biowarfare**.

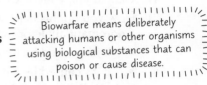

Biowarfare means deliberately attacking humans or other organisms using biological substances that can poison or cause disease.

Researchers using live pathogens have to follow **strict protocols**, which makes the chance of any of these things happening **very, very low**.

Genetically Engineered Organisms can be '**Owned**' by Big Companies

1) Many scientists around the world are working on techniques to improve and advance genetic engineering.

2) Scientists working for different institutions often share their knowledge and skills in this field so that, globally, beneficial genetically modified products can be created at a faster rate. The sharing of knowledge, skills and technology like this is called technology transfer.

3) Although they share information, a group of scientists or the company they work for may want to obtain legal protection for their genetically modified products, e.g. by getting a patent. This means, by law, they can control who uses the product and how for a set period of time.

4) This raises some positive ethical issues — it means that the owner of the patent will get money generated from selling the product. This encourages scientists to compete to be the first to come up with a new, beneficial genetic engineering idea, so we get genetically engineered products faster.

5) But the process raises many negative ethical issues too. For example, farmers in poorer countries may not be able to afford patented genetically modified seeds. Even if they can afford seeds for one year, some patents mean that they are not legally allowed to plant and grow any of the seeds from that crop without paying again. Many people think this is unfair and that the big companies that own the patents should relax the rules to help farmers in poorer countries.

Warm-Up Questions

Q1 What word is used to describe the process where animals are genetically modified to produce pharmaceuticals?

Q2 Give three negative ethical issues surrounding the genetic engineering of pathogens for research.

Q3 What is meant by the term 'technology transfer'?

Exam Question

Q1* Bromoxynil is a herbicide that many farmers spray on their crops to kill weeds. As well as weeds, bromoxynil also damages cotton plants. Some microorganisms, such as the bacterium *Klebsiella ozaenae*, naturally produce an enzyme that can convert bromoxynil to a harmless substance. A large company patented the gene responsible for this enzyme and, with the help of genetic engineering, bromoxynil-resistant cotton plants are now in existence.

Describe how genetic engineering may have been used in the creation of bromoxynil-resistant cotton plants and evaluate the ethical issues surrounding this crop. [6 marks]

* You will be assessed on the quality of your written response in this question.

Pig 'pharming' could produce some very useful oinkments...

Wow, scientists are really busy genetically engineering things aren't they? Plants, animals, microorganisms — they'll have a go at anything. And of course the reason they're doing it is to create products that can benefit our lives somehow, but there are also many negative ethical issues to consider. I reckon it's time to grab a cuppa and a biscuit while you ponder it all...

Gene Therapy

Genetic engineering doesn't have to stop at animals, plants and microorganisms — it could be done to humans too.

Gene Therapy Could be Used to Cure Genetic Disorders

Genetic disorders are **inherited disorders** caused by **abnormal genes** or **chromosomes**. **Gene therapy** could be used to **cure** these disorders — it **isn't** being used widely yet but there is a form of somatic gene therapy available, and other treatments are undergoing **clinical trials**.

1) Gene therapy involves altering alleles inside cells to cure genetic disorders.

2) How you do this depends on whether the genetic disorder is caused by a dominant allele or two recessive alleles:

See page 200 for more on dominant and recessive alleles.

- If it's caused by two recessive alleles you can add a working dominant allele to make up for them.
- If it's caused by a dominant allele you can 'silence' the dominant allele (e.g. by sticking a bit of DNA in the middle of the allele so it doesn't work any more).

3) To get the 'new' allele (DNA) inside the cell, the allele is inserted into cells using vectors.

4) Different vectors can be used, e.g. altered viruses, plasmids or liposomes (spheres made of lipid).

5) There are two types of gene therapy:

- Somatic therapy — this involves altering the alleles in body cells, particularly the cells that are most affected by the disorder. For example, cystic fibrosis (CF) is a genetic disorder that's very damaging to the respiratory system, so somatic therapy for CF targets the epithelial cells lining the lungs. Somatic therapy doesn't affect the individual's sex cells (sperm or eggs) though, so any offspring could inherit the disease.

- Germ line therapy — this involves altering the alleles in the sex cells. This means that every cell of any offspring produced from these cells will be affected by the gene therapy and they won't inherit the disease. Germ line therapy in humans is currently illegal though.

There are Positive and Negative Ethical Issues Surrounding Gene Therapy

Positive Ethical Issues

- It could **prolong the lives** of people with genetic disorders.
- It could give people with genetic disorders a better **quality of life**.
- Carriers of genetic disorders might be able to **conceive a baby** without that disorder or risk of cancer (only in germ line therapy).
- It could **decrease** the number of people that **suffer from genetic disorders** (only in germ line therapy).

Negative Ethical Issues

- The technology could potentially be used in ways **other** than for **medical treatment**, such as for treating the **cosmetic effects** of ageing.
- There's the potential to do *more harm* than good by using the technology (e.g. risk of overexpression of genes — see below).
- There's concern that gene therapy is **expensive** — some people believe that **health service resources** could be **better spent** on other treatments that have passed clinical trials.

There are other potential **disadvantages** of gene therapy too:

- The effects of the treatment may be **short–lived** (only in somatic therapy).
- The patient might have to undergo **multiple treatments** (only in somatic therapy).
- It might be **difficult** to get the allele into **specific** body cells.

- The body could identify vectors as **foreign bodies** and start an **immune response** against them.
- An allele could be inserted into the **wrong place** in the DNA, possibly causing **more problems**, e.g. cancer.
- An inserted allele could get **overexpressed**, producing too much of the missing protein.

Warm-Up Question

Q1 Give three negative ethical issues surrounding gene therapy.

(PRACTICE QUESTIONS)

Exam Question

Q1 A patient with cystic fibrosis was offered gene therapy targeted at his lung epithelial cells to help treat the disease.
 a) What does gene therapy involve? [1 mark]
 b) What type of gene therapy was the patient offered? [1 mark]

Germ line therapy — talking to a counsellor while in a queue at the doctors'...

Make sure you know about the two different types of gene therapy as well as all the positive and negative ethical issues.

Sequencing Genes and Genomes

Scientists have been able to sequence genes since the 1970s, but over time advancements in technology have made the process ever slicker. Some of the basic principles are still the same though, so it's helpful to take a look at how things used to be done before thinking about how things are done nowadays...

DNA can be Sequenced by the Chain-Termination Method

The **chain-termination method** was one of the first methods used to determine the **order** of **bases** in a section of **DNA**:

1) The following mixture is added to **four separate** tubes:

   - A **single-stranded DNA template** — the DNA to sequence.
   - Lots of **DNA primer** — short pieces of DNA (see p. 216).
   - **DNA polymerase** — the enzyme that joins DNA nucleotides together.
   - **Free nucleotides** — lots of free A, T, C and G nucleotides.

   - **Fluorescently-labelled modified nucleotide** — like a normal nucleotide, but once it's added to a DNA strand, **no more** bases can be added after it. A **different** modified nucleotide is added to **each** tube (A*, T*, C*, G*).

2) The tubes undergo **PCR**, which produces many **strands of DNA**. The strands are **different lengths** because each one **terminates** at a **different point** depending on where the modified nucleotide was added.

3) For example, in tube A (with the **modified adenine** nucleotide A*) sometimes A* is **added** to the DNA at point 4 **instead** of A, **stopping** the **addition** of any more bases (the strand is **terminated**). Sometimes A is added at point 4, then A* is added at **point 5**. Sometimes A is added at **point 4**, A again at point 5, G at point 6 and A* is added at **point 7**. So strands of **three different lengths** (4 bases, 5 bases and 7 bases) all ending in A* are produced.

4) The DNA fragments in each tube are separated by **electrophoresis** and **visualised** under **UV light** (because of the **fluorescent label**).

5) The **complementary base sequence** can be **read** from the gel. The **smallest** nucleotide (e.g. one base) is at the **bottom** of the gel. Each band after this represents **one more base** added. So by reading the bands **from the bottom** of the gel **to the top**, you can build up the **DNA sequence** one base at a time.

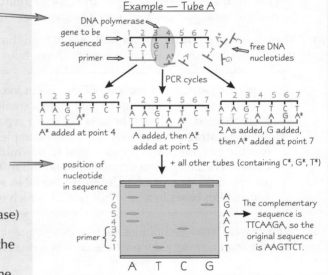

Gene Sequencing Techniques can be Used to Sequence Whole Genomes

The **chain-termination method** only works on fragments up to about **750 bp** long. So if you want to sequence the **entire genome** (all the DNA) of an organism using this method, you need to chop it up into **smaller pieces** first. The smaller pieces are **sequenced** and then **put back in order** to give the sequence of the whole genome. Here's how it's done:

1) A genome is **cut** into **smaller fragments** (about 100 000 bp) using **restriction enzymes**.

2) The fragments are inserted into **bacterial artificial chromosomes** (BACs) — these are **man-made plasmids**. **Each** fragment is inserted into a **different BAC**.

3) The BACs are then **inserted** into **bacteria** — **each bacterium** contains a **BAC** with a **different DNA fragment**.

4) The bacteria **divide**, creating **colonies** of **cloned** (**identical**) cells that all contain a **specific DNA fragment**. Together the different colonies make a complete **genomic DNA library**.

5) **DNA** is **extracted** from **each colony** and **cut** up using restriction enzymes, producing **overlapping** pieces of DNA.

6) Each piece of DNA is **sequenced**, using the **chain-termination method**, and the pieces are **put back in order** to give the full sequence **from that BAC** (using **powerful computer systems**).

7) Finally the DNA fragments from **all the BACs** are **put back in order**, by computers, to **complete** the **entire genome**.

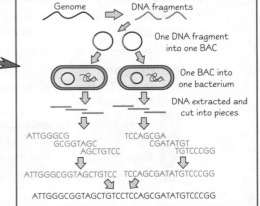

Sequencing Genes and Genomes

Faster, Whole Genome Sequencing Techniques Have Been Developed

1) Continued **research** and **improvements** in **modern technology** have led to **rapid advancements** in the field of gene sequencing.

2) The chain-termination technique described on the previous page is still commonly used but it has become **automated** and is **faster** — nowadays the tube contains **all** the modified nucleotides, each with a different coloured **fluorescent label**, and a **machine** reads the sequence for you. So instead of running a gel and determining the sequence from that, you get a **computer read-out**.

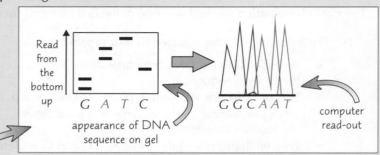

Read from the bottom up

G A T C

appearance of DNA sequence on gel

G G C A A T

computer read-out

3) Further advances in the field have also led to **high-throughput sequencing** — techniques that can sequence a lot **faster** than original methods (e.g. up to 1000 times more bases in a given time), at a **fraction of the cost**. For example, the chain-termination technique has been made high-throughput by new technology allowing up to 384 sequences to be run **in parallel**.

4) There are several **other, newer methods** of high-throughput sequencing being used too, some of which don't use electrophoresis. For example, **high-throughput pyrosequencing** is a **recently developed** technique:

> In **pyrosequencing**, a section of DNA is cut into **fragments**, split into **single strands** and then a strand from each fragment is attached to a **small bead**. **PCR** is used to **amplify** the DNA fragments on each bead, then each bead is put into a **separate well**. Next, **free nucleotides** added to the wells **attach** to the DNA strands via complementary base pairing. The wells also contain **specific enzymes**, which cause **light to be emitted** when bases are added to the DNA strand. **Computers** analyse the **occurrence** and **intensities** of the light emitted in the different wells, and process this information to **interpret the DNA sequence**. This technique can sequence around **400 million bases** in a ten-hour period (which is **super fast** compared to older techniques).

5) With **newer, faster** techniques such as pyrosequencing available, scientists can now sequence **whole genomes** much more **quickly**.

Sequencing Genes Shows Polypeptide Structure and Aids Synthetic Biology

1) You might remember from Module 2 that **amino acids** are coded for by **triplets of bases** in a gene.

2) This means that by sequencing a gene, the **sequence of amino acids** that a gene **codes for** and so the **primary structure** of a **polypeptide** can be predicted.

3) This has allowed us to create **biological molecules** from scratch and so has led to the development of an area of biology called '**synthetic biology**'.

4) Synthetic biology is a **large field** that includes:

- **building** biological systems from **artificially made molecules** (e.g. proteins) to see whether they work in the way we think they do.

- **redesigning** biological systems to **perform better** and include **new molecules**.

- **designing new** biological systems and molecules that **don't exist** in the natural world, but could be **useful** to humans, e.g. energy products (fuels) and drug products.

Synthetic biology is different from genetic engineering — genetic engineering involves the direct transfer of DNA from one organism to another, whereas in synthetic biology DNA is created from scratch.

> **Example:** **Artemisinin** is an **antimalarial drug** — until recently we got artemisinin by extracting it from a **plant**. Using **synthetic biology**, scientists have created all the **genes** responsible for producing a **precursor** to artemisinin. They've successfully inserted these genes into **yeast cells**, so we can now use yeast to help produce artemisinin.

Sequencing Genes and Genomes

Sequenced Genes and Genomes can be Compared

Gene sequences and **whole genome** sequences can be compared **between** organisms of **different species** and between organisms of the **same species**. This is a complicated process which is made easier with the use of computers — it involves **computational biology** (using computers to study biology, e.g. to create computer simulations and mathematical models) and **bioinformatics** (developing and using computer software that can analyse, organise and store biological data). There are many reasons why **biological research** can involve comparison of gene sequences and genomes, e.g.:

To study genotype-phenotype relationships

1) Sometimes it's useful to be able to predict an organism's **phenotype** by analysing its **genotype**.

2) For example, **Marfan syndrome** is a **genetic disorder** caused by a **mutation** of the *FBN1* **gene**. The position and nature of the mutation on the gene affects what **symptoms** a person with Marfan syndrome will experience (e.g. they could get a number of problems associated with their vision, cardiovascular system or muscles). Scientists have **sequenced** the *FBN1* gene of **many people** with Marfan syndrome and documented this along with details of their **phenotype**. **Bioinformatics** has allowed the scientists to **compare** all the data and identify **genotype-phenotype correlations** — this could help in the **treatment** of Marfan syndrome by using **gene sequencing** to predict what health problems the person is likely to face.

In epidemiological studies

Epidemiology is the study of **health and disease** within a population — it considers the **distribution** of a disease, its **causes** and its **effects**. Some gene mutations have been linked to a greater risk of **disease** (e.g. mutations in the *BRCA1* gene are linked to breast cancer). **Computerised comparisons** between the genomes of people that have a disease and those that don't can be used to detect **particular mutations** that could be responsible for the increased risk of disease.

To help understand evolutionary relationships

1) **All** organisms **evolved** from **shared common ancestors** (relatives). **Closely related** species **evolved away** from each other more **recently** and so **share more DNA**. Whole genomes of different species can be sequenced and then analysed using computer software to tell us **how closely related** different species are. E.g. the genomes of **humans** and **chimpanzees** are about **94**% similar.

2) Comparing the genomes of members of the same species can also tell us about evolutionary relationships. For example, when different groups of early **humans separated** and **moved** to different parts of the world, their genomes **changed** in **slightly different ways**. By using computers to **compare** the genomes of people from different parts of the world, it's possible to build up a picture of early human migration.

Look, when we stick our tongues out like this you can just TELL we're related, we don't need a genome comparison.

Warm-Up Questions

Q1 What is a bacterial artificial chromosome?

Q2 How can gene sequencing be used to predict a protein's primary structure?

Q3 Give three uses of synthetic biology.

Q4 What is meant by the terms 'bioinformatics' and 'computational biology'?

Exam Questions

Q1 To sequence a small DNA fragment using the chain-termination technique, a single-stranded DNA template is needed.
  a) Name the other four reactants needed for a sequencing reaction using this method. [4 marks]
  b) The chain-termination technique has been adapted to be high-throughput. Give two advantages of the high-throughput technique over the original technique. [2 marks]

Q2 Researchers are trying to establish how closely related two different bacterial species are. Suggest how they could do this. [2 marks]

Sequincing — so 80s...

Don't worry the buzzing in your head is normal — information overload. Have a break, then go over some of the difficult bits in this section again. Believe me, the more times you go over it the more things will click into place.

Plant Cloning

Plant cloning is probably more common than you think. These pages tell you all you need to know for your exam.

Some Plants can Produce Natural Clones by Vegetative Propagation

Cloning is the process of producing **genetically identical cells** or **organisms** from the cells of an **existing organism**. Cloning can occur **naturally** in some **plants** and **animals**, but it can also be carried out **artificially**.

Vegetative propagation is the production of plant **clones** from **non-reproductive tissues**, e.g. roots, leaves and stems. The table below describes some of the **natural vegetative propagation** methods that plants use:

Method	Description	Example of plant using method
Rhizomes	Rhizomes are stem structures that grow horizontally underground away from the parent plant. They have 'nodes' from which new shoots and roots can develop.	Bamboo
Stolons (also called runners)	Stolons are pretty similar to rhizomes. The main difference is that they grow above ground, on the surface of the soil. New shoots and roots can either develop from nodes (like in rhizomes) or form at the end of the stolon.	Strawberries
Suckers	Suckers are shoots that grow from sucker buds (undeveloped shoots) present on the shallow roots of a parent plant.	Elm trees
Tubers	Tubers are large underground plant structures that act as a food store for the plant. They're covered in 'eyes'. Each eye is able to sprout and form a new plant.	Potatoes
Bulbs	Bulbs are also underground food stores used by some plants. New bulbs are able to develop from the original bulb and form new individual plants.	Onions

Horticulturists (plant growers) use other 'natural' methods of **vegetative propagation** to produce **clones**. The methods include taking **cuttings** (see below), **grafting** (joining the **shoot** of **one plant** to the **growing stem** and **root** of **another plant**) and **layering** (bending a **stem** of a **growing plant** downwards so it **enters** the **soil** and grows into a **new plant**).

You Need to Know How to Produce a Clone From a Cutting

Growing plants from **cuttings** is a really simple way to make clones of a **parent plant**. You can take cuttings from **different parts** of a plant, e.g. a stem, root or leaf. Here's how a cutting can be taken and grown from a **stem**:

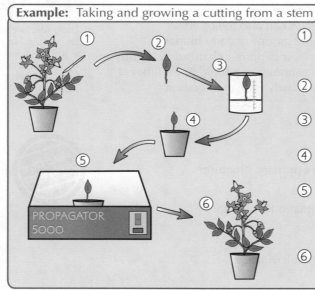

Example: Taking and growing a cutting from a stem

① Use a **scalpel** or **sharp secateurs** to **take a cutting**, between **5 cm** and **10 cm** long, from the end of a stem of your **parent plant**.

② **Remove** the **leaves** from the **lower** end of your cutting (if there are any), leaving just one at the tip.

③ **Dip** the **lower end** of the cutting in **rooting powder**, which contains **hormones** that induce **root formation**.

④ Then plant your cutting in a pot containing a suitable **growth medium** (e.g. well-drained compost).

⑤ Provide your cutting with a **warm** and **moist environment** by either covering the whole pot with a **plastic bag** or by putting it in a **propagator** (a specialised piece of kit that provides these conditions).

⑥ When your cutting has **formed** its **own roots** and is **strong enough**, you can **plant** it **elsewhere** to continue growing.

Here are examples of how you could take and grow cuttings from a **root** or **leaf**:

- To take a **root cutting**, cut a **piece** of root from the plant with a **straight cut** using a **scalpel** or **secateurs**. Then **remove** the **uncut** end of the root with a **slanted cut**. Dip the end of the cutting in **rooting powder** and **plant** it in a suitable **growth medium**. Then follow **steps 5** and **6** from the example above.

- A popular type of **leaf cutting** (known as a **split vein** cutting) involves **removing** a **complete leaf** and **scoring** the **large veins** on the **lower** leaf surface using a scalpel. You then put it **on top** of the **growth medium** with the **broken veins facing down** and then follow **steps 5** and **6** from above. A **new plant** should form from **each break** in the veins.

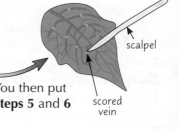

scalpel

scored vein

Plant Cloning

Plants can be Artificially Cloned using Tissue Culture

Plants can be **artificially cloned** from existing plants using a technique called **tissue culture**. Here's how it's done:

1) **Cells** are taken from the original plant that's going to be cloned.
2) Cells from the **stem** and **root tips** are used because they're **stem cells** — like in humans, plant stem cells can develop into **any type of cell**.
3) The cells are **sterilised** to kill any **microorganisms** — bacteria and fungi **compete** for nutrients with the **plant cells**, which **decreases** their **growth rate**.
4) The cells are placed on a **culture medium** containing plant **nutrients** (like **glucose** for **respiration**) and **growth hormones** (such as **auxins**).
5) When the cells have **divided** and **grown** into a **small plant** they're taken out of the medium and **planted in soil** — they'll develop into plants that are **genetically identical** to the **original plant**.

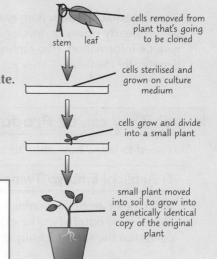

cells removed from plant that's going to be cloned

cells sterilised and grown on culture medium

cells grow and divide into a small plant

small plant moved into soil to grow into a genetically identical copy of the original plant

1) Tissue culture is used to clone plants that **don't readily reproduce** or are **endangered** or **rare**, e.g. British orchids.
2) It's also used to grow **whole plants** from **genetically engineered plant cells**.
3) **Micropropagation** is when **tissue culture** is used to produce **lots** of cloned plants **very quickly**. **Cells** are taken from developing cloned plants and **subcultured** (grown on another fresh culture medium) — repeating this process creates **large numbers of clones**. This technique is used extensively in **horticulture** and **agriculture**, e.g. to produce fields full of a crop that has been genetically engineered to be pest-resistant.

Agriculture and horticulture both involve cultivating plants — agriculture generally relates to farming (i.e. using land to grow crops for human use or consumption) whereas horticulture can involve the cultivation of any plant for any purpose, but usually on a smaller scale, e.g. for gardening.

There are Arguments For and Against Artificial Plant Cloning

You need to be able to **evaluate** the uses of **tissue culture** in **agriculture** and **horticulture** — this handy list of arguments **for** and **against** tissue culture should help you:

Arguments For
- **Desirable genetic characteristics** (e.g. high fruit production) are **always passed on** to clones. This **doesn't always** happen when plants **reproduce sexually**.
- Tissue culture allows plants to be reproduced in **any season** because the environment is controlled.
- **Less space** is required by **tissue culture** than would be needed to produce the **same** number of plants by conventional growing methods.
- It produces **lots** of plants **quickly** compared to the time it would take to **grow** them from **seeds**.

Arguments Against
- **Undesirable genetic characteristics** (e.g. producing fruit with lots of seeds) are **always passed on** to clones.
- **Cloned plant populations** have **no genetic variability**, so a **single disease** could **kill** them all.
- **Production costs** of tissue culture are **very high** due to **high energy use** and the **training** of skilled workers, so it's **unsuitable** for **small scale** production.
- **Contamination** by **microorganisms** during tissue culture can be **disastrous** and result in **complete loss** of the plants being cultured.

Warm-Up Questions

Q1 What is vegetative propagation?

Exam Question

Q1 A scientist wants to produce a whole plant from a genetically engineered plant stem cell. Describe how she could achieve this.

[4 marks]

Plant cloning is a cheap way to fill up your garden...

... as long as you don't like variety. Make sure you know the many different methods that can be used to clone plants (both naturally and artificially) and are clued up on the arguments for and against using tissue culture.

Animal Cloning

It's not only plants that can be cloned — there are plenty of genetically identical animals knocking about too...

Animal Clones can Occur Naturally...

During **sexual reproduction**, once an egg has been **fertilised**, it's possible for it to **split** during the very **early stages** of development and **develop** into **multiple embryos** with the **same genetic information**. The embryos can develop as normal to produce **offspring** that are all **genetically identical** — they are **clones**. For example, **identical twins** are natural clones.

... or They can be Produced Artificially

You need to know how animals can be **artificially cloned** using these **two methods**:

1) Artificial Embryo Twinning

This type of artificial cloning is **similar** to what happens when animal clones form **naturally**. The example below shows how this is done in **cows**, but the **same** technique can be used for **other animals**:

① An **egg cell** is extracted from a female cow and **fertilised** in a Petri dish.

② The **fertilised egg** is left to **divide** at least once, forming an **embryo** *in vitro* (outside a living organism).

③ Next, the **individual cells** from the embryo are separated and each is put into a **separate** Petri dish. Each cell **divides** and **develops normally**, so an **embryo forms** in **each** Petri dish.

④ The **embryos** are then **implanted** into female cows, which act as **surrogate mothers**.

⑤ The **embryos continue** to **develop** inside the surrogate cows, and eventually the **offspring** are **born**. They're all **genetically identical** to each other.

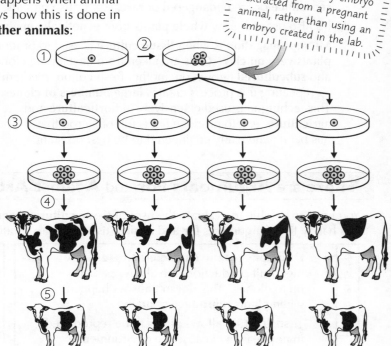

The process could also be done using an early embryo extracted from a pregnant animal, rather than using an embryo created in the lab.

2) Somatic Cell Nuclear Transfer (SCNT)

This method is a bit more **high-tech**. This is how it's done in **sheep**, but again the method's the **same** for **other animals**:

1) A **somatic cell** (any cell that isn't a reproductive cell) is taken from sheep A. The **nucleus** is **extracted** and **kept**.

2) An **oocyte** (immature **egg cell**) is taken from sheep B. Its nucleus is **removed** to form an **enucleated oocyte**.

3) The nucleus from sheep A is **inserted** into the enucleated oocyte — the oocyte from **sheep B** now contains the **genetic information** from **sheep A**.

4) The nucleus and the enucleated oocyte are **fused together** and **stimulated** to **divide** (e.g. by electrofusion, where an electrical current is applied). This produces an **embryo**.

5) Then the embryo is **implanted** into a **surrogate mother** and eventually a **lamb** is born that's a **clone** of **sheep A**.

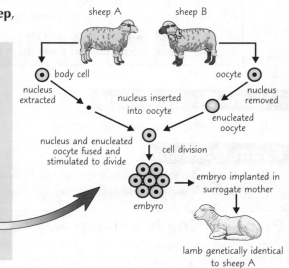

Animal Cloning

Animal Cloning has Many Uses

1) Scientists use cloned animals for **research purposes**, e.g. in the field of medicine they can **test new drugs** on cloned animals. They're all genetically identical, so the **variables** that come from **genetic differences** (e.g. the likelihood of developing cancer) are **removed**.

2) Cloning can be used to **save endangered animals** from **extinction** by cloning new individuals.

3) Cloning can also be used in agriculture so **farmers** can **increase** the **number** of animals with **desirable characteristics** to **breed from**, e.g. a prize-winning cow with high milk production could be cloned.

4) Animals that have been **genetically modified** (see page 222) to produce a **useful substance** that they wouldn't normally produce (e.g. a beneficial protein in their milk) could be cloned to produce **lots** of identical animals that all produce the same substance.

5) Cloning **doesn't** have to be used to make **whole** animals. Sometimes scientists only want the cloned **embryonic stem cells**. These cells are harvested from **young embryos** and have the **potential** to become **any cell type**, so scientists think they could be used to **replace damaged tissues** in a **range** of **diseases**, e.g. heart disease, spinal cord injuries, degenerative brain disorders like Parkinson's disease. If replacement tissue is made from cloned embryonic stem cells that are **genetically identical** to the **patient's own cells**, it **won't be rejected** by their immune system.

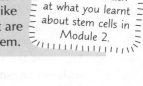

Take a look back at what you learnt about stem cells in Module 2.

There are Arguments For and Against Animal Cloning

You might have to **evaluate** the **uses** of **animal cloning**, so you need to be aware of the arguments **for** and **against** the process:

Mirrors — the budget way to clone.

Arguments For

- **Desirable genetic characteristics** are **always passed on** to clones (e.g. high milk production in cows). This **doesn't always** happen with **sexual reproduction**.
- **Infertile animals** can be **reproduced**.
- **Increasing** the population of **endangered species** helps to **preserve biodiversity**.
- **Animals** can be **cloned** at **any time** — you wouldn't have to wait until a **breeding season** to get new animals.
- Cloning can help us develop **new treatments** for disease, which could mean **less suffering** for some people.

Arguments Against

- Animal cloning is very **difficult, time-consuming** and **expensive**.
- There's no **genetic variability** in cloned populations, so **undesirable genetic characteristics** (e.g. a weak immune system) are **always passed on** to clones. This means that all of the cloned animals in a population are **susceptible** to the **same diseases**. Potentially, a single disease could **wipe them all out**.
- Some evidence suggests that clones **may not live as long** as natural offspring. Some think this is **unethical**.
- Using **cloned human embryos** as a **source** of **stem cells** is controversial. The embryos are usually **destroyed** after the embryonic stem cells have been harvested — some people believe that doing this is **destroying a human life**.

Warm-Up Questions

Q1 Describe how animal clones can occur naturally.
Q2 Describe how artificial embryo twinning is carried out.
Q3 Give three uses of animal cloning.

Exam Question

Q1 A team of scientists wants to create a herd of cloned alpacas from Alpaca A, which has particularly desirable characteristics for wool production.
a) Outline how they could create a clone of Alpaca A using somatic cell nuclear transfer. [4 marks]
b) Give two arguments against creating a cloned herd. [2 marks]

If you cloned yourself, you could be relaxing while the other you revised...

Unfortunately, that's not going to happen, so you should just get on with learning about how the different types of animal cloning are carried out, how cloning in animals is actually used and the arguments for and against it.

Biotechnology

The global biotechnology industry is humongous, but fortunately you've only got to learn a few pages about it...

Biotechnology is the Use of Living Organisms in Industry

1) **Biotechnology** is the **industrial use** of **living organisms** to produce **food**, **drugs** and **other products**.

2) The living organisms used are mostly **microorganisms** (bacteria and fungi). Here are a few reasons why:

- Their **ideal growth conditions** can be **easily** created — microorganisms will generally grow successfully as long as they have the right **nutrients**, **temperature**, **pH**, **moisture levels** and **availability of gases** (e.g. some need oxygen).
- Because of their **short life-cycle**, they grow **rapidly** under the right conditions, so **products** can be made **quickly**.
- They can be grown on a **range** of **inexpensive** materials — this makes them **economical** to use.
- They can be grown at **any time** of the year.

3) Biotechnology also **uses parts** of **living organisms** (such as **enzymes**) to make products.

4) Enzymes used in industry can be **contained within the cells** of organisms — these are called **intracellular enzymes**.

5) Enzymes are also used that **aren't contained within cells** — these are called **isolated enzymes**. **Some** are **secreted naturally** by microorganisms (called **extracellular enzymes**), but others have to be **extracted**.

You can find out how isolated enzymes are used in biotechnology on pages 236-237.

6) **Naturally secreted** enzymes are **cheaper** to use because it can be **expensive** to **extract** enzymes from cells.

Microorganisms are Used in a Wide Variety of Industrial Processes

Process	Role of Microorganisms
Brewing (making beer)	To make **beer**, **yeast** (e.g. *Saccharomyces cerevisiae*) is added to a type of **grain** (such as barley) and other ingredients. The yeast **respires anaerobically** using the **glucose** from the grain and produces **ethanol** (alcohol) and CO_2. (When anaerobic respiration produces ethanol, the process is called **fermentation**.)
Baking	Yeast is also the organism that makes **bread rise**. The CO_2 produced by **fermentation** of sugars in the dough makes sure it doesn't stay flat. Many flat breads, like tortillas, are made **without** yeast.
Cheese Making	**Cheese** production used to rely on a substance called **rennet**. Rennet contains the enzyme **chymosin**, which **clots** the **milk** — a key process in cheese making. Traditionally we used to get chymosin by extracting rennet from the lining of **calves' stomachs**, but now chymosin can be obtained from **yeast cells** that have been **genetically modified** to produce the enzyme. Cheese making also involves **lactic acid bacteria** (e.g. *Lactobacillus* and *Streptococcus*). These bacteria convert the **lactose** in milk into **lactic acid**, which makes it turn **sour** and contributes to it **solidifying**. The production of **blue cheeses** also involves the addition of **fungi** to make the characteristic blue veins.
Yoghurt Production	Just like cheese making, **yoghurt production** involves the use of **lactic acid bacteria** to **clot** the milk and cause it to **thicken**. This creates a basic yoghurt product and then any **flavours** and **colours** are added.
Penicillin Production	In times of **stress**, **fungi** from the *Penicillium* genus produce an **antibiotic**, **penicillin**, to stop **bacteria** from **growing** and **competing** for **resources**. Penicillin is one of the **most common** antibiotics used in **medicine**, so we produce it on a **massive scale**. The fungus (usually *Penicillium chrysogenum*) is grown under stress in **industrial fermenters** (see next page) and the penicillin produced is **collected** and **processed** to be used in medicine.
Insulin Production	**Insulin** is a **hormone** that's crucial for treating people with Type 1 diabetes. Insulin is made by **genetically modified bacteria**, which have had the **gene** for **human insulin production** inserted into their DNA (see page 220). These bacteria are grown in an **industrial fermenter** on a massive scale and the insulin produced is **collected** and **purified**.
Bioremediation	**Bioremediation** is a posh name for the process of using organisms (usually microorganisms) to **remove pollutants**, like oil and pesticides, from **contaminated sites**. Most commonly, pollutant-removing bacteria that occur **naturally** at a site are provided with **extra nutrients** and enhanced **growing conditions** to allow them to multiply and thrive. These bacteria **break down** the **pollutants** into **less harmful products**, cleaning up the area. For example, bioremediation using bacteria has been used to clean up **oil spills** at sea.

Biotechnology

Using Microorganisms in Food Production has Pros and Cons

1) As you can see from the previous page, **microorganisms** play a **key role** in the **production** of lots of **different** foods.

2) Some **microorganisms** can also be grown as a **source** of **protein** (called **single-cell protein**), which can act as a valuable **food source** for **humans** and other **animals**.

3) Examples of microorganisms used to make single-cell protein include the **fungus** *Fusarium venenatum* (which is used to make the popular meat substitute Quorn™) and the **bacteria** *Methylophilus methylotrophus*.

4) There are **advantages** and **disadvantages** of producing **food for human consumption** using **microorganisms**:

Advantages	Disadvantages
1) Microorganisms used to make single-cell protein can be grown using many different organic substrates, including waste materials such as molasses (a by-product of sugar processing). Production of single-cell protein could actually be used as a way of getting rid of waste products. 2) Microorganisms can be grown quickly, easily and cheaply. Production costs are low because microorganisms have simple growth requirements, can be grown on waste products and less land is required in comparison to growing crops or rearing livestock. 3) Microorganisms can be cultured anywhere if you have the right equipment. This means that a food source could be readily produced in places where growing crops and rearing livestock is difficult (e.g. very hot or cold climates). This could help tackle malnutrition in developing countries. 4) Single-cell protein is often considered a healthier alternative to animal protein	1) Because the conditions needed to grow the desired microorganism are also ideal for other microorganisms, a lot of effort has to go into making sure that the food doesn't get contaminated with unwanted bacteria, which could be dangerous to humans or spoil the food. 2) People may not like the idea of eating food that has been grown using waste products. 3) Single-cell protein doesn't have the same texture or flavour as real meat. 4) If single-cell protein is consumed in high quantities, health problems could be caused due to the high levels of uric acid released when the large amounts of amino acids are broken down.

Microorganisms are Grown in Fermentation Vessels

1) Biotechnology uses **cultures** of microorganisms. A culture is a **population** of **one type** of **microorganism** that's been **grown** under **controlled conditions**.

2) Cultures are grown in **large containers** called **fermentation vessels** to either **obtain lots** of the **microorganism** (e.g. for production of single-celled protein) or to **collect** lots of a **useful product** that the microorganism **makes**.

3) There are **two** main **methods** for **culturing** microorganisms:

- **Batch fermentation** — This is where microorganisms are grown in **individual batches** in a fermentation vessel — when one culture **ends** it's **removed** and then a **different batch** of microorganisms is grown in the vessel. This is known as a **closed culture** — see next page.

- **Continuous fermentation** — This is where microorganisms are **continually grown** in a fermentation vessel **without stopping**. **Nutrients** are put **in** and **waste products** taken **out** at a **constant rate**.

4) The **conditions** inside the fermentation vessels are kept at the **optimum for growth** — this **maximises** the **yield** of microorganisms and **desirable products**. Here's how it's done:

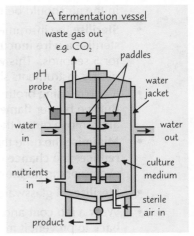

A fermentation vessel

Factor	How it's regulated	How it maximises yield
pH	Constantly monitored by a pH probe and kept at the optimum level.	Allows enzymes to work efficiently, so the rate of reaction is kept as high as possible.
Temperature	Kept constant by a water jacket that surrounds the entire vessel.	
Access to nutrients	Paddles constantly circulate fresh nutrient medium around the vessel.	Ensures that the microorganisms always have access to their required nutrients.
Volume of oxygen	Sterile air is pumped into the vessel when needed.	Makes sure that the microorganisms always have oxygen for respiration.
Vessel kept sterile	Superheated steam sterilises the vessel after each use.	Kills any unwanted organisms that may compete with the ones being cultured.

Module 6: Section 5 — Cloning and Biotechnology

Biotechnology

Closed Cultures of Microorganisms follow a Standard Growth Curve

1) A **closed culture** is when growth takes place in a vessel that's **isolated** from the **external environment** — extra nutrients **aren't added** and waste products **aren't removed** from the vessel **during growth**.

2) In a closed culture (e.g. in batch fermentation) a population of microorganisms follows a **standard growth curve**:

① **Lag phase** — the population size **increases slowly** because the **microorganisms** have to make enzymes and other molecules before they can reproduce. This means the **reproduction rate** is **low**.

② **Exponential phase** — the population size **increases quickly** because the culture **conditions** are at their **most favourable** for **reproduction** (**lots of food** and **little competition**). The number of microorganisms **doubles** at **regular intervals**.

③ **Stationary phase** — the population size **stays level** because the **death rate** of the microorganisms **equals** their **reproductive rate**. Microorganisms **die** because there's **not enough food** and poisonous **waste products build up**.

④ **Decline phase** — the population size **falls** because the **death rate** is **greater** than the **reproductive rate**. This is because food is very **scarce** and waste products are at **toxic levels**.

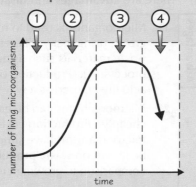

3) During the exponential growth phase, the number of cells in a culture of microorganisms **doubles** at **regular intervals**. You can work out how many individuals will be present in a population after a certain number of divisions using this formula: N (number of individuals present in population) $= N_0$ (initial number of cells) $\times 2^n$ (where 'n' = the number of divisions).

You Need to Know How to Culture Microorganisms in the Lab

1) Cultures of microorganisms can be grown in the **lab**.

2) A common way to do this is on an **agar plate** — a sterile **Petri dish** containing **agar jelly**.

3) Microorganisms are **transferred** to the plate from a **sample** (e.g. bacteria in broth) using a **sterile** implement like a wire **inoculation loop** or a **sterile pipette** and **spreader**.

4) You then **incubate** the plates and allow the microorganisms to **grow**.

5) **Nutrients** can be **added** to the agar to help **improve** the **growing conditions**.

inoculation loop

agar plate

microorganism spread on the plate

Aseptic Techniques Are Used when Culturing Microorganisms

An important part of culturing microorganisms is using **aseptic techniques**. These are used to **prevent contamination** of cultures by **unwanted microorganisms**, which may **affect** the **growth** of the microorganism being cultured. Contaminated cultures in **laboratory experiments** give **imprecise results** and may be **hazardous to health**. Contamination on an **industrial scale** can be very **costly** because **entire cultures** may have to be **thrown away**. Below are some **important** aseptic techniques that you should **follow** when culturing microorganisms in the lab:

- Regularly **disinfect** work surfaces to minimise contamination.

- Work near a **Bunsen flame**. Hot air rises, so any microorganisms in the air should be **drawn away** from your culture.

- **Sterilise** the instrument used to transfer cultures **before** and **after** each use, e.g. sterilise a **wire inoculation loop** by passing it through a **hot** Bunsen burner **flame** for 5 seconds. This will kill any microorganisms on the instrument. Pre-sterilised plastic instruments should only be used once and then safely discarded.

- If you're using broth, briefly pass the neck of the broth **container** through a Bunsen burner **flame** just after it's **opened** and just before it's **closed** — this causes air to move out of the container, preventing **unwanted** organisms from **falling in**.

- **Minimise** the time that the agar plate is open and put the lid on as soon as possible. This **reduces** the **chance** of **airborne** microorganisms **contaminating** the culture. You could even work in an **inoculation cabinet** (a chamber that has a flow of **sterile air** inside it).

- **Sterilise** all glassware before and after use, e.g. in an **autoclave**.

- Wear a **lab coat** and, if needed, **gloves**. **Tie long hair back** to prevent it from falling into anything.

When Lynda found a tiny copy of Pride and Prejudice embedded in the agar, she knew she had cultured bacteria.

An autoclave is a machine which steams equipment at high pressure.

Biotechnology

Factors Affecting the Growth of Microorganisms can be Investigated

You can **investigate** the **effects of different factors** on the growth of microorganisms by growing them on **agar plates** under **different conditions**. The example below shows how you can investigate the effect of **temperature** on the growth of **bacteria** (although the same method can be used for other microorganisms, such as **fungi**).

Example: Measuring the Effects of **Temperature** on the Growth of **Bacteria**

1) You should be supplied with a **sample** of **bacteria** (e.g. *E. coli*) in **broth**. Using a sterile pipette, add a **set volume** (e.g. 0.1 cm^3) of your sample to an **agar plate**. Discard your pipette safely after use.

2) **Spread** the broth across the **entire surface** of the agar using a **sterile plastic spreader**. Discard the spreader safely after use.

3) Put the **lid** on the agar plate and **lightly tape it shut** using two small pieces of tape.

4) **Repeat steps 1-3** so that you have **six plates** in total.

5) Place three plates in a fridge at **4 °C** and put three in an incubator at **25 °C**. If you don't have access to an incubator, just leave the plates at room temperature, somewhere where the temperature is most likely to remain constant. The plates should be incubated **upside down**. This stops any **condensation** forming on the **lid** from **dropping** onto the **agar**.

6) Put another **lidded agar plate** in each of the two different temperature locations — these plates should be **uncultured** (i.e. you shouldn't have added any bacteria to them). These plates will act as **negative controls** (nothing should grow on them).

7) **Leave** all the plates for the **same** amount of time (e.g. 48 hours) then observe the results.

8) If **bacterial growth** has occurred, you should see **colonies** of bacteria on the surface of the agar.

9) **Count** the number of **colonies** that have formed on **each plate** and **record** your **results** in a table.

10) Work out the **mean** number of colonies formed at **each temperature**.

Remember to use aseptic techniques when doing the experiment (see previous page).

You might find that you have so many colonies that they overlap and you can't count them. If this happens, try making serial dilutions of your bacteria in broth and plate them on agar. One of these dilutions will give you a more manageable number of colonies.

This experiment can be **adapted** to investigate the effects of **different factors** on the growth of microorganisms. For example, you could:

- investigate the effect of **pH** by adding buffers at different pH levels to the broth.

- investigate the effects of **nutrient availability** by using different preparations of agar, which contain different nutrients.

You could also investigate the growth of microorganisms directly **in broth** (without the need to spread a sample of the broth on agar) using a **spectrophotometer**. This is a machine that measures the **turbidity** (**cloudiness**) of the **broth**. **Higher** turbidity means that **more** cells are **present** and, therefore, **more replication** has taken place.

Warm-Up Questions

Q1 What is meant by 'biotechnology'?
Q2 What is bioremediation?
Q3 List two advantages and two disadvantages of the use of microorganisms in food production.
Q4 Give three ways in which growing conditions are optimised inside a fermentation vessel.
Q5 List the stages of the standard growth curve of microorganisms in a closed culture.

Exam Question

Q1 A scientist is plating *E. coli* bacterial cultures on agar to investigate the effects of pH on their growth.
    a) Why must he carry out the experiment using aseptic techniques? [3 marks]
    b) Outline three aseptic techniques that should be followed when culturing bacteria. [3 marks]

Calf stomachs, yeast and waste materials — biotechnology is sexy stuff...

Wow, biology and technology fused together... forget bionic arms, legs and eyes though — growing bacteria in a tank is where it's at. There's a lot of tough stuff to remember on these pages, but I promise you it's worth giving it the time.

Immobilised Enzymes

You might remember from page 232 that enzymes can be isolated from living organisms to be used in biotechnology. These pages tell you about how those enzymes can be immobilised for use in industrial processes. It's clever stuff.

Isolated Enzymes can be Immobilised

1) **Isolated enzymes** used in industry can become **mixed in** with the **products** of a reaction.

2) The **products** then need to be **separated** from this mixture, which can be **complicated** and **costly**.

3) This is **avoided** in large-scale production by using **immobilised enzymes** — enzymes that are **attached** to an **insoluble material** so they **can't** become mixed with the products.

4) There are **three main ways** that enzymes are **immobilised**:

1 Encapsulated in jelly-like **alginate beads**, which act as a **semi-permeable membrane**.

2 **Trapped** in a **silica gel matrix**

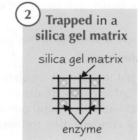

3 **Covalently bonded** to **cellulose or collagen fibres**

5) In industry, the **substrate solution** for a reaction is run through a **column** of **immobilised enzymes**.

6) The **active sites** of the enzymes are still **available** to **catalyse** the reaction but the solution flowing **out of** the column will **only** contain the **desired product**.

7) Here are some of the **advantages** of using **immobilised enzymes** in industry:

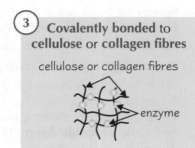

- Columns of immobilised enzymes can be washed and reused — this reduces the cost of running a reaction on an industrial scale because you don't have to keep buying new enzymes.

- The product isn't mixed with the enzymes — no money or time is spent separating them out.

- Immobilised enzymes are more stable than free enzymes — they're less likely to denature (become inactive) in high temperatures or extremes of pH.

8) There are **disadvantages** too:

- Extra equipment is required, which can be expensive to buy.

- Immobilised enzymes are more expensive to buy than free enzymes, so coupled with the equipment costs, they're not always economical for use in smaller-scale production.

- The immobilisation of the enzymes can sometimes lead to a reduction in the enzyme activity because they can't freely mix with their substrate.

Immobilised Enzymes are Used in a Wide Range of Industrial Processes

Conversion of Lactose to Glucose and Galactose

Some people are unable to digest lactose (a sugar found in milk) because they don't produce enough (or any) of the enzyme lactase. Lactase breaks lactose down into glucose and galactose via a hydrolysis reaction. Industrially, fresh milk can now be passed over immobilised lactase to produce lactose-free milk for use in the production of lactose-free dairy products.

Immobilised Enzymes

Production of Semi-Synthetic Penicillins

Penicillin is a useful **antibiotic**, but some bacteria have become **penicillin resistant**. Semi-synthetic penicillins can now be produced, which have the **same** antibiotic properties as natural penicillin, but are **effective** against **penicillin-resistant** organisms. **Immobilised penicillin acylase** enzyme is used in their **production**.

Conversion of Dextrins to Glucose

Glucose and glucose syrup are used in massive amounts in industry, e.g. they're used in the food industry to sweeten and thicken foods. Glucose can be derived from starchy foods, such as corn and potatoes, with the help of immobilised enzymes. Starch breaks down into dextrins (carbohydrate products), which are then broken down into glucose by the immobilised enzyme glucoamylase.

Conversion of Glucose to Fructose

Fructose is a sugar that's much **sweeter** than glucose. It's used as a **sweetener** in **food** — using fructose rather than glucose means that **less sugar** is needed to obtain the same level of sweetness in our foods. **Immobilised glucose isomerase** is used to convert **glucose** to **fructose** on an industrial scale.

Even though he eats your coursework and looks like a sultana, Doug is still even sweeter than fructose.

Production of Pure Samples of L-Amino Acids

Amino acids have two chemical forms (isomers) — L or D. Most amino acids utilised by the body need to be in the L form. Scientists are able to chemically synthesise amino acids, but end up with a mix of L and D forms. The enzyme aminoacylase separates them. Immobilised aminoacylase is used for the industrial production of pure samples of L-amino acids, which can be used for many purposes in the production of animal and human food, as well as in dietary supplements.

Warm-Up Questions

Q1 List three advantages of using immobilised enzymes in industry.

Q2 Name a type of product that involves immobilised lactase in its production.

Q3 Name an industrial process that relies heavily on the action of immobilised penicillin acylase.

Q4 Name the immobilised enzyme that converts glucose to fructose.

PRACTICE QUESTIONS

Exam Questions

Q1 Aminoacylase is used industrially in the production of pure samples of L-amino acids.
   a) The aminoacylase can be immobilised. What does this mean? [1 mark]
   b) Give three ways in which aminoacylase could be immobilised. [3 marks]

Q2 A team of food technicians is designing a protocol for the mass production of glucose syrup. The enzyme glucoamylase plays a key role in this process. They are deciding whether to use immobilised or free enzyme.
   a) What role does glucoamylase play in the manufacture of glucose syrup? [1 mark]
   b) Give two disadvantages of using immobilised glucoamylase, rather than free glucoamylase, in the production of glucose syrup on an industrial scale. [2 marks]

Here's another way to immobilise an enzyme — run over it with a steamroller...

Some industrial processes can really benefit from the use of immobilised enzymes, but they have their drawbacks too. Make sure that you're able to give a balanced account of the pros and cons of immobilised enzyme usage in industry. You also need to know the different ways that enzymes can be immobilised and some examples of how great they are.

An Introduction to Ecosystems

All this ecology-type stuff is pretty wordy, so here are a nice few definitions to get you started.
This way, you'll know what I'm banging on about throughout the rest of the section, and that always helps I think.

You Need to **Learn Some Definitions** to get you **Started**

Habitat — The **place** where an organism **lives**, e.g. a rocky shore or a field.
Population — **All** the organisms of **one species** in a **habitat**.
Producer — An organism that **produces organic molecules** using sunlight energy, e.g. plants.
Consumer — An organism that **eats other organisms**, e.g. animals and birds.
Decomposer — An organism that **breaks down dead** or **undigested organic material**, e.g. bacteria and fungi.
Trophic level — A **stage** in a **food chain** occupied by a particular **group** of organisms,
e.g. producers are the first trophic level in a food chain.

Ecosystems Are Always **Changing**

1) An **ecosystem** is all the organisms living in a certain area and all the non-living conditions (factors) found there. It's a **dynamic system** — this means it's **changing all the time**.

2) An ecosystem includes both **biotic** and **abiotic factors**:

   - **Biotic factors** — The **living** features of an ecosystem. For example, the presence of **predators** or **food**.

   - **Abiotic factors** — The **non-living** features of an ecosystem. E.g. the **temperature**, **rainfall**, shape of the land (**topology**) and **soil nutrient availability**. In an aquatic ecosystem these may also include the **pH** and **salinity** (salt content) of the water.

The undead can find it hard to identify themselves as a living or a non-living feature of an ecosystem.

Biotic and Abiotic Factors Have an **Impact** on **Ecosystems**

Ecosystems cover different areas. They can be **small**, e.g. a pond, or **large**, e.g. an entire forest. Whatever size they are, ecosystems are **influenced** by **biotic** and **abiotic** factors. Here are some examples:

Rock pools

- **Biotic factors** — Seaweed can be a **food source** for **consumers** such as limpets that graze on this **producer**. Intense **competition** for food (such as seaweed) can **limit** the **number** of **organisms** that are present in a small rock pool ecosystem.

- **Abiotic factors** — Rock pools are heavily influenced by the **tides**. At **high** tide they are completely **submerged** by the ocean so experience **similar** abiotic factors (e.g. **pH**, **salinity**, **temperature**, etc.) to the ocean ecosystem. However, at **low** tide they experience more **extreme abiotic** conditions (e.g. **higher** salinity and temperatures) — only **some organisms** can **tolerate** these conditions.

Playing field

- **Biotic factors** — **Producers** include grass and other plants such as daisies, clover and dandelions. The large amount of these plants might attract a large number of organisms that use them as a food source (e.g. rabbits, caterpillars).

- **Abiotic factors** — **Rainfall** and **sunlight** affect the **growth** of the **producers** in the ecosystem. In a very **wet** year, the soil may become **waterlogged**, making it **difficult** for plants to grow. Poor plant growth may **decrease** the number of **consumers** the ecosystem is able to support.

Large tree

- **Biotic factors** — Insects, such as caterpillars, can use the **leaves** of a tree as a source of food. However, if they consume **all the leaves** on a tree (defoliation) they can **slow** tree growth and even lead to its **death**.

- **Abiotic factors** — **Drought conditions** (e.g. when there are prolonged periods of very **low rainfall**) can **negatively impact** the **growth** of a tree. In severe cases it can result in the whole tree (or parts of it) **dying**.

An Introduction to Ecosystems

Energy is Transferred Through Ecosystems

1) The **main route** by which energy **enters** an ecosystem is **photosynthesis** (e.g. by plants, see p. 174). (Some energy enters sea ecosystems when bacteria use chemicals from deep sea vents as an energy source.)

2) During photosynthesis plants **convert sunlight energy** into a form that can be **used** by other organisms — plants are called **producers** (see previous page). They store energy as **biomass**. Biomass is the **mass** of **living** material, e.g. the mass of plant material.

3) After producers store **sunlight energy** as **biomass**, you can then think of the following **energy transfers** through ecosystems as **biomass transfers**. You might come across energy transfers being called biomass transfers in your exam — don't panic, they refer to the same thing (energy transfer).

4) Energy is **transferred** through the **living organisms** of an ecosystem when organisms **eat** other organisms, e.g. producers are eaten by organisms called **primary consumers**. Primary consumers are then eaten by **secondary consumers** and secondary consumers are eaten by **tertiary consumers**.

5) **Food chains** and **food webs** show how energy is **transferred** through an ecosystem.

6) **Food chains** show **simple lines** of energy transfer.

7) **Food webs** show **lots** of **food chains** in an ecosystem and how they **overlap**.

8) Energy locked up in the things that **can't be eaten** (e.g. bones, faeces) gets recycled back into the ecosystem by **decomposers**.

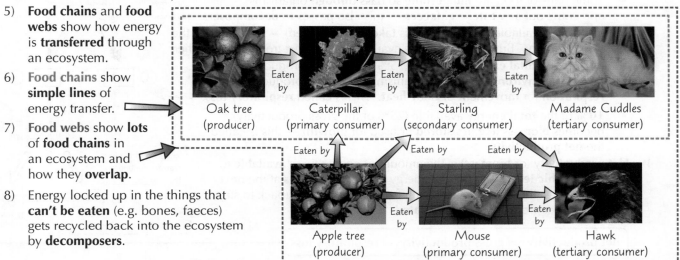

Oak tree (producer) → Eaten by → Caterpillar (primary consumer) → Eaten by → Starling (secondary consumer) → Eaten by → Madame Cuddles (tertiary consumer)

Apple tree (producer) → Eaten by → Mouse (primary consumer) → Eaten by → Hawk (tertiary consumer)

Warm-Up Questions

Q1 Define ecosystem.
Q2 Why are ecosystems described as being dynamic?
Q3 What is a biotic factor?
Q4 What is biomass?
Q5 How is biomass related to energy?

PRACTICE QUESTIONS

Exam Questions

Q1 Which of the following is **not** an example of an abiotic factor.

A The amount of rainfall in a forest ecosystem.
B Sufficient space on a rocky surface for barnacles to attach themselves to in a seashore ecosystem.
C The presence of other plants that are competing for light in a woodland ecosystem.
D The salinity of water in an aquatic ecosystem. [1 mark]

Q2 In an orchard ecosystem, if there's a frost once the trees have started flowering, it can mean that the fruit doesn't develop properly.

a) Describe the effect that this might have on the rest of the organisms in the ecosystem. [2 marks]
b) Frost is an example of an abiotic factor in an ecosystem.
Suggest two other abiotic factors that might influence an orchard ecosystem. [2 marks]

Food chains — apparently there's more to them than candy necklaces...

Don't be taken in by the pretty pictures — this topic is not as easy as it might appear. Ecologists use very specific terms for things so you have to learn them and then be really careful that you use the right one. Take biomass and energy for instance. Biomass is energy <u>stored</u> in living material. Had me stumped for ages that one...

Energy Transfer Through an Ecosystem

Energy is lost along food chains (how careless, they should put it in a safe place if you ask me).

Not All Energy gets Transferred to the Next Trophic Level

1) **Not all** the energy (e.g. from sunlight or food) that's available to the organisms in a trophic level is **transferred** to the **next** trophic level — around **90%** of the **total available energy** is **lost** in various ways.

2) Some of the available energy (**60%**) is **never taken in** by the organisms in the first place. E.g.

   - Plants **can't use** all the light energy that reaches their **leaves**, e.g. some is the **wrong wavelength**, some is **reflected**, and some **passes straight through** the leaves.

   - Some sunlight can't be used because it hits parts of the plant that **can't photosynthesise**, e.g. the bark of a tree.

   - Some **parts** of food, e.g. **roots** or **bones**, **aren't eaten** by organisms so the energy isn't taken in — they pass to **decomposers**.

   - Some parts of food are **indigestible** so **pass through** organisms and come out as **waste**, e.g. faeces — this also passes to **decomposers**.

The percentages used are general figures — real values for a given ecosystem will vary.

① 100% available energy

② 60% energy not taken in

③ 40% energy taken in (gross productivity)

③ 30% respiratory loss

④ 10% biomass (net productivity — energy available to the next trophic level)

3) The rest of the available energy (**40%**) is **taken in** (**absorbed**) — this is called the **gross productivity**. But not all of this is available to the next trophic level either.

   - **30%** of the **total energy** available (75% of the gross productivity) is **lost to the environment** when organisms use energy produced from **respiration** for **movement** or body **heat**. This is called **respiratory loss**.

   - **10%** of the **total energy** available (25% of the gross productivity) becomes **biomass** (e.g. it's **stored** or used for **growth**) — this is called the **net productivity**.

4) **Net productivity** (or **biomass**) is the amount of energy that's **available** to the **next trophic level**. The **flow** of energy transfer **continues** at the **next trophic level** — the process starts again from the beginning (back to step 1). Here's how net productivity is **calculated**:

energy and biomass transfer continues at the next trophic level

① ② 60% energy not taken in ③ 40% energy taken in (gross productivity)

net productivity = gross productivity − respiratory loss

EXAMPLE: The rabbits in an ecosystem receive **20 000 kJm⁻²yr⁻¹** of energy, but don't take in **12 000 kJm⁻²yr⁻¹** of it, so their gross productivity is **8000 kJm⁻²yr⁻¹** (20 000 − 12 000). They lose **6000 kJm⁻²yr⁻¹** using energy from **respiration**. You can use this to **calculate** the **net productivity** of the rabbits:

net productivity = 8000 − 6000 = 2000 kJm⁻²yr⁻¹

5) You might be asked to **calculate** how **efficient energy transfer** from one trophic level to another is:

The rabbits receive **20 000 kJm⁻²yr⁻¹**, and their **net productivity** is **2000 kJm⁻²yr⁻¹**. So the **percentage efficiency** of **energy transfer** is:

(2000 ÷ 20 000) × 100 = 10%

6) You can also calculate how **efficient** organisms from **one trophic level** are at **converting** what they **eat** into **energy** for the **next trophic level**. You work it out like this:

(energy transferred ÷ energy intake) × 100

'Energy transferred' here means the net productivity of the trophic level.

Energy Transfer Between Trophic Levels can be Measured

1) To **measure** the **energy transfer** between two trophic levels you need to **calculate** the **difference** between the amount of **energy** in each level (the net productivity of each level).

2) You can **calculate** the **amount of energy** in a trophic level by measuring the **dry mass** of the organisms (their **biomass**). Remember, energy is stored as biomass, so it indicates **how much energy** an organism **contains**.

3) First you calculate the amount of biomass in a **sample** of the organisms, e.g. a 1 m² area of **wheat** or a single **mouse** that feeds on the wheat.

4) Then you **multiply** the results from the **sample** by the **size** of the **total population** (e.g. a 10 000 m² **field** of wheat or the **number** of mice in the population) to give the **total** amount of energy in the organisms at that **trophic level**.

5) The **difference** in energy between the trophic levels is the amount of energy **transferred**.

Energy Transfer Through an Ecosystem

6) There are **problems** with this method though. For example, the consumers (mice) might have **taken in energy** from sources **other than** the producer measured (wheat). This means the difference between the two figures calculated **wouldn't** be an **accurate** estimate of the energy transferred between **only those two** organisms. For an **accurate estimate** you'd need to include **all** the individual organisms at each trophic level.

Human Activities can Increase the Transfer of Energy

Some **farming methods increase productivity** by **increasing** the **transfer** of **energy** through an **ecosystem**:

1) **Herbicides** kill **weeds** that **compete** with agricultural crops for **energy**. Reducing competition means crops receive **more energy**, so they grow **faster** and become **larger**, **increasing** productivity.

2) **Fungicides** kill **fungal infections** that **damage** agricultural crops. The crops **use more** energy for **growth** and **less** for fighting infection, so they grow **faster** and become **larger**, **increasing** productivity.

3) **Insecticides** kill **insect** pests that **eat** and **damage** crops. Killing insect pests means **less biomass** is **lost** from crops, so they grow to be **larger**, which means productivity is **greater**.

4) **Natural predators** introduced to the ecosystem **eat** the pest species, e.g. ladybirds eat greenfly. This means the crops lose **less energy** and **biomass**, **increasing** productivity.

5) **Fertilisers** are chemicals that provide crops with **minerals** needed **for growth**, e.g. **nitrates**. Crops **use up** minerals in the soil as they **grow**, so their growth is **limited** when there **aren't enough** minerals. Adding fertiliser **replaces** the lost minerals, so **more energy** from the ecosystem can be used to grow, **increasing** the **efficiency** of energy conversion.

6) Rearing livestock **intensively** involves **controlling** the **conditions** they live in, so **more** of their **energy** is used for **growth** and **less** is used for **other activities** — the **efficiency** of energy conversion is increased so **more biomass** is produced and productivity is **increased**. Here are a couple of **examples**:

> 1) Animals may be kept in **warm, indoor** pens where their **movement** is **restricted**. **Less energy** is **wasted** keeping **warm** and **moving around**.
>
> 2) Animals may be given **feed** that's **higher in energy** than their natural food. This **increases** the **energy input**, so **more energy** is available for **growth**.

Increasing productivity was not an issue that was easy to raise with Herbert.

The benefits are that **more food** can be produced in a **shorter** space of time, often at **lower cost**. However, enhancing productivity by intensive rearing raises **ethical issues**. For example, some people think the **conditions** intensively reared animals are kept in cause the animals **pain, distress** or restricts their **natural behaviour**, so it **shouldn't be done**.

Warm-Up Questions

Q1 What is the equation for net productivity?

Q2 What do you need to calculate to find the energy transfer between two trophic levels?

Q3 Give one example of how farmers increase the productivity of animals.

PRACTICE QUESTIONS

| Grass 13 883 kJm⁻²yr⁻¹ | → | Arctic hare 2345 kJm⁻²yr⁻¹ | → | Arctic fox 137 kJm⁻²yr⁻¹ |

Grass $13\,883\ kJm^{-2}yr^{-1}$ → Arctic hare $2345\ kJm^{-2}yr^{-1}$ → Arctic fox $137\ kJm^{-2}yr^{-1}$

Exam Questions

Q1 The diagram above shows the net productivity of different trophic levels in a food chain.
   a) Explain why the net productivity of the Arctic hare is less than the net productivity of the grass. [4 marks]
   b) Calculate the percentage efficiency of energy transfer from the Arctic hare to the Arctic fox. [2 marks]

Q2 A farmer grows cabbages in one of his fields.
   a) Suggest how you could calculate the energy that the cabbages in the field contain. [2 marks]
   b) The farmer wants to increase the productivity of his field.
      Describe two ways he could do this and explain how they would help increase productivity. [4 marks]

I'm suffering from energy loss after those two pages...

So farming's not just about getting up early to feed the animals then — farmers are manipulating the transfer of energy to produce as much food as they can. And it's really important to remember that this transfer of energy isn't 100% efficient — most gets lost along the way so the next organisms don't get all the energy. Interesting, ve-ry interesting...

Recycling in Ecosystems

Bin day is Monday for the secondary consumers. Actually, ecosystems have developed a much better system to make sure necessary elements like carbon and nitrogen can be re-used and they don't run out.

The **Carbon Cycle** shows how **Carbon** is **Passed On** and **Recycled**

All organisms need carbon to make **essential compounds**, e.g. plants use CO_2 in photosynthesis to make glucose. The **carbon cycle** is how carbon **moves** through **living organisms** and the **non-living environment**. The cycle includes processes that involve organisms (**photosynthesis**, **respiration**, and **decomposition**) and also chemical and physical processes such as **combustion** and **weathering**:

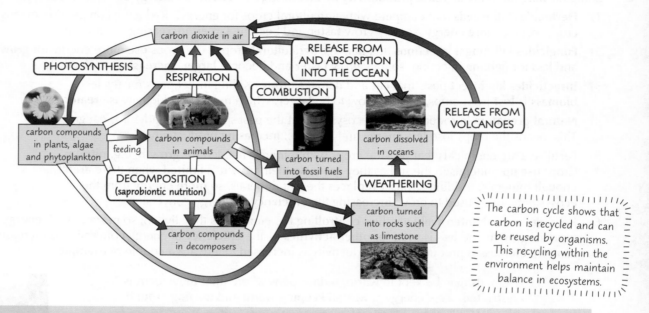

The carbon cycle shows that carbon is recycled and can be reused by organisms. This recycling within the environment helps maintain balance in ecosystems.

1) **Carbon** (in the form of CO_2 from **air and water**) is **absorbed** by plants when they carry out **photosynthesis** — it becomes carbon compounds in **plant tissues**.

2) Carbon is **passed on** to **primary consumers** when they **eat** the plants. It's passed on to **secondary** and **tertiary consumers** when they eat other consumers.

3) All living organisms **die** and the carbon compounds in the **dead organisms** are digested by **microorganisms** called **decomposers**, e.g. bacteria and fungi. Feeding on dead organic matter is called **saprobiontic nutrition**.

4) Carbon is **returned** to the air (and water) as **all living organisms** (including the decomposers) carry out **respiration**, which **produces CO_2**.

5) If dead organic matter ends up in places where there **aren't any** decomposers, e.g. deep oceans or bogs, their carbon compounds can be turned into **fossil fuels** over **millions of years** (by heat and pressure).

6) The carbon in fossil fuels (e.g. oil and coal) is **released** when they're burnt — this is called **combustion**.

7) As well as coal, other types of rock can be formed from dead organic matter deposited on the sea floor. For example, rocks such as **limestone** and **chalk** are mainly composed of **calcium carbonate** ($CaCO_3$). This comes from marine organisms like crabs, mussels, sea urchins and coral that utilise this compound in their development, e.g. to form **shells**.

8) One way carbon can be returned to the atmosphere from these rocks is by them being **drawn down** deep into the Earth's crust by the movement of **tectonic plates**. There they undergo chemical changes and release **carbon dioxide**, which is returned to the atmosphere by **volcanoes**.

9) The rocks can also eventually become **land**, which then is **weathered** (broken down by exposure to the atmosphere). This can happen **chemically** by **rainwater** (which is naturally slightly acidic due to the CO_2 dissolved in it) and **physically**, e.g. by plant roots, animals, etc. **Chemical weathering** causes **mineral ions** and **bicarbonate ions** (HCO_3^-) to be released from the rock in to solution and enter **groundwater**, from where they are transported into **rivers** and the **oceans**. There they **combine** to form carbon-containing compounds such as $CaCO_3$.

10) CO_2 can also **dissolve** directly into the **oceans** from the Atmosphere and be transported in the ocean by **deep underwater currents** (a physical process). CO_2 can remain in these slow-moving currents for hundreds of years before returning to the surface and being **released** back into the **atmosphere**.

Recycling in Ecosystems

The **Nitrogen Cycle** shows how **Nitrogen** is **Recycled** in **Ecosystems**

Plants and animals **need** nitrogen to make **proteins** and **nucleic acids** (DNA and RNA). The atmosphere's made up of about 78% nitrogen, but plants and animals **can't use it** in that form — they need **bacteria** to **convert** it into **nitrogen compounds** first. The **nitrogen cycle** shows how nitrogen is **converted** into a useable form and then **passed** on between different **living** organisms and the **non-living** environment.

The nitrogen cycle includes **food chains** (nitrogen is passed on when organisms are eaten), and four different processes that involve bacteria — **nitrogen fixation**, **ammonification**, **nitrification** and **denitrification**:

1 Nitrogen fixation

- **Nitrogen fixation** is when nitrogen gas in the atmosphere is turned into ammonia by bacteria such as *Rhizobium* and *Azotobacter*. The ammonia can then be used by plants.
- *Rhizobium* are found inside **root nodules** (growths on the roots) of **leguminous** plants (e.g. peas, beans and clover).
- They form a **mutualistic** relationship with the plants — they provide the plant with **nitrogen compounds** and the plant provides them with **carbohydrates**.
- *Azotobacter* are found living in the **soil**. They **don't** form mutualistic relationships with plants.

2 Ammonification

- **Ammonification** is when nitrogen compounds from **dead organisms** are turned into **ammonia** by **decomposers**, which goes onto form **ammonium ions**.
- Animal **waste** (**urine** and **faeces**) also contains nitrogen compounds. These are also turned into ammonia by decomposers and go on to form ammonium ions.

3 Nitrification

- **Nitrification** is when ammonium ions in the soil are changed into nitrogen compounds that can then be used by plants (nitrates).
- First nitrifying bacteria called *Nitrosomonas* change ammonium ions into nitrites.
- Then other nitrifying bacteria called *Nitrobacter* change nitrites into nitrates.

4 Denitrification

- **Denitrification** is when nitrates in the soil are **converted** into **nitrogen gas** by **denitrifying bacteria** — they use nitrates in the soil to carry out **respiration** and produce nitrogen gas.
- This happens under **anaerobic conditions** (where there's **no** oxygen), e.g. in **waterlogged** soils.

Other ways that **nitrogen** gets into an **ecosystem** is by **lightning** (which **fixes atmospheric nitrogen**) or by **artificial fertilisers** (they're **produced from atmospheric nitrogen** on an **industrial scale** in the **Haber process**).

Warm-Up Questions

Q1 Describe a chemical process that occurs in the carbon cycle.

Q2 Name the two groups of bacteria involved in nitrification.

Exam Questions

Q1 The diagram on the right shows the nitrogen cycle.
a) Name the processes labelled A and B in the diagram. [2 marks]
b) Name process C and describe the process in detail. [3 marks]

Q2 Cattle can be fed on silage (preserved grass) over winter months. Describe how carbon moves from carbon dioxide in the air to the formation of carbon compounds in cattle. [2 marks]

Nitrogen fixation — cheaper than a shoe fixation...

The nitrogen cycle's not as bad as it seems — divide up the four processes of nitrogen fixation, ammonification, nitrification and denitrification and learn them separately. Then before you know it, you'll have learnt the whole cycle.

Succession

The types of organisms in an ecosystem change over time, as does the environment itself...

Succession is the **Process of Ecosystem Change**

Succession is the process by which an **ecosystem changes** over **time**. The **biotic conditions** (e.g. **plant** and **animal communities**) change as the **abiotic conditions** change (e.g. **water** availability). There are **two** types of succession:

1) **Primary succession** — this happens on land that's been **newly formed** or **exposed**, e.g. where a **volcano** has erupted to form a **new rock surface**, or where **sea level** has **dropped** exposing a new area of land. There's **no soil** or **organic material** to start with, e.g. just bare rock.

2) **Secondary succession** — this happens on land that's been **cleared** of all the **plants**, but where the **soil remains**, e.g. after a **forest fire** or where a forest has been **cut down by humans**.

Succession Occurs in **Several Stages**

1) **Primary succession** starts when species **colonise** a new land surface. **Seeds** and **spores** are blown in by the **wind** and begin to **grow**. The **first species** to colonise the area are called **pioneer species** — this is the **first stage**.
   - The **abiotic conditions** are **hostile** (**harsh**), e.g. there's no soil to **retain water**. Only pioneer species **grow** because they're **specialised** to cope with the harsh conditions, e.g. **marram grass** can grow on sand dunes near the sea because it has **deep roots** to get water and can **tolerate** the salty environment.
   - The pioneer species **change** the **abiotic conditions** — they **die** and **microorganisms decompose** the dead **organic material** (**humus**). This forms a **basic soil**.
   - This makes conditions **less hostile**, e.g. the basic soil helps to **retain water**, which means **new organisms** can move in and grow. These then die and are decomposed, adding **more** organic material, making the soil **deeper** and **richer in minerals**. This means **larger plants** like **shrubs** can start to grow in the deeper soil, which retains **even more** water. As **more plants** move in they create **more habitats**, so **more animals** move in.

2) **Secondary succession** happens in the **same way**, but because there's already a **soil layer** succession starts at a **later stage** — the pioneer species in secondary succession are **larger plants**, e.g. shrubs.

3) At each stage, **different** plants and animals that are **better adapted** for the improved conditions move in, **out-compete** the plants and animals that are already there, and become the **dominant species** in the ecosystem.

4) As succession goes on, the ecosystem becomes **more complex**. New species move in **alongside** existing species, which means the **species diversity** (the number of **different species** and the **abundance** of each species) **increases**.

5) The amount of **biomass** also **increases** because plants at later stages are **larger** and **more dense**, e.g. **woody trees**.

6) The **final stage** is called the **climax community** — the ecosystem is supporting the **largest** and **most complex** community of plants and animals it can. It **won't change** much more — it's in a **steady state**.

This example shows primary succession on bare rock, but succession also happens on sand dunes, salt marshes and even in lakes.

Example of primary succession — bare rock to woodland

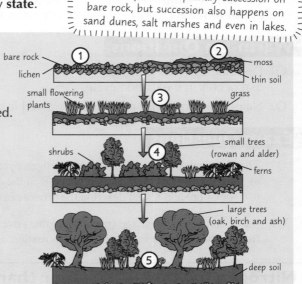

1) **Pioneer species colonise** the rocks. E.g. **lichens** grow on and **break down** rocks, **releasing minerals**.

2) The lichens **die** and are **decomposed** helping to form a **thin soil**, which thickens as more **organic material** is formed. This means other species such as **mosses** can **grow**.

3) **Larger plants** that need **more water** can move in as the soil **deepens**, e.g. **grasses** and **small flowering plants**. The soil **continues to deepen** as the larger plants die and are decomposed.

4) **Shrubs**, **ferns** and **small trees** begin to grow, **out-competing** the grasses and smaller plants to become the **dominant** species. **Diversity increases**.

5) Finally, the soil is **deep** and **rich** enough in **nutrients** to support **large trees**. These become the dominant species, and the **climax community** is formed.

Succession

Different Ecosystems have Different Climax Communities

Which species make up the climax community depends on what the **climate's** like in an ecosystem. The climax community for a **particular** climate is called its **climatic climax**. For example:

> In a temperate climate there's plenty of available water, mild temperatures and not much change between the seasons. The climatic climax will contain large trees because they can grow in these conditions once deep soils have developed. In a polar climate there's not much available water, temperatures are low and there are massive changes between the seasons. Large trees won't ever be able to grow in these conditions, so the climatic climax contains only herbs or shrubs, but it's still the climax community.

Succession can be Prevented or Deflected

Human activities can **prevent succession**, stopping the normal climax community from **developing**. When succession is stopped **artificially** like this, the climax community is called a **plagioclimax**. **Deflected succession** is when succession is prevented by human activity, but the plagioclimax that develops is one that's **different** to any of the **natural stages** of the ecosystem — the path of succession has been **deflected** from its natural course. For example:

1) A regularly mown grassy field won't develop woody plants, even if the climate of the ecosystem could support them.

2) The growing points of the woody plants are cut off by the lawnmower, so larger plants can't establish themselves — only the grasses can survive being mowed, so the climax community is a grassy field.

Humankind had been given a mighty weapon with which they would tame the forces of nature.

3) A grassy field isn't a natural stage — there should also be things like small flowering plants, so succession has been deflected.

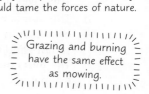

Grazing and burning have the same effect as mowing.

Warm-Up Questions

Q1 What is the difference between primary and secondary succession?

Q2 What is the name given to species that are the first to colonise an area during succession?

Q3 What is meant by a climax community?

Exam Questions

Q1 Which one of the following statements correctly describes deflected succession?

A When human intervention causes the natural climax community to form in an ecosystem.
B The process by which pioneer species change the abiotic conditions by forming a basic soil.
C A process that occurs on land that has been cleared but where soil remains.
D Where human activity has stopped the normal climax community from developing. [1 mark]

Q2 Succession occurs on sand dunes.
You can often see the different stages of succession as you move further inland from the sand dunes.

a) What type of succession is taking place when the first grasses start to appear on the dune? Give a reason for your answer. [2 marks]

b) Explain how the growth of grasses can lead to larger plants like shrubs becoming the dominant species on the sand dunes. [3 marks]

Revision succession — bare brain to a woodland of knowledge...

When answering questions on succession, examiners are pretty keen on you using the right terminology — that means saying "pioneer species" instead of "the first plants to grow there". If you can manage that, then you'll be just fine.

Investigating Ecosystems

Examiners aren't happy unless you're freezing to death in the rain in a field somewhere in the middle of nowhere.
Still, it's better than being stuck in the classroom being bored to death learning about fieldwork techniques...

You need to be able to **Investigate Populations** of **Organisms**

Investigating **populations** of organisms involves looking at the **abundance**
and **distribution** of **species** in a particular **area**.

1) **Abundance** — the **number of individuals** of **one species** in a **particular area**.
   The abundance of **mobile organisms** and **plants** can be estimated by simply counting the **number** of
   individuals in samples taken. **Percentage cover** can also be used to measure the abundance of plants
   — this is **how much** of the area you're investigating is **covered** by a species.

2) **Distribution** — this is **where** a particular species is within the **area you're investigating**.

You need to take a **Random Sample** from the **Area You're Investigating**

Most of the time it would be too **time-consuming** to measure the **number of individuals** and the **distribution**
of every species in the **entire area** you're investigating, so instead you take **samples**:

1) **Choose** an area to sample — a small area within the area being investigated.

2) Samples should be random to avoid bias, e.g. by picking random sample sites.

You'll have learnt more about random sampling in Module 4.

Finally! 26 542 981 poppies. What do you mean I didn't need to count them all?

3) Use an appropriate technique to take a sample of the population (see below and on the next page).

4) Repeat the process, taking as many samples as possible. This gives a more precise estimate for the whole area.

5) The number of individuals for the whole area can then be estimated by taking an average of the data collected in each sample and multiplying it by the size of the whole area. The percentage cover for the whole area can be estimated by taking the average of all the samples.

When you are recording species it's important to identify them correctly. An identification key (a tool that allows you to identify species by their features) can help you do this.

Frame Quadrats can be used to **Investigate Plant Populations**

1) A frame quadrat is a square frame divided into a grid of 100 smaller squares by strings attached across the frame.

2) They're placed on the ground at random points within the area you're investigating. This can be done by selecting random coordinates (see above).

3) The number of individuals of each species is recorded in each quadrat.

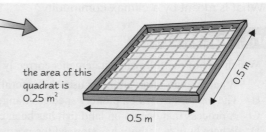

the area of this quadrat is 0.25 m²

0.5 m

0.5 m

4) The percentage cover of a species can also be measured by counting how much of the quadrat is covered by the species — you count a square if it's more than half-covered. Percentage cover is a quick way to investigate populations and you don't have to count all the individual plants.

5) Frame quadrats are useful for quickly investigating areas with species that fit within a small quadrat — most frame quadrats are 1 m by 1 m.

6) Areas with larger plants and trees need very large quadrats. Large quadrats aren't always in a frame — they can be marked out with a tape measure.

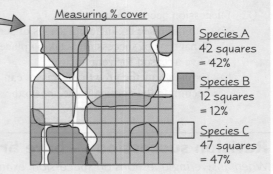

Measuring % cover

Species A
42 squares
= 42%

Species B
12 squares
= 12%

Species C
47 squares
= 47%

Investigating Ecosystems

Point Quadrats can also be used to Investigate Plant Populations

1) A **point quadrat** is a **horizontal bar** on **two legs** with a series of holes at set intervals along its length.

2) Point quadrats are **placed on the ground** at **random points** within the area you're investigating.

3) **Pins** are dropped through the holes in the frame and **every plant** that each pin **touches** is **recorded**. If a pin touches several **overlapping** plants, **all** of them are recorded.

4) The **number of individuals** of each species is recorded in **each quadrat**.

5) The **percentage cover** of a species can also be measured by calculating the **number of times** a pin has touched a species as a **percentage** of the **total number** of pins dropped.

6) Point quadrats are especially useful in areas where there's lots of **dense vegetation** close to the ground.

wood frame — *pins* — *hole to place pin*

multiple hits

Transects are used to Investigate the Distribution of Plant Populations

You can use **lines** called **transects** to help find out how plants are **distributed across** an area, e.g. how species **change** from a hedge towards the middle of a field. You need to know about **three** types of transect:

1) **Line transects** — a **tape measure** is placed **along** the transect and the species that **touch** the tape measure are **recorded**.

point quadrat

tape measure

line transect

Transects can be used in many different ecosystems, not just fields.
For example, along a beach or in a woodland.

interrupted transect

belt transect

frame quadrat

2) **Belt transects** — data is collected along the transect using **frame quadrats** placed **next to** each other.

3) **Interrupted transects** — instead of investigating the **whole transect** of either a line or a belt, you can take **measurements** at **intervals**. E.g. by placing **point quadrats** at **right angles** to the direction of the transect at **set intervals** along its length, such as **every 2 m**.

Warm-Up Questions

Q1 Define abundance.

Q2 What does percentage cover show?

Q3 Explain why samples of a population are taken.

Q4 Briefly describe how belt transects are different from line transects.

Exam Question

Q1 A student wants to sample a population of daffodils in a field.
   a) Describe a method she could use to avoid bias in her investigation. [1 mark]
   b) Describe how she could investigate the percentage cover of daffodils in the field using frame quadrats. [3 marks]
   c) Suggest how incorrect identification of plant species could lead to inaccuracies in the results. [1 mark]

What did the quadrat say to the policeman — I've been framed...

If you want to know what it's really like doing these investigations then read these pages outside in the pouring rain. Doing it while you're tucked up in a nice warm, dry exam hall won't seem so bad after that, take my word for it.

Factors Affecting Population Size

Uh-oh, anyone who loves cute little bunny-wunnys look away now — these pages are about how the population sizes of organisms fluctuate and the reasons why. One of the reasons, I'm sad to say, is because the little rabbits get eaten.

Population Size Varies Because of **Abiotic Factors**...

Remember — abiotic factors are the non-living features of an ecosystem.

1) **Population size** is the **total number** of organisms of **one species** in a **habitat**.

2) The **population size** of any species **varies** because of **abiotic** factors, e.g. the amount of **light**, **water** or **space** available, the **temperature** of their surroundings or the **chemical composition** of their surroundings.

3) When abiotic conditions are **ideal** for a species, organisms can **grow fast** and **reproduce successfully**.

> E.g. when the temperature of a mammal's surroundings is the ideal temperature for **metabolic reactions** to take place, they don't have to **use up** as much energy **maintaining** their **body temperature**. This means more energy can be used for **growth** and **reproduction**, so their population size will **increase**.

4) When abiotic conditions **aren't ideal** for a species, organisms **can't** grow as **fast** or reproduce as **successfully**.

> E.g. when the temperature of a mammal's surroundings is significantly **lower** or **higher** than their **optimum** body temperature, they have to **use** a lot of **energy** to maintain the right **body temperature**. This means less energy will be available for **growth** and **reproduction**, so their population size will **decrease**.

...and **Because of Biotic Factors**

Biotic factors are the living features of an ecosystem.

1 **Interspecific Competition** — **Competition** Between **Different Species**

1) Interspecific competition is when organisms of **different species compete** with each other for the **same resources**, e.g. **red** and **grey** squirrels compete for the same **food sources** and **habitats** in the **UK**.

2) Interspecific competition between two species can mean that the **resources available** to **both** populations are **reduced**, e.g. if they share the **same** source of food, there will be **less** available to both of them. This means both populations will be **limited** by a lower amount of food. They'll have less **energy** for **growth** and **reproduction**, so the population sizes will be **lower** for both species. E.g. in areas where both **red** and **grey** squirrels live, both populations are **smaller** than they would be if there was **only one** species there.

3) Interspecific competition can also affect the **distribution** of species. If **two** species are competing but one is **better adapted** to its surroundings than the other, the less well adapted species is likely to be **out-competed** — it **won't** be able to **exist** alongside the better adapted species. E.g. since the introduction of the **grey squirrel** to the UK, the native **red squirrel** has **disappeared** from large areas. The grey squirrel has a better chance of **survival** because it's **larger** and can store **more fat** over winter.

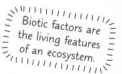

Plants compete for things like minerals and light.

2 **Intraspecific Competition** — **Competition Within** a **Species**

Intraspecific competition is when organisms of the **same species compete** with each other for the **same resources**.

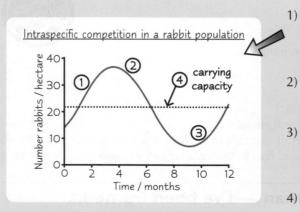

Intraspecific competition in a rabbit population

1) The **population** of a species (e.g. rabbits) **increases** when resources are **plentiful**. As the population increases, there'll be **more** organisms competing for the **same amount** of **space** and **food**.

2) Eventually, resources such as food and space become **limiting** — there **isn't enough** for all the organisms. The population then begins to **decline**.

3) A **smaller** population then means that there's **less competition** for space and food, which is **better** for **growth** and **reproduction** — so the population starts to **grow** again.

4) The **maximum stable population size** of a species that an ecosystem can **support** is called the **carrying capacity**.

Factors Affecting Population Size

③ Predation — Predator and Prey Populations are Controlled by Negative Feedback

Predation is where an organism (the predator) kills and eats another organism (the prey), e.g. lions kill and eat (**predate** on) buffalo. The **population sizes** of predators and prey are **controlled** by **negative feedback** (see p. 133):

1) As the **prey** population **increases**, there's **more food** for predators, so the **predator** population **grows**. E.g. in the graph on the right the **lynx** population **grows** after the **snowshoe hare** population has **increased** because there's **more food** available.

2) As the **predator** population **increases, more prey** is **eaten** — so the **prey** population then begins to **fall**. E.g. **greater numbers** of lynx eat lots of snowshoe hares, so their population **falls**. This is an example of **negative feedback** — the **prey population** is restored to a more **stable size**.

3) This means there's **less food** for the **predators**, so their population **decreases** (more negative feedback), and so on. E.g. **reduced** snowshoe hare numbers means there's **less food** for the lynx, so their population **falls**.

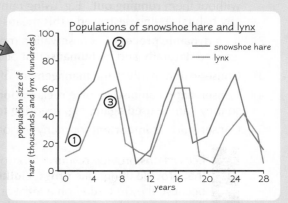

Predator-prey relationships are usually more **complicated** than this though because there are **other factors** involved, like availability of **food** for the **prey**. E.g. it's thought that the population of snowshoe hare initially begins to **decline** because there's **too many** of them for the amount of **food available**. This is then **accelerated** by **predation** from the lynx.

Limiting Factors Stop the Population Size of a Species Increasing

1) Limiting factors can be **abiotic**, e.g. the amount of **shelter** in an ecosystem **limits** the population size of a species because there's only enough shelter for a **certain number** of individuals.

2) Limiting factors can also be **biotic**, e.g. **interspecific competition limits** the population size of a species because the amount of **resources** available to a species is **reduced**.

3) Limiting factors determine the **carrying capacity** of an ecosystem.

Parasols and silk cushions were the limiting factors for Ralph's comfort.

Warm-Up Questions

Q1 What is interspecific competition?

Q2 What will be the effect of interspecific competition on the population size of a species?

Q3 Define intraspecific competition.

Q4 What does 'carrying capacity' mean?

Q5 What is a limiting factor?

Exam Question

Q1* The graph on the right shows the population size of a predator species and a prey species over a period of 30 years.

Using the graph, describe and explain how the population sizes of the predator and prey species vary over the first 10 years.

[6 marks]

* You will be assessed on the quality of your written response in this question.

Predator-prey relationships — they don't usually last very long...

You'd think they could have come up with names a little more different than inter- and intraspecific competition. I always remember it as int-er means diff-er-ent species. The factors that affect population size are divided up nicely for you here — just like predators like to nicely divide up their prey into bitesize chunks.

Conservation of Ecosystems

It's important that ecosystems are conserved, so the resources we use from them don't run out.

We Need to **Conserve Ecosystems**

1) **Conservation** is the **protection** and **management** of **ecosystems** so that the **natural resources** in them can be **used** without them **running out**. E.g. using rainforests for timber without any species becoming **extinct** and without any habitats being **destroyed**. This means the natural resources will still be available for **future generations**.

2) It's a **dynamic process** — conservation methods need to be **adapted** to the **constant changes** (caused **naturally** and by **humans**) that occur within ecosystems.

3) Conservation involves the **management** of ecosystems — controlling how **resources** are **used** and **replaced**.

4) Conservation can also involve **reclamation** — **restoring ecosystems** that have been **damaged** or **destroyed** so they can be **used again**, e.g. restoring **forests** that have been **cut down** so they can be used again.

5) Conservation is **important** for many reasons:

> **Economic**
> Ecosystems provide resources for lots of things that humans need, e.g. rainforests contain species that provide things like drugs, clothes and food. These resources are economically important because they're traded on a local and global scale. If the ecosystems aren't conserved, the resources that we use now will be lost, so there will be less trade in the future.

> **Social**
> Many ecosystems bring **joy** to lots of people because they're **attractive** to **look at** and people **use** them for **activities**, e.g. birdwatching and walking. The species and habitats in the ecosystems may be **lost** if they **aren't** conserved, so **future generations** won't be able to use and enjoy them.

> **Ethical**
> 1) Some people think we should conserve ecosystems simply because it's the **right thing to do**, e.g. most people think organisms have a **right to exist**, so they shouldn't become extinct as a result of **human activity**.
> 2) Some people think we have a **moral responsibility** to conserve ecosystems for **future generations**, so they can enjoy and use them.

Cast your mind back to Module 4 — the reasons for conservation are similar to the reasons for conserving biodiversity.

6) **Preservation** is different from conservation — it's the **protection** of ecosystems so they're kept **exactly as they are**. Nothing is **removed** from a preserved ecosystem and they're only **used** for activities that **don't damage** them. For example, **Antarctica** is a preserved ecosystem because it's protected from **exploitation** by humans — it's only used for **limited tourism** and **scientific research**, not **mining** or other **industrial** activities.

Woodland Ecosystems can **Provide Resources** in a **Sustainable Way**

Ecosystems can be **managed** to provide resources in a way that's **sustainable** — this means enough resources are taken to meet the **needs** of people **today**, but without **reducing the ability** of people in the **future** to meet their own needs. **Temperate woodland** can be managed in a **sustainable way** — for every tree that's **cut down** for **timber**, a **new one** is planted in its place. The woodland should never become **depleted**. Cutting down trees and planting new ones needs to be done **carefully** to be **successful**:

Temperate woodland is between the tropics and the polar circles.

1) Trees are cleared in **strips** or **patches** — woodland grows back **more quickly** in smaller areas between bits of **existing woodland** than it does in larger, **open areas**.

2) The cleared strips or patches aren't **too large** or **exposed** — lots of **soil erosion** can occur on large areas of **bare ground**. If the soil is eroded, newly planted trees **won't** be able to **grow**.

3) Timber is sometimes harvested by **coppicing** — **cutting** down trees in a way that lets them **grow back**. This means new trees don't need to be planted.

4) **Native tree species** tend to be planted in **preference** to non-native species. This is **better** for **biodiversity** because native species have long-established **interactions** with other native species (e.g. plants, fungi, animals), so their presence should help species **thrive** in an area. Also some species might not adapt to the presence of non-native tree species.

5) Planted trees are attached to **posts** to provide **support**, and are grown in **plastic tubes** to stop them being **eaten** by grazing animals — this makes it **more likely** the trees will **survive** to become mature adults.

6) Trees **aren't** planted too **close together** — this means the trees aren't **competing** with each other for **space** or **resources**, so they're more likely to **survive**.

Conservation of Ecosystems

Fishing can also Provide Resources in a Sustainable Way

Fish stocks are **declining** because we're **overfishing**. This means there's **less fish** for us to **eat**, the ocean's **food chains** are affected and some species of fish may **disappear** altogether in some areas. To tackle this problem, we need to **maintain fish stocks** at a level where the fish **continue to breed**. This is **sustainable food production** — having enough food without using resources faster than they renew. Here are two examples of how fish stocks can be conserved:

Using Fishing Quotas

1) **Fishing quotas** are **limits** to the **amount** of certain fish species that fishermen are **allowed** to **catch**.

2) **Scientists** study different species and decide **how big** their populations need to be for them to **maintain** their numbers. Then they decide **how many** it's **safe** for fishermen to take without reducing the population **too much**.

3) **International agreements** are made (e.g. the Common Fisheries Policy in the EU) that state the **amount** of fish **each country** can take, and **where** they're allowed to take them from.

4) Fishing quotas are supposed to help to **conserve** fish species by **reducing** the numbers that are **caught** and **killed**, so the populations aren't **reduced** too much and the species aren't at risk from becoming **extinct**.

5) There are **problems** with fishing quotas though — e.g. fish of the wrong species or size are **still caught**, but they end up being **thrown back** into the sea, often **dead** or **dying**, because the restrictions don't allow the fishermen to bring them ashore. However, **new rules** for the Common Fisheries Policy are **banning** the discarding of fish like this and the whole catch will have to be brought ashore to be counted against the quota.

Controlling Mesh Size of Nets

1) There are different **limits** to the **mesh size** of the fish net, depending on what's being fished.

2) This is to **reduce** the number of '**unwanted**' and **discarded fish** that are **accidently caught**, e.g. shrimp caught along with cod. Using a **bigger mesh size** will let the 'unwanted' species **escape**.

3) It also means that **younger fish** will **slip through** the net, allowing them to reach **breeding age**.

4) However, it can be difficult to determine exactly **how big** the mesh size should be in areas where **several different fish species** are fished for at the same time. And **two nets**, each of which meets regulations, could be used **one inside the other** — effectively **reducing** the **reported mesh size**.

Warm-Up Questions

Q1 How is preservation different from conservation?
Q2 What does managing an ecosystem in a sustainable way mean?
Q3 Give one way that fish stocks can be conserved in a sustainable way.

Exam Question

Q1 Some deciduous woodland in the UK is managed through a process called 'coppicing with standards'. The coppiced trees are cut down to the stump, and allowed to regrow from shoots which spring from the stump. The standards are trees that are not cut down and are left to grow and mature as normal.

a) Explain how coppicing allows woodland to be managed sustainably. [1 mark]

b) Suggest two benefits of not coppicing all the trees in a woodland. [2 marks]

c) It's recommended that only about 30% of the canopy is made up of standard trees. Suggest why it is necessary to restrict standard cover. [1 mark]

If I can sustain this revision it'll be a miracle...

Never mind ecosystems, I'm more interested in preserving my sanity after all this hard work. I know it doesn't seem all that sciencey, but you can still study Biology without a lab coat and some Petri dishes. Sustainability's a funny one to get your head around, but you need to know about how it applies to timber production and fishing.

Conservation of Ecosystems

Human activity can often come into conflict with conservation and preservation...

Conservation and Preservation can be Balanced with Human Needs

Areas can be **managed** to **reduce** the **conflict** between conservation and preservation, and human needs.

Example 1 — The Terai Arc

1) The **Terai Arc** is an area of **forest** and **grasslands** on the border between **Nepal** and **India**. A **variety** of **plants** and **animals** are found there, including **endangered species** like the **Bengal Tiger** and **Asian elephant**.

2) Nearly **7 million people** also live in this area and many of them depend on the **forest's resources** to survive.

3) Areas of the forest are also being **destroyed** to make way for **more housing** and **other development** — this **destruction of habitat** brings humans and animals into **closer contact** and **increases conflict** between the two. For example, **elephants** can **eat** and **trample crop fields** and **tigers** can **kill livestock**. This increases the likelihood of these animals being **shot** and **killed**.

4) Conservation charity the **WWF** has worked with **local people** to help **balance** their needs with conserving the forest and its wildlife. For example, the charity has provided people with things like **solar cookers** and **biogas generators**, so they **don't need** to use **wood** from the forest as **fuel**. Farmers are encouraged to plant **mint hedges** around their crops to **keep animals** (which don't like the taste of mint) **away**.

Example 2 — The Maasai Mara

1) The **Maasai Mara** is a national reserve in **Kenya**. It's a large area of **grassland** (**savannah**), which is home to huge populations of **wildebeest** and **zebra**, as well as **lions** and **cheetahs**. The Maasai Mara is named after the **Maasai people** who live in the area.

2) The Maasai people traditionally **earn a living** by raising **livestock**, such as **cattle**. This can bring them into **conflict** with conservationists — e.g. **overgrazing** by **livestock** can destroy grassland for **wildlife**.

3) Conservation trusts are working with the Maasai people to help them **make money** from their land through **conservation** and **ecotourism projects** rather than farming, and to **farm** in a **sustainable way**. So, the **economic needs** of the Maasai people are met, while still allowing the area to be conserved.

Example 3 — UK Peat Bogs

1) Lots of **upland** parts of the **UK** are home to **peat bogs** — areas of wet peat. These peat bogs **store water** and **carbon dioxide**, and are home to **lots of different plants** and **animals**, such as *Sphagnum* moss — these mosses actually help the peat bog form by retaining water.

2) Farmers use the peat bogs to **graze sheep** and **deer**. However, this can lead to **conflict** with conservationists because **overgrazing** causes **loss of moss species**, **soil compaction** (which increases **water runoff** down sheep paths, taking sediment with it) and general peat bog **erosion**.

3) Recent **government-funded programmes**, like the Environmental Stewardship Scheme, have given farmers **money** to use the peat bogs in a sustainable way, e.g. to carry out measures to **reduce water runoff**, to **lower** the **number** of **livestock** that use the peat bogs, and to **remove livestock** over **winter**.

Human Activities Affect Environmentally-Sensitive Ecosystems

The **animal** and **plant populations** in **important**, but **fragile**, **ecosystems** have been affected by **human activity**. Here are some examples, along with information on how these effects are being **controlled**:

1) The Galapagos Islands

The **Galapagos Islands** are a small group of islands in the **Pacific Ocean**. Many **rare species** of **animals** and **plants** have evolved there that **can't be found elsewhere**. In the past the islands have attracted **sailors**, **explorers** and **scientists**, but recently the number of **inhabitants** and **tourists** to the islands has increased considerably.

Effects of Human Activities:

1) **Non-native animals introduced** to the islands by humans **eat** some native species. This has caused a decrease in the populations of native species. E.g. non-native **dogs**, **cats** and **black rats** eat young **giant tortoises** and **Galapagos land iguanas**. **Goats** have eaten much of the **plant life** on some of the islands.

2) **Non-native plants** have also been introduced to the islands. These **compete** with native plant species, causing a decrease in their populations. For example, **quinine trees** are **taller** than some native plants — they **block out light** to the native plants, which then **struggle** to **survive**.

Conservation of Ecosystems

Methods of Control:

1) **Eradication programmes** have **removed wild goats** from some of the smaller islands and **wild dogs** from the largest island. **Quinine trees** are kept in check using **chemical herbicides** and by **uprooting** young trees.

2) When people visit the Galapagos National Park they are expected to follow a list of **rules**, which includes not bringing any **live plants** or **animals** onto the islands, or moving them between the islands. People are also only allowed to visit the Galapagos National Park in the company of a **licensed guide**.

2) Antarctica

Antarctica is the world's **southernmost continent**. It has a **unique icy landscape** with plants and animals that have adapted to its **harsh conditions**. For at least 200 years it has attracted **visitors**, e.g. research scientists and tourists.

Effects of Human Activities:

1) **Visitors** to Antarctica have caused **pollution** in the past by dumping **sewage** into the sea and leaving **rubbish**. **Shipping accidents** have lead to **oil spills**, which severely affect wildlife.

2) **Hunting**, **whaling** and **fishing** have all **reduced wildlife populations** in the area.

Methods of Control:

1) **All waste** apart from food waste and sewage must be **taken away by ship** for disposal in other countries. Many research stations now **treat** their **sewage** before releasing it, to reduce its effects on the environment.

2) **Ships** that use **thick oil** as a **fuel** are now **banned** from **Antarctic waters** — heavy oil spills are likely to cause more damage and be harder to clean up than spills of lighter fuels.

3) There are **tourist restrictions** — e.g. tourists are only allowed on land at **certain locations** for **a few hours**.

4) **Hunting** and **whaling** have been **banned** for some time now, although fishing still continues.

3) The **Lake District** and **Snowdonia National Parks**

The **Lake District** and **Snowdonia** are **beautiful national parks** — both are areas of **hills** and **lakes**, with the **Lake District** in North West England and **Snowdonia** in Wales. Both also attract **millions of visitors** per year.

Effects of Human Activities:

1) Many of the visitors to the Lake District go **walking** on the region's **footpaths**. This leads to the **erosion** of the footpaths and the **loss of soil** from **hillsides**. Soil that ends up in **waterways** and **lakes** can **disturb the pH** of the **water**, causing knock-on effects for wildlife. As the paths become harder to walk on, people can start to **trample** and **destroy** the **sensitive vegetation** either side of the paths.

2) It's a similar story in **Snowdonia** — a lot of **rain** falls in the Snowdonia hills, which leads to the **erosion** of the paths. Walkers often **trample the surrounding vegetation** as they try to walk around the floods.

Methods of Control:

1) Simple really — in the Lake District, conservation charities and the Lake District National Park Authority attempt to carry out **regular repair** and **maintenance work** on the paths and **encourage** the **regrowth** of **damaged vegetation**. Walkers are also **educated** about the importance of sticking to the paths and not taking short cuts, as these increase erosion.

2) In Snowdonia, volunteers have **dug drains** next to the paths to prevent them from flooding.

Warm-Up Questions

Q1 Give one effect of human activity on the Galapagos Islands and an example of how this is being controlled.

Exam Question

Q1 Compare the ways in which the economic needs of humans have been balanced with conservation in three named areas of the world. [4 marks]

All I know is that exams affect my environmentally-sensitive system...

Ecosystems can be managed so that the needs of humans in the area can be met, but human activities also need to be controlled to protect ecosystems. Make sure you know all of the examples on these two pages. Off. By. Heart.

Extra Exam Practice

That's the end of <u>Module 6</u> — now it's time to put your knowledge of the module to the test...

- Have a look at this example of how to answer a tricky exam question.
- Then check how much you've understood from Module 6 by having a go at the questions on the next page.

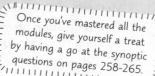
Once you've mastered all the modules, give yourself a treat by having a go at the synoptic questions on pages 258-265.

1 Epidermolysis bullosa simplex (EBS) is a skin disorder caused by a dominant allele. **Figure 1** shows the incidence of EBS in a family, over three generations. Horizontal lines between two individuals link mating parents and vertical lines link parents and offspring.

Figure 1

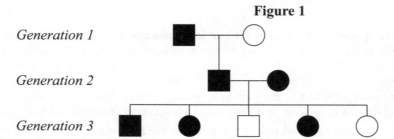

Generation 1

Generation 2

Generation 3

Key:
- ■ Male with EBS
- □ Male without EBS
- ● Female with EBS
- ○ Female without EBS

(a) Explain how **Figure 1** shows that the allele which causes EBS is dominant.

(2 marks)

(b) It is estimated that 1 in every 17 000 children that are born in the UK, will inherit EBS. The Hardy-Weinberg equations are:

$$p^2 + 2pq + q^2 = 1 \quad \text{where } p = \text{the frequency of the dominant allele}$$
$$p + q = 1 \quad \text{and } q = \text{the frequency of the recessive allele}$$

Calculate the percentage of people in the UK that are heterozygous for EBS. Show your working and give your answer to one significant figure.

(3 marks)

The son of Generation 1 could have inherited a recessive allele from each parent, or a dominant allele from his father — it's difficult to answer the question until you look at the offspring of Generation 2.

1(a)

Both parents in **Generation 2** have EBS but two of their children don't. The parents in Generation 2 must have, either, at least **one dominant allele** each, or **two recessive alleles** each.

If the allele which causes EBS was recessive then it would be **impossible** for two homozygous recessive parents to have any children without EBS, as each child would have inherited two recessive EBS alleles. As there are **two children without EBS**, it can be concluded that the allele which causes EBS is dominant.

1(b)

Use the information from the question to work out where to start.

EBS is **coded for by a dominant allele** so children with the disease could have the homozygous dominant genotype or the heterozygous genotype.

So, $p^2 + 2pq = 1 \div 17\ 000 = 5.88... \times 10^{-5}$

$p^2 + 2pq + q^2 = 1$, so $q^2 = 1 - 5.88... \times 10^{-5} = 9.99... \times 10^{-1}$

$q = \sqrt{9.99...} \times 10^{-1} = 9.99... \times 10^{-1}$

$p + q = 1$, so $p = 1 - 9.99... \times 10^{-1} = 2.94... \times 10^{-5}$

Heterozyotes $= 2pq = 2 \times 2.94... \times 10^{-5} \times 9.99... \times 10^{-1} = 5.88... \times 10^{-5}$

Percentage $= 5.88... \times 10^{-5} \times 100 = 0.00588...\% = 0.006\%$

You'd get 3 marks for the correct answer, but if your final answer was wrong you could still pick up 1 mark for correctly identifying $p^2 + 2pq$ as children with EBS, and 1 mark for correctly identifying $2pq$ as heterozygotes.

You'd pick up 1 mark for identifying that both parents in Generation 2 must carry a dominant allele and 1 mark for explaining how you know this based on the phenotypes of Generation 3.

Don't round until the end. You can use the 'Ans' button on your calculator to carry the result of one step over to the next.

You've been asked for a percentage so convert from a decimal by multiplying by 100.

Extra Exam Practice

2 **Figure 2** shows the biomass of three different types of plants during succession of a woodland.

Figure 2

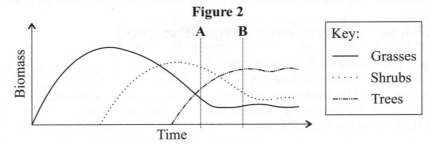

(a) **(i)** The grasses shown in **Figure 2** require soil in order to grow.
Explain why this means that **Figure 2** does not show primary succession.

(2 marks)

(ii) The carrying capacity of several shrub species in the woodland is lower at point **B** than it is at point **A**. Using **Figure 2**, explain why interspecific competition may be responsible for this.

(2 marks)

(b) Wildfires are rapidly spreading fires that can occur naturally in wild areas such as forests. Trees growing in areas with frequent wildfires often have thicker bark than trees growing in areas with very infrequent wildfires. The thicker bark helps to protect the trees when there is a wildfire. Explain the type of natural selection that may have acted on populations of trees frequently exposed to wildfires.

(3 marks)

3 Until the 1980s, the insulin used for treating Type 1 diabetes was extracted from the pancreases of pigs or cows. Now insulin can be produced by *E. coli* bacteria, by inserting the gene for human insulin into the bacterial cells.

(a) Suggest **two** advantages of using transformed *E. coli* as a source of insulin rather than pigs or cows.

(2 marks)

(b) **(i)** Once present in *E. coli* DNA, the human insulin gene is transcribed by the T7 RNA polymerase. The transcription of T7 RNA polymerase is controlled by a *lac* operon. Explain how the *lac* operon could allow scientists to control the production of insulin.

(4 marks)

(ii) Once *E. coli* has been transformed, the population size of the bacteria could be increased using fed-batch fermentation. This process is similar to batch fermentation, except that nutrients can be added to the fermentation vessel while the bacteria are growing. Explain why growing *E. coli* using fed-batch fermentation may delay the onset of the stationary phase of the bacterial growth curve, compared to batch fermentation.

(2 marks)

(c) A scientist investigating the transformed *E. coli* grew colonies of the bacteria on an agar plate.

(i) The scientist started with a solution containing 1.5×10^4 bacterial cells per cm^3 and added $1 \ cm^3$ of this solution to a test tube containing $9 \ cm^3$ of a sterile buffer. She mixed the contents of the test tube and then transferred $0.1 \ cm^3$ of the solution from the test tube to the agar plate. Calculate how many bacterial cells were transferred to the agar plate.

(2 marks)

(ii) The agar plate was incubated for 10 hours, during which time the number of bacterial cells doubled every 30 minutes. Each colony that formed developed from a single bacterial cell. Calculate the number of bacterial cells in each colony after 10 hours. Give your answer in standard form to three significant figures.

(2 marks)

How To Do Well in Your Exams

The reason for learning all the lovely facts and diagrams in this book is so that you can ace your exams and get yourself an A-level in Biology. So, now it's a good idea to find out exactly what you'll be in for exam-wise...

Make Sure You Know the **Structure** of Your **Exams**

It seems obvious, but if you know exactly what will be **covered** in each of the exams, how much **time** you'll have to do them and how they'll be **structured**, you can be better prepared. So let's take a look at the ins and outs of all the exams you'll be facing for **A-level Biology**...

All this exam info is **only relevant** if you're taking the A-level in Biology. If you're taking the AS-level, you'll be sitting a **completely different set of papers**, which are structured in a different way. There are two AS-level papers that both test Modules 1 to 4.

	Paper	No. of marks	Time	Modules assessed	Type of questions in paper	
01	Biological Processes	100	2 hrs 15 mins	1, 2, 3, 5	Section A (15 marks) — multiple choice	Section B (85 marks) — short answer and extended response
02	Biological Diversity	100	2 hrs 15 mins	1, 2, 4, 6	Section A (15 marks) — multiple choice	Section B (85 marks) — short answer and extended response
03	Unified Biology	70	1 hr 30 mins	1, 2, 3, 4, 5, 6	No multiple choice. Short answer or extended response throughout.	

As you can see from the table...

1) **All three papers** cover theory from **both years** of your course — this means you need to make sure you **revise** your **Year 1** modules (1-4) as well as your **Year 2** modules (5-6) for these exams. The papers will contain some **synoptic** questions, which **connect** and **test** different areas of Biology from Years 1 and 2.

2) For each paper you get **just over a minute per mark**. This means if you get stuck on a short question it's sometimes worth moving onto another one and then coming back to it if you have time. However, bear in mind that you might want to spend a **bit longer** on the **extended response** questions, in which case you'll have to spend **less time** on the multiple choice and short answer questions.

3) In **Section A** of the **Biological Processes** and **Biological Diversity** papers you'll have **15 multiple choice questions**. Each question will have four possible answers **(A-D)** but only one will be correct.

4) All three papers include **short answer** and **extended response** questions. Short answer questions may involve **problem solving**, **calculations** or a **practical context** (see next page). There's more about extended response questions below...

Julie had heard of multiple choice, but this just took the biscuit...

All of Your Exams Will Contain **Extended Response** Questions

1) In each of your three papers there will be **one** or **more extended response** questions.

2) These questions are worth **6** or **9 marks** and will require a **long answer**.

3) The questions are shown with an **asterisk** (*) next to their number.

4) You'll be awarded marks for the **quality** of your extended response as well as the **content** of your answer, so your answer needs to:

These questions often want you to use a source (such as some text or a diagram, table or graph) to help you answer the question.

- Be **legible** (the same goes for all your written answers).
- Have a **clear** and **logical structure**.
- Show **good reasoning** — i.e. show that you have thought about and understood the question, and can justify your answer.
- Include information that's **relevant** to the question.

5) You can gain **practice** at extended response questions by doing the exam questions marked with an asterisk in this book.

How To Do Well in Your Exams

Command Words Tell You **What You Need to do** in a Question

Command words are just the bits of a question that tell you **what to do**. You'll find answering exam questions much easier if you understand exactly what they mean, so here's a brief summary table of the **most common** ones:

Command word:	What to do:
Give / Name / State	Give a brief one or two word answer, or a short sentence.
Identify	Pick out information or say what something is.
Describe	Write about what something's like, e.g. describe the structure of fish gills.
Explain	Give reasons for something.
Suggest	Use your scientific knowledge to work out what the answer might be.
Compare	Give the similarities and differences between two things.
Outline	Write about the main points of a topic.
Calculate	Work out the solution to a mathematical problem.
Discuss	Write about a topic, considering different issues or ideas.

Even though you're taking an A-level in Biology, you'll still need to do some maths in the exams — but it'll be set in a biological context.

Some questions will also ask you to answer '**using the information/data provided**' (e.g. a graph, table or passage of text) or '**with reference to figure X**' — if so, you must **refer to** the information, data or figure you've been given or you won't get the marks. Some questions may also ask you to answer '**using your calculation**' — it's the same here, you need to use **your answer** to a particular **calculation**, otherwise you won't get the marks.

Not all of the questions will have command words, e.g. the multiple choice questions — instead they may just ask a which / why / what type of question.

Solving Problems in a **Practical Context**

Make sure you learn the language that goes with experiments too, e.g. precision, accuracy, validity — see page 4 of Module 1 for more.

In the exams, you'll get plenty of questions set in a 'practical context'. As well as answering questions about the **methods** used or the **conclusions** drawn (see Module 1), you'll need to be able to **apply** your **scientific knowledge** to **solve problems** set in these contexts. For example:

> Q1 A scientist is investigating the effect on plant growth of adding additional CO_2 to the air in a greenhouse. The results are shown in the graph.
>
> a) Explain the difference in the two curves shown on the graph. [3 marks]

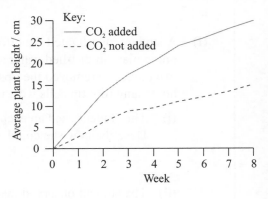

You should remember from Module 5 that plants use carbon dioxide to produce glucose by photosynthesis. The more carbon dioxide plants have, the more glucose they can produce (until something other than CO_2 becomes a limiting factor), meaning they can also respire more. This gives them more ATP for DNA replication, cell division and protein synthesis, leading to increased plant growth.

You might think you need your head examined for picking A-level Biology...

... because there's a lot to learn and three big exams to do. But let me just stop you right there... instead of worrying, just work through this book, including having a go at all of the questions, and you'll be well and truly prepped for the exams. Then re-read these pages to make sure you know what's coming. After that, all there is to say is... good luck.

Synoptic Practice

There's no denying that synoptic questions are tough — I reckon that's why examiners love them so much. You'll need a good knowledge of the whole course to answer these questions as each one pulls in different parts of the course to test you on. Luckily, these pages are chock full of synoptic practice...

1   Lectins are carbohydrate-binding proteins that are found in most plants.

(a)   Lectins secreted by the seeds of some plants can bind to the surface of some *Rhizobium* bacteria and assist the attachment of these bacteria onto the roots of the plants.
Explain how this action of lectins could be beneficial for plants.

(2 marks)

Some lectins can result in increased mitosis in their target cells.

(b)   An increase in mitosis can be linked to a loss of function of the cell cycle checkpoints.
Explain how the loss of function of the G2 cell cycle checkpoint could negatively affect protein synthesis in the resulting daughter cell.

(2 marks)

(c)   Explain the importance of the breakdown and formation of nuclear envelopes during mitosis.

(2 marks)

(d)   Lectins can result in increased mitosis in their target cells because they act as messenger molecules and pass signals to their target cells.
Suggest how lectins are able to communicate only with their target cells.

(2 marks)

(e)   An increase in mitosis in the cells of plant roots can damage the tissues in the root and reduce water uptake by plants. In response to a reduction in water uptake, plants may close their stomata.

(i)   Which chemical produced by plants is responsible for stomatal closure?

(1 mark)

(ii)   Explain why stomatal closure is a beneficial response to reduced water uptake.

(1 mark)

(iii)   Explain how prolonged stomatal closure could affect the amounts of ribulose bisphosphate and glycerate 3-phosphate in the chloroplasts of a plant.

(3 marks)

(f)   A student investigated the effect of lectins on the growth of roots of onion plants. She grew one onion plant in distilled water and another in a lectin solution. After leaving the plants to grow for two days, she removed the tips of the roots and observed them under a microscope to determine how many root tip cells were undergoing mitosis.

(i)   The student used an eyepiece graticule to measure some of the cells she observed.
Describe how she could have worked out the value of the divisions on the eyepiece graticule.

(1 mark)

(ii)   The student observed that more root tip cells were undergoing mitosis in the roots of the onion plant she had placed in lectin solution, compared to those in the roots of the onion plant she placed in distilled water. From these results, she concluded that lectin solution increased the rate of mitosis in onion plant root cells.
Explain one reason why this may not be a valid conclusion.

(1 mark)

Synoptic Practice

2   A simplified food chain is shown in **Figure 1**.

Figure 1

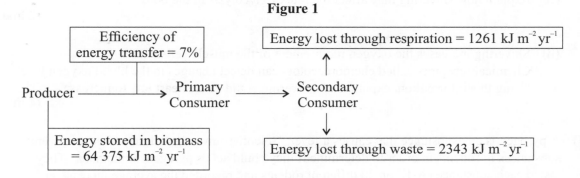

(a)   During summer, the energy stored in the biomass of the producer increases.
This is partly due to an increased activity rate of RuBisCO.
Explain how an increase in the activity rate of RuBisCO could lead to more energy being stored
in biomass.

(2 marks)

(b)   The secondary consumer in **Figure 1** does not ingest 10% of the material available in
the primary consumer.
Using this information and **Figure 1**, calculate the energy stored in biomass in the
secondary consumer. Give your answer to four significant figures.

(3 marks)

(c)   The breathing rate of the secondary consumer increases when it is hunting for food.
Explain how this helps to maximise the rate of ATP synthesis in the secondary consumer.

(3 marks)

(d)   A farmer wanted to introduce livestock into this ecosystem to feed on the producer.
In order to increase the growth rate of her livestock, she planned to introduce more individuals
of the secondary consumer. The secondary consumer is not a predator of the livestock species.
Explain why increasing the population size of the secondary consumer could increase the growth
rate of the farmer's livestock.

(2 marks)

3   Fever can form part of the immune response to a pathogenic infection.
A fever is characterised by an unusually high body temperature.

(a)   Explain how goblet cells could help to protect a person from developing fever.

(2 marks)

(b)   A person with a fever had their temperature recorded regularly over a 48 hour period.
The results are shown in **Table 1**.

Table 1

Time	3:00	9:00	15:00	21:00	3:00	9:00	15:00	21:00	3:00
Temperature / °C	38.4	37.3	38.8	37.8	37.9	36.8	39.6	39.5	37.7

Using the information in **Table 1**, explain whether body temperature associated with fever is
an example of negative or positive feedback.

(1 mark)

Synoptic Practice

(c) During a fever, the body shivers, which is the involuntary, rapid contraction and relaxation of muscles.

    (i) Explain how shivering may affect the rate of glycolysis in the body.

        (2 marks)

    (ii) Shivering increases the oxygen requirement of the muscle cells.
Chemical receptors called chemoreceptors can detect changes in the blood oxygen level.
Using this information, explain how shivering could cause heart rate to increase.

        (4 marks)

(d) A pyrogen is any substance that causes a fever. Scientists investigated the effects of several substances in rodents in order to determine if they could act as pyrogens in humans. They tested each substance (**A-E**) on 20 different rodents and recorded the average increase in body temperature they caused. Their results are shown in **Table 2**.

Table 2

Substance	Average increase in body temperature / °C	Range / °C	Standard deviation / °C
A	0.3	0.5	± 0.2
B	1.1	0.6	± 0.3
C	1.0	0.9	± 0.7
D	1.2	1.1	± 0.6
E	0.9	0.7	± 0.3

    (i) The range and standard deviation are both values that indicate how the results are dispersed. Explain which measure is better for judging the precision of the results shown in **Table 2**.

        (2 marks)

The scientists carried out a Student's t-test to determine whether there was a significant difference between the results for substances **A** and **B** at the 5% level.

    (ii) Suggest what the scientists' null hypothesis would have been.

        (1 mark)

    (iii) Calculate the t-value which the scientists would need in order to decide whether or not they could reject their null hypothesis.
Use the formula below and give your answer to two significant figures.

$$t = \frac{\bar{x}_1 - \bar{x}_2}{\sqrt{\left(\frac{s_1^2}{n_1}\right) + \left(\frac{s_2^2}{n_2}\right)}}$$

Where, $\bar{x}$ = mean
s = standard deviation
n = number of values in a group
$_1$ or $_2$ = the group being referred to

        (2 marks)

    (iv) Calculate the degrees of freedom the scientists would need to use when determining whether their t-value is significant.

        (1 mark)

    (v) Describe how the scientists would use their t-value and the degrees of freedom to determine whether or not to reject their null hypothesis.

        (2 marks)

Synoptic Practice

4 Huntington's disease is an inherited disorder for which there is currently no cure. The gene responsible for the disease is called *HTT*, which codes for the production of the huntingtin protein. A mutation in the *HTT* gene can lead to many additional CAG triplet repeats being added to the DNA sequence.

(a) Suggest why the mutation in the *HTT* gene leads to the formation of a defective huntingtin protein.

(2 marks)

(b) The mutated *HTT* gene results in the production of a huntingtin protein that can lead to degradation of the neurones in the cerebellum of the brain.

(i) Using this information, suggest **one** symptom of Huntington's disease.

(1 mark)

(ii) Brain tissue contains a dense network of neurones. Scientists can use tissue samples taken from the brains of deceased people who had Huntington's disease to help develop their understanding of the progression of the disease.
Evaluate the use of transmission electron microscopes and scanning electron microscopes for investigating the neuronal damage in the brain of a person who had Huntington's disease.

(4 marks)

(c) Scientists are researching the use of stem cells to treat diseases such as Huntington's disease. Suggest why stem cells could be used to treat Huntington's disease.

(2 marks)

(d) A genetic test can be used to determine if a person has a mutation in the *HTT* gene that would mean that they are at risk of developing Huntington's disease. During the genetic test, a blood sample is taken from the person and the DNA isolated. PCR can then be used to create many copies of the *HTT* gene present in the DNA.

(i) Explain why DNA needs to be temporarily heated to 95 °C during the PCR procedure.

(2 marks)

Electrophoresis can be carried out on the products of PCR, and the results used to help determine whether the person is likely to develop Huntington's disease.

(ii) Suggest how electrophoresis could be used to determine if a person is at risk of developing Huntington's disease.

(2 marks)

(iii) **Figure 2** shows the generic structure of a phosphate group.

Figure 2

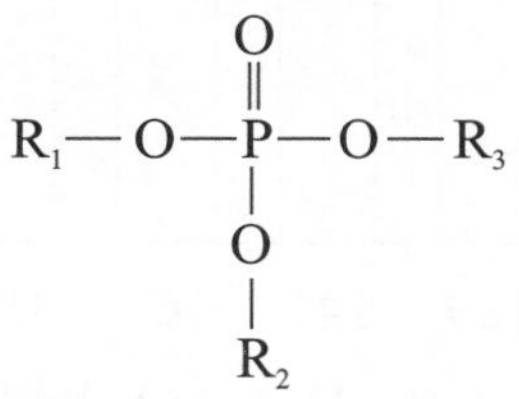

$$R_1 - O - \overset{\overset{\textstyle O}{\|}}{\underset{\underset{\textstyle R_2}{|}}{P}} - O - R_3$$

The R_1-R_3 variable groups indicate other atoms or molecules that can be bonded to the oxygen atoms, such as a hydrogen atom. If nothing else is bonded to any of the oxygen atoms then the molecule is called a phosphate ion. The presence of phosphate groups in DNA allows electrophoresis to be used in genetic tests such as the test for Huntington's disease. Using this information and your knowledge of the structure of DNA, suggest why DNA fragments move during electrophoresis.

(3 marks)

Synoptic Practice

5   Neuromuscular blockers are a group of muscle relaxant drugs often used to ensure patients do not move during surgery. The drugs act at neuromuscular junctions, where they can affect the nicotinic cholinergic receptors found on the postsynaptic membrane.

(a)   **(i)**   One such drug prevents acetylcholine from binding to nicotinic cholinergic receptors. Explain how this neuromuscular blocker would prevent muscle contraction.

(5 marks)

(ii)   Another type of neuromuscular blocker works by binding to nicotinic cholinergic receptors and generating an action potential. The drug remains bound to the receptors for a long time, resulting in extended depolarisation of the postsynaptic membrane.
Using your knowledge of how an action potential works, explain how this drug prevents a person from moving.

(2 marks)

(iii)   Other than binding to nicotinic cholinergic receptors, suggest **one** way in which a drug could act at a neuromuscular junction to prevent a person from moving.

(1 mark)

(b)   The administration of some neuromuscular blockers can prevent the contraction of the intercostal muscles. Explain why patients administered these types of drugs are at risk of low blood oxygen concentration.

(3 marks)

(c)   Scientists investigated how the dose of a neuromuscular blocker given to patients affected the force of muscle contraction. In their investigation, the scientists measured the force of contraction of one muscle in the body before the patient had been given any of the drug and again once they had received a dose of the drug. 80 patients were included in the investigation. The results are shown in **Figure 3**.

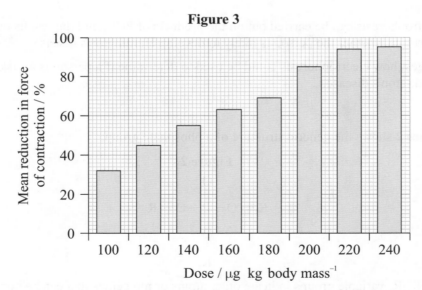

Figure 3

For the drug to be classed as suitable for use in surgery, the scientists recommended that the patient should have no more than 15% of their usual force of contraction remaining. Using this information and **Figure 3**, calculate the minimum amount of the drug in mg that should be given to a patient with a body mass of 75 kg.

(2 marks)

Synoptic Practice

(d) In the liver, there is a layer of endothelial cells between the hepatocytes and the sinusoids. Some studies have shown that old age may be associated with an increased thickness of these endothelial cells. Using the information provided, suggest why a neuromuscular blocker may have a prolonged effect in an elderly patient.

(3 marks)

(e) After surgery, patients can be given anticholinesterases to help overcome the effects of the neuromuscular blockers. Anticholinesterases have an inhibitory effect on the enzyme, acetylcholinesterase, which normally breaks down acetylcholine in the synaptic cleft. Suggest how anticholinesterases work to overcome the effects of the neuromuscular blockers.

(2 marks)

6 Familial hypercholesterolaemia (FH) is an inherited medical condition that is characterised by a high blood cholesterol level. Normally, low density lipoproteins (LDLs) carry cholesterol molecules through the blood and into body cells, by binding to LDL receptors present on cells. FH can be caused by many mutations that affect the LDL receptor gene and result in defective LDL receptors, causing cholesterol to remain in the blood.

(a) There are several mutations that can lead to the LDL receptor being defective. An individual was screened for mutations in their LDL receptor gene that would put them at risk of FH. They were found to have a mutation that resulted in a change from the triplet code CCG to CTG. No other mutations were detected. Explain why this mutation may have less harmful effects than a deletion mutation.

(4 marks)

(b) **Figure 4** shows the incidence of FH in some members of a family. Horizontal lines between two individuals link mating parents and vertical lines link parents and offspring.

Figure 4

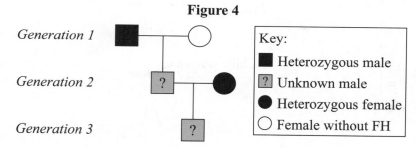

FH can be described as an autosomal dominant disease.
One student concluded that the Generation 3 male has a 50% chance of inheriting FH.
Evaluate this conclusion.

(3 marks)

(c) It is estimated that around 1 in every 1 000 000 people in the UK is homozygous for the FH allele.

(i) A city in the UK has an estimated population size of 9.62×10^6 people. Calculate an estimate of how many people in this UK city are homozygous for the FH allele.

(1 mark)

(ii) The Hardy-Weinberg equations are:

$$p^2 + 2pq + q^2 = 1 \quad \text{where } p = \text{the frequency of the dominant allele}$$
$$p + q = 1 \quad \text{and } q = \text{the frequency of the recessive allele}$$

Calculate the frequency of the heterozygous genotype in the UK.
Show your working and give your answer to two significant figures.

(2 marks)

Synoptic Practice

(d) People with FH can be given drugs, called statins, to reduce their blood cholesterol level. However, there are some side-effects associated with statins, such as an increased risk of developing Type 2 diabetes. Scientists hope that somatic gene therapy could eventually be used as an alternative treatment for FH.

(i) Statins can increase the expression of a protein complex called NLRP3 inflammasome. This protein complex can lead to the inflammation of β cells in the islets of Langerhans. Suggest an explanation for how this could lead to the development of Type 2 diabetes.

(5 marks)

(ii) Suggest **two** ethical reasons why people may disagree with research into somatic gene therapy for FH.

(2 marks)

7 Light is an important abiotic factor for optimum crop plant growth.

(a) Over several years, large areas of a farmer's crop fields have become more shaded. Rabbits are a pest species that feed on the farmer's crop plants. Explain how the increase in shade may have changed the carrying capacity of the rabbits living in the fields.

(3 marks)

Plant leaves contain photosynthetic pigments, which can absorb different wavelengths of light. **Figure 5** shows the absorption spectra for two photosynthetic pigments found in plant leaves, chlorophyll a and chlorophyll b.

Figure 5

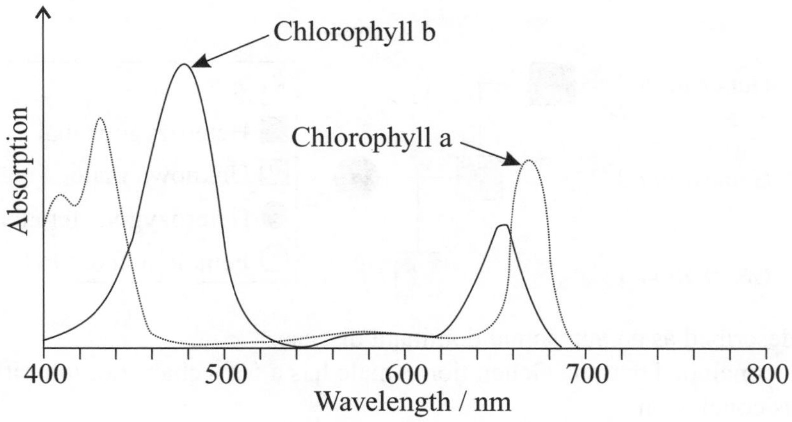

Far-red light is light with a wavelength of around 700-800 nm.

(b) (i) Using **Figure 5**, explain why exposure to only far-red light could limit plant growth.

(3 marks)

(ii) Far-red light is reflected off the leaves of plants. Plants can detect an increase in the amount of far-red light, which indicates that their environment may have become more shaded. Far-red light is detected by a photoreceptor called phytochrome. When phytochrome is exposed to far-red light, it is converted from an active form (Pfr) into an inactive form (Pr). Pfr inhibits the activity of a protein called TTA1, which is involved in the synthesis of the auxin indoleacetic acid (IAA). Suggest and explain how the detection of far-red light could help a plant to maximise growth as its environment becomes more shaded.

(3 marks)

Synoptic Practice

(c) When different individuals of the same plant species have been grown in either shaded or brightly lit environments, they have been observed to develop different phenotypes.
Explain why the binding of transcription factors to DNA can lead to differences in phenotypes between two organisms that have the same genome.

(3 marks)

(d) A scientist wanted to investigate whether the amount of shade or light a plant was exposed to had an effect on the photosynthetic pigments in the plant.

(i) She planned to gather plant samples from a field using a systematic sampling technique. Suggest how she could gather her samples using this technique.

(2 marks)

(ii) The scientist planned to carry out thin layer chromatography to separate the photosynthetic pigments from leaves exposed to shade and leaves exposed to light, and then use her chromatagram to identify each pigment present in the leaves. Explain why marking the solvent front on the chromatography paper would be an essential stage in the scientist's method.

(2 marks)

8 Including omega 3 in the diet is believed to be important for heart health.
A good source of omega 3 is oily fish, such as salmon.

(a) **Figure 6** shows a simplified diagram of the structure of omega 3.

Figure 6

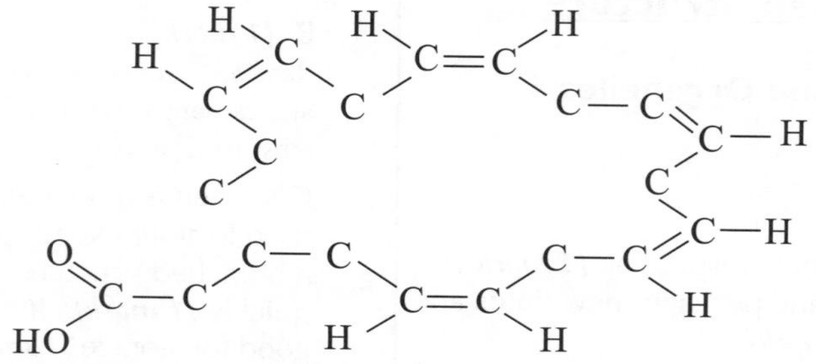

Omega 3 can form part of a macromolecule.
Name and describe the structure of **one** type of macromolecule that could contain omega 3.

(2 marks)

(b) As the human population increases, demand for seafood rises, which may be partly responsible for the decline observed in wild fish populations. Conservation methods, such as limits to the number of fish that can be caught, aim to protect the remaining populations from the effects of overfishing. Explain how this conservation method differs from preservation methods that could be used to protect wild fish populations.

(1 mark)

(c)* Some methods of salmon farming can help to meet the growing demand for salmon with little to no impact on wild salmon populations. Artificial selection and improved farming methods over nearly 50 years have led to farmed Atlantic salmon that grow faster than wild types, reaching the required weight for harvesting around 12 months faster than wild salmon.

AquAdvantage® salmon has been approved for human consumption in the USA. This salmon is a genetically modified Atlantic salmon, generated using a gene for a growth hormone from a Chinook salmon and a promoter sequence from an ocean pout. This genetic manipulation allows the AquAdvantage® salmon to grow all year round, meaning they can grow faster than standard farmed Atlantic salmon.

Describe the method that may have been used to generate AquAdvantage® salmon and evaluate the use of AquAdvantage® salmon to meet demand for salmon rather than artificial selection.

(9 marks)

* You will be assessed on the quality of your written response in this question.

Answers

Module 1 — Development of Practical Skills

Page 9 — Drawing Conclusions and Evaluating

1 a) E.g. light intensity — it could be controlled by using a lamp a set distance away from the apparatus *[1 mark]*.

b) 46 cm³ ÷ 480 s = **0.096 cm³ s⁻¹** (accept answers between **0.09 cm³ s⁻¹** and **0.11 cm³ s⁻¹**) *[2 marks for correct answer, otherwise 1 mark for correct working]*

c) The Student's t-test *[1 mark]* because two means are being compared *[1 mark]*.

d) i) (1 ÷ 48) × 100 = **2.1%** *[1 mark]*

   ii) E.g. by using a smaller measuring cylinder *[1 mark]*.
   A smaller measuring cylinder is likely to be more sensitive as it will have smaller increments, which will lower the uncertainty in the experiment.

e) At each temperature the rate of photosynthesis was high for the first few minutes of the experiment and then started to level off after that — at 20 °C the rate of photosynthesis levelled off after 2.5 minutes, at 15 °C after 4 minutes and at 10 °C after 7 minutes *[1 mark]*. Overall the rate of photosynthesis was higher at a higher temperature *[1 mark]*.

Module 2: Section 1 — Cell Structure

Page 13 — Eukaryotic Cells and Organelles

1 B *[1 mark]*

2 a) i) mitochondrion *[1 mark]*
   ii) Golgi apparatus *[1 mark]*

b) Mitochondria are the site of aerobic respiration *[1 mark]*. The Golgi apparatus processes and packages new lipids and proteins / makes lysosomes *[1 mark]*.

Page 15 — Prokaryotic Cells

1 a) Ribosomes *[1 mark]* because this is where protein synthesis occurs *[1 mark]*.

b) The rough endoplasmic reticulum *[1 mark]* and some vesicles *[1 mark]*.

c) Vesicles transport substances in and out of the cell and between organelles *[1 mark]*.

2 Any three from: supports the cell's organelles *[1 mark]*. / Strengthens the cell/maintains its shape *[1 mark]*. / Transports materials around the cell *[1 mark]*. / Enables cell movement *[1 mark]*.

Page 17 — Studying Cells — How Microscopes Work

1 Magnification = image size ÷ object size
                 = 80 mm ÷ 0.5 mm *[1 mark]*
                 = × 160 *[1 mark]*
Always remember to convert everything to the same units first — the insect is 0.5 mm long, so the length of the image needs to be changed from 8 cm to 80 mm.

2 Image size = magnification × object size
             = 100 × 0.059 mm *[1 mark]*
             = **5.9 mm** *[1 mark]*
Hint: To convert 59 μm into mm, divide by 1000.

3 a) mitochondrion *[1 mark]* and nucleus *[1 mark]*
The resolution of light microscopes is not good enough to show objects smaller than 0.2 μm *[1 mark]*.

b) All of the organelles in the table would be visible *[1 mark]*. The resolution of SEMs is good enough to resolve objects down to about 0.002 μm in size *[1 mark]*.

Page 19 — Studying Cells — Using Microscopes

1 a) 10 ÷ 6.5 = **1.5 μm** *[2 marks for the correct answer or 1 mark for the correct calculation]*

b) 14 × 1.5 = **21 μm** *[1 mark for multiplying 14 by answer to part a), 1 mark for an answer of 21 or 22 μm.]*

Module 2: Section 2 — Biological Molecules

Page 21 — Water

1 As the water evaporates from the surface of the elephant's body *[1 mark]*, some of the elephant's heat energy is used to break the hydrogen bonds which hold the water molecules together *[1 mark]*. This cools the surface of the elephant's body *[1 mark]*.

Page 23 — Carbohydrates

1 B *[1 mark]*
Remember a hexose monosaccharide is one with six carbon atoms and carbohydrates don't contain nitrogen, so the chemical formula must be $C_6H_{12}O_6$.

2 Glycogen is a polysaccharide of alpha-glucose, which is used to store excess glucose in animals *[1 mark]*. It has a branched structure, meaning glucose can be released quickly *[1 mark]*. It's also a very compact molecule, so it's good for storage *[1 mark]*.

Page 25 — Lipids

1 They arrange themselves into a (phospholipid) bilayer/ double layer *[1 mark]*, with fatty acid tails facing towards each other *[1 mark]*. This is because the fatty acid tails are hydrophobic (water-repelling), forcing them to face inwards, away from the water on either side of the membrane *[1 mark]*.

2 a) The flattened shape allows the cholesterol molecules to fit in between the phospholipids and affect how closely they pack together *[1 mark]*, which regulates the fluidity of the membrane *[1 mark]*.

b) The hydrophobic tails force triglycerides to clump together in the cytoplasm as insoluble droplets *[1 mark]*. This means they can be stored in cells without affecting the cell's water potential *[1 mark]*.

Page 28 — Proteins

1 keratin *[1 mark]*

2 *5-6 marks:*
The answer fully describes four different bonds that may be in the tertiary structure and explains clearly how the structure of HSA makes it suited to its role.
The answer has a clear and logical structure.
The information given is relevant and detailed.

Answers

3-4 marks:
The answer describes two or three of the bonds that may be in the tertiary structure and explains briefly how the structure of HSA makes it suited to its role.
The answer has some structure. Most of the information given is relevant and there is some detail involved.
1-2 marks:
The answer briefly describes one of the bonds that may be in the tertiary structure and there is an attempt to link the structure of HSA to its role.
The answer has no clear structure. The information given is basic and lacking in detail. It may not all be relevant.
0 marks:
No relevant information is given.
Here are some points your answer may include:
The tertiary structure may contain ionic bonds. These are attractions between negatively-charged R groups and positively-charged R groups on different parts of the molecule. It may also contain disulfide bonds, which form when the sulfur atoms in two nearby cysteine molecules bond. There may also be hydrogen bonds, which are weak bonds between slightly positively-charged hydrogen atoms in some R groups, and slightly negatively-charged atoms in other R groups on the polypeptide chain. The tertiary structure will also contain hydrophobic and hydrophilic interactions. Hydrophobic R groups clump together, meaning that hydrophilic R groups are more likely to be pushed to the outside. This will make HSA soluble in water, which makes it suited for its role of transporting molecules in the blood.

Page 29 — Inorganic Ions

1 hydrogencarbonate *[1 mark]*, HCO_3^- *[1 mark]*
If a H_2CO_3 molecule loses a hydrogen ion (H^+) it will become HCO_3^-. (You're told in the question an anion is made, so you should definitely know to add the minus sign.)

Page 31 — Biochemical Tests for Molecules

1 a) Solution C *[1 mark]*
Solution C has the lowest absorbance. It therefore has the least amount of Benedict's reagent <u>left</u> — so it had the most reducing sugar <u>before</u> the Benedict's test.
  b) Any two from, e.g: the amount of Benedict's reagent used in each test tube *[1 mark]*. / The concentration of Benedict's reagent used *[1 mark]*. / The length of time each solution is left for *[1 mark]*.

Page 33 — Biochemical Tests and Separating Molecules

1 a) A concentrated spot of the sugar solution was placed on the line at the bottom of the paper *[1 mark]*. The bottom of the paper was then dipped in a solvent *[1 mark]*. The paper was taken out when the solvent had nearly reached the top of the paper *[1 mark]*.
  b) The substances in the sugar solution travel different distances in the mobile phase *[1 mark]*.

c) R_f value $= \dfrac{\text{distance travelled by solute}}{\text{distance travelled by solvent}}$
  $= 2.5$ cm $\div$ 10.4 cm $= \mathbf{0.24}$ *[2 marks for 0.24 or 1 mark for the correct calculation]*
  Solute X is fructose *[1 mark]*.
  Fructose has a R_f value of 0.24 in the table of R_f values, so solute X is fructose.

Module 2: Section 3 — Nucleotides and Nucleic Acids

Page 35 — Nucleotides

1 a) A is cytosine and B is adenine *[1 mark]*. Cytosine is a pyrimidine base, so it only has 1 (carbon-nitrogen) ring *[1 mark]*. Adenine is a purine with 2 (carbon-nitrogen) rings *[1 mark]*.
  b) Any one from: hydrogen / oxygen / carbon *[1 mark]*.
  The carbon atoms aren't labelled in the diagrams on the page, but they're present at each corner of the rings (except where there's a N atom there instead).
2 a) AMP consists of a ribose sugar *[1 mark]*, an adenine base *[1 mark]* and a single phosphate group *[1 mark]*.
  Be specific with your answer here — make sure you write 'ribose' and 'adenine' instead of just 'sugar' and 'base' or you won't get the marks.
  b) phosphorylation *[1 mark]*
3 ATP contains the sugar ribose *[1 mark]* so increasing the heart's supply of ribose could help it to produce ATP faster *[1 mark]*.

Page 37 — Polynucleotides and DNA

1 a) Nucleotides are joined between the phosphate group of one nucleotide and the (deoxyribose) sugar of the next *[1 mark]* by phosphodiester bonds *[1 mark]*. This is catalysed by DNA polymerase *[1 mark]*.
  b) Two polynucleotide strands join through hydrogen bonding between the base pairs *[1 mark]*. Base pairing is complementary (e.g. A always pairs with T and C always pairs with G) *[1 mark]*. The two (antiparallel) polynucleotide strands twist to form a DNA double helix *[1 mark]*.
2 a) The detergent breaks down cell membranes *[1 mark]*.
  b) He could have added an enzyme/RNase to the mixture before adding the ethanol *[1 mark]* to break down any RNA present *[1 mark]*.
3 *5-6 marks:*
The answer describes the full process of DNA replication with correct references to the enzymes involved and bonding.
The answer has a clear and logical structure.
The information given is relevant and detailed.
3-4 marks:
The answer describes most of the process of DNA replication with some references to the enzymes involved or bonding.
The answer has some structure. Most of the information given is relevant and there is some detail involved.

Answers

1-2 marks:
One or two steps involved in the process of
DNA replication are referenced.
The answer has no clear structure. The information given
is basic and lacking in detail. It may not all be relevant.
0 marks:
No relevant information is given.
Here are some points your answer may include:
DNA helicase breaks the hydrogen bonds between the two
DNA strands. The DNA helix unzips. Each strand acts as a
template for a new strand. Individual free DNA nucleotides
join up along the template strand by complementary base
pairing. DNA polymerase joins the individual nucleotides
together, so that the sugar-phosphate backbone forms.
Hydrogen bonds then form between the bases on each
strand and the strands twist to form a double-helix. Two
identical DNA molecules are produced. Each of the new
molecules contains a single strand from the original DNA
molecule and a single new strand.

Page 39 — Genes and Protein Synthesis

1 C *[1 mark]*
2 a) 4 *[1 mark]*
  b) GUG = valine
     UGU = cysteine
     CGC = arginine
     GCA = alanine
     Correct sequence = **valine, cysteine, arginine, alanine.**
     [2 marks for all 4 amino acids in the correct order.
     1 mark for a minimum of 3 correct amino acids in the
     correct order.]
3 a) The mRNA sequence is 18 nucleotides long and the protein
     produced is 6 amino acids long *[1 mark]*. 18 ÷ 6 = 3,
     suggesting three nucleotides code for a single amino acid
     [1 mark].
  b) E.g. The sequence produced began leucine-cysteine-
     glycine. This would only be produced if the code is
     non-overlapping, e.g. UUGUGUGGG = UUG-UGU-GGG
     = leucine-cysteine-glycine *[1 mark]*.
     If the code was overlapping, the triplets would be, e.g. UUG-UGU-
     GUG-UGU, which would give a sequence starting leucine-cysteine-
     valine-cysteine.
     Also, this part of the DNA sequence produces 6 amino
     acids. This is only correct if the code is non-overlapping —
     the sequence of amino acids would be longer if the code
     overlapped *[1 mark]*.

Page 41 — Transcription and Translation

1 a) CGCUUCAGGUAC *[1 mark]*
  b) GCGAAGUCCAUG *[1 mark]*
2 The drug binds to DNA, preventing RNA polymerase from
  binding, so transcription can't take place and no mRNA
  can be made *[1 mark]*. This means there's no mRNA for
  translation and so protein synthesis is inhibited *[1 mark]*.
3 (10 × 3 =) 30 nucleotides long *[1 mark]*. Each amino
  acid is coded for by three nucleotides (a codon), so the
  mRNA length in nucleotides is the number of amino acids
  multiplied by three *[1 mark]*.

Module 2: Section 4 — Enzymes

Page 43 — Action of Enzymes

1 Dextran binds to the active site of the dextranase enzyme
  [1 mark]. As it does so, dextran makes the active site
  change shape slightly to fit more closely around it *[1 mark]*.
  Amylose is not able to fit into dextranase's active site and
  make it change shape in the right way, so dextranase won't
  catalyse its breakdown *[1 mark]*.

Page 46 — Factors Affecting Enzyme Activity

1 C *[1 mark]*
2 a) She could add a buffer solution of a different pH to each of
     the test tubes containing the milk powder solution *[1 mark]*.
  b) E.g. the volume of milk powder solution used in each
     test tube / the concentration of milk powder solution
     used in each test tube / the volume of trypsin used / the
     concentration of trypsin used / the temperature *[1 mark]*.
  c) Any four, valid points from: above the optimum pH, the
     OH⁻ ions in the alkaline solution *[1 mark]* will interfere
     with the ionic/hydrogen bonds that hold trypsin's tertiary
     structure in place *[1 mark]*. This will make the active site
     change shape *[1 mark]*, so the rate of reaction will decrease
     [1 mark]. The enzyme will eventually denature *[1 mark]*.
     [Maximum of 4 marks available.]

Page 49 — Cofactors and Enzyme Inhibition

1 C *[1 mark]*
  Galactose is a product inhibitor of ß-galactosidase. This means it's
  reversible, so it must bind to the enzyme via weak hydrogen or ionic
  bonds. Galactose is a competitive inhibitor because it binds to the
  active site of ß-galactosidase.
2 a) Magnesium ions are a cofactor for hexokinase *[1 mark]*.
     They help the enzyme and substrate bind together *[1 mark]*.
  b) Aluminium ions are an enzyme inhibitor for hexokinase
     [1 mark]. They bind to the enzyme and prevent the
     enzyme-substrate complex from forming *[1 mark]*.
  c) Because they inhibit respiration, which is a metabolic
     reaction *[1 mark]*.
3 Ritonavir will prevent the HIV virus from replicating
  [1 mark], because the virus will not be able to break
  down the proteins and use the products to make new
  viruses *[1 mark]*. The Ritonavir molecules are a similar
  shape to the protease enzyme's substrate so it will act as
  a competitive inhibitor *[1 mark]* / it will bind to the active
  site of the enzyme and block it so the substrate cannot fit in
  [1 mark]. *[Maximum of 3 marks available.]*

Module 2: Section 5 —
Biological Membranes

Page 51 — Cell Membranes

1 The membrane is described as fluid because the
  phospholipids are constantly moving *[1 mark]*. It is
  described as a mosaic because the proteins are scattered
  throughout the membrane like tiles in a mosaic *[1 mark]*.

Answers

2   Any two from: Proteins form channels in the cell membranes which allow small or charged particles through *[1 mark]*. / Carrier proteins transport molecules and ions across the cell membrane *[1 mark]*. / Proteins can act as receptors for molecules, e.g. hormones, which are important in cell signalling *[1 mark]*.

Page 53 — Cell Membranes

1 a) Cut five equal-sized pieces of beetroot and rinse them to remove any pigment released during cutting *[1 mark]*. Make up five test tubes with alcohol concentrations 0, 25, 50, 75 and 100% *[1 mark]*. Place a piece of beetroot in each test tube for the same length of time *[1 mark]*. Remove the piece of beetroot from each tube and use a colorimeter to measure how much light is absorbed by each of the remaining solutions *[1 mark]*.

   b) As the concentration of alcohol increased the absorbance also increased *[1 mark]*. This means that more pigment was released by the beetroot as the alcohol concentration increased, which suggests that the cell membrane became more permeable *[1 mark]*.

   c) E.g. Increasing the concentration of alcohol increases the permeability of the cell membrane because the alcohol dissolves the lipids in the membrane causing it to lose its structure *[1 mark]*.

Page 55 — Transport Across Cell Membranes

1 a) Any two from: e.g. the concentration of hydrochloric acid solution *[1 mark]*. / The temperature of the hydrochloric acid and gelatine cubes *[1 mark]*. / The concentration of cresol red in each gelatine cube *[1 mark]*.

   b) As surface area to volume ratio decreases, rate of diffusion decreases *[1 mark]*. *[Opposite explanation also gets 1 mark.]*
   You can see from the results of the experiment that as the surface area to volume ratio of the cubes gets smaller, the time taken for the gelatine cubes to turn yellow gets longer. Therefore the rate at which the hydrochloric acid is diffusing through the gelatine blocks is decreasing.

   c) Any one from: e.g. observing the colour change is a matter of opinion *[1 mark]*. / It is hard to say exactly when the colour change has occurred *[1 mark]*. / It would be difficult to cut the blocks to exactly the same size every time *[1 mark]*.

Page 57 — Transport Across Cell Membranes

1   Facilitated diffusion involves channel proteins, which transport charged molecules across the membrane *[1 mark]* and carrier proteins, which transport large molecules across the membrane *[1 mark]*. Both types of protein transport molecules down a concentration gradient *[1 mark]*.

2   Endocytosis takes in substances from outside the cell *[1 mark]* via vesicles formed from the plasma membrane *[1 mark]*. Exocytosis secretes substances from the cell *[1 mark]* via vesicles made from the Golgi apparatus *[1 mark]*.
   Make sure you don't get these two processes mixed up — try to remember endo for 'in' and exo for 'out'.

Page 59 — Transport Across Cell Membranes

1 a) The water potential of the sucrose solution was higher than the water potential of the potato *[1 mark]*. Water moves by osmosis down a water potential gradient / from a solution of higher water potential to a solution of lower water potential *[1 mark]*. So water moved into the potato, increasing its mass *[1 mark]*.

   b) The water potential of the potato and the water potential of the solution was the same *[1 mark]*.

   c) – 0.4 g *[1 mark]*. The difference in water potential between the solution and the potato is the same as with the 1% solution, so the mass difference should be about the same, but negative / mass should be lost not gained *[1 mark]*.
   A 5% sucrose solution has a lower water potential than the potato. This means that water will move out of the potato into the sucrose solution, decreasing the mass of the potato.

Module 2: Section 6 — Cell Division and Cellular Organisation

Page 61 — The Cell Cycle and Mitosis

1 a) C *[1 mark]* because the centromeres have divided and the chromatids are moving to opposite ends of the cell *[1 mark]*.

   b) X = Nuclear envelope *[1 mark]*.
      Y = Cell membrane *[1 mark]*.
      Z = Centriole *[1 mark]*.

Page 63 — Sexual Reproduction and Meiosis

1 a) Meiosis I because the homologous pairs have separated, halving the chromosome number *[1 mark]*.

   b) During meiosis I/prophase I, homologous pairs of chromosomes come together *[1 mark]*. The chromatids twist around each other and bits swap over *[1 mark]*. The chromatids now contain different combinations of alleles *[1 mark]*. This means each of the four daughter cells will contain chromatids with different combinations of alleles *[1 mark]*.

   c) Independent assortment means that the separation of homologous pairs of chromosomes (in anaphase I) is random/can happen in any way *[1 mark]*. So, the daughter cells produced by meiosis can contain any combination of maternal and paternal chromosomes with different alleles *[1 mark]*.

Page 65 — Stem Cells and Differentiation

1   It has many chloroplasts to absorb light for photosynthesis *[1 mark]*. It has thin cell walls, so carbon dioxide can easily enter *[1 mark]*.

2   Stem cells divide to make new, specialised cells *[1 mark]*. In animals, adult stem cells are used to replace damaged cells *[1 mark]*, e.g. stem cells in the bone marrow differentiate/become specialised to make erythrocytes (red blood cells)/neutrophils (white blood cells) *[1 mark]*.

Answers

Page 67 — Tissues, Organs and Systems

1   It's best described as an organ *[1 mark]* as it is made of many tissues working together to perform a particular function *[1 mark]*.

2   B *[1 mark]*

Extra Exam Practice for Module 2

Pages 68-69

2 a) i) glycosidic bond *[1 mark]*

ii) E.g.

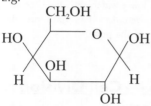

[1 mark]

You should know that lactose is made up of the monosaccharides glucose and galactose joined by a glycosidic bond. You should also know the structure of glucose, so you should be able to work out the structure of galactose from there.

b) The rate of flow of milk needs to be controlled because if it is too slow, then the concentration of galactose in the column would increase *[1 mark]*. The galactose molecules would compete with the lactose molecules for the active sites of the lactase enzyme *[1 mark]*, which would mean that fewer enzyme-substrate complexes would form, and less lactose would be broken down *[1 mark]*.

Lactose starts being broken down as soon as the milk enters the column. If the rate of flow is too slow then it takes more time for the galactose to leave the column at the other end, so its concentration in the column increases.

c) i) E.g. pH / enzyme concentration / substrate concentration / the length of time the reaction was left for *[1 mark]*.

ii) If immobilisation strengthens the tertiary structure, then the immobilised lactase would have been less likely than free lactase to lose its shape/denature as temperature increased *[1 mark]*. The relative yield of glucose produced by immobilised lactase declined less rapidly than for free lactase at increasing temperatures *[1 mark]*, which suggests that the tertiary structure/shape of immobilised lactase was less affected by increasing temperature, supporting the student's suggestion *[1 mark]*.

Module 3: Section 1 — Exchange and Transport

Page 71 — Specialised Exchange Surfaces

1   Any two from, e.g. they have thin walls *[1 mark]*. / They have a good blood supply *[1 mark]*. / They're well-ventilated *[1 mark]*. / They have a large surface area to volume ratio *[1 mark]*.

2   The microvilli give the cells a large surface area *[1 mark]*, so nutrients can be absorbed faster *[1 mark]*.

Page 73 — The Gaseous Exchange System in Mammals

1 a) The trachea will contain large C-shaped pieces of cartilage in its walls *[1 mark]*. The walls of the bronchi will contain smaller pieces of cartilage *[1 mark]* and the large bronchiole will not contain any cartilage *[1 mark]*.

b) E.g. the student will be able to see goblet cells / ciliated epithelium / smooth muscle in the tissue sample from the largest bronchiole, but not the sample from the smaller bronchiole *[1 mark or opposite argument accepted for 1 mark.]*

2 a) If the elastic fibres are destroyed, the walls of the alveoli may not recoil properly on breathing out *[1 mark]*. This may make it difficult for the person to exhale/breathe out fully *[1 mark]*.

Destruction of the elastic fibres means the alveoli can't recoil to expel air as well, so more air than normal remains trapped in the lungs.

b) Any two from, e.g. it could cause mucus to build up in the lungs/airways *[1 mark]*. / It could prevent dust/ microorganisms from being cleared out of the lungs/airways *[1 mark]*. / It could increase the chances of a lung infection developing *[1 mark]*.

Page 75 — Ventilation in Mammals

1   The external intercostal muscles contract *[1 mark]*, making the ribs move up and out *[1 mark]* and the diaphragm contracts/flattens *[1 mark]*. This increases the volume of the thorax *[1 mark]*, so the pressure inside decreases, drawing air into the lungs *[1 mark]*.

Page 77 — Ventilation in Fish and Insects

1 a) E.g. the liquid preservative has entered the grasshopper's tracheae, so they are no longer filled with air (and they would appear silver in colour if filled with air) *[1 mark]*.

b) To provide support *[1 mark]*.

2   The fish opens its mouth, which lowers the floor of the buccal cavity *[1 mark]*. This increases the volume of the buccal cavity *[1 mark]*, decreasing the pressure *[1 mark]*. Water then flows into the buccal cavity *[1 mark]*.

Module 3: Section 2 — Transport in Animals

Page 79 — Circulatory Systems

1   The blood flows through the body in vessels *[1 mark]*.

2   Beetles are insects, so they have an open circulatory system *[1 mark]*. The blood is pumped into the body cavity where it circulates freely *[1 mark]*.

3 a) It is a closed system *[1 mark]*.

b) It is a single circulatory system, not a double one *[1 mark]*.

Page 81 — Blood Vessels

1   D *[1 mark]*

2   The hydrostatic pressure in the capillary is greater than the hydrostatic pressure in the spaces around the cells *[1 mark]*, so fluid moves out of the capillary and into spaces around the cells *[1 mark]*.

Answers

Page 83 — The Heart

1 a) i) D *[1 mark]*
   The semi-lunar valve will only open if the pressure in the ventricle is higher than the pressure in the aorta (or pulmonary artery, if you're looking at the right side of the heart).

   ii) C *[1 mark]*
   The atrioventricular valve will be forced closed when the pressure in the ventricle becomes higher than the pressure in the atrium.

   b) The graph should increase and decrease at the same times as the graph for the left side (because both ventricles contract together) *[1 mark]*. The pressure should be lower than for the left side of the heart at all times *[1 mark]*. E.g.

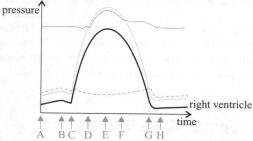

The left ventricle of the heart has thicker, more muscular walls than the right ventricle because it needs to contract powerfully to pump blood all the way round the body. The right side only needs to get blood to the lungs, which are nearby — this is why the pressure will always be lower in the right ventricle than the left.

Page 85 — Heart Activity

1 a) The sino-atrial node acts as a pacemaker/initiates heartbeats *[1 mark]*.
   b) The Purkyne tissue conducts electrical impulses through the ventricle walls *[1 mark]*.
2   The ventricles are not contracting properly *[1 mark]*. This could be because of muscle damage / because the AVN is not conducting impulses to the ventricles properly *[1 mark]*.

Page 87 — Haemoglobin

1   B *[1 mark]*
   You know that the Bohr effect means that as pCO_2 increases, more O_2 is released from the blood, so this removes A and C. If the curve shifts right this means that at a particular pO_2 the haemoglobin will be less saturated with O_2 at higher pCO_2. (This is true so the curve shifts right and the correct answer is B.) Try doing a sketch of the O_2 dissociation curve and experiment with the movement of the curve to help you remember this.

Module 3: Section 3 — Transport in Plants

Page 89 — Xylem and Phloem

1   Any two from: e.g. xylem vessel cells have no end walls *[1 mark]*, so they form an uninterrupted tube that allows water to pass through easily *[1 mark]*. / The vessel cells are dead and contain no cytoplasm *[1 mark]*, which allows water to easily pass through *[1 mark]*. / Their walls are thickened with a woody substance called lignin *[1 mark]*, which helps support the xylem vessels/stop them collapsing inwards *[1 mark]*. / The vessel walls have small holes called pits *[1 mark]*, which allow substances to pass in and out of the vessels *[1 mark]*.

Page 91 — Water Transport

1   When water evaporates from the leaf this creates tension that pulls more water molecules into the leaf *[1 mark]*. This then causes water to move through the xylem and into the leaf to replace water that has been lost from the plant *[1 mark]*. Cohesive forces between water molecules mean that they are attracted to each other *[1 mark]*. This means that when water molecules move through the xylem, they move as a continuous column *[1 mark]*.
2   Blocking the plasmodesmata would prevent water from travelling between cells via the symplast pathway *[1 mark]*. This would mean that water would only be able to travel via the apoplast pathway *[1 mark]*.

Page 93 — Transpiration

1   'Hairs' on the epidermis *[1 mark]* trap moist air round the stomata, which reduces the water potential gradient and so reduces transpiration *[1 mark]*. A thick waterproof cuticle *[1 mark]* stops water evaporating through it *[1 mark]*.

Page 95 — Translocation

1 a) Water enters at point A/the source by osmosis *[1 mark]*. This increases the pressure at the source end of the top tube *[1 mark]*, causing the sugar solution to flow along the tube from the source to the sink *[1 mark]*.
   b) i) phloem *[1 mark]*
      ii) xylem *[1 mark]*

Extra Exam Practice for Module 3

Pages 96-97

2 a) i) When the heart segment is contracting the pressure inside it will increase *[1 mark]*. When the pressure becomes greater than the pressure in the body cavity, the valve will shut, preventing blood from re-entering the contracting segment of the heart *[1 mark]*.

   ii) In mammals, haemoglobin binds to oxygen molecules to transport them in the blood to respiring cells *[1 mark]*. However, in insects oxygen molecules diffuse directly into respiring cells from the tracheoles, so they don't require haemoglobin *[1 mark]*.

   b) i) Solutes/sucrose/assimilates from the leaves will be loaded into the sieve tubes near site 2, meaning the water potential at this site will be relatively low *[1 mark]*. The water potential will increase as the phloem sap moves towards site 3 because the solutes/sucrose/assimilates will be removed from the sieve tubes to be used by cells *[1 mark]*.

   Because the question tells you to assume the plant is not in a growing season, you should realise that the majority of the transport in the phloem is taking place in a downward direction from site 2 to site 3. If the plant was in a growing season, lots of the translocation would be occurring in an upward direction, to move solutes from the roots to the leaves to provide the leaves with energy for growth.

Answers

ii) The stem at site 2 is connected to more leaves than the stem at site 1 *[1 mark]*. Therefore, the phloem sap at site 2 is likely to contain more solutes/sucrose/assimilates than the phloem sap at site 1 *[1 mark]*. This causes more water to move into the sieve tubes from the xylem and companion cells by osmosis *[1 mark]*. This results in the pressure of the phloem sap at site 2 being greater than at site 1, which forces a greater volume out through the stylet *[1 mark]*.

iii) The sucrose moves through the cytoplasm of neighbouring cells by passing through the plasmodesmata *[1 mark]*.

Module 4: Section 1 — Disease and the Immune System

Page 99 — Pathogens and Communicable Diseases

1   C *[1 mark]*
2 a) Indirect transmission, because the virus is being transferred via an intermediate (the gardeners' hands/tools) *[1 mark]*.
  b) E.g. they could wash their hands after handling infected plants/between handling one plant and another plant *[1 mark]*. / They could wash/disinfect their tools after using them on infected plants *[1 mark]*.
3 a) bacteria *[1 mark]*
  b) Any two from: e.g. more overcrowding (in low-income country) *[1 mark]* / more limited access to drugs (in low-income country, compared to wealthier country) *[1 mark]* / less likely to be diagnosed/treated (in low-income country) *[1 mark]*.

Page 101 — Defence Against Pathogens

1 a) Plant cells are surrounded by a cell wall, which forms a physical barrier against pathogen entry *[1 mark]*. When the cell wall is damaged, the barrier is broken and the virus can enter the cells *[1 mark]*.
  b) E.g. callose deposition at the plasmodesmata *[1 mark]*.

Page 105 — The Immune System

1   D *[1 mark]*
2   IgG can bind two pathogens at the same time, so the pathogens become agglutinated/clump together *[1 mark]*. This makes phagocytosis easier, so IgG also acts as an opsonin *[1 mark]*.
3   Any three from: e.g. the nucleus of the neutrophil will have three lobes *[1 mark]*. / The nucleus of the B lymphocyte will not have lobes and will take up most of the cell *[1 mark]*. / The neutrophil's cytoplasm will be grainy/contain granules, but the B lymphocyte's won't *[1 mark]*. / The B lymphocyte will be smaller than the neutrophil *[1 mark]*.
4   When the person caught chickenpox for the first time, her B and T lymphocytes produced memory cells *[1 mark]*. When she was exposed to the virus for a second time, the memory B lymphocytes divided into plasma cells *[1 mark]* to produce the right antibody to the virus *[1 mark]*. The memory T lymphocytes divided into the correct type of T lymphocyte to kill the virus *[1 mark]*. The secondary response was quicker and stronger, so got rid of the pathogen before she showed any symptoms *[1 mark]*.

Page 107 — Immunity and Vaccinations

1   Memory cells produced from vaccination with one strain of the influenza virus will not recognise other strains with different antigens *[1 mark]*. So a new vaccine is made every year to protect against the most recently circulating strains of influenza *[1 mark]*.

Page 109 — Antibiotics and Other Medicines

1   There was genetic variation in the *Staphylococcus aureus* population that meant some of the bacteria were resistant to meticillin. / Some *Staphylococcus aureus* developed a mutation that made them more resistant to meticillin *[1 mark]*. This made them more likely to survive and reproduce in a host being treated with meticillin *[1 mark]*. The bacteria passed the allele for meticillin resistance on to their offspring *[1 mark]*, so meticillin resistance became more common in the population over time *[1 mark]*.

Module 4: Section 2 — Biodiversity

Page 111 — Studying Biodiversity

1   Field A
    $D = 1 - ((80/400)^2 + (110/400)^2 + (210/400)^2)$
    $= 1 - 0.39$
    $= \mathbf{0.61}$ *[1 mark]*
    Field B
    $D = 1 - ((20/400)^2 + (50/400)^2 + (330/400)^2)$
    $= 1 - 0.70$
    $= \mathbf{0.30}$ *[1 mark]*

Page 113 — More on Biodiversity

1   $36/80 = \mathbf{0.45}$ *[1 mark]*
2   *5-6 marks:*
    The answer describes a variety of the impacts of population growth and monoculture on global biodiversity levels.
    The answer has a clear and logical structure.
    The information given is relevant and detailed.
    3-4 marks:
    The answer describes some of the impacts from population growth and monoculture.
    The answer has some structure. Most of the information given is relevant and there is some detail involved.
    1-2 marks:
    One or two points are given relating to either population growth or monoculture.
    The answer has no clear structure. The information given is basic and lacking in detail. It may not all be relevant.
    0 marks:
    No relevant information is given.
    Here are some points your answer may include:
    Human population growth leads to more human development, which destroys habitats, decreasing habitat diversity. There is a greater demand for resources, which can lead to over-exploitation / resources being used up faster than they can be replenished, decreasing genetic diversity and species diversity. Urbanisation can isolate species, meaning populations are unable to interbreed, decreasing genetic diversity. High amounts of pollutants can kill species or destroy habitats, decreasing biodiversity.

Answers

Monoculture leads to loss of habitats and habitat diversity as land is cleared for large fields. Local and naturally occurring plants and animals are destroyed with pesticides and herbicides, reducing species diversity. Heritage varieties of crops are lost because they don't make enough money and so aren't planted any more, decreasing species diversity.

Page 115 — Importance of Biodiversity

1 a) A keystone species is a species on which many of the other species in an ecosystem depend and without which the ecosystem would change dramatically *[1 mark]*.
  b) Because it is a predator *[1 mark]*.
2 Continuous monoculture is growing a single variety of a single crop in an area without interruption *[1 mark]*. Over time this leads to soil depletion, where the nutrients in the soil are used up and not replaced *[1 mark]*. This results in increased spending on fertilisers *[1 mark]* and decreased yields in the long run *[1 mark]*.

Page 117 — Conservation and Biodiversity

1 a) In situ methods could include protecting the turtles from hunters *[1 mark]* and protecting their nesting sites *[1 mark]*. A national park/protected area could also be established to restrict human usage of the area *[1 mark]*.
  b) It's only possible to conserve a limited number of individuals with ex situ methods *[1 mark]*. They can be very expensive *[1 mark]*. It may be difficult to sustain the environment for the turtle *[1 mark]*. They don't protect the habitat of the turtle *[1 mark]*.

Module 4: Section 3 — Classification and Evolution

Page 119 — Classification Basics

1 a) *Salmo [1 mark]*
    Remember that the genus is always the first part of the Latin name.
  b) Any two from: e.g. it must be eukaryotic *[1 mark]*. / It must be multicellular *[1 mark]*. / It must have no cell walls *[1 mark]*. / It must be heterotrophic/consumes plants or other animals *[1 mark]*.
2 a) Green monkey *[1 mark]* because it's the closest to humans on the tree *[1 mark]*.
  b) The following branch point should be circled:

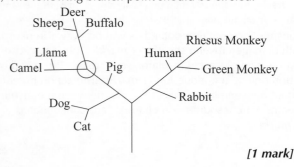

[1 mark]

Page 121 — Evolution of Classification Systems

1 E.g. scientists could compare the DNA base sequences of gibbons and humans *[1 mark]*. The more similar the sequences, the more closely related they are *[1 mark]*. / Scientists could compare the amino acid sequences of a protein found in both humans and gibbons (e.g. cytochrome C) *[1 mark]*. The more similar the amino acids sequences of the protein, the more closely related they are likely to be *[1 mark]*.
2 Any three from: e.g. RNA polymerase is different in the Archaea and Bacteria *[1 mark]*. / Archaea, but not Bacteria, have histones similar to Eukarya *[1 mark]*. / The bonds of the lipids in the cell membranes of Archaea and Bacteria are different *[1 mark]*. / The development and composition of flagellae are different in the Archaea and Bacteria *[1 mark]*.

Page 124 — Variation

1 a) For species A and species B, as the temperature increases the development time decreases *[1 mark]*. The development time of species B is less affected by temperature than species A *[1 mark]*.
  b) Individuals within a species have different forms of the same genes (alleles), which causes genetic variation *[1 mark]*.

Page 126 — Adaptations

1 a) Whales and sharks live in a similar environment (water) so have evolved similar adaptations to help them survive in that environment *[1 mark]*.
  b) E.g. humans don't need to be as efficient at exchanging oxygen as whales because they spend most of their time on land, where oxygen is readily available in the air *[1 mark]*.

Page 129 — The Theory of Evolution

1 a) E.g. the brown owls may be better camouflaged/blend in with the landscape better than the grey owls when there's no snow cover *[1 mark]*. This makes them less likely to be eaten by predators *[1 mark]*.
    Snow makes everything white, so lighter coloured owls blend in better when there's snow around. They stick out more when there's no snow though.
  b) The brown owls are more likely to survive and reproduce when there's less snow cover *[1 mark]* and pass on the allele for darker/brown colouring to their offspring *[1 mark]*. Over time, the allele for darker/brown colouring will become more common in the population *[1 mark]*.
2 a) Genetic mutations/variation would have resulted in some moths having alleles for DDT-resistance/being resistant to DDT *[1 mark]*. When the population was exposed to DDT (a selection pressure), only those individuals who were resistant would survive to reproduce *[1 mark]*. The alleles which code for resistance would be passed on to the next generation *[1 mark]*. Over time, the number of individuals with DDT resistance would increase and it would become more common within the population *[1 mark]*.
  b) Any two from: e.g. moth infestations would be harder to control *[1 mark]*. / Broader pesticides might be used, which could kill beneficial insects *[1 mark]*. / New pesticides might need to be developed if the moth develops resistance to all pesticides in use *[1 mark]*.

Answers

Extra Exam Practice for Module 4

Pages 130-131

2 a) Rhizostomae *[1 mark]*

   Phylogenetic trees show a hierarchy, with the taxa getting progressively smaller at each level. You should have realised that Cassiopea andromeda was a species due to its binomial name. By working backwards from its position on the tree you can identify the order it belongs to.

   b) According to the theory of evolution by natural selection, the alleles for advantageous characteristics gradually become more common in a population over time *[1 mark]*. *Cassiopea xamachana* and *Cassiopea andromeda* share a more recent common ancestor with each other than they do with *Cyanea capillata* *[1 mark]*. This means that the alleles (and therefore the DNA base sequences) found in *Cassiopea xamachana* and *Cassiopea andromeda* should be more similar to each other as there has been less time for changes to arise and become common in the populations *[1 mark]*.

   c) *Physalia physalis* and scyphozoans may have evolved in similar environments, which led them evolving similar adaptations/features to aid their survival, despite being from different taxonomic groups *[1 mark]*.

3 a) i) Any two from: e.g. the equipment/method used to sample the organisms. / The method used to identify the organisms found. / The time of day the organisms were sampled. / The date/date range in July when the sampling took place. *[2 marks]*

   ii) N = 18 + 15 + 11 + 22 = 66

   $$D = 1 - \left(\left(\frac{18}{66} \right)^2 + \left(\frac{15}{66} \right)^2 + \left(\frac{11}{66} \right)^2 + \left(\frac{22}{66} \right)^2 \right)$$

   $= 1 - 0.2649... = 0.7350...$

   $= \mathbf{0.74}$ (to 2 s.f.)

   [2 marks for the correct answer, otherwise 1 mark for correct working]

   Species richness is a measure of the number of different species in an area, whereas Simpson's Index of Diversity is a measure of the number of individuals of each species present in an area *[1 mark]*. The species richness remained at 4 in this study, while Simpson's Index of Diversity decreased from 0.74 to 0.58, so it could be concluded that the biodiversity of insect larvae in the area of the park studied fell between 2016 and 2017 *[1 mark]*.

   b) The insect larvae may be more common in some types of habitat than others *[1 mark]*. Stratified sampling would mean that all the different types of habitats in the park were sampled in proportion to their part of the park as a whole *[1 mark]*. Random sampling may provide less valid results because it may result in some of the different habitats in the park not being sampled at all / being sampled disproportionately in relation to their occurrence in the park due to chance *[1 mark]*.

Module 5: Section 1 — Communication and Homeostasis

Page 133 — Communication and Homeostasis Basics

1 a) The maintenance of a constant internal environment *[1 mark]*.

   b) Receptors detect when a level is too high or too low *[1 mark]*, and the information's communicated via the nervous system or the hormonal system to effectors *[1 mark]*. Effectors respond to counteract the change / to bring the level back to normal *[1 mark]*.

Page 135 — Receptors and Neurones

1 a) They convert the energy from the stimulus into another form/electrical energy *[1 mark]*.

   b) When a Pacinian corpuscle is stimulated, the lamellae/layers of connective tissue are deformed and press on the sensory nerve ending *[1 mark]*. This causes deformation of stretch-mediated sodium channels in the sensory neurone's cell membrane *[1 mark]*. The sodium ion channels open and sodium ions diffuse into the cell *[1 mark]*, creating the generator potential *[1 mark]*.

   c) Once the threshold level is reached an action potential/nerve impulse will travel along the sensory neurone to a relay neurone in the CNS *[1 mark]*. An action potential/nerve impulse will then travel from the relay neurone to a motor neurone, which carries the action potential/nerve impulse to effector cells *[1 mark]*.

Page 137 — Action Potentials

1 a) A stimulus causes sodium ion channels in the neurone cell membrane to open *[1 mark]*. Sodium ions diffuse into the cell, so the membrane becomes depolarised *[1 mark]*.

   b) The first action potential fired at 0.5 ms.
   If the second one fired at 4.5 ms, this means an action potential is fired every (4.5 − 0.5) = 4 ms.
   Number of ms in one hour = 60 × 60 × 1000 = 3 600 000.
   There is one action potential every 4 ms, so in one hour there will be 3 600 000 ÷ 4 = 900 000
   $= \mathbf{9 \times 10^5}$ action potentials.
   [2 marks for the correct answer, allow 1 mark for the correct calculation of 3 600 000 ÷ 4.]

   c) 30 mV *[1 mark]*
   This is the same as the maximum potential difference shown on the graph. Remember, action potentials always fire with the same change in voltage no matter how big the stimulus is.

2 Transmission of action potentials will be slower in neurones with damaged myelin sheaths *[1 mark]*. This is because myelin is an electrical insulator, so increases the speed of action potential conduction *[1 mark]*. The action potentials 'jump' between the nodes of Ranvier/between the myelin sheaths, where sodium ion channels are concentrated *[1 mark]*.

Answers

Page 139 — Synapses

1 A — voltage-gated calcium ion channels in the presynaptic membrane open *[1 mark]* / calcium ions diffuse into the synaptic knob *[1 mark]*
B — vesicles fuse with the presynaptic membrane and release neurotransmitter *[1 mark]*
C — neurotransmitter diffuses across the synaptic cleft *[1 mark]*
D — neurotransmitter binds with the specific receptors on the postsynaptic neurone *[1 mark]*

Page 141 — The Hormonal System and Glands

1 The cortex secretes steroid hormones, such as cortisol and aldosterone *[1 mark]*. Any two from: The hormones stimulate the breakdown of fats and proteins into glucose to make more energy available *[1 mark]*. / They increase blood volume and pressure by increasing the uptake of sodium ions and water by the kidneys *[1 mark]*. / They suppress the immune system *[1 mark]*.

2 Any three from: The medulla secretes adrenaline *[1 mark]*. Adrenaline binds to specific receptors on cell membranes *[1 mark]* and activates adenylyl cyclase *[1 mark]*. This catalyses the production of cyclic AMP from ATP *[1 mark]*, which activates a cascade of reactions including the conversion of glycogen into glucose *[1 mark]*. *[Maximum of 3 marks available.]*

Noradrenaline (secreted by the medulla) can also catalyse the production of cyclic AMP from ATP, but you need to know specifically about **adrenaline** *for your exam.*

Page 143 — Homeostasis — Control of Body Temperature

1 Peripheral temperature receptors/thermoreceptors in the skin detect a higher external temperature than normal *[1 mark]*. The peripheral temperature receptors/thermoreceptors send impulses along sensory neurones to the hypothalamus *[1 mark]*.

2 Snakes are ectotherms so they can't control their body temperature internally and depend on the temperature of their external environment *[1 mark]*. In cold climates, snakes will be less active *[1 mark]*, which makes it harder to catch prey, avoid predators, find a mate, etc. *[1 mark]*.
You need to use a bit of common sense to answer this question — you know that the activity level of an ectotherm depends on the temperature of the surroundings, so in a cold environment it won't be very active. And if it can't be very active it'll have trouble surviving.

3 Maximum of four marks available. 1 mark for each method, up to a maximum of 2 marks. 1 mark for the correct explanation of the method, up to a maximum of 2 marks.
Vasoconstriction of blood vessels *[1 mark]* reduces heat loss because less blood flows through the capillaries in the surface layers of the dermis *[1 mark]*. / Erector pili muscles contract to make hairs stand on end *[1 mark]*, trapping an insulating layer of air to prevent heat loss *[1 mark]*. / Muscles contract in spasms to make the body shiver *[1 mark]*, so more heat is produced from increased respiration *[1 mark]*. / Adrenaline and thyroxine are released *[1 mark]*, which increase metabolism so more heat is produced *[1 mark]*.

Page 145 — Homeostasis — Control of Blood Glucose

1 a) Negative feedback because the pancreas secretes hormones that return blood glucose concentration to normal if it is detected as being too high or too low *[1 mark]*.

  b) Any four from: Insulin is released when blood glucose concentration is too high *[1 mark]*. It binds to specific receptors on muscle and liver cells *[1 mark]* causing them to become more permeable to glucose so more is absorbed from the blood *[1 mark]*. Insulin activates glycogenesis so that glucose can be stored *[1 mark]*. Insulin also causes the rate of respiration of glucose to increase so that more is used up *[1 mark]*. *[Maximum of 4 marks available.]*

2 No insulin would be secreted *[1 mark]* because ATP wouldn't be produced, so the potassium ion channels in the β cell plasma membrane wouldn't close / the plasma membrane of β cell wouldn't be depolarised *[1 mark]*.

Page 147 — Diabetes

1 Any two from: It's cheaper to produce insulin using GM bacteria than to extract it from animal pancreases *[1 mark]*. Large amounts of insulin can be made using GM bacteria, so there's enough insulin to treat everyone with Type I diabetes *[1 mark]*. GM bacteria make real human insulin, which is more effective and less likely to trigger an allergic response or be rejected by the immune system *[1 mark]*. Some people prefer insulin from GM bacteria for ethical or religious reasons *[1 mark]*.

2 a) Any two from: Person A's blood glucose concentration is initially at a higher level than person B's blood glucose concentration. / Person A's blood glucose concentration reaches a much higher level than person B's blood glucose concentration. / It takes longer for person A's blood glucose concentration to start to decrease than it does for person B's blood glucose concentration to start to decrease. / Person A's blood glucose concentration decreases at a much slower rate than person B's blood glucose concentration. / Person A experiences a greater range of blood glucose concentration than person B. *[2 pieces of evidence for 1 mark.]*

  b) The insulin receptors on person A's cell membranes don't work properly / person A does not produce enough insulin, so their cells don't take up enough glucose *[1 mark]*. This means their blood glucose concentration remains higher than normal *[1 mark]*.

Answers

c) i)

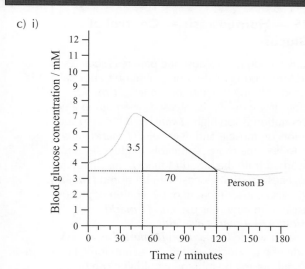

$$\text{Rate of decrease} = \frac{3.5}{70} = \textbf{0.05 mM min}^{-1} \textbf{\textit{[1 mark]}}.$$

ii) Person A has diabetes so they don't produce enough insulin or they are unable to respond to insulin properly, which means their body can't take up all of the glucose as quickly as person B *[1 mark]*.

d) Metformin acts on liver cells to reduce the amount of glucose that they release into the blood *[1 mark]*. It also acts to increase the sensitivity of cells to insulin so more glucose can be taken up with the same amount of insulin *[1 mark]*. This means that person A's blood glucose concentration would decrease much more quickly after taking the glucose drink if they did the test again *[1 mark]*.

Module 5: Section 2 — Excretion

Page 150 — The Liver and Excretion

1 central vein *[1 mark]*
2 B *[1 mark]*
3 *5-6 marks:*
The answer explains fully why there would be an increased concentration of urea in the urine, with a detailed description of deamination and the production of urea in the ornithine cycle.
The answer has a clear and logical structure.
The information given is relevant and detailed.
3-4 marks:
The answer explains briefly why there would be an increased concentration of urea in the urine, with some mention of the break down of amino acids into ammonia and the production of urea in ornithine cycle.
The answer has some structure. Most of the information given is relevant and there is some detail involved.
1-2 marks:
The answer includes a basic explanation as to why there would be an increased concentration of urea in the urine. The answer has no clear structure. The information given is basic and lacking in detail. It may not all be relevant.
0 marks:
No relevant information is given.

Here are some points your answer may include:
The protein would be digested, producing amino acids. Amino acids contain nitrogen in their amino groups, but the body can't usually store nitrogenous substances, so if a lot of protein is eaten there could be an excess of amino acids that will need to be used or broken down and excreted. Excess amino acids are broken down in the liver into ammonia and organic acids in a process called deamination. Ammonia is then combined with CO_2 in the ornithine cycle to produce urea. Urea is then released into the blood and filtered out at the kidneys to produce urine. So if a large amount of protein is eaten, there may be excess amino acids that are broken down by the liver, producing a large amount of urea that's excreted in the urine.
Don't forget to say that only excess amino acids are broken down.

Page 153 — The Kidneys and Excretion

1 a) C (loop of Henle) *[1 mark]*
b) Point C because glucose is reabsorbed in the PCT so by the time the filtrate reaches point C there will be no glucose remaining/the concentration of glucose will be much lower than at point B *[1 mark]*.
c) Ultrafiltration is when substances are filtered out of the blood and enter the tubules in the kidneys *[1 mark]*. Blood enters a glomerulus, a bundle of capillaries looped inside a hollow ball called a Bowman's capsule *[1 mark]*. The blood in the glomerulus is under high pressure because it enters through the afferent arteriole and leaves through the smaller efferent arteriole *[1 mark]*. The high pressure forces liquid and small molecules in the blood out of the capillary and into the Bowman's capsule *[1 mark]*. The liquid and small molecules pass through the capillary wall, the basement membrane and slits in the epithelium of the Bowman's capsule. But larger molecules like proteins and blood cells can't pass through and stay in the blood *[1 mark]*.

Page 155 — Controlling Water Potential

1 a) Strenuous exercise causes more water to be lost from the body (through sweating), which decreases the water potential of the blood *[1 mark]*. This is detected by osmoreceptors in the hypothalamus *[1 mark]*, which stimulates the posterior pituitary gland to release more ADH *[1 mark]*.
b) ADH increases the permeability of the walls of the distal convoluted tubule and collecting duct *[1 mark]*. This means more water is reabsorbed into the medulla and into the blood by osmosis, so a small amount of concentrated urine is produced *[1 mark]*.
2 Gerbils have longer loops of Henle than mice or rats *[1 mark]*. A longer ascending limb means more ions are actively pumped out into the medulla *[1 mark]*, which creates a very low water potential in the medulla *[1 mark]*. This means more water moves out of the nephron into the capillaries, giving very concentrated/a very low volume of urine *[1 mark]*.

Answers

Page 157 — Kidney Failure and Detecting Chemicals

1   E.g. Advantages, any two from: Kidney transplants are cheaper in the long term than renal dialysis *[1 mark]*. / Having a kidney transplant is more convenient for a person than regular dialysis sessions *[1 mark]*. / A patient who has had a kidney transplant won't feel unwell between dialysis sessions *[1 mark]*.
Disadvantages: A transplant means the patient has to undergo a major operation, which is risky *[1 mark]*. The patient also has to take drugs to suppress the immune system so it doesn't reject the transplant *[1 mark]*.

Module 5: Section 3 — Animal Responses

Page 159 — The Nervous System

1 a) Hypothalamus *[1 mark]*.
  b) Control of breathing rate and heart rate *[1 mark]*.
  c) Lack of coordinated movement / balance / posture *[1 mark]*.
    You know that the cerebellum normally coordinates muscles, balance and posture, so damage to it is likely to cause a lack of coordinated movement, balance or posture.

2 a) It helps to maintain posture and balance *[1 mark]*.
  b) Any four from: Stretch receptors in the quadriceps muscle detect that the muscle is being stretched *[1 mark]*. A nerve impulse is passed along a sensory neurone *[1 mark]*, which communicates directly with a motor neurone in the spinal cord *[1 mark]*. The motor neurone carries the nerve impulse to the effector/quadriceps muscle *[1 mark]*, causing it to contract and the lower leg to move forward quickly *[1 mark]*. *[Maximum of 4 marks available.]*

Page 161 — 'Fight or Flight' Response and Heart Rate

1 a) High blood pressure is detected by pressure receptors in the aorta called baroreceptors *[1 mark]*. Impulses are sent along sensory neurones to the medulla *[1 mark]*. Impulses are then sent from the medulla to the SAN along the vagus nerve *[1 mark]*. The vagus nerve secretes acetylcholine, which binds to receptors on the sinoatrial node/SAN *[1 mark]*. This slows the heart rate (reducing blood pressure) *[1 mark]*.
  b) No impulses sent from the medulla would reach the SAN *[1 mark]*, so the heart rate wouldn't increase or decrease/ control of the heart rate would be lost *[1 mark]*.

Page 164 — Muscle Contraction

1   Drawing number 3 *[1 mark]* because the M-line connects the middle of the myosin filaments *[1 mark]*. The cross-section would only show myosin filaments, which are the thick filaments *[1 mark]*.
   The answer isn't drawing number 1 because all the dots in the cross-section are smaller, so the filaments shown are thin actin filaments — which aren't found at the M-line.

2   The A-bands stay the same length during contraction *[1 mark]*. The I-bands get shorter *[1 mark]*.

3   Muscles need ATP to relax because ATP provides the energy to break the actin-myosin cross bridges *[1 mark]*. If the cross bridges can't be broken, the myosin heads will remain attached to the actin filaments *[1 mark]*, so the actin filaments can't slide back to their relaxed position *[1 mark]*.

4   The muscles won't contract *[1 mark]* because calcium ions won't be released into the sarcoplasm, so troponin won't be removed from its binding site *[1 mark]*. This means no actin-myosin cross bridges can be formed *[1 mark]*.

Page 167 — Muscle Contraction

1 a) Creatine phosphate is split into creatine and phosphate *[1 mark]*. The phosphate group combines with ADP to make ATP *[1 mark]*.
  b) Short burst of vigorous activity, such as a tennis serve (or similar example) *[1 mark]* because it is used up in a few seconds / very quickly *[1 mark]*.

2   Any four from: When an action potential arrives at a neuromuscular junction, it triggers the release of the neurotransmitter acetylcholine *[1 mark]*. This should bind to nicotinic cholinergic receptors on the postsynaptic membrane *[1 mark]* and trigger depolarisation in the muscle cell causing it to contract *[1 mark]*. If some of the nicotinic cholinergic receptors are damaged or blocked, the muscle cells won't be depolarised and won't contract *[1 mark]*. Fewer muscle cells working properly will lead to muscle fatigue *[1 mark]*. *[Maximum of 4 marks available.]*

Module 5: Section 4 — Plant Responses and Hormones

Page 170 — Plant Responses

1 a) Because auxins are made in the shoot tip, so removing the tip means that any effects caused by auxins will only be due to the auxins added in the experiment *[1 mark]*.
  b) To provide the shoots with the energy they needed to grow *[1 mark]*.
  c) They are a (negative) control *[1 mark]*. They show that it is the auxin having the effect and nothing else about the sponges *[1 mark]*.
  d) **5-6 marks:**
    The answer fully explains all the results for shoots A-C for each experiment, with reference to the movement of auxin and the effect of auxin on the shoot cells.
    The answer has a clear and logical structure.
    The information given is relevant and detailed.
    3-4 marks:
    The answer explains some of the results for shoots A-C, with some reference to either the movement of auxin or its effect on the shoot cells.
    The answer has some structure. Most of the information given is relevant and there is some detail included.
    1-2 marks:
    One or two results are described with little or no explanation.
    The answer has no clear structure. The information given is basic and lacking in detail. It may not all be relevant.
    0 marks:
    No relevant information is given.

Answers

Here are some points your answer may include:
In experiment A, shoot A, the auxin diffused straight down from the sponge into the left-hand side of the shoot. This stimulated the cells on this side to elongate, so the shoot grew to the right. In shoot B, the opposite occurred, making the shoot grow to the left. In shoot C, equal amounts of auxin diffused down both sides, making all the cells elongate at the same rate and the shoot grow straight up. In experiment B, the shoots were exposed to a light source. The auxin diffused into the shaded/left-hand side of the shoots regardless of where the sponge was placed, so the shoots all grew to the right/towards the light. In each experiment (A and B), shoots A, B and C all grew the same amount as their growth was equally stimulated by the auxin and glucose. Shoots in experiment B grew 2 mm more than the shoots in experiment A because they were exposed to light. This meant they were able to carry out photosynthesis, which allowed them to put more energy into growth compared to the shoots in experiment A, which were in the dark and not photosynthesising.

Page 173 — The Effects of Plant Hormones

1   A *[1 mark]*
2 a) ethene *[1 mark]*
  b) Ethene stimulates enzymes that break down cell walls, break down chlorophyll and convert starch to sugars *[1 mark]*.
  c) E.g. the tomatoes are less likely to be damaged in transport *[1 mark]*.
3   Abscisic acid/ABA triggers stomatal closure *[1 mark]*. This helps the plant to conserve water, by reducing water loss through transpiration *[1 mark]*.

Module 5: Section 5 — Photosynthesis

Page 175 — Photosynthesis and Respiration

1   C *[1 mark]*.

Page 179 — Photosynthesis

1 a) The thylakoid membranes *[1 mark]*.
  b) Photosystem II *[1 mark]*.
  c) Light energy splits water *[1 mark]*.
     H_2O *[1 mark]* $\rightarrow 2H^+ + \frac{1}{2}O_2$ *[1 mark]*.
     The electrons from the water replace the electrons lost from chlorophyll *[1 mark]*.
     The question asks you to explain the purpose of photolysis, so make sure you include why the water is split up — to replace the electrons lost from chlorophyll.
  d) NADP *[1 mark]*.
2 a) *5-6 marks:*
     The answer describes the full process of triose phosphate production, including the reactants and products of each step, and the roles of RuBisCO, ATP and reduced NADP.
     The answer has a clear and logical structure.
     The information given is relevant and detailed.

3-4 marks:
The answer describes most of the process of triose phosphate production, including most of the reactants and products of each step and gives some mention of the roles of RuBisCO, ATP and reduced NADP.
The answer has some structure. Most of the information given is relevant and there is some detail involved.
1-2 marks:
Only one of the steps in the process of triose phosphate production is mentioned. There may be some mention of the role of one of either RuBisCO, ATP or reduced NADP.
The answer has no clear structure. The information given is basic and lacking in detail. It may not all be relevant.
0 marks:
No relevant information is given.
Here are some points your answer may include:
Ribulose bisphosphate/RuBP and carbon dioxide/CO_2 join together to form an unstable 6-carbon compound. This reaction is catalysed by the enzyme RuBisCO/ribulose bisphosphate carboxylase. The compound breaks down into two molecules of a 3-carbon compound called glycerate 3-phosphate/GP. Two molecules of glycerate 3-phosphate are then converted into two molecules of triose phosphate/TP. The energy for this reaction comes from ATP and the H^+ ions come from reduced NADP.
  b) Ribulose bisphosphate is regenerated from triose phosphate/TP molecules *[1 mark]*. ATP provides the energy to do this *[1 mark]*.
     This question is only worth two marks so only the main facts are needed, without the detail of the number of molecules.
  c) No glycerate 3-phosphate/GP would be produced *[1 mark]*, so no triose phosphate/TP would be produced *[1 mark]*. This means there would be no glucose produced *[1 mark]*.

Page 181 — Limiting Factors in Photosynthesis

1   25 °C *[1 mark]*. This is because photosynthesis involves enzymes *[1 mark]*, which become inactive at low temperatures/10 °C *[1 mark]* and denature at high temperatures/45 °C *[1 mark]*.

Page 183 — Limiting Factors in Photosynthesis

1 a) The level of GP will rise and levels of TP and RuBP will fall *[1 mark]*. This is because there's less reduced NADP and ATP from the light-dependent reaction *[1 mark]*, so the conversion of GP to TP and RuBP is slow *[1 mark]*.
  b) The levels of RuBP, GP and TP will fall *[1 mark]*. This is because the reactions in the Calvin cycle are slower *[1 mark]* due to all the enzymes working more slowly *[1 mark]*.
2   *5-6 marks:*
     A full description of the method used to investigate how temperature affects photosynthesis in Canadian pondweed is given, including all the apparatus needed.
     The answer has a clear and logical structure.
     The information given is relevant and detailed.
     3-4 marks:
     A description of the method used to investigate how temperature affects photosynthesis in Canadian pondweed is given, with one or two steps missing. Most of the apparatus needed is included.
     The answer has some structure. Most of the information given is relevant and there is some detail involved.

Answers

1-2 marks:
Only one or two of the steps in the method used to investigate how temperature affects photosynthesis in Canadian pondweed are given. There may be mention of some of the apparatus needed.
The information given is basic and lacking in detail. It may not all be relevant.
0 marks:
No relevant information is given.
Here are some points your answer may include:
A sample of pondweed would be placed in a test tube of water. The test tube would be placed in a beaker containing water at a known temperature. The test tube would be connected to a capillary tube of water and the capillary tube connected to a syringe. The pondweed would be allowed to photosynthesise for a set period of time. Afterwards, the syringe would be used to draw the bubble of oxygen produced up the capillary tube where its length would be measured using a ruler. The experiment is repeated and the mean length of gas bubble is calculated. Then the whole experiment is repeated at several different temperatures.

Module 5: Section 6 — Respiration

Page 185 — Aerobic Respiration

1 a) A = CO_2 *[1 mark]*, D = acetate *[1 mark]*, E = acetyl CoA *[1 mark]*
   b) Compound B (NAD) is reduced — it collects hydrogen from pyruvate, changing pyruvate into acetate *[1 mark]*.
   c) mitochondrial matrix *[1 mark]*
2 C - A 2 carbon molecule that is the product of the link reaction and feeds into the Krebs cycle *[1 mark]*.
3 D — Only 1 *[1 mark]*.
4 *5-6 marks:*
The answer describes the full process of glycolysis, including correct references to all the intermediate molecules, as well as the number of ATP and reduced NAD molecules made or used at each stage.
The answer has a clear and logical structure.
The information given is relevant and detailed.
3-4 marks:
The answer describes part of the process of glycolysis, including correct references to some of the intermediate molecules. There is some mention of the either the number of ATP or reduced NAD molecules made or used.
The answer has some structure. Most of the information given is relevant and there is some detail involved.
1-2 marks:
The answer mentions at least one of the stages of glycolysis, but lacks correct reference to the intermediate molecules or the involvement of ATP and NAD.
The answer has no clear structure. The information given is basic and lacking in detail. It may not all be relevant.
0 marks:
No relevant information is given.

Here are some points your answer may include:
First, the 6-carbon glucose molecule is phosphorylated by adding two phosphates from two molecules of ATP. This creates one molecule of 6-carbon hexose bisphosphate and two molecules of ADP. Then, the hexose bisphosphate is split up into two molecules of 3-carbon triose phosphate. Triose phosphate is oxidised (by removing hydrogen) to give two molecules of 3-carbon pyruvate. The hydrogen is accepted by two molecules of NAD, producing two molecules of reduced NAD. During this step, four molecules of ATP are produced.

Page 187 — Aerobic Respiration

1 a) The transfer of electrons down the electron transport chain stops *[1 mark]*. So there's no energy released to phosphorylate ADP/produce ATP *[1 mark]*.
   b) The Krebs cycle stops *[1 mark]* because there's no oxidised NAD/FAD coming from the electron transport chain *[1 mark]*.
   Part b is a bit tricky — remember that when the electron transport chain is inhibited, the reactions that depend on the products of the chain are also affected.

Page 189 — Anaerobic Respiration and RQs

1 Because lactate fermentation doesn't involve electron carriers/the electron transport chain/oxidative phosphorylation *[1 mark]*.
2 RQ = $CO_2 \div O_2$ *[1 mark]*
So the RQ of triolein = $57 \div 80 = 0.71$ *[1 mark]*
Award 2 marks for the correct answer of 0.71, without any working.

Page 191 — Respiration Experiments

1 *5-6 marks:*
A full description of the method is given, making it clear how the effect of temperature should be investigated. It includes all the apparatus required, states any variables that should be controlled, and outlines any repeats and control experiments that are needed.
The answer has a clear and logical structure.
The information given is relevant and detailed.
3-4 marks:
A brief description of the method is given that shows how the effect of temperature should be investigated. However, full details about the apparatus required, variables that should be controlled or repeats and control experiments needed aren't included.
The answer has some structure. Most of the information given is relevant and there is some detail involved.
1-2 marks:
There is some description of the method, but it's not clear how the effect of temperature should be investigated. There is limited mention of the apparatus required, variables that should be controlled or repeats and control experiments needed.
The answer has no clear structure. The information given is basic and lacking in detail. It may not all be relevant.
0 marks:
No relevant information is given.

Answers

Here are some points your answer may include:
The respirometer should be set up in a water bath at one of the temperatures under investigation. In one of the tubes of the respirometer, a known mass of germinating mung beans should be placed on top of the gauze. The other tube should be set up as a control tube by placing glass beads, of the same mass as the mung beans, on top of the gauze. The syringe should be used to adjust the level of the fluid in the manometer to a known level. The apparatus should then be left for a set period of time (e.g. 20 minutes) with the tap closed. After this time, the distance moved by the liquid should be measured and used to calculate the volume of oxygen taken up by the mung beans per minute. Any other variables that could affect the results, e.g. light intensity, should be kept constant. The experiment should then be repeated at each of the temperatures under investigation several times and the mean results calculated.

Extra Exam Practice for Module 5

Pages 192-193

2 a) The calcium ions leave their binding site on troponin *[1 mark]*, which causes the tropomyosin molecules to move back so they block the actin-myosin binding sites again *[1 mark]*. Because there are no actin-myosin cross-bridges, the actin filaments slide back to their relaxed position, lengthening the sarcomere *[1 mark]*.

b) i) Thermoreceptors detect the rise in body temperature and send impulses along sensory neurones to the hypothalamus *[1 mark]*. The hypothalamus then sends impulses along motor neurones to the sweat glands, causing them to secrete more sweat *[1 mark]*.

ii) A person with diabetes insipidus would be more at risk of dehydration, because not as much ADH would be released when the fall in blood water potential was detected *[1 mark]*. This would mean that the permeability of the DCT and collecting duct wouldn't be increased as much as normal *[1 mark]*, so not as much water would be reabsorbed into the blood by osmosis from the glomerular filtrate *[1 mark]*. With less water being reabsorbed into the blood, it would be more difficult to increase the blood water potential, meaning the person would be more at risk of dehydration *[1 mark]*.

3 a) ABA binds to receptors in guard cell membranes *[1 mark]*. This causes ion channels inside the guard cells to open and ions to leave, which raises the water potential inside the cells *[1 mark]*. Water leaves the cells via osmosis, meaning that the guard cells become flaccid and the stomata close *[1 mark]*. This results in less carbon dioxide being able to enter the leaves, so there is less carbon dioxide available for the light-independent stage of photosynthesis *[1 mark]*.

b) i) Any two from: e.g. the temperature the seeds were germinated in. / The moisture levels of the substrate / humidity the seeds were germinated in. / The pH of the substrate the seeds were germinated in. / The species of plant used in the investigation. *[2 marks]*

ii) The rate of seed germination would have been lower in the genetically modified plants compared to the plants which had not had the *OsNCED4* gene inserted *[1 mark]*. This is because the enzyme would have led to more ABA being synthesised in the genetically modified plants, which would have resulted in a greater inhibitory effect on gibberellins *[1 mark]*. As gibberellins normally stimulate seed germination, this would have resulted in the genetically modified plants showing a reduced rate of seed germination *[1 mark]*.

4 a) i) The increased permeability of the membrane to ions will alter the potential difference of the membrane *[1 mark]*. This will lead to a generator potential big enough to trigger an action potential *[1 mark]*. Action potentials will travel along sensory neurones to the brain, which will interpret the impulses as feelings of pain *[1 mark]*.

ii) If the sensitivity of cell receptors to serotonin is reduced then this could result in the associated enzyme in the cell membrane not being activated when serotonin binds to these receptors *[1 mark]*. This would mean that the production of the signalling molecule/second messenger would not be catalysed *[1 mark]*. This could prevent cascade reactions from occurring in these cells, meaning that they may not be able to react properly to communication/signals from other cells *[1 mark]*.

b) **5-6 marks:**
The answer fully explains how sulfonylureas work as a treatment for Type 2 diabetes and suggests why doctors may be reluctant to prescribe them by referring to the link between Type 2 diabetes and obesity.
The answer has a clear and logical structure.
The information given is relevant and detailed.
3-4 marks:
The answer explains briefly how sulfonylureas work as a treatment for Type 2 diabetes and there is a basic suggestion as to why doctors may be reluctant to prescribe them.
The answer has some structure. Most of the information given is relevant and there is some detail involved.
1-2 marks:
The answer includes a basic explanation of how sulfonylureas work as a treatment for Type 2 diabetes. The answer has no clear structure. The information given is basic and lacking in detail. It may not all be relevant.
0 marks:
No relevant information is given.
Here are some points your answer may include:
Type 2 diabetes can occur when β cells in the pancreas don't produce enough insulin, meaning that the blood glucose concentration becomes too high.
Sulfonylureas cause the potassium ion channels in the β cells to close. This means that potassium ions cannot pass through the β cell plasma membranes so they build up inside the cells. This makes the inside of the β cells more positive so the plasma membranes of the β cells become depolarised.

Answers

Depolarisation triggers calcium ion channels in the plasma membranes to open, so calcium ions diffuse into the β cells. The influx of calcium ions into the β cells causes the vesicles containing insulin to fuse with the plasma membrane and release insulin. This increases the amount of insulin in the blood, meaning that more glucose can be taken up by the body cells, which reduces the blood glucose concentration.

Some doctors may be reluctant to prescribe sulfonylureas to patients because Type 2 diabetes is often linked to obesity, so many patients may already be overweight.

Module 6: Section 1 — Cellular Control

Page 195 — Regulating Gene Expression

1 The introns from primary mRNA (pre-mRNA) are removed in a process called splicing *[1 mark]*. This makes mature mRNA, which consists only of the exons *[1 mark]*.
2 When no lactose is present, the lac repressor binds to the operator site and blocks transcription *[1 mark]*. When lactose is present, it binds to the lac repressor *[1 mark]*, changing its shape so that it can no longer bind to the operator site *[1 mark]*. RNA polymerase can now begin transcription of the structural genes, including the ones that code for β-galactosidase and lactose permease *[1 mark]*.

Page 197 — Regulating Gene Expression

1 Insertion *[1 mark]*.
2 Because they all have similar genes called Hox genes, which control body plan development *[1 mark]*. These Hox genes contain homeobox sequences, which are highly conserved between different organisms *[1 mark]*.

Module 6: Section 2 — Patterns of Inheritance

Page 199 — Types and Causes of Variation

1 a) Coat colour — because it shows discontinuous variation *[1 mark]*.
 You can tell the variation is discontinuous because there are no intermediate categories of coat colour — puppies are either yellow, chocolate or black and nothing inbetween (like yellowy-black). Discontinuous variation is usually controlled by only a small number genes (or a single gene).
 b) Mass — because it shows continuous variation *[1 mark]*.
 c) 18.99 − 9.25 = **9.74 kg** *[1 mark]*

Page 202 — Inheritance

1 Parents' genotypes identified as RR and rr *[1 mark]*. Correct genetic diagram drawn with gametes' alleles identified as R, R and r, r *[1 mark]* and gametes crossed to show Rr as the only possible genotype in the offspring *[1 mark]*.
 The question specifically asks you to draw a genetic diagram so make sure that you include one in your answer, e.g.

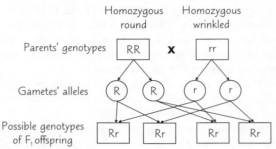

2 a) Because the alleles for red and white coats are codominant, so they are both expressed in the phenotype *[1 mark]*.
 b) Parents' genotypes identified as C^WC^W and C^RC^W *[1 mark]*. Correct genetic diagram drawn with gametes' alleles identified as C^W, C^W and C^R, C^W *[1 mark]* and gametes crossed to show two offspring with genotype C^WC^W and two with genotype C^RC^W *[1 mark]*. The phenotypes of the offspring are stated as two white and two roan *[1 mark]*.
 The question specifically asks you to draw a genetic diagram so make sure that you include one in your answer, e.g.

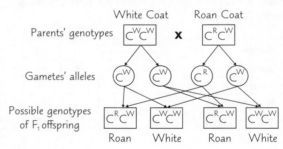

Page 205 — Linkages and Epistasis

1 a) Parents' genotypes identified as X^HX^h and X^hY *[1 mark]*. Correct genetic diagram drawn with gametes' alleles identified as X^H, X^h and X^h, Y *[1 mark]* and gametes crossed to show X^HX^h, X^HY, X^hX^h and X^hY as the possible genotypes of the offspring *[1 mark]*.
 The question specifically asks you to draw a genetic diagram, so make sure that you include one in your answer, e.g.

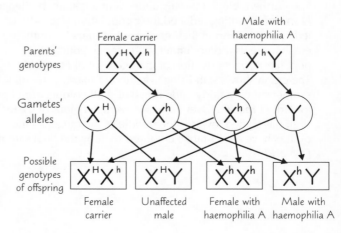

Answers

b) Men only have one copy of the X chromosome (XY) but women have two (XX) *[1 mark]*. Haemophilia A is caused by a recessive allele, so females would need two copies of the allele for them to have haemophilia A *[1 mark]*. As males only have one X chromosome they only need one recessive allele to have haemophilia A, which makes them more likely to have haemophilia A than females *[1 mark]*.

2 A cross between CCGG and ccgg will produce a 9 : 3 : 4 phenotypic ratio in the F_2 generation *[1 mark]* of coloured grey : coloured black : albino *[1 mark]*. This is because gene 1 has a recessive epistatic gene (c) *[1 mark]*, and two copies of the recessive epistatic gene (cc) will mask the expression of the colour gene *[1 mark]*.

You don't need to draw a genetic diagram to explain the phenotypic ratio that you'd expect from this cross. You can just state the ratio and explain it using your own knowledge.

3 The table shows that a cross between hhss and HHSS produces a 36 : 9 : 3 or 12 : 3 : 1 phenotypic ratio in the F_2 generation of bald : straight hair : curly hair *[1 mark]*. This is because the hair gene has a dominant epistatic allele (H) *[1 mark]*, which means having at least one copy of the dominant epistatic gene (Hh or HH) will result in a bald phenotype that masks the expression of the type of hair gene *[1 mark]*.

Page 207 — The Chi-Squared Test

1 a) *[3 marks]* for a correct answer of 3.81. Otherwise, allow *[1 mark]* for each of the $O-E^{-2}$ and $(O-E)^2/E$ columns correctly filled in.

Phenotype	Ratio	Expected Result (E)	Observed Result (O)	O – E	O – E²	$\frac{(O - E^2)}{E}$
Blue with white spots	9	135	131	–4	16	0.12
Purple with white spots	3	45	52	7	49	1.09
Blue with yellow spots	3	45	48	3	9	0.2
Purple with yellow spots	1	15	9	–6	36	2.4
						3.81

b) The χ^2 value does support the null hypothesis *[1 mark]* because it's smaller than the critical value *[1 mark]*.

Module 6: Section 3 — Evolution

Page 210 — Evolution by Natural Selection and Genetic Drift

1 The northern elephant seals underwent a genetic bottleneck *[1 mark]*. Hunting reduced their population size, which led to a reduction in their gene pool *[1 mark]*. Southern elephant seals did not undergo the same reduction in population size/reduction of their gene pool *[1 mark]*.

2 a) The graph shows stabilising selection *[1 mark]*. The initial sample shows a fairly wide range of shell colours from light to dark *[1 mark]*. Over time, the average colour of oyster shell has shifted towards the middle of the range, so more oysters have a mid-range coloured shell by the final sample *[1 mark]*.

b) Oyster shells at the extremes of light and dark are less likely to survive because they can be more easily seen by predators against the sand *[1 mark]*. This means that the mid-range coloured oysters have an advantage and are more likely to survive and reproduce *[1 mark]*. The advantageous alleles for mid-range coloured oysters are more likely to be passed on to the next generation *[1 mark]* leading to an increase in mid-range coloured oysters in the population *[1 mark]*.

Page 213 — Hardy-Weinberg Principle and Artificial Selection

1 Farmers could have selected a male and female with a high meat yield and bred these two together *[1 mark]*. Then they could have selected the offspring with the highest meat yields and bred them together *[1 mark]*. This process could have been continued over several generations to produce cattle with a very high meat yield *[1 mark]*.

2 q = 0.23
p + q = 1
so p = 1 – 0.23 = 0.77
The frequency of the heterozygous genotype = 2pq
= 2(0.77 × 0.23)
= **0.35 *[2 marks for the correct answer or 1 mark for p = 0.77 or 2(p × 0.23)]***

3 a) Frequency of genotype CC = p^2 = 0.14
So the frequency of the dominant allele = p = $\sqrt{0.14}$
= 0.37
The frequency of the recessive allele = q
q = 1 – p
q = 1 – 0.37
= **0.63 *[2 marks for the correct answer or 1 mark for $1 - \sqrt{0.14}$]***

b) Frequency of the homozygous recessive genotype = q^2
= 0.63^2
= **0.4 *[1 mark for the correct answer. Allow 1 mark for evidence of correct calculation using incorrect answer to part a)]***

Page 215 — Speciation

1 a) The new species could not breed with each other *[1 mark]*.

b) Different populations of flies were isolated and fed on different foods *[1 mark]*. This led to changes in allele frequencies between the populations *[1 mark]*, which made them reproductively isolated and eventually resulted in speciation *[1 mark]*.

c) Any two from: e.g. seasonal changes (become sexually active at different times) *[1 mark]* / mechanical changes (changes to genitalia) *[1 mark]* / behavioural changes (changes in behaviour that prevent mating) *[1 mark]*.

d) E.g. geographical barrier *[1 mark]* / flood *[1 mark]* / volcanic eruption *[1 mark]* / earthquake *[1 mark]* / polyploid organisms are formed *[1 mark]*.

Answers

Module 6: Section 4 — Manipulating Genomes

Page 218 — Common Techniques

1   **5-6 marks:**
The answer describes and explains the full process of PCR, including correct references to all the molecules and temperatures involved.
The answer has a clear and logical structure.
The information given is relevant and detailed.
3-4 marks:
The answer describes the full process of PCR including the molecules involved, but gives limited explanation of the process or detail of the temperatures involved.
The answer has some structure. Most of the information given is relevant and there is some detail involved.
1-2 marks:
The answer mentions at least one of the molecules involved in PCR and gives a basic description of the process, but lacks any explanation of the process or detail of the temperatures involved.
The answer has no clear structure. The information given is basic and lacking in detail. It may not all be relevant.
0 marks:
No relevant information is given.
Here are some points your answer may include:
The DNA sample from the hair is mixed with free nucleotides, primers and DNA polymerase. The mixture is heated to 95 °C to break the hydrogen bonds. The mixture is then cooled to between 50-65 °C to allow the primers to bind/anneal to the DNA. The primers bind/anneal to the DNA because they have a sequence that's complementary to the sequence at the start of the DNA fragment. The mixture is then heated to 72 °C and DNA polymerase lines up free nucleotides along each template strand, producing new strands of DNA. The cycle would be repeated over and over to produce lots of copies.
This question asks you to describe and explain, so you need to give the reasons why each stage is done to gain full marks.

Page 219 — DNA Profiling

1 a) DNA is isolated from all the samples *[1 mark]*. PCR is used to amplify multiple areas containing different sequence repeats *[1 mark]*. The DNA mixture undergoes electrophoresis to separate out the bands according to size *[1 mark]*.
   b) The blood is most likely to belong to missing person B because all of the bands on this DNA profile match that of the blood sample *[1 mark]*.

Page 221 — Genetic Engineering

1   C *[1 mark]*
2 a) Colony A is shown on the plate under UV light, whereas colony B isn't *[1 mark]*, which shows that colony A contains the YFP gene, so it contains transformed cells *[1 mark]*.

   b) The plasmid vector DNA would have been cut open with the same restriction endonuclease that was used to isolate the DNA fragment containing the YFP gene *[1 mark]*. The plasmid DNA and gene (DNA fragment) would have been mixed together with DNA ligase *[1 mark]*. DNA ligase joins the sugar-phosphate backbone of the two bits of DNA *[1 mark]*.
   c) A suspension of unmodified bacterial cells would have been mixed with plasmids containing the YFP gene *[1 mark]*. Then the mixture would have been put into an electroporator where an electrical field increased the permeability of the bacterial cell membranes *[1 mark]*. This would have been done to allow the bacterial cells to take in the plasmids *[1 mark]*.

Page 223 — Genetically Modified Organisms

1   **5-6 marks:**
The answer fully describes how genetic engineering could be used to create a bromoxynil-resistant cotton plant (including the use of restriction enzymes) and fully explains several ethical issues (both positive and negative) surrounding bromoxynil-resistant cotton plants.
The answer has a clear and logical structure.
The information given is relevant and detailed.
3-4 marks:
The answer briefly describes how genetic engineering could be used to create a bromoxynil-resistant cotton plant and explains some of the positive and negative ethical issues surrounding bromoxynil-resistant cotton plants.
The answer has some structure. Most of the information given is relevant and there is some detail involved.
1-2 marks:
The answer gives a basic description of how genetic engineering could be used to create a bromoxynil-resistant cotton plant and references one positive and one negative ethical issue surrounding bromoxynil-resistant cotton plants.
The answer has no clear structure. The information given is basic and lacking in detail. It may not all be relevant.
0 marks:
No relevant information is given.
Here are some points your answer may include:
The gene responsible for the enzyme that converts bromoxynil to a harmless substance could be isolated using restriction enzymes, and then inserted into a bacterial plasmid. The plasmid could be reinserted into the bacteria and then the cotton plant infected with the transformed bacteria.
The creation of bromoxynil-resistant cotton plants raises positive ethical issues. For example, it should reduce the amount of chemical weedkillers used by farmers, which can harm the environment. The patenting of the gene could also be seen as a positive ethical issue, as sale of the genically modified cotton plant seeds will generate money for the company that owns the patent and they could then use this money to research and develop other beneficial genetically modified products.
However, the creation of bromoxynil-resistant cotton plants also raises negative ethical issues. For example, it could encourage monoculture, which decreases biodiversity. Also, the patenting of the gene may mean that some farmers in poorer countries cannot afford to produce bromoxynil-resistant cotton plants year on year.

Answers

Page 224 — Gene Therapy

1 a) Gene therapy involves altering/supplementing defective genes (mutated alleles) inside cells to treat genetic disorders *[1 mark]*.
b) Somatic gene therapy *[1 mark]*.

Page 227 — Sequencing Genes and Genomes

1 a) DNA polymerase *[1 mark]*, DNA primer *[1 mark]*, free nucleotides *[1 mark]* and fluorescently-labelled modified nucleotides *[1 mark]*.
b) E.g. it's faster/more bases can be sequenced in a given time/ whole genomes can be sequenced more quickly *[1 mark]*, it is much cheaper *[1 mark]*.
2 They could sequence the genome of each bacterial species *[1 mark]* and then compare the genomes using computer software/bioinformatics/computational biology to establish how closely related they are *[1 mark]*.

Module 6: Section 5 — Cloning and Biotechnology

Page 229 — Plant Cloning

1 She could use tissue culture *[1 mark]*. The cell would be sterilised, to kill off any contaminating microorganisms *[1 mark]*, then placed on a culture medium containing nutrients and growth factors *[1 mark]*. The cell would then divide and grow into a small plant *[1 mark]*.

Page 231 — Animal Cloning

1 a) The nucleus from a somatic cell from Alpaca A *[1 mark]* is inserted into an enucleated oocyte taken from another individual *[1 mark]*. The host cell containing its new nucleus is stimulated by electrofusion to divide and produce an embryo *[1 mark]* and the embryo is implanted into a surrogate mother, where it develops into a clone of Alpaca A *[1 mark]*.
b) Any two from: e.g. any undesirable genetic characteristics from Alpaca A will be passed on to all the herd *[1 mark]*. / Animal cloning is a time-consuming, difficult and expensive process *[1 mark]*. / There is a risk that the cloned herd may have a shorter life-span than conventionally bred alpacas *[1 mark]*. / There is no genetic variability within the herd, which could make the entire herd susceptible to being wiped out by a single disease *[1 mark]*.

Page 235 — Biotechnology

1 a) Using aseptic techniques can prevent contamination of cultures by unwanted microorganisms *[1 mark]*. This is important because contamination could affect the growth of *E. coli*, which would reduce the precision of his results *[1 mark]* or allow the growth of microorganisms that could be harmful to health *[1 mark]*.

b) E.g. Minimise the time that the culture medium is open/ put the lid on the agar plate quickly/work in an inoculation cabinet to reduce the chances of airborne microorganisms from contaminating the culture *[1 mark]*. If the bacterial sample is in broth, briefly pass the neck of the container through a Bunsen burner flame just after it's opened and just before it's closed so that air moves out of the container and unwanted microorganisms are prevented from falling in *[1 mark]*. Sterilise equipment before and after use to kill any unwanted microorganisms *[1 mark]*.

Page 237 — Immobilised Enzymes

1 a) Immobilised means that the enzyme is attached to an insoluble material *[1 mark]*.
b) By being encapsulated in alginate beads *[1 mark]*, trapped in a silica gel matrix *[1 mark]* or covalently bonded to cellulose or collagen fibres *[1 mark]*.
2 a) Glucoamylase catalyses the conversion of dextrins to glucose *[1 mark]*.
b) Any two from: e.g. the extra equipment needed to use immobilised enzymes can be expensive to buy *[1 mark]*. / Immobilised enzymes are more expensive to buy than free enzymes *[1 mark]*. / The activity of immobilised enzymes can be lower in comparison to free enzymes *[1 mark]*.

Module 6: Section 6 — Ecosystems

Page 239 — An Introduction to Ecosystems

1 C *[1 mark]*
2 a) If the fruit does not develop properly there will be less food available for the consumers *[1 mark]*. If the primary consumers don't get enough food, fewer of them will survive so there will be less food available for the secondary consumers, and likewise for the tertiary consumers *[1 mark]*.
b) Any two from: e.g. rainfall/precipitation *[1 mark]* / shape of land/topology *[1 mark]* / soil nutrient availability *[1 mark]*.

Page 241 — Energy Transfer Through an Ecosystem

1 a) Not all of the energy available from the grass is taken in by the Arctic hare *[1 mark]*. This is because some parts of the grass aren't eaten, so the energy they contain isn't taken in *[1 mark]*, and some parts of the grass are indigestible, so they'll pass through the hare and come out as waste *[1 mark]*. Also, some energy is lost to the environment when the Arctic hare uses energy for respiration *[1 mark]*.
b) $(137 \div 2345) \times 100 = 5.8$ *[1 mark]*
Efficiency of energy transfer = **5.8%** *[1 mark]*
Award 2 marks for correct answer of **5.8%** without any working.
2 a) You could take a 1 m^2 sample area of his cabbage field and calculate the dry mass of the cabbages *[1 mark]*. You would then multiply the mass of the sample by the total area of the field *[1 mark]*.

b) One mark for suggestion and a second mark for associated explanation up to a maximum of four marks: e.g. he could use herbicides to kill weeds that compete with the cabbages for energy *[1 mark]*. Reducing competition means the cabbages receive more energy, so they grow faster and become larger, increasing productivity *[1 mark]*. / He could use fungicides to kill fungal infections that damage the cabbages *[1 mark]*. The cabbages would use more energy for growth and less for fighting infection, so would grow faster and become larger, increasing productivity *[1 mark]*. / He could use insecticides to kill insect pests that eat and damage the cabbages *[1 mark]*. Killing insect pests means less biomass is lost from the cabbages, so they grow to be larger, which means productivity is greater *[1 mark]*. / He could introduce natural predators to the field to eat cabbage pest species *[1 mark]*. This means the cabbages lose less energy and biomass due to damage caused by pest species, which increases productivity *[1 mark]*. / He could use fertilisers to provide the cabbages with all the minerals needed for optimum growth, e.g. nitrates *[1 mark]*. Adding fertiliser means the cabbages have all the minerals they need and this maximises the amount of energy they can use for growth/the efficiency of energy conversion *[1 mark]*.

Page 243 — Recycling in Ecosystems

1 a) A — nitrification *[1 mark]*,
B — nitrogen fixation *[1 mark]*
  b) Process C is denitrification *[1 mark]*. Denitrification is where nitrates in the soil are converted into nitrogen gas by denitrifying bacteria *[1 mark]*. The denitrifying bacteria use nitrates to respire anaerobically, which releases nitrogen gas *[1 mark]*.
2 Carbon (in the form of CO_2) is absorbed by grass when it carries out photosynthesis — the grass converts carbon to carbon compounds in its tissues *[1 mark]*. Cattle (primary consumers) eat the grass and they incorporate the carbon compounds it contains into their tissues *[1 mark]*.

Page 245 — Succession

1 D *[1 mark]*
2 a) Primary succession *[1 mark]* because the sand is freshly exposed and there is no soil or organic matter to start with *[1 mark]*.
  b) When grass dies, microorganisms decompose the dead organic material forming a soil *[1 mark]*. The formation of soil helps to retain water and makes the conditions less hostile, which allows larger plants (e.g. shrubs) to move in *[1 mark]*. The larger plants are better adapted for the improved conditions and out-compete the species already there, so they become the dominant species *[1 mark]*.

Page 247 — Investigating Ecosystems

1 a) Take a random sample of the population of daffodils in the field *[1 mark]*.
  b) Several frame quadrats would be placed on the ground at random locations within the field *[1 mark]*. The percentage of each frame quadrat that's covered by daffodils would be recorded *[1 mark]*. The percentage cover for the whole field could then be estimated by averaging the data collected in all of the frame quadrats *[1 mark]*.

c) Including plant species that aren't daffodils (or ignoring daffodil plants) could lead to inaccurate percentage cover estimates being calculated in frame quadrats *[1 mark]*.

Module 6: Section 7 — Populations and Sustainability

Page 249 — Factors Affecting Population Size

1 **5-6 marks:**
The answer fully describes and explains how the population sizes of both the predator and prey species vary over the first 10 years, using a range of figures taken from the graph. The answer has a clear and logical structure. The information given is relevant and detailed.
3-4 marks:
The answer partly describes how the population sizes of the predator and prey species vary over the first 10 years and offers some explanation for this. Some figures from the graph are included.
The answer has some structure. Most of the information given is relevant and there is some detail involved.
1-2 marks:
The answer outlines how the population size of either the predator or prey species varies over the first 10 years. No explanation is given. A figure from the graph may be included.
The answer has no clear structure. The information given is basic and lacking in detail. It may not all be relevant.
0 marks:
No relevant information is given.
Here are some points your answer may include:
In the first three years, the population of prey increases from 5000 to 30 000. The population of predators increases slightly later (in the first five years), from 4000 to 11 000. This is because there's more food available for the predators. The prey population then falls after year three to 3000 just before year 10, because lots are being eaten by the large population of predators. Shortly after the prey population falls, the predator population also falls (back to 4000 by just after year 10) because there's less food available.

Page 251 — Conservation of Ecosystems

1 a) It provides wood for people to use today without depleting the woodland/reducing the ability of people in the future to take wood from the woodland *[1 mark]*.
  b) Any two from: e.g. it maintains the woodland habitat for other organisms *[1 mark]*. / It allows new trees to grow from seeds produced by the mature standards *[1 mark]*. / The mature standards can be used to produce larger logs at a later date *[1 mark]*.
  You're not expected to know the answer to this question, just to be able to come up with sensible suggestions.
  c) So that the mature standard trees don't block out the light that the coppiced trees need to grow *[1 mark]*.

Answers

Page 253 — Conservation of Ecosystems

1 E.g. in the Terai Arc, farmers are encouraged to plant mint hedges around their crops to protect them from being eaten and trampled by elephants and to avoid the elephants being killed. In the Maasai Mara, conservation trusts have helped the local people to make money from conservation or ecotourism projects rather than farming / to farm in a more sustainable way. In peat bog areas of the UK, government-funded programmes have given farmers money to farm in a more sustainable way, e.g. by reducing the number of livestock that graze on peat bogs. These ways are all similar because they allow the economic needs of the farmer to be met/they allow the farmer to continue to make a living, whilst also conserving the areas in which they farm. *[1 mark per correct named example, plus 1 mark for a comparison of the examples.]*

Extra Exam Practice for Module 6

Pages 254-255

2 a) i) Primary succession occurs when pioneer species colonise new land surfaces that don't contain soil *[1 mark]*. As the grasses in Figure 2 require soil and begin growing from time = 0, soil must already be in the environment and so Figure 2 cannot be showing primary succession *[1 mark]*.

ii) E.g. at point B the biomass of trees is greater than it is at point A, which suggests that the shrub species face greater competition from trees at point B *[1 mark]*. Greater competition is likely to reduce the carrying capacity of shrub species, as there are not enough resources to maintain the population size of each species *[1 mark]*.

Remember, the carrying capacity is the maximum stable population size of a species that an ecosystem can support.

b) Directional selection is likely to have acted on the trees *[1 mark]*. Trees with the allele(s) for thicker bark would have been more likely to survive wildfires and to reproduce, passing on the allele(s) for thicker bark *[1 mark]*. Over time this increased the frequency of the allele(s) for thicker bark in the population of trees frequently exposed to wildfires *[1 mark]*.

3 a) Any two from: e.g. *E. coli* has a shorter life-cycle, compared to pigs or cows, meaning that more insulin could be produced from *E. coli* in a given time. / Growing *E. coli* doesn't require as much space or resources as rearing pigs or cows, so producing insulin from *E. coli* could be more economical. / There may be fewer ethical considerations from using *E. coli* compared to extracting insulin from pig or cow pancreases. / Using transformed *E. coli* produces human insulin, whereas using pigs or cows means using pig or cow insulin, which may not be as effective as human insulin / may cause unwelcome side effects. *[2 marks]*

b) i) In the absence of lactose, RNA polymerase would be unable to bind to the promoter region of the *lac* operon because the lac repressor protein would be bonded to the operator region *[1 mark]*. This means that the T7 RNA polymerase gene would not be transcribed and so the insulin gene would not be transcribed *[1 mark]*.

The scientists could add lactose to the *E. coli* when they want insulin to be produced *[1 mark]*, as this would bind to the repressor and change its shape so that it would no longer block the transcription of the T7 RNA polymerase gene and the insulin gene could be transcribed *[1 mark]*.

ii) Adding nutrients to the fermentation vessel could mean that the exponential phase is prolonged *[1 mark]* as conditions are maintained at more favourable levels/ nutrient availability is maintained at a high level for longer, which allows the bacteria to continue to reproduce for longer, delaying the onset of the stationary phase *[1 mark]*.

Remember, the stationary phase occurs when the population size stays constant — this happens when there's not enough food for bacteria to continue to reproduce and poisonous waste products build up and begin to kill the bacteria.

c) i) Concentration of bacterial cells present in the test tube solution = $1.5 \times 10^4 \div 10 = 1.5 \times 10^3$ bacterial cells per cm^3.
Number of bacterial cells transferred to agar plate = $1.5 \times 10^3 \div 10 = $ **150 cells**
[2 marks for the correct answer, otherwise 1 mark for correctly calculating the number of bacteria per cm^3 in the test tube]

By adding 1 cm^3 of the initial solution to 9 cm^3 of sterile buffer, the initial solution is diluted by a factor of 10. So to find the number of bacteria per cm^3 in the test tube you need to divide the starting concentration by 10. The scientist only transferred 0.1 cm^3 (a tenth of 1 cm^3) of the solution to the agar plate, so to find how many cells were transferred you need to divide by 10 again.

ii) $N = N_0 \times 2^n$
N_0 = initial number of cells = 1
n = number of divisions = $10 \div 0.5 = 20$
$1 \times 2^{20} = 1\,048\,576 = $ **1.05 × 10^6 bacterial cells in each colony** (to 3 s.f.)
[2 marks for the correct answer, otherwise 1 mark for 1×2^{20}]

Synoptic Practice

Pages 258-265

1 a) The *Rhizobium* bacteria could fix nitrogen gas in the atmosphere and convert it into ammonia *[1 mark]* for the plant to use for growth/to make proteins *[1 mark]*.

b) The G2 checkpoint checks whether all the DNA has been replicated without any damage *[1 mark]*. If there is loss of function of this checkpoint then this could mean that damaged/mutated DNA is passed on to the daughter cell, which could lead to the incorrect amino acids being coded for and therefore the incorrect proteins being synthesised *[1 mark]*.

c) During prophase, the nuclear envelope of the dividing cell breaks down to release the chromosomes so they lie free in the cytoplasm *[1 mark]*. After the sister chromatids have separated (in anaphase) the formation of new nuclear envelopes around each group of chromosomes means that each daughter cell contains its own nucleus *[1 mark]*.

d) Lectins could bind to glycoproteins/glycolipids in the cell membrane of their target cells *[1 mark]*. The lectins would only be able to bind to the glycoproteins/glycolipids that have a complementary shape to them, meaning that the lectins can only communicate with their target cells *[1 mark]*.

e) i) abscisic acid/ABA *[1 mark]*

ii) When the stomata are open, water diffuses out of the leaf into the surrounding air, so closing the stomata helps the plant to conserve water *[1 mark]*.

iii) Prolonged stomatal closure would lead to a lack of carbon dioxide in the leaf *[1 mark]*. This would mean there was less carbon dioxide present to react with ribulose bisphosphate/RuBP in the Calvin cycle/ light-independent stage of photosynthesis, so the amount of ribulose bisphosphate/RuBP in the chloroplasts would increase *[1 mark]*. The reaction between carbon dioxide and ribulose bisphosphate/RuBP is needed to produce glycerate 3-phosphate/GP, so with a lack of carbon dioxide in the leaf the amount of glycerate 3-phosphate/ GP in the chloroplasts would decrease *[1 mark]*.

f) i) She could have put a stage micrometer on the stage then looked down the eyepiece and used the divisions/scale/ units on the stage micrometer to determine the value of each division on the eyepiece graticule *[1 mark]*.

ii) E.g. it's unclear whether the student controlled all the variables that could have affected the results, and if she didn't control them all then the conclusion may not be valid *[1 mark]*. / The student only grew one plant in water and one in the lectin solution, so she would need to carry out repeats to make sure there were no variables associated with these individual plants affecting the results and making the conclusion invalid *[1 mark]*.

2 a) RuBisCO is an enzyme involved in the Calvin cycle/ light-independent reaction of photosynthesis *[1 mark]*. An increase in RuBisCO's activity would mean that more organic substances could be produced, which would increase the producer's biomass *[1 mark]*.

b) The efficiency of energy transfer from the producer to primary consumer = 7%

Energy transferred to primary consumer
= (64 375 ÷ 100) × 7
= 4506.25 kJ m^{-2} yr^{-1}

Energy intake of secondary consumer is 90% of 4506.25
= (4506.25 ÷ 100) × 90
= 4055.625 kJ m^{-2} yr^{-1}

Energy transferred to secondary consumer and stored in biomass
= energy intake of secondary consumer − energy losses
= 4055.625 − (2343 + 1261)
= 451.625
= **451.6 kJ m^{-2} yr^{-1}** (to 4 s.f.)

[3 marks for the correct answer, otherwise 1 mark for correctly calculating energy transferred to the primary consumer and 1 mark for correctly calculating energy intake of the secondary consumer]

c) By breathing faster, more oxygen will be available in the cells of the secondary consumer *[1 mark]*. Oxygen is needed as a final electron acceptor in the oxidative phosphorylation stage of aerobic respiration *[1 mark]*.

By increasing the amount of oxygen that is available, oxidative phosphorylation will be able to occur at a faster rate, increasing the rate of ATP synthesis / oxidative phosphorylation will be able to occur, reducing the need for anaerobic respiration, which produces ATP at a slower rate than aerobic respiration *[1 mark]*.

d) Increasing the population size of the secondary consumer would be likely to reduce the population size of the primary consumer *[1 mark]*. This would mean that more of the energy stored in the producer's biomass would be available to the farmer's livestock, so the livestock would be able to grow more quickly *[1 mark]*.

3 a) Goblet cells secrete mucus at mucous membranes/in the airways *[1 mark]*. Mucus is able to trap pathogens to prevent them from entering the body and causing infection, meaning the person is less likely to develop a fever *[1 mark]*.

b) Body temperature associated with fever is an example of negative feedback because the temperatures shown in Table 1 fluctuate around a set point rather than rising continuously/moving further and further away from a set point *[1 mark]*.

c) i) Shivering is likely to increase the rate of glycolysis as the muscles need more ATP for contraction *[1 mark]*, which is produced during glycolysis *[1 mark]*.

ii) As the muscles use more oxygen, the oxygen concentration in the blood may fall, which would be detected by chemoreceptors *[1 mark]*. Impulses would be sent from the chemoreceptors to the medulla oblongata *[1 mark]*, which would send impulses along the sympathetic neurones/the accelerator nerve *[1 mark]*. These would secrete noradrenaline onto receptors of the SAN in the heart, causing heart rate to increase *[1 mark]*.

d) i) Standard deviation is better for judging the precision of the results as this shows the spread of data around the mean *[1 mark]*, whereas the range just shows the total spread of the data *[1 mark]*.

ii) That there would be no significant difference between the average increase in body temperature for substances A and B *[1 mark]*.

iii)
$$t = \frac{0.3 - 1.1}{\sqrt{\left(\frac{0.2^2}{20}\right) + \left(\frac{0.3^2}{20}\right)}}$$

$$= \frac{-0.8}{\sqrt{0.002 + 0.0045}}$$

$$= \frac{-0.8}{0.08062\ldots}$$

$$= -9.92278\ldots = -9.9 \text{ (to 2 s.f.)}$$

[2 marks for the correct answer, otherwise 1 mark for the correct working. Allow marks even if minus sign is omitted.]

You were told in the introduction to the question that each substance was tested on 20 rodents, so both of your values for *n* should be 20.

iv) Degrees of freedom = (20 + 20) − 2 = **38** *[1 mark]*

Answers

v) The scientists would use a table of critical values to find the critical *t*-value at the degrees of freedom they had calculated and a probability level of 5% *[1 mark]*. If the *t*-value they had calculated was greater than the critical *t*-value then the scientists would reject their null hypothesis / was lower than the critical *t*-value then the scientists would fail to reject their null hypothesis *[1 mark]*.

4 a) As there are excess base triplets in the gene, there will be more than the usual number of amino acids in the protein that's produced *[1 mark]*. This will mean that the protein can't fold into its unique tertiary shape, which will affect its function *[1 mark]*.

b) i) E.g. loss of muscle coordination / posture / coordination of balance *[1 mark]*.

ii) E.g. a transmission electron microscope would produce an image with a higher magnification / resolution than a scanning electron microscope *[1 mark]*, so the detail of the neurones / organelles in the neurones could be investigated more easily *[1 mark]*. However, unlike a transmission electron microscope, a scanning electron microscope could be used to produce a 3D image *[1 mark]*, which may allow the overall structure of the dense network of neurones to be investigated more easily *[1 mark]*.

c) Stem cells can divide to make new, specialised cells *[1 mark]*, so they may be able to be used to regrow healthy neurones to treat Huntington's disease *[1 mark]*.

d) i) The DNA is heated to 95 °C to break the hydrogen bonds between the two strands of DNA and therefore separate them *[1 mark]*. This means that single DNA strands are created which act as templates to create the complementary strands of DNA *[1 mark]*.

ii) Electrophoresis separates out DNA fragments based on size, so copies of a *HTT* gene that have a larger number of CAG repeats would move a shorter distance than those that have a smaller number of CAG repeats *[1 mark]*. Therefore, if the PCR products of the genetic test only move a short distance (e.g. compared to a control/sample taken from a person known not to have a mutated *HTT* gene) it suggests that the person is at risk of developing Huntington's disease *[1 mark]*.

iii) A phosphate ion has a negative charge of 3– *[1 mark]*. In the sugar-phosphate backbone of DNA, two of the R groups on the phosphate group would be a (pentose) sugar/deoxyribose *[1 mark]*. This may result in the phosphate group having a negative charge of 1– in DNA, meaning that the DNA fragments would be attracted to the positive electrode in electrophoresis *[1 mark]*.

5 a) i) If acetylcholine didn't bind to the receptors then sodium ion channels in the postsynaptic membrane wouldn't open *[1 mark]*. With no influx of sodium ions the postsynaptic membrane would not become depolarised *[1 mark]*, meaning an action potential would not be generated in the target/muscle cells *[1 mark]*. This would mean that the sarcoplasmic reticulum would not be triggered to release calcium ions *[1 mark]* and so the actin-myosin binding sites would remain blocked by tropomyosin, preventing muscle contraction *[1 mark]*.

ii) The drug prevents the membrane from repolarising / returning to its resting potential *[1 mark]*, which prevents the generation of a new action potential and any further muscle contraction *[1 mark]*.

iii) E.g. it could prevent the influx of calcium ions into the presynaptic neurones so the vesicles containing acetylcholine are not triggered to release it. / It could increase the rate of acetylcholine breakdown in the synaptic cleft, so that it can't bind to receptors on the postsynaptic membrane/motor end plate and generate an action potential. / It could bind to acetylcholine in the synaptic cleft to prevent it from binding to receptors on the postsynaptic membrane/motor end plate and generating an action potential. *[1 mark]*

b) Contraction of the intercostal muscles is needed to increase the volume of the thorax *[1 mark]*, which reduces the pressure inside the thorax/lungs and causes air to be drawn in to the lungs *[1 mark]*. Without this action, there would be no air entering the lungs meaning gas exchange in the alveoli would stop and blood oxygen concentration would fall *[1 mark]*.

c) Minimum dose at which no more than 15% of usual force of contraction remaining (the mean reduction in force of contraction is no less than 85%) = 200 μg kg body mass^{-1}.
200 × 75 = 15 000 μg
15 000 μg ÷ 1000 = **15 mg**
[2 marks for the correct answer, otherwise 1 mark for 15 000 μg or for a correct conversion from μg to mg.]

d) In order to be excreted, the neuromuscular blocker/drug molecules may need to be broken down in the hepatocytes *[1 mark]*. Having thicker endothelial cells could reduce the rate at which drug molecules in the blood/sinusoids were absorbed into the hepatocytes *[1 mark]*. This could result in the drug molecules circulating in the blood for longer, where they could continue to act at neuromuscular junctions and affect muscle contraction *[1 mark]*.

e) If acetylcholinesterase was inhibited by anticholinesterases then more acetylcholine would remain in the synaptic cleft *[1 mark]*, and be available to bind to receptors on the postsynaptic membrane/motor end plate to overcome the action of the neuromuscular blocker *[1 mark]*.

6 a) A substitution mutation will not cause the number of bases in the gene to change, whereas a deletion mutation would *[1 mark]*. This means that the base triplets that come after a substitution mutation would be unchanged, but the base triplets would all be different after a deletion mutation *[1 mark]*. This means that only one amino acid in the sequence could be affected following a substitution mutation, but many amino acids could be affected following a deletion mutation *[1 mark]*. The fewer amino acids that are affected, the more likely it is that the function of the resulting protein will be unaffected, meaning that the effects of a substitution mutation are likely to be less harmful than the effects of a deletion mutation *[1 mark]*.

b) The Generation 2 male is either heterozygous or homozygous for the healthy allele *[1 mark]*. If the Generation 2 male is homozygous for the healthy allele then there is a 50% chance that the Generation 3 male will inherit the disease, meaning the student's conclusion is correct *[1 mark]*. However, if the Generation 2 male is heterozygous then there is a 75% chance that the Generation 3 male will inherit the disease, meaning the student's conclusion is incorrect *[1 mark]*.

It might be helpful to draw out a genetic diagram (e.g. a Punnett square) in your exam to help you get your head around what's going on.

Answers

c) i) Number of people in the city = 9.62×10^6 = 9 620 000. Number of people in the city homozygous for the FH allele = 9 620 000 ÷ 1 000 000
= 9.62 = **10 people** *[1 mark]*

Here you're working out the number of people that would be homozygous for the FH allele, so you need to round your answer to the nearest whole number (as you can't have 0.62 of a person).

ii) $p^2 + 2pq + q^2 = 1$
Frequency of the homozygous dominant genotype = p^2
so p^2 = 1 in 1 000 000
= 1 ÷ 1 000 000
= 1×10^{-6}
so $p = \sqrt{(1 \times 10^{-6})}$ = 0.001
p + q = 1, so q = 1 − p
= 1 − 0.001
= 0.999
Frequency of the heterozygous genotype = 2pq
= 2 × 0.001 × 0.999
= 0.001998
= **0.0020** (to 2 s.f.)
[2 marks for the correct answer, otherwise 1 mark for recognising that the frequency of the heterozygous genotype = 2pq]

d) i) Inflammation of the β cells in the islets of Langerhans could reduce the secretion of insulin into the blood *[1 mark]* due to glucose being unable to enter the cell to trigger insulin secretion / ion channels in the β cell membrane being unable to close to trigger depolarisation of the β cell membrane / vesicles containing insulin being unable to fuse with the β cell membrane *[1 mark]*. Insulin normally lowers the blood glucose level by increasing uptake of glucose by cells *[1 mark]* and increasing the conversion of glucose into glycogen *[1 mark]*. If insulin secretion is reduced then the blood glucose level can't be controlled properly/remains high, which could lead to Type 2 diabetes *[1 mark]*.

ii) Any two from: e.g. the technology used for somatic gene therapy could potentially be used in ways other than for medical treatment, which some people may be opposed to. / Some people may worry that somatic gene therapy could do more harm than good, e.g. there's a risk of overexpression of genes. / Somatic gene therapy is expensive and some people may think that the resources could be better spent on other treatments that have passed clinical trials. *[2 marks]*

7 a) The increase in shade means that the crop plants may not have access to as much light as before, so their growth rate may be reduced *[1 mark]*. This could mean that there is less food available for the rabbits *[1 mark]*, so the environment can no longer support the same number of rabbits as before, meaning that the carrying capacity will have been reduced *[1 mark]*.

b) i) Chlorophyll a or b can't absorb light beyond a wavelength of 700 nm, which could mean that ATP and reduced NADP aren't produced in the light-dependent reaction of photosynthesis *[1 mark]*. This could mean that there is less ATP and reduced NADP available for the light-independent reaction/Calvin cycle *[1 mark]*, so fewer products needed for plant growth (e.g. glucose) are produced *[1 mark]*.

ii) When far-red light is detected, TTA1 activity is no longer inhibited so the amount of indoleacetic acid/IAA/auxin produced will increase *[1 mark]*. Indoleacetic acid/IAA/auxin stimulates the growth of plant shoots *[1 mark]*, so an increase in the indoleacetic acid/IAA/auxin concentration could cause the plant to grow taller/bend further so that it is exposed to more light *[1 mark]*.

c) When bound to DNA, transcription factors control the rate of transcription of their target genes *[1 mark]*. If two organisms with the same genome have different transcription factors acting on their genes then there will be different amounts of various proteins produced *[1 mark]*, which will lead to the organisms having different phenotypes *[1 mark]*.

d) i) E.g. the scientist could gather the samples at fixed intervals along a line *[1 mark]* that ran from an area of shade to an area of light across the field *[1 mark]*.

ii) Marking the solvent front would allow the scientist to measure how far up the chromatography paper the solvent travels *[1 mark]*. This information is needed to calculate an R_f value for each pigment, which is needed in order to identify the pigments present in the leaves *[1 mark]*.

8 a) E.g. a triglyceride could contain omega 3 *[1 mark]*, which is made up of a glycerol molecule and three fatty acids *[1 mark]*. / A phospholipid could contain omega 3 *[1 mark]*, which is made up of a glycerol molecule, a phosphate group and two fatty acids *[1 mark]*.

b) Preservation methods would protect the ecosystem/habitat of the wild fish populations so that it remains exactly as it is, so fishing would not be allowed at all, even with limits to the number of fish that can be caught *[1 mark]*.

c) **7-9 marks:**
The answer clearly describes all of the steps in the process that may have been involved in the genetic engineering of AquAdvantage® salmon. The answer clearly discusses the practical and ethical advantages and disadvantages of using AquAdvantage® salmon to meet the demand for salmon rather than artificial selection.
The answer has a clear and logical structure.
The information given is relevant and detailed.
4-6 marks:
The answer describes most of the steps in the process that may have been involved in the genetic engineering of AquAdvantage® salmon. The answer discusses some of the practical and ethical advantages and disadvantages of using AquAdvantage® salmon to meet the demand for salmon rather than artificial selection.
The answer has some structure. Most of the information given is relevant and there is some detail involved.
1-3 marks:
The answer briefly describes parts of the steps in the process that may have been involved in the genetic engineering of AquAdvantage® salmon. The answer has little discussion of the practical and ethical advantages and disadvantages of using AquAdvantage® salmon to meet the demand for salmon rather than artificial selection.
The answer has no clear structure. The information given is basic and lacking in detail. It may not all be relevant.
0 marks:
No relevant information is given.

Answers

Here are some points your answer may include:
The growth hormone gene from the Chinook salmon and the promoter sequence from the ocean pout may have been cut out using restriction enzymes. These DNA fragments could have then been inserted into a vector. The vector DNA could have been cut open using the same restriction enzymes that were used to cut out the growth hormone gene and the promoter sequence. The sticky ends of the vector DNA would then be complementary to the sticky ends of the DNA fragments containing the growth hormone gene and the promoter sequence. The vector DNA and DNA fragments could have been mixed together with DNA ligase to join them together. The vector with the recombinant DNA could then have been used to transfer the growth hormone gene and the promoter sequence into the DNA of an Atlantic salmon.

AquAdvantage® salmon can grow faster than farmed Atlantic salmon produced via artificial selection. This would lead to higher yields, meaning that the farmers of AquAdvantage® salmon would be able to meet the demand for salmon more easily than the farmers of Atlantic salmon produced via artificial selection. Eventually, artificial selection may be able to produce a population of Atlantic salmon that grow as fast as AquAdvantage® salmon but this is likely to take a long time to achieve. Also, the genetic manipulation of the AquAdvantage® salmon means that the yield from each population may be more certain, as each fish will have the genes which allow it to grow faster. In the artificially selected Atlantic salmon population, sexual reproduction would create genetic variation. This means not all fish would possess the alleles required for faster growth, so the yields may be more uncertain.

The technology involved in producing the AquAdvantage® salmon is likely to have been very expensive, which may make the salmon more expensive than artificially selected Atlantic salmon.

There are negative ethical issues associated with both genetic engineering and artificial selection to meet the demand for salmon. However, there may be more ethical concerns surrounding genetic engineering as it is a relatively new method (so the long-term effects are more uncertain) and it is considered to be a less natural method than artificial selection. Examples of ethical concerns associated with AquAdvantage® salmon include concern that manipulating Atlantic salmon's genes could cause harmful side-effects for the AquAdvantage® salmon, concern that genetically engineering Atlantic salmon could reinforce the idea that they are merely assets for humans to treat however they like, and concern that the AquAdvantage® salmon could escape into the wild and negatively impact wild Atlantic salmon populations.

Some consumers could refuse to buy AquAdvantage® salmon as they could be concerned about how it could affect their health.

The company that generated AquAdvantage® salmon could patent the genes, which could mean that they were able to charge consumers very high prices for the salmon. It could also mean that some poorer salmon farmers would be unable to afford to buy and rear AquAdvantage® salmon, which would put them at a disadvantage compared to farmers who could afford to farm AquAdvantage® salmon.

Index

Index

Index

Index

Index

Index

Index